Word, Image, and Deed in the Life of Su Shi

Harvard-Yenching Institute Monograph Series 39

Word, Image, and Deed in the Life of Su Shi

RONALD C. EGAN

Published by the Council on East Asian Studies, Harvard University,
and the Harvard-Yenching Institute
and distributed by the Harvard University Press,
Cambridge (Massachusetts) and London   1994

The Harvard-Yenching Institute, founded in 1928 and headquartered at Harvard University, is a foundation dedicated to the advancement of higher education in the humanities and social sciences in East and Southeast Asia. The Institute supports advanced research at Harvard by faculty members of certain Asian universities, and doctoral studies at Harvard and other universities by junior faculty at the same universities. It also supports East Asian studies at Harvard through contributions to the Harvard-Yenching Library and publication of the *Harvard Journal of Asiatic Studies* and books on premodern East Asian history and literature.

Grateful acknowledgment is made to the following for permission to use quotations or reproduce illustrations: Oxford University Press, for James R. Hightower's translations of Tao Qian in Chapter Eight; The Research Center for Translation, The Chinese University of Hong Kong, for D. C. Lau's translation of Yan Shu in Chapter Ten; James R. Hightower, for his translations of Liu Yong in Chapter Ten; and The National Palace Museum, Taipei, for Figures 1, 3, 4, and 5.

Endpapers: Su Shi, attrib., *Tree, Rock, and Bamboo*. Handscroll. Location unknown. From *Zhongguo gudai huihua xuanji* (Beijing: Renmin meishu chubanshe, 1963), fig. 37.

Index by Susan Stone

Library of Congress Cataloging-in-Publication Data

Egan, Ronald C., 1948–
    Word, image, and deed in the life of Su Shi / Ronald C. Egan.
        p.   cm.—(Harvard-Yenching Institute monograph series; 39)
    Texts of Su Shi's poems in Chinese and English.
    Includes bibliographical references and index.
    ISBN 0-674-95598-6
    1. Su, Shih, 1036–1101.—Criticism and interpretation. I. Su,
Shih, 1036–1101. Poems. English and Chinese. Selections. 1994.
II. Title. III. Series.
PL2685.Z5E34   1994
895.1'142—dc20   93-46196
                                                                        CIP

For Susan and Louisa

Contents

Figures

Preface

Su Shi peers over the edge of a boat to see the reflection of his face in the water. Suddenly, waves disturb the image, and he watches as it spreads outward and multiplies, creating the illusion of a hundred Su Shis. But abruptly these disappear and a single face forms again in the stilled water, staring up at him.* Readers of Su Shi's works are likely to feel that they are witness to similar dazzling transformations. Given that Su was so broadly accomplished across separate fields (a fact that is invariably mentioned regarding him), he speaks with an array of distinct voices. Even a short list would have to include statesman, Buddhist, gastronome, alchemist, classicist, dissident, hydrology engineer, philosopher, and, above all, poet, calligrapher, and connoisseur of the arts. What, then, is the balance among these many Su Shis and how are they connected? The problem, moreover, goes beyond this multiplicity of voice and role. On many particular subjects Su Shi's writings are so voluminous and, given the conventions of his day, so occasional and piecemeal that divergences and apparent contradictions are numerous.

It has not been my goal to tie the diverse aspects of this life neatly and systematically together. Any account of Su Shi's life and works should accommodate a certain amount of disconnectedness and tangential interests, which are, after all, part of his richness and unique appeal. At the same time, there is a need for an updated comprehen-

---

* See pp. 205–206 below.

sive treatment of this remarkable person. The interests of history and biography alone justify a critical survey of the entire range of this most celebrated life, though no single volume could ever do justice to all of it.

My approach is intended to have special utility regarding Su's achievements in literature and the arts. This is not to deny the importance of other aspects of his life (on the contrary, I stress it), nor is it to question the usefulness of literary studies of Su that do not include the non-literary aspects of his life. Such studies have and will continue to enhance our appreciation of Su's poetry and its place in the literary tradition. However, the broader treatment of Su's accomplishments, as in this study, puts his artistic achievements in a different light. The first and simplest contribution such a treatment makes is to remind us that Su Shi was great not only in the field of poetry, and indeed, not only in literature and the arts generally. Inasmuch as this fact immediately distinguishes Su Shi from most earlier major poets, it deserves a place in literary history. There are also less obvious insights to be gained.

When the critic restricts himself to literary or stylistic analysis, questions of motivation (e.g., why did the poet develop a particular style or express himself a certain way?) are notoriously elusive. It happens that with Su Shi, a poet who also led a prominent and controversial life in the divisive politics of his day, connections can be discerned between political and intellectual disputes he engaged in and the directions he took as artist. Naturally, such connections between the poet and his times, in a vague and simple sense, may be discovered for many writers. But with Su Shi the situation is special.

It has been observed that just as one cannot imagine Du Fu without the An Lushan rebellion, so, too, one cannot conceive of Su Shi without the reform movement led by Wang Anshi and Su's opposition to it. But merely to say this is to understate Su's involvement in the momentous social and political events of his day and their relevance to his art. In Du Fu's case, the An Lushan rebellion is something that befell or overtook him. He was more of a witness to than participant in the military and political struggles that ensued. Su Shi, by contrast, became an important player in the drama of the New Policies and the struggles it brought about, which stretched over his entire career and, indeed, cast their shadow over virtually every aspect of late Northern Song intellectual and political history. Su's poetry, moreover, became a crucial part of his public persona as it matured through the contentious politics of the time. Su was imprisoned and brought to trial because of the political criticism his poetry contained. Years later, he became the leader of a political faction whose identity owed itself, in part, to the special interest its members took in poetry and related arts. As leader of this faction, Su was banished to the distant south (eventually even "across the sea"), where he remained until just before his death, continuing all the while to express himself in verse. There is good reason, then, to want to bring to a reading of Su's poetry knowledge of the non-literary controversies of his day, which he helped to define. That is why the chapters on Su's literature and art are saved for the latter part of this volume. These aspects of Su Shi remain the culmination of our study of him—as they will always be—and certainly they have value and meaning that transcend the biographical circumstances of his life. Yet, his art springs from those circumstances and is conditioned in countless ways by them, just as it, in turn, affected them. My goal is to analyze Su's art in this larger context of his life and thought.

The inclusive treatment of this many-faceted person also better prepares us to appreciate the apparent divergence between our perception of Su (inherited from late imperial times) and his own self-image. We think of Su Shi first as a poet, but his own mind seems filled with ambivalence and vacillation on this point. Occasionally, he states clearly that it is his achievements outside of literature and the arts that he considers primary (and his followers reiterate this opinion concerning him). No matter how we finally choose to think of him, the existence of this discrepancy itself has ramifications for our conception of his poetry. Attention to his work in non-literary fields sharpens our apprehension of this issue.

In recent years a prodigious amount of scholarship has appeared on Su Shi, greatly advancing our understanding of his life, politics, thought, and literary work. In China, five separate volumes of collected articles on Su have appeared, based on national Su Shi conferences held during the 1980s. These collections, some of which focus on a single genre of Su's writing or a single period of his life, have raised biographical knowledge of Su Shi and critical appreciation of his works to new levels. Several other volumes devoted to Su have also appeared, including biographies (e.g., by Zeng Zaozhuang), interpretative studies (Chen Yingji, Liu Naichang, Zhu Jinghua), collections of anecdotes and historical criticism (Yan Zhongqi, Li Fushun), and annotated anthologies of his works (Wang Shuizhao, Wang Siyu, Yan Zhongqi), as well as a study of the textual history of his writings (by Liu Shangrong). Special mention should be made of major new editions of Su's complete prose and poetry, which were published separately during the 1980s. The complete poetry reproduces the extensive and indispensable commentary by the Qing scholar Wang Wen'gao. The complete prose, in six volumes, edited by Kong Fanli, is the first fully and reliably punctuated edition of Su's prose, together with collation notes, that has appeared.

This country has likewise seen a dramatic increase in scholarly attention to Su Shi in the past twenty years, filling a heretofore conspicuous void, which stretched all the way back to Lin Yutang's biography of Su (1947), a remarkable achievement for its time. In the 1970s, a Ph.D. dissertation by Stanley Ginsberg on Su's Huangzhou exile, together with lengthy biographical and bibliographical articles written by George Hatch, brought critical scholarship in English on Su Shi to a new level. More recently, several dissertations have been devoted to Su, and books derived from those dissertations are beginning to appear. Important work has been done on Su Shi's thought by Peter Bol, on his borrowings from Buddhism by Beata Grant, and on various aspects of his poetry and aesthetics by Alice Cheang, Michael Fuller, Stuart Sargent, Kathleen Tomlonovic and Vincent Yang. I have benefited from all of these studies, even as I have developed my own understanding of the man.

A figure of the stature of Su Shi deserves to have a variety of critical treatments, and more focused studies (whose subjects may still be sizable) will continue to fulfill an important need. Given the wealth of the material available, including that produced by Su as well as that written by others about him, each of my chapters could easily be expanded to provide a fuller treatment and analysis. In what I have chosen to include, moreover, specialists will find much that is already familiar ground.

A fellowship from the National Endowment for the Humanities, in 1990–1991, gave me the time to rework the material presented here. Susan Bush, Chou Shan, and James T. C. Liu read portions of the work and offered valuable suggestions for improvement. Sabine Gross read several chapters of the manuscript and suggested numerous changes that benefited both style and substance. Kang-i Sun Chang, Alice Cheang, Patrick Hanan, Freda Murck, Hoyt Tillman, Timothy Wixted, and Anthony Yu all provided much-needed advice or assistance. I am grateful to Peter Bol for sharing chapters with me in manuscript form of his recent book on Tang and Song intellectual history, to Robert Hymes for a copy of his unpublished paper on Song-dynasty famine relief, to Paul J. Smith for his then unpublished analysis of Wang Anshi's reform program, and to Peter Sturman for allowing me to see drafts of his Ph.D. dissertation on Mi Fu. Critical comment on earlier presentations of my views was provided by Wm.

Theodore de Bary, Lin Shuen-fu, and Yu Ying-shih. My colleagues Pai Hsien-yung and Peter Pang alerted me to many relevant new publications. Katherine Keenum, as editor, brought clarity to numerous turgid passages and eliminated many other errors and oversights. My greatest debt for advice and criticism is to Susan Chan Egan.

CHRONOLOGY OF THE LIFE OF SU SHI

EMPEROR AND REIGN YEAR	DATE	EVENT IN THE LIFE OF SU SHI
Renzong		
Jingyou 3	1037	Born in Meishan
Zhihe 1	1054	Married Wang Fu
Jiayou 2	1057	Passed *jinshi* examination
Jiayou 2–4	1057–1059	In mourning for mother, returned to Meishan
Jiayou 6	1061	Passed decree examination
Yingzong		
Jiayou 7–Zhiping 1	1062–1064	Appointed notary in Fengxiang
Zhiping 2	1065	Recalled to capital, death of Wang Fu
Shenzong		
Zhiping 3–Xinging 1	1066–1068	In mourning for father, returned to Meishan, married Wang Runzhi
Xining 2–3	1069–1070	Returned to capital, protested against the New Policies
Xining 4–6	1071–1073	Appointed vice prefect of Hangzhou
Xining 7–9	1074–1076	Appointed prefect of Mizhou, took Zhaoyun as concubine
Xining 10–Yuanfeng 2	1077–1079	Appointed prefect of Xuzhou
Yuanfeng 2	1079	Arrested and charged with having slandered the emperor and Court
Yuanfeng 3–7	1080–1084	Exiled to Huangzhou
Yuanfeng 8	1085	Appointed prefect of Dengzhou
Zhezhong		
Yuanyou 1–3	1086–1088	Recalled to capital, appointed Hanlin academician
Yuanyou 4–5	1089–1090	Appointed prefect of Hangzhou
Yuanyou 6	1091	Recalled to capital as Hanlin academician
Yuanyou 6–7	1091–1092	Appointed prefect of Yingzhou and Yangzhou
Yuanyou 8	1093	Recalled to capital as minister of rites, death of Wang Runzhi, appointed prefect of Dengzhou
Shaosheng 1–4	1094–1097	Exiled to Huizhou, death of Zhaoyun

EMPEROR AND REIGN YEAR	*DATE*	*EVENT IN THE LIFE OF SU SHI*
Shaosheng 4–Yuanfu 3	1097–1100	Exiled to Danzhou (Hainan Island)
Yuanfu 3	1100	Allowed to return to the mainland
Huizhong		
Jianzhong jingguo 1	1101	Died in Changzhou

Word, Image, and Deed in the Life of Su Shi

First Fame and Remonstrations: The Decree Exam

Su Shi was brought to national prominence in his mid twenties by his performance on two examinations in the capital. In the *jinshi* exam of 1057, he placed second out of hundreds of candidates; and in the special decree exam for which he was recommended in 1061, he received a grade given only once previously in the hundred-year history of the dynasty. That his younger brother, Su Che, trailed not far behind him on both exams, and that his father, Su Xun, though not an examinee, won during those same years the acclaim of the most prestigious officials of the day, made Su Shi's successes seem all the more remarkable. The fame of the Three Sus spread quickly through the capital.

Su Shi and his younger brother had arrived in the capital in 1056, accompanying their father. Su Xun had been urged to make the long trip by Zhang Fangping, who was then serving as military intendant of the Chengdu circuits, which included the Su homeland of Meishan (in modern Sichuan).[1] Su Xun himself had failed to pass the *jinshi* or its equivalent on three previous trips to Kaifeng. After his last attempt, in 1046, Xun had returned home and burned all his practice essays, determined never to sit for the exams again. He remained secluded at home for some ten years.

Not long after this fourth journey to the capital was completed, Su Xun sent a letter introducing himself to Ouyang Xiu, who was then, as a special drafting official, one of the most powerful men in the government.[2] At this time, Xun passed on to Ouyang letters recommending him from Zhang Fangping and others, as well as copies of his own writings on statecraft. Ouyang must have been impressed by what he saw; for he proceeded to memorialize to the Court recommending that Xun be given a post without taking the exams, and he also formally presented Xun's writings to the Court.[3] Nothing, however, came of Ouyang's recommendation.

During the next several months, well into 1057, Su Xun occupied an odd niche among elite circles in the capital. He befriended several eminent officials beside Ouyang Xiu, including the grand councilors Fu Bi and Wen Yanbo, and the commissioner of military affairs, Han Qi. He was a frequent guest at their tables, and the singularity of a "commoner" thus socializing with such high-ranking officials excited comment.[4] Yet Su Xun was still given no post. Unlike Ouyang, the other officials seem to have done nothing to assist Xun in his ambition; and one source even says that Han Qi and Fu Bi disapproved of the military and border policies Xun strenuously advocated in his essays.[5]

In the meantime, and apparently by coincidence, it happened that Ouyang Xiu, Su Xun's strongest supporter, was appointed to oversee the *jinshi* examinations of 1057. The examination papers were graded "blind"—the authors' names not revealed to the examiners—so that Ouyang and the other examiners could not have known which were the Su brothers' papers. Three hundred eighty-six men passed the *jinshi* that year. Su Che passed in the highest of three ranks, but Su Shi did even better: his papers were graded second overall. We have it, moreover, from Su Che himself that his brother's papers would have won first place were it not that Ouyang wrongly suspected that they had been composed by Zeng Gong, Ouyang's own protégé, and deliberately withheld the highest grade to avoid the appearance of favoritism.[6]

Of the several essays Su Shi composed during the exams of 1057, the one that excited the most comment was that on the theme "Loyalty and Generosity in Punishments and Rewards," a title derived from a passage in an early commentary on the *Book of Documents*.[7] (It was specifically this essay that Ouyang Xiu thought must have been written by Zeng Gong.) Su adopts the traditional preference, found already in the passage from the *Documents* itself, for giving rewards in borderline cases and withholding punishments in the same, developing the ideas through several discrete sections, each of which considers the problem from a new point of view. It is precisely this multifaceted treatment, the twists and turns in the exposition, that traditional critics single out for praise.[8] One section of Su Shi's essay is particularly famous. Su relates how the sage-king Yao countermanded three times his minister's order that a certain man be put to death (an example of an admirable reluctance to use punishments). The passage is said to have puzzled the examiners, who could not remember the classical source in which the incident was recorded. Later, after the results of the examination had been posted and Su Shi came to pay his respects to Ouyang as was the custom, Ouyang asked Su about his source for this passage. Su answered, "I imagined he would have acted that way."

Whether or not this exchange with Ouyang took place, to judge from the frequency with which the story is told and retold in Song sources, the audacity Su showed in his essay by creating a new episode in the life of the sage Yao left a deep impression on those who heard of it.[9] After witnessing Su Shi's performance on the exam, and after reading formal letters of thanks Su sent to his examiners, Ouyang wrote in a note to his colleague Mei Yaochen, "I'm old now and should move aside to make room for this young man. How wonderful is his writing!"[10]

There was, however, to be a four-year period of silence before Su Shi was heard from again and before the story of his examination successes reached its climax. One month after the palace exam of 1057, word came to the capital that Su Xun's wife had died back in Meishan. Su Xun and his two sons departed hurriedly on the long journey back to Sichuan to bury the deceased and begin a period of mourning.

It was not until the spring of 1060 that the Sus returned to the capital. This time the whole Su family made the trip, including Su Shi's and Che's wives, young children, and their nursemaids. The family sailed down the Yangzi in several boats, making frequent stops along the way, and took some four months to reach the capital. In the autumn of 1060, Su Xun finally became a member of the government, and by direct appointment. His was a humble post, though, that of provisional collator in the imperial library (ranking in the ninth, i.e., the lowest, grade). Much grander things awaited his two sons. They were recommended for the decree examination to be held in 1061. Su Shi was sponsored by Ouyang Xiu himself, and Su Che by Yang Tian, an administrator in the Bureau of Policy Criticism.

The decree examination (zhice) was a special means used to find and honor men of exceptional talent. The exam was held irregularly and given only to men who had been sponsored by high-ranking officials. A candidate need not have passed the jinshi to be recommended (Su Xun sat for but failed a decree exam in 1046). On the other hand, the standards by which the examinees were evaluated were extraordinarily high. During the 170 years of the Northern Song, only thirty-nine men passed the decree exam, compared with some eighteen thousand *jinshi* recipients.[11]

The decree exam consisted of three parts. First, each candidate had to submit to the examiners a portfolio of fifty essays that he had prepared ahead of time. The only requirement here was that the papers be equally divided between *ce* ("policy papers"), that is, recommendations concerning current problems facing the realm, and *lun* ("disquisitions"), broad considerations of perennial issues in statecraft and history. The precise topics were left to each candidate. In the second part of the exam, candidates were required to write, all in one day, six essays on classical themes selected by the examiners. The third part was one long treatise (over three thousand characters) in response to a policy question put to the candidates by the emperor himself. Su Shi emerged from the ordeal with a grade in the third of five ranks. In fact, the first two ranks were never awarded, and in the entire Northern Song only four men placed as high as the third. Su Che placed in the fourth rank, the normal passing grade, together with one other candidate, Wang Jie. The Su brothers and Wang were the only three men to pass the examination that year.

It is the collection of essays Su Shi wrote for the first part of the decree exam that holds the greatest interest. In this portfolio of fifty essays Su, freed from the constraints of a set theme, holds forth on a wide range of historical, institutional, and philosophical problems. Here he displays a breadth of knowledge and brilliance of argumentation that could not be exercised in other parts of the exam. It was also this group of fifty essays that was subsequently copied over and widely circulated, spreading Su Shi's fame.

Su's twenty-five policy essays are grouped according to broad topic: on bureaucratic personnel (six pieces), on governing the populace (six pieces), on trade and finance (two pieces), and on military preparedness (three pieces). These four groups are preceded by five introductory essays on general principles of government, and succeeded by three essays on border relations and military strategy. The twenty-five disquisitions are mostly on famous historical figures: rulers (e.g., Han Gaozu, Cao Cao), advisors (e.g., the Duke of Zhou, Zhuge Liang), and thinkers (e.g., Mencius, Han Feizi, Han Yu). Chronologically, the topics of these essays range from the early Shang down through the Tang. Only five of the essays are not on individuals: three on the classic *Doctrine of the Mean* (*Zhongyong*) and two generalized essays on high-ranking ministers.[12]

Years later, during his Huangzhou exile, Su Shi wrote disparagingly of these examination essays, virtually repudiating them: "To hold forth brazenly on advantage and disadvantage, and to pass judgment irresponsibly on gain and loss—this is the practiced manner of all those who sit for the decree examination. They resemble seasonal insects or birds, which sing out for a time and then fall silent. What does it all mean?"[13] It is true that there is a certain amount of posturing and bluster in these essays. After all, the name decreed for the exams on this occasion was "forthright words and ardent remonstration" (*zhiyan jijian*). The emperor, Renzong, received from Su Shi this and more. The title of the exams suited the accomplished young writer perfectly, and there is every indication that he relished the opportunity, doing his best to leave a deep impression upon the emperor and his examiners.

That does not mean that we must accept Su Shi's later dismissal of these writings. The political, economic, and social problems that they address were certainly real ones. Su Shi, the aspiring official, was now given his chance to formulate solutions. In fact, with these essays he took his place among a long line of would-be reformers (including Fan Zhongyan, Ouyang Xiu, Zhang Fangping, Sima Guang, Shen Gua, and Li Gou) who had been vocal throughout recent decades. The Song faced serious military threats on its borders from the Tangut Xixia nation centered in the Kansu corridor and the Khitan Liao in the north (but already inside the Great Wall). Defense appropriations were rising steadily, consuming an ever larger part of the national budget; and this left the government severely hampered in its ability to respond to internal crises. Corruption was widespread at all levels of the enormous bureaucracy. For various reasons the government consistently recruited more men into the civil service than it had positions to fill. Wealthy clans and guilds dominated the private economy, controlling prices and bankrupting smaller merchants and farmers. In many respects these problems, all of which Su Shi addressed in his exam essays, were the very ones that contributed to the eventual loss of North China to the invading Jurchens seventy years later.

Su Shi uses his exam essays to sound a ringing alarm, an urgent call for reform. Above all he decries the lethargy and complacency into which the nation has fallen. We think we live in a time of peace and prosperity, Su warns, but we deceive ourselves and are pursuing a course that will lead to ruin. Surely, there is genuine concern expressed here, mixed as it is with the "practiced manner" of the examination candidate. Collectively, these essays are Su's earliest articulation of his views on key issues in the fields of statecraft and ethics. Preferences evident in these writings recur time and again in later years, even as they mature and transform. The exam essays constitute, then, the logical starting point for any inquiry into Su Shi's thought and action.

On Rites, Human Nature, and Governance

In his essay on the *Doctrine of the Mean*, the difficult chapter from the *Classic of Rites* that was such a favorite among Song intellectuals, Su Shi singles out the statement that even "the most foolish husband or wife" may participate in or live up to certain aspects of the Way of the sage, as obscure and difficult as that is often said to be, whereas a sage himself will be unable to master the most advanced or perfect levels of the Way.[14] Obviously, this is the sort of statement that lends itself to various interpretations. Su's is very one-sided. He stresses only the first half of the formulation, and treats it as an absolutely crucial tenet of the classical text. Confucius sought to teach, Su elaborates, that the highest of moral standards are rooted in actions that are simple and commonplace. Or, as Su puts the matter elsewhere in the essay, the Way has its origins in the emotions (*renqing*). This will be obvious to anyone who examines the matter from its roots or origins. But, Su goes on, there are those who approach the matter from the end or culmination instead. Looking only at the Way's highest manifestations, they conclude that realization of the Way comes from self-coercion, discipline, and effort. Thus they set anyone who listens to them off on an impossible quest.

This particular notion of the Way may serve to introduce a whole cluster of related concepts that inform Su's examination essays. If the Way is so intimately connected to natural emotions, then proper conduct, even that specified by the elaborate ritual and social codes of behavior (*li*, "rites"), must also grow out of universal human inclinations. Su argues this point, explaining that later ages have misunderstood the *li*, studying them too assiduously, exaggerating their importance as an ultimate goal, and insisting that only the superior man can live up to their demanding standards. Scholars have become obsessed with this or that commentary on the ancient texts, and insist that each type of behavior described by the classics must be mimicked down to the last detail. But originally, Su maintains, the *li* were not fixed and were not prescriptive. "The *li* had their origins in the emotions; then, in accord with what people took comfort in, codes of conduct were written down describing rank and role. Whatever the emotions take comfort in and also preserves role distinctions is part of the *li*." Su Shi paraphrases the *Classic of Rites* here, ignoring the possibility that in the original language the key term, *qing*, may have referred less to emotions than to "situations" or "actual circumstances." Su concedes that sometimes it was expedient to treat the *li* as if they were fixed and prescriptive, so that the common man would have something on which to model his behavior; but he insists that this was not the original significance or the highest understanding of *li*.[15]

So strongly does Su Shi feel the need to correct the widespread perception of *li* as being fundamentally at odds with human nature that he attempts to explain, in the following passage, how even the most seemingly unnatural sorts of behavior described by *li* can be reconciled with his view:

> Today I may say that standing all hunched over [a deferential posture, part of *li*] is not as comfortable as standing upright; but if comfort is all I want, no manner of standing can compare with sitting. Regular sitting, however, is not as comfortable as sitting with the legs extended, while that manner of sitting is not as comfortable as lying down all day. And if I am unsatisfied even with lying down, then let me take my clothes off and show no shame! But if I were to lie around naked, I myself should disapprove of it. Nor would it be only I: every common man and woman in the entire world would disapprove. As soon as there is such disapproval, it leads eventually to standing all hunched over and kowtowing a hundred times. With this in mind, we may say that standing all hunched over and kowtowing a hundred times has its origins in not wanting to lie around naked. And it is not just standing hunched over or a hundred kowtows, all the myriad kinds of conduct that the world considers coercive must have similar origins.[16]

Li must not be misconstrued as forced or unnatural, for they accord with universal human emotions. The primacy of the emotions is a related concept and one that bulks equally large in Su Shi's essays. His argument begins with the observation that certain feelings (e.g., hunger, cold, sexual urges) are indisputably fundamental to human life. Then he refers to the seven classically enumerated emotions (pleasure, anger, sorrow, fear, love, hate, desire) and asserts that they, too, are unavoidably part of life. Next, Su makes the more ambitious claim that these emotions are precisely the wellspring of Confucian morality and that without them such virtues as "humaneness" (*ren*) would not exist.

> There is no person alive who does not feel uncomfortable when hungry or cold and who has never experienced sexual desire. Would it be acceptable today for someone to say that eating when hungry, drinking when thirsty, or having sexual desires is not part of human nature? Everyone knows this is unacceptable. Lacking these emotions, the sage would have no means to be a sage, and the petty man would have no means to be

vile. The sage takes his seven emotions . . . and harnesses them so that they lead him to goodness, whereas the petty man harnesses the same seven and lets them lead him to what is vile.[17]

The Way of humaneness and rightness has its origins in love between husband and wife, father and son, and brother and brother, while the rites and regulations as well as punishments have their origins in the awe of minister for ruler and of subordinate for superior. Love ensures that men have that which they cannot bear to do, and awe ensures that they have that which they do not dare to do. Wherever these emotions of not being able to bear and not daring are combined, the Way of the sages will be found.[18]

In Su's view, not only are emotions essential for moral virtues, they are also inseparable from human nature (*xing*). This is a point that he returns to repeatedly in his essays, as he criticizes former Confucians who separate the two. The issue is itself tied to the perennial debate in Chinese thought over the nature of human nature: is it good, bad, or some combination of the two? In the ninth century, Li Ao had declared that human nature was essentially good but that the emotions, which he held to be separate from the nature, were capable of beclouding or overpowering it. The task of achieving sagehood thus consisted largely of suppressing or conquering emotions so that the good tendencies of the nature might prevail.[19] Li Ao's notion of the nature as good and emotions as bad was iterated, as we shall see, by prominent Northern Song philosophers. Su Shi strives to refute this view, calling attention to the good conduct that emotions may engender.

Because the assertion that emotions were not intrinsic to human nature was usually the first step in developing the kind of formulation credited to Li Ao (human nature good, emotions bad), Su Shi is particularly averse to it. Han Yu (one of Li Ao's mentors) had made the case for this view of the emotions, and Su Shi assails him for it in several essays.[20] Su Shi is likewise critical of all attempts to make pronouncements on the nature of human nature. Su maintains that human nature is neither good nor bad, nor any combination of the two. Human nature is simply beyond such labels: Confucius had wisely refrained from characterizing it, and later thinkers should be content to do the same.

Their pronouncements on human nature have always been a stumbling block for Confucians. [Han Yu] maintained that pleasure, anger, sorrow, and joy all spring from the emotions but are not part of human nature. Actually, it is only when first there is pleasure or anger that there can be humaneness and rightness, and only when first there is sorrow and joy that there can be the rites and music. To teach that humaneness, rightness, the rites, and music all come from the emotions but not from human nature is to lead people to reject the doctrines of Confucius. Laozi asked, "Can you be like the little babe?" To say that pleasure, anger, sorrow, and joy are not rooted in the nature but come instead from the emotions is to lead people to become Laozi's little babe![21]

In ancient times there were many who discussed human nature, and yet no consensus ever emerged. First Mencius said it was good, then Xunzi said it was bad, then Yangzi (Yang Xiong) said it was a mixture of good and bad. Later, Han Yu took up all three views and introduced Confucius's observation into them, dividing human nature into three levels and saying that persons in the middle level may move up or down, whereas people of the highest knowledge or the lowest stupidity cannot move out of their level.

Unfortunately, Han Yu did not understand human nature; what he was discussing was really innate material (*cai*, "talent"). Human nature and innate material are similar, but they are not the same; and the aspects of them that are different are as dissimilar as black and white. That which the sage and the petty man have in common, and which no person can escape, is human nature. But material varies from person to person. For example, all trees require soil to grow; and if they are nourished by rain and wind, they flourish and become luxuriant. This is true of all trees and is, in fact, the original nature (*xing*) of trees. But still there are differences between hard woods, which are made into hubs, and soft woods, which are made into rims, as well as differences between large trees, which are made into pillars, and smaller trees, which are made into rafters. Rafter lumber cannot serve to make a pillar, and rim lumber cannot serve to make a hub: is this the fault of the original nature of the tree? Scholars throughout the world who speak of human nature all mix it up with innate material. Consequently there is endless bickering and no final agreement.

When Confucius said that a person of the middle level might move up or down but the highest wisdom and the lowest stupidity could not move out of their level, he was talking of innate material. As for human nature, he never declared it to be either good or bad . . .

Moreover, [Han Yu] said, "People who speak about human nature today all mix it up with Buddhism and Taoism."[22] Yet Han Yu held that human nature has nothing to do with emotions and that pleasure, anger, sorrow, and joy are not part of human nature. Thus Han Yu himself had strayed into Buddhist and Taoist doctrines and did not even know it.[23]

Su Shi's vision of how the Chinese bureaucracy ought to function clearly shows the influence of his views on the philosophical issues examined above. His convictions about the primacy of the emotions, the capacity of ordinary people to approximate sagely or at least moral behavior, and the non-coercive nature of *li* show themselves in his ideas about governance. Su Shi never questioned the legitimacy of the imperial system, the need for elaborate hierarchies in social and political life, or even, as we have seen above, the usefulness of ensuring that subordinates have some degree of awe for their superiors. For his day, however, Su Shi's notion of how the government should work gave remarkable importance to the wants of the disenfranchised masses and to the desirability of the central government's responsiveness to the needs and opinions of the lower officials and people.

For example, on the need for redistributing the population more evenly through the country, Su bases his plan on the principles of "according with people's emotions" (*yin ren zhi qing*) and "according with the circumstances of the times" (*yin shi zhi shi*). Many of the Northern Song prefectures, especially those along the Yellow and Yangzi Rivers, had become overpopulated, with the result that land was almost impossible to acquire in them. But there were still certain prefectures, even within the central regions of the realm, that were sparsely populated. The problem was how to get people to move to them. Su points out that many bureaucrats, who were, after all, accustomed to relocation, might be persuaded to move to these prefectures if only they saw that they would not be isolated and alone. Were substantial numbers of these men, when they were approaching retirement, directed to move to a select number of these prefectures, the cultural backwardness of the places would be overcome and the bureaucrats would be quite happy to relocate. This would be an instance of "according with people's emotions." Unlike bureaucrats, however, the common people have strong ties to their homeland and are extremely reluctant to leave it. It would be a mistake to try to relocate them by directive. Instead, the government should wait for years of poor harvests and famine which, unfortunately, are experienced in all regions of the country from time to time. In such years, commoners would not object to quitting their homeland and the government could move them to the underpopulated areas. This would be "according with the circumstances of the times."[24]

For policymakers to be cognizant of the needs and preferences of their subordinates and the commoners, too, close contact and communication are essential. Some of Su Shi's sharpest criticisms are directed at forces that served to keep the rulers aloof, ignorant, and consequently unresponsive. First, there were the clerks, that large class of staff assistants, who often interposed between the officials and the people, cutting off the desired contact. Clerks tend to do this, Su observes, both because it is in their interests to do so (multiplying, for example, their chances to extort money) and because many officials are only too happy to yield up their own responsibilities to these underlings.[25] Second, misguided scholars have succeeded in convincing high officials that they ought to cultivate a severe and aloof manner. The reasoning is that an official's air of authority is enhanced if he remains distant and impassive. Many officials therefore make a point of not showing their emotions or speaking their minds in the presence of subordinates, hoping thus to intimidate and mystify them.[26]

The ideal Su Shi presents is one of thoroughgoing communication and responsiveness rather than of intimidation and estrangement, as he describes in the following elaborate analogy:

> A person's body has but a single heart and two hands. Nevertheless, whenever a pain or itch occurs in any part of the body, no matter how slight and inconsequential it may be, the hands move to relieve it. Is it that each time the hands move they await directions from the heart? Because the heart has long had such profound love for the body, and because the hands have long grown accustomed to following the directions of the heart, eventually the hands do not wait upon an order but move of their own accord. The way the sage governs the empire is similar. Despite the numerousness of the officials and the breadth of the territory, the sage ensures that the joints and arteries are all interconnected as one. Knock on any part and he will hear, touch it anywhere and he will respond. The entire empire is transformed into a single body. The ruler in his exaltedness and the officials and commoners in their lowliness all have a common bond of love and concern. Worries are shared between them and in crises they come to each other's aid.[27]

Even more striking, for the sanction it gives to the wishes of the people generally, is a passage in which Su Shi considers the values of good and bad. According to Su, in remotest antiquity the distinction between good and bad was unknown. But everyone began to pursue whatever he found pleasurable. Seeing that this was unwise, the sages established a principle: whatever the empire at large took comfort in was said to be good, whereas whatever a single person alone enjoyed was said to be bad. Now, it is true that Su Shi makes this point in the midst of a larger argument. He is, once again, building a case against declaring human nature to be either good or bad; and he touches on the origin of the two concepts, explaining that they were not first intended to be applied to human nature at all. Still, his statement here about the original distinction is exceptional. He does not define goodness according to the cardinal Confucian virtues (humaneness, rightness, loyalty, etc.), nor does he link it to "the Way of the ancients." Good and bad are defined solely in terms of communal versus individual happiness.[28]

At first sight Su Shi's examination portfolio seems to be filled with suggestions for changing administrative procedures and practices. He writes of relieving the Secretariat of responsibility for dealing with the recurrent border crises, of altering the bureaucratic recruitment process, of relaxing restrictions on long-term service within a single bureau, of reforming taxation and land distribution, and on steps the state should take to increase revenues and to cut expenditures. Running through these many calls for procedural change, however, is a deep antipathy for governance based primarily upon strict procedure. This distrust of inflexible regulation is consonant with the ideal of responsiveness to the needs of the people, discussed above. Referring to the age-old Chinese polarity of rule by set policy and rule by men, Su Shi says that the current government relies too heavily upon policy and neglects human initiative. (The Chinese word rendered as "policy" here is *fa*, a broad term whose meanings, depending on context, include "method," "procedure," "regulation," and "law.") Su allows that while there are flaws in current policies which should be corrected, the great failing of recent decades is that set policies have been relied upon too heavily and that human initiative and discretion in rule, as well as the issue of finding the right people to entrust with power, have been neglected.[29]

In ancient times there were no set policies, Su explains, and people simply followed their inclinations. This sometimes resulted in great accomplishments, but it could also disintegrate into chaos. Policies were established to avoid the chaos, but subsequent ages made the mistake of trusting entirely to the policies, growing wary of inclinations. They strayed from the ideal of a balance between the two.

> If people dominate policies, policies become an empty vessel. If policies dominate people, people become mere fillers of positions. But if people and policies proceed together without either dominating, the empire will be at peace. Today, all officials from the lowest ranking up to the grand councilor think that they fulfill their duty if they do nothing more than uphold policies and follow regulations. They fold their arms and entrust everything to policies, asking, "How could I ever be free to act on my own?" Once policies came to hold sway, people became fillers of positions. Thereafter, whether there was success or failure, order or chaos, everyone throughout the empire just said, "It is not me, it is the policy." Are the drawbacks of policies not extreme?
> . . . Why is it that the empire entrusts everything to policies? It comes from people being unsure of themselves, which in turn comes from

selfishness. If the empire were free of selfishness, then people could apply their insight and knowledge outside of policies and laws. Why? Their trust in themselves would be clear.[30]

In fact, a great many of the reforms Su advocates are intended to relax the force of policies and to make the bureaucracy more flexible, reasonable, and humane. One of the essays on officialdom, for example, calls for abolishing a sponsor's liability for wrongdoing by the man he had recommended.[31] Sponsorship was an important means by which men were promoted up through Song bureaucracy, a prime alternative to the other methods of promotion based on tenure or merit ratings. Sponsorship, however, carried with it a legal guarantee of the conduct of the person sponsored. If the man subsequently committed an offense, even years or decades later, his sponsor could be held liable and subjected to punishment. Su characterizes the liability as an essentially impossible demand (requiring that a person's conduct be vouched for years in advance), an instance of misguided regulatory rigidity.

In essays on the initial recruitment of officials into the bureaucracy, Su similarly criticizes mechanistic observance of policies. He suggests that there ought not to be automatic appointment of young men who have passed one of the several civil service examinations. Instead, the Bureau of Personnel should gather together all those who have passed an examination, as well as those who have been recommended through the regular channels, and evaluate and rank them one additional time, doing this by interview and character assessment rather than by any kind of objective test. Appointments would then be made from the top of the Bureau's list as needed to fill vacancies. The advantage of this, Su observes, is that it avoids following "a set procedure" and therefore allows human judgment rather than regulations to have the final say. Su recognizes that some people will be unsatisfied with his plan and will argue that it encourages favoritism, but he maintains that regulations should be nothing more than general guidelines and that their implementation must finally be "given over to men."[32] In another essay Su takes up the obverse issue of excluding certain types of persons from the higher levels of the bureaucracy. Here, too, Su challenges the inflexibility of blanket regulations, pointing out that truly talented men are to be found among those who began their careers as menial clerks and even those who have been implicated in criminal conduct in office. Why should such men be forever prohibited from advancement up the ladder of officialdom? After all, there is no inviolate rule about where men of worth originate. "Some of them emerge from the merchant and lowly classes, or even from among thieves. Meanwhile, scholars and members of high-ranking clans, whom the world expects to behave like superior men, often indulge in wanton and unprincipled conduct to which even commoners would not stoop."[33]

On Historical Figures

In the essays on historical figures (philosophers, statesmen, and generals), Su Shi delights in offering novel interpretations of the life or ideas of the man in question. The piece on Yue Yi is of special interest because it presents a relativistic approach to moral values that seems akin to the aversion to fixed standards discussed above. Yue Yi, a general of Yan in the Warring States period, led the combined forces of several states in an attack upon the state of Qi. He easily took control of most of the cities of Qi; but two cities held out defiantly against him, and he was stymied for five years. Eventually, a rift arose between Yue Yi and the new ruler of Yan, and Yue fled to Zhao and sought refuge there. Soon a general of Qi led a counterattack from one of the resisting cities, inflicted heavy damage upon the forces of Yan, and restored Qi to power.

Historians had traditionally looked with admiration upon Yue Yi and blamed his ruler for not trusting him. Su Shi adopts a different attitude. Su concludes that Yue never completed his conquest of Qi because he was unwilling to launch an all-out assault upon the defiant cities and was trying to win them over through a show of kindness and compassion. But these Confucian virtues had no place in that situation, Su asserts. Yue Yi made the mistake of using a petty version of "humaneness and rightness," and he tried to live up to moral standards that were inappropriate to his goals. After all, Su observes, this was the Warring States era, when states were devouring each other. If Yue had thrown his immense army against the two cites, "he could have obliterated them and then had a good meal. Who would say otherwise? The fact is, if you aspire to be a true king then you must act like one. But if that is not your aspiration, you must take stock of where you are. In this way you may avoid failing to reach either goal and being laughed at by the world."[34]

Many scholars of Su Shi's day must have had similar thoughts about the limitations of the old virtues, but few people voiced them. An essay like this comes very close to challenging some of the most fundamental assumptions of the Confucian tradition. Perhaps Su wrote it with his own dynasty's military woes in the northwest in mind. In that case Su would have been urging policymakers to take a clear assessment of the circumstances they faced and not to let their choices be distorted by values that were inappropriate to the situation. In any case, the relativistic suggestion that values are alterable according to circumstances is precisely the sort of notion for which Su was criticized throughout his life. His views reminded many of the opportunistic strategies of the very same Warring States period. Wang Anshi himself is said to have expressed this opinion of Su's examination essays.[35]

In evaluating statesmen and generals Su Shi reserves his highest praise for men whose service was, to his mind, free of self-interest or personal ambition. Yi Yin and Huo Guang, grand councilors of the early Shang and the Former Han, respectively, were such men.[36] Both had helped to remove an inept ruler and then acted as regent for a period but never sought to usurp the throne, and eventually relinquished power voluntarily, returning it to the ruling clan. What interests Su Shi most is not the achievements of these men, but the state of mind that made the achievements possible. Su stresses the indifference to personal gain evident in each man from early on in his career. He thus makes temperament (qi) the primary qualification for greatness, placing it even above innate talent (cai) and integrity (jie). The deeds of Zhang Liang, the advisor to Han Gaozu, were not comparable to those of the regents.[37] Still, he was instrumental in the founding of the great Han dynasty. Su interprets his entire career as a reflection of his virtue of "forbearance," that is, of being able to tolerate personal insult and frustration in order to achieve grander goals. By contrast, Su has little regard for Jia Yi, the would-be Han advisor.[38] Jia Yi was a man of genuine talent, but he did not know how to use it. He was unreasonably impatient for imperial recognition; and when it did not come, he isolated himself, casting himself in the role of the tragically neglected minister, Qu Yuan. Jia Yi lacked forbearance; his temperament was flawed by an excessive need for quick appreciation.

Despite all of Su Shi's talk in these essays of the virtues of patience, forbearance, and personal disinterestedness, it would be wrong to conclude that his ideal is a minister who is timid or unmotivated. On the contrary, Su calls for the empowerment of men who will boldly enact sweeping reforms. Using language drawn from the *Analects*, Su advocates the recruitment of "wild men" (*kuangren*), that is, men of action who will rush to set mistaken policies aright.[39] The virtues of patience are confined to matters of personal satisfaction. There ought to be no patience with regard to policy reform. Su's vision of governance is a distinctly activist one. On the analogy of the positive effects that activity and exercise have for the body, he argues that frequent "movement" (*dong*, i.e., political activism) is likewise good for the body politic.[40] Yet Su realizes that the government is full of officials who will be hostile to reform, officials who have a personal stake in preserving the status quo. Therefore Su predicts that truly able ministers will have to cope with hostility and even slander from those whose comfortable lives they will inevitably disrupt.[41]

Su Shi appropriates another term from the classics to designate the mediocre bureaucrats who are so numerous in the current government. They are "village honest men" (*xiangyuan*), of whom Confucius and Mencius had spoken disparagingly. These are men who cultivate an appearance of virtue, while actually their motives are self-serving. They strike an amiable manner and nurture a reputation for integrity and reasonableness, but their only real goal is to win the world's approval.

One cause of the abundance of these village honest men is that the world has come to accept what is to Su's mind a peculiar and inferior concept of the "middle way":

> In ancient times the middle way meant to realize completely the inherent Pattern (*li*) of the myriad things and to be free from error.[42] It was also called "the grand culmination." "Culmination" means realizing completely. However, in later ages the middle way was thought to entail following meekly along, doing whatever the crowd did. Is this really the middle way? This is what Confucius and Mencius called the way of the village honest man. The entire village praises him as an honest man, and he is perceived as an honest man wherever he goes. He shares with others the practices of his day and is in harmony with the sordid world, saying, "Why did the ancients walk along in such a solitary fashion? Being in this world, one must behave in a manner pleasing to this world. So long as one is good, it is all right." It is wrong to say that such a man is close to the middle way. He is an enemy of virtue.[43]

This passage is full of ideas and language drawn from Mencius's discussion of the middle way.[44] Su Shi has not created the notion of this particular "enemy of virtue," nor has he distorted Mencius's description of it. But he has put his own twist on the discussion. The passage leads directly into Su's call for "wild men" who will obliterate this inferior understanding of the middle way and go on to reform the nation. Actually, Mencius only considered "wild men" the second-best type of person with whom to work. Indeed, Mencius insists that Confucius still preferred men who kept absolutely to the middle way. That sort of person has dropped out of Su Shi's treatment of the issue.

In another essay Su likewise gives a new slant to a crucial phrase drawn from the text of the *Doctrine of the Mean*, one that also has the effect of introducing latitude and flexibility into the concept. The classic says that in conforming to the middle way, the superior man makes sure to "*shi zhong.*" The standard commentary explains this to mean that he regulates the middle way (*zhong*) according to the needs of "the times" (*shi*). But Su Shi interprets it to mean that the superior man "sometimes" (*shi*) conforms to the middle way, but sometimes he does not. This occasional conformity ultimately amounts, in Su's opinion, to the highest order of the middle way.[45]

The main target of Su's "forthright words" in these essays is the bureaucratic complacency, lethargy, and corruption he perceived all around him. As he would write years later, "Long ago when I was recommended for the decree examination during Renzong's reign, the policy papers and essays I submitted, together with my answers to the emperor's questions, were generally all intended to urge Renzong to make the administration more rigorous and efficient, to supervise the bureaucracy more stringently, and to be more decisive and act more forcefully."[46] Knowing as we do about the conflict that developed later on between Su Shi and Wang Anshi, we may be tempted to interpret Su's exam essays as an early reaction against Wang's approach to governance. After all, although Wang had not yet really come to power in 1061, he was already a presence in the capital (as a drafting official) and was widely recognized as a man with a potentially illustrious future before him. In 1058, Wang had submitted his famous "Ten Thousand Word Memorial" to Renzong, which blamed the nation's many problems on its failure to establish the right "regulating systems" or "institutions" (*fadu*). Su Shi's essays of three years later do certainly elucidate a divergent point of view, but it would probably be a mistake to conclude that Su was reacting specifically to Wang. The bureaucracy itself provided Su Shi with ample material for his remonstration, and Wang Anshi was not yet influential enough to single out for confrontation.

One particular theme in Su Shi's essays might, however be a reaction to an intellectual trend that both Wang Anshi and another future rival, Cheng Yi, were associated with. Cheng Yi had appeared at the imperial academy in 1051 and written an essay that caused a great stir. Entitled "To What Learning Was Yanzi Devoted?,"[47] it presented a restatement of Li Ao's contention that man's essential nature was good but the emotions bad. A person is born with all the five virtues (humaneness, rightness, etc.) complete in him, Cheng Yi maintained. But external things may assail him and cause commotion inside, which stirs up the emotions. Aroused emotions have the ability to puncture the inherent nature (with its virtues). In this view, the emotions are pitted against the nature. The cultivated man always keeps his emotions in check; he "turns his emotions into his nature," while the uncultivated man indulges his emotions, "turning his nature into emotions."

In the years to come, as we shall see below, Su Shi would identify Wang Anshi, even more than Cheng Yi, with the preoccupation on the part of intellectuals with inquiry into human nature and Heaven's decree (xingming). Unfortunately, because many of Wang Anshi's essays on philosophical issues are undated, we cannot reconstruct a satisfactory chronology of the articulation of his views, especially for this early period of his career. Nevertheless, certain writings that can be dated to this general period portend his later influence. There is, for example, an inscription Wang wrote in 1064, in which he says that the Way and virtue upheld by the ancient kings spring from the patterns of human nature and Heaven's decree (xingming zhi li).[48] Such a statement exemplifies an orientation toward what has been called "inner sageliness," and the same orientation encourages just the kind of speculation about human nature that Su deplored.

Regardless of the extent of Wang Anshi's (or Cheng Yi's) influence upon intellectual trends in 1061, it is clear that scholars in positions of prominence and their students had already begun the shift towards reflection on xingming that would later become even more pronounced. In other words, although it cannot be established that Su was taking issue in 1061 specifically with either of his two great later rivals, obviously he was not just engaging in a debate across the centuries with Han Yu, Yang Xiong, and other early thinkers. In a separate memorial, also composed in 1061, Su Shi inveighs against the current habit among scholars of setting their sights on the ultimate truths and, in the end, accomplishing nothing, instead of being content to master a single field or classic, as scholars in ancient times did. "Scholars today all discuss Heaven and man, and investigate human nature and Heaven's decree. Thus they arrive at questions that are impenetrable, and worldly teachings forever remain unclear. Their opinion of themselves is too high and they apply themselves to matters that are too broad."[49] Actually, on the issue of human nature Su Shi sounds much like Ouyang Xiu, who similarly complains about the contemporary debate over whether human nature is good or bad. Ouyang also holds that the question cannot be settled and distracts scholars from more important concerns.[50] But Ouyang had not worked this dissatisfaction with current intellectual discourse into so coherent a system of views and values as had the younger man he brought to prominence.

The Essay on Zhang Liang

As interesting as these views on historical figures, statecraft, and human nature may be, and as important as they undeniably are for Su's later intellectual development, the effectiveness of his essays comes as much from the power and ingenuity of their argumentation as from the extractable ideas themselves. What Su Shi displayed in his portfolio of essays, and what so impressed the elder examiners, was a gift for thought and exposition that enabled him even when he was restating conventional Confucian precepts (e.g., rule by "men" rather than by set policy) to sound forceful and new. The rhetorical and literary qualities of the essays are a crucial part of their success and the attention they attracted. On many of the issues, Su would modify or expand his views through the ensuing years. Nevertheless, already in these essays we glimpse something of the genius for structure, argumentation, and rhetorical effect (as in the fabrication of the Yao incident) that mark Su's prose throughout his career and carry over into his poetry.

The essay presented below, on the Han strategist Zhang Liang, should illustrate these qualities, as difficult as it is to do justice to them in translation. The essay will also serve to recapitulate some of the themes of Su's thought discussed earlier, including sensitivity to circumstantial exigencies, the crucial role of the ruler's advisors to guide and correct him, subordinating self-interest (in this case, a personal grudge) to grander long-range goals, and the importance of a highly cultivated temperament. The essay will, moreover, show that Su's endorsement of the emotions does not mean that he supports conduct based purely on impulse, whim, or unchecked emotional reaction.

Each of Su's historical essays assumes considerable knowledge on the reader's part of the facts and tradition of discourse that had become an integral part of each topic. The relevant background information for this essay will be briefly summarized here. Zhang Liang was known as a great military strategist, the man who guided Liu Bang (Han Gaozu), the founding emperor of the Han dynasty, to victory over his rivals. Zhang's biography in the *Records of the Grand Historian* (ca. 90 B.C.) tells, however, of an unpromising beginning, when as a young man he tried unsuccessfully to assassinate the first emperor of the Qin, intending to avenge Qin's subjugation of his ancestral state of Hann. The assassination attempt was bungled and Zhang Liang nearly lost his life in the process. Thereafter, an anecdote is told about him that purports to explain his subsequent mastery of the art of war.

Once when Zhang Liang was out walking in the Xiapei region, as he crossed a bridge he met an old man wearing coarse cloth. The old man approached Liang and deliberately dropped his shoe beneath the bridge. He turned and said to Liang, "Boy, go fetch my shoe." Taken aback, Liang's first impulse was to strike the man, but on account of his age Liang forced himself to forbear and climbed down and got the shoe. The old man said, "Put it on my foot." Since Liang had already retrieved the shoe, he knelt down to put it on. The old man stuck his foot out for Liang, then laughed and walked away. Liang was completely at a loss and watched the man go. He went some distance, then returned and said, "Boy, you show some promise. Five days from now, meet me here at dawn." Liang did not know what to think but he knelt and agreed.

Five days later Liang set out at dawn, but the old man was waiting for him by the time he reached the bridge and said angrily, "When you set a time with your elder, how dare you be the last to arrive!" The old man walked off, adding, "Five days from now meet me here early." Five days late, when the cock crowed, Liang set off. But once again the old man was already there and angrily demanded why Liang was late. Walking off, he said, "Five days from now, come earlier." This time, Liang set out before midnight. Soon after he arrived, the old man appeared. Pleased, the old man said, "This is how it ought to be."

The old man took out a scroll and said, "Read this and you will be teacher to a king. Ten years hence you will arise. Thirteen years hence you will see me in Jibei. I will be the yellow rock you see lying at the foot of Gucheng Mountain." The old man left without another word and Liang never saw him again. At dawn Liang examined the scroll. It was *The Grand Duke's Art of War*. Liang treasured it and studied it thoroughly.[51]

The scroll Zhang Liang receives is not otherwise known (the Grand Duke in its title presumably refers to the advisor to King Wen of the Zhou). Obviously, we are supposed to understand that the book is a magical, secret handbook on the art of war.

Later, Zhang Liang joins up with Liu Bang, who begins as just one of several local strongmen who rise up in rebellion against the tyranny of the Qin dynasty. As the Qin empire disintegrates, a rivalry develops between Liu Bang and his fellow general Xiang Yu, who have become the two most powerful leaders of the rebellion. During the famed struggle between the two, which rages over several years, Zhang Liang is ever at Liu Bang's side, counseling him, encouraging him, forestalling disaster and guiding him towards victory. Zhang Liang saves Liu Bang's life on more than one occasion, when his own foolish impulses or other advisors' poor strategies have endangered him, and he masterminds strategies that doom Xiang Yu's side by sowing rifts between Xiang Yu and his most gifted advisors. After his victory, Liu Bang himself acknowledges that his success is due entirely to the efforts of Zhang Liang and other trusted advisors. Su Shi's essay is translated below:

On the Marquis of Liu (Zhang Liang)

In ancient times men who were known as great heroes had principles of conduct superior to those of other men. There are provocations in the world that few can forbear. When a common fellow is insulted, he draws his sword and rises, stretching himself tall for a fight. But that is not real bravery. Those in the world who are truly brave are not frightened when suddenly confronted and are not angered when imposed upon for no reason. It is because the principles they hold to are grand, and the goals their minds are set upon are distant.

Zifang (Zhang Liang) received a book from an old man on a bridge. The tale is truly strange. And yet, how can we be sure that this was not some superior man who lived as a recluse during the Qin dynasty and came out to test Zifang? The ideas that the old man so subtly transmitted were, after all, advice with which the sages and worthies of old had admonished each other. But the world has not discerned this and has concluded that the old man was some kind of ghost or spirit. That conclusion cannot be justified.

Furthermore, the old man's intent was not upon the book. When the state of Hann perished and Qin was at the height of its power, Qin used the knife, saw, and cooking pots to deal with the scholars of the world. The innocent men who were put to death, together with their families, could not be numbered. Even with Ben and Yu one could not have done anything about it.[52] The fact is, the spears of those who enforce the law so stringently cannot be withstood; but they do have weaknesses that can be taken advantage of. At that time, Zifang could not bear his pent-up anger. He concentrated all of his strength—that of only an ordinary man—in a single assault. He was saved from death by only a hair's breadth. Truly, he put himself in danger!

A wealthy family's son makes certain that he does not die at the hands of robbers and thieves. Why? He prizes his life and feels that robbers and thieves do not warrant his death. In spite of his peerless talent, Zifang did not develop the strategies of a Yi Yin or Taigong.[53] Instead, he followed the plots of Jing Ke and Nie Zheng.[54] The result was that he escaped death only through a stroke of luck. That is why the old man on the bridge took pity on him and acted so arrogantly and haughtily to cut him down to size. The old man knew that only after he could forbear would he be able to achieve great deeds. In the end the old man said, "Boy, you show some promise."

When King Zhuang of Chu attacked Zheng, the Earl of Zheng met him with bared shoulder, leading a sheep. King Zhuang said, "This ruler is able to submit to others. He must be able to win the trust and employment of his people." With this he freed him.[55] When Goujian was surrounded at Kuaiji, he went as a slave to Wu and toiled there for three years without ever tiring in his determination.[56] Those who would avenge themselves upon others but who are unable to submit to others have only the resolve of ordinary fellows. The old man believed that Zifang had more than enough talent but regretted that his capacity was insufficient. Therefore, he took steps to break Zifang's youthful temperament of stubbornness and sharpness, ensuring that he would be able to bear petty grievances and thus achieve great things. How did he know Zifang's potential? The two of them were unacquainted and met by chance in the wilds. He ordered Zifang to perform a servant's task, yet Zifang was not provoked and did not think it amiss. This, then, was clearly a man the Emperor of Qin would not be able to frighten and Xiang Yu would not be able to enrage.

The causes of Gaozu's (Liu Bang's) eventual victory and of Xiang Yu's eventual defeat lie precisely in this difference between being able and being unable to forbear. Xiang Yu simply could not forbear. Consequently, although he won a hundred victories in a hundred battles, he used his forces impetuously. Gaozu could forbear, and so he nurtured his forces until they were complete, waiting until his rival was worn out. This was what Zifang had told him to do. When Huaiyin (Han Xin) conquered Qi and wanted to make himself king there, Gaozu became angry and his emotion showed on his face and in his words.[57] We can see from this that Gaozu still had a stubborn, headstrong temperament and that he could not forbear. Were it not for Zifang, who would have saved him?

The grand historian thought is strange that although Zifang was such a heroic and extraordinary man, his physique and face resembled that of a woman or girl, seemingly not matching his great character.[58] I venture to ask: was this not precisely what made him Zifang?[59]

The essay opens with the distinction Su draws between a higher and lower order of bravery. The key term "to endure, forbearance" (*ren*), which turns out to be the key to the entire essay, occurs right at the outset. Next, Su broaches the subject of Zhang Liang's encounter with the old man on the bridge, suggesting that, while it certainly seems strange, it might have happened after all. The suggestion anticipates the great significance Su discerns in the story and his emphasis on its psychological, rather than magical, dimension. That Su is interpreting the story a new way becomes obvious in the third paragraph, when he says that the book was not what was uppermost in the old man's mind. Previously, the passage had always been read primarily as an explanation of how Zhang Liang acquired his rare insight into the art of war (i.e., through the magical handbook).

From early on it was assumed that the old man was a supernatural being and that his manifestation and gift to Zhang Liang were signs that Heaven was on the side of Zhang's future lord, Liu Bang.[60] The momentousness of Zhang Liang's subsequent cause, the founding of a dynasty, was sufficient in this case to overcome what was already in Han times considerable skepticism about the very existence of spirits and ghosts. The story about the old man may also be understood as part of a cult of Zhang Liang as magician-general, a perennial figure in Chinese legend, that grew up around Zhang Liang soon after his military successes. There are other Taoist and supernatural motifs in Zhang Liang's biography: we are told that he would abstain from eating grains and that he practiced Taoist breathing exercises. We also read about sacrifices made jointly to Zhang Liang and the yellow stone (the form in which the old man reappeared), which Liang did encounter years later, as predicted.[61]

Su Shi was the first to see that the story about the encounter with the old man might be taken another way altogether, that it had a rightness in the larger context of Zhang Liang's life and accomplishments distinct from its supernatural element. The ingeniousness of Su's reinterpretation is shown by what immediately follows. The difference between Zhang Liang as a rash young man who nearly lost his life in a disastrous attempt to assassinate the first emperor of the Qin and the mature strategist who guided Han Gaozu to victory over of the more powerful Xiang Yu seems perfectly accounted for by Zhang's earlier lack and later acquisition of the virtue of "forbearance" (cultivated by the humiliation to which the old man subjects him). Not only is Su's reading of the old-man passage novel, in one stroke it put Zhang Liang's whole life in a new perspective.

In the next paragraph Su broadens his purview to include the entire struggle between Han Gaozu and Xiang Yu, attributing Gaozu's final victory to his tutelage, at Zhang Liang's hands, in the virtue of forbearance. The rivalry between Gaozu and Xiang Yu had always been understood as one that turned on the radically different personalities of the two leaders. Throughout the historical narrative that is the basic source for the period, Sima Qian's *Records of the Grand Historian*, Xiang Yu is depicted as a fearless but impulsive and untrusting leader, while Liu Bang, however prone to miscalculation, has the sense to listen to good counsel when it is offered. Xiang Yu is the abler warrior, both more daring and more skilled in the use of arms than Gaozu; but Liu Bang is better at capitalizing upon his advisors' talents. Xiang Yu, moreover, is loath to share his power or the spoils of his victories with his generals, whereas Liu Bang does this, even if only after Zhang Liang admonishes him to do so. Xiang Yu is given to fits of temper and can be ruthless and cruel. Liu Bang is reserved, by comparison, and must be persuaded by those around him to assume the role of leader. These differences in character, as traditionally perceived, may readily be linked to the presence or absence of Su's virtue of forbearance in each leader, respectively. Forbearance by itself may not account for every aspect of the personality contrast, as normally thought of, but it goes as far as any single concept might to characterize the difference between the two men.

In his final paragraph, Su alludes to the observation Sima Qian makes at the end of his biography of Zhang Liang about his unmanly and unimpressive appearance. Sima Qian's is little more than an offhand remark. He relates his surprise at seeing a portrait of the famous strategist and finding his demeanor to be so "womanly." To Sima Qian the discrepancy between Zhang's appearance and his great deeds is a curiosity, but one that has no particular significance. Su Shi, however, perceives that Sima Qian's comment suits his own purposes perfectly. Forbearance is, of course, not the same thing as meekness or timidity, the qualities that might be inferred from Zhang Liang's demeanor, but, again, it is close enough for the rhetorical point to be effective. Su thus ends his essay with a flourish that reiterates and clinches his main theme even as it introduces an unexpected twist.

Esteem for the virtue of forbearance must have lain within the heart of this examination candidate, and he used Zhang Liang's life as an occasion to hold forth on it. As it would turn out, the youthful Su, who fancied himself a budding advisor in the general tradition of Zhang Liang or, more precisely, Lu Zhi, who felt that his breast contained ten thousand books and that a thousand words hung on his brush tip, who boasted that "it should not be hard" to make his emperor into a Yao or Shun, would have ample opportunity to test his own capacity for forbearance in the coming years.[62]

CHAPTER TWO

National Politics: Opposition to the New Policies

Su Shi received his first appointment shortly after his success on the decree examination. He spent three years as a notary under the administrative assistant of Fengxiang (west of Chang'an). Soon after his tour had ended there, in 1066, his father died in the capital. Su Shi, together with his younger brother, accompanied the coffin on the long journey up the Yangzi River to Sichuan, and went into mourning. It was 1069 before the Su brothers returned to the capital, whereupon Shi was appointed to the staff of the Investigation Bureau (a branch of the Censorate).

It was a radically altered political situation that greeted Su upon his return. Emperor Yingzong had died in 1067 and his heir, Shenzong, had acceded to the throne. The young ruler was more of a mind than either his father or, more importantly, Renzong (r. 1023–1063) had been to try bold solutions to the nation's worsening problems. For decades, hostilities with the Tanguts and the Khitans had crippled the country's economy and weighed on the minds of the leading statesmen.[1] Heavy losses in warfare with the Tanguts in the early 1040s prompted a renewed call for military and economic reforms, led by Fan Zhongyan, but resistance was strong and the measures were abandoned. The economy suffered the consequences. By 1065, defense expenditures consumed 83 percent of the government's cash and 43 percent of its total income.[2] The Song had what has been called a "wartime economy," trying to support a regular army of 1.25 million men, most of whom were stationed on the western and northern borders.[3] Expenditures began to exceed receipts, and the government slipped into debt. It has been argued that the financial officers could not even measure the size of the debt, so incomplete was their knowledge of all the transactions within the enormous bureaucracy.[4] In 1066, warfare with the Tanguts flared up again.[5] Tangut armies invaded the northern prefectures of Qinfeng and Yongxingjun circuits and captured the city of Daxuncheng (150 miles northwest of Chang'an). In 1067, they lured the prefect of Bao'an to a treaty conference and murdered him, an act that gave rise to further attacks and counterattacks. Meanwhile, the new emperor asked Sima Guang to study the debt problem and to make recommendations. Sima reported that "administrative expenditures are extravagant, imperial rewards and gifts are unrestrained, the imperial household is excessively large, the bureaucracy is wasteful, and the military is inefficient."[6] Shenzong made some effort to cut back. Within a year, however, he had all but given up on this method of stabilizing the economy and turned instead to the measures suggested by Wang Anshi.

Beginning in 1069, when Wang Anshi was first appointed to the Council of State, and stretching on through the next two years, during which Wang was promoted to be grand councilor, the government adopted a whole series of reforms, which would come in time to be known as the New Policies (xinfa). These reforms touch upon virtually every aspect of the operations of the bureaucracy, altering many of them fundamentally. The general intent of the reforms was to improve the social, military, and fiscal condition of the realm, and to do this by 1) enhancing the quality of the bureaucrats and 2) greatly increasing state involvement in and stimulation of private and local economies. Other scholars have described and analyzed the reforms at great length—there is a considerable amount of material on them available even in English—and so only a brief account of the most important of them need be given here.[7]

Green Sprouts Policy (*qingmiao fa*): a crop loan system designed to augment agricultural production and prevent small farmers from losing their land during hard times. The government was to lend money to farmers to assist their spring planting and collect repayment at harvest time. Interest collected on the loans was set at 24 percent (2 percent per month), but this was justified as being a considerably lower rate than that demanded by private money lenders, whose influence and power the government sought to curtail.

Hired Service Policy (*muyi fa*): this abolished the corvée by which men had been drafted to fill menial sub-bureaucratic posts in local government offices. The corvée had been largely unpopular because it took young men away from their families for months or years at a time. All households were now assessed a graduated tax (the service exemption tax, *mianyi qian*), the revenues from which would allow local offices to hire personnel instead.

Tribute Distribution and Price Equalization Policy (*junshu pingjun fa*): this empowered fiscal intendants in the provinces to buy or sell local tribute, depending on market conditions, in order to stabilize prices and better supply both local and central government needs. This policy replaced a less flexible system by which fixed quotas of local tribute had to be transported annually from the provinces to the capital.

State Trade Policy (*shiyi fa*): government trade offices in principal commercial centers were authorized to buy directly from small merchants when there was insufficient demand in the marketplace, and to issue loans to them when needed. The government thus sought to make small merchants less dependent upon the wealthy guild merchants.

Civilian Security Policy (*baojia fa*): this organized households into groups of ten or more units, and each household was required to supply one adult male to a local security force. The forces were used for surveillance, law enforcement, and even tax collection. In border regions the *baojia* units contributed men as reserve soldiers to the standing armies.

Examinations Policies: the civil service examinations were changed to emphasize discussions of policy and the application of the classics to practical statecraft. The examinations in the "various fields" (*zhuke*) were abolished, including the popular one in the classics (*mingjing*) with its traditional stress upon memorization (*tie*) and on elucidation of particular passages (*moyi*). Likewise, poetry and rhapsodies (*fu*) were eliminated from the *jinshi* exam. In its new form the *jinshi* consisted of questions on the general significance (*dayi*) of the classics, as well as policy questions. A specialized examination in law and administration was subsequently instituted.

A new vision of the role of the state in managing finance, and in creating more wealth for the entire nation, was central to Wang Anshi's program. It is true that Wang was also committed to improving both the moral quality and the administrative expertise of the bureaucrats. These were key themes of his "Ten Thousand Word Memorial" of 1058. But once Wang came to power ten years later, the deluge of new policies that issued from his administration had more to do with finance, taxation, agricultural production, and hired service than with the nurturing of a new type of bureaucrat. Even Wang's examination reforms strayed from the approach he had advocated in 1058, when he had apparently been in favor of selecting men by other methods altogether.

Wang held that public finance lay at the heart of governance. He goes so far as to equate the task of managing finance with a hallowed Confucian virtue: "Governing consists of managing wealth (*licai*), and managing wealth is what is known as moral duty (*yi*)."[8] Wang arrives at this conclusion after quoting *Mencius* on how a good ruler knows to store grain away when it is plentiful and likewise knows to open up the granaries when people are starving. One may perhaps find the seed of Wang Anshi's idea in the classic, but Mencius himself would never have stated the conclusion as Wang does.

Not only did Wang recognize financial regulation as a key function of the government, he was confident that with proper management the empire's wealth could be increased. Wang rejects the view that the empire's debt has been brought on by excessive expenditures. The financial woes stem instead from a lack of expertise in fiscal management. We have, Wang asserts, forgotten how to use our fiscal resources. "[The ruler] relies upon the strength of the empire to produce the empire's wealth. He appropriates the empire's wealth to supply the empire's expenditures. Since ancient times governments have never been troubled by inadequate wealth. Their troubles come only from not knowing the Way of regulating wealth."[9]

Wang believed that if this Way were known, the economy would grow and wealth would be increased. Both the government and the people would be better off. Of course, there were men who disagreed with this view, men who thought that the empire's quantity of wealth was fixed. Wealth might be distributed in different ways, but it could never be increased. The sources record the following exchange between Wang Anshi and Sima Guang:

> Wang Anshi said, "The reason public revenues are inadequate is simply that we do not have officials who are good at managing wealth."
>
> Guang said, "Those who are 'good at managing wealth' do nothing more than take grain away from the people until the people's wealth is exhausted. In desperation the people turn to banditry. That is hardly good for the country."
>
> Anshi said, "No, those who are good at managing wealth make the public revenues adequate without increasing taxes."
>
> Guang said, "The myriad forms of wealth and goods that Heaven and Earth create are fixed in number. If they are not held by the people, they are held by the government. The situation is like that with rainfall: if

there is an overabundance in summer, there will be a drought in autumn. Anyone who claims he can make the public revenues adequate without increasing taxes is going to do nothing more than institute policies that covertly steal the people's profits, and that will do more harm than increasing taxes. These are the methods with which Sanghong Yang misled Han Wudi. The historian Sima Qian wrote about them to expose Wudi's folly."

They argued on with no resolution.[10]

Because Wang Anshi expected to augment the country's wealth, making the peasants better off and the central government solvent again, he did not hesitate to call for an expansion of the bureaucracy (just when Sima Guang and others were decrying its bloated size). A larger force of bureaucrats was needed to implement the new programs. We know, in fact, that the increase was considerable: the number of bureaucrats rose from 24,000 in 1067 to 34,000 in 1080, a jump of 41 percent.[11] In response to those critics who protested early on against this consequence of the New Policies, Wang maintained that the increase in revenues from the programs would dwarf the additional expenditures on bureaucratic salaries.[12]

In many respects what Wang hoped to put in place was a new corps of bureaucrats who would be empowered and motivated to take an active role in local economies. Paul J. Smith has described Wang's goal as a bureaucracy that would encourage local and regional officials to undertake entrepreneurial activity and compete with private interests in the marketplace.[13] A key aspect of Wang's plan was his desire to break the power and wealth of those he called "engrossers" (*jianbing*). Wang used the term to designate men who aggrandized wealth and exploited others, whether the exploiters were rich guild merchants in the capital or landlords in the provinces. The engrossers sapped the economy of its well-being. They were the landholders who issued usurious loans to small farmers in lean years and then confiscated their land when repayment was impossible. They were the merchants who controlled prices for their own advantage, operating monopolistically by buying and selling huge quantities of goods.

It was precisely such wealthy actors in the economy whom Wang wanted to cripple with several of his reforms, including the Green Sprouts, Tribute Distribution, and State Trade policies. But to compete with these private interests, the state had to become entrepreneurial itself. Wang insisted, therefore, that once the new bureaucrats were appointed they be entrusted with broad discretionary powers. They should be given exclusive authority over whatever task they oversaw. They should not be limited to fixed terms in office but should remain until their assigned goals were accomplished. They should have the power to choose their own subordinates, like-minded men with whom they could work effectively. Lastly, they should be encouraged to experiment and to try new methods to achieve their goals. Given such leeway, the new breed of bureaucrats should be able to overcome the power and corruption of the engrossers, liberating the stagnant economy and allowing it to flourish.[14]

Wang's critics, however, did not see these goals. Watching in frustration through the early years of Shenzong's reign, as the young emperor's confidence in Wang grew, all that the political opposition saw was a plethora of new regulations and an administration apparently obsessed with enriching itself. In a debate before the emperor in 1071, the senior statesman Wen Yanbo challenged Wang, saying, "Our founding emperor's policies and regulations are all still in place. They need not be expanded upon, turning the people against us."[15] Wang responded that if all of the necessary policies and regulations really were in place, the government would not be in debt and the nation's borders would not be threatened. Wen Yanbo said that nothing more was needed than to administer and enforce the old regulations conscientiously. Wang said that his reforms were intended to put such conscientious administrators in office and to facilitate their work. Wang went on to cite the case of Zhao Ziji, who had implemented Wang's Civilian Security program early on in the prefecture of Zhenliu. Zhao's measures exposed several serious cases of extortion and intimidation (presumably, by engrossers) that had previously gone unreported to the authorities. "Civilian Security is intended to root out just such crimes," Wang commented, "and yet critics say that it adds to regulations and disrupts people's lives. I do not understand them."

As Wang Anshi's New Policies were promulgated in a steady stream of imperial decrees, they gave rise to an equally persistent chorus of protest. One after another, high-ranking officials came forward to lodge their complaint. The New Policies were attacked on broad philosophical grounds: they were denounced as Legalistic, for they were said to put wealth and profit before humane administration, just as they valued rule by law over rule by moral suasion.[16] The reforms were also discredited in all their particulars: the Green Sprouts Policy, for example, was said not only to be unworkable, but to be a certain path to rural disaster. Local officials would overzealously force the loans upon farmers who did not need them and bankruptcy would be widespread. Also, the program would destroy the private moneylenders, whose function was useful and could never be fully replaced by the government.[17] Each of Wang's policies was criticized in turn.

The objections sometimes delayed the emperor's approval or limited the regions over which the policy was implemented, but always it seemed the result was the same: Wang's policies were eventually adopted anyway. Then one dissenting official after another was demoted at the urging of Wang and his allies; or the statesman removed himself in protest, requesting reassignment to the provinces. Sima Guang resigned and went to Luoyang, where he was eventually joined by the Cheng brothers; Ouyang Xiu retired to Yingzhou; Lü Gongzhu was demoted and sent as prefect to the same place; Fu Bi, the former grand councilor, left for Bozhou; Fan Chunren was demoted and sent to Hezhou; Fan Zhen retired; and Wen Yanbo was sent to Heyang.

Initial Dissent

Su Shi, being younger, was not so prominent as these senior leaders of the opposition. Yet he, too, was vocal in his criticisms of the reforms. In a series of memorials written during 1069 and 1070, he argued against virtually every one of the changes.[18] The centerpiece of Su's critique is his own "Ten Thousand Word Memorial," which identifies and discusses problems with Wang's plans.[19] Su Shi's writings attracted the attention of both sides in the ongoing debate. Impressed by the boldness of Su's objections, Sima Guang and Fan Zhen recommended him for appointment to the Bureau of Policy Criticism.[20] Conversely, Wang Anshi personally intervened to block commissions for which Su Shi was being considered, and denounced him to the emperor.[21] Wang is also said to have been behind some charges of misconduct that were now brought against Su. It was alleged that when he accompanied his father's remains back to Sichuan, Su had used the government boat to transport and trade privately in salt. The case against him was pressed by the censor Xie Jingwen, who happened to be Wang Anshi's in-law. Both Sima Guang and Fan Zhen defended Su before the emperor, saying that the charges were unfounded and stemmed from nothing more than Wang Anshi's enmity towards Su.[22] Fan Zhen even specified the injustice of the case against Su as one of the causes of his own retirement from government service. Nevertheless, because of the pressure of the investigation, Su Shi requested reassignment out of the capital in 1071, and was appointed vice prefect of Hangzhou.

Su Shi's string of dissenting memorials of 1069 and 1070 is filled with thoughtful objections to the particulars of Wang Anshi's reforms. Many of these repeat the substance of what other Conservatives, as they came to be known, were saying. Still, Su's arguments are marked by their thoroughness and appeal to pragmatic considerations. Here is Su on the shortcomings of Wang's Tribute Distribution and Price Equalization Policy, which put the government's fiscal intendants in competition with private merchants:

> The activities of merchants have many variables and are not easy to carry out successfully. Often they pay their money far in advance of a purchase or wait until long after a sale to collect their due. Thus they cooperate with each other in various ways and engage in complicated dealings to increase their wealth many times over. Now, if the government wants to purchase the same commodities, it must first set up offices and staff them. The expenses for record-keeping and salaries will be considerable. On top of that, the government will buy only goods of the highest quality and will pay only in cash. Therefore, the price the government pays will inevitably be higher than what the private merchants pay. When the government decides to sell, the same restrictions will apply. How can the government ever hope to make the kind of profits merchants make?[23]

Others of Su's disagreements with the New Policies are interesting for the candor with which their author views not only the proposed reform, but also existing practices, as in his comments on Wang's plan to remove poetry and rhapsodies from the *jinshi* examination. Su concedes that from a literary point of view the policy papers and essays that Wang favors are of greater utilitarian value than poetry and rhapsodies. As indicators of how effective a man will actually be in office, however, prose essays are just as useless as poetry. Su supports his point by recalling the early-Song statesman, Yang Yi, whose literary work was flowery and vapid, but whose conduct in office was highly principled. He also refers to the erudite scholars Sun Fu and Shi Jie. Their prose was esteemed for its forcefulness, but they were by temperament so eccentric and uncompromising that they would not have made good officials. Poetry and the rhapsody should be retained because they are traditional and are no worse, as barometers of potential, than other written forms. But Su's main argument is that examinations, whatever their form, ought to count for little in the entire process of deciding whom to place where in the bureaucracy. The purpose of exams should be merely to lay before the central government a pool of potentially able men. The real test of these men should be their performance early in their career. Men may be advanced for consideration on the basis of their words, but they should be employed on the basis of demonstrated administrative ability.[24]

Wang's Tribute Distribution Policy sought to institutionalize government regulation of the private economy; and his exam reform sought, in Su's interpretation at least, to solve the problems of the recruitment and assignment of officials through procedural changes. Su's objections to both policies may be linked to his criticisms of the New Policies generally. Wang's was a vision of government that smacked of mechanistic regulation. Both the means and the ends were wrong. Wang spoke abundantly of the need to enrich the state, and he set out to do so by expanding the bureaucracy and its regulatory role in virtually every sphere of life. For Su Shi, Wang's programs seemed bound to lead the nation even further in the wrong direction.

This, of course, was the basis of much of the disapproval of Wang's reforms. It did not matter that Wang also stressed, as James T. C. Liu has emphasized, the need to cultivate "human talent" (rencai) among the bureaucratic class.[25] This aspect of Wang's program went largely unnoticed by the Conservatives, probably because the tasks these talented men would be entrusted with struck the opposition as so fundamentally unnecessary and unsound. Yet while Su Shi's criticisms have much in common at this most general level with those of other opposition leaders, philosophically he was particularly qualified as a critic. As early as 1061, as we have seen, Su Shi had developed a whole series of positions on the emotions, human nature, and governance that virtually assured heated disagreement with Wang Anshi at the end of the decade. Most of Su Shi's positions on these larger issues were not commonplace among the Conservatives, and certainly not in the systematic form Su had presented them.

Although, given his general outlook, it is readily understandable why Su Shi should object to most of the New Policies, we still must ask why he was so categorically negative about them.[26] Was he not being unfair and partial to voice blanket disapproval? The New Policies, after all, were not presented all at once as a systematic restructuring of the government. They are often treated as if this were the case; but, in fact, the major policies were introduced piecemeal and adopted one by one after a period of debate on each. Why did Su Shi find not any of them to his liking?

The question becomes more troubling when we remember that Su himself had called for sweeping reforms just a few years earlier, in his exam essays of 1061. This was the man who had warned that complacency among officials was a grave threat to the nation, and that the realm's present course would, unless changed, lead to disaster. He had also said that boldly innovative officials were now needed. They would necessarily cause great turmoil as they did away with wasteful and self-serving bureaucratic procedures; they would be attacked and slandered by officials who sought to preserve things as they were. In the Southern Song, Zhu Xi raised this question about Su Shi's apparent inconsistency; and it has been brought up again in recent times.[27]

There is inconsistency, at least in the simple sense that Su Shi had changed from a would-be reformer in 1061 to an opponent of everything new that the government was considering in 1071. There is also partiality, that is, an unwillingness really to consider certain of Wang's programs on their own merits. This is easy for us to recognize and admit, for Su Shi himself admits it years later, as we shall see. The causes of Su's bias against Wang are more difficult to pinpoint.

The most distinctive section of Su Shi's "Ten Thousand Word Memorial" is not that which dissects the particulars of Wang's reforms, explaining the misconceptions on which they are based, or that which assails the harm that the reforms, with their emphasis on material gain and harsh regulation, will do to the "customs" (*fengsu*) of the nation. The most distinctive section is the third, in which Su Shi urges the emperor not to allow Wang to destroy the "ordering principles" (*jigang*) of the realm. The ordering principles Su Shi has in mind are specifically those embodied in the government's primary organ of policy evaluation and rectification, the Censorate. During the first hundred years of the Song, this institution was an extraordinarily powerful and effective agent for policy review.[28] Su Shi thinks that Wang Anshi has jeopardized the Censorate's function by packing it with his own men and by intimidating the other censors into silence. Aside from his pride in the institution itself, Su's comments reveal much about his estimate of Wang Anshi and his own commitment to ideological pluralism. The relevant sections of Su's memorial are excerpted below:

> From Qin and Han times through the Five Dynasties several hundred censors lost their lives because they spoke out against an imperial policy. However, from the Jianlong reign period [the Song's first] until today not a single censor has been incriminated for speaking out. Even when there was some slight blame, the man was soon allowed to rise again in officialdom. Censors are permitted to "receive complaints borne upon the wind" [i.e., protect the anonymity of plaintiffs], and the charges are considered without regard for the rank or demeanor of the man who lodges them. The censors do not care if the accused is high- or low-ranking. If the censor's words touch upon the actions of the throne, the Son of Heaven himself assumes a penitent expression; and if the issue concerns the halls of government, the grand councilors of state admit guilt . . .
>
> Now, the censors have not necessarily all been worthy men, and their opinions have not necessarily all been right. But rulers have nurtured

their aptitude for sharp criticism and have given them weighty powers. Why? To ensure that treacherous officials are rooted out just as they sprout, and to correct the problems inherent in a highly centralized administration. Today, our laws and regulations are strict and comprehensive, and the Court is free from corruption. We certainly do not have any treacherous officials. However, you raise a cat to catch mice. Just because right now you have no mice, you do not teach a cat not to catch them . . .

I remember hearing my elders say when I was young that what the censors said usually accorded with public opinion throughout the empire. What public opinion favored the censors also favored, and what public opinion attacked the censors also attacked . . . Today opinion everywhere is in tumult; rancor and outrage converge from all directions. The drift of public opinion is easy enough to see. And yet the censors look at each other and say nothing, leaving everyone, both here and in the provinces, disappointed. When the custom of challenging officials and policies is strong, even timid men may be roused to join in. But once the practice loses its vitality, the most daring of men will not be stirred to action. I fear that from today on our present manner will become customary. Censors will all be the executive official's own men, and the ruler will be isolated. Once this ordering principle is abandoned, what disaster will not follow? . . .

"Superior men unite harmoniously but do not have identical views. Unscrupulous men have identical views but do not unite harmoniously."[29] To unite harmoniously is like blending different flavors in a broth; to have identical views is like adding water to water.[30] That is why Sun Bao said, "The Duke of Zhou was the most lofty of sages, and the Duke of Shao was the most worthy of men. Still, the two were in disagreement with each other, as the classics record, but they did not try to harm each other."[31] . . . Let us imagine that everyone's speech is identical and everyone's opinions in agreement, so that when one person sings, everyone answers in turn—what is wrong with that? But what if by some slight chance an unscrupulous man infiltrates the group? How will the ruler ever know? This is my reason for urging that the ordering principles be preserved.[32]

Few of the memorials written to protest to the implementation of the New Policies at this time are argued at such a high level. But at the same time that he seems to be reflecting so dispassionately on the usefulness of the Censorate, Su Shi is dropping hints of his real feelings about the man behind the reforms. What if, Su keeps asking, an "unscrupulous man" or a "treacherous official" were to seize power when the Censorate was so weakened? This is precisely what Su believes has already happened, and to Su's mind there is no clearer proof of Wang's disingenuousness than his manipulation of the organs designed to assure policy criticism. (The term "executive official" [*zhizheng*] is not even a hint, it is an explicit reference to Wang Anshi. The term was used specifically to designate the vice grand councilor [*canzhi zheng-shi*], the position Wang held when this memorial was written.)

The word "treacherous" (*jian*) brings up a related but knotty problem. Su Shi's father, Su Xun, is the reputed author of an essay supposedly written in the early 1060s that warns against entrusting Wang Anshi with power. The essay, entitled "On Detecting Treach-ery" ("Bianjian lun"), never refers to Wang Anshi by name, but it has long been understood as a diatribe against Wang. The essay is adroitly written, developing arguments about foresight and inevitabil-ity; and it became widely anthologized as a model of expository prose. Su Xun's authorship was never questioned until the Qing dynasty, when some scholars suggested that the essay may have been composed in the Conservative camp during the factional strife of the 1080s and 1090s and anachronistically attributed to Su Xun to further discredit the man who had initiated the reforms.[33] The problem is for now in-soluble. External evidence supports the case for Su Xun's authorship, since other sources (including Zhang Fangping's tomb inscription for Su Xun and a letter by Su Shi) refer to the essay as Su Xun's own.[34] But when one returns to the essay itself, it seems too incredibly presci-ent to be believed. Those who cannot accept it as a document from the early 1060s (Su Xun died in 1066) conclude that the "supporting" sources were also tampered with.[35]

Whether or not Su Xun wrote "On Detecting Treachery," the essay is true to the spirit in which his son viewed Wang Anshi in 1070. Su Shi is categorically opposed to the New Policies because he does not trust the man who conceived of them, and he does not trust him because he sees him taking steps to silence all opposition. Su Shi was not alone in this perception,[36] but with Su Shi the issue of Wang's true intentions (his "treachery") and his intolerance of dissent are of fun-damental importance. As a consequence, it appears that Su Shi could never accept that the stated purpose of particular reforms was their real intent. Su Shi witnessed, for example, Wang's creation of bureaus that seemed designed to extract more money from the people, though Wang disavowed such a goal. A man, Su Shi says, sets into the forest with a pack of hunting dogs and falcons but claims he is not going to hunt. He should not be surprised when people do not believe him.[37] Su Shi did not believe Wang, especially when he decided that Wang was attempting to suppress all protest.

Protest Poetry from the Provinces

Su Shi's departure from the capital in 1071 began a new phase of his life. For the next several years he was moved from one eastern prefecture to another (Hangzhou, Mizhou, Xuzhou, Huzhou), where he served as prefect or vice prefect. These are rich years, in which Su's life, interests, and writings broaden perceptibly. Distanced from the capital, Su felt freer to let his energies flow outside of the issues around which national politics swirled. It is no accident that this is his first period of greatness as a poet, and also the period in which his interests in the other arts and in Buddhism flourished.

Nevertheless, there are certain aspects of his activities during these years in the prefectures that remain quite directly connected to national politics. The most conspicuous of them is Su's continued protest against the New Policies, which were in force throughout the decade of the 1070s. In the early years of the reforms, Su had used the formal memorial to express his dissent; now he turned to poetry and other literary forms to attack or satirize the reforms and their consequences. Although, numerically, these poems are but a small fraction of the literary work Su Shi produced during the 1070s, this small corpus of works is significant for two reasons. Its existence reveals traits of Su's personality—boldness, captiousness, and stubbornness—that made up an important side of him. Also, these poems led straight to a celebrated event in Su's life, and indeed in Song literary and judicial history: his arrest and trial in 1079 on charges of having defamed the emperor and Court. Today the trial may in retrospect seem to have its preposterous elements, but at the time it was a deadly serious business (Su came close to losing his life) and it affected Su Shi profoundly.

Years later Su Shi accounted for his protest poems this way: "Previously, our former emperor summoned me before the throne and questioned me about ancient and current affairs, charging me thereafter always to speak my mind on policy issues. Later, I repeatedly expressed my views [viz., in the memorials of 1069–1070], but they were not adopted. Then I turned to writing poetry, in which I expressed my criticisms obliquely, using subjects metaphorically. I hoped that these poems would be transmitted upward and eventually move and enlighten His Majesty."[38] Su Shi's poems did not have their desired effect. All they succeeded in doing was annoying the leading reformers in the capital. The offending poems were included and perhaps featured in collections of his poetry that were being printed then. Book printing was a technology new to Su Shi's generation (for poetry, at least), and the fact that Su's poems were being printed and widely disseminated figures prominently in the indictments against him.[39]

A series of five quatrains entitled "Mountain Villages," which Su Shi wrote in 1073, uses references to hardships in the lives of the commoners to comment sarcastically upon the effects of the New Policies. To judge from the frequency with which these particular quatrains are specified in the indictments against Su and other accounts of the charges, they must have been particularly offensive. One of them alludes to the ill effects that the Green Sprouts program of crop loans had upon peasant farmers:

杖藜裹飯去忽忽	With bramble staff and bundles of cooked rice he hurried off,
過眼青錢轉手空	Yet the copper coins passed through his hands in a flash.
贏得兒童語音好	What he's won is a son whose accent has improved,
一年强半在城中	More than half the year they've spent in town![40]

The crop loans required farmers to spend long periods away from their fields, making frantic trips to town first to obtain the loans in the spring and then to repay them in the fall. Once they arrived at the prefectural offices, bureaucratic procedures and unscrupulous clerks often kept the farmers waiting for weeks on end before they could complete their business.[41] Here, Su refers to improvement in a son's rustic pronunciation, brought on by such an extended stay in the city, as the only gain a farmer realized from the program. Su explains elsewhere that corrupt officials found ways to tempt and defraud the unworldly farmers of their loan money. Just when the loans were issued, the government wine shops would stage elaborate entertainments, including gambling and prostitution. Many farmers would squander all the cash they had just been given ("copper coins passed through his hands") and end up returning to the countryside with nothing left.[42]

Another of the quatrains concerns the salt monopoly that, tightened under the New Policies, had the effect of eliminating salt from the diet of many commoners who lived in rural areas:

老翁七十自腰鐮	An old man of seventy wears a sickle at his waist,
慚愧春山筍蕨甜	He's grateful the bamboo and bracken on spring hills are sweet!

豈是聞韶解忘味	Is it Shao music that made him forget the taste of food?
邇來三月食無鹽	It's been three months since he had salt for a meal.[43]

It was Confucius who upon hearing Shao music (the legacy of the ancient ruler, Shun) did not notice the taste of the meat he ate for the next three months.[44] But the old man has no such distraction. His meals have no flavor to forget.

Sarcasm of a different kind, combined with a frankly personal tone, accounts for the effect of a much longer poem that was also singled out by the censors as slanderous. It is a poem Su addressed to his brother, when Su was serving as vice prefect of Hangzhou and Ziyou (Su Che) was instructor in a provincial school in Chenzhou (Wan Hill). The poem opens with a reference to Ziyou's height and develops from it themes of moral loftiness and degradation:

戲子由	*Teasing Ziyou*
宛丘先生長如丘	The Master of Wan Hill is tall as a hill
宛丘學舍小如舟	But his Wan Hill study is as cramped as a boat.
常時低頭誦經史	He constantly lowers his head to recite his classics;
4　忽然欠伸屋打頭	When he suddenly straightens up, he knocks it on the ceiling.
斜風吹帷雨注面	Winds blow his curtains, rains splash his face;
先生不愧旁人羞	He is not ashamed, though others think it demeaning.
任從飽死笑方朔	So let overfed fellows laugh at Fang Shuo:
8　肯為雨立求秦優	Better to stand in rain than be the Jester of Qin.
眼前勃蹊何足道	The domestic squabbles before his eyes, what do they matter?
處置六鑿須天游	His senses in check, he roams the heavens.
讀書萬卷不讀律	He reads ten thousand scrolls but no regulations,
12　致君堯舜知無術	Knowing there is no way to make his ruler a sage.
勸農冠蓋鬧如雲	Agriculture inspectors' caps and canopies are as turbulent as clouds;

41

送老虀鹽甘似蜜	In older years pickled greens taste sweet as honey.
門前萬事不挂眼	The myriad affairs beyond his gate do not catch his eye,
16 頭雖長低氣不屈	Though his head is hung low his spirit's unbent.
餘杭別駕無功勞	The vice prefect of Hangzhou has not served with distinction,
畫堂五丈容旂旄	But his painted hall, fifty feet high, flies long banners.
重樓跨空雨聲遠	His storied house touches the sky, keeping rain's patter distant,
20 屋多人少風騷騷	Rooms many and occupants few, the wind rattles through.
平生所慚今不恥	Deeds he was always ashamed of now he routinely performs,
坐對疲氓更鞭箠	Sitting before weary refugees who are whipped in turn.
道逢陽虎呼與言	Meeting Yang Hu on the road, he calls him over to talk,
24 心知其非口諾唯	His heart knows it's wrong but his mouth utters "yes."
居高志下真何益	What good is living high if your aims are low?
氣節消縮今無幾	His spirit is worn down until there's little left.
文章小技安足程	Literature is a minor art, what does it count for?
28 先生別駕舊齊名	You, sir, and the vice prefect used to be equally acclaimed.
如今衰老俱無用	Now we are getting old both useless to our realm,
付與時人分重輕	Let the world decide which one's the greater poet.[45]

Line 7. Dongfang Shuo is the Han scholar and wit who once complained to the emperor that the dwarfs who tended the royal stables had the same grain stipend that he had: "The dwarfs are about to die from overeating, while I am about to starve."[46]

Line 8. Jester Zhan of Qin, who was himself a dwarf, made fun of the palace guards—tall, strapping fellows—because they had to stand out in the rain. The Jester here is analogous to ministers close to the emperor who would do anything to stay in favor.[47]

Line 13. The inspectors are the fiscal intendants (*tiju guan*) sent to the prefectures to implement the crop loans program.[48]

Line 23. Yang Hu is an official Confucius disapproved of. Once however, when he met Yang on the road, Confucius accepted, temporarily at least, Yang's invitation to join the local government.[49]

Lines 1–16 describe Su Che's humble but moral existence. Lines 17–26 describe Su Shi's exalted but compromised life. The last four lines suggest that there is at least one field in which the two men are comparable—literature—but it is of little importance, compared to the matters broached earlier.

The crucial contrast throughout this poem is between Su Shi's job as a vice prefect and Su Che's as a scholar. Su Shi's post necessarily involves him in the implementation of the New Policies, while Su Che in his non-administrative post can remain detached and uninvolved. He does not have to keep up with all the new regulations. There is an element of conventional humility here: Su Shi's implying that he has not stuck to his principles so well as his younger brother. But what distinguishes the poem is the strong sense of guilt it conveys, despite the pretense of jocularity. In letters to friends, Su described the anguish of having to preside as judge over offenders against the new laws, especially the salt laws in Hangzhou; and he records, almost unbelievably, that each year seventeen thousand persons in the Liangzhe circuit are incriminated for violating the stringent salt monopoly imposed under the reforms.[50] Here, Su evokes his anguish in a poem.

There was sometimes an obsessive quality to Su Shi's criticisms. He expresses them occasionally when we least expect them, that is, when he is in the midst of some quite unrelated subject. In 1072, for example, he wrote an inscription for a hall in which a friend, Zhang Cishan (Xiyuan), housed a large private collection of stelae. When Su Shi wrote about people's calligraphy or painting collections, he often addressed the problem of how to justify interest in these "mere diversions." This is the theme of his inscription for Zhang Cishan's building, Ink Treasures Hall (Mobao tang), in which Su develops at considerable length the idea that different men have different notions of what is worthwhile in life and that all of these are subjective. Moreover, since one can find pleasure in virtually any activity, no matter how seemingly insignificant, "it is wrong for people to laugh at what another person likes purely on the basis of what he himself likes." The argument suits the occasion. But then Su tacks on an unexpected paragraph:

> Mr. Zhang Xiyuan of Piling comes from a family that has for generations been fond of calligraphy. His collection of calligraphic works from ancient and modern times is extensive. Now he has carved them all onto stelae and has built a hall to house the stelae. He asked me to write an

inscription for the hall. I am a native of Shu, and in Shu there is a proverb: "Those who study calligraphy waste paper, but those who study medicine waste human lives." This saying may be trivial, but it illustrates a larger truth. There are men in the world who desire to become famous for great deeds. They take what they have studied, though it has never before been tested, and implement it in government policy. Will they not waste far more lives than the aspiring doctor? Today Mr. Zhang combines the abilities of several men in one man, but his position is not worthy of his talent. He lives at leisure throughout the year, with nothing to which he can apply his heart and knowledge. That is why he amuses himself with calligraphy. I myself can see that he will not continue in abandonment for long. If he maximizes his capabilities and communicates them to others, he is bound to be used prominently in the government. He should know that government policy can waste many more men than an aspiring doctor. I hope he takes my words as a warning.[51]

Clearly this ending, which really does not fit the piece it is attached to very well, is yet another expression of Su's disapproval of what he took to be the maliciousness of the New Policies government.

Finally, there is a distinct group of poems that concentrate on the personal shortcomings of the men leading the reform movement. There was, of course, a whole set of new ministers ushered in by Shenzong's adoption of Wang Anshi's policies. Wang himself resigned once briefly in 1074 over disagreements with his subordinates and criticisms of his policies. He resigned permanently in 1076 and retired to his estate outside of Jinling. But the New Policies, administered by Wang's one-time favorites, remained in effect for another ten years.

In poems written for his own friends and fellow Conservatives, Su Shi characterizes these reformers harshly. They are upstarts and opportunists; they are brash, insincere, and without compassion. It is hard to know what Su Shi hoped to accomplish with these poems. It seems most unlikely that they could have altered the emperor's trust in the reformers. Unlike Su's other poetic protests, exemplified above, these poems do not describe the sufferings of the masses or the dilemma of prefectural officials who, like Su, had to enforce the seemingly cruel laws. These compositions are personal attacks on a whole group of high officials. They are probably best understood as the literary overflow of Su Shi's frustration and indignation. The slurs are almost all contained in poems sent to friends.

The ingenuity and erudition of these poems save them from being bald and uninteresting insult. Su could afford, of course, to be indirect and allusive. His friends, who were like him embroiled in the exceptionally hostile and polarized politics of the day, would understand what he meant, no matter how vague or opaque Su's language might seem to us today. Here is a poem Su wrote matching one by Liu Shu:

仁義大捷徑	Virtue and duty are a handy shortcut;
詩書一旅亭	The Songs and Documents are a roadside inn.
相夸綬若若	They praise each other, tassels fluttering,
猶誦麥青青	And still they chant "The Wheat Is Green."
腐鼠何勞嚇	A rotting rat: why bother to shoo anyone away?
高鴻本自冥	The soaring goose disappears on its own.
顛狂不用喚	No need to wake them from their wild revelry,
酒盡漸須醒	When the wine is gone, they will sober up.[52]

This is the explication Su would later provide during his trial:

This poem criticizes the men whom the Court has recently promoted and employed. They look upon virtue and duty as a mere shortcut and consider the Songs and Documents as temporary resting spots. They are all seduced by the seals and tassels of office, as well as rank and salary. They avail themselves of the Confucian classics to advance and resemble the scholars who Zhuangzi said use passages in the Songs and Documents to justify robbing graves. That is why I referred to "The Wheat Is Green."[53] The poem also implies that these unscrupulous men are as attached to their official salary as the owl [in Zhuangzi] was to the rotting rat, when it needlessly shooed the wild goose away.[54] They are as inebriated with profit as other men are drunk with wine. But when the wine is exhausted they will sober up all by themselves.[55]

Su Shi could be more indirect than this. A gift of Fujian tea sent to him in 1073 prompted a lengthy poem of gratitude. His poem begins by cataloguing the fine points of various Fujian teas, using the physiological and moral terms common in evaluations of the arts and of human character (e.g., "Its bones are pure, its flesh glossy; it is harmonious and upright"). Then Su goes on to describe the inferior but popular varieties known as "scrub tea" (caocha), produced mainly in the Liangzhe region of the Yangzi Valley, where many of the reformers came from:

草茶無賴空有名	Scrub teas are unreliable, their fame undeserved.
高者妖邪次頑懭	The best kinds are beguiling and wicked; the rest are obdurate.
體輕雖復強浮沉	Light of substance, they can rise or sink at will;
性滯偏工嘔酸冷	Inert but clever by nature, they leave a sour aftertaste.

The poem returns then to the excellent qualities of the gift, with lines that speak quite matter-of-factly about the Fujian tea. Su ends his poem with this couplet:

| 此詩有味君勿傳 | This poem too has flavor; you must not pass it around. |
| 空使時人怒生癭 | In vain it would make some men break out in boils from anger.[56] |

In the confession Su Shi submitted during his trial, he admitted what the careful reader of the poem would have suspected: that these few lines, hidden among truly apolitical ones, were meant to denounce the opportunistic reformers.[57]

One last example is contained in a quatrain inspired by a peony tree that blossomed in the winter:

一朵妖紅翠欲流	A single blossom of bewitching red is bright enough to shimmer.
春光回照雪霜羞	Beside its glistening spring hues the snow and frost are ashamed.
化工只欲呈新巧	The Transformer seeks only to make a show of newness and ingenuity,
不放閑花得少休	And won't allow dormant blossoms their little rest.[58]

Such a poem may of course be taken at face value, and it makes perfectly good sense as a comment on the early peony. But in the politically polarized world of 1073, when this was written, a phrase such as *xinqiao*, "newness and ingenuity," had special significance that no one would miss, especially when found in a poem written by Su Shi and followed by a line about depriving something of its rightful rest. These were precisely the sort of terms used by the Conservatives to denigrate Wang Anshi's *New* Policies (Wang himself had tried to invest *xin* with positive connotations, but his success was not complete). Su Shi later confessed that the poem was intended as a criticism of the reform leaders who harassed the common people mercilessly.[59]

Arrest and Trial

It was not customary among the Conservatives to produce such poetry of political and personal attack. Su Shi stood alone as a literary dissenter. Furthermore, even Su's friends thought he was excessive and reckless in his poetic references to the New Policies and their administrators. It is recorded that in 1070, when his memorials against the reforms were going unheeded, Su Shi would return from his duties in the evenings and chat with friends. He would amuse everybody with jibes at the reformers. Wen Tong, the bamboo painter, repeatedly asked Su to stop but he paid no attention. When Su was sent out of the capital, to Hangzhou, Wen Tong urged him, in a farewell poem, to refrain from writing poetry in his new post and not to inquire about affairs back at the capital. Later, when several of Su Shi's Hangzhou poems were used as evidence in the case against him, people realized how farsighted Wen Tong's advice had been.[60] Another close friend, Huang Tingjian, made this observation in a letter of caution to his own nephew, "Su Shi's writing is the most marvelous in all the world. His only shortcoming is that he likes to rebuke people. In that you must not follow him."[61] A similar assessment is given by other contemporaries, and was echoed by several later critics, including Yuan Haowen and Wang Fuzhi, who remark coldly that Su had only himself to blame for the troubles that befell him.[62]

Su Shi was aware of his singularity as a critic. "By nature I am careless with words. When I write to someone, whether or not he is a close friend, I always express my innermost feelings. If I leave anything unsaid, it is just like a morsel of food stuck in my throat. I must spit it out before I can rest."[63] Years later, Su was delighted to find similar sentiments in a poem by Tao Qian. Su then rephrased his earlier account of himself. "Words are produced by the heart and are held in the mouth. Sometimes they will offend people if you spit them out, but will offend yourself if you swallow them. I have always thought it better to offend other people, and so I have always spat them out."[64]

Su Shi might have foreseen the consequences of his choice. In 1074, a certain Zheng Xia, who had served as a judicial inspector in Guangzhou, submitted a memorial to the throne that described disastrous consequences the New Policies were having on the commoners in his region. Zheng accompanied his memorial with a painting he drew of the miserable scenes of impoverished and vagrant peasants he had witnessed. The painting made a deep impression on Shenzong, who questioned Wang Anshi about it. Zheng's protest is said to have contributed to Wang Anshi's temporary resignation from the government that year. And yet two of Wang's powerful ministers, Lü Huiqing and Deng Guan, succeeded in having charges brought against Zheng Xia for having improperly gained access to the Court. Zheng was briefly incarcerated in the Censorate prison. The following year, the intrepid Zheng denounced Lü Huiqing in another memorial. Shortly thereafter, the censor Shu Dan arrested Zheng en route to a new post, searched his belongings, and found correspondence to friends (some of which appears to have been planted in Zheng's possession by his enemies) that touched upon the failings of the reforms. Zheng was again brought to trial, for having conspired against the government; and Lü Huiqing, who was now the vice grand councilor, demanded that he be put to death. Shenzong opted for leniency, however, and Zheng Xia was demoted and sent back to the prefectures.[65]

Su Shi's arrest came in 1079. It was precipitated by an obligatory memorial of gratitude Su submitted upon taking up his new appointment as prefect of Huzhou. In the memorial Su said that in giving him another post outside the capital, the emperor must have known that he did not understand current affairs and would be unable to keep up with "those who had newly been advanced."[66] The wording sounds much like the English term *upstarts*. The censor He Dazheng accused Su Shi of insulting the Court, and told of numerous other instances in which he had slandered the administration. "Today our institutions are not yet complete and customs are not yet unified. This is precisely the moment we should make clear to the empire the basis for imperial reward and punishment. Faced with such a vile person as Shi, can we simply desist and not take action?"[67]

Two other censors also filed indictments, citing well-known articles of the Song criminal code that prescribed the death penalty for such crimes as were now imputed to Su.[68] Shu Dan identified several offending poems, including those in the "Mountain Villages" series and the poem sent to Ziyou, discussed above. Su Shi had not only vilified the Court, he had committed lèse majesté by discrediting the emperor himself. Li Ding listed four crimes for which Su deserved punishment: 1) he had not, when given the chance, repented of his earlier slanderous writings; 2) he continued to produce arrogant and contrary statements; 3) his writings, false as they were, fomented unrest among the people; and 4) he knew that such gross disrespect was a crime punishable by death, but he had maligned the reforms anyway because he was embittered over not being employed at the Court.[69]

Su was arrested at the end of the seventh month, taken off under armed guard ("like a common criminal or thief," he said),[70] and escorted back to the capital.

> I said farewell to my wife and children, and left a letter for my brother Che, instructing him about my posthumous affairs, since I was certain I would die. When we crossed the Yangzi, I wanted to throw myself into the river. But the soldiers guarded me closely so that it was impossible. When I was first put in prison, I intended to starve myself to death. But

the emperor sent a special envoy to impose restraints, and thus the jailors did not dare to be particularly cruel to me.[71]

Su Shi's family proceeded up the Grand Canal to rejoin Su Che at the southern capital (Shangqiu, Henan). Their trip was interrupted when the Censorate issued an order to search Su's belongings for additional incriminating writings. The family's boat was surrounded and soldiers ransacked the possessions, terrifying young and old alike. The women, as Su would later record, reviled him in his absence: "This is what comes of all his writing. What good did it ever do us? It brings nothing but this fright." They burned many of the manuscripts the soldiers left. Su had the impression that 70 to 80 percent of his manuscripts were lost in the episode.[72]

Once he arrived in the capital Su was remanded to Raven Terrace, the Censorial prison, where he would remain for over four months while charges against him were considered. In the meantime, investigating officials were sent from the capital to Hangzhou. They searched the entire prefecture for poems that Su Shi had left (that is, with friends or inscribed on walls) and managed to find several hundred compositions, which they brought back to be used as evidence against him.[73] During his incarceration, Su was repeatedly interrogated about the meaning of specific poems and prose pieces.[74] At first he denied that any of them touched upon current affairs, except the quatrains in the "Mountain Villages" series. He also denied that he had exchanged poems with friends that were critical of the Court.[75] (It is obvious that Su tried at first to protect his friends. The "Mountain Villages" poems are almost the only ones in which a friend could not be implicated.) Gradually, however, Su began to change his plea. There is every reason to think that beatings accompanied the interrogations. Su himself says that he became convinced that he would die as a result of the jailors' "abuse"; and a distinguished fellow prisoner, locked in an adjoining cell, remarks that the sounds of "cursing and humiliation" that came from Su's cell, and which lasted through the night, were more than he could bear to hear.[76] Eventually, then, Su admitted that one after another piece did indeed contain remarks intended to disparage the government. By the end of the tenth month, when the case against him was finalized, Su had elucidated for his prosecutors political criticism in several dozen of his writings. Su's explications, together with the indictments filed against him, are preserved in a work known as *The Poetry Trial at Raven Terrace*.[77]

There was an element of overzealousness on the part of Su's prosecutors. One of the indictments against Su, for example, alleged that slanderous statements had been made in an inscription Su wrote for a friend's country estate and garden. Su had politely praised the selection of the site of the estate, not far from Kaifeng, as one that would allow future generations of the clan to serve in the government without forgoing the beauties of nature. This was preferable to having to choose between the two, as most men in the past had to do. "Superior men of ancient times did not necessarily serve in the government, nor did they necessarily refuse to serve. But if they chose to serve they forgot their persons, while if they refused to serve they forgot their sovereign."[78] Li Yizhi, a professor in the imperial academy, had charged, incredibly enough, that with these words Su sought to put an end to loyalty and respect for the emperor.[79]

An even more unfounded accusation is recorded, and even featured, in some accounts of the trial. Su Shi had written two poems describing a pair of juniper trees that grew outside the residence of his Hangzhou friend, Wang Fu. One of the poems, which uses the enduring grandeur of the trees and the imagined straightness of their roots as an analogy for Wang Fu's upright character, contains the couplet:

根到九泉無曲處　　The roots go down to Nine Springs
　　　　　　　　　　　　without any twist or bend;
世間惟有蟄龍知　　In all the world only
　　　　　　　　　　　　the hidden dragon knows.[80]

Grand Councilor Wang Gui pointed out to Shenzong that while His Majesty, an imperial dragon, soared gloriously through the sky, Su Shi concerned himself only with dragons hidden deep within the earth. He must have disloyal intentions. The interpretation drew the rebuff it deserved. Shenzong remarked, "How can you read poetry like that? He was just describing junipers. It has nothing to do with me."[81]

At times, Su Shi himself seems to be overzealous, though undoubtedly for very different reasons. Once he decided to plead guilty, he did so quite extravagantly. He began to identify even seemingly conventional lines in his poems—references to friends being unappreciated by the world or suffering impoverishment—as covert criticisms of the government.[82] At a drinking party one day Su had penned a couplet about sentencing anyone who mentioned politics to an additional cup of wine. Even this, Su now asserted, deserved to be considered as part of his offense.[83] Su had apparently come to the conclusion that he could not but improve his own chances, and those of his friends, by cooperating in incriminating himself.

But the excesses, on both sides, need not distract us from the central issue. Su Shi had angered the most powerful men at the Court by criticizing their policies and questioning their character. In printed poems that circulated widely, he referred sarcastically to the "benefits" of the reforms; he likened Court discourse to the croaking of frogs and drone of cicadas; he wrote of prefects beating and torturing their people to collect taxes; and he described recovering abandoned corpses beside a city wall.[84] He showed, moreover, no sign of letting up.

During the Yuanyou period, years later, Su was charged once again with having defamed the emperor in writing. This time he considered the charges totally unfounded, and in his defense he wrote revealingly about his earlier trial: then, he says, I expressed my disapproval of the New Policies in poetry, hoping to change the emperor's mind. Li Ding, Shu Dan, and He Zhengchen accused me of slander and eventually I was incriminated.[85] Nevertheless, there was at least some resemblance between what I had done and what I was charged with: political protest was taken as slander. Su's later sense of injustice made him realize that the accusations brought by Li Ding and others in 1079 had at least some basis.[86]

There was, of course, ample precedent in earlier dynasties for this use of poetry to express political protest. The tradition Su had in mind when he decided to use metaphors to express oblique criticism is one that could be traced back through the Tang all the way to the *Book of Songs*. Even the personal element in the protest, describing the leading ministers as frogs and insects, is well attested in earlier poetry. What is difficult to find a precedent for is such a fractious political situation that included such a brazen literary dissenter as Su Shi. It was because Su, despite the volatility of the politics of the era, persisted in composing poems of outspoken criticism that he was punished. Li Ding and the others surely intended to make an example of Su to intimidate the opposition into silence. They had tried to do just that with Zheng Xia a few years earlier, but their success was incomplete. Before the reform era, Northern Song officials took great pride in their dynasty's record of tolerance for remonstration. We have seen this in Su Shi's comments on the Censorate ("[for a hundred years] not a single censor has been incriminated for speaking out"), and similar sentiments are expressed elsewhere.[87] Officials had grown bold and were accustomed to speaking their minds. However, it was one thing for a Court official charged with remonstration to criticize policy, and another for a lowly prefect to circulate caustic poems. Moreover, Wang Anshi's administration, bent as it was upon "making customs one" (the phrase occurs in He Dazheng's indictment of Su), imposed less tolerant standards. Men like Zheng Xia and Su Shi ran up against a new reality. In Su Shi's case, the new technology of printing was also a factor, as the Qing-dynasty scholar Zhao Yi has pointed out.[88] Those in power were quick to recognize the enhanced potential of the written word, even in poems.

Naturally, Su Shi had his defenders. Soon after he was imprisoned, Zhang Fangping and Fan Zhen petitioned the emperor for clemency.[89] They allowed that Su Shi might have penned some ill-considered lines, but pleaded that these did not warrant the severity of the charges against him. Of course, Su Che also wrote on his brother's behalf, and offered to be punished in his place.[90] More significantly, even certain members of the reform government, including Grand Councilor Wu Chong and Wang Anli (Wang Anshi's younger brother) argued that the action against Su Shi was unwise. How, they asked Shenzong, would he like to be remembered as a ruler who was intolerant of criticism and could not make allowances for men of exceptional talent?[91] It is said that even the sickly Empress Dowager Cisheng commiserated with Su Shi's plight shortly before her death in the tenth month. Upon learning of Su's incarceration, she remarked to Shenzong that Su must have been the victim of unwarranted persecution. She also reminisced sadly about how pleased her husband (Renzong) had been when the Su brothers first passed their examinations, convinced that he had discovered two future grand councilors.[92]

Eventually and, it must be admitted, for reasons that are not entirely clear, the emperor decided to spare Su Shi. At the very end of the twelfth month, it was decreed that Su Shi be demoted and reassigned to the undistinguished mid-Yangzi prefecture of Huangzhou. There he was to hold the titular office of assistant militia commandant. Moreover, he was forbidden to memorialize or speak out on government affairs. This was not the punishment that the censors had hoped for, but it was severe nonetheless. Three of Su's closest allies—his brother, Wang Shen, and Wang Gong—were also demoted and banished to minor prefectural posts. Fines were imposed on twenty-five other men who had been implicated as recipients of Su's treasonous writings, including Zhang Fangping, Fan Zhen, and Sima Guang.

In the following year, Su wrote out a casual note on his vegetarian habits that provides some glimpse, despite its offhand tone, of the meaning his incarceration had for him. I have never been comfortable, Su explains, with the practice of killing animals for my table; but my craving for certain foods, especially clams, was such that I could not bring myself to desist. However, ever since my imprisonment I have not killed a single thing: "It is not that I hope for some reward. It is simply that having experienced such worry and danger myself, when I felt just like a fowl waiting in the kitchen, I can no longer bear to cause any living creature to suffer immeasurable fright and pain simply to please my palate."[93]

As much as his incarceration had frightened him, Su Shi could still occasionally be less than circumspect as a poet. On the way to his Huangzhou exile, Su stopped to see Chen Zao, the son of a man he had served under in Fengxiang. Chen Zao showed Su a painting he had of a rural marriage scene in a nearby Zhuchen Village. The village lay within the prefectural boundaries of Xuzhou, where Su had been prefect a few years before. Su wrote two poems. The first describes the idyllic life the village had traditionally enjoyed, as depicted in the painting. The second poem touches on the present circumstances:

我是朱陳舊使君	I myself am Zhuchen's 　　former prefect;
勸農曾入杏花村	To encourage agriculture 　　once I went to Apricot Blossom.
而今風物那堪畫	But the scene there today, 　　who could bear to paint it?
縣吏催租夜打門	County bailiffs demanding taxes 　　bang on doors at midnight.[94]

This is precisely the sort of poem that had nearly cost him his life.

CHAPTER THREE

Towards Theories of Knowledge and Self

Motivated largely by his disagreement with the reform government and the profound effect it had upon not only the politics but also the world of thought of his day, Su Shi went on in the 1070s, 1080s and, 1090s to develop a body of alternative thought. Su Shi was not content, in other words, simply to keep criticizing the reforms in memorials or to belittle the men behind them in his poems. Now he sought to engage them philosophically, arguing against several of Wang Anshi's underlying ideas and offering his own in contrast. He did this first in short prose pieces (essays, prefaces, and letters to friends) and later in voluminous commentaries on the Confucian classics. The origins of some of Su's ideas can be found in his examination portfolio of 1061; but the scope is more philosophically ambitious now, going far beyond issues of statecraft. Still, it is a distinctive mark of this philosophy that as wide-ranging as it is, and as detached from worldly problems as it may sometimes become, it is generally possible to discern a connection back to a contemporary view against which Su Shi was reacting. We will examine first here a broad theme or orientation that became prominent in Su's writings during the 1070s, and then turn to the further development of key ideas in his commentaries on the *Book of Changes* and *Book of Documents*.

On Analogies for the Sun

A man who was blind from birth did not know what the sun looked like and asked sighted persons. One told him it resembled a copper platter.

The blind man struck a copper platter and listened to the sound it made. Days later he heard a bell and concluded that it was the sun. Another person told him the sun glows like a candle. The blind man ran his hand along a candle to determine its shape. Days later he picked up a flute and concluded that it was the sun.

The sun is very unlike a bell or a flute; and yet the blind man did not understand the difference because, having never seen the sun himself, he relied on other people's descriptions. The Way is far more difficult to see than the sun, and a person who has not reached it is just like a blind man. When someone who has reached it tries to tell him about it, no matter how clever his analogy or wise his guidance, it will be no better than the platter and the candle. From platter to bell and from candle to flute, where will it ever end, this groping from one approximation to the next? Men who speak about the Way today, whether they are trying to name what they have seen or are trying to imagine that which they have never seen, are all going about it wrongly. Does that mean that the Way cannot be sought at all? Master Su says, "The Way may be caused to come, but it cannot be sought." What does "caused to come" mean? Sun Wu said, "Men skilled at warfare cause their enemy to come to them. They do not allow themselves to be brought before their enemy."[1] Zixia said, "The artisan perfects his craft by remaining in his workshop, and the gentleman causes the Way to come to him through learning (xue)."[2] Without seeking, it comes of its own accord. Is this not what is meant by "causing it to come"?

In the south there are many underwater divers who live in daily contact with the water. By the age of seven they wade into the water, by ten they float on it, and by fifteen they dive under it. That they are able to dive is no coincidence. They have acquired something of the Way of water. Because they live in daily contact with water, by age fifteen they have attained its Way. Even as an adult, however, a person who has never been around water will be frightened by the very sight of a boat. Furthermore, any brave northerner who asks a diver how he dives and then attempts the feat himself, relying simply on words for guidance, is bound to drown. All men who are bent on seeking the Way but do so without pursuing learning are like northerners who would thus learn the art of diving.

Formerly, officials were selected on the basis on their poetry and rhymed prose. They studied all sorts of things and did not set their minds on the Way. Today, officials are selected for their knowledge of the classics. They know to seek the Way but do not devote themselves to learning. Mr. Wu Yanlü of Bohai is a man whose mind is set upon learning. Now that he is seeking to be recommended to the Board of Ritual I have written this piece on analogies for the sun to instruct him.[3]

This is probably the most succinct statement Su ever wrote on his understanding of the Way and progress towards it. In the sizable

descent the piece makes in its closing paragraph, from the lofty philosophical issues to the situation of Mr. Wu, one sees how intellectually
developed Su Shi's opposition to the examinations, under the New
Policies, had become. Su's argument with the reforms has moved to a
new stage, one barely glimpsed in the memorials of 1069–1070. He is
still protesting, but his protests are supported now by a systematic
intellectual outlook. He is no longer attacking particulars of Wang's
program, and the larger ideas in his dissent are no longer merely those
of Confucian convention.

In almost any other context, the language Su uses to describe
how men used to study ("they studied all sorts of things and did not
set their minds on the Way": *zaxue er buzhi yu dao*) would be censo-
rious. But to Su this represents a desirable approach, and one vastly
preferable to that dominant at the present. What was it that people
formerly studied? In another piece Su provides a list that includes
"astronomy, geography, music, the calendar, palaces and temples,
clothing and implements," prescriptions for ceremonies, and sanctions
from the classics and histories.[4] We see from this that the swimming
analogy must be interpreted with care. The issue is not simply that of
reflective versus unreflective activity. The key point for Su is that the
skill or Way not be directly or deliberatively sought (as in the sun
analogy). The swimmer learns through constant exposure, but he does
not have his mind set on achieving that final mastery of skills. Those
who do are the northerners who drown.

On the New Learning and Other Fallacies

When we think of Wang Anshi, we think first of his ambitious program of institutional reforms. If we then consider where he fits in the
age-old tension in Confucian discourse between the two realms of the
inner and the outer (*nei/wai*), we naturally conclude that his preference must be for dealing with the latter. This, after all, was the basis
for many, if not most, of the objections Conservatives voiced to the
reforms. Wang Anshi was neglecting the transforming power of those
inner virtues and Confucian charisma. Instead, he intended to rely
upon external forces of policy, law, and institutional change. Hence
the charges of Legalism. However, there are serious flaws with any
such description of Wang Anshi's thought, flaws that prevent us from
understanding the alternative vision Su Shi developed.

Despite the abundant attention he gave to restructuring
bureaucratic institutions, when Wang wrote about the sage or superior
man (that is, the ones who would oversee the new order) he empha-

sized the inner approach to the Way. In fact, Wang suggests that this particular orientation is precisely what distinguishes superior from inferior men: "The sage looks inward, while men of the world look outward. Those who look inward delight in discovering their nature, while those who look outward delight only in gratifying their desires."[5]

It is a difficult task to try to reconstruct today Wang Anshi's philosophical views.[6] Most of the commentaries he wrote, including those on the Confucian classics (which were mandated for the examinations) and those on Buddhist and Taoist texts, were lost when his reforms fell into opprobrium.[7] Snatches of the lost commentaries survive as quotations. In addition, Wang's collected works contain some fifty essays on philosophical topics, most of which were probably written early in his career (before he came to power).[8] What does survive does not present a thoroughly systematic body of thought, and certain inconsistencies may be detected. Still, divergences on key points from the views Su Shi would articulate certainly can be identified and discussed.

In a letter to a friend, Wang tried to explain his beliefs about perception and innate knowledge, drawing upon Buddhist terminology to do so. The friend had suggested to Wang that *se* (appearance, color) is the basis for all living things. Wang replies that this merely explains the visual aspect of things.

> What you are talking about is like the shimmering heat waves that flicker in the air, or what is illuminated by sunlight entering through a crack. Living things combine *shi* [knowledge, discernment] and pure water together with this to achieve their form. Living things [ordinarily] have their perceptions obstructed by thinking. If there is no sunlight, they are unable to see. But once the thinking obstruction [*yin*: "darkness"] is removed, then the light of the mind shines forth. Even without sunlight everything is clearly perceived. This is what is called the basis of all living things.[9]

The language is obscure and the concepts are not entirely clear. But it is obvious that Wang believes in some type of innate knowledge or intelligence (the "light" of the mind or heart, *xinguang*) that is potentially so powerful and illuminating that even in darkness the mind perceives everything clearly. This intelligence, moreover, is universal but seems to be actualized only in a presumably small number of persons who succeed in overcoming the blockages brought on by cogitation and worry.

In another passage, Wang tells the story of a peasant boy, Zhongyong, who at the age of five suddenly began to write out poems though he had never studied reading or writing previously. Wang concludes, "Zhongyong's enlightenment was something he received from Heaven. Because he received it from Heaven, he was far more gifted than even an ordinarily talented man."[10] What makes this passage more than a curiosity are observations in Wang's essays that corroborate a belief in a supreme kind of knowledge that precedes sense perceptions and is not dependent upon worldly experience. In the course of explaining how Confucius could have equated "humaneness" with refusing to look at or listen to anything that was not in accord with the rites, Wang observes that "what [the sage] held on to was extremely restricted and what he adopted was extremely close to hand: all men who have a heart and body possess it."[11] Wang is speaking of human nature. He goes on:

> Before listening, there is a prior good hearing. Before looking, there is a prior good seeing. Before speaking, there is a prior speech. Before moving, there is a prior movement. Among Confucius's disciples, this could be said only of Yanzi. It is not the ear that makes for good hearing; and if you do not know what does, you will never hear all that there is to hear in the empire. It is not the eye that makes for good seeing; and if you do not know what does, you will never see all that there is to see in the empire. Clear hearing and clear seeing are processes the ears and eyes can engage in, but the causes for clear hearing and clear seeing are not brought about by the ear and eye.[12]

And elsewhere in the same essay: "To have good hearing without listening, to have good seeing without looking, to realize without deliberating, to arrive without departing, these are capabilities that human nature possesses intrinsically and through which the daimonic (*shen*) is born."[13]

We saw above that Wang Anshi holds that "the sage looks inward, while men of the world look outward." In different passages Wang's explanations of this vary, or rather the key terms vary, but his general preference remains the same. In one place Wang equates human nature, which lies within the individual and which he comes to understand by looking inward, with Pattern (*li*) in the world at large: "Those who devote themselves to study seek to master Pattern. Those who devote themselves to the Way seek to master the nature. In external things the nature is none other than Pattern; thus [those who are devoted to the Way] attain an understanding of Pattern throughout the world."[14] The suggestion here is that since Pattern is nothing more than human nature abroad in the world, the goal of understanding it may be attained simply by looking inward and mastering one's own nature.

In his essay on the "Hongfan" chapter of the *Book of Documents*, Wang presents another account of the Way and the sage. Several points are noteworthy. Wang divides people into three classes according to their understanding of the Way: the commoners, superior men, and one supreme sage ruler. The highest understanding or realization of the daimonic and quintessential principles of the universe, that acquired only by the sage ruler, empowers him to set the Way for the rest of the world. When we examine how that understanding is achieved, it seems to come entirely from a kind of mental discipline: focusing the mind until it arrives at One (the mystic unity that is the very first issue of the Way). The highest truths are discovered directly, without any mediating presence of the things of the world.

> To follow the Way and to obey [Heaven's] decree but not to understand, this is the condition of the commoners. To follow the Way and to obey [Heaven's] decree while understanding, this is the condition of the superior man. To guide [lit. "make the Way for"] the myriad things and follow nothing, to issue decrees to the myriad things and to obey none himself, it is only the most daimonic of persons in the empire who can attain to this ... The daimon follows the will; or if there is no will, it follows the intent. When the will arrives at the One, it is said to be quintessential. It is only the person who has achieved the perfectly quintessential who can combine all the daimons of the world. If the quintessential and the daimonic are united and not allowed to separate, then all the transformations of the world lie within me. That is why I will be able to guide the myriad things and follow nothing, to issue decrees to the myriad things and obey nothing.[15]

A word should also be said here about Wang Anshi's views of the relation between human nature and emotions (*qing*). There are several places in which Wang declares his opposition to the idea that the nature is either good or bad. There are also passages in which Wang describes the emotions as being an essential part of human nature and explains that they are as capable of leading to good as to bad conduct.[16] (In all of this, Wang's position is reminiscent of Su Shi's.) The situation is complicated, however, by passages in which Wang affirms the rightness of the Mencian view that human nature is good,[17] as well as by passages which go a step further to intimate that what is inherently bad, dangerous or undesirable in persons is their emotions. Wang thus makes certain statements that Su Shi never would have made, particularly when he associates the emotions with desires (*yu*). His observation about men of the world looking outward only to gratify their desires is part of this view. He also says:

> To nurture life is humaneness, and to protect the *qi* is rightness. By doing away with the emotions and resisting the desires, one can perfect human nature in the world; and by cultivating the daimonic and attaining insight, one enters into the domain of the sages.[18]

> By doing away with the emotions and resisting the desires, one gives rise to daimonic insight.[19]

The problem with emotions and desires seems to be that they direct the attention outward to the material and sensual world, whereas enlightenment is to be found in the inner realm, in fact, the realm of human nature.

Wang Anshi's philosophical views may be difficult to reconstruct or understand in their entirety, but it is less problematic to gauge the effect that his rise to power had upon the examinations and, consequently, the scholarship of the reform period. In 1071, Wang overhauled the format of the examinations, as we have seen. Poetry and rhapsodies were cut from the prestigious *jinshi* exam, and classics became the dominant focus. Students were questioned on the "general meaning" of the classics and were also required to write essays and policy papers on specified topics. The stated intent was that students "should strive to comprehend the larger meaning and not be allowed to stick completely to commentaries and subcommentaries."[20] At the same time, other exams, including a classics exam that had stressed memorization and one in the "various fields," were abolished. Wang also took the bold step of terminating the study of the *Spring and Autumn Annals*, a work in which he found little significance and is said to have repudiated as "worthless fragments of Court bulletins."[21]

But these changes were not enough. There were still too many different interpretations of the texts that remained on the exams.

> Today there is a shortage of talented personnel. Moreover, learning is not uniform. Divergent views contend with each other, and therefore the Way and virtue are not one.[22]

> In ancient times both the Way and virtue were made one to unify the customs of the empire. When scholars planned some action in the world, there were no divergent views. Today each school has a different Way and each person a different notion of virtue. Moreover, on the basis of their own likes and dislikes or delight and anger they transmit altered accounts of actual circumstances.[23]

To help eliminate the "divergent views" in 1073, a Bureau of the Meaning of the Classics was established, with the full support of

Shenzong.[24] Wang Anshi, Lü Huiqing, and Wang's son, Pang, were put in charge, and younger scholars were recruited as assistants. The bureau was to establish definitive interpretations of the three classics Wang considered the most important to his program: the *Songs*, the *Documents*, and the *Rites of the Zhou*. The commentaries were not yet complete when Wang resigned temporarily in protest the following year. Father and son withdrew to Jiangning, where they evidently threw themselves into the task. In the following year, when Wang returned to power, he submitted the three finished commentaries to the throne. He reminded the emperor again of the crucial role such scholarship had in ordering the nation: "I observe that the use of classical learning to mold scholars began with the eminent former kings, whereas to allow false doctrines to delude the people is the custom of ages of decline."[25] Wang himself had done the commentary on the *Rites*. Pang is credited with the other two. The three works, which came to be known as the *New Meaning of the Three Classics* (*Sanjing xinyi*) were printed by the imperial academy. Copies were distributed to schools in the prefectures. The *New Meaning* became the standard interpretations required on the examinations.

Wang Anshi's efforts to reform learning continued even after his permanent retirement in 1076. He turned his energies to a lexicographical study, which he entitled *Explanations of Characters* (*Zishuo*). When this work was eventually completed in 1082, it, too, was submitted to the throne and became part of the New Learning, as Wang's doctrines were called, complementing the classics commentaries. This work also was subsequently lost, although certain passages survive.

Explanations of Characters is premised on at least three beliefs: 1) The Chinese writing system is not an artificial system of signs devised subjectively by humankind. Instead, it is a system the sages developed in imitation of the forms and principles of nature. 2) Because of this origin, each graphic element of a character, as well as the relations between graphic elements, has its significance. Each element has a meaning that contributes to the meaning of the entire character. 3) The effect of clarifying the true meanings of the characters, and ensuring that they are adopted by all scholars, will be no less than to "make the Way and virtue one" (*yi daode*) throughout the realm.[26]

The idea that the writing system somehow imitated natural forms or patterns was, of course, an ancient one. However, no one before Wang Anshi, I believe, tried to extrapolate so much from the old tales of Cang Jie and the bird tracks. In a sense what Wang did in his study, as Winston Lo has pointed out, was to analyze every character as if it were formed in accordance with the ideographic principle (*huiyi*), where each graphic component of a character does have a meaning and each meaning contributes to the sense of the whole character.[27] But this is only one of the six principles governing the formation of characters, and the number of graphs it accounts for is very small.

The results of Wang's "explanations" were often imaginative, to say the least. Some examples follow:

Ginger 薑 : ginger is able to forcibly resist 彊禦 the myriad illnesses, that is why it is called 薑 .

Wealthy 富 : to share 同 fields 田 [i.e., to have many fields] is to be wealthy.

Poor 貧 : to divide up 分 your cowry shells 貝 [ancient currency] is to be poor.

Toad 蝦蟆 : it is popularly said that toads are attached to the place of their origin. If you take them to a distant place, in one night they will return. Even if you place them further away 遐 , by nightfall 暮 they will return. That is why they are called 蝦蟆 .[28]

Scholars from Song times down to the present have ridiculed Wang's study for this sort of false etymology.

Wang's book remains significant, however, both for the influence it had upon scholarship through the remainder of the Northern Song and for what it reveals about its author's thinking. As described here, *Explanations* is the fourth and final step in Wang's quest to facilitate access to Pattern and finally, of course, the Way itself. Before achieving power, Wang variously asserted in his essays that these ultimate truths were intimately connected with human nature and could be discovered by looking inward. Once in office, Wang recast the examinations to concentrate attention on the key texts that embodied these truths. He ensured, at the same time, that scholars would no longer be distracted by literary requirements. Later, his own commentaries on the key classics proved necessary to guide scholars toward the underlying meanings and to silence heterodox interpretations. Lastly, Wang nearly dispensed with the classics themselves, as he sought to demonstrate that the eternal truths were embodied even in individual characters. We have it from Cai Bian, Wang's son-in-law, that the *Explanations* represented the culmination of Wang's scholarship and that in it Wang had elucidated the "Patterns of Heaven and Earth and the myriad things."[29]

A twelfth-century scholar, Zhao Bingwen, observed that "once Wang's learning became dominant, scholars spoke of nothing besides the Way and virtue (*daode*) and human nature and Heaven's decree (*xingming*)."[30] This is the development that Su Shi is attacking in "On Analogies for the Sun." The notions that insight into the Way or into the secrets of the nature or Heaven's decree can be gained through concentration on just a small number of classical texts (interpreted by Wang's commentaries and his *Explanations of Characters*), that scholars do not need to "study all sorts of things," that historical study (e.g., the *Spring and Autumn Annals*) can be dispensed with, that literary accomplishment (e.g., poetry on the examinations) is unimportant—all these Su objects to, likening Wang's new brand of scholar to blind men who stray further and further from the truth, seizing as they do upon the wrong aspect of someone's analogy, and would-be divers who want to acquire the skill all at once from words rather than gradually from experience with the world. Elsewhere, Su Shi remarks on the irony that in his generation, as in no other before, printed books were abundantly available, and yet scholars "shut their books and don't look at them, indulging instead in baseless speculative chatter."[31] It is the same rush toward the Way that he has in mind.

There was more wrong with the New Learning than its choice of the wrong methods. It also imposed uniformity upon those who embraced it, so narrow was its focus and so rigid its delineation of what was correct. We recall Wang Anshi's concern that learning, the Way, and virtue were "not one," and his frustration over "divergent views" that prevented the empire from achieving a grand unity. But to Su Shi, Wang's attempts to thus unify learning and thinking were a kind of intellectual tyranny. In former times, Su Shi explains, people studied in order to enhance their native intelligence and to expand upon their knowledge. "But Mr. Wang's learning is just like making prints from a woodblock: they all come out looking exactly like the model." If you are content thus to fashion things without any differentiation or embellishment, Su asks, how will you ever produce anything of special value?[32]

In a letter to Zhang Lei, Su Shi changes the metaphor but reiterates much the same point:

> The decline of writing has never been as extreme as it is today. The cause may be traced to Mr. Wang. Now, Wang's own writing is not necessarily bad. The problem is that he wants to make everyone the same as he. Not even Confucius could make everyone the same: Yan Yuan was known for humaneness and Zilu for bravery, and the two never converged as one. Yet Mr. Wang wants to use his learning to make everyone in the whole world the same. Fertile lands all produce crops, but they do not all produce the same crop. It is only on infertile or salty fields that as

far as you can see there is nothing but yellow wildgrass and white reeds—that is Mr. Wang's sameness! Recently, Zhang Zihou told me that in his last years our former emperor was disturbed about the degeneration of letters and wished to reform the methods used to select scholars on the examinations. But he did not live to do so. Interested persons hold that the restoration of poetry and rhapsodies on the examinations together with the reestablishment of the *Spring and Autumn Annals* in the schools would be a great improvement.[33]

One of Su's supporters, Chao Yuezhi, went further in his criticisms of the dogmatism of the New Learning. With their efforts to "make the Way and virtue one," Wang and his followers had, according to Chao, hit upon a method of "stupefying the people" that was even more effective than that used by the first emperor of the Qin, who burned the books. Like the ancient tyrant, Wang Anshi sought to mandate a narrow intellectual orthodoxy that was incompatible with real inquiry or wisdom.[34]

The wider ramifications of Su's thinking on these issues also deserve some comment here. Towards the end of Su's 1069 memorial against the changes Wang had proposed for the examinations, the argument takes an odd turn as Su begins to warn against the growing popularity of Taoist and Buddhist doctrines among the scholarly class.

Long ago Wang Yan was fond of *Laozi* and *Zhuangzi* and the whole empire took him as their teacher. Customs deteriorated and eventually brought about the withdrawal southward [i.e., the loss of North China in 317]. Wang Jin was fond of Buddhism. He abandoned human affairs to practice his unorthodox teaching. Consequently the government of the Dali period [766–775] has been laughed at right down to today.[35]

Confucius seldom spoke about human nature, convinced that few could understand it. Zigong said, "One can hear about the Master's views on culture, but one cannot hear about his views on human nature and the Way of Heaven."[36] Beginning with Zigong, explanations of human nature and Heaven's decree (*xingming*) were not heard, and yet scholars today are ashamed if they do not speak about human nature and Heaven's decree. This is really so! Nowadays, all gentlemen consider the Buddha and Laozi to be sages, and booksellers in the marketplace sell nothing but books on Laozi and Zhuangzi. When you read their writings, they flow on and on, without saying anything apropos, and never stop. When you look at their faces, they appear transcendently blank and reveal nothing by which you might comprehend them. Yet these appearances are not even true! In fact, it is the nature of mediocre men to find comfort in lack of constraint and pleasure in irresponsibility.[37]

It may appear that Su Shi has lost sight of his memorial's proper subject, but that is not so. He is still criticizing Wang Anshi's proposal, but he is now criticizing it as being part of the regrettable drift of intellectuals towards Buddhism and Taoism. The fact that Su's two historical examples were both influential ministers and were both named Wang makes it very clear whom he has in mind. And Su repeats this particular criticism of Wang's New Learning in subsequent years, as do others.[38]

The great debate over whether Wang Anshi was really a Legalist or a Confucian has tended to obscure the importance of these other systems of belief in his thought. But Song scholars remark repeatedly upon this Buddhist and Taoist connection with the New Learning, especially as it shows itself in Wang's *Explanations of Characters*. In glossing the meaning of words in the Confucian classics, Wang had, they observe with disdain, drawn upon Buddhist or other "heterodox" schools.[39] In fact, Wang did more than that. He produced full-fledged commentaries on *Laozi* and the *Śūraṅgama Sutra* (*Lengyan jing*). But it is easy to overlook this aspect of his activities now because these commentaries have been lost, like most of his scholarly works.[40]

In his memorial of 1069, however, Su Shi probably has only a very general similarity between Wang and the non-Confucians in mind. The same interest in such topics as "human nature and Heaven's decree" that Su elsewhere identifies as characteristic of Wang's thought he here connects to Buddhism and Taoism. Both involve, for Su, turning away from human affairs and concentrating instead on questions of the great metaphysical truths. But to Su these are imponderables. They are the questions best left unasked because only unsatisfactory or even dangerously misleading answers are possible. Fascination with these problems is symptomatic, moreover, of intellectual sloth and deceit. Because men do not want to expend the effort necessary to gain understanding through experience of the world (like the would-be divers from the north), they give themselves up to hazy speculations, cultivating the appearance of profound transcendence. Su distrusts them on several counts.

Su Shi's own interest in and indebtedness to Buddhism is a large subject, and one to which we will keep returning. The passage translated above, written early in Su's career and addressed, after all, to an ostensibly Confucian emperor, gives no hint of the depths of Su's commitment to Buddhist values. But within that commitment there was room for Su to take exception to certain tendencies he noticed among believers (just as there was disagreement among the many Buddhist schools). Su's Buddhistic preferences turn out to be of a kind with the Confucian ones examined so far.

The two subjects of Buddhism and Wang Anshi converge again

in one of Su Shi's later colophons, in which his attitude towards the religion is much altered. A notice of Su's survives that was written on Wang's commentary on the *Avataṁsaka Sutra* (*Huayan jing*). Wang's commentary was restricted to a single chapter of the eighty-chapter sutra, the one in which the Buddha speaks. Wang had explained that this small section of the text contained its most profound statements and that the rest of the work was "merely the words of bodhisattvas." Su, of course, takes issue with this exclusionary approach. Actually, it moves him to recount a little story. Having once been told that pigs raised in Qianyang yielded the tastiest pork, Su dispatched a servant there to buy one. But on the return trip the animal somehow escaped and the servant substituted an ordinary pig in its place. At the banquet that followed, Su and his guests, unaware of the substitution, exclaimed over the special flavor of the meat. When the truth later came out, there was chagrin all around. Su concludes, "Today it's just that the truth has not yet come out about Wang's pig [his favored portion of the sutra]." Su continues: "Even the shouts of a butcher selling meat and the sound of a courtesan singing may bring about enlightenment. If the mind is pure and clean, even tiles and pebbles on the wall preach the supreme dharma. Yet he said that the Buddha's words are deeply profound and the bodhisattvas' words do not match them—he was speaking in a dream!"[41] Su is uncomfortable with the assertion that access to enlightenment is so textually exclusive.

Eventually, Su Shi would expand his view of knowledge until it encompassed far more than his disagreement with Wang Anshi. He comes to apply it, as a grand orientation, equally and freely to a range of topics. The following inscription, written to commemorate a huge sculpture of a thousand-armed Guanyin made by the Hangzhou monk Juze, suggests the breadth of Su's vision:

> Tasty dishes are made from lamb or pork, with the five flavors blended harmoniously in, and wine is made from glutinous rice combined with ferment. Everywhere the processes are the same. Now, the ingredients may be of the same quality, the amounts of water and heat constant, and the climatic temperature and humidity identical; but when two people make something, the results will not be the same. The fact is, recipes alone cannot guarantee tastiness. Nevertheless, cooks in ancient times never did away with recipes. Skilled cooks used recipes to produce marvelous dishes, while unskilled ones used them and produced at least an approximation of the desired result. The origin was the same for both, but they passed either through skilled or unskilled hands, and thus ended up either as excellent or crude. Seeing that the results were not the same, other people began to seek excellence without relying upon recipes

at all, hoping for marvelous results by rejecting past experience. "I know what makes for good wine and food," they said. They used an approximation of the correct ingredients and did away with measurements, believing that the result did not depend on these, and relied entirely upon their own ideas. It was, however, rare that the results they produced were not spat out by those who tasted them!

Today the defect in our field of studies is precisely this. Astronomy, geography, music, the calendar, palaces and temples, clothing and implements, the prescriptions for the capping ceremony and marriage as well as for burial and sacrifice, what the *Spring and Autumn Annals* approves of and rejects, what the *Rites* allows, what the punishments prohibit, the causes of the rise and fall of the dynasties, and the lives of worthy and unworthy men—these are the subjects to which all people who would study ought to devote themselves assiduously. But people say, "All these are not worth studying. We want to learn that which cannot be recorded in books or transmitted by teachers."

Zixia said, "To know each day that which you lack, and to remember every month that which you can do, that is devotion to learning."[42] Those who studied in ancient times could enumerate every day and every month what they lacked and what they could do. As for those who study today, who can say what they lack and what they are capable of? Confucius said, "Once I went the whole day without eating and the whole night without sleeping so that I could deliberate. It did no good. It is better to study."[43] From this we can see that to reject study and simply to deliberate is something that Confucius himself forbade, and yet it is something that people prize nowadays.

Moreover, this is true not just in our field of study. It is true in Buddhism as well. To fast and observe the monastic rules, to recite the scriptures, to construct pagodas and temples—these are the activities through which Buddhists should spread their teachings day and night. But presently many disciples consider it better to cultivate no-mind than to fast and observe the monastic rules, better to "be free of words" than to recite the scriptures, and better to "do nothing" than to construct pagodas and temples. Inside themselves they have no-mind, their mouths have no words, and their bodies no actions. All they do is eat to the full and relax. Thus they greatly cheat the true intentions of the Buddha.[44]

In the remainder of the inscription, Su praises the diligent efforts of Juze, who labored for thirty years on the enormous sculpture of Guanyin. We do not know whether Su Shi was personally close to this monk. But it is hard not to suspect that, personal ties aside, Su agreed to write this inscription largely because it provided him with an opportunity to hold forth on this favorite theme.

Another opportunity was given to Su a few years later, in 1078, when Zhang Zhifu asked him to compose an inscription for a studio he had built and earnestly named "Hall of Deliberation" (Sitang). One can imagine Su's delight. "No one in the world," Su's piece begins, "is as free of deliberation as I am. I spring into action whenever a situation arises and allow no time for deliberating."[45] In this piece, Su's aversion to cogitation (*wusi*) becomes, half jokingly, a way of explaining his proclivity for insulting people. He speaks his mind without first weighing the consequences. Whatever the special twist or application, and no matter how playful is his tone, Su keeps drawing on the same general commitment to knowledge gained through contact with the external world rather than through introspection. It came to be a commitment of such breadth and utility that one can, with the help of the opening lines of the inscription for Juze, picture Su pondering it even in his kitchen.

Commentaries on the *Changes* and *Documents*

In his two periods of exile (Huangzhou, 1080–1084, and Lingnan, 1094–1100), Su Shi wrote prolifically. The fact that writing was what had sent him into both exiles occasioned a certain amount of caution and no end of claims in statements to friends that he had given up the dangerous pursuit; but, in fact, the sheer volume of what Su produced during these years of confinement probably surpasses his output for any other comparable span of his life.

One of the types of writing he turned to in these exiles was commentaries on the Confucian classics. By the end of his second banishment Su had completed three lengthy commentaries: on the *Book of Changes*, the *Book of Documents*, and the Confucian *Analects*. It should be noted immediately here that these commentaries have never attracted much attention. They have always been considered minor works in the rich two-thousand-year tradition of classical exegesis. Indeed, one of them (the commentary on the *Analects*) was lost sometime during the Southern Song. The commentaries, moreover, have always been looked upon as a minor component of Su Shi's works. Su is remembered as a poet and also as a statesman, governor, and artist. No one thinks of him first as a classicist.

The irony of this is that sometimes, though certainly not all the time, Su Shi himself felt that his commentaries were his greatest achievement. In the final year of his life, for example, he confided to a relative that it was his commentaries (not his other writings) that made him think that his life had not been completely wasted.[46] A late entry from his autobiographical jottings yields a similar impression. At the end of his banishment to Hainan Island, when Su and his son, Guo, were making the sea voyage back to the mainland, the ocean became rough and Su sat up late into the night. It suddenly occurred to him that the manuscripts of his three commentaries were packed in his bags on board the boat. Since there were no copies deposited elsewhere, if calamity should befall the boat his interpretations of the classics would be lost to the world. The thought was too horrible to contemplate alone, and Su tried in vain to awake his snoring son to share his distress. But then Su realized that these circumstances actually ensured a safe ocean crossing: Heaven would not be so cruel as to arrange otherwise.[47]

For centuries scholars who sought to leave their mark had done so through commentaries on the classics. Reinterpreting the ancient canon was, and would remain, a primary method of presenting new modes of thought. Like many commentators, moreover, Su Shi in his journey back into these ancients texts was not just engaged in a scholarly enterprise unrelated to the controversies of the day. It is evident that his immediate motivation was to formulate his own alternative to the interpretations of the New Learning. This comes out clearly in several of Su's statements. Referring to his ongoing work on the *Documents* in Huizhou, Su observes how regrettable it is that "the New Doctrines [i.e., the New Learning] are dominant, while ancient traditions have disintegrated."[48] Likewise, several late poems present images of Su laboring away on the classical texts, oblivious of his miserable surroundings on the southern sea, determined still to combat the pernicious doctrines of the Han-dynasty usurper Wang Mang (i.e., Wang Anshi), or the heterodox philosophers Yang Zhu and Mozi.[49]

It is sometimes said that Su Shi completed his commentaries in Huangzhou, or that he finished his works on the *Changes* and the *Analects* there and wrote the one on the *Documents* in Lingnan. But from notes Su sent to his friends, it is obvious that he began all three commentaries in his first exile and took them all up again in the second. He continued to revise and expand upon them, and did not consider them complete until the last years of his life.[50] Actually, the *Changes* project is one that Su inherited from his father. Su Xun had been working on his own commentary on the *Changes* and had left it unfinished. There are occasional statements, by Su himself as well as his brother, that have the effect of minimizing Su's contribution to the project: Su is said merely to have continued his father's work, implying that the plan and gist were not his own.[51] This is almost certainly filial modesty. Su Shi worked on the *Changes* too long for it not to bear his stamp. Besides, most of his later references to the work make no mention of his father, suggesting that the son came to think of the commentary as his own.[52] Su Che was also active in this field. Che mostly tackled the classics his brother had not touched, producing commentaries on the *Spring and Autumn Annals*, the *Book of Songs*, and, stepping outside the canon, *Mencius* and *Laozi*.

A number of themes in both of Su's commentaries reflect quite plainly and unambiguously his continuing dispute with the New Policies. This antagonism is especially obvious in Su's work on the *Book of Documents*, whose focus on ancient political history lent itself to expressions of Su's dissenting views on statecraft.[53] As Su the commentator worked his way through this classic, he took advantage of the many opportunities its momentous speeches and historical narratives provided to iterate his positions on key issues of governance, such as reliance upon men rather than regulations, the importance of minimizing punishments (especially the death penalty), the respect that the ruler should have towards his people, and the crucial role that advisors should be given in policy formation.

Several of Su's comments on passages in the *Documents* allude with surprising specificity to the controversies of his day. A passing reference to the way land was distributed among the feudal lords by King Wu is seized upon by Su and used to challenge a divergent account of enfeoffment in the *Rites of the Zhou*. Su develops his commentary at this point into an attack upon the credibility of the text in the *Rites* generally, and upon "those scholars in recent years" who have sought to replicate the governmental structure it describes.[54] This is a transparent criticism of the reform movement and its heavy reliance upon the *Rites* (at the expense of attention to other classics, such as the *Spring and Autumn Annals*). Similarly, Su explains how "recent scholars" have misconstrued the words of the marquis of Yin, who in an exhortation to battle declared to his men that awesome sternness must prevail over compassion if affairs were to be satisfactorily concluded.[55] The words were appropriate on the eve of battle, Su points out; but they were not intended to serve as a general principle of governance, though they have in recent times often been adduced to justify harsh rule. Even Pan'geng's speech to his people on the necessity of moving their capital is seen to bear, in Su's interpretation, on issues facing the Song state.

> At the time, [Pan'geng's] people dared to gather together to express resentment and criticism. They suspected that he was going to establish

new policies and practice authoritarian rule, controlling them by means of unrelieved sternness. But Pan'geng was a humane ruler. What he used to instruct his people with was nothing other than constant and hallowed practices. He did not create *new regulations*.[56]

What Su admires in Pan'geng, and stresses about this event, is his appeal to ancient precedent, as well as the trouble he took to share with his people the reasons for his decision, and even to deliberate with them. Pan'geng's was not an administration that was as aloof and unpredictable as thunder or the gods.[57]

The *Book of Changes* is less singularly focused upon issues of statecraft. Still, Su takes advantage of those passages that do bear on such matters to convey his political philosophy.[58] The mention, for example, of the phrase "managing wealth" (*licai*) in "The Great Appendix" causes him to launch into a lecture that reflects his lingering hostility to the reforms, even though he does not refer specifically to them.[59] The topic of "managing wealth" was, after all, one of Wang Anshi's favorite themes. It is indeed the ruler's duty, Su asserts, to regulate the nation's wealth, and he should ensure that it circulates everywhere and is never blocked up. The great danger, however, is that instead of managing the country's wealth the ruler may actually appropriate it (the difference between *licai* and *qucai*). If he does this, he will lose the trust of the people and his laws will become unenforceable. Like many of the Conservatives, Su Shi seems always to have considered Wang's stated economic goals duplicitous. Wang's "management" was really designed all along to concentrate wealth in the hands of the imperial Court. And the consequences Su here describes are precisely those that he believed he had witnessed whenever the reforms were in place.

Su's commentary on the *Changes* also stresses the obligations of the ruler to his subjects. We recall that this orientation towards the will of the people was evident early on, in Su Shi's examination essays. But now, after what Su had witnessed in the intervening years, his articulation of it became insistent and extreme. A ruler must not force his people to do anything against their wishes. In Su's formulation, the people virtually determine the direction the nation will go. But the ruler is still essential; his role may in one sense be reactive—he responds to the desires of his subjects—but his subjects still need him as a center to rally around. Both of these functions of the ruler are brought out in Su's gloss on the *huan* hexagram, the symbol of scattering, in which he stresses the ideal ruler's composure and restraint in periods of civil disorder and unrest:

When the world is well governed, it resembles a great stream that flows peacefully and proceeds where it should. But when the world is in chaos, it is like a stream that overflows its banks in all directions and cannot be stopped. The water does not do this because it likes it. Something has appeared that obstructs the water's nature (*xing*), causing it to flood unceasingly. The obstructing force will eventually diminish, and the water will be able to recover its nature. It will select a course it is at peace with and return there. Ancient rulers who were good at governing never contended with their people. They allowed the people to choose their own course and thereafter guided them accordingly.

...The *tuan* explanation says, "The king goes to his ancestral temple," and the *xiang* explanation says, "The ancient kings presented offerings to the Supreme God and established the ancestral temple." Why? A ruler who takes action against the unrest and contends with his people is one whom the people dislike. But a ruler who takes his place amid the danger and does not seek fleeting comfort is one on whom the people rely. The ancient kings dwelled in the midst of scattering. They remained calm and did not contend but instead laid long-range plans. Once the ancestral shrines were established and the presentations to the Supreme God settled, the heart of the empire had that which bound and held it fast.[60]

Su Shi also expects the ruler to have a large capacity for self-denial, and a correspondingly strong commitment to improving the lot of his people. "The ruler looks upon his people as himself."[61] This is significantly different from the old Mencian notion of ruler as "father and mother" to the people. So sensitive is Su to the issue of abuse of power that when he comes to the *sun* hexagram (the symbol of lessening) and the *tuan* explanation that "the lower is diminished and the upper increased" (processes that are said to portend good), Su turns the text on its head, even though it is not at all certain that the original is meant to have political implications. First Su explains that there is really no such thing as diminution without increase. This particular hexagram just names one aspect of the dual process. But in case there are readers who might still suspect that the classic here implicitly sanctions exploitation of the commoners by the ruling class, Su observes: "The superior man strives to understand what is distant and grand. To him, diminishing those below to increase himself is to diminish himself, while diminishing himself to increase those below is to increase himself."[62]

References in the *Changes* to differentiations (between trigrams or the myriad things of the world) provide Su Shi with the opportunity to reiterate another tenet of his political views: that true harmony comes not from forced uniformity but from a blending of dissimilar views. We have seen this idea expressed in Su's opposition to Wang's suppression of dissent, and will meet it again in his experiences at the Yuanyou-period Court. Su must have been pleased by comments the classic offers on the *kui* hexagram (the symbol of strangeness and disunion), so many of which can readily be applied to this theme: "Heaven and Earth are separate and apart, but the work which they do is the same. Male and female are separate and apart, but with a common will they seek the same object. There is diversity between the myriad classes of beings, but there is an analogy between their several operations."[63] Su's gloss on such lines provides a decidedly political interpretation: "If people only want sameness and dislike difference, they will end up with disunion. Therefore, what I find beautiful is not necessarily congenial, and what I find vile is not necessarily hateful. He who follows along with me is not necessarily loyal, and he who resists me and goes off on his own is not necessarily disloyal."[64]

The Way and Human Nature

The Confucian classics also provided Su Shi with an opportunity to reexamine his understanding of key philosophical concepts and the relationships between them. It was, of course, particularly the *Book of Changes* and its appendices that encouraged this undertaking— the *Documents* seldom allowed Su to take leave of pragmatic issues of statecraft. There is much in Su's commentary on the *Changes* that sounds familiar—echoes of views expressed in earlier essays—and yet the nature of the classic pushes him towards the articulation of a grand cosmological scheme. It is, of course, a scheme that seeks to explain both the primal forces of the cosmos and human morality.

One of the ancient "Ten Wings" of the *Changes*, the "Treatise of Remarks on Trigrams," refers in passing to the classic's ability to help us acquire two kinds of knowledge: it allows us to overtake that which proceeds away from us, and to work our way back to the origins of that which proceeds toward us. Su Shi applies the idea to the sage: proceeding "upstream," he gradually gains insight into human nature and Heaven's decree. Then, enlightened by this knowledge, he goes in the opposite direction "downstream" to oversee and regulate all the myriad variations in human behavior and talent that spring from our quintessential nature. What is striking is the emphasis Su places on the starting point for these great quests: "The superior man prizes an understanding of human nature and Heaven's decree. Wanting to arrive at this, he knows that he must begin from what comes naturally (*qi suoyi ran zhe*) and proceed upstream to its origins. Now, the reason we eat is that we are hungry, and the reason we drink is that we are thirsty. The causes certainly are not external ones. People are able to eat and drink without studying how to do so. That they are naturally able is clear."[65] This is reminiscent of Su's old assertion that the *li* ("rites") have their origins in our natural inclinations. It is characteristic of Su to insist that any approach to the higher truths be rooted in, and accommodate, such unstudied behavior.

This entry in Su's commentary is amplified by another on the "Great Appendix." The classic simply says, "The alternation of yin and yang constitutes the Way. The extension of them is goodness, and their culmination is human nature." The passage raised two problems for Su Shi. First, it implies that the Way is knowable and describable: it turns out to be nothing more than the workings of yin and yang. Second, the passage posits much too close a link between the Way, goodness, and human nature for Su to be comfortable with or pass over it without comment. He reacts with this entry:

> The sage knew that the Way is difficult to describe, and so he borrowed the concept of yin and yang to describe it, saying "the alternation of yin and yang constitutes the Way." The phrase "alternation of yin and yang" refers to the stage before yin and yang have mingled and before material things have been generated. It is meant to illustrate a semblance of the Way and to make it less unfathomable. When yin and yang do mingle and generate things, the first one they generate is water. Water is at the juncture of existence and non-existence. It is what is present just as you leave non-existence and enter into existence. Laozi understood this. That is why he said, "The highest goodness is like water" and "Water is closest to the Way."[66] As for the virtue of the sage, although it can be named and described, it is not fixed in any single thing, just like water which does not have any constant form. This is the highest kind of goodness and the closest to the Way. Yet it is not the Way. Now, before water is generated, when the yin and yang have not yet mingled, there is a vast emptiness which contains no thing. But you cannot say there is nothing. This is truly the resemblance of the Way.
>
> Thereafter, yin and yang mingle and generate things, and then the Way comes into contact with things and generates goodness. Once things are generated, the yin and yang are hidden; and once goodness is established, the Way cannot be seen. That is why the classic says, "The extension of them is goodness, and their culmination is human nature." People who are humane see the Way and say it is humaneness, and people who are wise see the Way and say it is wisdom. Humaneness and wisdom are what the sage calls goodness. Goodness is the extension of the Way, but to label it the Way itself is not right.[67]

It is not difficult to see where this is leading. Su goes on to take issue with Mencius's pronouncement equating human nature with goodness. Why is Su Shi so obsessed with this famous opinion? One reason is that he sees it as a great impediment to learning. "It says 'The extension of them is goodness.' If one who would study the Way starts from its extension, then the Way [he learns] will never be complete."

This passage brings out more clearly than earlier ones Su's reservations about goodness as the focus for a program of self-cultivation or study. Goodness, as conventionally understood, is too fixed and abstract; and it is also incomplete. His digression about water above must be inspired by the first of these objections. It is only the highest kind of goodness that has no fixed form or manifestation. Lesser kinds are rigid. Indeed, they tend to be heavily prescriptive and therefore removed from immediate experience and impulse. And even the highest goodness is not as formless (i.e., unfixed) as the Way itself. Goodness is an effect or result of the dynamics of the Way, but it is only one result. Can eating when hungry be considered an example of goodness? And Su Shi will not accept a conception of the Way that is not broad enough to include such essential behavior as eating.

The cardinal virtues of humaneness and rightness (*ren, yi*) make a good test case. They are, of course, unassailable as exemplary manners of conduct; and yet Su Shi, true to his principles, maintains that in their highest form they are not dependent upon self-examination or even self-awareness: "[The sage] has a commiserating heart but never considers himself humane. He has a heart that knows to make distinctions [of merit and rank] but never considers himself to know rightness. He brings these to bear on everything he encounters. This is simply the way his heart meets things. It is other people, observing him from behind, who say that his commiserating heart is humane and that his heart that knows to make distinctions is one of rightness."[68] Su's inspiration for this, unlikely as it may seem, is the classic's account of how the forces in the trigrams generated the myriad phenomena of the world: "The strong and weak lines rubbed against each other and the eight trigrams moved each other. They excited the world with thunder and lightning, and moistened it with wind and rain. Sun and moon followed each other on their course, and cold and heat alternated. Those with the Way of the *qian* trigram became male, and those with the Way of the *kun* trigram became female." What Su seizes upon here is the idea of unreflective activity. He is not concerned here with the process of achieving sagehood, and it would be a mistake to think Su believes that one must be born a sage. He is simply trying to make the point that when the superior person appears to fulfill prescriptive norms of conduct, he does so unwittingly.

Involvement

The binary complementarity that is so fundamental to the *Changes* (e.g., unbroken and broken lines, the generative powers of the *qian* and *kun* hexagrams) gave Su Shi the opportunity to stress the importance of interaction or involvement in the human sphere. He reads the classic's descriptions of dynamic alternation between active (yang) and inactive (yin) phenomena in the cosmos or the trigrams and, extrapolating from them, affirms that the superior man will never permit himself to be solitary or aloof from the world in which he lives. This is probably the most original aspect of Su's interpretation of the classic. Also, although the theme appears in others of Su's writings, nowhere is it so prominent as in his commentary on the *Changes*. In fact, his interest in this classic may derive largely from its special suitability to the theme.

The following passage anticipates the drift of Su's position. Su begins with an account of the formation of the five phases or elements:

> Water is the most yin [of the phases] but it must await the One of Heaven to press upon it before it is generated. If its yin does not obtain a yang, there will be nothing to steam it and bring it to formation. Fire is the most yang [of the phases] but it must await the Two of the Earth to press upon it before it is generated. If its yang does not obtain a yin, then, with nothing for it to adhere to, it will never be manifest. All five phases behave similarly. All of them are generated by the pressing of yin and yang against each other. Yang pressing against yin generates water, wood, and earth. Yin pressing against yang generates fire and metal. If there is no pressing of one against the other, then although the resources of yin and yang may be present, the utility of the five phases will go unrealized.

Of course, yin-yang dualism had long before been projected onto the five phase scheme, reconciling the two systems. Su's description, however, assigns particular importance to the contact of yin with yang (*yinyang xiangjia*) rather than just the ascendancy of one over the other. But see how Su continues, jumping abruptly to human affairs:

> The *Changes* operates the same way. A man is endowed with a particular kind of "raw material" (*cai*), but at first it is just an unformed and uncarved mass and is not shaped into any useful implement. The *Changes*, opening it up, brings it to formation, and only then can the material be utilized. Everyone in the world cultivates his own technique of the Way, each believing that he has achieved perfection. But actually

each person remains separated, self-contained, and fixed, not partaking of the common middle. Only after the *Changes* covers him with its doctrines can he progress in the world. Therefore, the *qian* trigram is unyielding but never broken, while the *kun* trigram is yielding but never subjugated. The eight trigrams each have fully realized power yet none is ever permanently weakened. Were this not so, all things in the world would be wasted material, and all approaches to the Way would be wasted techniques.[69]

Su likens a person's innate "material" (*cai*) to the five phases. The similarity Su has in mind is that just as each of the phases results (and realizes its utility) from a meeting of yin and yang forces, so, too, a person's "material," to be useful, must be acted upon by the teachings of the *Changes* to be fully realized and useful. This is more than just a plug for the importance of the classic. The hexagrams, after all, are thought to symbolize dynamic configurations of opposing forces. This must be the aspect of the *Changes* Su Shi has in mind here, now with a human and social application. "Material" that is kept separate and aloof from opposing forces is not described in positive terms as being self-sufficient or uncontaminated. Instead, its aloofness guarantees that its full potential and usefulness will go unrealized.

The above may at first sight appear too vague to signify much; but when it is amplified by more concrete passages, we see at once the consistency and scope of Su's position. "What is esteemed about the sage is not that he remains still and has no contact with things. What is esteemed is that he proceeds together with things into the domain of good and bad fortune but is never disoriented by them."[70] This comment is inspired by the classic's description of the *gen* hexagram (the symbol of checking and stopping). The classic itself seems to offer a positive interpretation of the hexagram ("there will be no error"; "when one's movements and restings all take place at the proper time, one's way of proceeding is brilliant and intelligent"). But Su Shi's reading of the hexagram is much less favorable. Why? It consists of the same trigram above and below so that, as the classic itself says, "the upper and lower parts correspond to each other but do not interact." To Su Shi's way of thinking, this image is undesirable. Therefore, in a lengthy entry (introduced by the statement quoted above) Su distinguishes between two types of stopping. The first is that which brings an end to the current state of something (whether it be active or inactive). This is good because it ushers an opposing force or condition. The second, symbolized for Su by the *gen* hexagram, is that which freezes forever that which is already inert or inactive. This is bad because it is redundant rather than complementary. "It is for wheels that brakes are made, and for rivers that dikes are made. But now [this hexagram] would do differently. It would make brakes for a sedan chair and dikes for a mountain. Does not this verge upon stiffness?" The key term here, "stiffness" or "fixity" (gu) is the same one that occurs in the preceding passage. It is the term that so often in writings from this period has the positive meaning of moral steadfastness, firmness, or constancy. But to Su Shi in this context the term implies a kind of stubborn inertia and a refusal to participate in the great processes of change that the classic describes. The relevance all this has for Su to precepts for daily life is suggested by his opening comment. Su reiterates essentially the same point elsewhere in his commentary, approaching it from the other direction: "The top line [of the dui hexagram] is transcendent on the outside, not connected to any thing. This is the petty man's attempt to attain happiness through having no wants . . . His heart is hard to fathom and he will cause serious injury."[71]

The prominence of this theme in Su's commentary naturally suggests that it is a reaction to a contemporary school of thought. We might first suppose that Su has Cheng Yi in mind, since Cheng is the contemporary philosopher best known for emphasizing stillness and detachment as preconditions for inquiry into the nature of the Way. And if, for example, we check Cheng Yi's entry on the gen hexagram in his commentary on the Changes, we find remarks that seem a perfect foil to Su's interpretation:

> Changes (guaci): He stops with his back [turned] and loses all consciousness of his body . . . There will be no error.
> Cheng Yi: The reason people are unable to find peace where they stop is that they are stirred up by their desires. Desires tug at them from the front; and so even if they want to stop, they are unable to. Therefore the way of the gen hexagram is to stop them with their back turned. What people see lies in front of them, but gen turns them around so that their back faces it. Consequently they do not see it. Stopping where they see nothing, they no longer have desires that throw their minds into turmoil, and they find peace where they have stopped.[72]

As tempting as it may be to take such passages as the inspiration of Su Shi's contrary assertions, there is little support for doing so.[73] It is, as noted above, Wang Anshi and his New Learning, rather than Cheng Yi, whom Su Shi keeps murmuring against while laboring away on his classics commentaries in his exiles. During Su's lifetime Cheng Yi's thought did not have nearly the influence that Wang's had; and Su Shi had considerably less cause to go on the offensive against it, though he did attack Cheng Yi's conduct as imperial tutor.

Wang Anshi may, once again, seem an unlikely candidate for

the role of Su's antagonist in this. How could the great proponent of political activism possibly be identified with stillness and detachment? But we have seen something of precisely this contradiction already in Wang's philosophical interiority and his interest in "human nature and Heaven's decree." Wang Anshi may have called for unprecedented state intervention in the economic and social life of the nation; but when he wrote about the sage (that is, the man or men who should mastermind government policy), he emphasized transcendent insight facilitated by detached philosophic inquiry. In fact, the two need not be seen as contradictory at all, as Wang's opponents would have readily perceived. If one believes, as Su Shi did, that the New Policies were generally harmful to the welfare of the realm, and if one is convinced, as Su was, that the reform government remained, year after year, insensitive to the dire consequences its policies were having upon the commoners, then it would not be difficult to equate that political activism with a penchant for aloofness. Here, moreover, lies a connection between the theme of "involvement" in Su's commentary on the *Changes* and that of the intimacy of ruler with subjects in his work on the *Documents*. "The people may be treated intimately and may not be kept at a distance." "Ruler and minister are like two rulers."[74] The ruler and his subjects should take comfort in each other, and they should befriend each other.[75] Such statements in Su's commentary on the *Documents* are the fitting counterpart to his explanations of the interaction of cosmic forces in his glosses on the *Changes*.

In fact, advocacy of the disengagement of the sage from mundane matters is a theme that recurs in various guises in Wang Anshi's writings. There is no single ringing endorsement of this attitude. Instead it emerges as a consistent preference in Wang's descriptions of the highest knowledge. This is a preference that other scholars have noticed in Wang. Hou Wailu calls attention to the apparent contradiction between it and what he calls the "materialism" of Wang's politics.[76] As mentioned earlier, Wang maintains that the sage "looks inward" for wisdom. It is only the mediocre man whose search is directed outward. It is fitting, then, that in his account of cosmic forces Wang give highest place to stillness (*jing*). "Stillness is the master of movement (*dong*) . . . If movement does not know eventually to return to stillness, it loses its master."[77] "The Way has its substance and its application. The substance is made of the primal *qi* and does not move. The application is made of vacuous *qi* and circulates between Heaven and Earth."[78] "When things return to their roots they are said to be in stillness. Being in stillness, they may recover Heaven's decree."[79]

The connection between such views and Wang's notions of governance is suggested by Wang's commentary on the famous statement in *Laozi* that "Heaven and Earth are not humane and treat the myriad creatures as straw dogs; the sage is not humane and treats the people as straw dogs."[80] Straw dogs were items used in sacrifices. They are said to have been treated with utmost care before and during the solemn ceremonies, but trampled upon after they had served their purpose. It is evident that Wang Anshi finds the gist of the *Laozi* passage congenial:

> Heaven is able to generate things but cannot complete them. Earth is able to complete them but cannot put them in order, and so the sage must emerge to order them. For this reason, in his manifest form he shows himself to be humane; and as he emerges, he shares with all things their concerns over good and bad fortune. Consequently, in their generation the myriad things assist each other and nothing loses its proper place. But when the sage hides himself away to use things, then as he withdraws he does not share sorrows with any thing, even another sage. He obliterates his tracks, conceals his heart, and looks upon things as apart from himself. Now let me ask: as for the sage's relationship with Heaven and Earth, how could he ever permit humaneness and love to encumber his heart? . . . But later scholars cultivated a trivial sort of humaneness and forgot the great substance of the ancients. They lost other men by following the doctrine of universal love, and they lost themselves by seeking to be selfless.[81]

Even when Su and Wang chance to remark upon the very same passage in the classic, their comments go off in different directions that are consistent with the general divergences noted here. The "Great Appendix" to the *Changes* contains a turgid description of a program of self-cultivation: "By discovering the essence of what is right and entering into the daimonic, you apply yourself in the world; by taking advantage of such application and putting your person at peace, your virtue is increased." In his important early essay, "On Achieving Oneness," Wang Anshi assumes that the rightness in question here is an abstract truth that may be approached through quiet mental inquiry. He stresses the importance of "putting your person at peace" (*anshen*) as a preliminary step and one on which all else depends. At the moment of highest insight (entry into the daimonic and achievement of the Way), the person is described as "without thought, without action, quiet and motionless." Action in the world is treated as an afterthought and of secondary importance: "Nevertheless, as for worldly affairs, there are those that he may think and act on."[82]

Su Shi was ordinarily averse to speaking about such tasks as "discovering the essence of what is right." But as a commentator on the "Great Appendix" he had little choice but to provide some gloss on the famous passage. Yet the gloss he gives has an emphasis distinctly at odds with Wang Anshi's and shows how reluctant Su was to acknowledge that insight or moral progress could take place except as a result of the individual's engagement with things. Su resorts to a worldly analogy to explain the passage. And Su is plainly delighted that the wording of the classic allows for the view that the great culmination of the process is in "applying yourself in the world":

> To discover the essence of what is right is to master Pattern. To enter into the daimonic is to comprehend fully human nature and thus to achieve Heaven's decree. Could it be for no purpose that [the sage] "masters Pattern and comprehends fully human nature to arrive at Heaven's decree"?[83] He does this to apply himself in the world.
>
> It is like the boatman's relation with water. To know how it floats and how it sinks, to comprehend fully all the transformations of water and to be able to respond aptly to each one, this is to discover the essence of its rightness. To know how it floats and sinks and yet to become one with it so that you no longer realize it is water, this is to enter into its daimon. Now, a person who becomes one with water and no longer realizes it is water will in every case be an excellent swimmer. And how much easier will it be for him to handle a boat! This is what is meant by "applying oneself in the world."[84]

Lurking not far behind Su's image of the boat-handler in this passage is his ideal of the ruler, a man who is thoroughly familiar with the masses of people who support his government and who is able to respond aptly to their every transformation.

Selflessness

The theme of interaction is supplemented in Su's commentary on the *Changes* by ideas on the self. Primary among them is the doctrine of *wuxin* ("no-mind"), which describes a type of selfhood that is especially suited to the thoroughgoing involvement with the world that Su demands. Water is a prominent image in this notion, too; but here it is a metaphor for the ideal self rather than for the object of the sage's knowledge.

Explaining the *kan* hexagram (the symbol of sinking), the classic observes that water flowing through a defile does not lose its integrity or trustworthiness (*xin*). This is a perfect opportunity for Su, and he comments:

> The myriad things all have a constant shape; only water does not. Water shapes itself in accordance with the things it meets. The world holds that

things that have a constant shape are trustworthy, while those that do
not are untrustworthy. But something that is square may be chiseled
into a circle, and something that is crooked may be straightened into a
line. So it is that something with a constant shape cannot be relied upon
as trustworthy. Now, water may have no constant shape, but the fact
that it takes its shape from other things is something we all know in advance. That is why the carpenter uses it as a level, and why the superior
man models himself upon it. Because it has no constant shape, it can
come into contact with things but suffer no harm. And because nothing
harms it, it can flow through a defile and not lose its trustworthiness.
From this point of view, nothing in all the world is as trustworthy as
water.[85]

Several of the ideas in this passage may be traced back ultimately to
Laozi or to early descriptions of Taoist thought, including the notion
of "according with things" (*yinwu*), the desirability of having no
constant shape, and the use of water as a metaphor for wisdom. Su's
contribution is to introduce an unconventional conception of "trustworthiness," making a virtue of the inconstancy of water's form.[86]

When describing the self, Su Shi is more apt, as above, to speak
of what it should lack rather than what it should possess. The trait analogous to water's lack of a constant shape is the individual's lack of *xin*
("mind/heart"). The simplest sense of what Su means by no-mind is
that the individual should have no selfish motives in his dealings with
others. Indeed, the phrase *wusi* (to be free of selfishness) occurs early
on in Su's commentary on the *Changes* and seems to anticipate his
statements about no-mind later on. The phrase also occurs in Su's
commentary on the *Documents*: "the sage ruler possesses absolute
freedom from selfishness," and this enables him to accept the good
counsel of his ministers.[87] But Su Shi was not completely satisfied with
"freedom from selfishness." It sounds like commonplace morality, and
he sought to replace it in his commentary on the *Changes* with a more
radical notion of selflessness. Another phrase (used interchangeably
with no-mind) helps to clarify Su's notion. He says that the sage has
no intent (*wuyi*) towards things. He evidently means that 1) the person
should have no ulterior motives, 2) he should have no preconceived
notions about the nature of those things or how best to react to them
(that is supposed to be determined on the spur of the moment by the
shape of the things encountered), and 3) he should shed all sense of self
in his dealings with things.

Such absence of mind or intent or selfishness is regularly associated with the ideal of gaining insight into the Pattern (*li*) of things. It is
only the person who maintains no-mind who can attain such insight,

presumably because it is only such a person who is clear-sighted enough to perceive the ultimate nature of the world. Another way of putting it is that only a person who has emptied himself of intent will have room to contain the Patterns of the world.[88] A sampling of representative passages follows:

> How could the compliance of the superior man be anything but this: he conforms to Pattern and has no selfishness (*si*) ... The superior man has no intent (*yi*) in acting as he does. He conforms to Pattern and has no selfishness.[89]

> He who rides upon the perfect compliance of the world and proceeds in the direction of the people's delight is bound to be he who has no-mind. "The boat is empty" refers to his having no-mind.[90]

> He who has no-mind is One, and he who is One is trustworthy, so that all things [in their contact with him] will fully realize their innate Pattern. ... But if I were to have a mind, then things, being either favored or treated unjustly, would not be able to fully realize their Pattern.[91]

In another passage Su introduces different terminology, *shen* ("body, self") and *shen* ("daimon"), but the reader quickly perceives that the issue he is addressing and his position on it remain essentially the same: "The *xian* hexagram [the symbol of mutual influence] shows intermingling of daimons. He who would attain the daimonic must abandon his mind. How much the more must he so treat his body! When the body is forgotten, the daimon will be preserved. If the mind is not left behind, the body will not be forgotten; and if the body is not forgotten, the daimon will be forgotten. Daimon and body cannot both be preserved. One or the other must be forgotten."[92] Su is imagining a transcendent, spiritual mingling of the daimon in the self with the daimons above (and perhaps those of other people as well). But he insists that this ideal can never be attained if the individual does not first free himself from all consciousness of mind and body.

This raises the question of what is left to give identity and integrity to the self after it has been purged of mind and intent. Su rarely addresses this matter head-on. He speaks of the person's need to have that which he "maintains within himself" (*shou yu zhong*) to prevent him from being intimidated by external things.[93] But what is it that he preserves in himself?

One entry in the commentary on the *Documents* touches upon the issue. Su's statement is inspired by Yi Yin's injunction that the sage should have a oneness (of purpose or virtue). Su is disquieted by this and feels impelled to explain that the classic is not saying that conduct should be fixed and unchanging. He continues:

To have a ruler within (*zhong you zhu*) is what is meant by oneness. If there is a ruler within, the person responds appropriately as things confront him. And if a person thus responds, he is renewed daily. However, if there is no ruler within, external things take control. [In that case] pleasure, anger, sorrow, and joy will all reside with the things, and what will renew him? That is why Yi Yin said, "From start to finish he is one, and thus he is renewed daily." I have said that the sage is like Heaven, which takes life and gives it at the proper time. The superior man is like water which takes its shape according to whatever thing it encounters. Heaven never acts contrary to humaneness, and water never loses its property of being level. Because they are one, they are renewed daily.[94]

This is reminiscent of Su's statement in his commentary on the *Changes* that the sage is not aloof from things; he proceeds with them into the realms of good and bad fortune and yet is never disoriented by them. It must be something like "the ruler within" that allows him to keep his proper orientation. Nevertheless, Su has still not elaborated upon the nature of this inner guidance. He simply talks about the effects of its presence or absence. There is the suggestion here that the emotions are bound up inextricably with the "ruler within," inasmuch as, if the latter is lacking, the emotions become identified with the external things rather than with the person's inner nature. That amounts to a situation gone haywire, given Su's belief that it is precisely the experience of emotions that guides a person to proper conduct.[95]

Drawing on another passage from the *Documents*, Su develops two contrasting terms, "mind of man" (*renxin*) and "mind of the Way" (*daoxin*), to account more satisfactorily for, first, the source of inner constancy; second, the relations between such constancy and the emotions; and, third, for the relations between the emotions and conduct. The "mind of man" is the common mind, which is prey to unchecked emotions and, thus, to immoral conduct. The "mind of the Way," however, is the "original mind" (*benxin*). This is clearly an innate moral consciousness, which, however, must be nurtured if it is not to be overcome by the base "mind of man." Here, for once, Su recognizes a moral consciousness that is independent of the emotions. Indeed, the "original mind" is antecedent to the experience of emotions. Quoting the *Doctrine of the Mean*, Su allows that before the emotions arise, this original mind is in a state of harmony. Thereafter, if this mind remains in control, the experience of emotions is positive and leads to virtuous conduct. But if the "mind of man" is allowed to take control, then the same emotions result in selfish and wanton conduct.

There had always been a potential contradiction between Su's early affirmation of the centrality of the emotions and his later distrust

84

of the self-centered mind and its proclivity for selfish conduct. In his remarks on the two "minds," we witness Su backing away from his early faith in the inherent goodness of the emotions. This doctrine of the two minds allows Su to explain how the emotions may figure in immoral as well as moral conduct, depending upon the quality of the mind in which they arise. This is a significant refinement of his earlier views, and one informed by a more skeptical view of natural human inclinations. But this itself is really just an ad hoc explanation, presented here (because the classic refers to the two minds) and then dropped.

Su Shi's remarks on the self and its relation with the world seem unbalanced. He concentrates on the dynamics of the self's contact with the external world. He gives abundant attention to the goal of overcoming narrow self-centeredness, and never tires of describing the supreme adaptability and sensitivity that result. But he fails to provide more than a cursory account of what remains to direct and lend integrity to the self. He is content to allude to "the ruler within" or the "original mind," without examining the source or nature of the moral values that constitute them.

This unevenness in his treatment surely sprang from his place in the political and intellectual controversies of the day. There is a brief but revealing passage early in Su's commentary on the *Changes*. Explaining the first line of the *li* hexagram (the symbol of treading), the classic says that it shows "its subject treading his accustomed path. If he goes forward there will be no error." The *xiang* portion of the text further expands on the auspicious image: "Singly he carries out his long-cherished wishes." This may sound innocuous enough; but it strikes a nerve in Su Shi, who writes, "The reason that the Way of the superior man has many transformations and is not constant is that dissimilar things keep appearing before him. If he did not have contact with things, the superior man would only be carrying out his own wishes."[96] It is because Su believed that he lived in a world in which certain men had been allowed to carry out their wishes and remain aloof from the disastrous consequences that he insisted on this alternative vision of enlightened conduct and gave scant attention to the make-up of the self in isolation.

CHAPTER FOUR

National Politics Again: Yuanyou-Period Factionalism

When Emperor Shenzong died in 1085, the heir to the throne, Zhezong, was but ten years old. Consequently, Empress Dowager Gao took control of the government and ruled as regent on the boy's behalf. The empress dowager, who was the wife not of Shenzong but of his father, Yingzong, had long been opposed to the New Policies and now moved quickly against them. She recalled Sima Guang and other senior leaders of the Conservative party from retirement and persuaded them to accept high-level posts. Predictably, a struggle broke out between these newly returned Conservatives and the leaders of the old reform administration, including Grand Councilor Cai Que and his assistant, Zhang Dun, who at first were still a powerful presence at the Court. Over the next several months, however, the Conservatives gradually gained control. The reform leaders were relieved of their posts and reforms began one by one to be repealed. Thus began the Yuanyou reign period (1086–1093), a time often remembered nostalgically for its enlightened rule by gifted ministers, men who gave the nation a respite, however brief, from the harshness of the New Policies. In fact, the period ushered in its own manner of divisiveness.

Su Shi's four-year exile in Huangzhou had been ended in 1084. The abrupt change of government the following year brought Su back to the capital after fifteen years of undistinguished posts and exile in the prefectures. The return must have also rekindled Su's hopes for the kind of career that his performance two decades earlier on the exams had seemed to portend but which had never developed. Su Shi was one of many men who, upon Sima Guang's recommendation, were now recalled and asked to join the new government. Once in the capital Su Shi was promoted rapidly to be executive secretary of the Chancellery. By the second month of 1086, Su Che had also returned to Kaifeng, whereupon he was appointed to the Bureau of Policy Criticism.

The Split with Sima Guang

There is no question that Su Shi generally supported the succession of early Yuanyou-period initiatives to revoke the New Policies. Within the first months of the period, several keystones of Wang's program, including the Civilian Security system, the "reformed" examinations, the Green Sprouts policy, and the state trade policy, were all drastically altered or abandoned, all with Su Shi's support. When in the autumn of 1086 Fan Chunren urged that the Green Sprouts program be reinstituted in order to generate more income for the state, Su Shi vigorously objected. The memorial he wrote on this occasion ("A Plea against Distributing Green Sprouts Cash")[1] describes all the suffering caused over the years by the loan program and explains how open it was to abuse by corrupt officials. Sima Guang himself, who had been in favor of granting the loans with certain restrictions, was dissuaded by Su's argument and the initiative was dropped. Su Shi also drafted, in the summer of 1086, the imperial decree demoting a former vice grand councilor, Lü Huiqing (Wang Anshi's disloyal protégé). The decree castigates in the strongest language both Lü's character and the reforms he administered.[2]

There was, however, one issue on which Su Shi strongly disagreed with Sima Guang and other leading Conservatives. Sima Guang intended to abolish Wang Anshi's Hired Service System, under which households paid a tax to fund the hiring of menial help in local government offices, and reestablish the Assigned Service laws, under which local families were required, on a rotating basis, to staff those positions themselves. Su Shi felt that the Hired Service System was one part of the reform legacy that should not be lightly abandoned, and he was convinced, moreover, that a sudden and facile return to Assigned Service would be disastrous for the realm. So firmly did he believe that the Conservatives were misguided on this issue that, in effect, he staked his political career on the point and did not alter his stance even when it became obvious that he would lose the fight. His role as a champion of one of the now discredited reforms contributed directly to his removal from the capital in 1089, at the height of Conservative power, when so many of his former friends and associates enjoyed unprecedented honor. The man who had formerly been made an example of for his opposition to the reforms now became estranged from the leaders of the Conservatives during their heyday because he supported one of those reforms. Su Shi would never again have the chance to rise so high in the government as he could have at this time.

It would be wrong to suppose that the argument over the Hired Service policy was just one of many political squabbles in the early Yuanyou period. Actually, the rest of the New Policies were abandoned with rather little struggle (the reform leaders themselves had become disillusioned with some of them and favored their repeal), but around the issue of hired service there developed a major controversy.[3] Sima Guang declared that of all the reforms, this ought to be the first to go; and Sima's colleague, the censor Liu Ji, identified it as the most urgent matter facing the government.[4] Those reformers who were still vocal agreed that no issue so affected the lives of the general populace as did this matter of how the local administrations were to be staffed and supported, but they remained confident of the long-term benefits of their system.[5] Even the retired Wang Anshi, who is said to have stoically accepted the news that his program was being generally dismantled, could not contain himself when he heard that Hired Service had also been repudiated: "This one policy ought never be abandoned. I consulted with our former emperor for two years before enacting it, and we considered the matter from every possible angle."[6]

Su Shi's own position was complex and carefully developed. Actually, he had his own alternative to both systems and so could be said to favor neither. Still, he was set in his opposition to Sima Guang's proposal simply to replace hired with assigned service. Su Shi had written a lengthy and detailed memorial on the subject in the twelfth month of 1085, within a few days of his arrival in the capital.[7] Clearly, Su had been working out his thoughts on the matter even as he made his way to the capital. Su begins his memorial by reminding the throne that through all the years of the Hired Service system a surtax had been collected, on top of the service exemption tax itself, to support the system in case of deficits in times of hardship. However, none of the funds collected through the surtax had ever been spent, or needed, for the designated purpose. Su suggests that this money now be used to buy up "public lands" (that is, the lands of bankrupt or dissolved estates) and that these in turn be used to recruit local service personnel. The service personnel would thus be volunteers who, in exchange for the use of the land by themselves and their families, would serve for extended periods in whatever capacity the local government required. As Su envisioned it, the practice of buying and using public lands this way could be gradually phased in while either the Hired Service or the Assigned Service law was in effect. If the former, for every recruit obtained the local government would save one hired man's wages and the service exemption tax could be correspondingly lowered. If the latter, for every recruit the government would be able to function with one less conscripted person and the man's family would not have to go without his labor. Su hoped that in time his public-lands plan would supply all the personnel local bureaucracies needed and local governments would thus be virtually self-supporting. He saw other benefits in his plan: 1) It bound the volunteers, people who presumably were destitute and had no other means of support, to government lands and was apt to make them law-abiding and keep them from becoming refugees or outlaws in times of distress. 2) It would improve the value of farmland which, because there were now few buyers, was practically worthless. 3) It would give local governments a way to spend their surplus cash and thereby stimulate the economy. 4) It would be an act of good faith on the government's part to thus put tax revenue to use in a manner that would benefit the people who paid the tax in the first place. Additionally, Su points out that such a plan had been briefly tried during the reform period and had the enthusiastic support of the late emperor, but it was ruined by short-sighted bureaucrats who insisted on diverting the tax revenues for other purposes. Su also reveals that when he was governor of Mizhou, he adopted a similar plan to support the local militia there, and it worked well.

There is no evidence that Su's memorial attracted any of the attention it deserved. Instead, Su was abruptly appointed to a commission charged with determining conscription quotas for the Assigned Service System, soon to be reestablished. The deliberations of this group must have been heated to the point of unpleasantness. Su Shi kept insisting that the concept of assigned service was wrong and that men ought to be paid for their work, one way or another, rather than drafted. He perceived, of course, that his differences with the other members of the commission were irreconcilable; and he sought to be relieved of his appointment. He memorialized to the throne on four separate occasions, asking to be taken off the commission. For whatever reason his request was not granted for several months, until well into the autumn of 1086. By that time other members of the commission had grown so impatient with his dissent that they had complained about him to the throne.[8]

Su Shi's dispute with the other Conservatives involved more

than disagreement over the merits of the Hired Service System. That was the specific issue over which discord arose; but what lay behind it, and is in its way more significant, was Su Shi's willingness to question the opinions and leadership of his sponsor Sima Guang, the new grand councilor. Put another way, what is noteworthy is that Su Shi was now willing to drop his own formerly categorical opposition to the New Policies.

This altered attitude towards the reforms appears to have been reached through reflection and even a degree of self-reproach. A letter that Su Shi probably wrote shortly before his return captures his feelings. This brief letter was sent to his close friend, Teng Dadao, evidently on the eve of Teng's own return to the capital:

> What I had hoped to say to you face to face was this: At the start of the New Policies era, we and our party all had a biased view of things and that is what caused our dissent. Although our hearts were steadfast and never swerved from loyal concern for our nation, our words were in error and little of what we said was reasonable. Today sagely virtue is daily renewed and a grand transformation is occurring in all quarters. When I look back on the course we formerly adopted, I see all the more how misguided it was. As for changing one's principles to gain advancement—I would never dare suggest you do that. But if we continue to carry on as we did before, the distress and problems we'll cause will be even more extreme.
>
> This journey of yours signifies great wisdom. Not being content to withdraw from the world, your loyal heart simply wants, despite your old age and infirmity, to gaze once more upon His Majesty's bright countenance. This being so, I believe you are certain to be rewarded with a response. Is that not your true intention? Because of my deep affection for you, I have here let my brush write freely and convey such pointed advice. I beg your forbearance on this matter.[9]

The date of this letter is uncertain; but a strong case can be made for 1085, the year Emperor Shenzong died.[10] The document sounds as if it were composed during such a transitional period; and it is during that period that the recipient, who was known for his opposition to the reforms, might well have decided to travel to the capital in search of a new appointment.

During his Huangzhou years, Su Shi hardly wrote anything, even privately, that broached contemporary politics. Yet it is clear that he engaged in a considerable amount of reflection upon the events that led up to his exile. His writings from Huangzhou are full of references to solitary hours he spent in self-examination. It is plausible that the new view of the reforms controversy that we find in the letter to Teng Dadao grew out of this process of reexamining his past.[11]

Another potential influence may also be mentioned, intriguing as it is. After years of dispute and mutual suspicion, Su Shi and Wang Anshi had their first direct contact in 1085. Their meetings together were private and, by all indications, extremely cordial. But we do not have enough information about what took place to gauge with any certainty the true significance of the event.

The origin of the personal relationship between the two political antagonists can be traced back to the late 1070s, and it began with poetry.[12] In the winter of 1076, while serving in Mizhou, Su Shi had witnessed a great snowstorm and had written two poems about it, emphasizing the hardship it caused for the commoners.[13] Su's poems circulated and eventually reached Wang Anshi, who had by then resigned permanently from the government and was living in seclusion at Zhong Mountain, outside Jinling (Nanjing). Wang was impressed by Su's snow poems, and he praised and explicated them to his son-in-law.[14] Then Wang wrote several poems in response and evidently sent them to Su Shi. The poems that survive compliment Su on the intricacy of his verses and present images of Wang poring over and savoring them in his study.[15]

Su Shi answered Wang with more verses of his own. Su's poems, the collective title of which avoids identifying the man they are written for ("Thanking Someone for Matching My Rhymes"),[16] are polite and sympathetic. One of them may make a veiled reference to the inconstancy of Wang Anshi's assistants (e.g., Lü Huiqing, Zeng Bu), who proved to be personally disloyal to Wang, but not to the reforms, after he had brought them to power.[17] In his closing lines Su solicitously encourages Wang to enjoy his leisure while he has it and anticipates that he will be summoned back to the Court before long, which was not to happen.

By the time Su Shi was indicted in 1079, Wang Anshi had been in retirement for three years. Wang had nothing to do with the charges brought against Su by those to whom the leadership of the reform party had passed. Actually, it is said that Wang was shocked to hear the news of Su's arrest. How could any age that considered itself enlightened, Wang asked, bear to send a talented man to his death?[18] When Su's exile ended in 1084, he stopped at Jinling for two months while en route to his new assignment in Ruzhou. During the layover he paid several visits to Wang Anshi in his seclusion outside the city. This was apparently the first and only time the two men ever met. Su

Shi wrote to his friend Teng Dadao, "Since arriving here, I have met Jinggong [Anshi] and am delighted with him. We recite poetry together and discuss Buddhism."[19]

Poems the two men wrote during this visit celebrate the quiet joys of Wang's retreat. One of Su's lines reads, "I realize now that I am ten years late in befriending you,"[20] and there is even talk of Su Shi's making plans to buy land in the Jinling area so that he could settle near Wang's retreat.[21] Neither man refers directly to any conversation they had together about politics, though it is unimaginable that they could have avoided the subject altogether. Su Shi would later write back to Wang, "I have long been a disciple at your gate, but never had such a satisfying meeting with you as we recently had. Morning and evening I got to hear things I had never heard before. I was greatly comforted and consider myself extremely fortunate."[22] The observation about long being Wang's disciple is obviously formulaic politeness, but the other statements cannot be lightly dismissed. Su may well have opened himself up during their conversations to points of view he had never considered. One source plausibly describes how Su persuaded Wang during these visits to voice his opinions on current politics that both men disapproved of,[23] and it would be strange if such persuasion and compromise were entirely one-sided.

Nevertheless, despite all this evidence of private cordiality and mutual respect, Su Shi could still be harsh in his characterizations of Wang's performance as a political leader. Memorials Su wrote during the Yuanyou period refer to Wang's "trickery," "deceit," and "wickedness" when he had control of the government.[24] It is contradictions such as this that should make us wary of accepting Su's private expressions of respect for Wang at face value. It is impossible to know the extent to which these expressions were encouraged or required by polite custom.[25]

Su Shi's willingness to disagree with Sima Guang complemented, as noted above, his new open-mindedness about the reforms and prepared the way for the serious rift that developed within the Conservative point of view. This willingness likewise involved more than just a second opinion on the Hired Service policy.[26]

When Su Shi was recalled to join the new government, he knew that all he had to do was to go along with the dismantling of the New Policies and his career would soar. Yet he was unable to bend his views on certain points to conform to the new consensus; and the new consensus itself became, for Su Shi, the primary issue at stake. Interestingly, Su drew a distinction here between Sima Guang and his followers. The leader he characterized as tolerant of disagreement, but not so his underlings. And it was, in fact, not until after Sima Guang's untimely death in the ninth month of 1086 that Su Shi's troubles began. This is the way Su Shi himself described the situation:

> Although I am not as worthy as our late grand councilor, Sima Guang, our friendship was deep and sincere. After Guang came to power, I, too, was promoted rapidly. In the nature of things, why should I have expressed any disagreement? But I truly believed that the Assigned Service System Guang instituted, that one policy, was unwise and I could not but protest vigorously. The members of the Censorate sought only to concur facilely with whatever Guang said, in order to win advancement. After Guang died, these same men wrongly concluded that the ruler took Guang's words as his standard. They banded together as a faction and tried to block all divergent opinions. If anyone disagreed with them, they attacked him jointly. They never understood that Guang had genuinely sought what was best for the people and did not want other ministers to concur in a facile fashion with him. Nor did they realize that our ruler has an open mind and lacks any predetermined preferences of his own—how could he have adopted a single point of view as his standard?[27]

Su Shi came to believe that a new rigidity and uncritical compliance had replaced the old one, and that the new was virtually as undesirable as the old had been. The current censors, Su observes, "seek only to repeal the policies of the Xining period. They do not take account of a policy's benefit or harm, nor are they willing to retain the better aspects of the old program."[28] In a letter to a friend, Su confides, "In years past all gentlemen took Jing (Wang Anshi) and him alone as their master. Nowadays all gentlemen follow no one but Wen (Sima Guang). The person they follow has changed, but the way they follow him is the same. I myself am on the most intimate terms with Wen. Nothing has ever come between us personally, and yet I often do not follow him."[29]

The Dispute with Cheng Yi

The enmity against Su Shi during the Yuanyou era had a second source, which must have been linked to the split with Sima Guang described above but remains distinguishable from that split. This was the friction between Su Shi and Cheng Yi, the man known to history as a major Neo-Confucian philosopher.

After appearing at the National University in the early 1050s, some thirty-five years before, when he so impressed the scholars there with his essay on Yan Hui, Cheng Yi had returned to his native Luo-yang and pursued his studies privately. He had repeatedly been recommended for positions but declined all offers. Sima Guang had gotten to know him well during his own withdrawal to Luoyang during the New Policies period; and when Sima returned to power, he and his colleague Lü Gongzhu arranged to have Cheng Yi summoned to the capital.[30] In the spring of 1086, as befit his high repute for learning, Cheng Yi was appointed lecturer of Chongzheng Palace, that is, tutor to the ten-year-old emperor.

Su Shi was soon to become Hanlin academician and reader-in-waiting, in which capacity he, too, would sometimes attend upon the young emperor (with the apparent approval of Empress Dowager Gao). Coincidence, then, brought these two leading figures, with their vastly different personalities and values, into the same imperial room. Viewing back across the centuries, one hardly knows whether to envy or pity the boy ruler.

The simplistic version of what ensued is that the ebullient Su Shi could not endure Cheng Yi's pomposity, with all of his attention to ancient rites and reverence. The animosity that developed between the two men is the subject of numerous stories.[31] When Sima Guang died, Cheng Yi was put in charge of his funeral; and he insisted that everything be done according to ancient standards. One day Su Shi and other officials attended a state ceremony in the Hall of Brightness to celebrate the recent accession of the new emperor. Music was part of the ceremony. Later, Su went to where Sima Guang was laid out to mourn for him. Cheng Yi tried to stop him from entering the room, citing the observation in the *Analects* that on the day he mourned the Master never sang. Su Shi ignored him and observed, as he proceeded inside, that he had heard of not singing after you mourn, but had never heard of not mourning after you sing. Everyone laughed at Cheng Yi.[32] On another occasion, an anniversary of Shenzong's death, Cheng Yi instructed the assembled officials that they should refrain from eating the meat dishes, though the custom had long been to include meat in the ceremonial meal. Su Shi, who was well aware of Cheng's antipathy towards Buddhism, asked him if he were not now adopting the vegetarian habits of the monks. Cheng Yi countered that such an anniversary was really an extension of the mourning period, and that in mourning one was prohibited from taking meat or wine. Oblivious, Su Shi helped himself to the meat dishes and encouraged the others to follow suit. Many did.[33]

These anecdotes hint at philosophical differences between the two men. Cheng Yi, as mentioned earlier, firmly believed that in its native and quiescent state human nature was good. He, more consistently than Wang Anshi, equated human nature with the "Pattern of Heaven" (*tianli*), which is moral, and counterpoised against these the human desires (*renyu*). If a person loses sight of the Pattern, he is no different from an animal. And it is precisely human desires that are apt to take control of the individual and lead him astray. Thus the goal of sagely teaching is "to overcome human desires and rediscover the Pattern of Heaven."[34] Such a position runs counter to Su Shi's views on the centrality of the emotions to human nature.

The polarity of inner and outer also figures in Cheng Yi's thought. Study, Cheng Yi explains, directs us to seek the truth within. Anyone whose focus is "outer" is not pursuing the learning of the sages.[35] In fact, mental reflection and interiority are the keys to curbing desires. "How does one contain his desires? By deliberation (*si*) and nothing else. Nothing is more important in study than deliberation . . . Zengzi examined his conduct three times daily: this was the way he contained his desires."[36] Cheng Yi and his elder brother, Cheng Hao, are also known for their stress upon *jing* ("reverence"), the mental attitude essential for progress in the lifelong task of moral cultivation. Reverence is achieved by "gathering in" the body and mind. If reverence is lost, the myriad selfish desires will arise.[37] But if reverence is maintained, the individual may devote himself to the One. "Then he will not move to the east or to the west; he will remain in the Mean. If he does not go this way or that, he will proceed nowhere but within. And if he can maintain this, then the natural Pattern of Heaven will become clear to him."[38] Much of this is strongly reminiscent of Wang Anshi's interiority, and Su's objections would apply equally well. "No one in the world," Su had boasted, "is as free of deliberation as I am."

On some issues Cheng Yi exceeded Wang Anshi. Cheng's commitment to the search "within" led him to be positively hostile to literary work. Within this elite "literati" culture, it would be hard, in fact, to find anyone more negative about literary composition than Cheng Yi. While other philosophers differed over the manner in which writing serves or transmits the Way, Cheng Yi came out and declared that writing is positively harmful to the Way (*wen yi hai dao*).[39] Why? Writing epitomized misdirectedness: it is the clearest indication that the individual is devoted to the outer rather than the inner. This may sound odd to us, habituated as we are to think of writing in psychological terms, but for Cheng Yi writing betrayed preoccupation with externals (words, the world out there). These he also calls the branches; the roots lie within. Consequently, Cheng Yi characterized literary talent as one of life's three great misfortunes (the other two were youthful eminence on the exams and gaining office through family influence).[40] Su Shi had two of the three.

There was still more to Su Shi's conflict with Cheng Yi, more than these philosophical differences. Su Shi subsequently refers to Cheng Yi's "treachery" (*jian*) during this period.[41] That is not a word that anyone used lightly. What did Su have in mind? Cheng Yi was a peculiar presence in the early Yuanyou period Court. Here was a man who had no prior history of official service, who arrived at the capital in his fifties, and quickly became the future ruler's primary tutor. And it was not just the boy emperor who listened to him. He is said to have attracted a large following of admirers, including several of the most prominent and outspoken members of the Censorate (e.g., Wang Yansou, Zhu Guangting, and Jia Yi). His prestige grew to the point that he was perceived as having powerful influence over the advancement and demotion of ministers of state.

In the eyes of his supporters, Cheng Yi was victimized by less worthy men who were envious of his intimacy with the imperial family and his fearless manner. This is how Zhu Xi describes what happened: "The officials of the age who flocked to [Cheng Yi] were many; and he, for his part, took the whole empire as his responsibility. As he lectured and adjudicated praise and blame, there was no subject on which he held back. Consequently, officials in the Court who were known for their skill in letters came to despise him as an enemy, and together with their partisans they fabricated slanderous remarks about him."[42] Likewise, Fan Zuyu wrote, "In his tutorial sessions Yi was most anxious that the emperor make progress in his studies. Therefore his lectures and discussions often went on and on. This man, a commoner from the hinterlands, had in one day gained entry to the Court. In his dealings with the other officials, he showed no restraint; and he was not versed in normal Court etiquette. As a result, people said he was a great deluder and a wicked man."[43]

Naturally, this is not the only point of view. Su Shi does not elaborate upon his judgment of Cheng Yi; but from the words of others of his detractors, it is obvious that it was more than his style or origins that concerned them. In short, Cheng Yi was suspected of attempting to isolate the young emperor and to abuse his unique position. If one looks, moreover, at some of the recommendations Cheng Yi made, it is easy even from our remove today to see how onlookers could arrive at this conclusion.

When the appointment of imperial tutor was first offered to

him, Cheng had asked that should he accept, he be allowed to lecture the emperor sitting down rather than standing. This was no small change, for it meant that Cheng would be seated on the dais or throne together with the emperor. Cheng hoped that this arrangement would "nurture the ruler's respect for Confucianism and his dedication to the Way, at the same time it would keep him in awe and apprehension."[44] Later, Cheng asked that the location of the lessons be changed from Miying to the Yanhe Palace. The reason Cheng gave was that Miying Palace was too hot and crowded; but somehow other officials decided that his real motive was to be able to lecture sitting down (how the shift of palaces would have facilitated this is unclear), and they protested the proposed move.[45] Cheng Yi suggested still other modifications of the routine: He wanted to increase the frequency of the tutorial sessions, and not allow so many days off in between sessions.[46] He wanted to shorten the traditional summer break from the lessons, suggesting that a suitably cool spot might be found in an inner palace or the palace garden.[47] He sought to restrict the attendance of other officials (such as the grand councilors and Court historians) at the tutorial sessions, arguing that their presence was distracting and inhibiting to the young student and that there was no need, in any case, to have everything that occurred written down. He suggested that a curtain be hung at the back of the room so that the empress dowager herself might listen in on the lessons whenever she wanted. She, too, might benefit from the instruction; and, besides, if the lecturer wanted to communicate something to the empress dowager, this would make it easy for his words to reach her. Finally, although the other members of the Court urged that Cheng Yi be given other concurrent duties, outside the palace, he refused, insisting that he devote all his energy to his tutorial.[48]

In the autumn of 1087, the second year of his appointment, the emperor fell ill and was unable to attend his lessons for several days. When Cheng Yi came upon the grand councilors, he asked them about the emperor's condition and was shocked to discover that they had not even heard of His Majesty's indisposition. Cheng Yi admonished the councilors for being so remiss in their loyalty.[49] That was apparently the last straw. Whether deservedly or not, Cheng Yi was viciously denounced by the policy critic Kong Wenzhong shortly thereafter. Kong, who was a friend of Su Shi, accused Cheng Yi of seeking to ingratiate himself with and manipulate the emperor, of presenting wild and groundless interpretations of the classics before His Majesty, and of plotting deviously together with members of the Censorate to grab power.[50] Cheng was removed from his post and sent back in shame to Luoyang. He never returned to the capital and spent his remaining years in and out of the National Academy in Luoyang.

"Saying White Is Black and West Is East"

Compared to Cheng Yi, the difficulties Su Shi was to face during the Yuanyou period were more protracted and, at the same time, less ambiguous. We are in a better position to judge the nature of complaints against Su Shi; for they are based mostly on specific writings he composed, rather than speech and actions concealed behind palace walls, and these writings survive for us to read and evaluate. The image of the Song high bureaucracy conveyed by the events that will be summarized here is not an attractive one. But it is the bureaucracy in which Su Shi found himself and in which he tried to function.[51]

In the last months of 1086, Su Shi was called upon to draft questions for an examination administered by the Bureau of Academicians. One of Su's questions described two alternative philosophies of governance, that based on humaneness and that on strictness, and called attention to the dangers or potential consequences of each (inefficiency and cruelty, respectively). The point of the question was to challenge the examinees to describe how an administration could avoid both failings. In developing his point, Su Shi referred in passing to the last two reigns: "Today the Court wishes to emulate Renzu's [Emperor Renzong's] magnanimity but worries that the bureaucrats may not fulfill their duties and this would lead to laxity and complacency. The Court wishes to imitate Shenkao's [Emperor Shenzong's] activism and intensity but fears that the supervisory and prefectural officials may not understand the intent and that might lead to harshness."[52] Within a few days, the policy critic Zhu Guangting charged in a memorial to the throne that Su Shi had, with these sentences, slandered two of the dynasty's emperors and should be punished as a disloyal subject. Zhu Guangting's charges were reiterated by the head of the Censorate, Fu Yaoyu, and his assistant, Wang Yansou.[53]

There is a tradition that all of this activity has its origins in the mutual dislike Su Shi and Cheng Yi had for each other. Zhu Guangting is known to have been a follower of Cheng Yi, and his accusations against Su come not long after the celebrated quip about mourning after singing with which Su had humiliated the imperial tutor. Many sources, therefore, represent the charges that were now lodged against Su as coming from the hostility between the "Luo faction" (Cheng Yi's, of Luoyang) and the "Shu faction" (Su Shi's, of Sichuan).

Su Shi's most thorough biographer, Wang Wen'gao, has already pointed out the unlikelihood of this representation of events.[54] At this particular moment, the hostility towards Su Shi came primarily from his insistent disagreement with Sima Guang over the replacement of the Hired Service policy. As early as the summer of the same year, members of the special commission appointed to look into service alternatives were complaining to the emperor about Su Shi's stubborn refusal to accept Sima Guang's view of the matter. One of those commissioners was the censor Fu Yaoyu, who now argued for Su's impeachment over the exam question.[55] As long as Sima was alive (through the eighth month of the year), no one took serious action against Su; but when the elder statesman was gone, frustration with Su erupted in such an attack. And this is precisely how Su Shi, in defending himself against the charges of disloyalty, describes the sequence of events:

> Moreover, it is not just a matter of this one examination question. Let me here set forth the whole story of my refusal recently to shrink from controversy. When I was recalled last year from Dengzhou and met again with the late grand councilor, Sima Guang, he discussed with me the crucial issues facing the realm, explaining how he planned to handle each one of them. I said to him, "The policies you are planning all accord with Heaven's desires and match the peoples' wishes—that is beyond question. However, the service policy, this one matter, ought not to be decided hurriedly . . ."[56]

Su goes on to relate his troubles on the special commission, not ever mentioning Cheng Yi.

Of course, Su Shi also refutes the specific charge against him. He freely admits that in composing the exam question he intended to remind everyone of the need to strike a balance between the two previous administrations, for he was worried by the current tendency to find fault with the entirety of Shenzong's rule (and to permit no disagreement on this point). He insists, quite rightly, that he used the words "laxity" and "harshness" to describe shortcomings that might conceivably develop in the current government and that he had not applied the words to the former administrations (much less to the emperors themselves). Any fair reading of his question would exonerate him: "The logic of the writing is perfectly clear, as plain as black and white."[57]

Why should the censors have supposed that they might succeed? It must be that they believed Su to be particularly vulnerable to accusations of disloyalty and slander. Su Shi's past dogged him. Having once been arrested and tried for slanderous writing, he stood to be an easy target now. Even a flimsy case against him might succeed. This time the empress dowager herself saw that the accusations were based on a distorted reading of the exam question, and the charges were dropped.[58]

This was just the start of attempts by Su Shi's various enemies, and he had them in just about every camp, to implicate him in wrong-doing. The censors continued to complain about him to the empress. Early in 1088, Su Shi asked to be relieved of his duties as Hanlin academician, citing the censors' hostility towards him, and to be given some innocuous position instead.[59] This spring, Su explains, when he supervised the examinations, the censors protested that he would show favoritism to certain candidates, and they did so before the exams even began. By the end of the year, Su Shi started formally to request that he be reassigned out of the capital to the provinces, also to escape his detractors.[60] Su lists the sources of his troubles: his disagreement with Sima Guang, charges by Han Wei that Su and Lu Tao (a friend and fellow native of Sichuan) had banded together to form a "faction," and the long-standing hatred that the censor Zhao Tingzhi has had for him. This last item is interesting. We normally think of the Yuanyou-period government as one that had been purged of New Policies reformers, but Zhao shows that this is not entirely true. Su traces Zhao's rancor against him back to the reform period, when Zhao enthusiastically implemented the State Trade Policy in the poor county he administered and was criticized for it by Huang Tingjian (Su's supporter). Later, Su himself had tried to prevent Zhao's recall to the capital but had failed. There was thus a strong personal element in Zhao's enmity. (Su Che had even once memorialized against Zhao's father-in-law). In the years to come, this same man, who was now a censor, would rise to even higher office when the reformers returned to power. For now, however, he had set his sights upon Su Shi and would use, Su believed, every ounce of his mortal strength to bring him down.

Su complained that within a brief two years he had been slandered on several separate issues, and he cited passages from his recent writings that were being used unfairly against him (the exam question, again, and a line from the *Book of Songs* about the suffering of the people that Su had included in an appointment decree he drafted).[61] It was at this moment that Su contrasted his current situation with that he had faced in 1079. Zhao Tingzhi, Su explained, was more venomous than Li Ding, Shu Dan, and He Zhengchen combined. The charges formerly brought against him at least had some semblance of validity. There really was political protest in his reform-period poems. It was just that Li Ding and the others insisted that his protests were defamatory. This time, however, the charges against him were utterly without foundation: Zhao Tingzhi "is saying that white is black and west is east. There is not the slightest semblance of truth in his accusations."[62]

In 1089, Su Shi was finally granted his wish. He was sent out of the capital to be prefect of Hangzhou. Before that happened, though, one more charge was initiated against him, this one particularly bizarre. Some years before, Su had been urged by the throne to recommend instructors for the prefectural schools. One of the names Su responded with was that of a certain Zhou Zhong, who was assigned to the school in Yunzhou (Shandong). Now, without warning, Zhou Zhong memorialized to the Court, suggesting that the spirit tablet of the late Wang Anshi be installed in Emperor Shenzong's shrine. Not only was it a violation of procedure for a lowly prefectural instructor to broach a matter of imperial ancestor worship, the proposal itself was outrageously inappropriate. Wang Anshi's reforms had been officially discredited, his living ministers ignominiously removed. Besides, a spirit attendant had already been selected for Shenzong (the Conservative minister, Fu Bi).

Sponsorship for appointment carried with it the sponsor's legal guarantee of lawful conduct. If Zhou Zhong were convicted of wrongdoing, Su Shi could also be punished. Su Shi suspected that Zhou had not acted on his own, that someone had planted the idea in his head or somehow forced him to act.[63] It is plausible that one of Su Shi's enemies was the hidden manipulator (especially because Su Shi seems to be the only person aside from Zhou Zhong himself who was endangered by the proposal). But which one, or which camp? It might have been embittered reformers, who were still a presence, especially in the provinces, and were still hoping they might return to power (as Su warns the throne in his own defense). Or it might have been any of the various groups among the anti-reformers, who had also grown impatient with Su Shi. Su Shi asked for a full investigation, thinking, no doubt, that with it the exact nature of the scheme might come to light. But apparently none was ever undertaken. The case was not prosecuted, but neither was it forgotten. As with many of the accusations leveled against Su Shi at this time, the charges and their aspersions lingered in the political background. And with each new campaign against him, the old charges would be brought to the fore again to add to the weight of the new ones, even though guilt had never been determined.

Su Shi's two years in Hangzhou will be discussed in the next chapter. As difficult as they were, Su had no desire to return to the capital; and when he was recalled, he immediately asked for another prefectural governorship. In fact, he predicted that if he were to return, his enemies would move against him again.[64] His plea was ignored and his prediction came true. Now it was Jia Yi, disciple of the outcast Cheng Yi, who led the attack upon him. Su Shi traced the history of the animosity this way:

> Originally, there was no bitterness between Jia Yi and me. But Cheng Yi's treachery always vexed me, and I showed it in my speech and on my face. That is how stubborn and narrow I am! Jia Yi is blindly loyal to Cheng Yi and was determined to avenge his master. Cheng Yi had used his doctrines to try to delude Kong Wenzhong, hoping to get him to discuss state policy from his own selfish point of view, and was eventually indicted by Kong. When Cheng Yi was incriminated, Jia Yi was also implicated and removed to the provinces. In his memorial of gratitude, Jia Yi falsely charged that my younger brother, Che, had leaked secret imperial edicts, and for this Jia Yi was demoted a second time and made prefect of Guangde. Therefore, his hatred of my brother and me became extreme. Because of my various hardships I have aged quickly, and I have no more interest in seeking advancement. Why should I want to nurture this trivial grievance? But Jia Yi is absolutely determined to have revenge and never forgets about me even for a single day.[65]

When Su Shi did return to the capital, in 1091, Jia Yi, who was then a censor, promptly charged him with having exaggerated reports of flooding and rice shortages during his tenure at Hangzhou; and he renewed charges that Su Shi had improperly punished certain silk merchants, named Yan, there.[66] Next, Jia Yi attempted to get Qin Guan, whom Su Shi had recommended for office, convicted of wrongdoing.[67] When these direct and indirect attacks upon Su failed to achieve their desired result, Jia Yi, like others before him, turned back to Su Shi's writings.

In 1085, after his release from Huangzhou, Su Shi had received permission to withdraw to a farm he had recently acquired in Yixing (Changzhou, near Lake Tai). On his way there, when he thought he would be retiring permanently, Su Shi wrote the following quatrain, entitled "Returning Home to Yixing, Inscribed on Zhuxi Temple":

此生已覺都無事	Already I feel this life is free of all concerns,
今歲仍逢大有年	This year again the harvest will be abundant.
山寺歸來聞好語	Returning from the mountain temple, I hear joyful words;
野花啼鳥亦欣然	Wildflowers and singing birds are cheerful, too.[68]

This poem was written on the first day of the fifth month. Emperor Shenzong had died in the third month. Jia Yi asserted that the third line referred to Su's receipt of the news of the emperor's death and was, of course, defamatory.

In his defense Su Shi asked why, if that is what he had meant, he would have been so reckless as to inscribe the poem on the temple wall? Su had his own explanation of the second couplet. Not only had everyone already learned long before of Shenzong's death, people were already discussing what they had heard about Zhezong, the boy emperor who succeeded him. Along the roadside on this occasion Su Shi listened to a group of commoners as they spoke about Zhezong. One man adamantly declared that Zhezong was by all accounts "a fine young officer." Although these words were coarse, Su explained, he was touched by them and wanted to somehow incorporate them into his poem.[69] Su's explanation is plausible, although it is also possible that originally Su had some other words he had heard that day in mind. Jia Yi's reading is, by contrast, so improbable that it is remarkable it could be taken seriously. But evidently the danger from this charge was real. In less than a month Su Shi was removed from the Court to be prefect of Yingzhou.

Each time Su Shi came back to the capital, at the end of a stint as prefect outside, the same sequence of events recurred. He would return to a high post (Hanlin academician, special drafting official) and soon find himself accused of some misdeed. He would demand an investigation and not long thereafter request to be sent out to the prefectures again. Thus did those set against him ensure that he would never wield real influence at the Court. In 1093, it was the censor Huang Qingji who led the attack. Su was accused of having slandered Shenzong's government in the decree he had drafted demoting the reform minister Lü Huiqing. When Su wrote the decree, at the Court's direction early in the Yuanyou era, it was welcomed as a just denunciation of a wicked minister; but now it was used against its author.[70] Huang marshaled other charges as well, including one that Su Shi had taken advantage of the man from whom he had purchased his Yixing farm years before. Su Shi defended himself on each point, and observed to the Court that this tactic of finding slander in his various writings "had its origins with Zhu Guangting, matured with Zhao Tingzhi, and culminated with Jia Yi. Now Huang Qingji has adopted it once again."[71] Su Shi was reassigned to Dingzhou, in central Hebei, later in the year.

This time there would be no more struggles; or at least the next conflict would be of a different order, in which Su Shi was just one player and no longer the primary target. In the autumn of 1093, the

empress dowager died and control of the government passed to Zhezong, now eighteen. In spite of the empress dowager's preferences, it
was widely recognized that her grandson might listen to those who
wanted Wang Anshi's reforms reinstituted—the new emperor could
then claim to be loyal to the policies of his father (Shenzong). The
empress dowager herself summoned Fan Zuyu and other ministers she
trusted to her sickbed, and urged them loyally to resist the pressure for
change she expected after her death.[72] When Su Shi left the capital for
Dingzhou, the new ruler had declined Su's request to see him. Such an
imperial audience was customarily granted to officials leaving for distant posts. Su expressed his disappointment in a farewell memorial and
went on to urge the emperor, as he probably wanted to do in person,
not to effect sweeping changes in the government without first appris-
ing himself of current conditions. Su suggested that three years (the
mourning period) would be an appropriate time to wait and observe.[73]
Within weeks it would be obvious that Zhezong had no such intention.

Before the year's end, at the recommendation of Yang Wei,
who had himself recently been promoted as executive of the Board of
Rites, several key members of the defunct reform government were returned to prominent posts, including Zhang Dun, An Dao, Lü Huiqing, Cai Bian, Deng Runfu, and Li Qingchen. In the *jinshi* examination the following spring, the candidates were asked in a question
devised by Li Qingchen to comment on the unfavorable results of
dismantling the reforms. Yang Wei saw to it that any candidate who
sought to defend the Yuanyou policies failed. In the meantime, Su
Che, who was then executive of the Chancellery, protested the question itself in a long memorial that went on to argue generally against
the wholesale condemnation of the previous eight years of administration. The emperor was said to be displeased, and Su Che was removed
from his post and exiled from the capital as governor of Ruzhou (south
of Luoyang).[74]

By the summer of 1094, a full-scale purge of Yuanyou policies
and ministers was in operation. Virtually any member of the former
government could now be found guilty of having "slandered our
former emperor (Shenzong)" by virtue of having participated in the
process of revoking the reforms. So deep was the rancor of those who
led the purge that Zhang Dun, Cai Bian, and others now persuaded
the emperor to demote the two Yuanyou leaders, Sima Guang and Lü
Gongzhu, posthumously. Still unsatisfied, Zhang and Cai requested
that these men's tombs be opened, their coffins smashed, and their
corpses exposed. This proposal was supported in the highest ministries;
but one lone dissenter, Xu Jiang, persuaded the emperor that such an

action would set a dangerous precedent. Those in power had to content themselves with the destruction of the two men's tomb inscriptions.[75]

In the fourth month of 1094, members of the Censorate including Su Shi's old nemesis Zhao Tingzhi reiterated the charge that Su had defamed Shenzong in Lü Huiqing's demotion decree. This time there was no hope of a successful defense. News soon reached Su in Dingzhou that he had been reassigned to Yingzhou (at the other end of the empire, one thousand miles south) and demoted in rank and grade. En route he learned that he had been demoted further, was now ordered to proceed to the more remote Huizhou, on the coast of Guangdong, and was forbidden to speak out on matters of state.

Su Shi was to remain in Huizhou two and a half years, until the summer of 1097. At that time the persecution of Yuanyou and other prominent officials led by Zhang Dun and Cai Bian intensified. Sima Guang and Lü Gongzhu suffered, posthumously, another demotion in rank. Some thirty of the still living Yuanyou leaders were exiled to the distant south, where many would die in the succeeding years. Su Shi received what appears to have been the harshest of all these new or increased exiles: he was sent to Hainan Island (off Guangdong's Leizhou Peninsula), and was kept there for three years. His health deteriorated steadily during this confinement to the malarial island. Su lived for only one year after the general reprieve of the Yuanyou officials issued in 1100, which allowed him to return to the mainland.

That reprieve, moreover, exemplified just a brief hiatus in the persecution of Yuanyou leaders, brought on by the death of Zhezong. During the short regency of Empress Dowager Xiang (before Huizong acceded to power), an attempt was made to find a middle course between those of the "new" and "old" factions. But this effort at reconciliation failed to satisfy either side. Soon after Su's death in 1101, the supporters of the reforms regained ascendancy, Cai Jing began his infamous tenure as grand councilor, and the persecution began anew. A stele was erected outside the Wende Palace inscribed with the names of one hundred twenty-eight Yuanyou leaders (including Su), who were denounced as members of "the faction of traitors." Hundreds of lesser officials connected with these leaders were found guilty and punished for having slandered the reform administration in memorials. Special distinction was given to Su and his associates in this campaign. Su's literary works, together with those of his father and brother, were proscribed and the printing blocks ordered destroyed wherever they could be found (though this command seems to have had little effect, to judge from the wide circulation of Su's writings early in the Southern Song). The writings of Huang Tingjian and Qin Guan were likewise banned.[76] This time it would take dynastic catastophe—the loss of the entire northern half of the nation and imperial flight south in 1125—before the reform party would be discredited.

The story of Su Shi's southern exile, which occupied the last seven years of his life, and his death belongs to another chapter. In concluding this one, I shall quote Su's own account of his role and motives through four decades of prominence in national politics. This was written soon after his split with Sima Guang over the Hired Service policy, and after accusations were brought against him concerning the examination question he composed. In defending himself, Su reflects here upon three crucial episodes in his career: his success in the decree examinations, his denunciation of the New Policies under Shenzong, and his current role as a critic of Yuanyou-period policy:

> I have heard that in ruling over the empire the sage relies both on leniency and severity, and that between the ruler and ministers approval and disapproval enhance each other. If ministers, without questioning the correctness of a policy, approve of whatever their ruler approves of, or if they disapprove of whatever he disapproves of, without considering its rightness, this amounts to what Yanzi called "trying to enhance the taste of water by adding more water—who will want to drink it?"[77] and what Confucius referred to when he said, "When others all agree with what I say and never disagree, this will suffice to bring the state to ruin."[78] Long ago when I was recommended for the decree examination during Renzong's reign, the policy papers and essays I submitted, together with my answers to the emperor's questions, were generally all intended to urge Renzong to make the administration more rigorous and efficient, to supervise the bureaucracy more stringently, and to be more decisive and act more forcefully. Later, I served Shenzong and was summoned to respond to his questions. I withdrew and submitted several tens of thousands of words, all of which were meant to encourage Shenzong to be forgiving and magnanimous, to be tolerant of what was vile and degrading, and to bend to accommodate others. I did not reflect upon my own insignificance; rather, in all of this I hoped to emulate the ancient worthies, making approval and disapproval enhance each other.
>
> Ever since our two sages came to power [i.e., since the empress dowager's regency on Zhezong's behalf] our sagely government has been renewed daily, being wholly dedicated to magnanimity. In general, it has followed Renzong's precedent . . . Although Your Majesty has opened wide the paths of policy discussion, prohibiting nothing from consideration, today the censors attack no one but members of the previous administration and they denounce nothing but the previous administration's policies. This is truly "trying to enhance the taste of water by adding more water," and it gives me great concern. It was, then,

with these purposes in mind that I composed the examination question referred to earlier. In fact, the question was intended to criticize the present Court's censors and grand councilors. I hoped that when Your Majesty saw it, you might be persuaded to try to combine together the magnanimity and the rigorousness of our two former sage emperors.[79]

Reading this, we recall the particular aversion Su felt to Wang Anshi's efforts to emasculate the Censorate at the start of the New Policy's era and the pride with which he described, on that occasion, the earlier history of that institution during the Song. It is no small irony that so many of Su Shi's later battles would be fought against censors who had given up policy criticism themselves in favor of vilifying those who sought to voice it.

In national politics Su Shi always represented an alternative viewpoint to that which held sway. It was a role he self-consciously adopted, believing as he did that "approval and disapproval enhance each other." That his belief turned out to be particularly ill-suited to his times seems, if anything, to have hardened his resolve to act on it.

CHAPTER FIVE

Provincial Activism In and Out of Office

Su Shi was appointed prefect of Hangzhou in 1089, having been forced by the censors' attacks upon him to petition for reassignment to the provinces. As we have seen, this was the first of several times during the Yuanyou period that Su sought refuge away from the capital. Su arrived at Hangzhou in the summer, his first visit to the area since his tour as vice prefect ended there in 1074. "I return one more time to drink wine in West Lake rains / Having not glimpsed bouncing pearls for fifteen years."[1] Su would remain in Hangzhou less than two years before he was recalled to the capital. But these were eventful years, during which Su managed to do considerably more than just enjoy Hangzhou's scenery. Of all of Su's provincial posts, this one at Hangzhou is the most celebrated. An examination of what he accomplished and the methods he used in instituting two major relief efforts will serve to introduce his legacy in provincial government.[2]

Famine Relief in Hangzhou

Within a few months of his arrival, Su Shi began to memorialize to the throne about a problem that was to cast a shadow over his entire tenure as prefect and consume his energies. He asked that measures be taken to relieve the food shortage in the seven prefectures of the Zhexi circuit (the western division of Liangzhe, "the two Zhes"), which included Hangzhou.[3] Su pointed out that in the preceding winter and spring the region had experienced extensive flooding and that the waters had not receded until late in the spring, preventing the planting of the early-ripening rice. To make matters worse, later that summer the region had suffered from drought. By the winter the price of a *dou* of rice had risen to 90 *wen*, compared with the norm of 60–70 *wen*, and there were commoners who were going hungry. Su expressed his fear that if no action were taken, there would be widespread rice shortages, starvation, and banditry by the coming summer, before the next harvest was in. Hinting of how bad conditions could get, he reminded the throne of the famine that had devastated the region in the early 1070s (which Su had witnessed), when the price of rice rose to 200 *wen* and half the population of the circuit ("over 500,000" people) starved to death.[4]

To prevent further increases in the price of rice and the ensuing spread of starvation, Su proposed that the central government decrease its own demand of Zhexi rice for the coming year, leaving more rice available locally. Specifically, Su asked that the quota of rice Zhexi was required to deliver to the capital for official use (which was set at 1,600,000 piculs) be diminished by one-third to one-half, with the understanding that the shortfall would be made up over the following two years if regional harvests improved. With the same end in mind, Su also asked that the government suspend its purchase of Zhexi rice to stock the various kinds of granaries it maintained (including those in the capital, military storehouses, and the regional Ever Normal Granaries). Finally, to ease the shortage of cash in the circuit and to stimulate the local economy, Su urged the government to use the cash it had planned to spend on Zhexi rice to buy up local silver and silk instead.

The Song government had developed a variety of different strategies to provide famine relief.[5] Some of these were designed to give rice directly to starving masses in times of famine (by distributing it freely from the government's Relief Granaries [*yicang*], or by initiating public works projects that would recruit and feed starving laborers and their families, or by encouraging wealthy families to dole out rice to the masses), while others were intended primarily to influence the price of rice on the open market, and hence its availability. The Ever Normal Granary (*changping cang*) was an institutionalized, and venerable, example of the latter type of policy. The idea was that in years of abundant harvests the Ever Normal Granary would buy up quantities of surplus rice in order, first, to protect the farmers against falling prices (by increasing demand) and, second, to accumulate reserves for lean years. In times of poor harvests, then, the Ever Normal Granary would sell its stores on the open market but would sell them at lower than market price, which would be rising as a region experienced shortages of rice, and thus keep the price of rice down. Another strategy used to counteract a rise in the price of rice during lean years was the reduction of various forms of taxes in kind (to be paid in rice) or tribute that each region owed to the central government. Naturally, a decrease in the central government's demand of local rice for a given year would increase the local supply and work against rising prices, just as the sale of rice from the Ever Normal Granary was designed to do.

In his memorial Su Shi sought to anticipate and avoid rice shortages that he feared would develop in the coming year if nothing were done. It is typical of Su's conduct as prefect that he tried to anticipate the shortages before they developed rather than just react to them after they had become serious. Typical, too, is that in matters of famine relief Su consistently favored policies designed to control the price of rice over those intended to put rice directly in the hands of starving commoners. He points out that once starvation is allowed to become widespread, the granaries never contain enough rice actually to feed more than a fraction of all the hungry people. If, however, through government influence the price of rice is kept down, everyone in the region benefits as their ability to purchase rice is maximized. Su assumes that in the meantime merchants will ship rice into an area of shortage to take advantage of the increased demand, so long as the government does not inhibit this movement of rice by imposing transport taxes, whose repeal or suspension Su repeatedly calls for.[6] Price stabilization achieved through relief sales of rice by the government is thus the key to Su's strategy for alleviating shortages (and the efficacy of this method is singled out for praise by Dong Wei, the Southern Song author of a handbook on famine relief).[7] The practical problems of alternative approaches, including the free distribution of rice and the use of public works projects to provide famine relief, were widely recognized. Free distribution often gave rise to riots and theft. It also tended to be inequitable, favoring the residents of urban areas and ignoring those in the outlying countryside. Consequently, such distribution often caused refugees to flock to the cities from their farms. Also, corrupt local officials were known to demand bribes before making the rice available. Public works projects were subject to similar abuse. Often no work was accomplished (how could starving men, Su wondered, be expected to accomplish anything as laborers?).[8] Hordes of hungry people descended upon the site and left it as soon as the food was exhausted.

This time the Court agreed to the three main requests Su had laid before it, although it decreased the Zhexi quota of rice by only one-third rather than the one-half Su had hoped for (and only agreed to this amount reluctantly and after some additional prodding from Su).[9] Still, these measures seem to have had good effect. In the autumn of 1090, when he was requesting further assistance for the following year, Su referred to the benefits of the measures enacted earlier that spring as an exemplary instance of anticipating and avoiding food shortages. He notes that as soon as the government curtailed its purchases, the price of rice fell back to its normal level with the result that starvation was averted.[10]

Although the Court had given Su Shi much of what he had asked for, and although these measures appear to have had their desired immediate effect in the Zhexi circuit generally, by the end of 1089 Su Shi became convinced that one more step had to be taken in his own prefecture of Hangzhou to tide it over until the next harvest. Su had done all he could do to meet his first priority, to keep the price of rice from rising exorbitantly throughout the region. But it now occurred to him that in Hangzhou there would still be more demand for rice than the open market could supply, because of the poor harvest in 1089, and that the current reserves in the Ever Normal Granary were inadequate to satisfy this demand. He anticipated that he would have to open the granaries from the second through the sixth month of 1090, when he would sell government rice to those who needed it. He had already made arrangements to have adequate supplies available in the city of Hangzhou itself, but he calculated that the granaries in the outlying districts of Hangzhou would fall some 30,000 piculs short of the demand.[11] To obtain this amount, Su turned to another of the government's resources, ordination certificates (dudie). These were documents that the government began to issue in 1068 in recognition of a person's ordination as a Buddhist monk or nun. The bearer was exempted from government corvée obligations, and so the certificates came to be in high demand and sold at exorbitant prices. (In fact, many monks and nuns could not afford the purchase price themselves and had to rely upon a merit-seeking donor who bought the certificate for them.) The issuance of the certificates increased sharply during the New Policies era, and they soon became a principal instrument used by the government to generate emergency funds.[12] Shortly after Su had arrived in Hangzhou in 1089, he had asked the central government to issue 200 ordination certificates to him to raise money to rebuild the dilapidated government quarters he found waiting for him there. His request had not been granted, nor apparently had it been denied. Now, facing shortages in the granaries, Su returned to his earlier proposal, asking that he be given the 200 certificates to issue to local church-supporting merchants or families who had their own private stores of rice. The cost of the certificates would be paid in rice rather than cash. Su estimated that he could add 25,000 piculs of rice to the granaries this way, nearly all he would need. Stretching his argument, and unwilling to relinquish his earlier plan, he added that when this newly acquired amount of rice was subsequently sold (since his plan was to sell the granary rice at a low price rather than give it away), it would still generate enough cash to renovate the Hangzhou government buildings, even if not so extensively as he had originally hoped.

Su proposed this idea two times, first in a letter to the Court ministers (mentioned above) in the last month of 1089, and again in a memorial sent in the second month of 1090.[13] In the meantime, and possibly as a result of Su's letter, the Court had already decided to issue 300 certificates for famine relief to Zhexi Circuit (and another 300 to neighboring Huainan Circuit). Zhexi's portion of the certificates, however, were sent directly to the circuit's fiscal intendant, Ye Wensou, who took it upon himself to decide the allotment that would be given to each of Zhexi's seven prefectures. Although Hangzhou was by far the most populous of these prefectures, he allotted to it only 30 of the 300 certificates.

When Su Shi heard the news, he was furious. On the very next day he sent a memorial to the Court entitled, "On Ye Wensou's Inequitable Distribution of Ordination Certificates."[14] The memorial attacks Ye both for failing to consult with his colleagues (the assistant fiscal intendant, the judicial intendant, and Su himself as the military administrator of the circuit) in determining how to distribute the certificates, and for distributing them in an unreasonable manner. Su points out, for example, that although the population of Runzhou was only 10 or 20 percent that of Hangzhou, somehow Ye had decided that Runzhou should receive 100 certificates, even though there had been no report of rice shortages there. Su asks the Court to rescind Ye's distribution and to see that Hangzhou is given 150 of the certificates (still 50 short of the number Su had originally requested).

Little is known about Ye Wensou, Su's antagonist in this event. It is recorded that he and Su had long been at odds with each other, and it is probable that Ye was associated with one of the political factions that considered Su its enemy. A defense of Ye's handling of the certificates was subsequently written by Ye Mengde, the grandson of Wensou's brother.[15] Predictably, it says that Wensou was attempting to balance the needs of all of the prefectures in his circuit, whereas Su Shi was simply trying to get the most he could for his own Hangzhou.

This defense leaves much unanswered since it does not address Su's specific objections to the inequities he perceived.

The resolution of this disagreement over the ordination certificates led directly to another episode in Su's Hangzhou governorship, his famous West Lake project, which he began two months after his outburst against Ye Wensou. In the preceding decades Hangzhou's West Lake had shrunk to barely half its former size, choked by weeds and aquatic grasses, which local residents had been planting and cultivating for their own consumption. It was felt that if action were not taken, the entire lake would turn into a swamp within a few years. Su proceeded to dredge the lake and clear it of the grasses that were choking it. At the same time, he hit upon the idea of using the fill that resulted from the dredging to construct a causeway that cut across the lake, for the convenience of local residents.[16] Su's recovery of West Lake, and his construction of "Su Dike," which remains a prominent feature of the lake to this day, is ordinarily treated by historians as a separate undertaking, unrelated to his efforts to minimize the Hangzhou famine. Su himself, however, links the lake project to the famine, representing it occasionally as an undertaking that would support people through difficult times. Moreover, his funding for the work was not only of the same kind as he had requested for the famine relief (that is, the ordination certificates) but actually was generated by the very certificates that were given to him to augment the local granaries.

The Court evidently found Su's protestations against Ye Wensou persuasive, for subsequently it directed that Hangzhou's allotment of the Zhexi certificates be increased to 100 (still 50 short of Su's latest request). Our source for this is a memorial Su wrote in the early summer of 1090 describing the importance of saving West Lake.[17] In presenting his case, Su calls attention to the many benefits the lake provides to the city: it provides water for irrigation and to keep the canals navigable; it keeps fresh water in the wells nearby (which would otherwise turn briny from seawater); and it supplies the brewers of alcoholic beverages with their water, thus contributing to the city's tax revenue. At the same time, and seemingly to convince the authorities that he knew what he was doing, Su sent a separate petition to the leading ministers of state, explaining in detail how he would manage the dredging, how he would enlarge and regulate the feeder rivers and canals to keep the lake well supplied with water, and how he would prevent repetition of the current problem by prohibiting people from planting anything along the shore except for water chestnut, the harvesting of which would keep the waters clear of weeds.[18] Su represents his plans as having been developed in consultation with local experts, especially farmers and city elders who had witnessed the shrinking of the lake over the past decades and who knew best how to restore it to its former condition. Then Su makes a revelation: he has already begun the work. In fact, it is half completed. He explains that when he sold at a nominal price the rice that he had obtained from issuing the 100 monk's certificates given to him, he acquired 10,000 cash. With this money he hired 100,000 laborers to dredge and clear the lake. As he reveals this, Su requests that another 100 certificates be given to him, assuring the Court that with the money brought in from these additional certificates he would be able to complete the task and ensure the lake's preservation.[19]

It is probably no coincidence that the total number of certificates Su requested (200), now to complete the dredging of West Lake, matches the number he had originally asked for to supplement the rice in the granaries. Why had famine relief seemingly given way to water conservancy? Su must have perceived that the Court simply would not do anything more, whether in the form of tax abatement or the issuance of ordination certificates, for famine relief in Hangzhou. Consequently, he decided to request aid for another purpose, one he felt the Court might be more sympathetic towards (saving West Lake), and then to use that aid as best he could to accomplish both the acquisition of the granary rice he felt he would need and the project he had specified. By starting the West Lake project before making this latest request for 100 additional certificates, Su evidently hoped to pressure the Court into compliance, since he pointed out that if the West Lake work were left uncompleted, within a short time the weeds would reclaim large sections of the lake and all the dredging that had been done would be wasted effort.

Why was the Court unwilling to do more to avert a famine? Not, it turns out, because it lacked the resources, but because it was being informed by Su's superiors in the region that there was no crisis. At the end of the fifth month of 1090, Su learned that both the fiscal intendant (Ye Wensou) and the judicial intendant of Zhexi, as well as the judicial intendant of Western Huainan circuit, had written to the Ministry of Finance in the capital, explaining that there was no shortage of rice in their circuits, that the upcoming harvest would be bountiful, and that there were no refugees or dispossessed persons. Consequently, they said that the ordination certificates that had already been issued were unnecessary. As a result, the Ministry actually initiated the process of recalling the certificates. Su memorialized again, asking that this recall be halted and charging his superiors with dishonesty and opportunism.[20] Here, as in an earlier letter to the Court officials,[21] Su bluntly confronts a familiar bureaucratic malaise. Most prefects and circuit intendants would, Su maintains, never report food shortages because they did not want to be the bearers of unwelcome news. The Court might hold them responsible, blaming them for inadequate oversight or contingency planning. Consequently, the local authorities report what they know the Court officials want to hear, and the Court tends to accept the news because it is pleasing. But when the commoners learn of this decision to recall the ordination certificates, Su warns, "they will conclude that the Court does not care about its starving masses but cares instead about a few hundred paper certificates."[22] Aside from demanding that the recall be stopped, Su concludes by asking for 50 additional certificates (whereas earlier he had asked for twice that amount) to finish the work on West Lake. Both of his requests were granted.[23]

Several times in his memorials about West Lake, Su Shi connects the project with famine relief. In others of his writings Su voices skepticism over the value of such measures, but in this case he appears to have been forced into invoking this justification. He does so, one senses, with reluctance, mentioning it always as an afterthought or an ancillary benefit.[24] However, because public works was one of the standard Song government responses to famine, Su evidently believed that the mention of this aspect of his plan would strengthen his case.

Having weathered the rice shortages of the spring and summer of 1090, in the autumn Su turned his attention to the likely recurrence of the problem in the following year. It happened that the harvest of 1090 in Zhexi was far from abundant. Su saw that this would be so early in the seventh month, for the region had been beset by heavy rains and flooding. Inasmuch as the granaries were already dangerously depleted and many commoners were already struggling against food shortages and debts, Su likened the region to a patient facing a second outbreak of a serious disease: "Although the illness is the same, with his strength so sapped it will be difficult for him to survive this time around."[25] The situation deteriorated further later in the month, while most of the crops were still in the fields, when the region was struck by a storm of heavy winds and rains that lasted three days and nights and caused extensive flooding in the Taihu Lake area.

From the autumn of 1090 until the spring of 1091, when he was recalled from Hangzhou to the capital, Su memorialized no fewer than eight times, at an average length of one thousand words, to urge the Court to take steps to avoid a famine in Zhexi before the harvest of

1091. It must be said that, on the whole, Su was less successful with this round of requests and proposals than he had been in the preceding twelve months; for when he finally left Hangzhou, little had been done to ease the residents' plight. As Su's frustration increased through this period, with the Court's silence in the face of his requests, or its outright rejection of them, and as the situation grew more desperate with each month that no action was taken, we can see him alter his arguments and his recommendations. As thoroughgoing and persuasive as his proposals are, ultimately it is Su's doggedness in his cause that emerges as its most memorable element.

Su first requested that Zhexi's quota of rice for the capital be cut by one-half and that whatever rice could be spared from nearby prefectures be shipped to the Hangzhou granaries to prepare for the large-scale sale of granary rice that would be necessary in the spring and summer of 1091.[26] Once again Su stresses how crucial it is that the government act before widespread famine actually sets in. If officials allow circumstances to deteriorate to the point at which granary rice must be rushed to a region of starvation and distributed freely, the government empties its granaries and loses the potential revenue from the orderly sale of Ever Normal Granary supplies; and, if the starving masses abandon their fields and become refugees, wandering to other areas in search of food, it also loses tax income from the uncultivated fields. Su did not hesitate to represent the measures he was urging as being in the central government's own fiscal interest, aside from being in the tradition of humane governance.

What is striking about Su's request is the effort it makes to anticipate and eliminate skepticism over the accuracy of his account of the crisis, skepticism fanned by contrary reports. Obviously, Su has come to expect a struggle over the veracity of his description and he alters his rhetoric accordingly. He cites the words of other witnesses to the floods and poor harvests in Zhexi, quoting from officials who have toured the region and filed reports. He asks that each prefecture be directed to determine whether or not it will need to sell Ever Normal Granary rice in the coming spring. If a need is foreseen, it should begin buying up rice for the granaries right away. And if no need is anticipated, the prefectural officials, Su urges, should be required to guarantee, on penalty of their own impeachment, that no need will develop.

In the ninth and tenth months of 1090, having received no reply from the central government, the tone of Su's memorials became more urgent and his split with the circuit intendants, his supervisors, grew more apparent. Su discloses that he has been trying to buy up rice for the Hangzhou granaries, anticipating great need in the new year, but notes with dismay that not a single person has come forth with rice to sell. The problem was that merchants could get a better price for their rice on the open market, where the price had already begun to rise, than from the government. Su asks for permission to raise the amount that he is allowed to spend, pointing out that doing so does not mean that the government will actually lose money, since it will be able to sell the rice at the same price in the spring, when the price on the open market will be considerably higher.[27] This request was apparently never answered. Instead, the judicial intendant of Zhexi specifically ordered the prefects of his circuit, including Su Shi, not to pay higher prices. Su, by his own admission, ignored this directive and continued to purchase rice at the moderately inflated price of 70 *wen*. Still, he complains that he has not been able to purchase as much rice as the granaries would need, and notes that other prefectures, which were paying less than Su's, were doing even worse. This scrimping on expenditures made no sense to Su, who warned that the government expenses would be ten times as high if it allowed famine to engulf the region.[28]

Su Shi also attacked the opportunism of wealthy local clans, who saw in this crisis an opportunity for large profits:

> I have heard that the wealthy families in these prefectures, who all realize that the price of rice will be inflated next year, are all buying up and hoarding their own private supply, planning to sell it later at a huge profit. If the price the government is currently willing to pay is attractive, then the farmers' rice will all end up in the government's hands. In that case these wealthy men would not be able to take advantage of the situation to reap large gain and swallow up the impoverished and weak. That is why they are spreading false accusations now to unnerve the officials, saying how regrettable it is that the officials are wasting the government's money. If we reduce the price we are willing to pay or curtail our purchase of rice, we fall right into their trap.[29]

Probably Su intends to hint here at collusion between the wealthy clans and the local officials.

All through the autumn of 1090 Su had been asking that, in addition to the steps he was recommending for Zhexi Circuit and Hangzhou itself, the Court direct the exchange intendants of nearby circuits (Jiangdong and Huainan) to buy up 500,000 piculs of rice from prefectures that had good harvests and store it in Zhenzhou and Yangzhou. If, as Su feared, the reserves in Zhexi's own Ever Normal Granaries ran out the following spring, this backup supply could readily be shipped in. When it became obvious to Su that, for the reasons cited above, the Zhexi granaries were not being adequately stocked, he reiterated the importance of securing additional rice outside of the circuit.[30] In this instance, Su's request was granted. An imperial decree was issued to the exchange intendants, authorizing the purchases and providing funds with which to make them. But what happened, as Su discovered in the third month of 1091, was that the exchange intendants refused to buy more than a fraction of the 500,000 piculs. They reported back to the throne that the price of rice was high in their circuits and it was not a good time to buy. Exasperated, Su repeated his argument about false economy and also pointed out that, in justifying their inaction to the throne, the intendants had quoted the highest prices of rice that could be found in their circuits rather than the price found in prefectures where supplies were abundant.[31]

Su Shi was recalled to the capital at the end of the second month of 1091. On his journey northward Su made a point of touring the Taihu Lake region. While still en route he sent another memorial to the throne, saying that he had now witnessed the flooded counties himself, and pleading once again for surplus rice to be transported to them from other prefectures. "How should I dare, just because I have left my office, pass the worry on to my successor and bear no more responsibility myself?"[32] After Su arrived at the capital, he continued to show his concern. He submitted a detailed and comprehensive plan for flood control throughout the southeastern region, a plan that had been devised by local expert, Shan E.[33] In the seventh month, after he had assumed his new duties as drafting official at the Court, he memorialized again on Hangzhou's behalf, asking for immediate famine relief. One of Su's former subordinates had written to him, reporting that the granary rice in Hangzhou would be completely exhausted at the end of the month and thereafter famine was unavoidable. Su requested the central government to ensure that the granaries would be kept open by shipping rice in from other regions, right through the autumn of the following year if necessary. He briefly reminded the Court of the intendants' non-compliance with its earlier edict, which ought to have prevented such a crisis from arising.[34]

Two days after Su Shi submitted this last of his memorials on Zhexi, two imperial censors called for an investigation into the whole matter. What the censors were questioning was not the handling of famine relief efforts, but the reports of food shortages themselves. Su Shi is not mentioned by name in the censors' memorials, but there is little doubt that he was their principal target. The censors challenge the veracity of the claim that Zhexi, and Hangzhou in particular, was in distress. Technically, the censors are only calling for an investigation and so they do not say outright that the Court has been lied to. But their language implies as much. The people of the Zhe region, they assert, "are habitually arrogant and untruthful, and they make much of minor grievances. They have always been this way."[35] The censors also cite certain inconsistencies in the reports that have been filed, mentioning that some accounts have it that the flooding has been confined to the Taihu Lake area and has not affected Hangzhou. They urge that careful assessment should be made of the extent of the damage, so that local officials do not collude together to "engage in deceit and false reporting."[36] If it were concluded that there had been false reporting, the officials in charge would have been severely punished. Thus the investigation the censors were calling for amounted to an impeachment initiative against Su Shi, who had been and continued to be the chief and tireless reporter of the Zhexi crisis.

The censors' charges raise a problem for us today. In discussing Su's string of Hangzhou memorials, I have assumed that he was telling the truth. But what if he was not? Su's memorials are the principal source on the floods and food shortages in the region. There is little else to which we can turn for verification. What would Su's motives have been for misrepresenting local conditions? Presumably, he might have been trying to enhance his reputation as a capable and humane prefect. If he exaggerated the gravity of the crisis, not only would he stand a better chance of securing ample famine relief from the central government, but once famine had been successfully averted, he would appear in the Court's eyes as an unusually able local administrator.

As difficult as it may be to verify the accuracy of Su's reports, the problem loses much of its urgency when we consider the source of the allegations against him. The censor who led the attack upon Su Shi was Jia Yi, the supporter of Cheng Yi who had both his mentor's and, as we have seen, his own reasons for enmity towards Su Shi. In fact, when Su first received his recall from Hangzhou, he resisted the idea of returning to the capital specifically because he expected that Jia Yi would move against him.[37] Later, a week before Jia Yi's call for an investigation into the Hangzhou reports, Su had again memorialized about Jia Yi's rancor towards him, describing Jia as a man so obsessed with revenge that "not a day goes by that he does not plot against me."[38] And after the accusation concerning Hangzhou proved ineffectual, it was Jia Yi who tried to incriminate Su for his poetic line about "hearing good news."

The veracity of Su's representation of circumstances in Hangzhou was defended in a lengthy memorial by Fan Zuyu, one of the few high officials known for keeping aloof from any political faction.[39] Fan's support for Su on this matter was unequivocal. In his memorial

Fan never mentions the personal aspects of the dispute—in fact he never mentions Su by name at all. He addresses himself solely to the matter of the accuracy of the reports about Hangzhou and to the question of what action should be taken.[40] Fan stresses the obligation of the government to the welfare of its people, and he refutes point by point the assertions made by Jia Yi and his associate, Yang Wei. Fan allows that exaggerated reports of shortages may sometimes occur, but points out that in the present case the calamitous circumstances are well known and widely documented. The Zhexi prefectures have had to distribute rice freely for months and have also had to set up stations to serve gruel to starving crowds. Many different sources, which Fan quotes, attest that refugees roam the land and have fought over food (in one food riot, forty people were trampled to death).[41] To speak of exaggerations in such a case, Fan asserts, is perverse. The proposed investigation would only further delay essential aid and would have the effect of further intimidating local officials, making them even more reluctant to report bad harvests in the future.

Fan Zuyu's argument was accepted by the Court and the investigation was dropped. One more document pertaining to these events might be cited here, a document that is as important for its tone as for its message. It is a private letter Su Shi wrote from Hangzhou in the autumn of 1090, after the storms of the seventh month had dimmed prospects for a decent harvest. The letter was sent to a fellow prefect, Qian Mufu (Si), in the neighboring prefecture of Yuezhou. The man referred to as Zhongyu is Ma Sheng, who was the judicial intendant of the Zhedong and Zhexi circuits, and thus one of Su's (and Qian's) immediate superiors and one who was responsible for overseeing the agricultural as well as the judicial administration in the region.[42]

Today I received the official proclamation cautioning us that the Min bandits may in time reach Qu and Mu, but I believe the danger is not imminent. However, the several prefectures in Zhedong have experienced severe flooding; and from the twenty-first to the twenty-third of the seventh month, there was heavy rain and violent wind, which ruined nearly all the crops. The disaster is no less than last year's, but this time the reserves in the Ever Normal Granary have already been depleted. Responsibility for dealing with this crisis rests entirely with Zhongyu and me. I need to discuss the matter in person with him and cannot deal with it fully in letters. I have asked him to come here repeatedly for this purpose, but he has not paid any attention to me. Winter has just begun and although Zigong will arrive in Zhexi any day,[43] we can achieve success with matters as weighty as these only if all of us reach a consensus together. The burden of his trip here, past the few post-stations,[44] would be no worse than when he comes to observe the tidal bore, which itself is pleasant enough. Try to persuade Zongyu with this argument, but do not say I told you so. Would you? Would you? When a member of our group undertakes something, he must go about it with all possible care and thoroughness if he is to succeed. If the smallest detail is left unattended to, our critics will be unrelenting. Right now the price of rice is stable, but one month from now it will rise again. Day and night I wait for Zhongyu to come. If I set loose my subordinates to buy up 100,000 piculs of rice, and then if the fiscal intendants vie to purchase more for the army's rations and our contribution to the central government, the price of rice will jump dramatically. It may not be easy to discuss one by one all the other measures that should now be taken. I hope that you will think this over and speak out on whatever matters you feel you can address. Thank you! Thank you! I myself have already memorialized twice on this matter. Although the various ministers may not be pleased, there is no choice but to take action.[45]

Su Shi is trying to get his colleague and peer, Qian Mufu, to persuade their superior to visit Hangzhou, so that Su can present his case about the crisis there in person, and so that Ma Sheng will see the situation firsthand. At this point Su Shi is still hopeful of enlisting the support of this particular circuit intendant to persuade the central government to cut Zhexi's quota of rice to be supplied to the capital by one-half, so that Su can buy rice to restock the Ever Normal Granaries (the 100,000 piculs referred to in the note). But Su is worried that Zhongyu is ignoring his pleas to visit Hangzhou.

If Su Shi were engaged in an elaborate deception about the situation in Hangzhou, it is hardly likely that he would be trying, through private communications, to arrange for his superior to visit him there. Everything about a note such as this, and especially its tone, supports the case for the veracity of Su's official reports.

From various sources one gleans stray and mostly grim indications that the catastrophe Su had warned against became a reality in the ensuing years. In 1091, a censor reported gross mismanagement of the rice distribution in the Liangzhe (Zhedong and Zhexi) area. Merchants were conspiring together with corrupt local officials so that most of the rice was being distributed to them rather than to starving commoners, and there had been many deaths.[46] In the winter of the same year, by which time Su Shi had been transferred to Yingzhou, the prefectures adjoining Zhexi and Huainan witnessed a sizable influx of refugees from the starvation there. Su had to ask the central government for help in providing for these displaced commoners.[47] The famine apparently continued through at least the next two years. In 1092, Su, writing from Yangzhou (in Eastern Huainan Circuit) mentions in passing that he has heard that fully one-half the population in the three prefectures of the Taihu Lake region has died of starvation.[48] And in the summer of 1093, the intendants of Liangzhe, saying that food shortages were still rampant, asked for authorization to give, in addition to the rice that had already been distributed, one *dou* of rice to each person who came to ask for it at the government offices.[49] This pathetic gesture (the amount would have provided only about ten days' worth of rice to each person) probably reflects how desperate circumstances had become.

Other Undertakings as Prefect

Su Shi's efforts at famine relief in Hangzhou, whatever their degree of success, are the most fully documented of any of his undertakings as prefect. (His memorials on this one subject alone take up some fifty pages in the modern, typeset edition of his prose writings). The episode has been reviewed at some length here to convey a sense of Su's commitment to his responsibilities, the conceptual sophistication of his thinking, and the tenacity with which he represented his views to his superiors. But famine relief, and the recovery of West Lake that went with it, was by no means the only initiative Su took as prefect of Hangzhou. And if one looks, moreover, at Su's record in the other places he served as prefect (Xuzhou, Mizhou, Yangzhou), one finds other projects of a similar nature. A few of these will be briefly described here.

Debt abatement was a cause Su took up in Hangzhou and later in Yangzhou, as he tried to persuade the central government to reduce or cancel the commoner's burden of indebtedness because of fees and taxes. Most of the debts had been incurred during the New Policies era, when the central government had imposed new taxes on the people, and levied new fees on merchants, in its effort to increase revenues. When the people proved unable to pay these taxes, especially during lean years as at the end of the Xining era, the government recorded their indebtedness and thereafter tried to collect payment whenever it thought there was a chance of doing so. Su argues that circumstances had degenerated to the point where the farmers dreaded abundant harvests more than meager ones. Farmers, Su records, have said to him, "Although the people will experience food shortages in years that natural calamities occur, if they cut back on clothing and restrict their meals, they can get by. But in years of good harvests, when payment is demanded of their debts, as the people see the clerks stand in their doorways and feel the cangue and club on their bodies, they hope only to die."[50]

In some instances the commoners were certainly not blameless. However, inept policies adopted by local bureaucrats, who were under pressure from higher authorities to collect on the debts, exacerbated the situation. One kind of debt Su specifically addressed in his Hangzhou memorials grew out of a quota of silk that the prefecture had to supply to the central government.[51] After the silk had been purchased by local authorities, a large amount of it was discovered to be of unacceptable quality and was rejected. The local authorities tried to sell it in the public market, to recover their expenditure, but no one would buy it. Clearly, some private suppliers had successfully defrauded the prefectural government, and evidently the government could not locate them to hold them responsible. Instead, and acting in fear of their own supervisors, local bureaucrats simply imposed debts upon households it could identify and somehow implicate. Ten years later a sizable amount of the debt was still outstanding, and the government was still trying to collect it. But its efforts, Su charged, were directed either towards impoverished families who would never be able to comply, families that had long since been frightened out of the prefecture, or even fictitious households that had been concocted by the bureaucrats themselves to fill their books.

Even worse than such hapless efforts, in Su's eyes, was the deliberate perversion of imperial will by local clerks to prolong the commoners' debts. In fact, early in the Yuanyou period several kinds of debts had already been canceled by imperial decree. But in many instances clerks and local officials had altered the spirit or even the letter of these acts of clemency as they administered them. So regular was this practice that the people had coined the saying, "Yellow papers forgive the debts but white papers still demand them," yellow being the color of imperial decrees and white the color of the clerks' notices requiring payment.[52] Su cites the example of a decree that canceled the debts incurred in Liangzhe Circuit under the salt regulations implemented during the New Policies era. The decree acknowledges that the debtors are impoverished and have no means to extricate themselves. But the local officials rewrote the decree as they published and administered it, giving themselves the authority to decide which families qualified. It had originally been thought that hundreds of families would benefit by this decree, but after some five years only twenty-three families had their debts erased.[53] It was, as Su points out, in the clerks' own interests to prolong the debts. Indebtedness gave the clerks power over the people and must have provided them with endless opportunities to extort and demand bribes. Su estimates that each prefecture throughout the country had five hundred clerks whose primary activity was to try to collect these old debts. Confucius had said that harsh policies were more injurious to the people than a tiger; and so, Su observes, the government has now loosed, in all, some two hundred thousand tigers amid its populace and could hardly expect anything but catastrophe.[54]

Su Shi memorialized several times from Hangzhou about the debts but never received a response. He took up the matter again two years after he left Hangzhou, when he was reassigned to Yangzhou, where he found the same problem. In two documents, running to eight thousand characters, he presented his arguments again. This time he diminished the scope of his request, hoping no doubt to make it more palatable, and asked only that the collection of the debts be suspended for one year, so that the commoners would have some chance to improve their circumstances. This request was finally accepted. In the sixth month of 1092, the emperor, citing the impoverishment of the people in Huainan and Liangzhe (Su's Yangzhou and Hangzhou), decreed a temporary suspension of debts.[55]

Fiscal matters aside, as prefect Su Shi embarked upon several construction projects. He liked, in short, to build things. Mention has already been made of the West Lake project and the famous Su Causeway or Dike, as well as his attempt to reconstruct the prefectural offices in Hangzhou. Years before, when the Yellow River breached its banks at Chanzhou and threatened the prefectural seat of Xuzhou, Su, as prefect, mobilized the troops and residents of the city to fortify the wall against the rising waters. Su himself camped out on top of the wall until the waters receded, and was commended for his leadership by the emperor. Perhaps even more important than these heroics, however, was Su's subsequent determination to build a new fortification wall to protect the city against any recurrences of such a flood. Over a period of several months, Su repeatedly sent memorials to the Court describing his plan and specifying the funds and manpower necessary, stressing that such a fortification would protect Xuzhou for the foreseeable future. He received no response because, as he himself realized, available resources were being used first to repair the breach at Tanzhou. Su cut back on the size of the wall he planned, and wrote privately to high officials in the capital, urging them to see that the project was approved. In the following year the Court finally allocated 24 million cash, which was to be supplemented by additional revenue raised by the sale of Ever Normal Granary supplies—enough to hire some seven thousand laborers to build the wall. When the work was completed Su felt that the city was now secure and commemorated the undertaking by building Yellow Tower along the wall (named for the pounded earth of which it was made).[56]

Likewise, during his brief tenure at Dingzhou in 1093, Su developed a plan to build new barracks for the soldiers stationed there. Located strategically close to the northern border, Dingzhou was home to several detachments of imperial troops assigned to the Hebei Circuit. The troops were a bane on the local population, however, because of their incessant drinking and gambling, which often led to fighting and petty crime. Su came to the conclusion that the wanton behavior of the men could be traced in large part to the horrendous conditions in which they were forced to live, which resulted in turn from years of corruption in the military command. The men were housed in tiny rooms with dirt floors and roofs that leaked. "Apart from a single bed and a single stove, there is not even room enough to turn around."[57] Of the men who were married, 50 to 60 percent of the wives and children were found to be suffering from hunger and cold. Su submitted a plan to bring to justice those commanders who had diverted subsistence funds for the men into their own pockets. At the same time, he proposed the construction of new barracks with 7,971 rooms (the exactitude of the number is typical of his methods), calculating the cost down to the last *wen*. He suggested, once again, that the construction be financed by an issue of ordination certificates from the central government.

We might suppose that the kinds of measures described above (famine relief, debt abatement, flood control, housing) fell well within the normal concerns of the prefect, who was expected to look after the general welfare of his people. It is clear, however, that Su Shi's record of provincial activism was extraordinary. Furthermore, his efforts to alleviate suffering frequently extended beyond the normal concerns of the Confucian magistrate. From Xuzhou, for example, Su memorialized to the throne proposing that medical care be given to prisoners throughout the empire.[58] There had been a regulation, decreed in 1067, mandating punishments for jailors who had more than one prisoner die in their jail in a year's time. The regulation was very unpopular with prison officials, and it had been relaxed during the New Policies era so that jailors were only held responsible for deaths brought about by their own cruel treatment of prisoners or starvation. Jailors were no longer liable to punishment for death by sickness. Su Shi did not approve of either regulation, and pointed out the unreasonableness of even the earlier and apparently more humane policy. People die of sickness all the time. How can one demand, in effect, that it never happen in prison?

Su's solution was to provide regular medical care to all prisoners, and his plan comes with an incentive system for the doctors (rather than a punishment program for the jailors). Each prefecture and subprefecture throughout the realm would select one doctor and one bureaucrat (his secretary) who would, for twelve months, have no other duties than to look after sick prisoners. At the outset a list would be drawn up of all sick men, and the doctor and his assistant would be given one-third of their potential salary for the year. At the end of the year, the doctors would be ranked according to the survival rate of their patients. Doctors with the highest ranking (those who lost no more than one patient in ten) would be given the full amount of their remaining salary, but those with lower rankings would be given only a portion of the money that had been set aside for them. This would encourage conscientiousness on the part of the doctors and make them care for the prisoners "as if they are caring for members of their own family." The program would be financed by surplus funds generated by the surtax (*kuansheng qian*) paid under the Hired Service policy, funds which Su says were substantial and going unused.

The briefest of notes from Su Shi to a certain Zhang Jiafu complements his memorial on medical care for prisoners. The note, translated here in its entirety, allows us to glimpse in a more personal way Su Shi's involvement with the problem taken up by the complex and formal memorial: "I humbly address you: Today you are a prison officer. Nothing is more important than human life, and I hope you give it your closest attention. When it is extremely hot or cold, prisoners want only to die. If many of them fall sick and the officers and guards pay no attention, even those who were not sick at first end up perishing. That is why, wherever I have been prefect, I have always gone personally to examine the prisoners. If you keep this in mind, far-reaching blessings will come to you."[59]

Su evidenced a similar sort of concern during his tour as prefect of Hangzhou. Using a combination of personal and government funds, there he established a public hospital or infirmary which is said to have saved a thousand lives in the first three years it operated. The Song government had a long tradition of providing some forms of medical assistance to commoners. In earlier decades these included sending doctors to circulate through regions in which disease was rampant, and establishing and stocking local pharmacies for the distribution of medicines. But government hospitals appear generally to have been a Southern Song innovation. They are said, moreover, to have first appeared in Hangzhou (the capital) and nearby Shaoxing, and then gradually to have spread to other prefectures.[60] Su's hospital in Hangzhou was certainly among the earliest established by a prefectural administration during the Song, and it may have been one of the inspirations of the Southern Song policy (which is what a Southern Song gazetteer of Hangzhou implies).[61] Su says little himself about the hospital, and the details of how it was supported are sketchy. We do know that Su raised 2,000 strings of cash from private donations to first establish the institution; then he installed a Buddhist monk to run it and arranged to have it supported by 50 *hu* of rice from local taxes annually.[62] Su Che mentions that his brother also gave 50 *liang* (nearly two thousand grams) of his own gold to the hospital; this odd fact is clarified by a letter that has recently been discovered. A man named Xuande had sent an amount of gold and silver to Su right before Su left Hangzhou. Su did not think it proper to accept this gift and so he turned it over to the hospital, explaining in his reply to Xuande that would be a more beneficial use of the money.[63] The hospital evidently was well enough endowed to last long after Su left. Its continued presence in the city is attested not only by Su Che, but also by the Southern Song writer Zhou Hui, who records a conversation he had with a monk who had worked there.[64]

Private Initiatives

Thoroughgoing "involvement with things" (*jiwu*), that is, engagement with social problems, became for Su Shi an essential part of the criteria by which a man's performance as official and his moral cultivation were judged. ("Any official, regardless of his rank, who is able to involve himself with things as circumstances demand yet have nothing to be ashamed of is a man who has perfected himself.")[65] It is evident that the ideal carried over into private life as well, for no less remarkable than his record as a prefect is the list of initiatives Su Shi took in an unofficial capacity to improve local conditions wherever he was. This is an aspect of Su's conduct that has attracted comment both in Song and modern times.[66] Scholars point out that while certain of Su's efforts on behalf of his people as prefect may fall within traditional Confucian ideals of benevolent governance, the similar actions he took as a private person do not. The tradition, after all, stressed social obligations primarily for those men empowered by the emperor. When one was not so empowered, when in the common parlance of the literati one was "at odds with the times," the typical response was, as Mencius had said, "to improve oneself in solitude" (*du shan qi shen*), that is, to pursue study and self-cultivation. But that Su was not content to do. "Involvement with things" had become too pervasive a conviction to permit it.

Two instances of Su's private initiatives will be briefly described here, his efforts to end infanticide in Huangzhou and the various social projects he encouraged or contributed to in Huizhou. Both instances date from periods of exile. In other words, both times Su Shi had been confined to an outlying area, stripped of all bureaucratic authority (though he retained a low nominal rank since he had not retired), and was, in fact, specifically prohibited from memorializing or "speaking out" on government affairs.

The infanticide initiative is described in a long and moving letter Su sent from Huangzhou to the prefect of neighboring Ezhou, one Zhu Shouchang, who was an acquaintance:

> Humbly, I address you: I imagine that the several letters I have recently sent have reached you by now. Lately the spring has brought cold weather—I wonder how you are getting on? Yesterday a scholar living for now in Wuchang, Wang Tianlin (Dianzhi), visited me. He happened to mention something that so startled and upset me when I heard it that I could no longer swallow my food. It is only to someone as worthy as you that I would broach this matter, and that is why I have sent this messenger to you today. Such an insignificant fellow as I hardly has the time to correct the errors he makes in his own personal affairs. How should I have the strength or power to deal with matters beyond my ken?
>
> Tianlin said that the peasants of Yue and E have a practice of raising no more than two sons and one daughter. If they have any additional children, they kill them. They are especially averse to raising extra daughters, with the result that there is a shortage of marriageable girls in these regions and many unmarried men. As soon as the babies are born, they are drowned in cold water. The parents cannot bear to watch, and so they regularly close their eyes and turn their backs, holding the baby down in a tub of water. Its cries and gulps last for a long time, and then finally it dies. A certain Shi Kui in Shenshan Village had killed two of his babies. Then last summer his wife gave birth to quadruplets. The pain and suffering was intolerable, and mother and children all died. Such is the divine retribution for this killing, and yet the ignorant commoners do not know to reform their ways. Whenever Tianlin hears of an imminent killing nearby, he rushes off to try to save the baby, giving the family money for clothes and food. He has saved several children this way. After a week passes, even if childless parents ask for the baby, its own parents will not give it up. It is obvious from this that the love of parent for child is innate and universal. It is just that some parents are led astray by local practices.

I have heard that in E there is a man named Qian Guangheng, who has received the advanced degree and is now serving as judicial inspector in Anzhou. When he was in his mother's womb, his maternal uncle, Chen Zun, dreamed that a little boy came up to him and tugged his clothes, as if pleading with him. He saw this on two successive nights, the boy appearing increasingly agitated. Zun could think of no explanation except that his elder sister was due to give birth and she did not want any more children. Could the dream be a response to that? He hurried off to investigate, and found the baby boy already submerged in a tub of water. He pulled the child out and it survived. Everyone in E knows this story.

Under the law the punishment for deliberately killing one's child is two years of labor. Each case, then, is something that the local authorities should prosecute. I urge you to give clear orders to each subprefect and assistant in the subprefectures under your jurisdiction, and have them summon the various village wardens under them, informing them of the law, teaching them about the good and bad fortune involved, and requiring that they enforce the regulations. Have them return to their villages and circulate the news; have them copy the laws on walls for public display; and have them establish rewards for people who inform the authorities of such killings. The reward money should come from fines imposed on the guilty persons and their neighborhood guarantors or, if the offender is a tenant farmer, his landlord. A wife's pregnancy lasts several months. It is impossible that the guarantor or landlord should not know about it. If later the parents kill the baby, the circumstances require reporting. If the guarantor or landlord keeps silent and does not report, it is right that the reward money should be collected from them. If you deal with a few people according to this regulation, the practice will come to a stop. You should also direct the magistrates and assistants to go and enlighten the landlords and wealthy families with high-minded thoughts: if a family is really so poor that it cannot raise a newborn, those who are better off should provide some assistance. People are not made of wood or stone. They will be happy to comply. If the newborn's family can be kept from killing the infant for the first few days, thereafter, though you may encourage them to put the child to death, they will never do it. If you adopt these measures today, the number of lives you shall save now and in the future will be more than can be counted.

Buddhism teaches that the killing of a fetus or egg is the worst kind of killing. If this is so for animals, how much more must it be so for humans? Children who are sick are colloquially called "guiltless," but this is really a case of guiltlessness. If children or the elderly commit murder, they are not killed—how then could we allow completely innocent children to be killed? If you are able to save these babies from a fate of certain death, the hidden virtue you will accumulate will be ten times that of saving grown men . . .[67]

We learn from another of Su's writings that his efforts did not stop with this letter. His own Huangzhou was afflicted with the same problem, and Su took steps similar to the unofficial ones he suggested to Zhu Shouchang. Together with his friend Gu Gengdao, Su solicited donations from wealthy local families, asking that each contribute 10,000 cash annually, to purchase supplies of rice and cloth. A monk at the Anguo Monastery was put in charge of the books; and whenever he heard of poor families with newborn children, he would provide for them. Su estimates that in a year some one hundred infants were saved.[68]

One of the tasks Su Shi turned his attention to years later in Huizhou was bridge building. East of the prefectural seat was a confluence of rivers. The bridge that had once stood at the site had collapsed, and for a hundred years the people had been forced to cross the treacherous waters in small boats. Capsizings and loss of life had become commonplace. West of the city lay Feng Lake. That lake, too, had lost the bridge that once facilitated passage across it. During Su's confinement in Huizhou, solutions to both problems were found. A floating bridge was constructed at the eastern site, fashioned from forty boats lashed together. The bridge rose and lowered with the water level, and those who used it felt "as safe as if they were in their hall or bedroom." A towering new bridge was constructed over Feng Lake, supported by nine towers of rock and wooden pilings driven more than ten feet deep into the mud. A special type of lumber was brought to Huizhou from the Luofu Mountains to the north, "rock-salt lumber" (shiyan mu), the only kind that was resistant to the insects of the tropical forests. (One suspects from this that the previous bridge had succumbed to bugs and rot.)

Su Shi's poetry collection contains two pieces commemorating the completion of the new bridges.[69] The preface Su wrote to the poems gives all the credit for the construction to two local religious figures: the Luofu Taoist Deng Shouan for the floating bridge and the Buddhist monk Xigu for the Lake Feng bridge. The poems contain only fleeting reference to any part Su himself played in the projects. Mention is made of his donation of an ivory belt towards the cost of the work, as well as a cash gift sent by Su Che. But Su Shi's informal letters suggest that his role was much more than that of a small donor.

It happened that one of Su Shi's maternal cousins, Cheng Zhengfu (Zhicai), was judicial intendant of the Guangdong Circuit when Su was in Huizhou. In the numerous letters he wrote to Cheng, Su mentions the bridge projects frequently, as he tries to persuade this powerful circuit official to take steps to ensure their successful completion. In one letter Su complains that the funds on hand at the prefectural office for the floating bridge are insufficient by 40,000–50,000 cash (one-half the total estimated cost), and argues that in such cases it is always the circuit administrations that make up the difference.[70] Su goes on to warn that unless a capable man (Deng Shouan?) is appointed to oversee the entire project, 40 to 60 percent of the allocated funds will end up in the hands of corrupt Huizhou clerks and officers: that, he suggests, is the outcome in most such undertakings. We do not know for certain whether Cheng Zhengfu was persuaded by any or all of Su's pleas. That level of detail is not preserved in the historical record. But we do know that the bridges were completed, and that in later notes to Cheng, Su referred to them with pride in his voice.[71] I suspect that he would not have done so if his appeals had been completely ineffective.

Bridge building was by no means the only public project Su Shi concerned himself with in Huizhou. He arranged to have the remains of corpses that had not been given a proper burial gathered up and interred in tiled pits dug into a mountainside.[72] He developed a plan, reminiscent of his Dingzhou days, for constructing new army barracks, and asked Cheng Zhengfu to lend his support. Su had discovered that fully half the troops stationed in Huizhou had no government barracks. Moreover, the barracks that existed were made entirely of wood, with no tile roofs, and were a terrible fire hazard. To make matters worse, the soldiers had no reliable supply of water coming into their compound to supply their daily needs.[73] When the harvest was abundant in Huizhou and the central government demanded a higher than normal tax, specifying that a certain percentage (different for each type of household) be paid in cash, Su wrote in protest to Cheng. He pointed out that cash shortages ("cash famines," *qian huang*) were widespread in the southern prefectures, and the requirement of cash payment was unreasonable. In fact, the government ought to adopt a policy of allowing the poorer households to remit their taxes either in grain or in cash, whichever suited them best as their circumstances changed from year to year.[74] On New Year's Day in 1095, a fire broke out in Boluo (a subprefecture outside Huizhou), leveling the town and leaving its residents homeless. The circuit authorities had been slow to respond to the crisis; and Su wrote once again to his cousin, urging that steps promptly be taken to provide shelter, avert starvation, and restore civil order.[75]

Apparently, the greater Huizhou region was not large enough for Su Shi's energies. He wrote to the prefect of the neighboring prefecture, Guangzhou, about the problems with the drinking water there.[76] The city had only a briny supply of water, and that turned particularly bad during the summer months. Together with his Taoist friend, Deng Shouan, Su devised a plan whereby spring water from the Bujian Mountains, some eight miles away, could be piped into the city. Su's description of the project includes, aside from estimates of the total number of bamboos needed for the pipe and the initial construction cost, details on how to ensure that a continuous supply of new bamboo (to replace sections of the pipe annually) would be available, how much such maintenance would cost, and how to finance the cost with new forms of tax revenue. The prefect, Wang Gu (Minzhong), evidently put Su's and Deng's plan into operation. Delighted, Su would later write back to him, adding a detail he had neglected to mention at first. A small hole must be drilled in the side of each bamboo, and a small stick inserted into it which could be used to check for blockages. Blockages were inevitable over such a long distance, and this step would facilitate the process of locating them. It would be less likely, then, that perfectly good sections of the pipe would be needlessly discarded in the effort to get the water flowing again.[77]

It is not only the variety of plans and the meticulousness of their detail that is noteworthy. It should be borne in mind that through all of this Su Shi was officially in disgrace and was formally prohibited from speaking out on matters of government policy. He himself was certain cognizant of his unenviable status. This is the tone in which he couches his suggestions, contained in private letters to local officials: "I hope you will give this some thought," Su writes about changing the taxation policy in Huizhou, "but keep it secret. Don't let anyone know that the plan comes from me. You must not, you must not!"[78] On the plan for new barracks, he cautions, "Whatever you do keep this secret. If there is the slightest leak, I will not be able to live in peace here anymore."[79] On the floating bridge, he suggests, "When you speak with Caiyuan about it, just say it is your own idea."[80] Finally, on the plan for fresh water for Guangzhou, Su ends with these words, "Knowing that you are fond of doing good works, I now tell you this plan in secret. Whether it is acceptable or not is for you to consider carefully. But you must not let anyone know it originated with me."[81]

The Southern Song scholar Fei Gun remarked on the singularity of these activities undertaken by Su during his Huizhou exile. His comments may serve to conclude this account: "When Lu Xuangong [Lu Zhi, the Tang statesman] was exiled to Zhongzhou, he closed his door and turned away all visitors, and concerned himself with nothing but the compilation of his materia medica. He knew that if he emerged and had contact with others, the merest action or word might result in further slanderous attacks upon him. That is why he took such precautions. In later times, most men who were incriminated and sent into banishment followed his example. But East Slope was different." Fei Gun describes Su's Huizhou initiatives, including the construction of army barracks, the taxation plan, the Boluo fire relief, the bridge projects, and the fresh water for Guangzhou. He concludes, "Most of these undertakings involved matters of government policy, and thus might easily have inspired further complaint against him. But East Slope threw himself into them nonetheless and showed no hesitation. Such was his courage in doing good deeds."[82] Actually, there was some hesitation, as we have just seen. Su Shi tried to keep his involvement in these matters secret from officials other than the few who were trusted friends. One aspect of Su's complex motives in all of this will be considered in the following chapter.

CHAPTER SIX

A Thousand Arms and Eyes:
Buddhist Influences

When Su Shi wrote to Zhu Shouchang and urged him to take steps to stop the practice of infanticide in his prefecture, he made reference to the particular abhorrence with which Buddhism views the killing of a fetus or newborn. The Buddhist component in Su Shi's thought and action generally is a subject that requires attention; in fact, it is the largest omission in the account of Su's thought presented thus far. It will be convenient to take up the subject here, beginning with the possibility that Buddhism played some part in Su's record of good deeds that has just been described.

The goal here is to suggest the richness of Buddhism's influence upon Su Shi—the immensity of his indebtedness to the doctrines of Chan and other schools—rather than to attempt to classify the precise nature of his faith. *Was* Su Shi a Buddhist, and if so, what kind of Buddhist was he? The difficulty anyone will discover in attempting to answer those questions alerts us to the fact that they are inappropriately phrased. In Northern Song times, "Buddhism" was terribly diffuse, and faith and practice among laymen were not necessarily bound to a particular school or lineage. Su Shi call himself a "lay Buddhist" (*jushi*), but he left no single identification of his location on the bewildering terrain of Song-dynasty Buddhism. What he left instead are countless passing references to monk friends, temple visits, diverse sutras he read, and specific Buddhist doctrines that he embraced or criticized. It is obvious that Su and most literati of his age looked with special favor upon the Chan school. But which Chan was he closest to? There were heated rivalries within the Chan movement, and these have not been fully mapped out by scholars. Moreover, as important as Chan was for Su, he certainly also learned from texts and from monks who stood outside the Chan tradition.[1]

The Centrality of Compassion

We return here to a point implicit in Fei Gun's comments on Su Shi's activities in Huizhou, with which the preceding chapter ended. When they experienced the calamity of exile, most men "closed their doors" and scrupulously avoided any political or social contact, fearing further incrimination. One can live up to Confucian ideals in such circumstances by pursuing solitary study and self-cultivation. The Confucian virtue of "humaneness" (*ren*), in other words, undergoes a transformation upon the termination of official service. A "humane prefect" would, of course, be cognizant of the people's needs and be energetically involved in ministering to them. He might well throw himself into such tasks as famine relief and debt abatement. Such conduct is the legacy of the "reasonable provincial bureaucrats" (*xunli*) of the Han dynasty. But that sort of commiseration with the plight of the people, that sort of benevolent activity, typically ends when the person leaves office. Then we do not expect to find him rushing off to build bridges, clean the water supply, or try to reform popular customs. The Confucian historian, moreover, certainly does not require such conduct of the exile or retiree before pronouncing him to be a virtuous man.

I am assuming, however, that it is legitimate to lump all of Su Shi's humane initiatives together, and to look for common underlying motives. But what if they do not really belong together? What if, for example, his reasons for so vigorously pursuing famine relief and debt abatement as prefect of Hangzhou stem from values and standards that were quite independent of his reasons for trying as a private person to stop infanticide or to secure better shelter for the soldiers in Huizhou? The strongest objection to this possibility is that Su Shi himself seems to think of the activities as one. A poem that celebrates the construction of the floating bridge in Huizhou opens with these lines: "In my prime I longed to involve myself with things / Old and at leisure now, the urge is still there."[2] The bridge is an example of his old determination to involve himself with things (*jiwu*), that is, social and political projects. The first line evokes Su's long list of accomplishments as a prefect (and even his frustrations as a Court official). From the use of the word "leisure" (*xian*) in line 2, we understand that the first line must refer to his former activities as a government official. Line 2 then notes the persistence of his commitment to involvement, exemplified by the bridge, even after his removal from power.

What other evidence, aside from Su's letter to Zhu Shouchang, suggests Buddhist influence upon these activities of his? All that is proposed here, it should be stressed, is a degree of influence. There is no need to deny that values and motives that had nothing to do with Buddhism were also involved. It is probable, for example, that Su's frustrations at the Court had an impact. As Su saw his chances of guiding national policy diminish, he threw himself all the more into his duties as prefect, the only arena left open to him. Even here one can imagine a host of motivating factors: he wanted to make a name for himself, to prove his detractors wrong, and to dramatize the adverse effects the reforms were having at the local level. My argument is that Buddhist beliefs were just one component of Su's conduct in and out of office in the prefectures. Yet the interesting thing about this component (besides its being generally neglected in accounts of Su's life) is that evidence for it actually exists, whereas we can only speculate about other motives. Su said nothing that tangibly points to their impact upon his deeds. The establishment of the Buddhist influence will, moreover, lead naturally to a reconsideration of several of the key values in Su's thought that were discussed earlier. Buddhist preferences and Buddhist debates will be seen to occupy a significant place in a wide range of Su's concerns.

We may begin with some of the simple facts and statements that hint at the role of Buddhist compassion in Su's conduct. In Huizhou Su Shi wrote to a monk that since arriving at that place, he had busied himself with burying exposed bones, building bridges, dispensing medicine, and providing shelter, all to "dispel my impure obstruction."[3] The term used, *chen zhang*, is Buddhist: *chen* ("dusty") refers to the defilements of the phenomenal world, and *zhang* to delusions or obstructions that hinder enlightenment. A similar representation of his undertakings is implied in poems Su wrote at the time. The efforts of any individual may be insignificant, Su admits, and certainly cannot "save all living beings," but he does what he does because he cannot stand not to.[4]

It will be recalled that when Su founded a hospital in Hangzhou, he put a Buddhist monk in charge of it. When he raised private funds to discourage infanticide in Huangzhou, it was again a monk whom he chose to keep the accounts and administer the welfare. When a pitiful seventy-six-year-old man, who had no family and no one to live with, appeared one day at Su Shi's door in Huizhou, begging for help, it was a monk to whom Su wrote, asking that he take the man in and care for him: "Sir, you are compassionate and seek to save all living things. Why not set aside one mat of space within your grove and share a single serving of rice gruel daily with him? Care for this ill-fated scholar and let him live out his natural span, so that he does not end up stiff along the road: is this not the primary intent of dharma teaching?"[5]

So numerous and varied were Su Shi's humane initiatives that it may be easy to overlook one goal that the majority of them share: the saving of life. Su's floating bridge, for example, was not primarily intended to facilitate transportation. He was distressed by the needless drownings in the rough Huizhou river and sought to end them.[6] His plan to provide medical care to prisoners, likewise, was not mainly intended to relieve minor illnesses or discomfort. It was supposed to decrease the numbers of men who perished while in confinement. The note Su sent to a jailor (translated earlier) urging him to look after his prisoners' health refers in passing to the "blessings," that is, karmic reward, he will realize from doing so. Even Su's suggestions for improving Guangzhou's water may owe something to this same concern: he refers to the many fatalities that occur there in the summer months, attributing them in part to the impure water.[7]

Su's interest in saving life extended beyond human beings. He banned the slaughter of animals from his household, although he still relished meat and fish and would occasionally prepare dishes using them if the animal had "died of its own accord."[8] In Huangzhou Su criticized his friend Chen Zao for continuing to allow slaughter in his kitchen and shamed him by making him write a poem to the rhyme "sauce."[9] On Hainan Island Su was shocked by the prevalent sacrifice of oxen in shamanistic healing rituals. His condemnation of this practice is interesting for the way it broaches a number of related themes: medicine, killing, and the difference between Buddhist piety and shamanism.

> Everywhere south of the Ling Mountains the common people are fond of sacrificing oxen, but in Hainan the practice is extreme. Travelers embark from Gaohua on their voyage across the sea, carrying as many as a hundred oxen in their boat. If the wind is against them, innumerable animals collapse and die from hunger and thirst. When they first board the boat, the oxen low moaningly and snivel. Once they arrive at Hainan, half are used for plowing and the other half are sacrificed.
>
> Sick persons there do not drink medicine. Instead they sacrifice oxen

in supplication of the gods. A wealthy family may sacrifice more than ten animals at one time. If the patient dies, nothing more is said; but if he is lucky enough to live, credit for saving him is given to the shaman. Shamans are their doctors and oxen are their medicine! If a sick person does drink medicine, a shaman will say, "The god is angry with you. Your illness cannot be treated." Then his family will take the medicine away from him and prohibit his doctor from entering the door. There is no end to it until both oxen and patient die.

The region produces aloeswood incense, and the incense is exchanged for oxen by the aborigines. When the aborigines obtain an ox, they invariably sacrifice it to a demon. No animal ever escapes this fate. Now, people of the central empire use aloeswood incense when they pray to Buddha or the Supreme God (Di) for blessings. The people here, by contrast, roast ox meat. What blessings can they ever obtain that way? How regrettable it is! I myself cannot stop them, and so I have copied out Liu Zihou's "Rhapsody on the Ox" to give to a Buddhist monk of Qiongzhou, Daoyun, so that he may use it to instruct those among the local people who have some understanding. He may thereby diminish this practice somewhat.[10]

Liu Zihou is the Tang writer Liu Zongyuan, and his rhapsody is an allegorical complaint about the world's cruel indifference to those creatures that bring it the most benefit (i.e., scholars like himself).[11] Su Shi is interested in real oxen, not allegorical ones; and he forces Liu's piece to become a literary precedent for his concern.

Su is annoyed by what he perceives as the ignorant superstitiousness of Hainan culture, which substitutes shamanistic healing rituals for medical attention. Sick persons die as a result. But he is also aggravated by the cruel and senseless killing of the oxen. Sympathy for the animals runs through this colophon. The final paragraph suggests, furthermore, that the crucial difference in his mind between Buddhism and various shamanistic cults was the avoidance in the former of sacrificial offerings.

The importance of compassion in Su's understanding of Buddhism is suggested by his reaction to an early description of the religion he once came across. It was contained in the relatively obscure history, *Records of the Later Han (Hou Han ji)*, written in the fourth century by Yuan Hong. Yuan had given a very simple description of Buddhism, obviously intended for readers who had no idea what it was. To an eleventh-century scholar, familiar as Su Shi was with abstruse and complex aspects of Buddhist doctrine, not to mention acrimonious debates between the various sects, Yuan Hong's description had the appeal of a pristine and essential account. Su Shi was so moved by it that he copied it out and added his own praise. This is Yuan Hong's passage:

> *Futu* is Buddha. The country of India in the western regions believes in the Way of Buddha. "Buddha" is what the Chinese would call "enlightenment." The goal is to enlighten all living creatures. The teaching is based on cultivating goodness and compassion: believers do not engage in killing, and devote themselves to purity and quietude. The most devout among them are the *śramaṇa*. "Śramaṇa" is equivalent to "to rest" in Chinese. The meaning of "to rest" is to do away with desires and return to non-action. They also believe that when a person dies, his essence and daimon are not destroyed but acquire, in turn, a new material form. All good or bad deeds performed while alive thus result in retribution. Therefore, believers strive to do good and cultivate themselves, to purify their essence and nurture their daimon to the point where they are not reborn and become Buddhas.[12]

Su commented,

> These words were written when China was just beginning to learn about Buddhism. Although they seem shallow and commonplace, their general drift is correct. When men of the countryside first caught deer, they roasted and ate it just like that. Later, venison was sold to city folk; and eventually it made its way into the kitchens of noblemen, where it was prepared with a hundred different recipes. However, the deliciousness of venison was never increased by the tiniest bit over the way it tasted when first roasted in the countryside.[13]

Su's analogy may seem poorly chosen, but there is little doubt that part of what made Yuan Hong's passage so appealing to him is the prominent place it attributes to compassion in the religion. "The teaching is based on cultivating goodness and compassion . . ." Of all the ways Buddhism might be characterized, this is the one that struck a cord in Su Shi.

Some passages concerning Su Shi's first sponsor and mentor, Zhang Fangping, bear on this discussion. Zhang is an example of a man much more prominent in his time than in the historical memory of that time. Like Su Shi, Zhang was honored with recommendation for the decree examination. His youthful promise was subsequently borne out by his scrupulous conduct in eminent posts, including academician, censor, and vice grand councilor. Zhang acquired a reputation for fearless remonstration and fairness. He was known for his policy papers on defense of the northern borders, and for his effectiveness as a provincial administrator. Some sources say that no official of his generation was so highly regarded by colleagues and emperors alike.

One aspect of Zhang's life that goes unreported in the standard accounts is that he was also a devout Buddhist and even entertained the idea that in a former incarnation he had been a monk. A story is told about his tour as prefect of Chuzhou during the 1040s. One day he wandered into the library of a Buddhist monastery outside the city and suddenly ordered his attendants to climb a ladder to the roofbeams. Behind one beam an incomplete copy of the *Laṅkāvatāra Sutra* was found. Zhang turned to the place where the text ended and began to write out the continuation. Everyone was amazed to see that Zhang's calligraphy matched that of the incomplete manuscript perfectly. Zhang turned back to the beginning of the sutra and read the opening *gāthā*:

世間離生滅	The world takes leave of birth and death,
猶如虛空華	Life is no more than a flower in a void.
智不得有無	Wisdom sees neither existence or non-existence,
而興大悲心	And gives rise to boundless compassion.[14]

Tears flowed from his eyes as the truth dawned on him. In a former life he had been the monk in charge of this library, had started to copy out this sutra but never finished.[15]

What makes this more than just a quaint story is a related passage that comes from Su Shi himself. When Su visited Zhang Fangping in his retirement in 1085, Zhang gave him this very manuscript copy of the sutra (which he still had in his possession) together with 300,000 cash and asked Su to arrange to have it copied over and circulated throughout the southeast. Zhang, like Su, believed the *Laṅkāvatāra* to be a key scripture that had fallen into neglect. Foyin, the abbot of the Jinshan monastery, heard of the plan and suggested an alternative: the money should be used to have the sutra carved on woodblocks and printed, because many more copies could be produced that way. Su Shi consented, and wrote out the entire text in his own calligraphy. This clean copy of the text, done in Su's own hand, was to be turned over to artisans who would inscribe it on woodblocks for printing. In the colophon he wrote on the text, Su refers indirectly to the claim that Zhang had been a monk in a former life. More important for our purposes is that Su's colophon confirms the special significance the sutra's opening *gāthā* on compassion had for Zhang Fangping. Su Shi's remarks revolve largely around this aspect of Zhang's personality and piety:

> The grand protector of the heir apparent, Zhang Fangping, Master of Delight in Completion, has with his boundless heart attained pure en-

lightenment. During the Qingli period, while prefect of Chuzhou, he visited a monastery and happened to come upon this sutra. He fell into a daze as he picked it up, for it seemed he had recovered an old possession. Before he finished reading the scroll, his old impediments broke away like ice. Looking closely at the calligraphy, the marks of his own hand were clearly preserved. He sighed, overcome with emotion, and at that moment became enlightened. Thereafter he always used the four-line *gāthā* at the opening of the sutra to express the central tenet of his mind (*xinyao*). For some thirty years I have been calling at this gentleman's door. This year [1085] in the second month, when I passed through the southern capital, I visited him in his private residence . . .[16]

Su's colophon puts Zhang Fangping's career and values in a new light (of which the reader of Zhang's official biography would have no inkling) and equates the *gāthā*, with its emphasis on the "boundless compassion" that springs from insight into non-duality, with the most fundamental of Zhang's values. This suggests a perhaps unexpected degree of compatibility between Buddhist virtues and the conduct and standards of the most prestigious of Northern Song statesmen.

Several others of the highest officials shared aspects of Zhang Fangping's Buddhist faith, including Wen Yanbo, Fu Bi, and Han Qi.[17] But not all did. There were also eminent statesmen and literati who were hostile to Buddhism in any form. Three of these were men Su Shi knew well and respected: Fan Zhen, Ouyang Xiu, and Sima Guang. In one colophon, Su Shi performs the arabesque of transforming these very men into upstanding believers (even though he knows they would object):

I note that Fan Jingren (Zhen), Ouyang Yongshu (Xiu), and Sima Junshi (Guang) all disliked Buddhism; and yet when you consider the wisdom they possessed by virtue of their accurate perception of the world and the good deeds they accomplished because of the power of their humaneness, these things were nothing other than Buddha's dharma. Emperor Wudi of the Liang [who claimed to be a devout Buddhist] once raised a levee at Foushan to flood Shouchun so that he might conquer the central plains.[18] In one night he thus killed thousands upon thousands of people, and still he proceeded to sacrifice with noodles [instead of an animal offering] at the imperial shrine. How could he be said to understand Buddhism? From this it can be seen that those in the world who are truly devoted to Buddhism are not necessarily many, while those who truly dislike it are not necessarily few.[19]

Once again, it is compassionate conduct towards other people (as well as accurate perception of the world) that is the key in gauging a person's fidelity to Buddhism. The result is that even individuals who see themselves as enemies of the religion may, by virtue of their "humane-ness," be spoken of as upholders of the dharma.

Chan, Pure Land, Bodhisattvas

Su Shi's friendships with Buddhist monks are everywhere evident in his poetry and prose. Although some of these monks were of the Tian-tai school, most belonged to one or another Chan lineage, Chan being the school that has the most visible presence in the lives of Northern Song literati. Consequently, scholars have often written, and justifiably so, about Su's interest in Chan and the influence that Chan doctrines had upon his thinking and aesthetics. What has been less widely appreciated, particularly in Chinese and Western scholarship, is the in-fluence that Pure Land Buddhism, or rather the southeastern amalgam of Pure Land and Chan, had upon Su and other leading officials.

We know that throughout the southeast and particularly at Hangzhou, it was common by the eleventh century for Chan and Tiantai monks to incorporate Pure Land beliefs and practices, such as invocations of the name of Amitābha Buddha, into their regimens. The blending of Pure Land with Chan is normally traced back to Yanshou, author of *Mirror of the Source* (*Zongjing lu*), a Hangzhou Chan master of the tenth century.[20] The impact that Yanshou's ideas on harmoniz-ing the two schools had upon Song-dynasty Chan in Hangzhou is well documented in Song-dynasty writings, such as *Longshu's Treatise on Pure Land* (*Longshu zengguang jingtu wen*), by Wang Rixiu, and *Clas-sified Writings on Paradise* (*Lebang wenlei*), by Zongxiao. Eleventh-century monks associated with the Yunmen lineage of Chan, which had centers at Lu Mountain and Hangzhou, seem to have had a special affinity for Pure Land doctrine. The Yunmen lineage was that of the syncretist Qisong, who died in Hangzhou in 1072, after journeys to the capital and interviews with leading officials, and also that of Foyin, the Lu Mountain monk who would become Su Shi's close friend. Yun-men masters known for their particular interest in Pure Land include Tianyi Yihuai and his disciple, Zongben (Huilin Yuanzhao). It is re-corded that all of the Chan monks who studied under Yihuai devoted themselves wholeheartedly to Pure Land.[21] In Hangzhou, the physical center of the movement seems to have been Jingci (Yongming) Monas-tery, where Yanshou and later Zongben resided.

The developments within Yunmen-lineage monasteries had their parallels outside the temple walls. Buddhist societies (*fashe*) that were influenced by Pure Land practices appeared at Lu Mountain (organized by Foyin), and at Hangzhou. Calling themselves "Pure Land disciples," the members of these societies assembled in the streets on religious festivals to sacrifice and pray. The membership was predominantly laymen, and laymen were even chosen as presiding officers. Several of such leaders were high-ranking government officials, such as Grand Councilor Wang Dan, and his vice grand councilor, Su Yijian, who together headed up a Hangzhou association in the early years of the Song. Wen Yanbo seems to have been connected to a similar Pure Land association in the capital.[22]

This hybrid Chan was characterized, both in the monasteries and in lay life, by a strong belief in karmic reward and retribution, which might come either in this life or in the next (the ultimate reward being, of course, rebirth in Pure Land). The activities of the devotees included the normal invocations of the name of Amitābha, who presided over that paradise, and of prayers to the bodhisattva Guanyin, who was commonly linked to that deity; but, belief in karmic reward also led the members to go far beyond verbal affirmations of their faith. In Hangzhou the Buddhist societies regularly sought to minister to the needs of the city's impoverished residents. "Nothing compares to the Buddhist societies," wrote the Southern Song monk Zongjian, "for relieving social needs and performing good works."[23] Fayun of the Jingci Monastery, for example, followed a precedent set by Zongben and maintained an eating hall that could feed one thousand, which was supported entirely by lay donations.[24] Similar acts of charity became an important part of the annual Water and Land Assembly (*shuilu hui*), which had its origins in the *yulan pen* (*avalambana*) ritual of prayers for the dead. Over the centuries this festival, a particularly popular one in Hangzhou, had broadened in scope. The Tang *yulan pen* featured filial prayers and sacrifices offered to deliver one's ancestor from hell. But during the Northern Song, monasteries and lay religious societies used the festival to support charitable measures toward the living as well as the dead.[25]

The emphasis upon charity, good works, and social welfare comes through as a primary theme of *Longshu's Treatise on Pure Land*, one of the main texts of the Song Pure Land revival, produced by a twelfth-century layman, Wang Rixiu. "If you do not have compassion," Wang writes, "you will never become a buddha; and if you do not save living things, you will never become a buddha."[26] Wang offers separate advice to all manner of persons (e.g., filial sons, literati, wives, servants, doctors), but to each he stresses the importance not just of faith but of good works. He is very open about the rewards a person might expect. Why is it, he asks, that some literati who do not study hard pass the civil service examinations, and others, who are diligent in their studies, do not? They are being rewarded or punished for conduct in their former life. And much greater than a pass on the examinations is the supreme reward of deliverance to Pure Land that will come to the person who excels in his conduct.[27] The path, according to Wang, that men who hold office should follow to accumulate merit is to practice all sorts of expedient means to "show love for others and to bring increase to things" (airen liwu).[28] Now, Wang's concept of "alms-giving" (bushi, dāna) is broad enough to include spiritual gifts, such as spreading faith or imparting religious courage. But the giving of wealth (shicai), either in donations to monasteries or directly to persons who need help, also ranks as one of the primary forms of alms-giving.[29] As Wang explains it, this is precisely the difference between ordinary persons and superior ones. The ordinary person is uninterested in contact with others unless it will immediately enhance his own prestige or bring him material increase. But the "worthy or noble man" has no such precondition, and he enters freely into the kind of contact that brings increase to the other person. The model for this unselfishness is, of course, the conduct of the two bodhisattvas Amitābha and Guanyin, who deliver the faithful to the western paradise.[30]

Su Shi was certainly exposed to these developments in Chan, particularly within the Yunmen lineage in the southeast. Actually, Su's family already had a history of contact with that lineage in their native Meishan, where one of Su's cousins, who became a monk (Baoyue Weijian), studied with the Yunmen dharma heir Yuantong Juna.[31] However, it is during Su's first assignment to Hangzhou, in the early 1070s, that his liaison and dialogue with monks becomes a conspicuous part of his life. There he was instructed by Tiantai and Chan masters and was a frequent visitor to the city's famous monasteries (e.g., Lingyin, Jixiang, Lin'an Pure Land, and Tianzhu). Su had interviews with the ailing Qisong, who had written so much on the compatibility of Buddhism with Confucianism, in the months before he died. He corresponded with Huailian, another Yunmen syncretist who had instructed emperors and high officials. He also befriended Zongben, who was practicing at Jingci Monastery.[32]

Writings that Su produced during these years, and later, attest to his involvement with Pure Land beliefs. He offered prayers, for example, to Amitābha on behalf of his late mother: "The monk Yuanzhao (Zongben) of Hangzhou has always encouraged laymen to devote themselves to Amitābha of the paradise in the Western Regions. Now, I, Su Shi of Meishan, respectfully offer as alms hairpins and earrings left by my late mother, née Cheng, Lady of Shu Prefecture."[33] The jewelry was to be used to commission a portrait of Amitābha, possibly to hang in Jingci Monastery. The prayer Su offered to the bodhisattva accompanying this gift ends with these lines:

願我先父母	May my mother and father
與一切眾生	Together with all living beings
在處為西方	Reside in the Western Regions,
所遇皆極樂	Knowing supreme joy in all they meet.

Years later, Su would similarly direct his sons to commission a painting of Amitābha in memory of his second wife (the boys' mother).[34]

Su took a personal interest in Water and Land Assembly that had grown so popular in Hangzhou. In fact, the hospital he would establish during his second tour at Hangzhou was specifically intended to treat contagious diseases that spread through the masses of people who gathered to observe this religious festival and which left many dead. Hangzhou, Su realized, had the dubious distinction of losing more people to epidemics during this festival than did any other city in the empire.[35] Such risk aside, when Su left Hangzhou for the northern prefecture of Dingzhou in 1093, he sought to propagate the Hangzhou Water and Land Assembly observances in the new region. He commissioned sixteen paintings of deities, demons, and hells, hoping that they might "arouse a moment of compassion, and thereby bring immediate relief to all within the four seas."[36] He turned the paintings over to Fayong, a Chan monk, and urged him to observe this festival regularly and to "practice forever unimpeded charity."

Beyond such acts and donations, the clearest mark of Pure Land influence upon Su's Buddhism is the special place that bodhisattvas, particularly Guanyin, and the ideal of self-sacrifice have in Su's works. He writes often about these subjects, and always with great reverence. From distant Huizhou, Su's youngest son, Guo, once wrote out a copy of the *Suvarnaprabhāsa (Golden Light) Sutra* and sent it to the Kaifeng monastery in which his mother's remains had been placed. But Guo still felt that he had not done enough on his mother's behalf. He asked his father what other pious acts he ought to perform, and he also asked if the words of the sutra were literally true or were intended as parables. Now, this sutra is known for two stories it contains of bodhisattvas. Flowing Waters, the first, used elephants to transport water to a pond that was drying up and thus saved innumerable fish from death. Thereafter he fed the fish with food taken from his own household, and also preached to them, so that they were reborn in Trayastrimśat Heaven. Mahāsattva, the second, was once traveling through the woods with his brothers and came upon a tigress that was weak and emaciated from having recently borne a litter of cubs. So desperate was the mother that she was on the point of eating her own offspring. Mahāsattva was moved to profound pity by the sight and, determining that there was no time to go foraging for food, decided to give himself in sacrifice to the tigress. He slit his throat and lay down before her.[37]

In answering his son, Su Shi refuses to characterize the two stories as mere parables, taking recourse to the doctrine that the teachings of the Buddha are beyond the distinction of literal versus figurative truth. Su Shi uses the occasion to lecture his son on the bodhisattva ideal. He quotes, from the *Śūraṅgama Sutra*, a general description of how the bodhisattva delays his own entrance into nirvana to save other beings, and goes on to urge Guo to break free of the selfish motives and attachments common to all four categories of creatures (*caturyoni*). You should, he concludes, be like Flowing Waters: "expend great effort and have elephants bring out unhindered dharma water to save your waterborne fish that are in danger of going dry . . . Be self-sacrificing like Mahāsattva: be filled with pity for even the most vile of creatures, driven as it is by its karma, and perform acts of charity towards it."[38] Su Shi wants to leave no doubt in Guo's mind that the deeds described in the sutra may be emulated in his own life, and he records his injunction separately as a colophon on Guo's copy of the scripture.

The twenty-fifth chapter of the *Lotus Sutra* is commonly known as the *Guanyin Scripture*, because it is given entirely to a description of the benefits that devotion to the bodhisattva brings. Su Shi shows his particular attention to this text and to the bodhisattva ideal in a short colophon. The bodhisattva Akṣayamati had asked Buddha about the significance of Guanyin's name (lit., "the one who observes the sounds of the world"). Buddha explains that Guanyin always heeds the voice of anyone in distress who calls out the name. Buddha proceeds to give a long list of examples: people who fall into a fire, who are swept off in a great river, who are lost at sea, who are about to be murdered, who are captives of their own lust, who want to bear a son—all these will be delivered from their torment if they are mindful of Guanyin ("Sound-Observer") and call out to the deity. At the end of the chapter the list is resumed in verse:

> Or, one might be surrounded by enemies,
>   Each carrying a knife and intending to inflict harm.
> By virtue of one's constant mindfulness of Sound-Observer
>   All would straightway produce thoughts of good will.

Or, one might encounter royally ordained woes,
Facing execution and the imminent end of one's life.
By virtue of one's constant mindfulness of Sound-Observer
The knives would thereupon break in pieces.[39]

The litany of examples goes on and on. Contained within it is one and only one instance in which the deliverance enjoyed by the believer involves an element of vindictiveness or revenge:

When either by spells, or by curses, or by various poisonous herbs,
[Someone] wishes to harm his body, the victim,
By virtue of his constant mindfulness of Sound-Observer
Shall send them all back to plague their authors.

This one verse bothered Su Shi for its departure from the pattern of rescue without harm to the threatening agent. This is what Su chose to write about. "Guanyin," he observed, "is known for mercy and compassion. Yet here [we read of] a person who encounters spells and curses and, owing to the power that comes from being mindful of Guanyin, causes those spells to be visited back upon their authors. How could that represent the heart of Guanyin?" Having concluded that the text distorts, however briefly, the true spirit of Guanyin's influence in the world, Su proposes rewriting the scripture. This, Su says, is how the second half of the verse should read: "By virtue of his constant mindfulness of Sound-Observer / No harm comes to either him or the authors of the spells."[40] Not only does Su's colophon attest to his careful reading of this portion of the *Lotus Sutra*, it also suggests that he felt secure enough in his understanding of the bodhisattva to challenge the scripture itself on this one verse.

Su also asserts his special affinity with Guanyin in a hymn of praise he wrote for an image of the bodhisattva kept at a Chan monastery in Jinling. The hymn touches upon distinctions between apparently similar Buddhist and Confucian virtues, with Su identifying himself with the Buddhist versions. Su begins by listing four pairs of similar concepts: Buddhist *ci* ("mercy") and Confucian *ren* ("humaneness"), Buddhist *karuṇā* ("pity") and Confucian *yi* ("duty"; i.e., to do one's duty towards others), Buddhist *kṣānti* ("forbearance") and Confucian *yong* ("courage"), and Buddhist *you* ("sorrow") and Confucian *zhi* ("knowledge"; i.e., commiserating awareness of the world beyond the self). But for all their apparent similarity, Su explains, ultimately the two sets of virtues remain distinct. The essential difference between them can be traced to the Buddhist belief in a single, pervasive unity—

Buddha-nature—that permeates and joins all things. "The greatest perfect enlightenment recognizes universality in all things and has no other" (*wuer*). Then Su redefines the Confucian virtues in terms inspired by this Buddhist insight about *wu* ("not having"): "Having no enemies he is 'humane,' having no relatives he is 'dutiful,' recognizing no other people he is 'courageous,' and having no self he is 'knowledgeable.'" Because the Confucian virtues are based on *you*, "possessing things," such as distinctions of rank, status, and familial ties, their existence is precarious and impermanent: if the thing possessed is used up or absent, there is no longer any basis for the virtue and it, too, disappears. But the Buddhist virtues are based upon *wu* ("having nothing"), and therefore they are enduring and inexhaustible. Su concludes his hymn this way:

吁觀世音	Oh, Guanshiyin,
淨聖大士	Holy Master of all purity,
徧滿空界	Who fills the entire realm of emptiness
挈携天地	And grasps both Heaven and Earth.
大解脱力	Your great power of deliverance,
非我敢議	I do not dare discuss.
若其四無	But as for your four "nothings,"
我亦如此	I am that way myself.[41]

This is much more than a conventional paean to the deity of mercy. Su uses the occasion to offer a comparison of values between the two rival systems of belief. Not only does his comparison favor the Buddhist values, he injects himself into the discussion as a devotee and follower of Guanyin. The same devotion (though without the argumentation) is evident in a short encomium Su wrote upon awakening from a dream of Guanyin.

稽首觀音	I bow to Guanyin,
宴坐寶石	Resting on the precious stone.
忽忽夢中	While I was lost in a dream,
應我空寂	The deity responded to my emptiness.
觀音不來	Guanyin did not come,
我亦不往	I did not go.
水在盆中	Water sits in the basin,
月在天上	The moon in the sky above.[42]

These last passages bring us to a cluster of themes in Su Shi's thought, all concerned with the issue of worldly action, which are heavily influenced by Buddhist concepts. Before going on to examine these, the gist of the foregoing pages may be briefly summarized here. During his years in the provinces, Su Shi amassed an extraordinary record of activism in benevolent initiatives, both while serving as prefect and when stripped of office as an exile. Because it is difficult to see how Confucian "humaneness" could fully account for this behavior, naturally we look to other supplementary causes. Buddhist compassion is an obvious possibility but remains somewhat problematic. There is little doubt that Buddhist sentiments had a role in certain of Su Shi's initiatives (e.g., those on infanticide, burial, and bridge building) because he says so himself in personal letters. But what about his efforts as prefect to relieve the suffering of the commoners through famine relief or debt abatement? Here the argument is less certain because Su does not refer explicitly to Buddhist notions to justify his actions. Moreover, we are not accustomed to crediting Buddhist motives to the exemplary local official. We ought to bear in mind, of course, that when he was acting in a traditionally Confucian role, it would have been incongruous for Su Shi explicitly to cite Buddhist influences upon his conduct. Therefore, the absence of such references cannot be taken as proof that they did not exist. Ultimately, the point is not the kind that can be established by argument. Probably, as I have said, Su's frustrations in national politics also played their part in his local activism in complex ways. Still, the Buddhist thread in all of this is one that keeps resurfacing. As one reflects upon Su Shi's many expressions of admiration for Buddhist sympathy for the plight of others, his injunctions on emulating the ways of the bodhisattvas, his fond evocations of Guanyin, it is hard not to suspect that the Buddhist factor in his conduct was a significant one. Chikusa Masaaki has shown how centrally involved Buddhist monasteries were in assisting local governments in bridge building, water conservancy, and famine relief in the Fujian region during the Song.[43] By some accounts, monks shouldered more responsibility for such social projects than did the local bureaucrats and were also more trustworthy. Here the argument is the other way around: that the same religious ideals had considerable effect upon the layman Su Shi, both when he was prefect and when he was out of office. Actually, the point about Su Shi is one that has been made before. But it was made in what many persons interested in Su would consider an out-of-the-way place (Abe Chōichi's history of Chan Buddhism),[44] and made without reference to most of the documentation cited above. The case for Buddhist influence upon Su's actions should become even stronger as Su's indebtedness to Buddhist ideas of worldly involvement is examined in the subsequent section.

No-Mind and Responding to Things

Earlier chapters have discussed Su Shi's aversion to *xingming* and the New Learning of Wang Anshi, his criticisms of Cheng Yi, his own theory of knowledge, the importance of dynamic interaction in his cosmological thought, and the consequences of this for his notion of the self. Now, we have occasion to reexamine many of the same topics, but in the context of Buddhism rather than that of his disagreement with Court policies. Buddhism casts these issues in a new light. Reconsidering them in it, we see both the persistence of Su Shi's intellectual concerns and the profound contributions that Buddhist doctrines made to his preferences as he developed them in opposition to the New Learning.

It is difficult to know when significant influence began. It is normally supposed that Su's first period of residence in Hangzhou marked the start of his sustained participation in Buddhist circles and discourse. His writings convey this impression: beginning with his arrival in Hangzhou, suddenly Buddhist topics and friends seem everywhere in his works, whereas earlier they are seldom seen. Yet there are also references (from Su himself) to his parents' devotion to the religion and specifically to adoration of bodhisattvas.[45] We know, as mentioned above, that a member of Su's family who entered the monastery in Meishan was trained by a Yunmen master. It is intriguing, then, to note the similarities of Su's early criticisms of Han Yu on human nature to those of the Yunmen dharma master Qisong (who had befriended Zhang Fangping in Hangzhou before Zhang sponsored the Sus, father and sons, in Chengdu in 1056).[46] Without explicit statements from Su, however, the nature and extent of Buddhist impact upon his early thought is impossible to gauge, and a chronological account is not feasible.

Buddhism is often thought of as a faith that generally fosters withdrawal from society, epitomized by the location of temples on remote mountain peaks. But to Su Shi, as to many believers, the influence of Pure Land/Chan doctrines could be entirely different: they could be drawn upon to justify thoroughgoing engagement with the world and to explain how it could be undertaken without corruption or compromise. The opening of an inscription Su wrote for a Buddhist pavilion in Chengdu, the Pavilion of Great Compassion, broaches several key issues. The pavilion contained a sculpture of a thousand-armed Guanyin bodhisattva, with an eye in each hand. Su took the opportunity this offered to write about Guanyin's responsiveness to the world:

. . . If I tell someone to wield an axe with his left hand and hold a chisel in his right, use his eyes to count geese in flight and his ears to keep track of a beating drum, and nod his head to a person beside him and use his feet to climb a ladder, no matter how intelligent he was he would leave something undone. So how could a thousand arms each wield a different implement, and a thousand eyes each watch a different object? But when I sit at leisure and remain quiet, my mind and thoughts grow still and silent: everything appears as clearly to me as in a large bright mirror. People, ghosts, birds, and beasts are arrayed before me; sights, sounds, smells, and flavors come in contact with my person. Although my mind does not arise, there is nothing it does not receive, and it receives each according to the Way. Then as for a thousand arms extending or a thousand eyes turning, the pattern for this is fully established even if no one ever sees it happen. The bodhisattva is just this way. Even though the body remains one and does not become two bodhisattvas, still this one bodhisattva can cover as many countries as there are sands in the Ganges. There is no other reason than this: the bodhisattva is not confused when coming into contact with things and responds to whatever arrives. This is a natural consequence, so why should the bodhisattva have any difficulties in maintaining all-encompassing compassion?[47]

Next, Su explains the history of the Chengdu sculpture and how he came to be asked to write an inscription for the pavilion in which it was housed. He concludes with a rhymed encomium that restates his basic theme:

吾觀世間人	I observe men of the world
兩目兩手臂	With their two eyes and two arms.
物至不能應	Things approach and they cannot respond,
狂惑失所措	So bewildered they know not what to do.
其有欲應者	Even those who wish to respond properly
顛倒作思慮	Are all inverted and engage in thinking.
思慮非真實	But if their thinking is not real or true,
無異無手目	They may as well have no arms or eyes.
菩薩千手目	The bodhisattva has a thousand arms and eyes,
與一手目同	Yet it is like having but one.
物至心亦至	When things arrive, the mind meets them;
曾不作思慮	The bodhisattva never engages in thinking.
隨其所當應	In whatever way it is right to respond
無不得其當	The bodhisattva always does so correctly.
引弓挾白羽	A drawn bow and white arrow,
劍盾諸機器	A sword and shield or other weapons,
經卷及香花	A sutra scroll and incense flowers,
盂水青楊枝	A finger basin of green willow branch,
珊瑚大寶炬	A large jeweled censor made of coral,

白拂朱藤杖	A white whisk, a crimson wisteria staff,
所遇無不執	The bodhisattva holds onto whatever is encountered,
所執無有疑	Doing so without any doubts.
緣何得無疑	How can the bodhisattva be free of doubts?
以我無心故	Because the deity's self has no-mind.
若猶有心者	If there were still a mind,
千手當千心	A thousand arms would mean a thousand minds.
一人而千心	If a single person had a thousand minds,
內自相攫攘	They would fight with each other inside him,
何暇能應物	What time would he have to respond to things?
千手無一心	But when a thousand arms have no single mind,
手手得其處	Every arm attains its proper place.
稽首大悲尊	I bow to the Revered One of Great Compassion,
願度一切衆	Desiring also to save all living beings.
皆證無心法	May each actualize the way of no-mind,
皆具千手目	And each acquire a thousand arms and eyes.

In his remarks on the sculpture Su Shi combines two well-established Buddhist concepts. The first is that of "response" (*ying*), or more properly *nirmāṇa* (*yinghua*) or *nirmāṇakāya* (*yingshen*). This is the doctrine that Buddhas and especially bodhisattvas accord their teaching to the different needs of individuals. There are as many methods of instruction, and as many manifestations of the bodhisattva, as the number of different needs in the world. Thus the bodhisattva is commonly said to "dispense medicine in accordance (*ying*) with the sickness." The idea is really part of the doctrine of *upāya* or "expedient means" (*fangbian*) that is pervasive in the Mahayana schools, and a prominent theme of the most popular sutras in China, including the *Lotus*, the *Vimalakīrti*, the *Laṅkāvatāra*, the *Sūraṅgama*, and the *Avataṁsaka* (all of which we know Su was familiar with). The notion of "according" is found, for example, in this passage from the *Avataṁsaka Sutra*:

> Buddhas know beings' minds,
> Their natures each different;
> According to what they need to be freed,
> Thus do the Buddhas teach.
> To the stingy they praise giving,
> To the immoral they praise ethics;
> To the angry they praise tolerance,
> To the lazy they praise effort.[48]

The phrase Su Shi uses to describe Guanyin's responsiveness is *yingwu* ("responding to things"). Now, *wu*, despite the translation "things," is commonly used in Buddhist and even non-Buddhist writings to refer to creatures or persons (in distinction to *wo*, "the self"). We find, in fact, the same phrase used in sutra passages on Buddha's deliverance of all living creatures, as in the *Golden Light Sutra*: "The Buddha's embodiment of truth and the dharma is like an empty void. Responding to things it manifests itself, like the moon in the water."[49]

The second notion crucial to Su Shi's remarks on Guanyin is that of *wuxin*, "no-mind." This is a concept more exclusively associated with the Chan school, and was developed primarily in Tang and Song sutras and treatises.[50] *The Platform Sutra of the Sixth Patriarch* identifies the analogous phrase "no-thought" (*wunian*) as its primary doctrine. "No-thought" in Huineng's teaching liberates the individual from what might be called the tyranny of things. "No-thought" means being able to transcend both objective things and the subjective mind, so that all attachments dissolve.

> To be unstained in all environments is called no-thought . . . If you stop thinking of the myriad things, and cast aside all thoughts, as soon as one instant of thought is cut off, you will be reborn in another realm . . . The Dharma of no-thought means: even though you see all things, you do not attach to them, but, always keeping your own nature pure, cause the six thieves [fields of the senses] to exit through the six gates. Even though you are in the midst of the six dusts, you do not stand apart from them, yet are not stained by them, and are free to come and go.[51]

Later Tang treatises such as *Essentials on the Transmission of the Mind*, compiled by Pei Xiu (797–870), developed the similar concept of "no-mind."[52] An anonymous Dunhuang text entitled *Discourse on No-Mind* makes an important clarification. "No-mind" does not mean that one is mindless like a rock or tree. "No-mind" means that one is freed from false anxieties and cravings so that one's "true mind" may be recovered.[53]

Su Shi's inscription on the thousand-armed Guanyin sculpture combines these well-established Mahayana and Chan doctrines. Su may have been the first to develop at such length a discussion of how the two concepts are so perfectly manifested in the thousand-armed Guanyin, filling out his essay with the memorable counter-example of the fumbling two-armed mortal; but the idea that no-mind and responsiveness complement each other, and lead to ideal sensitivity to the phenomenal world, was already widespread in Chan circles. No doubt the Chan movement included a broad spectrum of beliefs, and a sizable segment of its members might have had no interest in either the intellectual question of sensitivity to the phenomenal world or the practical one of involvement in Chinese society. There was, however, an element within Song dynasty Chan, especially in the southeastern amalgam of Pure Land and Chan described above, that was interested in the problem of how to retain the ability to act in the world. It is anticipated by discussions of no-mind found in earlier Chan texts. The Tang *Discourse on No-Mind*, quoted above, treats the matter in a simple and straightforward manner: "Although you have attained no-mind you are still perfectly able to comprehend the true aspect of all things; your true *prajñā* three-fold Buddha-nature is still extant, and you respond and act with no impediment."[54] The point is not always this plainly stated. Moreover, as in the passages quoted below from Yanshou's *Mirror of the Source*, the language and the analogies keep changing. But the basic theme remains the same: no-mind serves to enhance rather than to diminish the individual's responsiveness to the world.

> A person who has no body has a large body. He who has no mind has a large mind. With a large mind comes a wisdom that covers all the myriad things. With a large body he can respond and react without end. So it is that someone who holds onto his body as his own loses this great responsiveness, and one who holds onto his mind as his own loses this great knowledge. That is why all the sutras and treatises teach that one must take leave of the body and mind and break free of all holding and attachment before entering into what is true and real. It is like how a goldsmith must smelt ore to obtain gold before he can fashion it into implements for use. If you have a body, you have bodily impediments. And if you have bodily impediments, your dharma body is obscured by your outer shell. If you have a heart, you have impediments of the heart. And if you have impediments of the heart, your true wisdom will be obscured by your thinking and apprehensions.[55]

> As for no-mind, how could it require that the mind be darkened and put to no use? Instead, no-mind resembles a bright mirror that reflects things: does it have a mind? You should know that all living creatures first had no-mind. Their mind and body were originally still. Being still, they were in constant use. Being in constant use, they remained still. They reflected and distinguished whatever situation they encountered, and what they reflected was always the true nature. It is not that one must have a mind before one can be of use. But most living things do not understand that their mind is first still, and foolishly they scheme to have a mind . . .[56]

By Su Shi's time, such formulations that link no-mind or a synonymous phrase with responsiveness to the world had evidently became commonplace. For example, Su's close monk friend, Canliao, says in praise of another monk that "his heart being empty, he is able to respond to things" (*xuhuai neng yingwu*).[57] (I take "heart being empty" to be virtually the same as "no-mind.") Likewise, when Huihong, a Chan monk of the succeeding generation, writes about Guanyin sculptures, he is apt to take the same approach Su did, using the same key phrases (*yingwu, wuxin*) to account for her special powers.[58]

The Guanyin that Su Shi wrote about was for him a model of one kind of interaction with the world: to be profoundly involved in affairs, responding to every need and circumstance that arises, and yet to remain in some sense aloof. Here we see that the selflessness of "no-mind" really has a dual function. It rids the individual of self-interest, making him all the more sensitive to external circumstances; but it also ensures that for all his immersion in worldly affairs, his heart and mind remain detached and calm. When speaking of Guanyin, Su emphasizes the first of these functions of no-mind; but when describing mortals (Chan monks, friends, and himself), he emphasizes the second.

We have encountered a version of this model before. It appears in Su Shi's commentary on the *Book of Changes*, where it is a key theme of his remarks on the relation of the self to the cosmos. "What is esteemed about the sage is not that he remains still and has no contact with things. What is esteemed is that he proceeds together with things into the domain of good and bad fortune but is never disoriented by them." The term *wuxin* "no-mind" also occurs in the commentary, where it describes the trait that permits the sage to enter into supreme harmony with the cosmos and the ruler to act in compliance with the desires of the people. The concept, like the term itself is, as George Hatch has aptly remarked, "without basis in the text" of the classic.[59]

Su Shi's commentary on the *Changes*, like that on the *Documents*, is part of his response to the New Learning of Wang Anshi and, specifically, to the new interpretations of the classics that were mandated for the examinations as part of Wang's reforms. In other words, the context in which Su's interpretations of the *Changes* must be viewed is that of his long-standing intellectual and political dispute with the reform movement. The notions that Su develops in his commentaries form a logical and consistent alternative to the New Learning positions on such matters as the nature of the sage ruler and his relation to the world. Certainly, there are strands of thought in these commentaries, such as the ideal of responsiveness or of responding to things, that may be traced back to *Laozi, Zhuangzi,* or other ancient philosophical works. Still, a reading of Su's Buddhistic writings suggests that Buddhist thought as it had been articulated during the Tang and early Song was a more immediate inspiration of key components of Su's reaction to the New Learning than was ancient Taoism.

There are two points that support the view that this model of interaction with the world was something Su Shi borrowed from Buddhist, and particularly Chan, discourse. First, this was a notion that had already been developed in earlier Chan writings and with precisely the terminology that Su would later use. Second, Su himself is most apt to mention the model when writing about Chan monks he knew; that is, he praised them as they would have liked to be praised. This, for example, is what Su writes to eulogize the life of Guanghui, a Chan monk who resided in the Donglin Monastery at Lu Mountain:

> Loyal ministers do not fear death, and so they accomplish the greatest deeds in the world. Courageous scholars have no thought for their own lives, and so they achieve the greatest fame in the world. However, such men have still not fully mastered the Way. It is just that their sense of duty is weighty and their self-interest is light. Nevertheless, they are still able to manage such accomplishments. What then may be accomplished by him who leaves the three realms behind, who comprehends the myriad dharmas, who experiences neither birth nor aging, who knows not sickness or death, and who responds to things and has no emotions?[60]

Su goes on to credit Guanghui with having transformed the whole Lu Mountain region with "the palace of Indra, Brahma, Nāgārjuna and Vasubandhu." This is Guanghui's great deed, one that Su wants us to think of as greater than any a loyal minister might accomplish, and one made possible by his no-mind. (There has been a slight change in Su's language here: Guanghui is said to "respond to things and have no emotions," but here again *wuqing* is surely synonymous with *wuxin*, "no-mind.")

Even within the life of the sangha there were certainly worldly affairs that had to be attended to. The problem of how monks who had "renounced the world" might yet oversee the administrative affairs of the sangha and its on-going contact with the Song government is one that interested Su Shi. The solution implicitly pointed to techniques Su might adapt to his own needs, enabling him to maintain mental and emotional distance from the bureaucracy even as he participated in it. Su writes about the problem in a eulogy for Haiyue, a Hangzhou monk. Hangzhou, Su explains, has the largest registry of monks of any prefecture in the nation. Therefore the administration of the monasteries is particularly complex. Recognizing this, most of the institutions established a special post, apart from the normal ones of principal abbot and assistant, which they called "overseer." The monk appointed as overseer was to take care of registration, government certification, administrative errands, and receiving visitors. But who was fit to discharge such tasks? "A lofty and remote type of man, the kind who withdrew to the mountains and abhorred the vulgar, would not be capable of doing it. It would have to be someone who was pure and upright, who could cross over into the world externally but remain free of things internally. Only such a person could do it."[61] In his verse encomium, Su considers the dilemma created by unworldliness:

人皆趨世	If everyone rushes into the world,
出世者誰	Who will be left to renounce it?
人皆遺世	But if everyone leaves the world behind,
世誰為之	Who will run the world?
爰有大士	Then came a great man
處此兩間	Who lived right between the two.
非濁非清	He was not impure or pure,
非律非禪	Did not follow *vinaya* or *chan*,
惟是海月	Such a man is Haiyue
都師之式	A model of the monk overseer.

For Su Shi, the Buddhist layman, the predicament that arose from the apparent necessity of having to choose between pure and impure was more acute than it was for this administrating monk. But Su found that within the monasteries, where one might least expect to find it, men like Huibian had charted a path between the two extremes that might be emulated by those on the outside.

Non-Attachment

A related theme in Su Shi's thinking is that of non-attachment, that is, not allowing oneself to become attached to things or possessive about them. The attitude is mentioned most frequently in Su's writings on art, for it bears both on connoisseurship and artistic creativity; but he also applies it to all sorts of other possessions and comforts, and even to place. The attitude helped Su to accept a lifetime of forced wandering from one post to another. No place should be singled out as preferable, and "home" might as well be anywhere. It also helped Su to search for contentment in very undesirable places. If you do not allow yourself to become attached to an attractive place like Hangzhou, you are more likely to find contentment even in desolate places like Mizhou (not to mention Hainan Island). Beyond this, the utility of the notion may also be seen in the degree of detachment Su Shi maintained from the very activities and struggles into which he threw himself. The ideal of always remaining in some sense detached from events fortified Su Shi through the decades of his political and social activism, making it easier for him to adapt to the vicissitudes of his career. Ironically, then, "non-attachment" served to sustain him in his involvement with human affairs. "Do not look upon me as a prefect," Su urged his friends in one poem, "On the outside I may resemble one, but inside I am not."[62] It was in part because Su could claim that in some ultimate sense he was aloof from the obligations and controversies of office that he was able to immerse himself so thoroughly in them.

Non-attachment is another notion whose immediate source is to be found in Buddhist literature. Because, according to Mahayana belief, all phenomena are illusory and impermanent, it is wrong to allow one's mind dwell upon them, or to suppose that one can possess them. Such misguided attitudes are associated with the egoistic views of the unenlightened. From these concepts springs the notion of "non-abiding" or "non-attachment" (apratiṣṭhita; wusuozhu, buzhu, buliu), the attitude the individual should maintain towards the phenomenal world. We have already seen that in the *Platform Sutra* non-attachment is closely associated with the ideal state of no-thought. No-thought means that no single thought abides in any dharma, and this results in "freedom from bondage."[63] It is an often-repeated story in Buddhist writings that the Sixth Patriarch became enlightened upon hearing his master recite this passage from the *Diamond Sutra*, "You must not be attached to things, and must produce a mind that stays in no place."[64] Non-attachment to worldly things, even while remaining in their midst, was also, of course, a fundamental tenet of the bodhisattva ideal. As the *Sūraṅgama Sutra* states, the bodhisattva possesses "dedication to the salvation of all living beings while avoiding the conception of saving them."[65]

Non-abiding, non-attachment, and non-possessiveness coordinate with the notions of no-mind and response to things. Achievement of the state of no-mind ensures that the self-centered desire to possess things, or to crave and be attached to them, has likewise been eliminated. Because the mind is in that sense unencumbered, it is free to respond selflessly to any and all phenomena as they are encountered. The following passage from *Longshu's Pure Land Treatise*, which sounds uncannily like Su Shi, shows how intimately these concepts are linked:

> Liezi said, "Confucius abandoned his mind and used his body."[66] He meant that he was able to abandon his mind because it was no longer dependent on things. In responding to things he used nothing but his body. I love this saying dearly. It is because of this that even when I find myself suffering and destitute, I do not consider it frustrating; and even when I have honors, wealth, and support, I do not find it satisfying. The

fact is, my mind is not attached to things. I recall that once the bodhi-sattva came to understand life and death, he entrusted himself to live amid the myriad living beings in order to spread his teaching. Because the bodhisattva's heart was not attached to things, he could respond to things merely by using his body. In this sense, Confucius himself seems to have been a disciple of the bodhisattva.[67]

Su Shi took this cluster of concepts, which was already common-place in descriptions of the bodhisattva and the monk, and applied it to literati life. His phrases for "non-abiding" (buzhu, buliu) he lifted directly from Buddhist works, while he coined his own terms to de-scribe the alternative, that is, the special attitude of the enlightened being toward the world, terms that are, however, synonymous with the "entrusted himself" (tuoshen) in the passage above. In Su's lan-guage, the enlightened one does not abide in things, he "lodges" in them. Su uses two words interchangeably to express this idea: yu ("to lodge or put up temporarily in") and ji ("to lodge, avail oneself of, or make use of temporarily").

Su's best-known statement on these issues is his repudiation of the possessiveness of the art collector. Su had been asked to write an inscription for Wang Shen's painting collection. This is how he began: "The noble man may lodge (yu) his mind in material things, but he must not let his mind abide (liu) in them. If he lodges his mind in things, then even the most trifling of things will suffice to bring him pleasure, and even the most alluring of things will not become an afflic-tion. However, if he lets his mind abide in things, then even the most trifling of things will be able to become an affliction, and even the most alluring of things will not bring pleasure."[68] Su goes on to explain how he overcame his own obsession with collecting works of art, which ruined whatever enjoyment they might have brought him, so that now if he loses or is forced to part with a painting, it no longer bothers him. (Su's friends corroborate this claim.) He urges Wang Shen to adopt the same attitude.

It may have been a painting collection that occasioned Su Shi's most eloquent treatment of the theme, but it is apparent that Su embraced it as a general principle broadly applicable in life. Writing about his recluse friend Wu Ying, Su says, "All his life he lodged in things but did not abide in them; / Living at home he mastered the Chan ideal of forgetting one's home."[69] There is no higher compliment that Su might offer. Though he never renounced the material world or his family, Wu was transcendent.

The indebtedness such notions had to currents of Chan dis-course is suggested by the following playful inscription Su Shi wrote for the Pavilion of Refreshing Winds of the Chan monk Yingfu. Here, we see Su develop such themes as non-possessive possession, lodging, and wisdom, and he explicitly says that he is using Buddhist language as he does so.

Master Wenhui, Yingfu, lives on top of Jade Ravine in Chengdu. He has built himself a pavilion there called Refreshing Winds, and he sent me a letter asking that I compose an inscription for it. I declined five times but he became all the more insistent. Having no choice, now in jest I use Buddhist words to ask him this question:

Fu, what you call your body is something that you temporarily lodge in, and what you call your pavilion is something in which you temporarily lodge what you temporarily lodge in. You cannot permanently possess either your body or your pavilion. What is the purpose then of naming the building? And if it is not to be named, why should it have an inscription? Nevertheless, out of consideration for you I will now free my mind, forget my form, and force myself to speak. You free your mind, forget your form, and force yourself to listen.

Trees grow on mountains, and brooks flow from underground springs. Neither the mountains nor the springs get to possess the trees or brooks. If a person were to say that he could, would it not be a delusion? Heaven and Earth grind against each other, the void and material things push on each other, and wind is born in their midst. Try as you might you can never grasp onto it. Hurry as you might you can never overtake it. But now you build a residence and name it after the wind, and I record it in an inscription: is this not an even greater delusion? Still, there are instances in which people possess things without being deluded, though they do not differ in outer appearance from cases of delusion. If your kind of possession is like that, then there is no harm even in saying that you possess the wind, and there is likewise no harm even in building a pavilion and naming it after the wind, or in my writing an inscription for your name. There is no delusion involved.

The wind arises in the remotest corners of the world. It circulates through the hills and marshes, then wafts across embankments and roads, always expanding and permeating, until it finally flows against your windows, railings, and inner curtains, never to depart. When you lean back on your chair and observe it, is there not something to be learned from it? Its force comes from whatever it runs up against. It does not exert itself and so is never tired. Its shape comes from what it encounters. It does not take on its own shape and so is never exhausted. Try looking at it this way.[70]

By the end of the piece the wind is endowed with traits congruent with the ideal of non-attachment. The wind becomes a model of unpossessive and responsive activity.

Equipped with this doctrine of non-attachment, Su Shi returned once to an old problem that had troubled Ouyang Xiu. Ouyang had prided himself on holding in disdain the material goods and riches that most men of the world eagerly pursue. Ouyang claimed to be content with but five "things," all of them high-minded ones: his books, his collection of ancient rubbings, his zither, his chess set, and his jug of wine. But it had occurred to Ouyang that he was still open to the charge of being dependent upon things. He had just substituted culturally sophisticated for vulgar ones. Ouyang really did not have a response to this criticism.[71] Su Shi inherited the concern from him, but Su had a response. Some people, Su writes, ask why, if Ouyang had really attained the Way, he still clung to his five beloved things? The question is misguided, Su explains. Ouyang would indeed have been deluded if in order to find peace, he had to cling to his five things. But it is equally a delusion to insist he must relinquish the five things to be called a man of the Way. The fact is, these five things did not encumber Ouyang's mind, because he never considered that he "possessed" them. And if one does not make the mistake of thinking that he can possess things, "then even the official's robe and jade insignia cannot encumber one, how much less may these five things."[72] This is another application of Su's doctrine.

A word should be added here about Su's well-known "Tower of Transcendence" ("Chaoran tai") inscription. The piece commemorates the tower that Su, as prefect, reconstructed on top of the city wall at Mizhou. The name Su chose for the tower was intended to evoke his own transcendent attitude towards his assignment to this decidedly dismal prefecture, which was so impoverished, unsightly, and uncultured compared to the Hangzhou he had just left. "My friends," Su explains, "felt that I must certainly be unhappy here." Actually, he was quite content, and he explains in the inscription how he managed it.

> All things have some attractive aspect that is worth looking at; and anything that is worth looking at may bring happiness, not just things that are extraordinary, imposing, or ornate. One can become gaily drunk even on weak wine or dregs, and the appetite may be satisfied even by vegetables, berries, and nuts. Extrapolating from this, where in the world might I go that I could not be happy?
>
> The reason people seek good fortune and avoid calamity is that good fortune brings happiness while calamity brings grief. However, people's desires are infinite, and yet the things in the world that can satisfy those desires are finite. Therefore, valuations of good and bad fight inside us, and the problem of which things to acquire and which to reject hangs before us. Consequently, our moments of happiness are few, while our moments of grief are many. This amounts to seeking calamity and avoiding good fortune. How could that be human nature?

The fact is, people let themselves be overwhelmed by things. People move about inside the realm of things, rather than outside it. Now, it is true of all things, whether big or small, that if we look at them from the inside, they seem towering and huge. With all this hugeness towering over us, we become befuddled and are at a loss. It is like watching a fight through a crack in the wall. How can you tell which side is winning? So it is that notions of good and bad are haphazardly created, with happiness and sorrow following upon them. Is it not regrettable?[73]

When Su Che learned of the name his brother had chosen for the reconstructed tower, he wrote a rhapsody on it. That piece emphasizes the ethereal nature of the tower, its soaring rise toward the aerial precincts of immortals and abandonment of the sullied world of vulgar men.[74] Su Shi's inscription, written after his brother's rhapsody and partly in response to it, gives a discernibly different twist to the "transcendence" involved.[75] In effect, Su denies that his is a transcendence that cuts him off from "things." In fact, Su Shi's inscription goes on to describe how from the tower he can look out over, and reflect upon, historical sites that lie just outside the Mizhou wall. It is clear, then, that when he ascends the tower, he does not do so to leave the world behind. Nevertheless, the distinction that Su Shi develops in his inscription between the two modes of existence (inside the realm of things, and outside it) is one that he specifically rejects in later writings.[76] Why? It is too detached, and too close to the complete aloofness that he never accepts. I take the "Tower of Transcendence" inscription as an early treatment of Su Shi's perennial concern with the problem of worldly involvement versus detachment. In the piece he is obviously moving towards the solution upon which he eventually settles. But in this moment he does not yet fully grasp the utility of the Buddhist concept of transcendence that is concurrent with involvement, and thus not "outside things" at all. Once he does, that becomes the dominant theme of his writings on worldly action.

Lingering Reservations

For all of the influence that Chan and Pure Land belief and practice had upon Su Shi, he continued to express unease with important aspects of these faiths. In one moment he might call himself a "lay Buddhist," or even playfully suggest that in a former life he had been the Sixth Patriarch,[77] or tell us that the a copy of the *Sūraṅgama Sutra* was always at his bedside.[78] But in the next he was apt to describe how little real understanding he has of Buddhist doctrine, taunt his monk friends about their strictures, or air his misgivings about the methods monks used to advance towards "the Way." The reservations that will be discussed here are intellectual positions Su developed in his deliberations on Chan. They are different, then, from what might be loosely referred to as temperamental factors, epitomized by Su's self-description in a poetic line: "I don't want to avoid people, so how could I avoid the world?"[79] As important as matters of temperament may be—ultimately, they may be the most important—they cannot readily be measured or analyzed.

We begin with Su's objections to meditation when practiced exclusively, that is, as the sole approach to the Way. It was pointed out earlier that Su was dissatisfied with the New Learning's assertion that the Way could be approached directly, without the mediating presence of history and the world, and that his dissatisfaction carried over into his remarks on Chan beliefs. We recall also Su's remarks about recipes (i.e., how misguided it is of people to throw them aside), and the statement they lead to, decrying the apparent arrogance and exclusivity of the New Learning. These remarks are, after all, part of an inscription Su wrote on a Buddhist sculpture, and in it Su eventually gets around to criticizing an analogous tendency he sees in Buddhist circles: withdrawing from the world, being selfishly content with vacant meditation rather than doing works and spreading the faith. The huge sculpture, which took thirty years to complete, is treated as a welcome departure from this trend.[80] (Because Su's inscription thus broaches secular as well as religious issues, the poor monk for whom it was written, Juze, was, like many other recipients of Su's writings, subsequently incriminated.)[81]

It has recently been suggested by Robert Gimello that when Su Shi made such comments about Buddhist practice, he was in effect joining a debate that was already being waged within the monasteries.[82] In the mid and late eleventh century, many monks, especially proponents of the "lettered Chan" (*wenzi chan*) movement, were reacting against the proud disregard of textual doctrine and worldly involvement that had distinguished Chan for recent generations. Lettered Chan, which was influenced by the new openness to Pure Land beliefs, was essentially a conservative retrenchment that sought to find grounds for reconciling Chan belief with the textual legacy both of other Mahayana schools and of high secular culture. Monks like Faxiu, Canliao, and Huihong displayed their broad learning and extraversion without reluctance. It was precisely such monks who befriended eminent literati like Su Shi, exchanged poems with them, and produced, aside from their Chan treatises and commentaries, literary collections.

There is no reason to question this account of Su's participation in the Chan debate. Nor is it even necessary to insist that the influence was entirely in one direction: that Su's dispute with the New Learning predetermined his stance on the Buddhist controversy. The problem of how to advance toward the Way, and specifically the rivalry of broad learning and worldly contact versus inner exploration, is one that seems to have been a prominent part of the intellectual climate of the age, as Gimello has pointed out. Certainly, in Su Shi's biography his dispute with Wang Anshi bulks larger than does his participation in the Chan debate. But influence may have proceeded in both directions, as Su worked out positions that he was satisfied with in the two very different contexts. It should be noted, however, that Su Shi does not use the term "lettered Chan" in his comments on Buddhism. He was associating with the monks who came to be identified with that movement, but he may not have been aware of it as a movement nor had a strong sense that his particular monk friends constituted a separate group.

In the course of a letter to Bi Zhongju, Su Shi provides one version of his dispute with "Buddhist" practice. As is typical of him, here he does not single out this or that school, but speaks as if all Buddhists were one. The essential statement is contained in the third paragraph below, but it is interesting to see how he leads into it. Bi had mentioned in his own letter that he was engaged in studying Buddhist texts.

> . . . I myself used to read Buddhist writings; but since my mind is all obstructed, I have been unable to penetrate to their marvelous truths. From time to time I simply use their most shallow teachings and analogies to cleanse myself. I am like a farmer weeding: now I clear it away, and now it grows back again. Although it seems that there is no lasting benefit, still it is better than not doing it at all. But as for the superior men of the world, those who are said to be transcendent and to have attained enlightenment, I know nothing whatever about them.
>
> Formerly, Chen Shugu was fond of discussing Chan, and felt that he himself had arrived, whereas he denigrated what I said as shallow and crude. Once I said to Shugu, "What you talk about is like dragon meat.[83] What I study is like pork. Now, there is a great difference between a dragon and a pig, but your talking all day about dragon meat is not nearly so filling or tasty as my dining on pork." I wonder what it is that you obtain from Buddhist works? Have you left the realm of life and death behind, transcended the three vehicles, and become a buddha? Or are you still milling around in this world with the likes of me?
>
> Those who study Buddhism do so because they hope eventually to achieve quietude and liberating insight. But quietude resembles laziness, and liberating insight resembles self-indulgence. Before they ever attain

their final goal, some students settle for the resemblance instead. The harm caused by this is considerable. I always have doubts about my own Buddhist cultivation on this score, and now I mention it for your consideration.

In your letter you say that if you can live in this world in peace and be free from illness, have coarse clothing and an adequate supply of food, and do not sow bad karma, you will be perfectly satisfied. I read and re-read these words, moved deeply by their beauty. But you must know that virtually everything a person does in this world, every step or thought, produces such karma. You do not have to kill innocent creatures or take what does not belong to you to accumulate bad karma. Having no way to discuss these matters in person with you, I send you this to give you one good laugh.[84]

There are several themes here: Su's lack of progress in self-cultivation, the difference between intellectual sophistication (Chen Shugu) and simple practice (Su), the dangers of the meditative approach, and insistence upon a stringent definition of wrongful acts. So while Su protests that he is a novice, it is evident that he is conversant with many of the crucial issues that Buddhists faced.

We see that Su was deeply suspicious of meditation when it was practiced to the exclusion of other sorts of conduct, and his concern that quiet sitting may lead to sloth and self-indulgence must echo worries voiced by Chan monks themselves. Now, this letter dates from Su's Huangzhou period, when he himself was practicing meditation regularly. Shortly after he arrived in Huangzhou, Su began a lengthy process of self-examination and reflection, to take stock of his conduct and the reasons for his incrimination and exile. As part of this undertaking, he would go "every second or third day" to the Anguo Monastery south of the city to meditate. "I would burn incense and sit silently, reflecting deeply on my conduct. Eventually, distinctions between myself and things were completely overcome, as my body and mind became empty. Then when I looked for the seeds of my wrongdoing, there were no longer any to be found. My whole consciousness was purified, and defilement fell of its own accord from me."[85] Here, in an inscription written for the monastery, Su describes the benefits of meditation. But his letter to Bi Zhongju shows that he was uncomfortable with the prospect of meditation being more than an occasional practice. Su's letter is reminiscent of part of the inscription he wrote for Juze:

To fast and observe the monastic rules, to recite the scriptures, to construct pagodas and temples—these are the activities through which Buddhists should spread their teachings day and night. But presently many disciples consider it better to cultivate no-mind than to fast and observe the monastic rules, better to "be free of words" than to recite the scriptures, and better to "do nothing" than to construct pagodas and temples. Inside themselves they have no-mind, their mouths have no words, and their bodies have no actions. All they do is eat to the full and relax. Thus they greatly cheat the true intentions of the Buddha.[86]

Now we see that there is a negative sense of "no-mind" in addition to the positive one examined above. Su is not really contradicting himself, he is just using the term in different contexts. "No-mind" is a virtue when it means selflessness in the world. In this sense no-mind is a pre-requisite of the heightened sensitivity to the world and the ability to respond appropriately to "things" that Su so extols. But "no-mind" is undesirable when it connotes nothing more than mental emptiness inside the walls of the meditation cell, especially if the devotee has no interest in ever going back out into the world to act. In this instance no-mind is subject to abuse. Indeed it is often disingenuously invoked to justify sloth and self-indulgence.

Su Shi's attitude is informed by more than common antipathy to laziness. He returns always to his conviction that the diverse "things" of the world, all that may be "observed" (*guan*, a favorite word of his, and the same word that figures in the name of the bodhi-sattva Guanyin), are the best means to knowledge. Images of clear-sightedness surface time and again in Su Shi's diverse treatments of the problem. In one he likens the goal of doing away with the "common mind" (*fanxin*), that is, a mind filled with self-centered notions and material attachments, to that of clearing away a film or cataract over the eye.[87] Once the film is removed, the eye will naturally be clear-sighted: it will require no other treatment or improvement. Most people mistakenly think that Buddhist cultivation leads in an entirely different direction. They hold that the accomplished Buddhist "looks sullen and has no knowledge or perception." If this is the goal, Su goes on, how does the perfect Buddhist differ from a dog or cat that has eaten to the full and lies sleeping soundly? The pets in that state have no thoughts either: are we to say that they have entered nirvana?

Su's preferences lead him to challenge the common Mahayana notion of the three vehicles or learnings: prohibitions or discipline (*jie*), composure or meditation (*ding*), and wisdom (*hui*). The three were thought of as a sequential course of self-cultivation that led ideal-ly to enlightenment. One began by observing the standard prohibitions regarding personal conduct (e.g., not eating at improper times, not drinking, not lusting, not craving wealth). This allowed one's mind to become settled or composed. It was only with such composure that one could attain insight into universal Buddha-nature, which was preparation for enlightenment. Su Shi questions this process in a farewell he wrote for another Hangzhou Chan monk, Sicong, who had apparently begun to concentrate on "composure" and meditation, as Chan monks typically did, and disavowed his earlier interests in worldly activities.

Su's prose farewell opens with very obscure language, drawing upon ancient native numerology, five-phases theory, and ethics, as Su struggles to find precedents in the Chinese classics for the concepts he wants to discuss.

> Heaven brought forth water from one and earth completed it with six. It was only after one and six were combined that water could be seen.[88] Thereafter, even the great Yu could not have said which part was the one and which the six. Master Zisi said, "It is human nature that allows one to attain clear-sightedness (*ming*) through integrity (*cheng*), and it is teaching that allows one to attain integrity through clear-sightedness. Integrity is clear-sightedness, and clear-sightedness is integrity."[89] It was only after integrity and clear-sightedness were joined together that the Way could be seen. Thereafter, even the Yellow Emperor and Confucius could not have said which part was integrity and which clear-sightedness.[90]

With the Zisi quotation the reader may begin to glimpse the gist of Su's reasoning. He wants to contrast inward with outward orientations. Finally, Su gets around to stating the problem in Buddhist terms: "Buddhists say, 'Prohibitions produce composure, and composure produces wisdom.' But cannot wisdom likewise produce composure?" One can imagine Sicong being brought up short by this reversal. What kind of wisdom could Su Shi mean, a kind that produces mental quietude rather than springing from it? Su continues, "When a man who is sighted walks, even if he lifts his robe to hurry along he normally reaches the great way. However, a blind man needs to be guided; and even if he holds on to a cart-wheel and shuffles along slowly, he frequently ends up tripping over a mound or hole. In fact, wisdom produces composure more readily than composure produces wisdom." Su is redefining Buddhist "wisdom" (*prajñā*). In Su's usage the term denotes clear-sightedness toward the world around one. In effect, Su is equating *prajñā* with the native Chinese concept of *ming*, "clear-sightedness, perspicacity" (mentioned in the Zisi quotation). Su's "wisdom" is not reached through the solitude or emptiness of the meditation cell. On the contrary, it seems to be dependent upon continual and accurate perception of the world. Su's immediate purpose is to urge Sicong not to abandon his earlier practice of the arts. The monk, Su explains, had even as a boy become an accomplished zither player, calligrapher, and poet. But recently he had turned away from those pursuits, devoting himself entirely to Buddhist studies and meditation. Su wants to persuade him that he need not repudiate his earlier skills.

This piece is an important source for Su's thinking about the arts, and we will return to it in a subsequent chapter. But Su Shi has more than just the arts in mind. It is really worldly pursuits of virtually any kind whose importance Su is arguing for. Here is his conclusion: "None of the persons who in ancient times studied the Way attained it through emptiness and vacuity (*xukong*). Wheelwright Bian hewed wheels, and the hunchback caught cicadas.[91] If it suffices to release one's proficiency and knowledge, no thing is too lowly." Knowledge may in some sense be innate, at least that is what Su suggests here, but at the same time it cannot be released (*fa*) or realized without contact with some worldly thing. The crux of Su's misgivings about Chan was that it so often guided men onto the path of "emptiness and vacuity," which Su believed led nowhere.

CHAPTER SEVEN

The Mirror in the Mind: Poetry in the Shi Form

What follows below is an essay on Su Shi's poetry in the *shi* form, the dominant form of his day. The sheer volume of his output in this genre (over twenty-four hundred poems survive) makes it exceedingly difficult to generalize about. Yet that same volume, and the richness of subject and mood that sustain it, may also be said to enhance the need for a summary account of its distinctive traits. Su's *shi* poetry is treated here without regard to chronology or the important questions of stylistic development through time.[1] However, poetry from Su's two extended periods of exile (1080–1084, 1094–1100) requires a chapter of its own. The poetry discussed here excludes the exile verse and its special problems. The poems that remain are primarily those of the 1070s, when Su established himself during his prefectural assignments as the greatest literary figure of the day, and those of the Yuanyou era (1086–1093).

The Uses of Play

It will be convenient to begin with a kind of poem that is conspicuous in Su Shi's collection but which might readily be dismissed as unimportant: poems written in jest or in apparent playfulness. Su's fondness for jokes, palindromes, and poetry games of various kinds is well known and was frequently commented on, often disapprovingly, by his contemporaries.[2] Here it will be argued that playful verse has its serious meanings in Su's works. Furthermore, the concept of play can be used to introduce a number of other traits of Su's poetry generally, and thus it has a significance that goes far beyond the special subset of poems that most obviously embody it.

Although Su wrote poems in jest in all periods of his life, the great age for this type of composition is the early years of the Yuanyou period. The account of those years provided in an earlier chapter concentrates on political factionalism and the resultant attacks upon Su. A reading of Su's poetry from the period yields a very different impression. This seems to be a time that Su was surrounded by intimate friends and confidants (most of whom were, in fact, his political supporters). Su Shi was, as a member of the Hanlin Academy, the highest ranking of them all and was responsible for recommending or placing many of them in their new positions in the capital soon after the formation of the Yuanyou administration. Huang Tingjian and Chao Buzhi were appointed to the Palace Library, where they were commissioned to compile the *Veritable Records* of Shenzong's reign. Qin Guan took the decree exam and became an erudite in the Imperial Academy. Kong Wuzhong worked as a collator, and Zhang Lei held a variety of similar literary posts in the Library and Bureau of History. Su Che, who was serving as vice-minister of the Ministry of Revenue, was also, of course, a member of the group.

There was a constant exchange of poetry among these men, all known as gifted writers, who visited each other regularly and sent poems back and forth by courier between visits. Many of the poetic exchanges took the form of "matching rhymes," that is, poems written with the very same rhyme words (and in the same order) that the first writer had used. The exchanges might continue back and forth through several rounds or expand outward to include more than the initial two poets.

There was friendly competition in these poetic exchanges, and the exercise of wit and ingenuity that we associate with such competition. The general tone of this poetry was one of lightheartedness, whether or not the words "written in jest" (*xizuo*) appear in the titles. A summary of one exchange is provided below. (The rhyme words, which occur at the end of the even numbered lines, are: *shu*, "book"; *zhu*, "pearl"; *ru*, "to resemble, compare to"; and *hu*, "lake." The English equivalents are italicized in the translations.)

Someone had sent to Huang Tingjian some choice tea produced in his native Hongzhou (Jiangxi). Huang set some aside for Su Shi (Zizhan) and presented this poem to him along with it:

雙井茶送子瞻	*Sending Twin Wells Tea to Zizhan*
人間風日不到處	The wind and sun of the common world never venture there:
天上玉堂森寶書	Jade Hall in Heaven, a forest of precious *books*.
想見東坡舊居士	I imagine East Slope's layman of former times,
4 揮毫百斛瀉明珠	Flailing his brush, a hundred gallons of bright *pearls* pour forth.
我家江南摘雲腴	From my home in the Southland the sleekness of clouds was plucked,
落磑霏霏雪不如	See the specks fall from the mill, whit*er* than snow.
為君喚起黃州夢	May it summon up for you a Huangzhou dream,
8 獨載扁舟向五湖	Alone in a small boat you'll sail Five *Lakes*.[3]

Line 2. Jade Hall was another name for the Hanlin Academy, located within the imperial city ("Heaven"), where Su served.

Line 3. During his Huangzhou exile, Su built a studio for himself at East Slope and began calling himself its resident layman.

Line 6. Tea leaves were commonly ground into a powder before infusing, hence the mention of the mill. Lightly colored leaves were highly prized, and Twin Wells tea was known for its "whiteness," which accounts for the comparison to snow.[4]

Lines 7–8. The logic is that the tea, being a product of the Southland, should inspire a dream of Su's former residence. Five Lakes alludes to Fan Li, who left his high office to live out his years as a recluse sailing the Southland's lake district.[5]

Su Shi expressed his gratitude for the gift with this poem:

黃魯直以詩饋雙井 茶次韻為謝	*Huang Luzhi Sent a Poem with a Gift of Twin Wells Tea, and I Matched the Rhymes to Thank Him*
江夏無雙種奇茗	Jiangxia has no twin to such rare tea;
汝陰六一誇新書	Liuyi of Ruyin praised it in a recent *book*.
磨成不敢付僮僕	The grinding cannot be trusted to any servant;
4 自看雪湯生璣珠	I watch the snowy broth produce white *pearls*.

列仙之儒癯不腴	A scholar ranked among immortals is too thin for any sheen;
只有病渴同相如	Only in having the illness of thirst does he resemble Xiang*ru*.
明年我欲東南去	Next year I plan to roam the southeast;
8 畫舫何妨宿太湖	What harm if my painted boat calls at Taihu *Lake*?[6]

Line 1. Jiangxia (Wuchang) is the region of Huangzhou, the site of Su's exile in the years before the Yuanyou period.

Line 2. Liuyi is Ouyang Xiu, who retired to Ruyin (Yingchou). There he wrote *Notes on Retiring to the Farm*, which mentions the excellence of Twin Wells tea.[7]

Lines 5–6. The scholar is Su Shi himself, who ranked among the "immortals" of the imperial Court. Only in having unquenchable thirst does he resemble the great Han poet, Sima Xiangru, who suffered from diabetes.

Line 8. According to Su's own note on the poem, this alludes to the famous teas of Guzhu (on the shores of Taihu Lake). There Su hopes to find a product similar in excellence to what Huang has given him.

Huang wrote back to Su Shi, thanking him for his poem ("The Academician sent me lines about the southeast; / Sitting in silence beside the window, I received his dark *pearls*")[8] and apologizing for an illness that had prevented him from visiting Su for the past month. The illness was eye trouble, which became the subject of Su's next poem to Huang.

次韻黃魯直赤目	*Matching the Rhymes of* *Huang Luzhi's Poem on Red Eyes*
誦詩得非子夏學	Is not this poetry reciting Zixia's tradition of learning?
紬史正作丘明書	Truly, you compile documents to write Qiuming's *book*.
天公戲人亦薄相	The Lord of Heaven teases men, playing tricks,
4 略遣幻翳生明珠	Causing an obscuring film to cover your bright *pearl*.
賴君年來屏鮮腴	Fortunately, in recent years you have abstained from tasty meat;
百千燈光同一如	The light of a million lamps is its *equal*.
書成自寫蠅頭表	When the book is complete, write a memorial in fly-head script,
8 端就君王覓鏡湖	Asking His Majesty immediately to grant you a Mirror *Lake*.[9]

Lines 1–2. The lines refer obliquely to Huang's poetry writing and his work on the *Veritable Records* as well as to his eye complaint. Zixia, who was supposed to have written the preface to the *Books of Songs*, is said to have gone temporarily blind as a result of crying over the death of his son. Zuo Qiuming, author of the history *Zuozhuan*, is said to have resolved to write the work after losing his sight.[10]

Lines 5–6. Huang Tingjian had sworn a layman's oath of abstinence from wine, meat, and sex in 1084. The "light" is the Buddhist merit of Huang's abstinence.

Lines 7–8. "Fly-head script" is script written in tiny characters (which Huang should be capable of when his work is complete and his ailment disappears). Mirror Lake alludes to the Tang poet He Zhizhang, who upon retirement was given that lake so that he could perform the Buddhist deed of saving fish by releasing them into it.[11]

The humor in Su Shi's historical comparisons was not lost upon Huang Tingjian, who replied with yet another poem, entitled: "Zizhan Jested with Me about Zixia and Qiuming, and I Answer Him Again in Jest."[12] The opening lines dwell wryly on his present duties:

化工見彈太早計	The Transformer saw a bow and laid plans in advance,
端為失明能著書	Knowing that loss of sight would improve my *book*.
邇來似天會事發	Recently it seems Heaven reacts knowingly to circumstances;
淚睫見光猶隕珠	If teary eyelashes saw the light, they would continue to weep *pearls*.

Line 1. An allusion to a passage in *Zhuangzi* about premature expectations ("at the sight of the egg, you expect the cock-crow; at the sight of the bow, you expect a roasted owl"), but Huang uses it without any nuance of disapproval.[13]

Huang seems to be sarcastically suggesting that it would be better to be "blind" to recent political history (of the reforms) than to have to face the truth, which would cause too much grief.

These are certainly not the poems on which Su Shi's (or Huang Tingjian's) eminence in literary history is based. And yet, as inconsequential as they may be, they do merit attention. Play may be seen to serve several distinct, if related, purposes in this verse. Jocularity used to veil political comment is perhaps the most obvious kind. An example is Huang's references to the usefulness of his "blindness" in his duties as Court historian, an official who is supposed to place particular value on perspicacity, objectivity, and truthfulness. These men were fully aware of the dangers of political criticism, even in poetry. The memory of what had happened to Su Shi in 1079 must have been sharp in their minds. But politics was so central to their lives that the subject would have been difficult to avoid altogether in any form of speech or writing. Most of the men in Su's circle had just been recalled from provincial posts (or exile) upon the dramatic change in rulership and Court policy at the start of the Yuanyou period. Quickly, however, the new administration degenerated into rival cliques; and hostilities developed among the anti-reformers, as well as between them and the ministers who remained as holdovers from Shenzong's reign. Su and his friends sensed the precariousness of the situation. This was a climate, as we have seen, in which remarks that were genuinely and plainly devoid of political criticism could be represented as treasonous by one's enemies. It was natural, then, that when Su and the others succumbed to the temptation to express an opinion in their writings to each other about Court politics, they would do so under some guise; and frivolity was one of the most common choices. Thus a painting of a well-fed imperial steed by Li Gonglin became for Su Shi an occasion for a poetic satire ("written in jest") on the subject of pampered imperial favorites.[14] Actually, the label "written in jest" attached to a poem from this period is one of the clearest indications that the piece may have quite serious, albeit veiled, political intent.

Playfulness in these poetic exchanges may also be taken as a sign of the intimacy of the relationships involved. These were friends who knew each other well enough, and who were confident enough of their mutual respect, to be able to poke fun at themselves and each other. Su Shi belittles himself as being comparable to the great writer Sima Xiangru only in the respect that he can never satisfy his thirst (i.e., for Huang's special tea). Because Su speaks of himself this way, it is not insulting for him to joke with Huang about being a latterday Zixia or Zuo Qiuming. Huang's eye trouble may be comparable, but his accomplishments in poetry and, even less, in history are not. Huang was to continue the joking (still using the same rhymes) in a tea poem addressed to his colleague Kong Wuzhong, which opens:

校經同省並同居	We collators of the same bureau live behind adjacent doors.
無日不聞公讀書	Not a day passes I don't hear you reciting your *books*.
故持茗椀澆舌本	So I'm sending a bowl of tea to moisten the base of your tongue,
要聽六經如貫珠	Hoping the six classics will sound like a string of *pearls*.[15]

Such gentle kidding reinforces the friend's sense of cohesiveness and the separateness of their group from others.

The image of men who do not take their serious duties seriously is an important part of these poetic exchanges. Su Shi is secluded, in Huang Tingjian's description, within "divine" precincts, surrounded by precious books, as he drafts decrees on the emperor's behalf; but what he dreams of is the antithesis of all this imperial power and glory: wandering the Southland's lakes. Su's own poetic response seems to confirm the preferences Huang attributes to him, as he looks forward to "roaming the southeast" in the following year.

There may be more than merely the conventional distaste for the drudgery of office in such utterances, as it is easy to believe when we recall the particular nastiness of the politics of the period. Su's observation that the Lord of Heaven just teases men and is a trickster, written in sympathy for Huang's eye ailment, seems significant in this regard. References to the fickleness of the Lord of Heaven (*tiangong*) or the Fashioner of Things (*zaowuzhe*) became, as Yamamoto Kazuyoshi has noted, a recurrent motif in Su's poetry.[16] He used it in lamenting the death of a friend (much as he used it to express his sympathy for Huang Tingjian's illness): "The Fashioner of Things is but a child playing; / The wind is his sighs, the thunder and lightning his laughter."[17] He repeated the idea in a line addressed to an impoverished friend, Wang Shi, "The Fashioner of Things himself is merely play-acting."[18] And he complimented a Taoist, who had lived to a venerable age, by asking, "What can the child Fashioner of Things do to you?"[19]

It was not only misfortune or the threat of it that elicited this idea from Su. He broadened it to apply to the accidental quality of life in general:

人人走江湖	Many men wander the rivers and lakes,
一一操網釣	Each carrying a fish net.
偶然連六鼇	By chance someone catches six turtles at once,
便謂此手妙	Everyone says his skill is superior.[20]

Su means that the catch has nothing to do with skill. Even the landscape is said to be nothing more than the Fashioner's playful creation (on the reverse analogy of artificial miniature mountains made by man): "How like a little boy does the Fashioner play!"[21]

If the supreme power in the universe goes in for self-amusement, and is oblivious—or worse—of the consequences of his play, why should a mere mortal take the world seriously? That is the atti-

tude Su adopts in these lines: "Who can understand all the transformations made by the Craftsman of Heaven (*tiangong*)? / I myself
play like a child writing little poems."[22] The inspiration for this is the
blossoms of the so-called wax-plum (*lamei*), which looked as if they
had been fashioned from wax. Bees take nectar from flowers to make
wax, Su observes, and then the divine Craftsman takes wax and molds
flowers out of it. What could be more appropriate? The implications
of Su's thinking go far beyond his immediate subject. The ingenious
poetic lines that Su keeps crafting are in some sense modeled on this
image of a supreme power that is essentially whimsical, does not take
the world seriously, and is given to clever play.

A world that is presided over by such a prankster has a streak of
madness to it. Su's many protestations that he himself is mad (*kuang*)
are, of course, a reflection of his feeling of alienation from that
world.[23] One of the two (Su or the world) must be mad because their
perceptions were utterly incompatible. Here the influence that Su's experience in politics had upon his thinking is unmistakable.

嗟我本狂直	I, alas, am mad and forthright,
早為世所捐	Early on the world rejected me.[24]

Su wants us to understand that his fearlessness in voicing criticisms of
the New Policies, which verges on "madness" and is so perceived by
the world, led directly to the frustrations in his career. In a longer
treatment of the same issues Su is a bit less obvious about the pride he
takes in his conduct. He contrasts a friend's enviable traits with his
own:

	懶者常似靜	Laziness may often resemble quietude,
	靜豈懶者徒	But would quietude ever be disciple to laziness?
	拙則近於直	Clumsiness is close to forthrightness,
4	而直豈拙歟	But are the two actually the same?
	夫子靜且直	You possess quietude and forthrightness,
	雍容時卷舒	Adjusting yourself calmly to the times.
	嗟我復何為	How, alas, do I conduct myself?
8	相得歡有餘	Befriending you brings particular joy.
	我本不違世	Originally, I did not go against the world,
	而世與我殊	The world and I were simply different.
	拙於林間鳩	More clumsy than the pigeon in the woods,
12	懶於冰底魚	Lazier than fish in a frozen lake,
	人皆笑其狂	Everyone laughs at me as mad;
	子獨憐其愚	You alone pity my stupidity.[25]

Line 11. The pigeon is clumsy because it is not a good nest-builder.

The pragmatic strategy of adjusting oneself to meet changing circumstances had become repugnant to Su Shi. That is not to say that he was forever unchanging. If anything, he deliberately adjusted himself to be out of sync with the changing times, believing in the great benefits of dissent. Thus finding himself at odds with the world, Su played at being lazy and mad.

The madness that Su affected must have its precedents; but in literary history, the dominant tradition of madness and disaffection had a rather different tone. Each "madman of Chu" may have mocked his Confucius, but how many of them also mocked themselves?[26] In poetry the conviction that one was hopelessly out of step with one's times was first represented by Qu Yuan, whose influence on later writers cannot be overemphasized. Qu Yuan did not call himself mad, but he certainly believed that the political world from which he so proudly withdrew was deranged; and his own obsession with purity and transcendence will strike many readers as bordering on delirium. But the tone of Qu Yuan's lyric poetry is self-righteous and self-pitying, completely unlike what we find in Su Shi. In the intervening centuries Du Fu had also pronounced himself to be mad. But in Du Fu the sense of enmity towards an unjust world remains plainly evident. Right before he calls himself mad ("This madman laughs at himself for growing madder the older he gets"), Du Fu wrote these grim lines: "My amply salaried friends have stopped sending letters; / My constantly hungry children have joyless faces."[27] This is certainly not Su Shi's version of madness either. Li Bo emulated the original madman of Chu and claimed to disdain all worldly ambitions. As outlandish and humorous as Li Bo can be, there is still in his wild unconventionality a strong sense of self-esteem. Moreover, it is one thing to affect the madman when setting off "in search of immortals on the five sacred peaks" and quite another to pose as crazed while in office. The latter is what Su Shi does, as illustrated by this better-known poem:

登雲龍山	*Climbing Cloud Dragon Mountain*
醉中走上黃茅岡	Drunk, I race up Yellow Grass Hill.
滿岡亂石如羣羊	The hill is strewn with rocks, like a herd of sheep.
岡頭醉倒石作牀	On top I collapse in a stupor, a rock my bed,
仰看白雲天茫茫	To stare at the white clouds in the boundless sky.
歌聲落谷秋風長	My song drifts down to the valley on far-reaching autumn winds,

路人舉首東南望　　Passersby look up
　　　　　　　　　　and gaze to the southeast,
拍手大笑使君狂　　Clapping their hands, they burst out laughing,
　　　　　　　　　　"The prefect's gone mad!"[28]

By saying that Su's manner of madness is freer of bitterness or recrimination than that of many earlier poets, I do not mean to imply that his disillusionment with the world was any less profound. In fact, it may well be that because his disillusionment was particularly thorough he was able to remain in the world while adopting the literary guise of madness. The eminent scholar Li Zehou has suggested as much in a recent essay on the poet: "Su never became a recluse, nor did he ever 'return to the farm,' but the sense of the meaninglessness of worldly striving conveyed by his poetry and prose is deeper and more profound than that of any earlier writer, including both those who merely paid lip service to the idea of withdrawing and those who actually did become a recluse or return to the farm."[29]

The significance of playfulness, self-parody, and "madness" in Su Shi's literary work lies in its pervasiveness. While some of it may be linked directly to his experiences in politics ("I, alas, am mad and forthright"), as a pose and persona it became for Su much larger than that particular inspiration. Su adopted it as a literary tone through which he would present himself to the world. There is a telling contrast here with Huang Tingjian, Su's literary friend. As long as the two men were exchanging poems in friendly competition, Huang could write with fully as much humor and playfulness as his colleague. But when Huang was separated from Su and wrote on his own, his tone changed dramatically. He becomes brooding, bookish, and somber. A poem such as the one by Su translated immediately above would then be completely out of character for Huang.

Su Shi permitted the spirit of play to carry over into his literary work generally, not just in those pieces he wrote as poetic games with his friends and political allies. A large part of this literary tone comes from not taking the self seriously (or, at least, not doing so explicitly). To help to account for Su's flair for this, we may refer back to the themes of his philosophical views on the self and its relation to the world. His notions of selflessness (*wuxin*), of avoiding deliberation (*wusi*), and even of the desirability of immersing the self in contact with "things," to which it is ever responding, would all seem to be relevant. Of course, there must also be matters of temperament involved, immeasurable and unarticulated. But it is remarkable how congruent Su's carefully developed positions on the self are with this aspect of his literary work. Water cannot be said to have the human characteristic of playfulness, but there is a sense in which its infinite adaptability may be said metaphorically to show that it does not take its "self" seriously. Su's intellectual positions were shown earlier to draw heavily upon Buddhist doctrines. In Su's literary sportiveness there is, indeed, much of the Chan monk's taste for the absurd and nonsensical, a fact often highlighted in the works Su addressed to his monk friends, such as his Refreshing Winds inscription for Yingfu. And Su's poetic "madness" certainly has greater affinity with the profound mirth of the Chan monk than with the dolorousness of Qu Yuan.

Imaging the Poet in the World

A disinclination to take the self all that seriously can be seen to have its influence on a variety of other traits of Su Shi's verse and shows itself in the vast number of poems that are not, unlike those cited above, explicitly jocular. As those traits are discussed in turn below, it will be possible to discern the impact of this particular attitude on each of them.

Discursiveness

Characterizations of Su Shi's poetry customarily list discursiveness as one of its distinctive features. The terms used to designate this trait vary from critic to critic, with some preferring terms such as "philosophical" or "intellectual." But whatever term is used, the critics seem to have much the same trait in mind (hence they tend to quote the same poems as illustrations).[30] Nor is the identification of this trait unique to modern critics. Traditional commentators were fond of calling attention to the preponderance of *lun* ("argument") and *yi* ("thought") in Su's poetry, and of observing that Su had "fashioned poetry out of prose," by which they meant in part that his verse presented a density of thought customarily borne only by prose.[31] Often, indeed, scholars call attention to this trait to express their disapproval. There have always been critics who are uneasy with intellectual poetry, believing that argumentation is best left to the prose forms.

An example of a discursive poem is translated below:

泗州僧伽塔   *Samgha's Pagoda in Zizhou*

我昔南行舟繫汴   Long ago I traveled south
                    and moored on the Bian.

逆風三日沙吹面	Headwinds blew three days; sand pelted my face.
舟人共勸禱靈塔	The boatmen all urged me to pray at this sacred pagoda;
4　香火未收旆脚轉	Before the incense finished burning, the flags turned around.
回頭頃刻失長橋	As we looked back in a moment, Long Bridge was out of sight;
却到龜山未朝飯	We got all the way to Tortoise Hill before breakfast.[32]
至人無心何厚薄	The enlightened man has no-mind: what is good or ill luck to him?
8　我自懷私欣所便	I clung to selfish interests, delighted to have them met.
耕田欲雨刈欲晴	Sowers want rain, reapers want clear skies,
去得順風來者怨	Favorable winds for men departing make those arriving complain.[33]
若使人人禱輒遂	For every person's prayer to be answered,
12　造物應須日千變	The Fashioner would have to effect a thousand changes a day.
今我身世兩悠悠	Today both my person and the world are insubstantial to me.
去無所逐來無戀	I pursue nothing when I go nor crave anything when I come.
得行固願留不惡	Being able to proceed is my wish, but delay does not cause resentment.
16　每到有求神亦倦	If I prayed each time I passed by, the god himself would grow tired.
退之舊云三百尺	Tuizhi once said, "It stands three hundred feet high."
澄觀所營今已換	But the tower Chengguan constructed has already disappeared.
不嫌俗士污丹梯	If a vulgar scholar may be permitted to defile cinnabar stairs,
20　一看雲山繞淮甸	I shall take one look at the cloudy hills encircling the lands of the Huai.[34]

Title. "Samgha" names a Tang-dynasty Buddhist monk, who had resided at the temple.

Lines 17–18. Samgha's pagoda was reconstructed in the eighth century by the monk Chengguan, and the project was celebrated in a poem by Han Yu (Tuizhi).[35]

Line 19. The phrase "cinnabar stairs" is also used in Taoist contexts to denote the path to immortality.

This poem was written in 1071, during Su Shi's journey from the capital to his post in Hangzhou. Su Shi had passed the same site five years earlier, when he was transporting his father's coffin back to Sichuan. It was then that he had the experience recounted in the opening lines of the poem.

The movement in the poem is from the particular events that Su recollects to a meditation upon their larger meaning. This sort of development of abstract reasoning out of concrete and, indeed, everyday circumstances is typical of Su Shi's intellectual verse. There is more to the thought here than simply the jump to omniscience, which sees that one man's convenience is another man's complaint. Su Shi is also thinking about time, the theme brought out in the closing lines. There are, in effect, two kinds of fixity under consideration, both of which are in the poet's mind undesirable. The first is basically spatial, that is, viewing things either as one who is departing or one who is arriving. The second is temporal: this is the delusion of supposing that anything manmade (or identified with *this* lifetime) may be truly great or eternal. The alternative to thus seeking to withstand the effects of time—the effort is doomed to failure, just as the towering pagoda would inevitably fall—is to transcend it altogether, as for example in Taoist immortality.

The poem is reminiscent of the prose inscription Su Shi wrote for the hall in which Zhang Cishan housed his calligraphy collection.[36] That piece opens with an extended reflection upon divergent ways of life and values. Su Shi is aware that to many people a life devoted to calligraphy connoisseurship, such as Zhang's, is a life of frivolousness. Naturally, he wants to argue against this, and he does so by calling attention to the subjectivity of all sets of values. Most men yearn for little else than to eat and dress well. Men of culture disparage these goals and pride themselves instead on their polite accomplishments in music, chess, and the arts. Men of letters similarly belittle the art connoisseurs, believing that the cultivation of skill at writing is the only worthwhile activity. But men of action look down upon the lettered gentlemen, and point instead to the impact that their deeds as officials have upon the world. Then there are the recluses, who maintain that the supreme deed is to renounce action in the world. Su concludes that the only real mistake a person can make is to think that his own preferences (or point of view) have more objective validity than those of anyone else.

The theme of praying to the gods, mentioned in the Samgha poem, comes up again in a poem on an ocean mirage that appeared off the Shandong coast. Just before he was recalled to the capital at the start of the Yuanyou era, Su was sent to the coastal prefecture of Dengzhou. His tenure as prefect there was ridiculously brief (he was recalled five days after he arrived), but it lasted long enough for him to catch a glimpse of the famed mirage of a city floating distantly out upon the sea. Su had asked in a prayer that he might see the mirage; and when his prayer was answered, he used the occasion to air his views on the relation between men and the gods. One venerable and widespread notion of the relationship held that Heaven was remote and tended toward hostility in its dealings with humankind. Thus Heaven regularly visited hardship and misfortune upon mortals. According to this fatalistic view, the origins of our sufferings was likely to be Heaven rather than ourselves, and it was only extraordinary virtue that could ever move Heaven to act beneficently on a mortal's behalf. This view is sympathetic to humankind or anthropocentric in that it tends to absolve mortals of responsibility for misfortune while it credits their virtue whenever good fortune prevails.

Su Shi proposes a very different account of the relationship between mortals and gods. The gods are fundamentally benign, and regularly assist us in achieving our goals. Because of this divine predilection, in Su's mind responsibility for hardship in this world is shifted back upon mortals: "My plea, though shallow, was not rejected; / Truly man's troubles are not inflicted by Heaven."[37] Here, Su Shi turns again to Han Yu to contrast his views with those of the great Tang writer. Han Yu had once passed by Heng Mountain (Hengyang, Hunan)—Su misremembers the precise occasion, thinking that it happened when Han was on his way into exile in Chaozhou—and was disappointed to find the famous peaks shrouded in clouds. Han offered a prayer to the mountain gods, and soon the clouds dispersed, revealing the mountain in all its grandeur. Han supposed that his own virtue was what had prompted the gods to grant his wish, but Su has a different idea: "He said his own uprightness moved the mountain spirit, / Not realizing the Fashioner pitied him in his distress."

The two sightings, Su's of the mirage at sea and Han's of Heng Mountain, both occurred after prayers and apparently, divine intervention. But the similarity ends there, as Su takes issue with what he considers Han Yu's inflated opinion of the effects of human virtue. The themes of this poem are not the same as in Su's Samgha poem: there Su reflects on multiple viewpoints among mortals, whereas here he challenges an understanding of man's place in the cosmos that champions his importance and goodness. Different though the two themes may be, they share an aversion to self-importance that makes them recognizable as the product of a single intellectual orientation. In poems on diverse other subjects, it is often this same interest in reconsidering a matter from multiple points of view that propels the reasoning. The "intellectual" or discursive character of Su Shi's verse is due in large part to this effort to overcome the subjectivity of experience.

Social and Spatial Perspectives

Translated below is a poem in which Su takes a giant step outside the view of society that was conventional for the official class. This is the well-known poem that Su wrote on a New Year's Eve in the early 1070s, when as vice prefect of Hangzhou, he was kept late at his office by the need to decide pending charges against prisoners before the old year expired.[38] Su complains elsewhere during this period that the salt regulations under the New Policies, which restricted the private marketing of salt, had resulted in thousands of arrests each year in the Hangzhou region.[39]

除日當早歸	New Year's Eve, I should go home early
官事乃見留	But official duties keep me behind.
執筆對之泣	Holding my brush, I face them with tears,
哀此繫中囚	Grieved for these prisoners in chains.
小人營餱糧	Petty men, looking for some food,
墮網不知羞	Fell into the net, knowing no shame.
我亦戀薄祿	I, too, cling to my meager salary
因循失歸休	Continuously missing chances to retire.
不須論賢愚	Don't talk of noble and base,
均是為食謀	Each of us schemes for a meal.
誰能暫縱遣	Who could set them free for a time?
閔默愧前修	I am silent, humiliated before the ancients.

For the Song dynasty official to reflect this way upon the circumstances that drove desperate men to steal is uncommon enough. For him to go on to compare his own means of livelihood with that of the criminal is virtually unheard of. The closing couplet refers to the humane practice, attributed in the dynastic histories to various earlier governors, of allowing prisoners to return home briefly during New Year to observe the festival with their families.[40]

This particular poem was not used as evidence against Su Shi in his 1079 trial for treason, but nearly all of those that were display in one way or another the same fondness for considering social circumstances from the viewpoint of those below the administrative class. We recall the quatrain that satirizes the effects of the crop loan policy. The claim of the reformers was that the policy would benefit the farmers by making them less dependent upon unscrupulous private money-lenders. But the poet dwells on the bureaucratic delays and corruption that first kept the farmer away from his fields for weeks on end (so that his son's speech became citified) and then helped to deprive him of the loans soon after they were finally issued to him.

The point here is that the poems of political criticism and dissent are merely one part of Su Shi's interest in exploring perspectives other than that which might be expected of a man of his status. Other effects of this interest have nothing to do with Su's positions in the political controversies of his day. Su is fond, for example, of the poetic conceit that attributes a human "viewpoint" to some inanimate element in a scene, and reconsidering events from it. That is what happens toward the end of the following poem, which was written as he departed from Xuzhou, where he had been prefect:

罷徐州往南京馬上
走筆寄子由五首
（其一）

Leaving My Post at Xuzhou and
Setting Out for the Southern Capital.
I Write Hurriedly on Horseback
and Send to Ziyou (No. 1)

	吏民莫扳援	Don't let the people hold me back,
	歌管莫淒咽	Don't let singers and flutes play mournfully.
	吾生如寄耳	My life is like a brief stay,
4	寧獨為此別	Will this be my only farewell?
	別離隨處有	Departures occur everywhere;
	悲惱緣愛結	Grief comes from too much love.
	而我本無恩	Besides, I am not a benevolent man—
8	此涕誰為設	For whom are these tears shed?
	紛紛等兒戲	All this commotion is childishness,
	鞭鐙遭割截	The whip and stirrups being cut away.
	道邊雙石人	That pair of stone statues along the road,
12	幾見太守發	How many prefects have they watched depart?
	有知當解笑	Were they sentient, they would start laughing,
	撫掌冠纓絕	Clap their hands and snap their capstrings.[41]

Line 14. On the day that Yao Chong (8th c.) was replaced as prefect of Jingzhou, the adoring commoners surrounded his horse, grabbed his whip away from him, and cut his stirrups off to prevent him from leaving.[42]

Line 14. When the advisor and jester Chunyu Kun heard how few gifts his king was prepared to send to a neighboring king to secure defending troops, he threw his head back and roared with laughter until the strings that held his cap in place broke.[43]

On this particular occasion, Su keeps attempting different ways of distancing himself both from those he depicts as his loyal subordinates and from his acclaim for having saved Xuzhou from the flooding Yellow River. In another poem in the series, a commoner stops Su's horse on the road to express his gratitude. Su's answer: "The flood's arrival was not my fault; / It's receding was not to my credit." In still another piece, Su focuses on the Bian River, which winds through the landscape of his journey, so that he keeps losing and reencountering it. The river becomes his friend who sees him off and is there again to welcome him onto the next leg of his journey. But finally the river stays behind as the poet proceeds to his distant destination. At the poem's close, Su thinks back to the river, which must still be flowing beside the Yellow Tower that he built in Xuzhou. But the person who so enjoyed listening to the river in the moonlight there is gone.

Su's interest in confronting the subjectivity of experience goes beyond this heightened awareness of his own place or social role in particular settings. He is equally intrigued by the larger thought that all perceptions themselves are subjective and that therefore nothing has but a single appearance. Even something as seemingly fixed and unchanging as a mountain turns out to constantly alter its looks:

朝見吳山橫	Mornings I view Wu Mountain's breadth,
暮見吳山縱	Evenings I view its distant reach.
吳山故多態	Wu Mountain assumes many appearances
轉折為君容	Turning about to pose for its lover.[44]

The clever elaboration in the second couplet of a common conceit (landscape as woman) is made possible by the earlier realization that the mountain's looks change as the day progresses. Here the poet is presumably referring to the effect of altered lighting (the sun's movement through the sky) rather than to his own movement through the landscape, which would have a similar effect. The latter possibility is treated in the well-known quatrain Su wrote about Lu Mountain:

題西林壁	Inscribed on the Wall of West Forest Monastery
橫看成嶺側成峰	From the side it's a mountain wall, from the end a single peak,
遠近高低總不同	Near, far, high, low— each view is different.
不識廬山真面目	I do not know Lu Mountain's true face,
只緣身在此山中	Because I find myself in the mountain's midst.[45]

And in another play upon the effect that his own movement, of a different sort, has upon the appearance of a mountain, Su writes, "My waterborne pillow makes the mountains rise and fall." Seen from his bed on a bobbing boat, the landscape appears to move. It is a line Su uses, with variations, in three separate poems.[46]

A concept that is central to Su's treatment of perceptions is *xiang* ("image, form, semblance"). "The ten thousand *xiang* all come from my own eyes," Su Shi proclaims, reminding us that our perceptions of the world are inevitably affected by our physical vantage point as well as our psychological stance.[47] Thus, the "true face" of Lu Mountain could not ever be glimpsed by any human eye (whether located on or outside the mountain). This manner of thinking clearly has much in common with Buddhist doctrines on the illusory nature of worldly phenomena and the limitations of sense perceptions. Two points concerning this overlapping may be borne in mind. First, while certain aspects of this thinking are certainly not new, Su Shi wove them more thoroughly into his literary work than any earlier major poet had ever done. Su is the first to explore the expressive force these well-established doctrines acquire when incorporated into the tradition of personal, lyric poetry. It is really the unlikely wedding of the two (an intellectual challenge to the validity of the individual's sense perceptions and a literary tradition rooted in the self) whose power is at work in these poems. Second, the direction Su Shi takes with these thoughts has a peculiar emphasis. We are familiar with Buddhist metaphors intended to illustrate the unreality of worldly phenomena: the moon reflected in a pool, images appearing in mirrors, and so on. The simple purpose of such illustrations is to counsel us to cast aside our preoccupation with worldly illusions and devote ourselves instead to the higher reality that transcends the phenomenal world. But there are also teachings on techniques for "receiving" sensory impressions without being fundamentally affected by them. That is what interests Su as a poet. Your mind, he tells us, should be like the water in a well, allowing the ten thousand *xiang* (images) to appear and disappear in it as they will.[48] This is a rather different use of *xiang* from that in the assertion that "the ten thousand *xiang* all come from my own eyes." There, the *xiang* are the deluding images our sense organs present to us. But in the statement about the mind as well water, there is nothing untoward or unwelcome about the appearance of the *xiang*. The mind accepts them without allowing them to have a lasting impact. The mind has this capacity because it is as clear and reactive ("empty") as the surface of the water, or as transparent as the *mani* gem, which takes on the color of whatever is behind it.[49] In a poem about poetry, Su counsels his monk friend Canliao, "With emptiness you admit the ten thousand scenes."[50] Then poetry and devotion to Chan present no contradiction.

Time

Time figures as frequently as space in the poet's treatment of his limitations as an observer of the world. Let us begin with time on a large or historical scale. The poem below was written during Su's second year at Xuzhou at the Yellow Tower he constructed on the city wall to commemorate the residents' victory over the floodwaters that nearly engulfed the city the year before.

送鄭戶曹	*Seeing Off Revenue Officer Zheng*
水繞彭祖樓	Waters encircle the Pengzu tower,[51]
山圍戲馬臺	Mountains surround Sporting Horses Terrace.
古來豪傑地	On this ancient land of heroes
4　千載有餘哀	Melancholy persists a thousand years later.
隆準飛上天	He with the prominent nose has flown to Heaven,
重瞳亦成灰	The double pupils have likewise turned to ashes.
白門下呂布	At White Gate did Lü Bu surrender,
8　大星隕臨淮	A great meteor felled Linhuai.
尚想劉德輿	One can still imagine Liu Deyu
置酒此徘徊	Setting out wine and tarrying here.
爾來苦寂寞	Since then the land grew desolate,
12　廢圃多蒼苔	Abandoned gardens are covered with moss.
河從百步響	The river echoes from Hundred Paces,
山到九里回	The mountains circle back from Nine Miles,
山水自相激	Mountains and river dash against each other,
16　夜聲轉風雷	At night the sounds become wind and thunder.
蕩蕩清河堧	How vast are the fields beside the clear river
黃樓我所開	Where I myself built Yellow Tower.
秋月墮城角	Tonight the autumn moon sets behind the city wall,
20　春風搖酒杯	Spring breezes ripple the wine in the cup.
遲君為座客	While we wait for you as guest at our banquet,
新詩出瓊瑰	Your recent poems show forth their bright gems.
樓成君已去	The tower complete, now you must depart,
24　人事固多乖	So contrary are human affairs!
他年君倦游	In future years, tired of your travels,
白首賦歸來	With white hair you will sing "The Return."
登樓一長嘯	Climbing this tower, you will heave a long sigh and ask,
28　使君安在哉	"Where is the prefect now?"[52]

Lines 1–2. Pengzu is the legendary figure who lived over seven hundred years. The sage king Yao enfeoffed him at Xu, which was also known thereafter as Pengcheng (Peng City). The tower referred to here was part of a shrine in his honor. Sporting Horses Terrace was a building overlooking the field in which Xiang Yu, who overthrew the Qin dynasty, exercised his horses.

Lines 5–6. It was the founding emperor of the Han dynasty, Han Gaozu, who had a prominent nose and who was a native of Pei (within Xuzhou). "Double Pupils" was Xiang Yu, Gaozu's great rival after the demise of the Qin dynasty. Early in his career, when he declared himself king of Chu, Xiang Yu based himself at Pengcheng; and he was eventually defeated by Gaozu not far from it, at Gaixia.

Lines 7–8. Lü Bu was the Later Han general who, when prefect of Xuzhou, found himself besieged by Cao Cao at nearby Xiapei, where he surrendered at White Gate and was hanged. Line 8 refers to the Tang general Li Guangbi, who had been enfeoffed as prince of Linhuai and who died at Xuzhou soon after a comet fell to earth there.[53]

Lines 9–10. Liu Deyu was Song Wudi, the founding emperor of the Southern Dynasties' Song. He was a native of Pengcheng.

Su Shi is not exaggerating the historical importance of his location. Xuzhou (Pengcheng) and the Huai River Valley had indeed been a land of great heroes and events, especially during the Chu-Han and Three Kingdoms period. As befits any *huaigu* poem ("cherishing the past"), the memory of these men is inseparable from the landscape. As the poet gazes out upon the now desolate scene, he is filled with nostalgia for them.

Yet in this poem the landscape is more than a setting or stage for grand deeds. From the very opening couplet the mountains and river are subtly juxtaposed with the human world. After the list of perished heroes the mountains and river reassert themselves, dominating the next few lines with their willfulness and self-generated noise that fills the scene at night. The landscape is the only enduring actor here. Humans are no match for it.

When the poem finally gets to the present situation (as announced in the title) we anticipate some parallel to this representation of the past. Yellow Tower was, after all, a symbol of Prefect Su's victory over the Yellow River floods. But how long could the prefect or his tower be expected to last or prevail over the timeless forces of nature? The striking feature of the conclusion is the tone in which Su acknowledges his impermanence upon the scene. He shows little emotion over the prospect of his own vanishing, and this makes the ending unlike what we expect in a poem of historical nostalgia. (The countless poets who shed tears over Yang Hu's tablet on Mount Xian were largely weeping for their own mortality, whether or not they got around to saying so.) Instead, Su puts emotion into the words of his friend, Zheng Jin, whose future return to Xuzhou and the tower he imagines. There is something slightly humorous about this ending, and it must be deliberately so. It is, of course, presumptuous of Su to describe this nostalgia for himself. It is a mark of his confidence in Zheng Jin's friendship that he can do so at all, but it remains too arrogant not to be uttered tongue-in-cheek. Where indeed will the prefect be? I leave that, Su thinks, for my friend to reflect on. Let it not concern me now. The mix of detachment and wistfulness with which Su contemplates his own slide into obscurity, paralleling that of the ancient heroes, is what distinguishes this poem and others Su wrote like it.[54]

Time on a smaller scale is likewise apt to be treated in ways that call attention to the transitory nature of mood and feeling. Su is intrigued by the thought of how short-lived particular scenes and experiences may be. Unlike so many earlier poets, Su is not content simply to assert this fact about experience. He takes pains to depict it in his poems, as in this example:

舟中夜起	*Awaking on a Boat at Night*
微風蕭蕭吹菰蒲	A light breeze soughs quietly, blowing river grasses.
開門看雨月滿湖	I open the hatch expecting rain; moonlight fills the lake.
舟人水鳥兩同夢	Boatmen and river birds share the same dream;
大魚驚竄如奔狐	A large fish suddenly jumps and dives like a darting fox.
夜深人物不相管	Late at night people and creatures are oblivious of each other,
我獨形影相嬉娛	While in my case alone, form and shadow delight each other.
暗潮生渚弔寒蚓	The dark tide appears at the bank, pity the cold crawlers,[55]
落月挂柳看懸蛛	The setting moon hangs in the willow, see the spider suspended.
此生忽忽憂患裏	In this hurried life, spent amid worries and troubles,
清境過眼能須臾	Pure scenes pass before the eyes— how long can they last?
雞鳴鐘動百鳥散	Cocks crow, bells sound, flocks of birds take flight.
船頭擊鼓還相呼	Drums beat on the bow, shout answers shout.[56]

Listening from inside the cabin, Su first mistakes the swishing of the gentle breeze through the rushes for rain. Only when he looks out, expecting to see rain, does he realize it is a clear and moonlit night. The beauty of the scene arrests him and he proceeds to record his minute observations.

Arising in the middle of the night and listening to or watching things that other men are unaware of is a recurrent motif in Su's writing.[57] It is a type of occasion perfectly suited to his fondness for detached observation. Here, the "pure scene" lasts for him right through until dawn, when the loud noises of the workaday world intrude and obliterate it. The evocation of a quiet, undisturbed scene is, of course, often encountered in earlier poetry. But in distinction from so many poems that build towards a final image of quietude, Su's piece continues on until the stillness has been broken. He is as interested in depicting the transitory nature of the quiet scene as the scene itself.

If experiences are fleeting, especially desirable ones, it is some consolation to think that they might at least be captured in poetry. The author will later be able to return to the poem to remind himself of the flavor of the occasion, however long ago it happened. This is the justification for writing poetry that appears in one of the earliest statements Su ever made on the subject,[58] and it reappears in a poem from his first Hangzhou tour:

臘日遊孤山訪惠勤惠思二僧	*On Winter's Day I Go to Lone Hill to Visit the Two Monks Huiqin and Huisi*
天欲雪　雲滿湖	The sky threatens snow, Clouds cover the lake.
樓臺明滅山有無	Pavilions and towers appear and vanish— are the mountains there?
水清石出魚可數	Rocks jut out from clear waters, you can count the fish;
林深無人鳥相呼	The forest is deep and deserted as birds call back and forth.
臘日不歸對妻孥	On Winter's Day I do not go home to be with my family;
名尋道人實自娛	I say I'm visiting men of the Way, it's really to enjoy myself.
道人之居在何許	These men of the Way, where do they dwell?
寶雲山前路盤紆	Below Precious Cloud Peak the road twists and turns.
孤山孤絕誰肯廬	Lone Hill is a lonely place— who would live there?

道人有道山不孤	But men of the Way possess the Way, their hill is not lonely.
紙窗竹屋深自暖	Paper windows and bamboo roofs, yet they are perfectly warm,
12 擁褐坐睡依團蒲	In coarse cloth they sit or doze on rush meditation mats.
天寒路遠愁僕夫	The cold weather and long road worry my servant;
整駕催歸及未晡	He readies the carriage to hurry me off, anxious to be home before dusk.
出山迴望雲木合	Down the hill I look back to where clouds meet the trees,
16 但見野鶻盤浮圖	All I see are wild hawks circling the pagoda spires.
茲遊淡薄歡有餘	The subtle flavor of this outing yields abundant joy;
到家恍如夢蘧蘧	Back home I am in a daze like a dreamer startled awake.
作詩火急追亡逋	Write a poem—emergency!— before it escapes:
20 清景一失後難摹	A pure scene once lost is hard to replicate.[59]

Title. Winter's Day was a twelfth-month holiday. The monk Huiqin had been recommended to Su Shi by Ouyang Xiu, which probably explains why Su visited him within the first month of his arrival at Hangzhou.[60] Lone Hill is a spit of land that sticks out into West Lake (which lay outside the city wall of Song-dynasty Hangzhou).

Line 17. Aside from the "flavor" of the monastery itself, Su may also be referring to absence of any literati companions or courtesans on this particular outing.[61]

Pure scenes are in the nature of things short-lived. A poem can be sent chasing after them. But what this poem finally captures, once again, is as much an awareness that the moment is always fleeting as it does the "subtle flavor" of the outing. Many previous poets had written about just such one-day retreats into the mountains. Usually they saw fit to end their poems at the site of their journey's destination. But Su brings us back out, even as his gaze is turned back to the monastery spires, and does not stop until he raises the possibility that the whole feeling inspired by the sojourn may be lost. Nor does Su always sound so confident that the poetic attempt to overtake and capture the experience will be successful. At the end of the Dengzhou sea-mirage poem mentioned earlier, it is suggested that the poem itself will be as ephemeral as the experience it records (that of glimpsing, fittingly enough, a mirage):

斜陽萬里孤鳥沒	In sunset rays stretching countless miles, a lone bird disappears.
但見碧海磨青銅	All I see is the emerald ocean like a burnished bronze mirror.
新詩綺語亦安用	This new poem with colorful phrases— what use is it?
相與變滅隨東風	It, too, will transform and vanish on the east wind.[62]

Wang Wen'gao put his finger precisely on what makes this ending distinctive. Other poets, he observed, would have been content to end the poem with the first couplet above.[63] But Su wants to question the poetic effort itself, acknowledging that it, too, is tied to a certain moment and can make no claim of immortality.

Metaphor

Ever since Su's own time, readers have remarked on the prominence of metaphor in his poetry. It is both the sheer number and the striking quality of Su's metaphors that attracts comment. In modern scholarship the richness of Su's metaphorical language is invariably mentioned in summary descriptions of his poetic style, and it has also been the subject of specialized studies.[64] However, critical writings have not progressed much beyond the point of labeling metaphor, especially extended metaphor, as a trait of Su's style.

We have already encountered, even in the few poems quoted above, some examples: Wu Mountain posing as a woman does for her lover, stone statues laughing until their capstrings break, the magistrate as a common criminal, the mountains bobbing up and down, the moon hanging in a willow like a spider in its web. (It will be obvious here that I am using "metaphor" in the broadest sense, to designate all kinds of tropes that name or describe one thing in terms of another. This is, in fact, consistent with traditional Chinese comments on Su's poetry, which typically do not discriminate between these various sorts of figures of speech, calling them all *yu*.) Some additional examples further illustrate the range of figures under consideration. On snow that fell overnight, for example:

| 青山有似少年子 | The green hills bear some resemblance to a young man |
| 一夕變盡滄浪髭 | Whose whiskers, overnight, have turned completely white.[65] |

On calligraphy styles:

短長肥瘦各有態　　Short, tall, plump, thin,
　　　　　　　　　　each has its beauty:
玉環飛燕誰敢憎　　Jade Bracelet and Flying Swallow—
　　　　　　　　　　who could dislike either of them?[66]

On being in prison:

夢繞雲山心似鹿　　My dreams encircle the cloudy hill,
　　　　　　　　　　my heart like the deer.
魂驚湯火命如雞　　My soul is frightened of the boiling pot,
　　　　　　　　　　my life like the chicken's.[67]

On a rock taken from a seacoast cliff:

我持此石歸　　As I carry this rock away,
袖中有東海　　　　My sleeves contain the eastern sea.[68]

On a pump, first moving and then at rest, that lifts water through a trough by means of a chain of moving wooden pallets:[69]

翻翻聯聯銜尾鴉　　Flapping in a continuous line,
　　　　　　　　　　ducks flying mouth to tail;
犖犖确确蛻骨蛇　　Jagged and spiny,
　　　　　　　　　　a snake that has shed its skin.[70]

On reading Meng Jiao's poetry:

初如食小魚　　At first it's like eating tiny fish:
所得不償勞　　What you get is not worth the effort.
又似煮彭螁　　It's also like boiling little crabs:
竟日持空螯　　You end up holding empty pincers.[71]

And on various other topics:

欲知垂盡歲　　What is the departing year like?
有似赴壑蛇　　A snake slithering down a hole.
修鱗半已沒　　Its scaly body has half disappeared:
去意誰能遮　　Who can prevent it from vanishing?
況欲繫其尾　　You may attempt to grab onto its tail—
雖勤知奈何　　Try as you might, what good will it do?[72]

忽逢佳士與名山　　Suddenly to meet such a fine gentleman
　　　　　　　　　　　　amid famous mountains
何異枯楊便馬疥　　Is like how the withered willow
　　　　　　　　　　　　suits a horse with an itch.[73]

人生到處知何似　　What is it, finally,
　　　　　　　　　　　　that life is like?
應似飛鴻踏雪泥　　It must be a wild goose
　　　　　　　　　　　　treading on snow and mud.
泥上偶然留指爪　　In the mud, by chance,
　　　　　　　　　　　　it leaves claw prints,
鴻飛那復計東西　　Then flies away,
　　　　　　　　　　　　who knows where?[74]

嶺上晴雲披絮帽　　Sunlit clouds on mountain peaks,
　　　　　　　　　　　　they wear a cotton cap.
樹頭初日挂銅鉦　　The dawn sun through the trees,
　　　　　　　　　　　　a copper gong suspended.[75]

我生天地間　　My existence between Heaven and Earth
一蟻寄大磨　　Is like an ant on a millstone.
區區欲右行　　It struggles to crawl to the right,
不救風輪左　　But the wind wheel carries it to the left.[76]

微風萬頃靴文細　　Light wind on the vast river,
　　　　　　　　　　　　tiny wrinkles in leather boots,
斷霞半空魚尾赤　　Sunset clouds in half the sky,
　　　　　　　　　　　　a crimson fish tail.[77]

仰看雲天真箬笠　　The cloudy sky above me
　　　　　　　　　　　　is really my rain hat.
旋收江海入蓑衣　　I allow the rivers and seas to
　　　　　　　　　　　　flow into my coat of reeds.[78]

The list might easily be expanded. The first observation to make about such figures is that they are for the most part novel. A significant percentage of metaphors in Chinese verse is based in one way or another on a small store of stock associations, for example, flowing water with the passage of time, celestial bodies with the emperor and the Court, the exceptional horse with the talented man, the neglected woman with the rejected minister, and so forth. Su Shi's poetry does, of course, contain figures of speech that are derived from these stock associations—it would be impossible to avoid them. But what is immediately noteworthy about many of his metaphors, especially the drawn-out and celebrated ones, is that they establish an unconventional pairing. Not only are the comparisons novel, the elements being compared, whether implicitly or explicitly, are often quite disparate (e.g., a fleeing snake with the old year, a horse's itch with Su's longing for a friend.) Critics have sometimes objected to this ambitiousness evident in Su's figures of speech, finding certain of them far-fetched or jarring.[79]

A related matter is that of emotion. Often in earlier poetry the most prominent metaphors carry a heavy load of emotive force. The poet uses the special power of metaphorical language to convey powerful feelings. Given this tradition, it is interesting to notice that so many of Su Shi's figures of speech are emotively quite flat, as in "Sunlit clouds on mountain peaks, they wear a cotton cap; / The dawn sun through the trees, a copper gong suspended." The poem in which these lines occur is autobiographical, but these figures of speech are barely engaged in the sentiment of the poem. They simply describe the scene through which the poet moves. One reason Su Shi's metaphors are so quotable, so readily extracted from their context, is that they tend towards the emotionally neutral. They are offered up as interesting and novel ways of seeing something, but then they are apt to be dropped as the poet turns his attention elsewhere. Even where the poet himself is part of the analogy that is fashioned, the metaphor is liable to remain highly intellectual, as in the image of the ant on the millstone. Rather than focusing in on the autobiographical predicament and its attendant anguish, the effect of Su's lines is to remind us of the larger human or cosmic context and, indeed, to make something of a joke of the poet's insignificance and haplessness. (Compare Du Fu's famous analogy: "Fluttering about, what do I resemble? / A lone gull caught between Heaven and Earth," which is not supposed to be the least bit amusing.)[80]

Recent studies by Zhang Sanxi and Beata Grant have called attention to a peculiar use of space in Su Shi's poetry: his fondness for upsetting our normal understanding of size and spatial relation.[81] A great many of Su's figures of speech hinge on precisely this technique. Zhang divides his examples into categories, such as: 1) lodging the large in the small (e.g., "My sleeves contain the eastern sea"), 2) placing the small in the large (e.g., "The reeds and lotuses are as vast as an ocean / Now and then I see a single leaf of a boat"),[82] and 3) seeing the large in the small (e.g., "When even a short space separates us, / It is a thousand miles to me").[83] Actually, even metaphors that are not so obviously or primarily "spatial" are apt to show traces of the same technique. Many of the examples cited above feature a startling spatial transformation in addition to some other figurative device (e.g., personification). By projecting faces onto the landscape, leather boots onto the river's surface, and female body types in calligraphy, Su presents us with unexpected incongruities of space and size.

This topic has much in common with the shifting visual perspectives discussed above. There, the relevance of Buddhist doctrines of non-attachment was pointed out. Related doctrines concerning space and time may be mentioned here. Of course, there was an older, native influence as well. Su's manipulations certainly owe something to the *Zhuangzi*'s fascination with the relativities of space and time and with contradicting ordinary perceptions (e.g., Pengzu was short-lived, Mount Tai is tiny). The more immediate source, however, must have been the Chan monks and their favorite sutras, which are such a ubiquitous presence in Su's life.

Given the Buddhist doctrine that all worldly forms are produced by misapprehensions, perpetrated by the senses, it follows that spatial and temporal relations as normally perceived are invalid. The *Śūraṅgama Sutra* says:

> All living things, from the time without beginning, have disregarded their own Selves by clinging to external objects, thereby missing their fundamental Minds. Thus they are being turned round by objects and perceive large and small sizes. *If they can turn objects round,* they will be like the Tathāgata, and their bodies and minds will be in the state of radiant perfection; from their immutable holy site, the end of each of their hairs will contain all lands in the ten directions [emphasis added].[84]

> . . . [Y]our eyes, ears, nose and tongue as well as our body and mind, are the six decoys which a thief uses to steal the treasures of your house. For this reason, since time without beginning, living beings and this world have always been interlocked [in time and space] hence you are unable to leap beyond the material world.[85]

The enlightened being has transcended false distinctions of time and space. We hear much in the *Vimalakīrti Sutra* about the miracles that bodhisattvas can perform, manipulating spatial and temporal relations:

> The bodhisattva who lives in the inconceivable liberation can put the king of mountains, Sumeru, which is so high, so great, so noble, and so vast into a mustard seed. He can perform this feat without enlarging the mustard seed and without shrinking Mount Sumeru . . . The bodhisattva who lives in the inconceivable liberation, for the sake of disciplining those living beings who are disciplined through immeasurable periods of evolution, can make the passing of a week seem like the passing of an

aeon, and he can make the passing of an aeon seem like the passing of a week for those who are disciplined through a short period of evolution.[86]

Thus, when Śāriputra complained that Vimalakīrti's home had not a single chair for the visiting bodhisattvas to sit in, Vimalakīrti focused himself in concentration and effected the transport of thirty-two hundred thousand enormous thrones from the universe Merudhvaja into his room. The thrones descended from the sky and "arranged themselves without crowding and the house seemed to enlarge itself accordingly."[87] The bodhisattvas then transformed themselves to a height of forty-two hundred thousand leagues so that they could sit upon the thrones.

Not only was Su Shi familiar with the sutras in which such passages are found, he specifically records his instruction in these concepts by his friend Foyin. Discoursing on a monk's robe with which the emperor had honored him, Foyin pointed out that when viewed with the "dharma eye," every tiny needle hole in the garment contains innumerable worlds.[88] In fact, the robe is not large and is not small, it is not short and is not long, it is not heavy and it is not light, and so on. Su Shi continues in his own words: when the robe is put in its case, he sees the robe but not Foyin. When Foyin wears it, he sees the monk but not the robe. The monk and the robe are neither one nor two. When you look at the numinous aspect of things, lice and nits are dragons and elephants.

As a poet, Su Shi often tries to replicate with words such feats as the bodhisattvas could accomplish, collapsing the normal dimensions of space and time, or otherwise offering up novel ways of envisioning familiar events or things. Underlying all the wit and fun that are obviously present in the effort is a serious idea about the unreliability of the senses.

The Problem of the Emotions

The subject of the emotions raises itself here: in the midst of this effort to temper subjectivity, which shows itself in so many ways in Su Shi's poetry, what place is left for the poet's feelings, which presumably are closely identified with the self? Criticisms, mentioned earlier, of the discursive bent of Su Shi's verse fault it by implication for being deficient in emotion. The belief that the emotions (*qing*) are fundamental and intrinsic to poetry was too well established for the question to go unasked. Indeed, it has never ceased to be brought up (and never will be) in the ongoing debate over the relative worth of Song versus Tang poetry. That debate hangs largely on perceived differences in the relative weight of intellect and emotion (Song intellect, Tang emotion), and everyone recognizes Su Shi's role in helping to establish the new style.

Su Shi should be given his own say at this point, if only to demonstrate that he was conscious of the issue as a theoretical problem. The statement quoted here (another example of his discursive verse) is not necessarily Su's final word on the matter, since it is obviously tailored to suit an occasion. Once again it is an opinion of Han Yu's that Su singles out to disagree with. More than any other Tang writer, it was against Han Yu that Su and other Northern Song intellectuals felt they had to measure and define themselves.

Han Yu once wrote a farewell piece to a monk, Gaoxian, who had aspirations to become a great calligrapher.[89] Han Yu doubted that this was possible. Good calligraphy, like good poetry, he thought, had to be rooted in powerful emotions. It is precisely because Zhang Xu, the master of the cursive style, was able to lodge his strong emotive reactions to worldly circumstances in his writing brush that his calligraphy was great. But Gaoxian's training in the monastery taught him ways to transcend sentiment. Han Yu concludes with the condescending observation that since Buddhists are known to excel at "magic and illusion," Gaoxian may yet achieve some fame as a calligrapher. Su Shi's monk friend Canliao, with his interest in poetry, presented Su with a parallel to Han Yu's Gaoxian and an opportunity to restate the matter. Su's poem, a farewell piece written in Xuzhou, begins by noting the apparent contradiction of a poetry-writing monk and then compliments Canliao on the elegance of his verse. The crucial lines are these:

退之論草書	Tuizhi [Han Yu] said that cursive script
萬事未嘗屏	May reflect any human concern.
憂愁不平氣	All sorrows and feelings of disquiet
一寓筆所騁	May be lodged in the darting of the brush.
頗怪浮屠人	But he wondered about the Buddhist
視身如丘井	Who looks upon his body as an abandoned well.
頹然寄淡泊	Timidly he avails himself of the placid and plain:
誰與發豪猛	Who will elicit boldness and fury from him?
細思乃不然	When I reconsider, I see this is not right:
真巧非幻影	True skill is not a matter of illusion.
欲令詩語妙	If you want to make your poems marvelous,
無厭空且靜	You need not shun emptiness and quietude.
靜故了羣動	With quietude you comprehend the myriad movements,

空故納萬境	With emptiness you admit the ten thousand scenes.
閱世走人間	You observe the world as you go among men
觀身臥雲嶺	And examine yourself when resting on cloudy peaks.
鹹酸雜眾好	What the crowd longs for is the salty or sour;
中有至味永	The true and lasting flavor lies in between.
詩法不相妨	Buddhism is not incompatible with poetry:
此語更當請	I submit this view to complement the other.[90]

Su Shi was not the first Song-dynasty literatus to express misgivings about the older emotive theory and practice of poetry. Ouyang Xiu and scholars associated with him had, in the generation before Su Shi, shown themselves to be uncomfortable, specifically, with poetry of frustration and bitterness. They also criticized Han Yu, whom they otherwise regarded highly, for writing poetry of complaint (*yuanshi*) when he fell from power. The reasons for their disapproval were moralistic rather than literary. A properly cultivated mind that is concentrated upon moral virtues ought to remain unaffected by life's vicissitudes.[91] But the challenge for Ouyang's generation was phrased in terms of avoidance: stoically, the writer should refrain from self-pity. Su Shi takes this detachment a step further and phrases it positively, suggesting in this poem that it might lead to a kind of verse distinguished by its sensitive and comprehending observation of the "myriad movements." Elsewhere, when Su does phrase the point negatively, as one of avoidance, he is still true to this new conception of the issue. He writes to a friend: "When you compose poetry, do not make the [sorrowful] sounds of the autumn insect; / The Lord of Heaven will disapprove of you for being hooked upon things (*wu*)."[92] Su is urging a kind of liberation, not just forbearance.

The "sounds of the autumn insect" implies lugubrious verse of enmity against the world. That kind of poetry Su Shi certainly did avoid, even when in exile (as we shall see). Yet other emotions, even heartfelt and "serious" ones, are hardly absent from Su Shi's collection. In practice, in other words, Su Shi often did not follow the counsel he offered to Canliao. "Emptiness and quietude" (*kongjing*) do not begin to suffice as a characterization of much of Su's work. In this light, the remarks Su addressed to Canliao appear to be extreme. They are, in other words, a particularly bold manifestation of Su's eagerness to question the legitimacy of the self and self-indulgence, and one that was encouraged by the identity of this particular friend.

As a group the most sentimental poems Su wrote are those addressed to his younger brother, Su Che (Ziyou). These poems are important in literary history, as the first instance of an extensive body of fraternal verse by a major poet, as well as being a significant subset in Su's collection. One example is given below. It is one of the many mid-autumn moon festival poems Su addressed to Ziyou, when the sight of the moon sharpened Su's sense of loneliness for his distant brother. This poem was written in Xuzhou in 1078.

中秋月寄子由	The Mid-Autumn Moon, Sent to Ziyou
六年逢此月	In six years the moon I see tonight
五年照離別	Has shone five times on our separation.
歌君別時曲	Whenever I sing your parting song,
4 滿座為淒咽	Everyone in the room begins to weep.
留都信繁麗	The auxiliary capital is truly magnificent—
此會豈輕擲	The holiday won't be wasted there!
鎔銀百頃湖	Molten silver, the hundred acre lake.
8 挂鏡千尋闕	A round mirror hung from soaring palace towers.
三更歌吹罷	At midnight when the singing and flutes cease,
人影亂清樾	Revelers' shadows crisscross beneath the trees.
歸來北堂下	As you return to your home before North Hall,
12 寒光翻露葉	Cold moonbeams reflect off dew-soaked leaves.
喚酒與婦飲	You call for wine to drink with your wife,
念我向兒說	Telling the children stories of me.
豈知衰病後	How could you know? Aged and sickly,
16 空盞對梨栗	I face pear tree and chestnut with empty cup.
但見古河東	All I see, east of the old canal,
蕎麥花鋪雪	Are buckwheat flowers fallen like snow.
欲和去年曲	I wanted to match your song of last year
20 復恐心斷絕	But was afraid my heart would break.[93]

Line 3. The *ci* that Ziyou wrote to bid farewell to his brother the year before.[94]

Line 5. Ziyou was serving as a notary in the southern capital (southeast of Kaifeng), which was presided over by an imperial regent (*liushou*).

Lines 7–8. Aptly enough, both of these lines, with their images of moonlight and the moon, are derived from lines in Tang moon-gazing poems.[95]

Line 17. Xuzhou was located along a section of the Old Grand Canal (the Sui Canal).

There is a certain rootlessness in the lives of leading Northern Song literati that has often been commented on. Their connection to their ancestral home seems to count for little. Once they embarked upon their careers, they seldom, if ever, returned to their family's native place; and when they retired, they chose other locales to settle in.[96] Su Shi seems ambivalent about his hometown. He does sometimes write fondly of Meishan and speak of his longing to go back, but mostly in letters sent to hometown friends and relatives. Su grew to be so fond of the Jiangnan region that elsewhere he explicitly rejects the thought of returning to Sichuan ("I have no permanent home, where should I reside? / My native place does not have such beautiful lakes and hills.")[97] From the early 1080s on, it is clear that Su planned to retire to Changzhou (on Taihu Lake), and he purchased a farm to support his family there.[98]

Amid this fluidity of geographic allegiances, this lessening of the supremacy of "my homeland" over all other places, in his poetry Su Shi emphasizes his yearning to be reunited with Ziyou. Functionally in these poems, Ziyou becomes for Su Shi something of a substitute for his native place. "Only our hearts of yesteryear," Su observes to his brother, "Stand fast in their old place."[99] Often, when Su writes on the familiar theme of longing to retire and to leave the drudgery of bureaucratic life behind, the happy prospect that is contemplated once this step is taken is not "returning home" but reunion with Ziyou. Seeing that Ziyou fulfills this special function in Su Shi's poetry helps to account both for the large number of poems addressed to him and their particular poignancy. It is clear, in any case, that when writing to Ziyou, Su shows no reluctance to indulge his emotions of affection, loneliness, and even a touch of self-pity.

Perhaps the emotions are expressed but not profoundly experienced. This is one solution to the problem of the emotions that suggests itself because it was a notion, indeed an ideal, that was widespread in contemporary Buddhist and literati discourse. One "lodges" the mind in emotions, reacting as circumstances warrant; but there remains a sense of detachment, an awareness that the feeling is but temporary and not fundamental to one's being. Su Shi himself evokes this doctrine in remarks to monks. Emphasizing Canliao's capacity to have feelings, he writes of him, "His body was withered and his mind ashen, and yet he enjoyed writing phrases [i.e., poems] that were moved by the times, took delight in things, and did not neglect human emotions."[100] At the same time, Su praises Canliao for keeping his emotions superficial:

吳山道人心似水	Wu Mountain's man of the Way has a mind like water,
眼淨塵空無可埽	His eyes clear, so free from dust there's none to sweep away.
故將妙語寄多情	That's why he can lodge powerful emotions in marvelous phrases,
橫機欲試東坡老	Using this leveling device to test old East Slope.[101]

The obscure phrase "leveling device" is derived from a passage in the *Liezi* that refers to a technique by which a Taoist master "levels" his *qi*, emptying himself of all thought and emotions.[102] Canliao's emotions are just something he avails himself of or toys with, tempting his friend. Canliao maintains his impassivity even as he writes poetic lines apparently full of feeling.

Unfortunately, this line of reasoning takes us out of the realm of literature and into historical psychology. Any statement about the nature of Su's experience of the emotions expressed in his poetry is, of course, sheer speculation. The goal here is a more modest and feasible one: to describe Su's distinctive handling of self and emotion in his verse.

Yamamoto Kazuyoshi has noted the peculiar force of the recurrent line, "My life is like a brief stay" (*wu sheng ru ji er*) in Su's poetry. Yamamoto points out that the line, or variations on it, goes back at least to late-Han and Jian'an-period poetry.[103] In that earlier verse, the line is typically used as an expression of despair over mortality. One of the "Nineteen Old Poems" contains the passage:

浩浩陰陽移	Endlessly the yin and yang progress;
年命如朝露	Our allotted span is like morning dew.
人生忽如寄	Life is as quick as a brief stay;
壽無金石固	Age has not the durability of gold or stone.[104]

Similarly, Cao Zhi wrote:

日月不恒處	The sun and moon have no constant place;
人生忽若寓	Life is as quick as a brief stay.
悲風來入懷	Sad winds blow into my bosom,
淚下如垂露	Tears descend like falling dew.[105]

Su Shi puts the line to a very different use. We have already seen one example ("Don't let the people hold me back; / Don't let singers and flutes play mournfully. / My life is like a brief stay— / Will this be my only farewell?"), and others have a similar import:

吾生如寄耳	My life is like a brief stay:
何者為禍福	What does good or bad fortune matter?
不如兩相忘	Better to forget them both—
昨夢那可逐	Can yesterday's dream be recovered?[106]

During the Jian'an period, cognizance in poetry that one's sojourn in the world was but a brief stay or temporary lodging brought sorrow.

To Su Shi, Yamamoto argues, the same thought occasions release from sorrow for it helps him to transcend subjectivity.

However, so long as Su Shi remains such a visible presence in these assertions ("*my* life is . . ."), these lines project the very image of a subjective persona that their paraphrasable sense tends to deny. Actually, this line typifies a straddling of the issue of self and emotion that is pervasive in Su's poetry. He may constantly strive for a relatively objective vantage point on the world, one that begins to transcend subjectivity; but he remains the lyric poet as he does this, a vivid, human, and unforgettable presence in his verse. Su Shi did not produce a corpus of verse in which we must search hard for traces of the poet's persona.

Su's dilemma as a poet may be tied to intellectual issues he grappled with, and to divergent statements he made outside the field of poetry. Early on, Su came to the conclusion that self-centeredness was at odds with knowledge. The greatest challenge for anyone who would apprehend the Way, he observed, was to be *wusi* ("without selfishness"). Thus he wrote about the delusion of self-importance, about the validity of diverse values and self-images, and the folly of supposing that introspection alone (that is, looking within for wisdom), when not balanced by observation of the world, could lead to real knowledge. No doubt Wang Anshi's New Policies and his positions on a host of intellectual issues were the impetus for Su to pursue and develop his contrary ideas. Su suspected that Wang's entire program was essentially self-serving, not only personally so for the mastermind of the reforms but also institutionally (and fiscally) so for the Court that adopted it. In Wang's effort to pack the Censorate and otherwise silence dissent, Su saw further confirmation of his suspicions. And in the reform administration's indifference to the hardships its policies brought about in the provinces, which he witnessed firsthand, Su saw an embodiment of self-importance. In time, however, Su broadened his views on these matters until they became larger than his stance on political controversies. His distaste for whatever smacked of self-centeredness could eventually be applied to virtually any aspect of life. In his misgivings about Chan meditation, his comments on those who cooked without recipes, his mockery of Han Yu for supposing that his uprightness had moved the mountain god, and in his playful self-mockery, we glimpse the broad impact of this manner of thinking.

From the start Su Shi had also affirmed the primacy and goodness of human emotions. This is a major theme of his examination essays, where it is linked to the idea that the *li* ("rites") are rooted in the nature and natural inclinations, and that the emotions are themselves an intrinsic part of human nature. These positions are all part of Su's call in those essays for a bureaucracy that was less dependent upon mechanistic regulation, which gave greater discretionary powers to bureaucrats, and which was more responsive to the desires of the people. The subsequent empowerment of Wang Anshi only deepened Su's commitment to these values, for in the reforms Su saw a program that contradicted the wishes of the people and that relied upon fixed regulation rather than humane adaptability. Therefore, in his commentaries on the classics Su reiterates the positions on these issues that he had staked out years before.

Between these two complex bodies of ideas there lay a potential for contradiction. Normally, it did not arise or seem particularly pressing, although we have seen some evidence of it before, as in Su's effort in his commentary on the *Book of Documents* to modify his endorsement of the emotions. But the aesthetic impulse was especially likely to bring the problem to the fore. How could one fully experience the emotions without being self-indulgent? Put the other way around, how avoid self-centeredness while still being free to follow whim and impulse? Poetry had always been the written form preeminently associated with the *qing*. Su's early statements on the primacy of the emotions would seem to bode well for his future devotion to poetry. But years later we find him holding forth on the utility of "quietude" for the would-be poet, and explaining that emotions are not essential for great verse after all. These were issues that could not be readily resolved. They constitute the crux of the problem and challenge that Su set for himself as a poet.

The identification of these divergent interests helps to account for the special traits of poems addressed to Ziyou and close friends. The overt expression of strong emotions was easiest to allow when the emotions were outwardly directed, that is, when they took the form of affection and admiration for a loved one. It would have been more difficult to justify the display of strong emotions that did not move immediately outward from the self.

To Canliao, Su described the poetic project this way: "You observe the world as you go among men / And examine yourself when resting on cloudy peaks." Actually, it is common in Su's poetry to find some coalescence of the two operations—observation of the world and self-scrutiny—rather than one or the other exclusively. That is what takes place in the poems below, which are cited as concluding examples of Su's distinctive handling of these ideals. The first was written outside Hangzhou in 1073, the second when Su was prefect of Yingzhou in 1091.

自普照游二庵	A Journey from Puzhao to Two Cloisters
長松吟風晚雨細	Tall pines chant in the wind, rain falls lightly at dusk.
東庵半掩西庵閉	East Cloister is half-shut, West Cloister is locked.
山行盡日不逢人	I walked through mountains all day yet met no people;
4　裊裊野梅香入袂	The perfume of wild plum blossoms fills my sleeves.
居僧笑我戀清景	The resident monk laughs at me for being so enamored of pure scenes.
自厭山深出無計	He dislikes the remoteness of mountains, but he cannot leave.
我雖愛山亦自笑	Though I love the mountains, I, too, laugh at myself.
8　獨往神傷後難繼	Solitary withdrawal harms the spirit, it would be hard to carry on.
不如西湖飲美酒	How much nicer, on West Lake, to drink fine wine,
紅杏碧桃香覆髻	The scents of red apricots and green peaches covering coiffured hair.
作詩寄謝採薇翁	I write this poem to apologize to the old men who gathered thorn-ferns,
12　本不避人那避世	I don't want to avoid people, so how could I avoid the world?[107]

Line 11. The old men are Poyi and Shuqi, the loyal Shang ministers who withdrew to Mount Shouyang upon the Zhou conquest, where they fed on thorn-ferns and eventually starved.

泛潁	Floating on the Ying River
我性喜臨水	By nature I enjoy viewing water;
得潁意甚奇	When assigned to Ying, I was overjoyed.
到官十日來	In the ten days since assuming my post
4　九日河之湄	I have spent nine on the river bank.
吏民笑相語	My clerks smirk and murmur together,
使君老而癡	"The prefect is old and foolish."
使君實不癡	Actually I am not foolish,
8　流水有令姿	The flowing waters have a lovely appearance.
遶郡十餘里	Encircling the city over ten miles,
不駛亦不遲	They are neither hurried nor sluggish.
上流直而清	The upper reaches are straight and pure,
12　下流曲而漪	The lower are winding and rippled.

	畫船俯明鏡	In a painted boat I lean over the bright mirror;
	笑問汝為誰	Smiling, I ask "Who are you?"
	忽然生鱗甲	Suddenly my image grows scales,
16	亂我鬚與眉	Blurring my whiskers and eyebrows.
	散為百東坡	It spreads out to form a hundred East Slopes,
	頃刻復在茲	In a moment it is at hand as before.
	此豈水薄相	Is the river playing tricks on me,
20	與我相娛嬉	Teasing me this way?
	聲色與臭味	Music and gowns, aromas and flavors
	顛倒眩小兒	These invert and befuddle common fellows.
	等是兒戲物	Water, too, is a thing of amusement,
24	水中少磷緇	But it does not grind down or taint.
	趙陳兩歐陽	Zhao, Chen, and the two Ouyangs
	同參天人師	All are teachers of devas and men.
	觀妙各有得	Each is able to observe the numinous,
28	共賦泛潁詩	Together we chant poems on floating on the Ying.[108]

Lines 25–26. The men were guests of Su, the prefect: Zhao Lingzhi (Jingkuang), Chen Lüchang, Ouyang Fei, and Ouyang Bian (sons of Ouyang Xiu). "Teachers of devas and men," an epithet commonly used to designate a buddha, refers to their achievements in Buddhist learning and practice.

The two poems move in opposite directions, the first leading eventually to an affirmation of the poet's place in society, and the second to the implication that enlightened men see through the folly of "music and gowns" (whereas the first poem ends with these), see through the illusion of self, and find contentment in truths that transcend the phenomenal world. The fact that the poems are in this sense contradictory presents no difficulty. Su Shi never made a final choice between "pure scenes" and the mundane world, any more than he could remain comfortable for long with the ideal of a heart/mind that was as intrinsically blank as a mirror. More important than the different directions the two poems take is their common method. In each the poet confronts and reexamines, virtually as an outsider and with considerable amusement, his initial impulse or self-image.

CHAPTER EIGHT

The Literature of Exile

One might suppose that several early cornerstones of Su Shi's personal philosophy, including "non-attachment," "no-mind," and "responding to things," would have been the perfect preparation for his subsequent periods of exile, fortifying him against its hardship and despair. Had not he written, as early as 1075 in Mizhou, "where could I go that I would not be happy?" The boast was rooted in his claim that he resided "outside the realm of things." There is, moreover, a sense in which Su's successive provincial appointments in the 1070s were themselves a kind of minor exile. They kept him at distant remove from the capital, and some them at least were in distinctly unattractive places. What was so much worse, then, about formal exile? When we add to these considerations the fact that in most of Su's literary works that date from his two exiles (Huangzhou, 1080–1084, and Lingnan, 1094–1100) he seems contented, it would be easy to conclude that banishment was no more than a small setback to him and that he took it in stride. Shortly after he went into his first exile, for example, we find him writing in poems and other literary works about what a pleasant place Huangzhou is and how abundant and delicious are the local foods. And he says much the same things upon his removal to the distant south in the 1090s. His "punishments" may appear very light.

However, if we look at Su's non-literary writings (such as his informal notes to friends and relatives) as well as collateral sources, a very different picture emerges, one in which the experience of exile appears to have been dramatically unlike anything that Su knew in other periods of his life. Our primary interest here is to understand the rich corpus of literature that Su produced in his two exiles—to explore how its greatness, universally acknowledged, may be linked to the fact of his banishment.[1] But there is a danger of naively equating Su's literary representations of his life in exile with the actual circumstances. To do so would hamper the attempt to properly contextualize and understand the literary work. Exile proved to be the greatest challenge Su was ever to meet to his interest in overcoming narrow subjectivity as a poet. It forced him to respond to that challenge in new ways, and his literary work took new directions. Yet it will be useful first to review, without reference to his literary representations, the circumstances of his two exiles.

The Circumstances of Exile

Huangzhou Exile

Su's trial for treason came to an end in the twelfth month of 1079. Instead of being put to death, as his accusers requested, he was demoted in rank and removed to Huangzhou, an insignificant prefecture seventy miles down the Yangzi from Ezhou (Wuhan, Hubei). He was forbidden to speak out on matters of government policy. Su did retain a title and thus, technically, a place in the bureaucracy, as was the convention for banished officials. He was now assistant militia commandant of Huangzhou. But there were no duties to go with this title and, more importantly, no salary. Su is clear on this point, repeating it in several letters and poems. For the first time since he had entered government service nearly twenty years before, Su had no income. Also, since his confinement was not for a specified time, he had no idea when a stipend might come to him again.

Su's most visible response, contained in a lengthy and much anthologized letter to Qin Guan, was to insist that he was unconcerned and to project his optimism in an amusing method of budgeting:

> When I first arrived in Huangzhou since my salary had been cut off and my household was large I was extremely worried. My only choice was to limit my expenditures severely, making sure that each day I spent no more than 150 cash. On the first of each month I would take out 4,500 and divide it into thirty bundles, which I then hung from the rafters inside my house. Every morning I would use a picture-hanging rod to take one bag down, then hide the rod away. I stored whatever was not spent that day in a large bamboo chest, to save for entertaining guests. This was the method Jia Yunlao taught me. I figure that the cash I have

left should last a year or so. When it is all gone, I'll make other plans. "Water digs its own ditch," so there's no need to worry about it now. Because I think this way, my breast is free from all concerns.[2]

But Su did not always face his financial uncertainties with such lightheartedness. When he first reached Huangzhou, accompanied only by his eldest son, Mai, he lodged in Dinghui Monastery, where he was content, he says, to live simply and eat vegetarian meals together with the monks. But the imminent arrival of Ziyou, who was to bring the rest of Su's household to join him (at least ten persons, not counting Ziyou's own dependents), weighed upon his mind. In letters to friends Su confided that he almost dreaded Ziyou's arrival because he did not know how he would provide for everybody, noting that Ziyou himself had "debts like mountains."[3] It is also clear that Su thought long and hard about economizing. He wrote to Li Gongze, "It is not easy to restrain oneself and restrict expenditures. I was fifty years old before I learned how to manage my own affairs. The most important thing is to be tightfisted, but we give it a more attractive name, calling it 'living economically and simply.'"[4] To another friend he revealed his discovery that if you wait to eat until you are ravenous, then even cabbage soup will seem a rich meal.[5] Of course, some of Su's friends tried to help. The fiscal intendant Cai Chengxi used his influence to get new rooms built for Su and his family at Lin'gao Pavilion, presumably because Su was unwilling to pay for additional space himself.[6] Another sympathizer sent Su a gift of 2,000 cash, which Su promised to repay the following spring.[7]

What are we to make, then, of the impressive sounding sums of money Su wanted to spend to acquire a farm somewhere in the lower Yangzi region? This longing to acquire land and a permanent dwelling (he had none, except for his share of the ancestral home back in distant Sichuan) is a new theme that enters his writings at Huangzhou, where it becomes almost obsessive. It appears that the experience of exile made him acutely aware that he lacked any secure haven for his dependents, and no private income to fall back upon. Hence his resolve to buy agricultural land, to provide food and income. Several times Su contemplates spending as much as 600,000 cash for such land, though it seems that he was prepared to put only one-third of that amount down on a purchase, with the rest possibly to come from the sale of a residence he still had back in the capital.[8]

The acquisition of a farm turned out to be a long and frustrating process for Su.[9] For four years he considered several plots of land in various locales, but for one reason or another these transactions all fell through. There was, for example, land in Luoshi Village, some thirty *li* south of Huangzhou, that Su was interested in and went to look at. But he found the land to be of poor quality and withdrew his offer.[10] There was also a certain Ren family farm in the Jingnan area, which his friend Chen Jichang had written to him about. Another friend, however, reported to Su that there was a hefty tax assessed on this land, and subsequently we hear no more about it.[11] Also, Su's friend Yang Yuan-su wrote to him about a Hu family farm in Dingxiang (Jiangling, Hubei) and introduced to him a local scholar there who would act as Su's intermediary in acquiring the land.[12] Su contemplated leasing the land first and buying it later, but this transaction, too, was eventually abandoned. From the regularity with which Su's plans went awry, as well as from the excitement he shows whenever someone informs him of another possible acquisition, one gets the impression that land was very hard to find, at least at the price Su was willing to pay. At times, Su despaired of ever finding what he was looking for: "I no longer have any ambitions in the world. All I need are two *qing* of rice fields to keep my family supplied with gruel. Wherever I go, I make inquiries about such a plot of land; but I have had no success. Is it because I am now in difficulties that nothing at all can go right for me?"[13] Su did not finally succeed in purchasing land until a few months after his Huang-zhou exile ended, in 1084. He seems to have retained this land, in Yi-xing, near Taihu Lake in Zhejiang, for the rest of his life (in the South-ern Song certain of his descendants were still living there);[14] and it was eventually to that same prefecture that Su would return to die.

Upon his banishment to Huangzhou, Su must have earmarked the bulk of his life savings (whether in cash or in the value of his resi-dence in the capital) for the purchase of a farm and decided that he would not to dip into it for daily living expenses. The sum, as we can surmise from the above, was at most barely adequate for the use to which he wanted it put. His resolve not to diminish it further would explain his preoccupation with being parsimonious in Huangzhou.

In his letter to Qin Guan, written soon after his arrival in Huangzhou, Su calculates that his ready cash will supply his needs for "a year or so." He had no idea how long he would be kept in Huang-zhou, and he might have hoped that some good news would come by the end of twelve months. None did; and early in the second year of his exile, a friend, Ma Mengde, approached the prefect of Huangzhou and asked that Su be allowed to farm an abandoned plot of land out-side the city. This was East Slope, from which Su took his new literary epithet, "layman (i.e., lay Buddhist) of East Slope" (Dongpo jushi). This was the phrase that would eventually become the best known of

Su Shi's many appellations, inseparable from the man and his celebrated reaction to exile.

Su says that Ma Mengde acted on his behalf because he was
worried that Su and his family would soon find themselves without
adequate food. Su describes how he personally cleared the land of
rubble (it had once served as a militia camp), bought a plow, and began
to farm, planting rice, wheat, fruit trees and mulberry trees.[15] Subsequently, Su would purchase a building on an adjoining piece of land,
which he converted into a studio for himself, naming it Snow Hall (because the renovation was completed during a snowstorm). Su may have
stayed in this structure occasionally; but his primary residence, where
his family stayed, remained inside the city.

East Slope is remembered mostly for the happy leisure hours Su
spent there. In his poetic evocations, Su transformed East Slope into a
rustic idyll, a place where he would gather his friends to drink and
view the blossoms, a place to which he would return in dreams long
after he departed from Huangzhou. It is important to remember,
nevertheless, that before this literary transformation took place, East
Slope was first a place for Su to grow his own food.

We will never know how much of the actual farm work Su did.
There was, of course, a literary tradition of the gentleman farmer, the
poet who wrote about planting and harvesting, but who rarely if ever
touched a farm tool himself. In Su's case, however, the descriptions of
labor are not confined to poetry but occur as well in informal notes he
sent to friends. In one he says, "I have bought an ox and plow and personally till the land. This year it has been dry and rice is extremely ex-
pensive. In the last few days we have had rain. Day and night I work
to prepare the field, intending to plant wheat. Although the labor
is hard, it, too, has its flavor."[16] This sounds like more than literary
pretense. But even if Su's farming was entirely supervisory, which is
unlikely, certainly this was a new stage in his life, one he probably
had never anticipated and for which he had no preparation.

The newness of psychological factors, aside from material ones,
also deserves some brief comment here. However frustrated Su might
have been with his provincial appointments through the 1070s, his confinement to Huangzhou was of a different order. Now he had suffered
disgrace and denunciation in full view of the emperor and the Court,
and had subsequently been demoted in rank. His career must have
seemed close to ruin. To make matters worse, his brother and his
closest friends (twenty-eight in all) had been implicated in his trial,
being the recipients of allegedly defamatory writings Su had sent them.

Three of them were likewise sent into exile; and one, Wang Gong, received a punishment even more harsh than that given to Su. He was banished to Binzhou in the distant southwest (modern Guangxi). In letters to Wang Gong, Su's sense of guilt and remorse is unmistakable.[17]

Reflecting these developments, the general mood of Su's writings (outside of poetry) changes perceptibly during his first weeks and months in Huangzhou. He becomes more withdrawn, apprehensive, introspective, and self-critical than he had ever been before. He speaks repeatedly of "closing his door and refusing to receive guests." He declines requests for new poems, and claims that he does not compose literary works anymore.[18] Several letters sent to close friends end with the admonition that the letter be burned once it has been read.[19] He secluded himself inside a Taoist temple for the standard forty-nine-day period to engage in self-reflection.[20] More regularly ("every two or three days"), he would go to the Buddhist Anguo Monastery south of the city for quiet self-scrutiny.[21]

In a letter to Li Zhiyi that dates from this period, we glimpse one of the consequences of this process of reevaluation. This is the document in which Su virtually repudiates all of his past writings, especially those on statecraft and government policy. Su traces the history of his erroneous ways back to the decree examinations. "To hold forth brazenly on advantage and disadvantage, to pass judgment irresponsibly on gain and loss—this is the practiced manner of all those who sit for the decree examination. They resemble seasonal insects and birds, which sing out for a time and then fall silent. What does it all mean?"[22] But people wrongly concluded that there was real substance in his essays, he explains, and from that came both celebrity and endless trouble. These thoughts are followed by this passage:

> Wood that has knots, rocks that have colored markings, and rhinoceros horns that have lines running through them are all highly prized by people, and yet in fact these knots, colors, and lines are all flaws in the substances in which they appear. Living in exile with no demands on my time, silently I have been examining myself. When I look back on what I have done for the past thirty years, I consider that it is entirely such a flaw. What you have seen is the old me, not the new me.

The implicit analogy is between the markings in the three materials and the "markings" Su has created throughout his life, that is, his writing. (The analogy is based on a pun on the word *wen* "marking, writing.") Just as the knot and colors and lines are really a flaw or weakness in their material, so, too, is Su's writing nothing more than a flaw in his character. The "old me" that Su refers to is that displayed in his writings, which Li had praised in his letter to Su, and which Su now disavows.

We know, of course, that Su hardly gave up writing, as he here implies he will. Actually, Huangzhou was to be a particularly prolific period for him (though not for writings on explicitly political topics). Still, this letter cannot be dismissed as either false modesty or an attempt to repulse an unwanted friend. The statements Su makes here are too elaborate and carefully crafted for them to be offhand remarks. Su had been reflecting deeply on his lifelong conduct, and we sense from a document such as this the pressures he felt to change and explore new types of expression. The differences that so many readers have noticed in his Huangzhou writings must be linked to these ruminations.

Lingnan Exile

The political events that led to Su Shi's Lingnan exile have been described earlier. There is no need here to repeat the details of the persecution of the Yuanyou-period officials that began with the change of government in 1093, when the reform faction regained imperial favor upon the death of the empress dowager and the empowerment of Zhezong, and which grew more intense in 1097. It will suffice to offer some general remarks on Su's circumstances during his years of confinement to Huizhou (1094–1097) and Hainan Island (1097–1100).

This was a much harsher banishment than Huangzhou had been. As remote as Huangzhou had seemed, it was after all a Yangzi Valley prefecture and had a history, culture, and amenities that were thoroughly familiar to Su. But in 1094, for the first time in his life, he was sent south of the Ling Range, which stretches across modern Guangxi and Guangdong, and was considered in Su's day the southern cultural border of the nation. Now, Su Shi found himself in a strange sub-tropical region that was to his eyes barely Chinese. Later, Su was driven even further away, across the sea to the jungles of Hainan Island. Su Shi was to die in 1101, a year after returning from these years "south of the Ling." It was essentially the exile that killed him, which is precisely what his enemies intended it do. Su was sixty-four by the time he returned, and his years in what the Chinese referred to as the "pestilential south" had left him weak and in poor health.

Su Shi was among the first of the many Yuanyou officials (including some who were already dead) whom the new reform administration of Zhezong denounced and demoted in 1094. The first news he received, while serving as prefect of the northern prefecture of Dingzhou, was that he had been reassigned to Yingzhou (a thousand miles south, just north of Guangzhou) and demoted in rank and grade. During Su's journey, on which he was accompanied by his sons and their families, it was decided that his eldest son, Mai, should take part of the clan and settle upon the land Su still owned in Yixing, Changzhou.[23] It would be easier to provide for the many family members there than in their father's southern exile. Along the way, Su petitioned the emperor to provide a boat to carry him south. He complained that he could not afford to hire a boat and that land travel, by horse and cart, was more than he could endure at his age. Su mentions that while the prospect of dying in his Yingzhou post did not disturb him, he did dread the thought that he might die during his journey at some way-station, be hastily buried beside the road, and become for ever after "a sojourner's ghost."[24] Soon after he reached the Yangzi river, Su heard that his banishment had been made more severe: he was now to proceed to the more remote Huizhou (east of Guangzhou); he was demoted again and now held a purely titular post (assistant military governor); and he was forbidden, as he had been at Huangzhou, to speak out on matters of state. Faced with these new deprivations, Su decided that his middle son, Dai, should also take his family to Yixing, to join Mai.[25] Su would go alone to his new destination, accompanied only by his youngest son, Guo (who was not married), and Zhaoyun, Su's concubine of nearly twenty years. Zhaoyun was to die in their third year there.

One of the puzzling aspects of Su Shi's stay in Huizhou is that he seems constantly to be changing residences. In fact, he moved no fewer than four times during the two-and-a-half years. There appears to be little logic or sense to these moves. When he first arrived at Huizhou, he put up at a pavilion attached to government offices, Hejiang lou. After a mere sixteen days, he moved out of the city entirely and lodged at a building that was part of a Buddhist monastery, Jiayou si, west of Huizhou. Five months later he moved back into Hejiang lou. Eleven months after that he went back to the monastery again. This last move is particularly perplexing since, by the time it happened, construction had already begun on what was to be Su's own residence at White Crane Peak (east of the city). Why not simply remain at Hejiang lou until the new residence had been completed?

Each move is recorded in one or more of Su's poems, but he breathes hardly a word about the reasons for this constant dislocation. Reasons have been proposed in a persuasive recent study by Wu Shiduan.[26] Wu finds in each move evidence of an ongoing struggle between local bureaucrats over the treatment of Su. That Su was both renowned, well-connected, and in official disgrace explains why there were among local bureaucrats men who were sympathetic to his plight as well as those who shunned any contact with him. Drawing upon Su's writings, as well as other documents, Wu proposes that Su was initially allowed to stay at government lodgings because of the goodwill of the Huizhou prefect, Zhan Fan. Su does refer several times to the special kindness of this official. According to this interpretation, Su was soon forced out of the comfortable lodgings because other bureaucrats feared reprisals from the grand councilor, Zhang Dun, should he learn of the privilege Su was enjoying. Su may not even have been free to choose which monastery he withdrew to, since there were others closer to the city and probably less humble that he passed over. It happened that Su's maternal cousin, Cheng Zhengfu, was serving at this time as judicial intendant of Guangdong, stationed in Guangzhou. From Su's voluminous correspondence with this relative, we know that he frequently sent gifts and inquiries after Su's living conditions. Cheng made his first visit to Huizhou to see Su in the second month of 1095, and it was in the very next month that Su returned from Jiayou Monastery into the city and Hejiang lou. It appears that the two events may well be related. Su refers to his cousin as the man "who liberated this prisoner of Chu"; and after Cheng goes back to Guangzhou, Su makes a point of telling him in a letter the exact date he will be able to move back into the government quarters.[27] Cheng made a second visit to Huizhou later in the year, but thereafter he never returned again (and may have been transferred away from the region altogether). By that time, Prefect Zhan had also been replaced, so that Su had no one powerful to speak on his behalf. That, Wu suggests, is why he had to remove himself to Jiayou Monastery again, in 1096, even though with the White Crane residence already under construction, this move made little sense.

The hard information that can be gleaned from Su's writings about his finances at this time is sketchy and incomplete. We do not know how he was supporting himself or the rest of his clan. The cost of building his White Crane house forced him to write to friends in Guangzhou, where he had deposited a bond or promissory note, part of his former salary. So desperate was his need for cash that he wanted to sell the note privately, at a considerable discount.[28] But the person with whom Su had left the note wrote back to say that it could not be located, and months passed as Su continued his inquiries. (It is unclear whether the document was ever found.) We also know that local officials provided Su with gifts of rice on more than one occasion. Naturally, when Su broaches these kindnesses in poems of gratitude addressed to the benefactors, he does so discreetly and by means of literary allusion. But commentators have elucidated the meanings of his lines and called attention to their grim implications for his circumstances.[29]

Su had no idea how long he would be forced to remain in Huizhou. He says that he has given up all hope of ever returning north—perhaps he had heard that Zhang Dun was asking that Yuan-you officials be denied any consideration of future reprieve—yet he also writes to friends in the circuit administration asking anxiously if they have heard any rumors about his future.[30] Even more frequently than in Huangzhou, his correspondence from this period often ends with the injunction that secrecy be maintained or that the letter or poem be destroyed once it has been read.[31] Su Che had written to his brother pleading with him in the strongest language to stop writing poetry. It is not enough, Che insists, merely to keep whatever verse you produce to yourself. You must desist from writing poetry altogether, and burn your brush and inkstone.[32]

There is a tradition concerning the even harsher banishments that were decreed in 1097, when the persecution of Yuanyou officials reached its height, that is memorable for its senseless cruelty.[33] Rather than select exile sites that preserved even the pretense of appropriateness to the severity of the alleged offense, it is said that Zhang Dun amused himself by selecting disagreeable places whose names bore graphic resemblance to the polite name (zi) of the official in question. Thus, Su Che was exile to Leizhou (on the Guangdong Peninsula) because the bottom of the character lei 雷 has a graphic element similar to the you 由 in Ziyou; Huang Tingjian was exiled to Yizhou (Guangxi) because yi 宜 resembles zhi 直 in his polite name, Luzhi; and Su Shi was exiled to Danzhou (on Hainan Island) because the character for dan 儋 has graphic elements in common with zhan 瞻 in Zizhan. This was Zhang Dun's little joke. In all, over thirty Yuanyou officials were banished, and many of them, including Lü Dafang, Fan Zuyu, Liu Zhi, Liang Dao, and Qin Guan, would die in the next few years in distant southern locales. Still, it seems likely that an effort was made to find a particularly odious place for Su Shi. He was the only one of the group who was sent "across the sea."

Soon after Su Shi arrived in Danzhou, he purchased wood for his coffin and wrote to his eldest son, Mai, telling him that if he were to die on Hainan Island, he should be buried there and not transported back to a family grave. (Presumably, he wanted to avoid imposing the expense of such removal upon his heirs.) He says at this time that he has given up hope of ever returning to the mainland.[34] As at Huizhou, he first stayed at government quarters. The prefect of Danzhou, Zhang Zhong, befriended Su and fixed up rooms for him to lodge in. But this arrangement lasted only a few months. The Court had dispatched a certain Dong Bi, tea and salt supervisor of Hunan, to check up on the exiled officials. Word came to Dong Bi, who was touring Guangxi, of Su's circumstances; and he sent a representative to Hainan to have Su evicted. Zhang Zhong was incriminated for his kindness, and the circuit general of Guangxi, Cheng Jie, was likewise demoted for not having detected the crime himself.[35] Su makes just the briefest of references to his eviction in a poem: "My former dwelling was not even one mat in size / But still this exiled official was rebuffed."[36]

Su built a dwelling for himself south of the city. He describes the task in a letter: "Recently, together with my youngest son I have built a thatched hut of several rooms to live in. It is barely enough to protect us from the wind and rain, yet the labor and expense were more than we could afford. We had to rely on the help of a dozen students to complete it. I myself toiled in the water and mud—the humiliation was more than I could describe."[37]

During the years Su spent on the island, his health deteriorated. He suffered from bouts of malaria and experimented with various herbal cures.[38] But the necessary ingredients were in short supply and he wrote to friends on the mainland, asking that they send even small amounts of any medicine at all ("it doesn't matter what it's called").[39] To a grand-nephew back in his native Meishan, Su sent this account of his life in Hainan:

> This old man is still living beyond the seas as before; but recently I have become sickly and thin, so that my health is not what it used to be. I wonder whether I will get to see you again in my remaining years. No letter has reached me from either Xunzhou or Huizhou for some time. The despondency of such a sojourn as this I hardly need to dwell on. Moreover, Hainan has not had a harvest for years on end so that all varieties of food and drink are in short supply. Furthermore, ocean-going vessels from Quanzhou and Guangzhou have stopped coming. Consequently, there is no medicine, condiments, or sauces of any kind. Finding ourselves in such straits, there is nothing to do but resign ourselves to fate. I sit facing my son Guo, the two of us like deprived Buddhist monks.[40]

Of course, Su's hardship and loneliness did not go completely unrelieved. He had occasional callers. Jiang Tangzuo came from Qiongzhou, on the north side of the island, to study with Su. Su's old friend, the Taoist Wu Fugu, who had visited Su in Huizhou, made the ocean crossing to be with him. A provincial examination graduate, Zheng Qingsou, also made the voyage to Hainan to pay his respects to Su and to be tutored by him.[41]

Emperor Zhezong died at the young age of twenty-four in 1100, and with the transition of power a general reprieve was granted to the exiled Yuanyou officials. However, the attempt to bring about a genuine reconciliation between the rival factions was short-lived. Within two years, after Cai Jing began his notorious tenure as grand councilor, the persecution of the Yuanyou leaders entered a new stage. Su would not be alive to witness this new campaign of denunciation, though his works would be proscribed by imperial decree.

The reprieve of 1100 permitted Su to return from Hainan Island. There was a flurry of directives issued to him as he began his journey northward, the last of which granted him titular office as overseer of a Taoist temple in Chengdu and permitted him to reside wherever he chose. Indecision over where he should now settle seems to have occupied him virtually until he died in the summer of 1101. He spent these months moving fitfully northward on boats, fighting illness, and changing his mind about his destination. He had trouble hiring boats, and watched with dismay as several of the boathands he did succeed in retaining died of malaria themselves.[42] At first Su says that he will try to settle in Changzhou, the same Taihu Lake region prefecture in which he had acquired land years before (in Yixing). But he no longer had a house there, and so he asks friends to locate one for him. If no house can be found, he says he will proceed instead to Shuzhou (Anqing, Auhui) or to Zhenzhou (Yizheng, Jiangsu), both lower Yangzi River valley prefectures.[43] Later, he allows his plan to be altered by the urgings of his brother and prepares to join Ziyou up north at his residence in Yingchang (Xuchang, Henan). But then he reconsiders, and comes to the conclusion that Yingchang is too close to the capital. Friends had reported recent developments at the Court to Su and cautioned him that there were many officials who were determined to strike out at him again. Reluctantly, Su explains to his brother: "If I were to proceed north and approach [the capital], there would be no peace for me . . . We shall not be reunited after all. It is not what I had wanted, but it will permit me to conserve my strength and avoid harm."[44]

Finally, Su Shi reverted to his first plan and proceeded to Biling in Changzhou. By the time he arrived there, in the middle of the sixth month, he was virtually bedridden, suffering from attacks of fever and intestinal disorders. He petitioned the throne for permission to retire from government service. He died at the end of the following month.

Su Che buried his brother in 1102 outside of Ruzhou (Linru, Henan), where his own sons resided. The remains of Su's first wife, who had died in 1065 in the capital, were reinterred beside his grave. The site chosen was a hillock named Emei, for the Sichuan mountain at Su's native place.[45]

The facts of exile in Su's life may seem relatively simple and straightforward (we know exactly where he was sent, how long he was confined, and how far down in rank he was demoted); but the meaning of the experience in his life was complex, to judge from the many different ways he reacted to it in his literary work. Before examining those reactions, we might consider briefly here a few of the more easily identified psychological challenges or consequences the experience occasioned for him.

Exile was certainly a challenge to Su's moral fortitude and self-sufficiency. It had long been a central tenet of Confucian thought that one's fortunes in the world ought not to affect one's moral values: usually, this meant that deprivation or frustration in a career was no excuse for any compromise of values or of one's commitment to continued self-cultivation ("learning"). The example of Yanzi, Confucius's beloved disciple, who did not let miserable circumstances diminish the joy he took in self-cultivation, is cited extensively in eleventh-century writings. Perhaps the influence of Buddhist doctrines on aloofness from material concerns helped to make this ancient idea particularly compelling during the Northern Song. In any case, we glimpse the importance Su assigned to it in a passage such as the following. After Su was removed to Huangzhou, a friend, Li Gongze, wrote to him to express his sympathy for his reduced circumstances and all that he had been through. Su wanted none of Li's pity and responded with this admonishment: "Your letter and new poems are filled with remorse over our distant separation. Why is it that while you show such deep love for me, I have reciprocated with a heart of iron and bowels of stone? Although we and our friends are old now and in straits, the Way and Pattern run through our hearts and livers, and loyalty and rightness fill the marrow of our bones. Therefore, we are able to chat and laugh in the face of death. If upon seeing me in dire circumstances you express pity, your conduct is not far removed from that of a man who has never studied the Way."[46]

Su Shi was certainly not the first exiled Song dynasty official who insisted upon chatting and laughing in the face of death, but the challenge of doing so must have been particularly acute for him. Su was repeatedly singled out among members of the political opposition and given the harshest treatment. During the 1070s, he had been the only prominent member of the anti-reformers whose protests caused him to be arrested and tried for treason. Twenty-odd years later, he was the only one of the Yuanyou officials who was banished to Hainan Island. It would seem that Su had more reason than his colleagues to revert to the tradition of the wronged poet in exile.

A second consequence of exile was that it brought certain kinds of liberation. It may at first sound odd to thus characterize removal and confinement by imperial command, but the experience certainly did have its liberating aspects. The simplest kind of freedom it provided was freedom from the drudgery of bureaucratic responsibilities. No wonder Su's literary productivity was so high when he was in exile, despite all the reasons he had just at such times to resist the impulse to write. These were the only times of his adult life (except for his early mourning periods, when it was not proper to be prolific as a poet) that he did not face the considerable daily administrative and documentary duties of the minister or provincial bureaucrat. We have seen, moreover, as in his conduct as prefect of Hangzhou, that Su Shi was hardly a bureaucrat who took his responsibilities lightly or who avoided taking initiative.

The deeper kind of liberation Su now enjoyed was that from the self-image of the loyal advisor and remonstrating official. Su had cast his public self, whenever he was not in exile, in the tradition of Jia Yi, Lu Zhi, Fan Zhongyan, and Ouyang Xiu—all high-ranking advisors famous for their writings and counsel on statecraft. But when his career was in apparent ruin, as it was in Huangzhou and Lingnan, he could no longer keep those aspirations. As mentioned above, in Huangzhou Su denigrated his own writings on statecraft and policy. He was ready now to explore new roles and modes of expression. He experimented with a range of them. He became a Confucian scholar, that is, a commentator on the classics. He took up an interest in medicine and alchemy, trying both internal and external techniques for improving health and prolonging life. He began to keep a diary or notebook (*Dongpo zhilin*) and filled it mostly with records of strange events, dreams, outings, and longevity techniques. He became a gentleman farmer and imitated, at first sporadically and then methodically, the poetry of the Tao Qian. All of these were new directions, and all are associated with his two exiles. Banishment not only provided Su Shi with more leisure time, it also freed him from having a single dominant orientation in life, that towards the service of his ruler.

Lastly, exile was an affront to Su Shi's sense of justice. It undermined his confidence in the institutions and principles of the huge bureaucracy (such as the protection of loyal dissent), and it challenged

PHILOSOPHY AND ITS LIMITATIONS

his commitment never to be intimidated into silence. The difference between this consequence of exile and the first cited above is that here
the problem is not essentially an internal one (can Su maintain his
integrity and self-assurance in the midst of deprivation?) but external:
how ought Su react to those who would suppress him, and how does
his predicament affect his understanding of fairness in the world? Such
questions became particularly prominent during his second exile. It
will be recalled how, with great exasperation, Su distinguished the
political attacks against him in the Yuanyou period from those of the
1070s. It was the difference between distortion of fact and outright lie.
And Su came to feel that way even before the real persecution began in
1094. Even as he explored new kinds of conduct and self-identities in
his exiles, Su never forgot the injustices that he believed had been done
to him.

Philosophy and Its Limitations

Discussion of the literature Su Shi produced in exile may begin with
what is probably the best-known of all these writings, the first of two
rhapsodies set at Red Cliff (Chibi), on the Yangzi river at Huangzhou.
Some background must be provided both on the historical significance
of Red Cliff and on the form of the rhapsody.

The place is known in Chinese history as the site of a momentous battle fought in A.D. 208, when the Han empire was disintegrating
and regional kingdoms emerging. Cao Cao, the most powerful of the
Han generals, led his huge army southward in an attempt to suppress
warlords in the Yangzi valley and reunite China under his own and,
nominally, the Han emperor's control. He had already received the
surrender of a powerful rival in Jingzhou and was proceeding down
the Yangzi to attack the kingdom of Wu in the southeast. The Wu
forces, led by Zhou Yu, met Cao Cao at Red Cliff, where they routed
him, destroying his armada of warships by intercepting it with a string
of barges that had been set afire. The battle marked the end of Cao
Cao's quest to reunite China and brought on sixty years of political division known as the Three Kingdoms period. Now, as commentators
on Su's rhapsody are fond of pointing out, the Red Cliff of the famous
battle was actually some one hundred miles further up the Yangzi from
Huangzhou. But it is not that Su Shi was grossly mistaken. In fact, he
was well aware of the dubiousness of what must have been local claims
that the Huangzhou Red Cliff was the battle site.[47] But he evidently
chose to suspend his skepticism in his rhapsody so as to lend to his
surroundings the kind of historical and nostalgic appeal he required.

The rhapsody (or prose-poem, *fu*) had a long and varied history in Chinese literature. In its classical, Han period it featured lavish descriptions, often bordering on the fantastic, of imperial palaces and capitals. Later, during the Six Dynasties period, more personal and lyrical rhapsodies were written; but always the distinctive mark of the form was embellished description (now of animals, emotional states, or small gardens). During the Tang and early Song the rhapsody had been used extensively on the civil service examinations. Candidates were required to write on set themes and to use prescribed rhymes. They were judged on their performance within rigid prosodic requirements. Late in his own writing career Ouyang Xiu rescued the rhapsody from the stultifying atmosphere of the examination hall and created a new style, personal in tone and flexible in prosody. In time Ouyang's compositions would come to be known as the first of the "prose rhapsodies" (*wenfu*), so called because of their changeable, prose-like rhythm. Su Shi's efforts in the form followed Ouyang's lead and moved it even closer to prose. Su's rhapsodies are still written primarily in couplets and use a succession of rhymes. However, the line-lengths vary so widely and so many extra-metrical syllables and lines are admitted that at times the writing is quite indistinguishable from prose (and is translated as such below). Su Shi wrote rhapsodies throughout his life, but his two Red Cliff pieces are his most ambitious and interesting by far.[48]

Rhapsody on Red Cliff

In the autumn of the Renxu year [1082], during the full moon in the seventh month, Master Su and his guests went boating beneath Red Cliff. A cool breeze blew gently and the river had no waves. I raised a toast to my guests and recited "Bright Moon" and sang "The Fair Lady."[49] Shortly, the moon rose over the eastern hills then moved leisurely among Dipper and Ox. White dew fell across the river, and the gleam of the water reached to the sky. Letting our little reed go where it would, we drifted out onto the vast expanse of water. We flew along as if we were borne by the wind up into the sky, not knowing where we would stop; we soared freely as if we had left the world behind, sprouting wings and rising aloft like immortals.

Then we drank wine and enjoyed ourselves, knocking time on the gunwales and singing:

> Cassia boat and orchid oar
> Strike the water, propelling us through shimmering
>   moonbeams.
> How deep is my longing!
> I gaze towards the beautiful one at the edge of the sky.

One of my guests could play the flute, and he joined in with the song. His music was plaintive, as if there was something he resented or yearned for, as if someone were weeping or complaining. He continued with frail and tremulous notes, which stretched on and on like a thread. It was music that would stir the hidden dragon in a lost valley and make the widow on a lone boat cry.

Master Su grew solemn and, straightening his robe and sitting upright, asked the guest why he played that way.

The guest replied, "'The moon is bright and stars are few / Magpies fly past us southward.' Are these not lines by Cao Mengde [Cao Cao]?[50] We gaze towards Xiakou in the west and Wuchang in the east. The mountains and river encircle each other, the landscape a dark and luxuriant green. Is this not where Mengde was routed by Master Zhou? After he conquered Jingzhou and took Jiangling, he proceeded eastward down the Yangzi. Bow to stern, his warships stretched a thousand miles; and his banners blocked out the sky. He poured wine as he gazed across the river and composed poetry with his halberd lying across his lap. Without a doubt he was the greatest warrior of his age, and yet where is he today? And what about you and me, we fishermen and woodcutters of the river islets? We keep company with fish and befriend deer. We ride a leaf of a boat and toast each other with gourdfuls of wine. We are May flies caught between Heaven and Earth, a speck of grain in the boundless sea. Grieved by the brevity of our lives, I envy the inexhaustibility of the Yangzi. I would like to grasp a soaring immortal to wander far and wide or embrace the bright moon and live on for all time. Knowing how difficult such feats are, I consign my fading notes to the sorrowful wind."

Master Su answered, "Do you not know about the river and the moon? The former flows on and on but never departs. The latter waxes and wanes but never grows or shrinks. If you look at the things from the viewpoint of the changes they undergo, nothing in Heaven or Earth lasts longer than the blink of an eye. But if you look at them from the viewpoint of their changeless traits, neither the objects of the world nor we ever come to an end. What is there to envy? Furthermore, all objects between Heaven and Earth have their master. As for something we do not own, we do not presume to take the smallest amount of it for ourselves. But as for the Yangzi's cool breeze and the bright moon that shines between the mountains—when our ears are exposed to them, they hear sounds; and when our eyes meet them, they see images. We are not prohibited from taking these for our own, and we can use them without ever exhausting them. They are, in fact, the Transformer's inexhaustible treasuries, given freely for us jointly to consume."

The guest smiled with delight and rinsed our cups and poured some more wine. By the time our snacks were eaten up, our wine cups and plates lay strewn about. We lay down in the boat and pillowed our heads on each other. Before we knew it, the east grew light.[51]

It is the last section of the rhapsody that is its climax and contains its most celebrated passage. As for the thought itself, "Master Su's" musings on impermanence, with which he consoles his guest, are not original. There are precedents for this special understanding of impermanence as permanence. Earlier discussions of the concept of change in the *Book of Changes* constitute a precedent, and others have been identified in Buddhist discussions of non-transference.[52] It is the appropriation of the old idea in a dramatized literary work that is new and striking. On top of that, the sanguine reassurance that Su finds in the underlying thought of an ongoing human consciousness and community, greater by far than any single life, yet linking separate lives together, as Su is linked to the Red Cliff warriors and later readers are, in turn, linked to Su is a special and memorable resolution of the problem raised so often by encounters with ancient sites in Chinese poetry. It is this evocation of human continuity, in the face of which individual possessiveness is meaningless, that makes the ending of the rhapsody so immensely satisfying.

Of course, the appeal of the rhapsody comes from more than the concluding section. One thinks of how often the scene was painted in later centuries, with all the essential elements (the cliff, the river, the small boat with Su Shi and his guests) rearranged by artist after artist (see Fig. 1). The piece has, aside from its philosophy, a strong narrative line (unusual in rhapsodies) as well as vivid descriptions of the moonlit river scene and the pleasure it gives the boaters. The sections are deftly arranged and seem to follow naturally from each other: the initial exhilaration of boating, Su Shi's plaintive song, the more melancholy flute-playing, explained by the conventional but elegantly presented reflections on history and mortality, and finally Su's gentle refutation of his guest's recourse to sorrow.

The piece bears comparison with Su's earlier inscription for the Tower of Transcendence, of which it is faintly reminiscent. Differences between the two may reflect some of the consequences of the liberating aspect of exile mentioned above. For all its philosophizing, the Tower essay leaves the impression of a frustrated provincial official struggling to reconcile himself to his unattractive assignment. Determinedly, he claims to have found a technique that will allow him to be happy even in the most wretched of places. However, the exiled author of the Red Cliff rhapsody, ironically enough, has moved beyond dissatisfaction with the place in which he finds himself. The problem he considers is the universal one of mortality, not the particular one of an undesirable assignment. Furthermore, for all the similarity between the goal of dwelling "outside of the realm of things" (the Tower inscrip-

FIGURE 1. Wu Yuanzhi (late 12th c.), *The Red Cliff*. Section of a handscroll. Collection of the National Palace Museum, Taiwan, Republic of China.

tion) and the exhortation not to cling to what is transient (the rhapsody), the moods that the two pieces project are quite unlike each other. In the earlier piece, the author boasts of his unique achievement ("where could I go that I would not be happy?"), whereas in the latter the author finds consolation in the thought that his finite life is part of an infinite flow ("neither the objects of the world nor we ever come to an end"). The broader perspective is that adopted by the exiled official.

Nevertheless, it would be wrong to conclude from the rhapsody's ending that Su Shi had reasoned his way, once and for all, to a philosophical acceptance of change and mortality, even in the midst of his frustration in exile. Familiar as its concepts are to the reader versed in Su's earlier writings, the first Red Cliff rhapsody may be considered the culmination of several strands of his thought, and probably their most satisfying literary embodiment. Yet, while the rhapsody itself presents the image of a poet who is perfectly resigned to his circumstances and mortality, there is every indication that the real Su Shi was less completely reconciled.

A song lyric (ci) that Su wrote on the Red Cliff theme, which is nearly as well known as the rhapsody, yields a very different impression of the poet in exile. The song focuses on Zhou Yu (Master Zhou, Gongjin), the Wu general who was responsible for Cao Cao's defeat at the site.

念奴嬌 赤壁懷古	*To the tune "Recalling Her Charms,"* *Cherishing the Past at Red Cliff*
大江東去	The great river flows east,
浪淘盡	Its waves scouring away
千古風流人物	The dashing heroes of a thousand ages.
故壘西邊	West of the abandoned fortifications,
人道是	People say, is
三國周郎赤壁	Master Zhou's Red Cliff of the Three Kingdoms.
亂石穿空	Crags and boulders poke through the sky,
驚濤拍岸	Frightening waves pound the bank,
捲起千堆雪	Enveloping a thousand piles of snow.
江山如畫	The river and mountains are like a painting,
一時多少豪傑	How many brave warriors were here!
遙想公瑾當年	Dimly I picture Gongjin then:
小喬初嫁了	He had just married Little Qiao,
雄姿英發	Valor shone everywhere in his bearing.
羽扇綸巾	His fan of plumes, kerchief of silk—
笑談間	As he chatted and laughed,

檣艣灰飛煙滅　　Masts and hulls became flying ashes and smoke.
故國神遊　　　　My soul wanders the ancient realm,
多情應笑我　　　So full of feeling, others will laugh at me,
早生華髮　　　　My hair turns grey prematurely.
人生如夢　　　　Life is like a dream,
一樽還酹江月　　Let me pour a libation to the river moon.[53]

In this song, the poet casts himself in a role like that filled by the flute player in the rhapsody. Here, it is the persona of the poet who is overcome with sentiment for the vanished heroes of a glorious past. Moreover, there is no recourse to philosophy here, no attempt to relieve the longing and loneliness.

How may this be explained? One possibility is that the song was written before the rhapsody, that the song represents an earlier stage of Su's thinking, before he was able to contemplate with calm detachment the steady flow of the past and human greatness into oblivion. In fact, we do not know the date of the song. It is generally assumed that the song was written about the time of the rhapsody, but the sequence of the two pieces is impossible to determine. Therefore, we cannot account for the apparent contradiction between the two works by means of chronology. And even if it could be demonstrated that the rhapsody postdated the song, the claim that the difference between them reveals some absolute and irreversible psychological "development" would be problematic (not to mention other dated poems that could be adduced to challenge such a claim). It might be supposed that the difference of literary genre has some bearing upon these divergent treatments of the Red Cliff theme. It is to be expected, this reasoning would say, that the song lyric would be more sentimental and that the prose-like rhapsody would be more intellectual. However, Su Shi's songs are known to be uncharacteristically full of thought, just as his rhapsodies may be charged with emotion. The disposition of the two Red Cliff pieces is not satisfactorily explained by genre alone.

It is preferable to understand the sanguineness of the first Red Cliff rhapsody merely as one possible reaction to the contemplation of the past and mortality. It represents one response, but not a final or dominant one. During his exiles, Su Shi must have given considerable thought to questions of the worth and lasting significance of individual effort, as well he might. Doubts and sorrows, however unwelcome, must have kept intruding, much as do the remarks of the unidentified friend in the rhapsody, which threaten the serenity of the evening. There were times when, as a poet, Su marshaled concepts that had become stock ideas of his (on non-attachment, on selflessness) to create a literature of consolation, but there were other times when those ideas did not quite suffice.

The identity of the historical figures featured in the two pieces may go far towards explaining their differences. When his focus is the fearsome Cao Cao, warrior and usurper, Su Shi remains detached and objective enough to attempt a philosophical response to the problems of mortality and mutability. But so great is the appeal of Zhou Yu, and so deep is Su's sympathy and identification with this figure, that any pretense of detachment becomes impossible, and Su gives himself over to much the kind of sentimentality and self-pity that he had resisted in the rhapsody, although he still makes an effort to view his own emotions objectively ("My soul wanders the ancient realm, / So full of feeling, others will laugh at me").

A literatus does not at first sight seem to have much in common with the general Zhou Yu. But Su had aspired to become a national leader, if not a general, a man the ruler could entrust with the fate of the state, just as Sun Quan had entrusted Zhou Yu with saving Wu from Cao Cao's advancing armies. It is the way Zhou Yu is described that suggests that the comparison was in the poet's mind. It is not his prowess as a fighter that is emphasized, but his youth, virility, and promise (hence the mention of his bride, Little Qiao), as well as his dashing manner and wit. "As he chatted and laughed, / Masts and hulls became flying ashes and smoke" (this alludes to the clever stratagem by which Zhou Yu set fire to Cao Cao's superior navy). So should Su Shi, by means of brilliant strategies, have liked to come to his nation's rescue. Thereafter the song jumps immediately to the poet and his profound nostalgia. It is commonplace in pieces written "longing for the past" not only to think fondly back upon the past, but to use the past as a gauge by which to measure present decline. Su Shi is doing just that here. He chooses at this moment in his life to write about Zhou Yu because he now sees that he will never become a modern Zhou Yu. Not only has historical time "scoured away" all traces of the ancient hero, Su's own chance for a career comparable in service to Zhou Yu's has also been lost. Chinese critics have long recognized the special relationship the song posits between Su and Zhou Yu, and anticipate this interpretation of the song in comments such as the following: "In his Red Cliff song Su Shi playfully compares himself with Zhou Yu" (Yuan Haowen). "The title is Red Cliff but the content is really about the poet himself. Master Zhou is the guest and the poet is the host. The song utilizes the guest to establish the host, it lodges the host in the guest . . . It is not right simply to recite the song and not realize wherein the poet's intent lies" (Huang Liaoyuan).[54]

East Slope, Tao Qian, Determined Contentment

The strategy of concentrating on the changeless aspect of things, and of finding satisfaction in nothing more than the bright moon and the cool breeze, was not always sufficient to overcome the special frustrations and doubts of exile. In one moment of depression, on his third Cold Food festival in Huangzhou, Su Shi likened himself to the dead embers of the extinguished cooking fires that could not be fanned back to life.[55] In response to such moods, Su began to explore other modes of expression, modes that could be used, together with the philosophy of selflessness, to keep sorrow and self-pity in check. One of those was to write the poetry of a gentleman farmer, describing the joys to be found in the new task of growing his own food, which circumstances forced upon him.

It does not follow that simply because Su's finances required him, during his second year in Huangzhou, to begin to plow and plant that he would necessarily write about that experience in poetry. He might well have avoided the subject in verse, as no doubt he avoided many others. It must be that he now found it congenial to write about his toil at East Slope. By doing so, he demonstrated to himself and others that the work could be endured (mentally and physically) and that it could even be transformed into a source of comfort. "Day and night I work to prepare the field, intending to plant wheat. Although the labor is hard, it, too, has its flavor." Su sought to capture that flavor in his poems. The best are a series of eight, entitled "East Slope" and preceded by a preface describing how Ma Mengde secured use of the abandoned plot of land for him. The poems then recount in considerable detail the challenge of transforming the rubble-strewn plot into a crop-yielding field, which, though humble, will supply Su and his family with food. The first five are translated below:

其一	*No. 1*
廢壘無人顧	An abandoned camp that no one tends,
頹垣滿蓬蒿	Toppled walls overgrown with grasses.
誰能捐筋力	Who would waste his muscles on it?
4　歲晚不償勞	At year's end the effort won't be repaid.
獨有孤旅人	Only a lone wanderer
天窮無所逃	Whose fate of hardship has no escape.
端來拾瓦礫	So he comes to gather up the broken tiles,
8　歲旱土不膏	A year of drought, the soil poor.
崎嶇草棘中	Hard-pressed amid weeds and brambles,

	欲刮一寸毛	He hopes to scrape off an inch of crop.
	嗒然釋耒歎	Putting down the plough, he sighs,
12	我廩何時高	"When will my grain be piled high?"

其二 — *No. 2*

	荒田雖浪莽	These neglected fields are now overgrown
	高庳各有適	But each plot, high and low, will have its use.
	下隰種秔稌	I'll plant rice on the lowland marshes
4	東原蒔棗栗	Jujubes and chestnuts on the eastern rise.
	江南有蜀士	A Shu gentleman living south of the river
	桑果已許乞	Has promised to send mulberry seeds.
	好竹不難栽	Good bamboo is not hard to transplant,
8	但恐鞭橫逸	But watch it does not spread out of control.
	仍須卜佳處	Finally I must choose a good spot
	規以安我室	On which to build my house.
	家僮燒枯草	My servant boy, burning dead grasses,
12	走報暗井出	Runs to say he's found a hidden well.
	一飽未敢期	I don't dare set a date for a hearty meal,
	瓢飲已可必	But at least my drinking gourd is assured!

其三 — *No. 3*

	自昔有微泉	There used to be a small stream
	來從遠嶺背	That came from behind the distant peak.
	穿城過聚落	Flowing through the city and past the settlement,
4	流惡壯蓬艾	It carried filth away, made wormwood thick.
	去為柯氏陂	It continued on to Ke Embankment,
	十畝魚蝦會	Ten *mu* of fish and shrimp.
	歲旱泉亦竭	In the drought this year the stream dried up,
8	枯萍黏破塊	Dead duckweed stuck to cracked clods of earth.
	昨夜南山雲	Last night clouds came from the southern hills,
	雨到一犁外	Rain soaked the soil deeper than a plowshare.
	泫然尋故瀆	Trickling along, it found the old streambed,
12	知我理荒薈	Knowing I mean to cultivate this weedy plot.
	泥芹有宿根	Muddy celery still had its dormant roots,
	一寸嗟獨在	See there, a single inch-long stalk appears.
	雪芽何時動	When will the snowy sprouts poke through
16	春鳩何可膾	So I can prepare braised spring dove?

其四 — *No. 4*

	種稻清明前	I plant rice before the Qingming Festival
	樂事我能數	The happy event to come—I can count the days.
	毛空暗春澤	Fur in the sky will darken the spring marsh,
4	針水聞好語	Needles in the water will bring shouts of joy.

分秧及初夏	Transplanting will last until the start of summer,
漸喜風葉舉	Happily I'll watch the wind-blown leaves rise.
月明看露上	In bright moonlight I'll see dew climb the plants,
8 一一珠垂縷	Pearls strung one by one on a silken thread.
秋來霜穗重	In autumn when the stalks are heavy with frost,
顛倒相撐拄	They'll bend low and knock against each other.
但聞畦壟間	All I'll hear, from among the dikes and paths,
12 蚱蜢如風雨	Will be grasshoppers whirring like a storm.
新春便入甑	Freshly husked rice will go right into the steamer,
玉粒照筐筥	Jade kernels will glow in the wicker bin.
我久食官倉	For years I've eaten from the government granary,
16 紅腐等泥土	Reddish rotting rice no better than dirt.
行當知此味	Finally I'll know a new taste,
口腹吾已許	I've already promised my mouth and belly.

其五	*No. 5*
良農惜地力	Good farmers do not wear out their land,
幸此十年荒	Luckily, this plot has lain fallow ten years.
桑柘未及成	The mulberry trees are not yet mature,
4 一麥庶可望	But I'm already looking forward to a crop of wheat.
投種未逾月	It's less than a month since I did the sowing,
覆塊已蒼蒼	Even now the tilled soil shows some green.
農父告我言	An old farmer came and told me,
8 勿使苗葉昌	"Don't let the sprouts get thick with leaves;
君欲富餅餌	If you want ample noodles and dumplings,
要須縱牛羊	Let sheep and oxen in to graze."
再拜謝苦言	I bow twice in thanks for this frank advice,
12 得飽不敢忘	When my stomach's full, I won't forget him.[56]

No. 3, Line 16: A note by Su explains, "Natives of Shu like to eat braised meat with celery shoots. It is dove meat that is used to make this dish."

No. 4, Line 4: Su explains, "Natives of Shu call fine rain 'furry rain,' and when rice plants begin to sprout farmers call to each other, 'The rice needles have appeared.'"

No. 4, Line 12: Su explains, "In Shu when rice is ready for harvesting, grasshoppers swarm in the fields just like locusts; but they do not harm the crop."

Su starts out in this series with a hopeless tract of land and gradually improves it until he has rice plants started on it. In remaining poems in the series he entertains the idea of planting fruit trees to benefit him in the years to come; and he writes of the friendships he has formed in Huangzhou with less-than-prominent men, and of the deep satisfaction he derives from their loyalty and company.

Much of the interest and impact of these poems can be attributed to all that goes unsaid in them, or rather from the gulf between what is said and what might have been said. No Chinese reader could work his way through the poems without a strong and constant sense of the significance that accrues to them because they were written by Su Shi in exile. At every line we are aware that the man who is carrying out all this humble labor is a celebrated poet and leader of the political opposition, and we marvel at his self-control. There is hardly a trace of bitterness, hardly a reference to anything at all outside the immediate concerns of the crops and society of East Slope. He gets on with his farming work and seems, as we progress through the series, to find more and more contentment in it. He alludes then only once to his past career—the reference in the fourth poem to the moldy rice he used to eat from government granaries (that is, his stipend). But he broaches this aspect of his past not to complain so much as to emphasize his eagerness now to nourish himself with fresh rice from his own fields. He seems to have succeeded remarkably in putting his tumultuous past behind him.

Critics are fond of praising Su Shi's East Slope poems as being reminiscent of the fourth-century poet Tao Qian.[57] The comparison has a certain validity and is, in fact, one that Su Shi thought of himself at the time. Su goes so far as to say that he is Tao Qian reborn.[58] By the end of the Northern Song, Tao Qian came to be thought of as the earliest and greatest poet of simple rustic pleasures, the founder of the poetic tradition of the gentleman farmer. But there are two senses in which Su Shi's accomplishment departs significantly from Tao Qian's precedent. First, for all his fame as a poet of "fields and gardens," Tao Qian did not write about the actual procedures of farming with anything approaching the detail of Su's works. The farming in Tao's poems is limited to an occasional and usually vague line or two (e.g., "When we meet we talk of nothing else / Than how the hemp and mulberry are growing").[59] Tao Qian's poems remain essentially intellectual and philosophical. He uses the fact of his farming to reflect on the ramifications of his decision to withdraw from government service. But he does not dwell on the details of his farming and certainly does not take pains to document his familiarity with the work, as Su does here. The second divergence is that while Tao Qian had never risen higher than the post of provincial magistrate, Su Shi was a figure of national renown, especially after his arrest and trial. It is considerably more unexpected and ironic that Su Shi would have to start growing his own food than that the comparatively lowly Tao Qian did.

Su's emulation of Tao Qian began at Huangzhou, but it became virtually obsessive during his Lingnan exile. There, he embarked upon a formidable Tao Qian project: he resolved to write matching poems (that is, using the same rhyme words) to every piece in Tao's corpus, some 120 works. Su was of course fully aware of how singular a project this was. Exchanging "matching poems" was an enterprise common among friends in the Northern Song. But it had never been done across the centuries on anything like the scale that Su now undertook to do, as he himself points out.[60]

The significance Tao Qian held for Su seems also to have deepened by the time of his Lingnan exile. He was more than just a gentleman farmer or poet of "fields and gardens." He was a man who had been forced to live out his life in obscurity because he was unwilling to compromise his principles to get on in a corrupt world. And yet, in his rural obscurity, he expressed no bitterness. Su Shi had discovered a remark that Tao had addressed to his sons, "When I was young, we were in straits; and on occasion I wandered abroad because of my family's difficulties. But with my stubborn nature and mediocre talents, I was often at odds with the world. Taking stock, I decided for my own sake I would have to give up practical concerns and somehow or other retire from the world."[61] Su comments, "I have precisely the same flaw myself, but for the longest time I did not realize it. I spent half my life serving as an official and ran up against all the troubles in the world. That is why now I stand in such awe of Yuanming [Tao Qian] and want to try, in my old age, to emulate even a tiny part of his example."[62]

However, even as Su's admiration for Tao increased, so that he now replaced Du Fu as Su's favorite poet,[63] and as his self-identification with Tao intensified, the gulf between the experiences of the two men widened. If it was willful for Su Shi in his Huangzhou exile to claim to be a latterday Tao Qian, it was patently strained to repeat the claim years later while the grand councilor of the realm was arranging for his banishment to the jungles of Hainan Island. The incongruity of the comparison Su now drew (and, in effect, reiterated with each new matching poem) was noted by his own brother: "Yuanming [Tao Qian] was unwilling, for a mere five pecks of grain, to tie on his sash and go see the petty men of the village yamen. But Zizhan [Su Shi] went out and served for more than thirty years. He was imprisoned and abused by jailors at the Censorate prison. Still unable to mend his ways, he eventually fell into great hardship. Then, in the twilight of his years, he decided to model himself upon Yuanming—who would ever believe it?"[64]

Taken in its entirety, the corpus of poems Su produced matching Tao Qian's constitutes a complex subject. Virtually every poem, as we would expect, presents a new variation on the dialogue across the centuries that Su has established. The dynamics of the exchange warrant further study.[65] Here, I intend only to call attention to certain aspects of Su's responses to Tao. There are among Su's matching poems some that may seem to reproduce quite closely the emotions and tone of Tao's originals, or what we may imagine Tao to have written. Consider the following poem, from the series Su wrote matching Tao's famous set entitled "Returning to the Farm to Dwell":

窮猿既投林	The desperate gibbon has hid in the forest,
疲馬初解鞅	The weary horse has been relieved of its halter.
心空飽新得	My mind vacant, I am sated on new acquisitions;
境熟夢餘想	The land familiar, I give my thoughts to dreams.
江鷗漸馴集	River gulls flock tamely beside me,
蜑叟已還往	Dan boatmen sail back and forth.
南池綠錢生	Green coins grow on the southern pond,
北嶺紫筍長	Purple bamboo shoots are tall on the north peak.
提壺豈解飲	How could the raise-a-gourd know how to drink?
好語時見廣	Yet his welcome call eases my heart.
春江有佳句	The river in spring inspires fine poetic lines
我醉墮渺莽	As I drink, I slip into the vast emptiness.[66]

Many of Su's lines are reminiscent of lines found in Tao's originals, such as the first (compare Tao's "For long I was a prisoner in a cage / And now have my freedom back again") and the third (compare Tao's "From time to time through the tall grass / Like me, village farmers come and go").[67] Still, the overall effect of Su Shi's poem is distinctly different from Tao's. Within Su's poem, one finds a degree of insistence upon contentment in the new surroundings that is unexampled in Tao's originals. Tao's poems freely express his apprehensions, in addition to his joy, over the new course he has chosen—supporting himself by farming. Thus Tao's second poem (the model for this one by Su) concludes with the lines, "My constant worry is that frost may come / And my crops will wither with the weeds"; and his third poem ends, "Wet clothes are no cause for complaint / If things will only go as hoped." Nor are crops Tao's only worry. He broods over time, history, and his own mortality ("Man's life is like a conjuror's illusion / That reverts in the end to empty nothing"), as he does in so many of his poems. But such worries have largely been removed from Su Shi's matching poems, where it is the joy of rustic life that predominates.

In other matching poems as well, Su Shi keeps outdoing Tao Qian in the virtue Su associates with him. Tao had written a set of poems in praise of impoverished gentlemen, in which he tries to comfort himself in his poverty by reflecting on the high repute of principled recluses of the past. These poems are full of reminders of Tao's hardship, and they hint that his wife and family sometimes did not bear it patiently. There is talk in the pieces of men who were, despite all the deprivations, able to find contentment in their humble circumstances; but the emphasis is on the sacrifices they had to make to keep their integrity intact ("And then one day his life was done, / His rags too short to cover him")[68] and, consequently, on what unusual men they were. Tao himself expresses a mixture of discouragement and resignation:

凄厲歲云暮	Sharp and chill the year draws to a close;
擁褐曝前軒	On the porch I clutch my coat and sun myself.
南圃無遺秀	The southern garden holds no sprig of green
枯條盈北園	Withered branches fill the northern orchard.
傾壺絕餘瀝	I tilt the bottle and no drop comes out
闚竈不見煙	I glance at the stove but see no smoke.
詩書塞座外	The classic books lie piled beside my seat
日昃不遑研	The sun declines, and leaves no time for study.
閑居非陳阨	Without a job is not a "crisis in Chen,"
竊有慍見言	But with me too are those who show resentment.
何以慰吾懷	What consolation is there left for me?
賴古多此賢	All those gentlemen since ancient times.[69]

The emphasis is different in Su Shi's matching poems. In his lines about Tao Qian, Su dwells on Tao's self-sufficiency:

誰謂淵明貧	Who says Yuanming was poor?
尚有一素琴	He still had one plain zither.
心閑手自適	His mind idle, his hand too was at ease,
寄此無窮音	So he lodged in the boundless melody.[70]

Su does refer to his own deprivation, but always on analogy to Tao's, which, Su believed, never affected Tao's inner peace. More directly, Su contrasts his own situation with those of his sons, scattered about in four different prefectures. They are the ones who are truly poor, Su asserts, while I am simply "at leisure."[71]

A similar recasting of a verse by Tao Qian is evident in a poem that broaches the crucial issue of resentment or bitterness. Tao had written a "Song of Resentment" in which he recorded several of the hardships he had suffered through his life (e.g., born into "troubled times," lost his first wife when she was young, saw his house burn down, experienced hunger).[72] Towards the end of the poem, Tao exculpates Heaven of any blame for this hard life, but he had no such kind words for his fellow man or society in general. In fact, the poem implicitly blames society for Tao's exceptionally hard life; and fittingly it concludes with a reference to Zhong Ziqi, the model friend who was the only person fully to understand Bo Ya's zither playing.

Su Shi's matching poem makes it sound as if Tao Qian had no resentment (despite the title of his song). It begins,

當歡有餘樂	In good times be more than happy,
在戚亦頹然	In distress be acquiescent.
淵明得此理	Yuanming knew this principle
安處故有年	And so had years of dwelling at peace.

Su concludes by regretting that he had not "discovered" the principle earlier on, but takes comfort in the thought that still it is not too late to "extol the worthiness of Yuanming."[73]

These transformations of Tao Qian, for that is what they amount to, are one consequence of Su Shi's commitment to avoiding sorrow and self-pity in exile. What began in Huangzhou with the poetry of farming reached its culmination in Huizhou and Hainan with the re-creation of Tao Qian, with Su Shi echoing a Tao Qian who was truer to Su's own aims and needs than he was to the historical poet.

There are other striking results of this same attitude, aside from the poems inspired by Tao. Su refers, for example, to his confinement on Hainan Island as a *you*, that is, a pleasure outing, observing as he returns to the mainland that the island exile has been "the finest pleasure outing of my whole life".[74] Elsewhere he says that he is, in fact, a native of Hainan,[75] and goes so far as to characterize Huizhou and Hainan as a land of immortals, Penglai, or even a Peach Blossom Spring.[76]

The following short prose piece is another instance of this determined optimism. It was written shortly after Su was forced to leave the mainland.

> When I first came to the southern sea, I gazed at the horizon and saw that the sky came right down to the ocean in all directions. This gave me great sorrow and I asked myself when I should ever be able to leave this island. But later I reflected on my situation: Heaven and Earth float upon a vast pool of water, and the nine continents sit amid the Great Ocean. China itself is surrounded by the Minor Sea—so who does not live upon an island?
>
> You empty a basin on water onto the ground. A blade of grass floats

in the water and an ant clings to the blade. The ant is terrified, not knowing how it can get back to dry ground. After a while the water dries up and the ant crawls away. When it meets other ants, it weeps, saying, "I thought I would never see you again. It never occurred to me that in just a short time I could stand here again at this great crossroads that leads in all directions." Thinking of this brought a smile to my face.

On the twelfth day of the ninth month of Wuyin [1098] I was drinking some weak wine with guests and became slightly drunk. I gave free rein to my brush and wrote this page.[77]

Few readers will not share in Su Shi's smile upon encountering this little piece. Here, rather than to transform the disagreeable place into a congenial refuge, Su contemplates an easy escape. All that needs to happen is for the southern sea to evaporate.

These discoveries of sources of consolation and even joy in the midst of deprivation have, of course, become a central part of Su Shi's fame. Whether by virtue of his emulation of the serene voice of Tao Qian or his transformation of malarial wastelands into paradises (or, at the least, harmless sites for pleasure outings), Su Shi may seem never to have given himself up to discouragement. Understandably, this has earned him the admiration of countless readers through the centuries. The achievement, moreover, seems especially remarkable in the Chinese literary tradition, where the archetype of the forlorn and self-righteous banished minister is so well established.

It should be borne in mind, nevertheless, that such moments of optimism represent only one of several reactions Su Shi had to the experience of exile. Among others, to be examined below, there are also moments of muffled rancor and defiance. Besides, the very willfulness of Su's apparent contentment in exile should alert us to its complexity. Su Shi, as mentioned before, was no Tao Qian—a man who was obscure even when he was in office and then retired voluntarily and farmed in the shadows of the culturally central Lu Mountain. The effort required for Su Shi to become, in his poems, a Tao Qian, a gentleman farmer of East Slope, or an undiscouraged "native of Hainan Island" must have been enormous. That effort is something that lies beneath or behind the surface meaning of his poems of contentment. Still, it is an essential part of those poems, imparting depth and resonance at every turn to seemingly simple lines about the new-found joys of rustic life.

Transcending the World of Men

There were times when Su Shi was unable to sustain his accommodating attitude or pretense of his own rusticity and sought instead to escape from the world and the devices of men. Writings from his exile periods that feature a cluster of subjects (including meditation, alchemy, breath control, and Taoist immortality) exemplify this yearning. Ultimately, the temptation of blocking the mundane world out to pursue various techniques of transcendence is one that Su Shi rejects, as we would expect him to. But he has to keep rejecting it, which shows how strong a temptation it was during his confinements.

In Huangzhou Su Shi built himself a studio, Snow Hall. The name signifies more than the fact that the structure was completed during a snowstorm; for once it was finished, Su proceeded to cover the walls inside with paintings of snow. Not an inch of wall was left unpainted. "Wherever you situate yourself and whichever way you gaze, turning round or glancing sideways, all you see is snow."[78] Su would sit alone inside this remarkable environment and "lose his body and lose his mind." He would feel as light as the fluttering butterfly, and experience profound stillness. He speaks of his skin becoming chilled from the visions of snow, and of the purifying effect this had upon his vexations and pent-up feelings. The desensitizing effect of coldness becomes, in his account of the hall, an antidote for the heat of worldly contention. Men accustomed to rushing along the paths of profit and loss, or wandering through the realms of worry and doubt, should find the numbing coldness provided by the hall as welcome as a bucket of water is to the man who has burned his hand.

Snow Hall was used for meditation. The goal was first to leave behind worldly concerns ("the devices of men")[79] through immersion in this oblivion of snow, and then to use this liberation to achieve insight into the great truths of the world. "I shall find between my eyebrows and eyelashes the flavor of the eight distant regions."[80] "When the myriad stillnesses become active again, great wisdom will arise."[81] It is noteworthy that even here, in describing the insight to be gained, Su avoids using such terms as "Pattern" or "human nature." Moreover, he is clearly full of misgivings, even as he celebrates the use of the hall. His essay on the hall is presented as a debate between himself and an unidentified visitor, who accuses Su of not being truly liberated or transcendent if he must still withdraw into his peculiar room to acquire wisdom. Su concedes the validity of the criticism.

At other times Su Shi did not stop with meditation alone. He often combined mental discipline with various techniques derived from the rich traditions of *yangsheng* ("nurturing life") and inner and outer alchemy. He practiced and wrote knowledgeably about a host of techniques, including breath control ("embryonic breathing," "tortoise breathing"), purification of the saliva, avoidance of grains, and the ingestion of longevity drugs, including water lily, pills derived from mother's milk, and, of course, cinnabar. He experimented with the alchemist's furnace, not only in the hope that he might actually produce a pill to delay the aging process, but also simply because he enjoyed, as he says, observing "the transformations of things."[82] He wrote to friends, asking that they send more ingredients for his experiments.[83] In fact, Su's protracted interest in these matters dismayed his Buddhist friends. The monk Huihong, who held Su in high regard, identified this pursuit of Taoist arts and the inability to accept death that it implied as Su's only shortcomings.[84]

One of Su's Huizhou writings clearly states the connection between his own history of frustrations in the world of ordinary men and his interest in leaving it behind. He first provides, for his younger brother, a detailed description of an inner alchemy procedure he has learned. He continues:

> This account is rare and penetrating, marvelous and simple, and can certainly be trusted. However, I have one great disappointment: during my life I have intended to follow it at least a hundred times, but each time it was an empty wish that went unfulfilled. I now know that unless I "discard my body" in pursuit of it, "hollow out my heart" to receive it, and "give up my life" to preserve it, I shall never succeed.
>
> I am now sixty years old. My reputation and position have been ruined, I am separated from my brother, and my sons are scattered about. I live among southern aborigines and have no date for returning north. The paltry flavor the world holds for me does not need to be described. If my interest in this turns out once again to be an empty wish, what kind of man am I? Therefore, during the past few days I have sworn an oath: I shall be like the ancients who took refuge from difficulties in inaccessible mountains, or who went on missions to deserted wastelands, where they munched weeds and sucked snow. What manner of men were they?
>
> I have had a meditation bench made, and two large tables, which I arranged beside a bright window, so that I may devote myself to this discipline. I have also made a hundred dry steamed buns. Starting on the first day of the second month, I will cease all involvement in worldly affairs. When hungry I will eat a bun. I will drink no warmed water and take no other foods. I will chew the buns slowly to increase my saliva . . .[85]

The technique that Su had been taught by an unidentified recluse was called the "dragon and tiger formula." Its goal was to cause the forces associated with the heart and kidneys to be joined together and nourished rather than separated and spent. The terminology includes animal symbolism and five phases correlations that are well known in inner alchemical texts.[86] The dragon and mercury are associated with semen and blood, and are produced by the kidneys. Tiger and lead are associated with the "breath" (*qi*) and effort (*li*), and are produced by the heart. Normally, the dragon appears inside the body in conjunction with water (its corresponding phase in nature): the kidneys secrete their liquids and the dragon slips away, leaving the kidneys' mercury insubstantial. Likewise, the tiger normally appears in conjunction with fire: the heart's passions are stirred and the tiger races through the body, leaving the heart's lead parched. The technique Su had learned was designed to prevent these developments, to reverse or confound the normal correlations, so that the animals would not flow away but would instead be commingled with their complementary phase. This was what was called "the dragon appearing in conjunction with fire, and the tiger being born amid water." The result was that the forces of the metals (mercury and lead) already present within the body would become increasingly refined and potent.

The methods used to effect this, as Su describes them, include breath control and saliva swallowing. Holding the breath for long periods causes a warming of the lower cinnabar field. Gradually, the whole body is filled with heat and "fire." But the heat has no outlet or application because the practitioner keeps his senses completely closed. As fire builds within the body, water increases correspondingly, as it must to balance the fire. Water and fire are united in steam and vapor: this is the dragon appearing in the midst of fire. Meanwhile the adept blocks the rear entrance to his mouth by curling his tongue back towards his uvula (and actually trying to touch it). His saliva, thus protected from any mixing with the mercury coursing through his body, is gathered and purified by "steaming" in the mouth. Eventually, the saliva is forced down, followed by pure air, into the cinnabar field, where it is nourished through meditation and transformed into lead. This is the tiger being born amid water.

One might suppose that such regimens that Su adopted were intended first and foremost to improve his health. Especially during his Lingnan exile, he complains frequently about the unavailability of medicine; and he refers often to various ailments he suffered, including eye problems, fever, boils, and digestive disorders. We also know that there was no absolute distinction drawn in much of *yangsheng* thought between improving health, delaying the onset of old age, and actually achieving immortality. Techniques that might lead to physical immortality if carried to perfection and practiced over many years might also have the short-term effect of simply improving one's health. Thus it seems that the Taoist master Deng Shouan, who befriended Su at

Huizhou, served both as Su's pharmacist for common ailments and his tutor in arcane longevity techniques.[87] The whole subject is further complicated by the belief in some quarters in the possibility of post-mortem physical immortality, as explained in the concept of "release from the corpse" (which Su Shi also wrote about).[88] Thus the adept might not be seeking to avoid normal death.

As tempting as it may be to say that Su's interest in alchemy and other *yangsheng* practices was entirely mundane and medical (in our sense), his own words suggest otherwise. No doubt he did hope to improve his health, but from time to time he also entertained the prospect of far greater benefits. He tells his brother that people who allow their "dragon and tiger" to slip away are those who die, whereas those few who follow the technique he describes and retain the forces are the people who become immortals.[89] Likewise, comments that he hopes soon to be "not far removed from becoming an immortal" and talk of "taking leave of the mortal world" echo through his writings on alchemy and breath control.[90] Still, Su remains ambivalent. About the ingestion of cinnabar pills, in combination with Taoist meditation (*zhiyi*), he writes to Ziyou, "Your older brother has no understanding of these matters. I only want to stick to them stupidly to become an immortal. It's all ridiculous, and yet it's also worth trying."[91] His ambivalence was not only over the question of whether physical immortality was possible to achieve—though certainly he has his doubts about that and discusses them in a note about long-lived Taoists who, disappointingly, end up dying.[92] He also had misgivings about the urge to embark upon the quest itself, and his own fascination with it.

It helped to represent this interest in transcending time and re-nouncing interest in the ordinary "world of men" as something that comes only after frustration in worldly striving and dutifulness. That is the stance Su adopts in the lengthy quotation above, concerning him-self; and he repeats it in a Hainan poem he wrote about the Han dynasty immortal Anqi Sheng. What Su stresses in the poem is not Anqi's achievements in the Taoist arts (what he was famous for), but rather a passing reference made in the Han history to how, before he ever withdrew from the world, Anqi had approached the rebellious general Xiang Yu "with a plan."[93] Xiang Yu proved unwilling to use Anqi, and that is why he embarked on a wholly different course. Su Shi is clearly delighted to have discovered this little-known fact about the immortal. "Thus we know that scholars who would bring order to the world / May, if they withdraw, 'mount the dragon.'"[94] This back-ground to an interest in immortality was one Su found appealing.

Ultimately, Su Shi could not sustain the effort to "mount the dragon," whether through meditation alone or in combination with inner or outer alchemy. His friend Huang Tingjian observed that Su "was fond of the Taoist arts and, upon hearing of a new technique, would immediately begin to practice it. Before long, however, he would abandon it."[95] A similar reluctance to follow through may be seen in Su Shi's literary treatments of Taoist themes, which form a substantial portion of his exile literature.

There are, to be sure, poems that never do descend from the aerial ecstasy of immortality. Many of these are pieces that Su wrote on visits to legendary Taoist mountains, as when he climbed White Waters Peak outside Huizhou in the company of his cousin Cheng Zhengfu.[96] But these are largely set pieces, the kind that could be found among almost any poet's works. More singularly Su's own are poems that vacillate in their attitudes towards the pursuit of immortality. During his Lingnan years, for example, Su frequently invoked the name and legacy of Ge Hong, the fourth-century poet, alchemist, and philosopher (the author of *Baopuzi*). Ge Hong had lived atop Luofu Mountain, just north of Su's Huizhou. In the sense that Ge Hong was one of the few literary figures associated with the region, it may seem easy to understand the many references to him in Su's poems.

Su's use of Ge Hong, however, goes far beyond the expedient use of local history. He adopts Ge Hong as a model for himself. Ge Hong comes to exemplify and validate Su Shi's own interest in the Taoist arts. He even takes his place next to Tao Qian as one of Su's primary teachers and friends:

無糧食自足	Without grain there's still enough to eat—
豈謂穀與蔬	Why talk of millet and greens?
愧此稚川翁	I'm ashamed before old Zhichuan [Ge Hong],
千載與我俱	Who remains with me across a thousand years.
畫我與淵明	Paint him together with Yuanming and me,
可作三士圖	We can be a "Three Scholars Portrait."
學道雖恨晚	I am late, I know, to study the Way,
賦詩豈不如	But is not my poetry as good as his?[97]

These lines are from the first in a series of thirteen poems that matches a series written by Tao Qian. Tao's series was inspired by his reading of the *Classic of Seas and Mountains* (*Shanhai jing*), the ancient repository of geography and mythology. Su announces in a preface to his matching set that he will take Ge Hong's eclectic treatise on alchemy and philosophy as his inspiration. Su has two models, then: Tao the poet and Ge the master of the Taoist Way (who transcended the need of millet and greens). Thus it is appropriate that the three be painted together in one portrait. The final poem in the series repeats this image of the closely bound threesome: "I hold hands with Ge and Tao— / Return home! Oh, let us return!," echoing Tao's famous celebration of his resignation from office.

Nevertheless, in the intervening poems Ge Hong comes in for a certain amount of criticism as Su's initial enthusiasm gives way to doubts and qualifications. Here is the second poem:

稚川雖獨善	Although Zhichuan sought to cultivate his self in isolation,
愛物均孔顏	He was actually as attached to things as Kong and Yan.
欲使蟪蛄流	He wanted to cause cicada-like creatures
知有龜鶴年	To know the longevity of tortoise and crane.
辛勤破封蟄	Hard toil could barely reduce a little mound,
苦語劇移山	But heartfelt speech moved an entire mountain.
博哉無窮利	How far-reaching, the boundless benefit!
千載食此言	The words nourish us across a thousand years.

Ge Hong's "attachment to things" (aiwu), to which Su objects, is his quest for immortality. Foolishly, Ge Hong sought to prolong his "cicada-like" life. He was obsessed both with his physical existence and the elixirs (also "things") that might prolong it. Thus, despite his identification with Taoism, he turned out to be just as "worldly" as Kong and Yan (Confucius and Yan Hui), whom he denigrated. The alternative to Ge Hong offered in this poem is, unexpectedly, derived from a story in Liezi about Mister Simple (Yugong) who succeeded in moving mountains. When, at age ninety, he decided to remove Taixing and Wangwu Mountains from his locale, he led his sons out to start carting earth and stones away. Old Wiseacre laughed at the futility of the undertaking. But Mister Simple replied that although he himself might not live to see the task through to completion, "my sons will beget me more grandsons, my grandsons in their turn will have sons, and these will have more sons and grandsons. My descendants will go on for ever, but the mountains will get no bigger."[98] The Lord of Heaven, moved by his sincerity, quickly ordered subordinate divinities to move the mountain for the man, and it was done. The story presents a different notion of "immortality," one resulting from the continuity of clan and inherited purpose rather than that of the alchemist and his elixirs.

The more we read of Su Shi's series of poems the more ambivalent does his stance regarding Ge Hong and what he represents appear to be. Several times Su refers to infamous fakirs in the annals of

Chinese alchemy—men who falsely claimed to have acquired special powers—and manages to imply that there is something specious about the whole long-life tradition. Ge Hong himself is once labeled "a narrow person" for having recorded the words of these impostors.[99]

Both Su Shi's fondness for Ge Hong and his doubts return in a later poem, written in his first year at Hainan

博大古真人	How grand were the True Men of antiquity
老聃關尹喜	Lao Dan and Guanyin Xi.
獨立萬物表	They stood alone on the edge of things,
長生乃餘事	To them long life was secondary.
稚川差可近	Zhichuan was close to them
倘有接物意	But he still longed for contact with things.
我頃登羅浮	Recently I climbed Luofu Mountain
物色恐相值	And worried that things would confront me.
徘徊朱明洞	I wandered about in Chuming Grotto
沙水自清駛	Where Sha Stream runs clear and fast.
滿把菖蒲根	I filled my hands with roots of sweet flag,
歎息復棄置	Then sighed and abandoned them again.[100]

The first half of the poem states unambiguously Su's preference for the Taoism of the ancient philosophers (Lao Dan is Laozi) to that of the longevity Taoists. Once again Ge Hong's (Zhichuan's) preoccupation with "things" is said to diminish his stature. The last four lines concern Su's visit to Ge Hong's former haunt. If this were just a simple ascent of a mountain peak, we would understand "things" in line 8 to refer to the scenery. Instead, I suspect that Su is thinking of the places and the substances found on the mountain associated with Ge Hong. Su is apprehensive that once there he will be attracted again by Ge Hong's pursuit of immortality. The particulars of the ensuing lines must be all bound up with that pursuit. Sweet flag was considered a long-life drug, and we know from another poem by Su that it grew in Chuming Grotto.[101] Also, I would not be surprised if Sha Stream, apparently "Sandy Stream," were really "Cinnabar (*dansha*) Stream," that is, a place where the precious mineral could be found. In any case, it is clear that Su is first attracted to the herbal drug but then has second thoughts and decides to cast it aside (he uses the word *qi* "to reject, abandon" rather than other words that mean simply to put down). The poem seems to dramatize nicely Su's occasional impulse to emulate Ge Hong and, ultimately, his refusal to do so.

It appears that even while Su Shi can sometimes visualize taking his place next to both Tao Qian and Ge Hong, it is usually not long before he expresses a final preference for the one who renounced public service and society but not the world itself. As drawn as Su Shi was to Taoist pursuits (and Buddhist salvation), it was Tao Qian who provided the model about which he had fewest reservations. On Hainan Island he wrote:

莫從老君言	Do not follow the words of Laozi,
亦莫用佛語	Do not adopt Buddha's teachings either.
仙山與佛國	Immortals' mountains and Buddhists' realms—
終恐無是處	There are probably no such places.
甚欲隨陶翁	I fervently wish to follow Old Tao [Qian]
移家酒中住	And take up residence amid a supply of wine.
醉醒要有盡	Drunkenness and sobriety may come to an end,
未易逃諸數	But it is hard to escape one's fate.[102]

In this poem, the goal that Su cherishes is simply to achieve anonymity in the world and with it freedom from any need for deliberation or value judgments:

所至人聚觀	Wherever I have gone, crowds gawked at me;
指目生毀譽	Their stares gave rise to praise and blame.
如今一弄火	Today let me light a great fire
好惡都焚去	To burn away all likes and dislikes.
既無負載勞	I will have no more heavy burden to shoulder
又無寇攘懼	And no fear of the bandit or thief.

This was a kind of "liberation" that Su ascribed not to Ge Hong, but to Tao Qian.

Su's vacillation during his Lingnan years concerning the pursuit of longevity, and all that it entailed, sheds light retrospectively on another major work from his Huangzhou period. This is his second rhapsody on Red Cliff, which he composed just a few months after the first rhapsody. There is little in the first piece to prepare us for the direction in which the second develops:

Later Rhapsody on Red Cliff

On the fifteenth of the tenth month of the same year (1082) I set out on foot from Snow Hall, intending to return to Lin'gao. Two guests accompanied me as we passed Yellow Dirt Hill. Dew had fallen and the trees had shed all their leaves. Our shadows lay on the ground, and we gazed up at the bright moon. Delighted by our surroundings, we sang back and forth to each other as we walked.

After some time, however, I heaved a sigh. "I have guests but no wine; and even if I had wine, I have no foods to go with it. The moon is bright and the wind fresh. Are we going to waste such a fine evening as this?"

One of my guests said, "Today at sunset I caught a fish in my net. It has a large mouth and tiny scales and looks just like a Song River bass. But where can we get wine to go with it?"

We returned to my house and consulted my wife. She said, "We do have one jug of wine I hid away, keeping it for just such an emergency."

Taking the wine and the fish, we went boating again below Red Cliff. The river made noise as it flowed, and the sheer cliff rose a thousand feet. The peak was towering and the moon tiny. The water level had fallen and rocks on the bottom were exposed. How many months had it been since my last visit? And yet the landscape seemed completely unfamiliar to me. So thinking, I picked up my robe and began to climb. I stepped over jutting rocks, pushed back undergrowth, squatted on tigers and leopards, and climbed along scaly dragons until I could pull myself up to perilous nests of the hawks and look down into the River Lord's palace in the depths.[103] My two guests were quite unable to follow me. All at once I let out a long, low whistle. The trees and grasses shook; the mountains sang out and the valleys answered; a wind arose and the water surged. I grew apprehensive and melancholy, humbled and fearful, and felt so cold that I knew I could not remain there long. I climbed down and got back into the boat. We rowed out into the middle of the river, then let the boat drift freely about and come to rest wherever it would. By that time it was nearly midnight and there was no sign of life anywhere around us. Just then a lone crane appeared, cutting across the river from the east. Its wings were as big as cartwheels, and it wore a black skirt and white robe. It let out a long, grating screech and swooped down over our boat before continuing westward.

A short while later the guests departed, and I, too, went home to sleep. I dreamed of a Taoist dressed in a fluttering feather robe who passed before Lin'gao.[104] He bowed to me and said, "Did you enjoy your outing to Red Cliff?" I asked his name, but he dropped his eyes and made no reply.

"So! Aha!" I said, "Now I understand. Last night it was you who flew screeching over my boat, wasn't it?"

The Taoist turned away with a smile, and just at that moment I woke up. I opened the door to look, but he was nowhere in sight.[105]

Traditionally, this latter rhapsody has not been greeted with nearly the enthusiasm readers have shown for the first rhapsody or the Red Cliff song. It is not so widely anthologized as the other two pieces, and has not generated nearly so many effusive remarks by literary critics. What comments have been made tend to be vague references to otherworldliness in the piece or attempts to explain its relationship to the first rhapsody. Yuan Hongdao says, "The second rhapsody carries within its narration of events boundless scenic description. As for the ending, even Zizhan [Su Shi] himself would not be able fully to explain its marvelousness." Wang Wenru comments, "The first rhapsody is substance (*shi*) while the second is emptiness (*xu*)." Jin Shengtan seems to say much the opposite, noting that the first piece conveys philosophical enlightenment while the second shows its application in the world (though he does not explain how).[106]

This shortage of critical appreciation and insight must stem from several factors. The first rhapsody speaks reassuringly to us, but the second is vaguely disquieting. The philosopher of the first piece, who was so magisterial and confident, now comes across as being both brash and unsure of himself, so that he finally becomes the butt of a Taoist's prank. Even when the author and his friends first arrive at Red Cliff in the second piece, what is stressed is how very different and unfamiliar the scene looks. The reader is being prepared for a different experience of the historical site from that presented in the first rhapsody. The crux of the problem is that throughout the remainder of the piece, unlike the opening, the speaker's motives and thoughts go largely unreported. We do not know why he begins his ascent up Red Cliff, why he abandons his friends almost without a thought, or what accounts either for his long whistle once he has gained the summit or his sudden feeling of fright. As for the concluding section of the piece, it is obvious enough that the Taoist who visits Su in his dream is one and the same as the crane that swoops over Su's boat after his descent from the cliff (cranes are conventionally associated with Taoists), but again it is not immediately clear why the bird behaves as it does or what the encounter is intended to signify.

The interpretation of the piece offered here is informed by the foregoing discussion of Su's ambivalence towards the longevity pursuits that he took up each time he was in exile. The philosophizing contained in the first rhapsody was not a final solution to the problems of mortality, insignificance, and failure that are treated therein, as we have seen in Su's song lyric on the Red Cliff theme. In the second rhapsody he attempts yet another solution, seeking, in effect, to step outside of time and mortality altogether. It is crucial to see that this piece is set against different issues in Su's thought from those in the first.

When Su jumps out of his boat and begins his climb up the cliffs, it is the eternity of the mountain peaks that he has in mind more than the fleeting glory of the naval battle below. We know that he sometimes explored these cliffs. He mentions having visited Xu Grotto there, named evidently after a recluse or immortal, and also refers several times to the hawks that nested on the cliffs' summit.[107] Su's climb is an impulsive but purposeful withdrawal into this landscape. It is entirely fitting that, intent as he is upon scrambling up the hill, Su leaves his companions behind. This is not a social outing or excursion. Su is off to experience the height as the immortals experience it, and this goal precludes accompaniment by his everyday acquaintances.

Once Su gains the summit, he lets out "a prolonged whistle" (*chang xiao*). This is a well-known method, associated with Taoist practices, by which the devotee prepares his own mind for the experience of nature and, simultaneously, attempts to elicit a sympathetic reaction. When Li Bo climbed to the top of Mount Tai, he emitted a prolonged whistle and immediately a clear wind began to blow toward him. Soon, immortal maidens from Heaven appeared and favored him with a cup of divine liquor.[108] Another scenario, one that Su Shi frequently describes, is that of nature responding in kind to the adept's noise, emitting its own sounds in a show of unity and harmony with the person (an idea often linked with *Zhuangzi*'s "pipes" of man, Earth, and Heaven.) In praising his friends, Su sometimes uses this motif to describe a man's extraordinary relation with nature and, by implication, his supreme cultivation: "One sigh from him causes the pipes of earth to sound; / The echoes reach far enough to hang from Heaven's belt."[109]

Su Shi's whistle from atop Red Cliff certainly gives rise to a response. But it is an overpowering, and for Su overwhelming, response. Immediately, Su scrambles back down the cliff and returns to his friends in the boat. Now, there is a tradition that one's level of accomplishment in this special kind of whistling reflects the degree of one's spiritual cultivation. A story about Ruan Ji (3rd c.) describes how he once went to visit a Taoist Realized Man and, upon finding the man squatting on the edge of a cliff, presented a speech to him on abstruse issues of Taoist learning. When Ruan Ji asked for a reply, the man stared fixedly ahead and did not utter a word. Juan, whose whistling was celebrated and was said to carry several hundred paces, then turned to the man and emitted a prolonged whistle. "After a long while the man finally laughed and said, 'Do it again.' Ruan Ji whistled a second time, but as his interest was now exhausted, he withdrew. He had returned about halfway down the ridge when he heard above him a shrillness like an orchestra of many instruments, while forests and valleys reechoed with the sound. Turning back to look, he discovered it was the whistling of the man he had just visited."[110] In Su Shi's case it seems to be the landscape itself (if it is not the Taoist, who subsequently appears, working through the landscape) that carries out the humiliation, reacting so violently that Su is intimidated. His own whistling, aside from appearing puny and pathetic by comparison, seems to have been an affront that called forth this angry response.

The encounter that follows, between the crane and the boat, reinforces the impression that Su's climb was an act of trespassing and of laying claim to something he was not entitled to. The crane, described ominously ("wings as big as cartwheels" is a phrase normally used to describe malevolent, monster birds), acts in a threatening manner, swooping down low to throw a fright into the boaters. Surely, this behavior cannot be unprovoked. The bird must be retaliating for what it took as Su's invasion and disruption of its rightful nesting area at the top of the cliff. But it is not only birds that occupy those mountain ridges. They share them with immortals and recluses. So when it becomes clear that the crane was, in fact, a transformation of the Taoist, who visits Su in his dream later, we are not much surprised. Su's scramble up the cliff was, after all, a bid to experience, however briefly, the immortal's oneness with nature, his aloofness from the world of men. The Taoist sees effrontery in this and determines to teach Su a lesson.

If the rhapsody, in its outline at least, were something that had been concocted and circulated by others to ridicule Su Shi for his amateur interest in immortality, it would not be so remarkable. But this degree of detachment from self and, indeed, self-parody is peculiar, even for Su Shi. As Su Shi began in Huangzhou to withdraw from the world of men—as he secluded himself in Snow Hall or experimented with various longevity techniques—he must have had misgivings about this new course. Years earlier Su had felt the tug of visions of transcendence and immortality; but he dismissed them upon a moment's reflection, settling for transcendent moments here in this world. Gazing up toward the mid-autumn moon, he had written:

不知天上宮闕	In those Heavenly palaces, I wonder,
今夕是何年	What year it is tonight?
我欲乘風歸去	I long to mount the wind and return there
又恐瓊樓玉宇	But fear those jeweled balconies and jade roofs
高處不勝寒	So high aloft will be too cold.
起舞弄清影	I stand up to dance with my clear shadow,
何似在人間	How could this be the world of men![111]

In Huangzhou, however, Su's interest in withdrawal and immortality was more than a passing fancy. He gives that interest free rein in the second Red Cliff rhapsody and lets it run full course. He follows it all the way to the top of the cliff, where his doubts—not so much about immortality as about his own suitability for the task—finally reassert themselves.

Poetry of Resentment and Defiance

Su Shi could not always contain his rancor against those who were responsible for his banishment, and sometimes he allowed it to show through in his poetry. Once he even broached the issue of self-delusion, an issue raised by the determination with which he kept asserting his contentment: "A forced song," he once acknowledged in Huizhou, "is not true happiness— / Why must we emulate Zhuang-zi?"[112] There were, then, times when he must have wearied of the obligation to appear carefree and allowed very different emotions to show at least dimly through his verse.

Irony is a useful rhetorical strategy for Su to employ, because it allows him to vent his frustrations even while preserving a thin pretense of innocence. "Do not object that Qiong and Lei are separated by clouds and sea; / Our ruler graciously allows us to gaze across at each other." He addressed these lines to his brother before setting sail for Hainan Island (Qiong). Ziyou had just had his own banishment made more severe and was to take up residence on the Leizhou Peninsula, jutting out southward toward that island. Ziyou would have understood that Su was not thinking of imperial graciousness at all. Similarly, in Huangzhou Su had "playfully" written this quatrain on the occasion of the first-month bathing ritual of his son, Dun:

人皆養子望聰明	In raising a son, 　　everyone hopes for cleverness.
我被聰明誤一生	But cleverness has plagued me 　　my whole life long.
惟願孩兒愚且魯	All I want for my boy 　　is to be doltish and dumb,
無災無難到公卿	Free from disaster and hardship, 　　he'll rise to be minister of state.[113]

It was too risky to write this way often. Most of Su's expressions of resentment are considerably more muted than this. In his Huangzhou exile, for example, Su Shi devoted several poems to the theme of flowering fruit trees whose beauty is isolated in wastelands or which are at the mercy of the elements and in danger of being stripped prematurely of their blossoms. The self-identification of the poet with this image of ill-fated purity is perhaps clearest in a long narrative poem about an encounter he has with a crab apple tree, which the locals, he says, "do not know to appreciate." The poem begins with several lines on the feminine loveliness of the crab apple (in the tradition of *yongwu* verse), but then abruptly becomes narrative as Su tells of how he happened unexpectedly upon the tree in all its splendor:

	先生食飽無一事	Having eaten, one day, and with nothing to do,
16	散步逍遙自捫腹	This gentleman strolled out, patting his belly as he went.
	不問人家與僧舍	Not asking if it was a private home or the residence of monks,
	拄杖敲門看修竹	I knocked at a gate to see the tall bamboo inside.
	忽逢絕艷照衰朽	All at once this matchless beauty shone upon my haggard form,
20	歎息無言揩病目	I sighed, speechless, and rubbed sore eyes.
	陋邦何處得此花	Where did a crude region obtain such blossoms as this?
	無乃好事移西蜀	Did some connoisseur transplant them from Western Shu?
	寸根千里不易致	To transport seedlings a thousand miles is no easy task,
24	銜子飛來定鴻鵠	It must have been a wild goose that flew here with the seed in its mouth.
	天涯流落俱可念	Cast adrift at the edge of the world, this we both have known;
	為飲一樽歌此曲	I drink a toast to you and sing this song.
	明朝酒醒還獨來	Tomorrow when I'm sober I'll come again alone—
26	雪落紛紛邢忍觸	But if your snowflakes are fluttering down how shall I bear the sight?[114]

We keep expecting the poem to turn back upon the poet himself and to develop into an explicit lament for his own removal to this crude and unfamiliar region. The poet, too, hailed from Western Shu, and line 24 alludes through a pun (*zi*: seed, son) to having been brought by his father out of Shu to central China.[115] But Su never allows the expected transition to happen. He keeps the poem focused on the tree, making sure that it retains its claim to our attention and not letting his own predicament eclipse it completely.

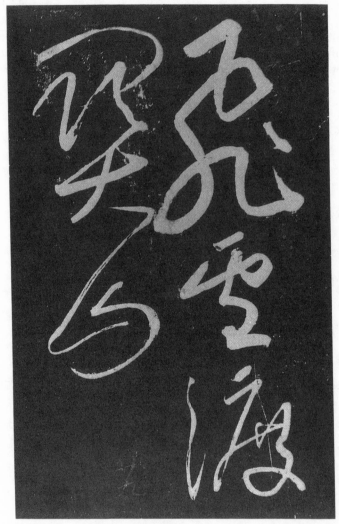

FIGURE 2. Su Shi, "Plum Blossoms," no. 1. In *Xilou Sutie*.

With such a poem in mind it will be easier to detect somewhat less obvious expressions of frustration in others of Su's poems on blossoms. The plum is more common in these than the crab apple. On his way to Huangzhou, Su wrote this quatrain about a flowering plum where he spent a night at Guan Mountain:

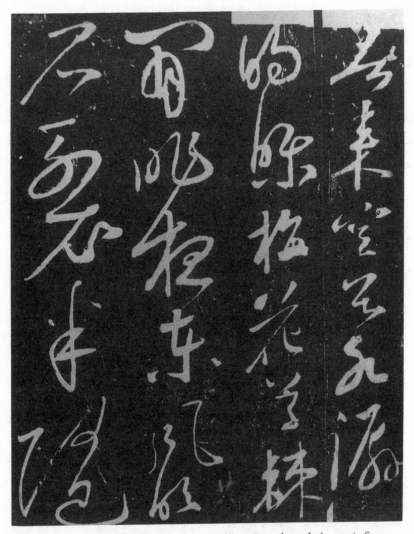

From *Zhongguo shufa quanji*, vol. 33 (Beijing: Rongbao zhai, 1991), fig. 47.

春來幽谷水潺潺	Spring comes to the hidden valley, the stream gurgles along,
的皪梅花草棘間	Bright plum blossoms stand amid wild grasses and brambles.
一夜東風吹石裂	As the east wind howls all night, splitting boulders apart,

半隨飛雪度關山   Half the blossoms follow the flying snow
                           across Guan Mountain.[116]

Since the poet, too, is in the process of crossing the mountain, proceeding into exile, the identification of the blossoms with him is unmistakable. (The second quatrain in the series ends with the line: "[The
blossoms] do not decline to accompany me distantly to Huangzhou.")
An inscription of this first quatrain written out by Su himself, preserved in a Southern Song period collection of rubbings, provides evidence of another kind of the depth of emotion contained in the poem.
The inscription, which is one of the few surviving examples of Su's
draft script calligraphy, begins in a small and tight "running draft"
style. But this gradually gives way to larger and bolder characters, and
ends with a remarkable flourish of "wild draft" in the line about the
wind-blown blossoms (see fig. 2). In this way did the calligrapher's
brush express the emotion implicit in the concluding poetic image of
beauty blown off into the wilds.

One year later, to the day, Su harked back to the sight: "This
day last year on the Guan Mountain road / Fine rain on plum blossoms truly broke my heart."[117] And when he was passing his third
spring in Huangzhou, on a rainy Cold Food Festival he drew an analogy between himself and another crab apple tree in blossom.

卧聞海棠花   From my bed I listen to the crab apple blossoms;
泥汚燕脂雪   Mud stains their rouge and snow.
暗中偷負去   In the darkness they are stolen away,
夜半真有力   Truly, this thief in the night is strong.
何殊病少年   The tree is like a sickly young man
病起頭已白   Who rises from his illness to find his hair gone
                   gray.[118]

It is worth noting that a copy of this and the second poem written on
the same occasion is preserved in another remarkable calligraphic inscription done by Su (see fig. 3). As befits the words of the poems and
their significance in Su's Huangzhou period, the calligraphy of these
Cold Food Festival poems is widely considered the most powerful and
expressive of any done by Su that survives.

Whatever form the reference takes, there is always some suggestion in these exile-period treatment of blossoms of the poet himself
growing old in a hostile environment, the poet assailed by adverse
forces, the poet dwelling unaccountably in deprived circumstances.
Su's poetic use of these fruit trees is not limited to conventional wist-

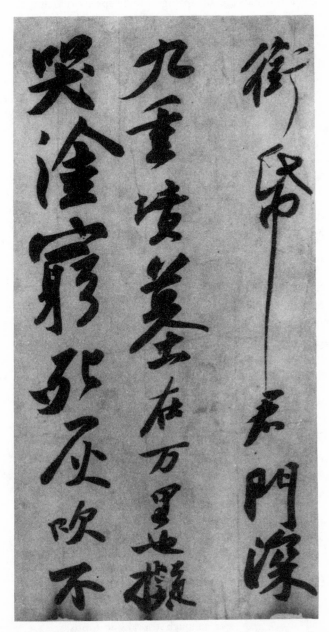

FIGURE 3. Su Shi, "Cold Food Festival," no. 2. Section of a handscroll. Collection of the National Palace Museum, Taiwan, Republic of China.

fulness over the passage of spring. He keeps associating them with specific circumstances that beg comparison with his personal situation. They become a vehicle for his peculiar kind of lament in exile, attenuated as it may be.

Having established this motif during his Huangzhou years, Su Shi reverts to it upon banishment to Huizhou. Now, the force is greater as the poet goes out of his way to remind the reader not only how unsuited the environment is, but also that he has suffered this deprivation before:

十一月二十六日
松風亭下梅花盛開

On the Twenty-Sixth Day of the
Eleventh Month
a Plum Tree Blossomed Fully
in Front of Pine Winds Pavilion

春風嶺上淮南村

On Spring Wind Peak
in a Huainan village

昔年梅花曾斷魂

Years ago plum blossoms
once broke my heart.

豈知流落復相見

How could I know, in my wanderings,
I would see them again

蠻風蜑雨愁黃昏

Where Man winds and Dan rains
grieve the sunset?

長條半落荔支浦

The long branches droop
half over the lichee bank,

臥樹獨秀桄榔園

The leaning trunk has unmatched grace
in the coir-palm garden.

豈惟幽光留夜色

Not only does their radiance in obscurity
detain the night,

直恐冷艷排冬溫

Their chill beauty, I suspect,
may dispel the winter's warmth.

松風亭下荆棘裏

Before Pine Winds Pavilion,
amid thorns and brambles,

兩株玉蕊明朝曉

The jade petals of the two trunks
will gleam in the bright dawn light.

海南仙雲嬌墮砌

Goddess clouds from the southern seas
waft gently down to my steps,

月下縞衣來扣門

In a white gown illumined by moonlight
she comes to knock at the door.

酒醒夢覺起繞樹

Awaking from drunken slumber,
I arise and encircle the tree;

妙意有在終無言

Its marvelous intent is clear,
though it speaks no words;

先生獨飲勿歎息

"Sir, though you drink alone
do not sigh:

幸有落月窺清樽　　　By good fortune the setting moon
　　　　　　　　　　　peeks into your clear cup."[119]

The injunction at the end of this poem leads to a related point. Caught as he is in exile, still feeling that he, like the plum blossoms, has no business in such a rank and unfamiliar place, the poet directs himself not to be sad and to appreciate what there is that is attractive in the scene (the moon shining on his wine cup). At this moment we can almost hear the poet prepping himself, preparing to utter one of his famous claims that he is, after all, a native of this place, that he has never so enjoyed a trip, that in fact he has discovered a Penglai. In much of Su Shi's exile poetry, hints of resentment and assertions of contentment appear side by side. This is possible because the two are really complementary rather than contradictory. They may be understood as two aspects of the same determination not to allow the spirit to be crushed. The insistent quality of Su's poetic emulation of Tao Qian—traceable to the great disparity between their circumstances—was discussed above. But in addition to consolation and self-encouragement, there is also in each assertion of pleasure found in banishment an element of defiance, however controlled and quiet it may be.

Two of Su's Lingnan poems and a story that concerns them will help to illustrate the point. In Huizhou in 1096 Su composed the following quatrain and entitled it "Written with an Unrestrained Brush" (*zongbi*):

白頭蕭散滿霜風　　　My white hair, wispy and tangled,
　　　　　　　　　　　is filled with frosty wind;
小閣藤牀寄病容　　　To a rattan bed in a small dwelling
　　　　　　　　　　　I entrust my sickly frame.
報道先生春睡美　　　When he is told the gentleman's
　　　　　　　　　　　spring slumber is sweet,
道人輕打五更鐘　　　The monk strikes but lightly
　　　　　　　　　　　the dawn temple bell.[120]

Tradition has it that this poem made its way back to the capital, where it was eventually recited in front of the grand councilor, Zhang Dun. When Zhang heard the last two lines he was furious and remarked, "So Su Shi is still enjoying himself!" It was then that Zhang decided to make Su's banishment even more severe and had him sent across the sea to Hainan.

The reliability of the story is open to question. It appears in twelfth-century texts,[121] but that does not prove that the incident

actually happened or, even if it did, that this particular poem was solely responsible for Su's reassignment. The historicity of the anecdote
aside, there is good reason to suspect that Su Shi himself heard it in the
ensuing years. He was in constant correspondence with friends in all
parts of the empire, and also had visitors from the mainland. In his
third year on the island he wrote three more quatrains to the same
title, a title he had never used previously. (One can imagine Su
Che's reaction when he learned that his brother was writing more
"Unrestrained Brush" poems.) The first of them reads:

寂寂東坡一病翁	Solitary East Slope is a sickly old man,
白鬚蕭散滿霜風	His white whiskers, wispy and tangled, are filled with frosty wind.
小兒誤喜朱顏在	My young son is pleased to see my ruddy complexion remains.
一笑那知是酒紅	I smile—how would he know it's red from drinking?[122]

The second line is virtually identical to the opening line of the 1096
quatrain (and there is a textual variant, "hair" for "whiskers" that
makes it identical). Such a borrowing from his own poetry, without
some explanatory note or identification, is extremely rare in Su's corpus. One explanation is that Su had indeed heard the story of Zhang
Dun's anger and responded by echoing the very poem responsible for
his removal. It was a gesture of defiance, Su indicating that he would
not be intimidated into silence. This is the interpretation of the odd
borrowing that some modern scholars have proposed, and it is a
plausible one.[123]

Particularly during his Lingnan years, Su Shi kept finding ways
in his poetry to allude to his long history of struggles with the Court
and to voice his discontent. Some pieces treat generalized issues of
loyalty and service. In a poem on the set theme of the "three dutiful
ministers" of ancient times who heeded the bidding of their lord, Duke
Mu of Qin, and agreed to be buried alive with him, Su distinguishes
between loyalty to a person and a higher loyalty to the best interests of
the realm.

我豈犬馬哉	Am I a dog or horse,
從君求蓋帷	Hoping only for a blanket when I die?
殺身固有道	There is a Way in giving one's life:
大節要不虧	The highest principles must not succumb.
君為社稷死	If my lord dies for the altars of state,

我則同其歸	I shall follow him to the grave.
顧命有治亂	But commands may be correct or confused,
臣子得從違	A minister may follow or disobey.[124]

Su is carving out for himself a protected space in which the validity of dissent and disobedience is recognized. The space should not be found solely on an island in the southern seas. Not only does this poem contradict the piece by Tao Qian it "matches," which praises the unfortunate ministers for their dutifulness, it also goes directly against a treatment of the same theme Su himself had written early on in his career.[125]

More often, Su broaches his sense of the injustice done to him in more personal terms. He calls himself a Yu Fan, that is, a minister who was slandered and wrongfully banished to the south, and who never received the pardon he deserved.[126] He also manages to produce poems that call attention to his past and to the aimlessness and disorientation he feels where he is now:

縱筆其二	*Written with an Unrestrained Brush, No. 2*
父老爭看烏角巾	Peasants vie for a glimpse of my raven cornered cap,
應緣曾現宰官身	It was fated once to appear upon the person of a minister of state.
溪邊古路三叉口	On an old road beside a stream where three ways converge
獨立斜陽數過人	I stand alone in the sunset counting passersby.[127]

被酒獨行遍至子雲 威徽先覺四黎之舍	*I Go Out Alone after Drinking and Call at All Four Dwellings of Lis, Ziyun, Wei, Hui, and Xianjue*
半醒半醉問諸黎	Half sober, half drunk, I look for the several Lis.
行刺藤梢步步迷	Bamboo spikes, wisteria twigs— more lost with every step.
但尋牛矢覓歸路	I can only follow the ox turds to find my way back.
家在牛欄西復西	My home is west of the ox pen and further west again.[128]

This last poem has been criticized by the Qing scholar Ji Yun for the crudity in its third line.[129] But Su Shi is deliberately flouting such aesthetic standards as Ji Yun would apply, in order to emphasize the crudeness of his surroundings. (Su has already called attention in his title to the fact that his friends are members of the Hainan ethnic group, the Li.)

The analysis offered above suggests at least one reason Su Shi never stopped writing poetry, despite the advice—even insistence—of his family and friends. Once poetry became for him not only a source of consolation, giving proof that he really could find contentment in obscurity, but also a way of showing that his spirit and outrage over what had befallen him were undiminished, he had to keep writing. To stop would have been tacitly to admit either that he no longer saw any injustice or that he no longer dared to call attention to it. This particular motive for writing poetry bears some resemblance to the reasons Su had for returning to his commentaries on the classics whenever he was sent into exile. For all their obvious differences, and despite the ways in which both transcend the politics of the day, both types of writing are informed at one level by Su's resolve to keep answering back against the persons and policies that sent him into exile.

CHAPTER NINE

Calligraphy and Painting

Su Shi was the first Song literatus known for his interest and accomplishments in the arts of the brush in addition to his literary work. In calligraphy he is known as one of the four masters of the Northern Song (the others are Cai Xiang and Su's friends, Huang Tingjian and Mi Fu). Samples of his brushwork, many of which survive as rubbings or fragmentary manuscripts, have always been among the most highly prized examples of that art throughout East Asia. The fate of Su Shi's paintings has been far less fortunate. Few if any of them are extant. What is amply documented, however, both in Su's own writings about painting and in contemporary records, is that Su was at the center of a movement, joined by many late-eleventh-century literati, that redefined the meaning of that art and enhanced its prestige. It was Su Shi and other men closely associated with him who formulated the principles of what came to be known as *wenren hua* (literati or amateur painting), which altered forever the history of painting in China.

The examination of Su Shi's involvement with these arts of the brush undertaken here will focus on his contributions to theory and criticism rather than his practice as a calligrapher or painter.[1] The voluminousness of Su's writings on the subject is worth mentioning at the outset. Any doubts about the depth of Su's interest in these arts, or his eagerness to promote a new image of them, will be quickly dispelled by a glance at the sheer bulk of his writings on the subjects. These writings, which consist of hundreds of poems, essays, colophons (*tiba*), and appreciations (*can*), are scattered through Su's collected works. When they are extracted from their normal locations and gathered together (as they have been in a recent publication),[2] it becomes evident that Su Shi wrote far more not only than had any previous Song scholar, but than even most of the major theorists and critics of earlier periods. Su's productivity alone would have secured him some place in the history of criticism of these arts, even if his ideas had not been innovative.

I have described elsewhere the interest that scholars of the generation preceding Su Shi's showed in calligraphy, as well as the ways their attitudes diverged from those of Tang calligraphy critics, and will briefly summarize that account here.[3] Dissatisfaction with current standards in calligraphy had gradually led, by mid century, to the coalescence of a reform movement that sought to alter both how calligraphy was practiced and how it was perceived. The scholars who expressed this desire for change were generally associated both with the political reform movement of the 1040s, led by Fan Zhongyan, and the related "ancient-style prose" (*guwen*) revival spearheaded by Ouyang Xiu. It happened that Ouyang was also the most prolific calligraphy critic of his generation (as Su would become of his). Ouyang had assembled a personal collection of upwards of a thousand ink rubbings of ancient inscriptions, which he called *Collection of Antiquities*, and wrote notices on the provenance and contents of some four hundred of them. His notices, which eventually circulated under the same name, are generally regarded as the beginnings of epigraphy in China. Many of them are entirely concerned with historiographical issues: Ouyang calls attention to the use that neglected inscriptions have in supplementing or correcting the documentary historical record. But he also frequently comments on the calligraphic style of the inscriptions, so that his notices constitute a convenient repository of *guwen* views on calligraphy.

Two contemporary issues inform Ouyang's remarks about the calligraphy of the inscriptions. The first is the prevailing opinion that to cultivate a comely hand one did not need to look beyond the example of just a small number of earlier calligraphers, especially those of the two Jin-dynasty calligraphers, Wang Xizhi and his son Wang Xianzhi. This way of thinking about calligraphy had been encouraged by the Song imperial house, which in 992 had commissioned the compilation of an anthology of model calligraphic inscriptions (*fatie*) from centuries past. Fully 50 percent of the anthology, the *Chunhua Pavilion Calligraphy Models* (*Chunhua ge fatie*), is devoted to the Two Wangs. Through the eleventh century, copies of the anthology

were presented by the emperor to newly promoted officials; and by
Ouyang's time, pirated copies of the work had begun to circulate
widely. Consequently, what might be called the copybook approach to
calligraphy became commonplace. Scholars sought only to duplicate
one or another of the hallowed styles. Ouyang would never have criticized the Two Wangs, for he recognized the greatness of their achievement. But he had harsh words for his own contemporaries who were
content merely to emulate them. Ouyang called these men "slavish"
and pointed out that their painstaking imitations lost all the freshness
and spontaneity of their models.[4] He also observed that the Two
Wangs themselves had not, after all, relied upon models.

The second, and related, influence upon Ouyang's views was
the cluster of beliefs associated with his promotion of *guwen* and, in a
broader sense, with the aims of the reform movement in politics and
thought. *Guwen* advocates maintained that what was important about
writing was that it convey the values of the Way of the Confucian
sages, not that its prosody be euphonic or its diction ornate. Likewise,
writings transmitted from earlier centuries were valuable insofar as
they embodied the moral principles of their authors. Ultimately, what
the latterday reader "gets" from earlier writings should be exposure to
or immersion in the principles that guided the lives of these upright
men. The modern reader who merely savors the literary elegance of
earlier writings is going about his studies incorrectly.

It did not prove difficult for Ouyang and his colleagues to ex-
tend this manner of thinking to calligraphy. To be sure, calligraphy
occupied a small place in the program the *guwen* scholars set for themselves. But when they did consider it, they treated it much as they
treated writing. It would have been inappropriate to argue that the
content of an inscription was more important than the beauty of its
calligraphy: that would be to move outside of the field of calligraphy
altogether and to disregard the fact that the calligrapher often was not
the author of his inscription. Instead, in their appreciations of surviving inscriptions, *guwen* scholars emphasized qualities they discerned in
the calligraphy that could be traced back to the personality of the calligrapher. Inscriptions were praised for exuding qualities of "forcefulness" and "integrity," or criticized for appearing to be "ingratiating" or
"clever."

Particular attention was given to the Tang statesman Yan
Zhenqing, whose squarish characters in the *kaishu* script and unmodu-
lated brushstrokes were seen as a perfect counterpart to the forthright
and heroic conduct he had shown in office, which led him first to resist
the advance of the rebel armies of An Lushan and eventually to be

martyred at the hands of the would-be usurper, Li Xilie. Ouyang possessed more rubbings of Yan Zhenqing's work, and that of Yan's follower, Liu Gongquan, than he did of any other calligrapher. Ouyang wrote effusively about Yan's style, and linked it frequently to Yan's conduct: "Yan's loyalty and integrity shone as brightly as the sun or moon. In his actions he was reverent, severe, steadfast, and forceful, just like his calligraphy."[5] Ouyang was not the only mid-eleventh-century statesman to show enthusiasm for Yan Zhenqing's brushwork. Han Qi expressed his admiration for it and encouraged others to study it; Cai Xiang interpreted it in his own imitations; and Song Minqiu, aided by Liu Chang, compiled a collection of Yan's surviving works.[6] In a real sense, the calligraphic style of Yan became the signature for this generation of intellectual and political reformers, embodying as it did for them the moral rectitude they sought to spread through the realm.

The distinctive appearance of Yan's work, and Liu Gongquan's after him, derived from several decisions concerning the arrangement and composition of the characters, the manipulation of the brush, and brush grip. In Yan's style the vertical axis of the characters is kept more or less at right angles to the horizontal axis, with a minimum of slanting toward the right. The elements of each character are also evenly spaced within an imaginary square, rather than more loosely spaced on the right than on the left, as was conventional in earlier styles ("left tight, right loose"). During execution the tip of the brush is turned under or "concealed." This makes the ends of the strokes rounded rather than pointed or angular as when the brush tip is exposed. Finally, the brush itself was kept "upright" or perpendicular to the page, rather than "slanted" or tilted towards the writer. This minimizes the modulation and variation of the line.[7]

The weightiness and predictability of Yan's calligraphic style, coupled with what was known of his illustrious behavior, held immense appeal for the Northern Song *guwen* scholars. Suspicious as they were of shallow beauty and aestheticism, these scholars saw Yan's calligraphy as the embodiment of personality traits to which they themselves aspired and which they believed their realm required if it was to avoid the disasters that befell the late Tang. They also saw Yan's style as a welcome alternative to that of the Two Wangs. Yan's "upright" characters, signs of his forthrightness, contrasted with the elegance, modulation, and sweep of the Wangs. Especially because the Wangs' style was being promoted by the Court, it was always suspect of insincerity. Its very beauty and grace meant that it might easily degenerate into mere cleverness or ornament: the ingratiating appearance that sought to hide ignoble intent.

Ouyang and others in his circle established what was really a new way of thinking about the calligraphic tradition. It was no longer just aesthetically appealing brushwork that could be viewed with appreciation and adopted as a stylistic model for one's own writing. Instead, it became part of the legacy of "the ancients." Collecting, connoisseurship, and even practice took on deeper meaning than either aesthetic enjoyment or the practical need to cultivate a comely hand could account for. The collector showed through his activity that he was devoted to antiquity (*haogu*), and could speak as he practiced with his own brush of communing with the spirits of the ancients.

For all that he wrote about calligraphy and dabbled in practicing it, Ouyang Xiu was not known in his own day or thereafter as a great calligrapher. Su Shi was, and the difference is historically significant in tracing the advancement of the art among eleventh-century literati. Ouyang Xiu promoted interest in calligraphy by writing about it. Su Shi went a step further, developing his interest into active mastery. The difference between Ouyang and Su in this regard is also characteristic of each man's generation. Although the *guwen* literati of Ouyang's time gave unprecedented attention to calligraphy, some degree of specialization remained, some gap between the fields of letters and calligraphy. The most prestigious calligrapher of Ouyang's age, Cai Xiang, was not known for his poetry or prose. Likewise, the famous poets, Ouyang and Mei Yaochen, were not known as calligraphers. In the next generation, however, with Su Shi and his admirer Huang Tingjian after him, this gap was completely, if not permanently, closed.

Su Shi was, of course, well aware of his accomplishment as a calligrapher. He knew how eagerly samples of his brushwork were sought out, though he professed not to understand why.[8] He must also have realized how unusual it was for a poet to be so accomplished in calligraphy. Huang Tingjian, for one, makes this point explicitly about Su. Literary men, he notes, have never been celebrated for their calligraphic skills, and that is one reason why Su Shi's brushwork is so much in demand.[9] Su Shi also makes claims about his ability both as a calligrapher and a critic that Ouyang Xiu never would have made. He boasts of the originality of his calligraphic style, comparing it to the innovations of Yan Zhenqing and, speaking as a critic, claims that "no one understands calligraphy as well as I do."[10]

Su Shi's writings about calligraphy are in three forms: prose essays (most of them written to commemorate friends' collections of calligraphy), poems, and colophons. The colophons are by far the most numerous. A late-Ming edition of Su's works contains 119 of his colophons on calligraphy drawn from various earlier sources (some known to us now only by title).[11] It was only in the Northern Song that literati began to produce large numbers of colophons on calligraphy, painting, and poetry. It must be no accident that three of the most prolific writers in this form, Su Shi, Huang Tingjian, and Mi Fu, were themselves great calligraphers. One reason they wrote so many colophons is that they were asked so often—their brushwork being in high demand. Typically, these colophons would be collected together and printed posthumously. Su Shi's colophons on calligraphy are the most important single source for his views on calligraphy. However, they are an extremely uneven and, at times, inconsistent source. The tone, focus, and values vary widely depending on the occasion and inscription involved. Certain persistent concerns and values may be extracted from these writings. Such analysis tends, however, to over-emphasize the coherence of Su's views and to underrepresent the impression the colophons give that in them Su is trying to work out his views on the subject. Su never wrote a systematic treatise on calligraphy, as so many pre-Song critics had done. He must have been more comfortable with the role of the occasional commentator on particular works than with that of the formal theorist or specialized critic.

Broadening *Guwen* Views on Calligraphy

In many of his statements about calligraphy Su Shi remains true to the values promoted by Ouyang and his generation of *guwen* scholars. But there is also a discernible shift in the overall drift of Su's remarks towards an understanding of calligraphy that is broader, more flexible, and more ambitious in its claims both for his own accomplishment as a calligrapher and for the meaning of the art. We see a simple instance of this greater breadth in Su's insistence that true accomplishment in the art involves mastery of all the script types (clerical, regular, running, and draft, if not the seal scripts and flying white as well). This had not been an important theme in Ouyang's remarks on calligraphy. But it becomes one with Su, who maintains that one cannot really be good at the cursive scripts (running, draft) unless the non-cursive, regular style is mastered first.[12] Su is suspicious of specialization, especially in the cursive scripts, where the liberties of the form might mask lack of real skill. But he also has a principle in mind. Doctors who treat only one kind of malady (or one kind of patient), and painters who paint only one subject are inferior members of their profession. A person who has truly grasped the Pattern (*li*) or meaning (*yi*) of calligraphy will be good at any script type.[13]

Su extends this broadened perspective on the art to a number of other issues, altering the *guwen* tenets he has inherited. On the matter of calligraphy and personality, he concurs in many colophons that brushwork does reflect the moral nature of the calligrapher. He also frequently affirms the related principles that a man's calligraphy ought not to be evaluated independently of his deeds and that the calligraphy of a good man deserves to be valued even if the brushwork is not particularly skillful.[14] The moral worth of the person is the uppermost consideration. Still, there are occasions on which Su Shi raises some questions concerning aspects of these beliefs. In the two colophons below, Su wonders about the basis of judgments that are made of calligraphy. Is it really the brushwork itself that conveys admirable (or objectionable) personality traits, or is it that our prior knowledge and opinion of the man affects our perception of his brushwork? To raise the question, Su refers in both notices to an ancient *Han Feizi* story (actually, it is in *Liezi*) about a man who lost his axe and suspected that the boy next door had stolen it.[15] He observed the boy and saw in everything about him—his gait, his speech, his facial expressions—signs that he was the thief. Soon afterwards, the man discovered the axe in his own garden. Thereafter, he observed the boy again and found that "nothing in his behavior or manner suggested that he would steal an axe."

> Second Preceptor Liu's [Liu Gongquan's] calligraphy derives from that of Yan [Zhenqing], and yet he was able to develop a novel style. "One character is worth a hundred pieces of gold"; these are not empty words.[16] His saying, "If the heart is upright, the brush will be upright," is not merely a clever admonition.[17] It is so in the nature of things. The mean-minded men of the world may write characters skillfully, but in the end the spirit and feeling of their calligraphy has a fawning and obsequious manner. I do not know if one's perception that this is so follows upon how one thinks about the calligrapher, as in the case of Hanzi's so-called axe thief, or whether the manner is really there in the calligraphy. However, if you have someone else look at the calligraphy and he also despises it, then there is no doubt about the character of the calligrapher.[18]

> If from examining a person's calligraphy one can tell what kind of man he is, then the character of superior men and mean-minded men must both be reflected in their calligraphy. This would appear to be incorrect. To select people on the basis of their face is considered improper—how much worse, then, to do so on the basis of their calligraphy! Whenever I

look at Master Yan's calligraphy, I invariably think of his manner and bearing. It's not that I merely learn what kind of man he was. It is as if I see him—so awe-inspiring!—berating Lu Qi and denouncing Xilie.[19] Why? The principle is no different from Han Fei's argument about the man who "stole the axe." And yet, each person's calligraphy conveys, quite apart from its skill or clumsiness, a certain drift, and it is said that it also shows whether the calligrapher was wicked or upright.[20]

As doubtful as Su is in these passages about the proposition that calligraphy can, all by itself, reveal a man's character, the proposition is obviously still attractive to him, and he is reluctant to relinquish it entirely. Thus both passages return to a restatement of it in their conclusion.

Su has introduced an important modification here to the idea that calligraphy reveals the man, or at least that he is working towards an important and useful refinement of the idea. He contrasts *qi weiren* (the way a person acts or his nature as shown through his actions) with something more vague and elusive, which he characterizes as his "spirit and feeling" (*shenqing*), "his manner and bearing" (*fengcai*), and his "drift" or "flavor" (*qu*). The modification has two advantages. First, it allows Su to tone down the claim about revelation without abandoning it altogether. All that calligraphy reveals is a certain feeling or "flavor." Second, it deemphasizes the connection between calligraphic style and deeds while it strengthens the connection between calligraphic style and the "style" of the man.

This prepares the way for a mode of appreciation—one that is still essentially moralistic—of a wide range of ancient calligraphers who had no great deeds to their credit. Here is what Su Shi says about Wang Xianzhi: "He did not have a particularly distinguished career. But when Xie An hoped he would write out the name of a palace, Xie never dared to ask him directly. The loftiness of Wang's spirit and integrity was certainly worthy of admiration. This single scroll [of his calligraphy] is especially endearing."[21] Su Shi can find greatness only in something Wang Xianzhi indirectly declined to do. Yet it is enough to confirm the impression that Su Shi seems already to have formed, on the basis of Wang's calligraphy, that he was a man worthy of admiration. There is a telling shift in attitudes here. Ouyang Xiu was apt to imagine, upon encountering an attractive rubbing of some obscure person's calligraphy, what a meritorious man the writer must have been. ("I imagine that Chuntuo must have been a scholar of repute in his day, but today no one remembers him.")[22] Su Shi was more likely to think only of the man's elevated bearing or "flavor," and leave speculations about accomplishments and renown aside.

Corresponding to this broader understanding of how calligraphy might reflect or embody the nature of the calligrapher, Su Shi adopted a more eclectic taste for earlier styles. Ouyang Xiu certainly held the Two Wangs in esteem: he never termed theirs "an ingratiating style," as Han Yu had done.[23] Still, Ouyang looked with disfavor upon styles said to derive from the Two Wangs', in which he thought innovative elegance gave way to affected beauty. He wrote the following notice on what purported to be a Southern Dynasties inscription, rejecting the attribution because he considered its brushwork too powerful to have been done during that degenerate age: "The mores of scholars of the Southern Dynasties were lowly and unmanly. Those who were skilled at calligraphy all thought the finest style was one of slender intensity and unblemished gracefulness. No one wrote with such imposing and wide brushstrokes as seen here. This makes it all the more likely that this stele comes from a later age."[24]

Su Shi makes more of an effort to accept a variety of approaches. In a poetic account of calligraphic history, he takes issue explicitly with Du Fu for having said that only one type of stroke "partakes of the daimonic." Su's criticism follows upon lines in which Su characterizes several historically famous styles, emphasizing their distinctiveness: the characters in Wang Xizhi's "Orchid Pavilion Preface" have the appearance of soaring dragons; Yan Zhenqing's brushstrokes are bones barely covered with skin, like the hawk in autumn; the writing of Xu Hao is graceful and hides all sharp corners; Li Si's style embodies ancient rules and has recently been duplicated by Li Yangbing. Su is referring in these lines not only to different styles but to different script types as well (e.g., cursive, regular, seal). Next, Su considers Du Fu's pronouncement, contained in his celebration of the seal script of Cai Yong:

杜陵評書貴瘦硬	In calligraphy Duling valued only the thin and taut,
此論未公吾不憑	His view is an unfair one I do not accept.
短長肥瘦各有態	Short, tall, fleshy, thin— each has its appeal,
玉環飛燕誰敢憎	Jade Bracelet and Flying Swallow, who could dislike either of them?[25]

Jade Bracelet is Yang Guifei, Emperor Xuanzong's portly concubine. Flying Swallow, said to have been slender, served Chengdi of the Han. It required some boldness on Su's part to contradict so openly the opinion of the great Tang poet. Su's assertion in these lines seems to have gained some notoriety among his friends.[26]

In another piece, Su suggests that even a single style ought to be flexible enough to encompass a range of stroke types and nuances:

貌妍容有矉	A charming face can tolerate a frown,
璧美何妨橢	What harm if a jade disk is slightly oblong?
端莊雜流麗	The sturdy may admit some gracefulness,
剛健含婀娜	The resolute may yet be lithesome.[27]

Su's openness to a variety of styles has an analogue in his view on brush grip and composition. Yan Zhenqing and his followers were, as mentioned above, associated with the "upright brush" technique. Owing in part to a famous quip, this method had come to be thought of as more than just a technical option. Emperor Muzong of the Tang had once asked Liu Gongquan the secret of his calligraphic skill. Liu, who was not pleased by the question and sought to direct the emperor's attention back to matters of statecraft, which he had been neglecting, replied, "If your heart is upright (correct) then your brush will be upright (correct)." Liu was trying to get the emperor to concern himself with matters other than brush grip, but ever after calligraphers who were moralistically inclined hastened to adopt the "upright brush" (zhengbi) method lest it be said that their hearts were less than upright. In the generation before Su's, Ouyang Xiu, Cai Xiang, and Han Qi had all followed suit.

As we have seen above (in Su's colophon on Liu Gongquan's calligraphy), Su Shi likewise could affirm the soundness of this method. Naturally, he is most apt to do so when writing, as there, about the connection between personality and calligraphy. But elsewhere he expresses reservations about sticking solely to this technique and makes arguments, once again, for variation.

吾聞古書法	Calligraphy of old, I have heard, preferred
守駿莫如跛	Being limp to always the perfect steed.
世俗筆苦驕	Everyone strives to make his brushwork imposing,
衆中强鬼駊	The crowd vying to be massive and towering.
鍾張忽已遠	Zhong and Zhang are distantly abandoned,
此語與時左	But my views are contrary to the times.[28]

Here, it is not clear whether bo, "limp" (or possibly "slanted"), refers to the vertical axis of the characters or to the position of the writing brush. But Su's lines on the prevailing fashion certainly call to mind the imposing, four-square kaishu that became the hallmark of the *guwen* generation, which utilized Liu Gongquan's upright brush. Su identifies himself, by contrast, with even more ancient styles (and more ancient than the Two Wangs as well): those of the Zhong Yao (151–230) and Zhang Zhi (Later Han), masters of regular, *bafen*, and cursive scripts.

There is no question about the import of another passage by Su on brush technique:

> In holding the brush there is no set method, the important thing is to make it "empty" but "substantial." Ouyang Wenzhonggong told me, "You should make the fingers move without the wrist's knowing it." This advice is superb. When the brush is in motion, going left and right and forward and backward, some slanting cannot be avoided. But when it comes to rest it should be as straight up and down as a rope with a weight on it. That is what is meant by the "upright brush." Liu Chengxuan's [Gongquan's] advice was most correct.[29]

Here, Su provides his own novel interpretation of the dictum about brush grip, and he even finds a way of indirectly associating Ouyang Xiu with his understanding of it.

In these many ways, whether through his remarks on the connection between calligraphic style and the "style" of the man, on the virtues of a variety of styles (or even complex, synthesizing styles), and on brush technique, Su Shi softens the views of Ouyang and other members of the preceding generation. Ouyang and his circle were struggling to establish a new standard that was to be an alternative to the Court-sponsored style. Perhaps in part because they had already succeeded, and in part because his inclinations were simply different, Su Shi struck off on his own. In the remarks of his considered thus far, he seems reluctant to recognize the supremacy of any standard. Even on the technical matter of brush grip, what he says is that there is "no set method." This contrasts nicely with Ouyang, who sees in his discovery that even brush grip "has its method" (*youfa*) further support for the generalization he wants to make that "there is a method for all things."[30]

It is easy to see how Su Shi's modifications of his mentor's views could support the cultivation, in practice, of greater versatility, greater openness to influences from a range of historical styles, and, consequently, a more varied and idiosyncratic result. That is precisely what extant examples of Su Shi's calligraphy show, which helps to explain their acclaim. Su's brushwork, for example, does indeed show signs of combining the disputed "slanted brush" with its more reputable counterpart. Huang Tingjian admitted as much, and sought to defend Su from scholars who could not accept such flexibility.[31] It has recently been argued by Amy McNair that even when Su Shi once "copied" Yan Zhenqing's famous *Letter on the Controversy over Seating Protocol*, the style he adapted was actually that of an unorthodox (and perhaps spurious) sample of Yan's work, a piece marked by dramatic alterations of character size, the mixture of cursive with running script forms, and a highly expressive use of the slanted brush and exposed tip.[32] This was the "Yan Zhenqing" that Su admired most, despite his many bows to the opinions of the elder *guwen* advocates.

Expressing New Meaning

The modifications discussed above that Su introduced culminated in his interest in stylistic innovation. In an art dominated by ancient models and the tradition of imitating them, Su Shi stressed the virtue of novelty. "My own calligraphy," he observed, "may not be very good, but it expresses new meaning and does not follow in the footsteps of the ancients. That is a source of pride to me."[33] Few calligraphers had ever spoken so openly of the uniqueness of their work. Su's understanding of the precise nature of his newness and what it entailed warrants some attention here.

The phrase that Su normally uses to refer to stylistic innovation is, as above, "expressing new meaning" (*chu xinyi*). (This is more commonly used by Su than the more conventional *zicheng yijia*, which also occurs.)[34] The term *yi* is a complex one and the rendering "meaning" is not entirely satisfactory. Obviously, the *yi* referred to is not the semantic meaning of the words in the calligraphic inscription, for more often than not those words are not the calligrapher's own. His act of copying out a standard passage from a classic or sutra may be said to contain as much of his *yi* as any piece that he himself had composed. *Yi* resides first within the heart/mind of the calligrapher. It is the "meaning" or "intent" that he possesses before ever picking up the brush, and it clearly is not a kind of "meaning" or "idea" that is restricted to what can be put into discursive language. It is his artistic intent or aesthetic mood, which the finished inscription embodies. But we must take care not to describe it with words that connote emotion, for one of the most significant features of *yi* is how emotively neutral the term is. There is a telling contrast here with earlier accounts of calligraphic expression. In earlier, and especially Tang, treatises, it was common to speak of calligraphy as an art that expressed emotions (*qing*), and strong ones at that.[35] But Su Shi and his colleagues prefer to posit this other kind of inspiration, which, indescribable as it may be, is intimately linked to character and personality. (Su Shi's insistence that the passionless monk could still create marvelous calligraphy will be recalled.) The modifying term in the phrase is also significant. One can speak of giving expression to "strong emotions" (*qiangqing*), but not to "new" ones. The Song preference, that is, for *yi* also encourages a focus upon the uniqueness of what is being expressed, its individuality.

As mentioned above, Su Shi's innovations did not go unnoticed or uncriticized. A lengthy defense that Huang Tingjian wrote on Su's behalf is worth quoting here for the issues it raises:

Colophon on East Slope's Water and Land Encomium

This calligraphy by East Slope is rounded, forceful, and fully realized. The so-called angry lion that breaks through rock and thirsty horse that gallops to the stream are probably not to be found in Kuaiji's brush after all;[36] rather they are in East Slope's hand. These several dozen columns also combine all the fine points of Kuaiji's inscription on filial son Dong and his Yu Temple poem.

Many scholars today criticize East Slope's brushwork for not conforming to ancient standards. But such people do not understand how those standards came to be. Du Zhou said, "Where did the three-foot tablets [which proclaimed the laws] come from? What former kings considered right they made into regulations, and what later kings considered right they made into ordinances."[37] Once I made the same argument about calligraphy, and East Slope himself was overcome with admiration. Formerly, Liu Zihou and Liu Yuxi criticized Han Tuizhi's inscription on pacifying Huaixi. At the time, most who heard and discussed their criticism considered it valid, but how does it look today?[38]

Some say that East Slope's *ge* [right-slanting] strokes show defective brushwork and others say that since he rests his wrist on the paper and lets his brush lean over, the left side of his characters is graceful but the right side is withered. This is to look at a leopard through a tube and fail to see the complete form.[39] Don't they know that when Xi Shi pounded herself on the breast and scowled, even in her imperfect condition she was beautiful? People today do not know how to cherish and respect East Slope's calligraphy. A hundred years hence a just evaluation will emerge, but I regret that those who resemble Feng Deyi will not live long enough to witness it.[40] My own calligraphy is not skillful, but I am fond of discussing calligraphy. Although I cannot bring myself to act like the examination candidates, who use compass and square to imitate the Wangs, I do appreciate the meaning and flavor of their work and befriend them across a hundred generations. That is why I have written out this definitive statement on the matter.[41]

Although Huang's derisive reference to the examination candidates is reminiscent of Ouyang's disapproving remark about "slavish" calligraphers, Huang goes on to affirm his affinity for the style of the Two Wangs, even as he separates himself from their mechanical imitators. Huang's account of what it is that the critics object to in Su's style (his brush grip and character composition) suggests that the critics were not such people as the examination candidates but instead were followers of the *guwen* aesthetic that Ouyang had helped to formulate. Such was Su Shi's commitment to innovation that he could not stick to any prescribed method even if it had been extolled and practiced by the elders whom he most admired.[42]

In the course of his defense Huang touches upon the general issue of ancient models. The cleverness of Huang's reference to the Han-dynasty official Du Zhou comes from the pun involved: Du Zhou had been challenging the suggestion that laws (*fa*) have universal and eternal validity. His contention is that laws merely reflect the subjective notions of what is right held by the person who codified them. Huang applies the same logic to calligraphic models (also *fa*). The implication is that there is nothing authoritative about the ancient models and, in fact, that each age ought to be free to develop its own standards. Actually, this brand of extreme relativism is anticipated in comments made by Ouyang Xiu. However, such an extreme stance is probably further than any of these literati, including Su, intended to go in distancing themselves from the masterworks of the past, except to make a rhetorical point. Huang himself withdraws from the position at the close of his defense of Su Shi, with his reference to the "meaning and flavor" of the Wang style.

Huang speaks of "befriending" the Wangs across the centuries, though he is not about to try to reproduce their brushwork. The idea that one could be inspired by an ancient style yet end up producing calligraphy that was in formal terms quite different is a favorite theme of Huang and Su.[43] It is linked to the conviction that "meaning and flavor" in brushwork are not wholly determined by formal features. It also helps to make the concept of *xue* ("study") quite unconstraining. And "study" does remain important in the process of becoming an adept calligrapher. We know of course that Huang Tingjian was intensely interested in ancient rubbings, and the influence that the partly obliterated and unorthodox *Yihe ming* inscription ("Memorial on a Dead Crane") had upon his brushwork is widely recognized.[44] Mi Fu was the premier connoisseur among Su's associates and the best exemplar of the commitment to learning from a range of ancient works (although Su, predictably, criticizes Mi for being too attached to his collection).[45]

In fact, Su Shi's concept of "expressing new meaning" is closely tied to the concept of transforming earlier models (*bian gufa*). The two are virtually one for Su Shi: the way the artist manages to innovate is by effecting a transformation of an ancient style or styles.[46] If it is the latter, we may characterize the transformation as a kind of synthesis, but it is not always so. In Su's mind the greatest transformer of earlier calligraphic styles was Yan Zhenqing. For all his enthusiasm over Yan's calligraphy, Ouyang Xiu was more apt to link it to Yan's unbending integrity than to comment on its novelty. Su Shi, with whom innovation emerges as a primary virtue in calligraphy, reverses the emphasis: "Yan Lugong's calligraphy is robust, elegant, and entirely his own. All at once it transformed all earlier models, just as Du Zimei's poetry did. The power of its forms comes directly from Heaven, and it combines in one style the dashing beauty of all the works of the Han, Wei, Jin, Song and later periods. Later calligraphers found it difficult even to pick up a brush."[47] The statements Su Shi makes about his own calligraphy echo this attention to stylistic innovation, though of course he cannot claim such a degree of achievement for himself. "My own calligraphy," Su continues, "is like Lugong's [in its novelty]; it is just that it does not supplant that of earlier masters."[48]

It is precisely this notion of *bian* ("transformation") that distinguishes on the theoretical level Su's determination to be distinctive from that of the "wild" cursive script calligraphers of the Tang dynasty, such as the monk Huaisu. Those scholars had viewed the tradition with considerably more disdain, even contempt. Unlike Su Shi and his friends, they were quick to claim images found in nature as their true inspiration.[49] (Su expresses his doubts about such claims, scoffing at the idea that a calligrapher might learn from viewing a swirling river or fighting snakes.)[50] These Tang masters could be positively hostile towards ancient models, boasting of how they obliterate or sneer at them.[51] At the opposite pole, in Su's mind, were the early Song calligraphers who could never get beyond the studied approach, men like Zhou Yue and Zhong Yi, whom Su criticizes for writing even cursive script slowly and painstakingly.[52] Su's values placed him between these two extremes. His notion of transformation gave him a way, intellectually, of reconciling the weight of the tradition with his quest for novelty.

The theme of stylistic novelty, so prominent in Su's colophons, is reflected in his practice and in that of the literati associated with him. Su Shi, Huang Tingjian, and Mi Fu, the three masters of the late Northern Song, each developed idiosyncratic styles. Su and Huang were particularly close friends in life; and their theoretical and critical views on calligraphy, as exemplified in hundreds of colophons each wrote, overlap on all the key issues. The brushwork of the three, however, even within the same "running-standard" script, is so different that the work of one man is instantly distinguishable from the others.

Su's and Huang's comments on each other's calligraphy show that they were as tolerant of the gulf between their styles as they were sensitive to it. Huang was quick to defend the "unorthodox" elements in Su's style. Su, for his part, gave the ultimate commendation to Huang's singular methods: he should not be faulted for having departed from the ways of the Two Wangs; rather, the Wangs are themselves less great for not having anticipated Huang's methods.[53] Su also called attention lightheartedly to "contradictions" in Huang's style. With his "balanced and impartial" viewpoint (a Buddhist phrase for non-attachment), he writes asymmetrical and slanted characters (a reference to the tilting of his characters to the right). And though his own demeanor was "genuine and substantial," he expresses himself with techniques that are playful.[54]

As with poetry, play is a crucial aspect of the "meaning" of this art. A well-known exchange typifies the jocular attitude with which calligraphy was often approached, while it also reminds us of how cognizant and tolerant Su and Huang were of each other's novelty. Su once complimented Huang on the vigor of his brushstrokes but added, "Sometimes they are too thin, almost like snakes dangling from treetops." Huang responded that while he would not presume to be disrespectful, Su should know that his own brushstrokes are often flat and squat, like a frog caught under a rock. "The two men laughed out loud, feeling that their comments had described each defect perfectly."[55] In this exchange the mythic animal images that are so commonly invoked in earlier descriptions of calligraphy—leaping dragons, soaring phoenixes, and writing serpents—reappear as caricatures. Beneath the humor lies appreciation for each man's development of a style of his own.

The Moment of Execution

Su also occasionally hints, in his diverse comments on calligraphy, at his thoughts about the larger meaning of practicing the art. We have touched upon one kind of significance: calligraphy as the embodiment of the moral qualities of the calligrapher. The context in which this significance is discussed is normally that of the appreciation of finished works. The connoisseur values his collection for what the brushwork suggests to him of the moral rectitude of the men who did it. But there is another significance attributed to the art, one that has mostly to do with the creative process itself. Su concerns himself with the meaning of involvement in the art as practitioner, the state of mind of the active calligrapher, and the relation between his activity and knowledge of the world.

There is more than one level at which these matters are discussed. At the least ambitious level, calligraphy is characterized as a pleasurable but largely unimportant diversion. It allows one temporarily to forget nagging worries just as games such as chess, to which it is likened, do. This manner of thinking about calligraphy owes something to ancient views of it as a mere craft and its long association with bureaucratic clerks. Calligraphy had not completely extricated itself from this old stigma of being no more than a clerical skill. What Su emphasizes, however, is the delight that engagement with this craft can bring, rather than its drudgery.

The focus on pleasurableness grows out of the *guwen* aversion to a host of "vulgar" practices, including specialization in script type, copying ancient models, and stress upon technical mastery of the brush. It had long been noticed that calligraphers could readily become slaves to the excruciating technical demands of the art. Many of the early stories about would-be calligraphers are obsession stories. A pond is turned black from the repeated rinsing of an inkstone; a family's silks are covered with writing before they can be made into clothes;[56] piles of worn-out writing brushes are given a burial;[57] and a tomb is violated to obtain a calligraphy model.[58] Northern Song *guwen* scholars thought they witnessed the same sort of perversions in the efforts of career-minded scholars to outdo each other in perfecting the styles that were promoted by the *Chunhua Pavilion Calligraphy Models*. Therefore, when Ouyang Xiu wrote about his own practice of calligraphy, he referred always to the enjoyment it gave him rather than to the effort it took. Su Shi, following this lead, applied his own notion of "lodging" (*ji, yu*) to the practice of the art (as well as to collecting): "For pleasing oneself momentarily, for temporarily lodging the mind, thereby forgetting worries and the onset of old age, calligraphy is at least a more worthy pursuit than chess."[59] Ever wary of the dangers of this diversion, Su advised an enthusiast not to get carried away: "You need not stand beside a [blackened] pond, practicing arduously. / Take all your family's cloth and use it for blankets!"[60]

Ouyang Xiu had been content to write about the quiet joy he found in practicing calligraphy alone in a sparsely furnished room, with one table placed beside a bright window.[61] But Su Shi develops the theme of the pleasurableness of calligraphy further, until it becomes quite a serious matter. Su is intrigued by the calligrapher's complete, if short-lived, immersion in his activity. In one colophon Su reinterprets an old story about Wang Xianzhi. It is said that when Xianzhi was a young boy, one day his father came up behind him while he was writing and was delighted to find that when he tried to grab the brush out of his son's hand, he could not do so. He predicted then and there that the boy would grow up to be a great calligrapher. Most people, Su observes, assume that the father's delight came from finding his son's grasp of the brush to be so firm. But it must really have been the boy's singleminded concentration, which made him unmindful of the attempted interruption, that so pleased the old man.[62] If it were just a matter of firm grip, any strong man might become a great calligrapher. Su writes with pride in another colophon about his own ability to lose himself in calligraphic execution. He tells how he and his companions were once caught in a storm while out in a boat. The other scholars were terrified as they watched the boatmen struggle to keep control of the craft. Su, however, sat in the cabin and practiced calligraphy. He says that he experienced no fear at all.[63]

Self-absorption in the art leads to transcendence of ordinary circumstances and concerns, and it also leads to obliviousness of the rules of the art itself. Su is absolutely insistent on this point, asserting time and again that there must be no conscious thought about what the hand is doing, or deliberate attempt to produce skillful work, once the brush has started to move. Of Wen Tong's execution of draft script, Su wrote, "His brush moved as fast as the wind; / From the first he gave it no thought."[64] The ideal was not only applied to cursive scripts. Of a copy of the *Prajñāpāramitā Sutra* written in lesser seal script, he says, "The mind forgot the hand and the hand forgot the brush; / The brush moved on its own, not guided by the self."[65]

There is ample precedent for such remarks in earlier treatises on calligraphy. It was conventional to speak of getting beyond the rules and of wielding the brush without thinking of formal appearances. Still, Su Shi takes an extreme position. He singles out an example of draft script by Yan Zhenqing and pronounces it to be even more extraordinary than the central part of his oeuvre in the running and regular scripts. Su assumes that it is so fine because it was executed with unusual freedom and spontaneity: "He entrusted his hand to write naturally, so that with each movement an attractive appearance was created. From this we see that even for this gentleman it was true that 'you shoot more skillfully when wagering tiles than when wagering pieces of gold.'"[66] Actually, Su Shi seems to connect such "natural-ness" and spontaneity with stylistic innovation. In its negative sense, *xue* ("study") refers equally to uninspired imitation of past masters and to painstaking execution:

> In calligraphy it is when you have no intent to produce excellent work that it turns out to be excellent. Although the draft script must be studied for a long time before it is mastered, when it is written it must be done quickly. The ancients said, "I am rushed now and have no time, that is why I am using draft script." That is wrong. To say "I am rushed now and have no time" implies that under ordinary circumstances you would still prefer to do it studiously. The height of this folly was reached with Zhou Yue and Zhong Yi [the early Song calligraphers who wrote draft script methodically]. It is little wonder! My own calligraphy may not be very good, but it expresses new meaning and does not follow in the footsteps of the ancients. That is a source of pride to me.[67]

There is yet a loftier significance than pride in establishing a style all one's own and the pleasures of spontaneous execution. Su Shi does not broach this highest meaning of the art often, but he does so enough to show that it was more than a chance occurrence in his writings. Here is a colophon he wrote on a calligraphic sample by his colleague Qin Guan (Shaoyou): "The draft script done recently by Shaoyou captures the flavor of that from the Eastern Jin, and his po-etry has likewise become increasingly extraordinary and beautiful. One can see that this is a man who cannot remain at leisure, but instead he will gradually gain command of all the hundred skills. Now, to ad-vance in skill without also advancing in one's mastery of the Way is something that never happens. Today Shaoyou is advancing both in skill and the Way."[68]

What does Su mean when he posits this connection between calligraphy as a skill (*zhi*) and attainment of the Way? The passage takes us back to Su's prose farewell for Sicong, the monk who had turned away from his precocious accomplishments in calligraphy and other arts to devote himself to meditation. Su had offered for Sicong's consideration a new concept of "wisdom" (*prajñā*), equating it with clear-sighted apprehension of the world. He returned, then, to the issue of involvement with worldly activities: "None of the persons who in ancient times studied the Way attained it through emptiness and vacuity. Wheelwright Bian hewed wheels, and the hunchback caught cicadas. If it suffices to release one's proficiency and knowledge, no thing is too lowly."[69] "Thing" (*wu*) here subsumes "activity," such as Sicong's previous artistic pursuits. These pursuits act, in Su's understanding, like a trigger to release (*fa*) one's innate but latent abilities and wisdom. The crucial point is not that wisdom or one's potential to grasp the Way is innate (as we might expect), but that the potential cannot be realized "through emptiness and vacuity," by which Su means inactivity, introspection, and meditation.

Specifically, we may identify at least two ways in which the practice of calligraphy triggers, in Su's estimate, the attainment of a kind of supreme wisdom. First, the moment of calligraphic execution, when it is done correctly, is more than merely pleasurable or liberating in some conventional sense. It is a model of spontaneous accord with the Way: "[Huaisu] did not seek to be accomplished, and so his calligraphy was accomplished. He was like a pearl-diver steering a boat, who has no concern over whether or not the craft will make it safely to shore. So it is through all the reverses, overturnings, and transformations, he remains unshaken in his movements. Is this not close to one who possesses the Way?"[70] The image evoked here is of a person who is so unconcerned with either failure or success that he can submit himself to incalculable turmoil without becoming flustered. It serves to account for the seemingly superhuman brushwork in Huaisu's calligraphy. But it also describes calligraphy as the projection of a mind that can immerse itself in a complex task and yet remain unaffected and aloof. As for the calligrapher of the manuscript in lesser seal script, Su had remarked that his mind forgot his hand and "the brush moved on its own, not guided by the self (*wo*)." This, he says, is true *prajñā* (also the subject of the text). In such colophons Su appears to be promoting calligraphy as a manifestation of the ideals of selflessness (*wuwo*) and no-thought (*wusi*) that are central tenets of his philosophical views. Su has found in calligraphy, in other words, a model of activity in the world which, as an alternative to "vacuity," is immediately recognizable from other areas of his thought.

Second, Su speaks of the skilled calligrapher's being able to replicate with his brush the myriad appearances (*tai*) or images (*xiang*) of the natural world. We have seen similar statements about the function of poetry: the poet empties his mind so that it can admit the myriad images or scenes of the world. But it was not just poetic phrases that could be used to describe the appearances of things. The calligraphic line might do so, too: Wen Tong's "flying white script" alternately evokes for Su wispy clouds covering the moon, a banner flapping in the wind, and water caltrop bobbing on a wavy river.[71] There is the suggestion in such statements that calligraphy is being thought of, and validated, as an activity that mediates between the self and the world, or one that allows the self to create its own replica of the world on the page. This might be another sense in which the activity releases wisdom. The ability of the self to thus embody the world is what will bring improvement both to the practice of the art and to the person's command of the Way. That is what Su Shi tells Qin Guan. Elsewhere he tells Sicong: "If you are able to be like a pond or a mirror and contain the ten thousand [images] in the one, then your calligraphy and poetry will both become even more extraordinary." And these arts will be indicators of Sicong's progress towards the Way.[72]

Comments that anticipate both of these claims about calligraphy may be found in earlier treatises on the art, such as Sun Guoting's (late 7th c.) *Calligraphy Catalogue (Shupu)* and Zhang Huaiguan's (late 8th c.) essays, "The Meaning of Calligraphy" ("Shuyi") and "On Writing" ("Wenzi lun"). However, the identity of Su Shi is crucial in appraising the significance of his developments of the earlier statements. Unlike Sun Guoting or Zhang Huaiguan, Su Shi was not a specialist in calligraphy or a scholar known primarily for his practice or criticism of that one art. His statements about calligraphy are set in a broader context and are more remarkable because of it. Likewise, before Su Shi, as Huang Tingjian had observed, "scholars of letters" were not known for their achievements in calligraphy. Ouyang Xiu may have been fond of collecting rubbings, but he did not make nearly the claims for the meaningfulness of the actual practice of calligraphy that Su Shi did.

Two Approaches to Painting

Su Shi's views on painting are, like those on calligraphy, expressed in dozens of short writings he produced throughout his life rather than in systematic treatises. The most numerous type are colophons he wrote on or about paintings, both ancient and modern (done mostly by his friends). Su also wrote dozens of colophons in verse. These, known as a special poetic subgenre called "poems on paintings" (*tihua shi*), are scattered through his collected poems. Finally, Su wrote a few dedicatory inscriptions for buildings that were to house private collections of paintings. As with Su's writings on calligraphy, some contradictions may also be uncovered among these diverse writings on painting, but more important is the impression the writings collectively impart that in them Su was still seeking to clarify his thoughts on the meaning and purposes of painting, as well as its relationship to other arts.

If there is any principal notion, around which others are clustered, it is Su's insistence that painting should not be concerned solely with formal likeness. This is Su's disapproval of preoccupation with form (*xing*) to the exclusion of all else, an attitude we associate with Su and with the whole *wenren* approach to painting he helped to define. Of all of Su's comments on painting, the best-known one epitomizes this attitude: "Anyone who judges painting in terms of verisimilitude (*xingsi*) / Has the understanding of a child."[73] A fuller exposition of Su's ideas, as they bear upon portraiture, is contained in the following colophon:

Written on a Portrait by Chen Huaili

The difficulty of portraiture lies in the eyes. Gu Hukou [Kaizhi] said, "Painting a portrait and drawing a likeness are first a matter of these [i.e., the eyes] and second the cheeks and jaw." Once when I noticed that a lamp cast the shadow of my cheeks upon a wall, I had somebody trace them but not add any eyes or eyebrows. People who saw the drawing all burst out laughing, recognizing it immediately as me. If the eyes or the cheeks and jaw are right, then everything else will be right as well. Even approximations of the eyebrows and nose will seem right.

Portraiture is based on the same principle as physiognomy. The goal is to find the person's nature (*tian*); and to do it, you must secretly observe his mannerisms when he is together with others. If you have him don his robe and cap and make him sit and pose, staring at something, he will compose his expression and freeze. How then could his nature ever show through?

Everybody's personality manifests itself in a certain place: with some it is in the eyes and eyebrows, while with others it is in the nose and mouth ... Once I saw the Buddhist monk Weizhen painting a portrait of Zeng Lugong. At first it was not quite right, but later Weizhen went to see Lugong and, upon his return, he was overjoyed and exclaimed, "I've got it." Beside the eyebrows he added three lines, which could just barely be seen. It made Lugong appear to have his head lifted in an upward gaze, his eyebrows raised and his forehead furrowed, just as in real life. Likewise, Chen Huaili, of the southern capital, has painted my portrait and everyone thinks he has captured me completely. Huaili's practice resembles that of these other masters: quiet and calm, his intent lies beyond the brush and ink. That is why I have sought to help and inspire him here with what I have heard.[74]

There is much in this passage that is not new. For centuries, starting with pre-Tang texts on painting, Chinese artists had been exhorted to make their images lively and vital as well as formally convincing. This commitment to an animating spirit within the image is expressed in the first of Xie He's "laws" (*qiyun shendong*) and it is broached in many of Gu Kaizhi's remarks as well, including those that Su quotes. Still, Su obviously felt that the early exhortations were commonly overlooked by the painters of his day, and there is exasperation in his words when he speaks of what was evidently the widespread reliance upon posing in contemporary portraiture.

Actually, Su's fundamental conviction about painting, exemplified here, is less important and original than the ways he applied and developed it. In a colophon on a friend's landscape painting, for example, Su draws a distinction between the works done by scholars (*shiren*) and those by men who specialize in painting (*huagong*).[75] If judging painting is like judging horses, Su observes, then to look upon a scholar's work is like finding an extraordinary horse. What sets it apart, and what the viewer immediately appreciates, is "the measure of its intent and vitality" (*yiqi*). Looking at the work of "artisan painters" is like gazing upon an ordinary horse: one may find some interest in its mane or in the things surrounding it (the stable, feed, horsewhip, etc.); but since the animal itself has no greatness, the viewer is only temporarily diverted.

This particular application of the distinction between liveliness and formal likeness lies at the heart of the aesthetics of "literati painting" (*wenren hua*), as it was later called, expounded by Su Shi and his followers in the late Northern Song. Before Su, differentiation between the two approaches and types of painters was seldom made. Ouyang Xiu had, in brief and unelaborated comments, suggested that the *yi* ("mood or meaning") of painting was ultimately more important than the forms depicted (*xing*), and he even professed lack of interest in such technical matters as "the effect of height and depth, distance and recession," saying that these are the business of the artisan-painters and that the connoisseur need not concern himself with them.[76] However, Ouyang appears to be talking more about the difference between appreciation and execution than about alternative approaches to execution of the art.

We have seen how in calligraphy an antipathy developed in the mid eleventh century towards preoccupation with form and the emphasis on technique associated with it. Now, the extensive involvement that Ouyang Xiu and scholars associated with him had with calligraphy is readily understandable: all scholars and officials had to write, and the act of writing and the matter of cultivating a calligraphic style were virtually inseparable. The mid-century *guwen* intellectuals were, however, considerably further removed from the art of painting. Painting was not required of them and not part of their daily activities. Their involvement with it was slight. They evidence glimmers only of interest in it and its aesthetic issues. In the succeeding generation, nevertheless, Su Shi showed himself to be immensely interested in painting. Then Su, in turn, extended to painting certain of the key terms and concepts his own mentors had applied to literature and calligraphy. But painting had its own set of problems, and it altered somewhat the dynamics of the debate. In the most rudimentary formulation, as in the colophon above, Su's emphasis on *yi* over *xing* in painting shows itself as interest in the animating vitality of the object depicted rather than attention only to the formal likeness. Unlike with calligraphy, the issue is not described in terms of imitation versus transformation of past styles, or the choice of a moral as opposed to an aesthetic model; for the legacy of the past seems to have been less potentially inhibiting in painting than in calligraphy. Instead, what is at issue is truth to nature. Su, like some of the earliest painting critics, is saying that there is a higher order of representation than that which can be achieved by formal likeness alone. (Su is not certain what term he wants to use to designate the animating spirit: Above he uses both *tian*, "nature," and *yisi*, "thoughts, intellect, personality." In other passages he uses *qi*, "breath, vitality"; *zhen*, "truth, essence"; and *huo* "liveliness, animation.") The people being criticized for the misguided approach have also changed. In calligraphy it was first the scholarly class at large that was belittled as "slavish," while the *guwen* adherents, a small and self-conscious group, stood proudly apart. Subsequently, Su Shi expressed reservations about the *guwen* approach itself, which had its own narrowness, even as he remained dissatisfied with the Court-sponsored orthodoxy. But in his remarks on painting Su takes on a small group of specialists whose prestige was not that high to begin with, men known only for their painting (*huagong*). At the same time Su coins a term for a phenomenon that hardly yet existed: "scholar's painting."

It should be stressed here that Su really is, in these remarks at least, concerned with the lifelikeness of the painting. Therefore to say, as modern scholars occasionally have, that Su sought to shift the painter's goal from verisimilitude to some higher artistic truth may be misleading. His goal is to point out the deficiencies of a certain type of verisimilitude, that which relies wholly on formal likeness and painterly technique. But at the same time he calls for what is, in his mind, a superior kind of lifelikeness. If we fail to recognize this aspect of his thought, we will be perplexed by colophons in which he emphasizes the importance of detailed observation of nature. For example, in colophons on paintings of animals Su quotes with approval criticisms that have been made of unfaithful details. A painting of fighting oxen by Dai Song has the tails of the animals extended. When a herdboy sees the painting, he bursts out laughing, explaining that when oxen fight their tails droop over their buttocks.[77] A sparrow painting by Huang Quan depicts the birds in flight with necks and legs both extended. It is pointed out that actually the two are extended alternately as the bird flies. Su comments that the artist's "observation of things" (*guanwu*) was insufficient.[78] Likewise, when Su inscribes poems on paintings, one of his favorite themes and methods of giving praise is to remark on how alive or real the painting seems. There are various ways this compliment may be delivered. Su may say that the painted image actually fooled him into thinking he was looking at the real thing; or, with landscape paintings, he may borrow a line from Tang landscape poetry and use it to describe the painted landscape; or he may project himself into the painted scene, treating it as real, and make up a little story about events that take place in it.[79] In each case it is the artist's convincing representation of nature that is being celebrated.

Signification of the Painted Subject

The demand that the painter go beyond the goal of depicting simple formal likeness anticipates others of the themes of Su's remarks on the art, which consistently have the effect of elevating painting above the level of a mere craft or technical skill. One of his favorite treatments of particular paintings is to elucidate the moral significance of the subject and then to link that, in turn, to the character of the painter. This interpretation of painting is reminiscent of the impulse to connect calligraphy with the personality of the calligrapher. Actually, painting lent itself even more readily than calligraphy to such an enterprise, since its excellences were not confined to the beauty of abstract line. Moreover, many of the conventional subjects of painting, though taken from the world of nature, had a long history of association with human values outside of painting criticism.

The great catalysts in Su Shi's development of this interpretation of painting seem to have been first his friendship with Wen Tong, the calligrapher and bamboo painter (see Fig. 4), and later his acquaintance with Li Gonglin, whom Su thought of primarily as a horse painter. Wen Tong was, like Su, a native of Sichuan and would eventually become father-in-law to one of Su Che's daughters (the match was encouraged by Su Shi). Wen was twenty years Su Shi's senior and died in the middle of Su's career, in 1079. The two men first met in the capital early in the Xi'ning period. After a few months they parted, never to meet again; but they kept in touch through the next ten years, with obvious high mutual regard, and often exchanged letters and gifts. Su Shi wrote poems for Wen Tong's gardens, and requested, in turn, Wen

FIGURE 4. Wen Tong, attrib., *Bamboo*. Hanging scroll. Collection of the National Palace Museum, Taiwan, Republic of China.

Tong's calligraphy and paintings to hang in halls he built.[80] The fullest statement of the correspondence in Su's mind between Wen Tong's specialty, bamboo painting, and his personality is contained in the inscription Su wrote for the hall in which Wen kept the paintings, translated below:

Ink Gentleman's Hall

In addressing people, to show respect for someone's rank you call him "lord," to show respect for someone's worthiness you call him "gentleman," while lesser persons are simply referred to as "him" or "you." As for many of the highest ranking nobleman and ministers, people cower before them but do not in their hearts submit to them, so that in their presence they address them as "lord" or "gentleman," but once they withdraw they refer to them as "him." However, after Wang Ziyou called bamboo "gentleman," the whole nation followed suit and referred to it that way, and no one called it otherwise. Today, Yuke (Wen Tong) is able to represent this gentleman's form with ink, and has built a hall in which to lodge him. He has requested an inscription for the hall from me to praise this gentleman's virtues. Yuke's affection for this gentleman is truly abundant!

In his conduct Yuke is solemn yet elegant, wise and loyal. More than one of his contemporaries cultivates and educates himself, polishing and cleansing morning and night, all in the hope of befriending him. Yet Yuke has affection for this gentleman only. This gentleman is simple yet unyielding; he does not have sounds, beauty, or fragrance to delight the onlooker's senses. Therefore, Yuke's affection for this gentleman must be based on his moral worth. Of all of the phenomena in the world that can chill or heat a person, none penetrate the skin so deeply as snow and frost or wind and rain, so that there are few men who do not lose control of themselves when afflicted by them. As for plants, the changes that the four seasons bring to them are considerable, but this gentleman alone remains unaffected. Even without Yuke, who in the world would not consider this gentleman worthy? Still, Yuke's appreciation of this gentleman is especially profound, for he understands what it is that makes him so worthy.

When Yuke is at leisure, chatting and laughing, he brushes and splatters ink rapidly yet captures this gentleman's virtues completely. His appearance may be either youthful or elderly, either standing tall or bending low: in driving wind and snow his character is revealed, and cliffs and rocky crags bring out his integrity. When he achieves his desires, he is luxuriant but not arrogant; and when he is frustrated, he is frail but not ashamed. When he dwells together with others, he does not lean on them; and when he stands by himself, he is not afraid. As for Yuke's appreciation of this gentleman, one could say that he has fully grasped his feelings and has mastered his nature. Although I myself am not worthy to know this gentleman, I hope to ask Yuke for the portrait of one of his brothers, descendants, or friends to keep in my own study, so that it might be a place this gentleman visits occasionally.[81]

There is ample precedent for many of the associations of bamboo described here. Wang Ziyou (Wang Huizhi, another son of Wang

Xizhi) had, as Su notes, called bamboo a gentleman centuries earlier, and thereafter numerous writers expanded upon the plant's virtues. What had not been done before, with anything approaching the elaborateness seen here, is to find those same qualities in bamboo painting. Su manages to skirt entirely the issue of the relation between Wen Tong's paintings and reality or nature as he moves directly from the painted images to the virtues they embody. Painting seems in Su's formulation not a whit inferior to reality. Actually, as a reflection of a person's character, painting is superior to nature: a man may express fondness for real bamboo and surround himself with them, as Wang Ziyou did; but only a painter can create bamboo, giving tangible physical form to his hidden inner qualities. It is, of course, because Wen Tong created these bamboos that his relationship with the plant is said here to be so exclusive.

Once he has given such an elaborate account of the analogous virtues of Wen Tong and his subject matter, Su does not need to keep repeating it. "Look at [the bamboo on] the sheer cliff, / Its gaunt joints (*jie*, also "integrity") coursing like serpents." "[Wen Tong's] body fused with the bamboo / To express boundless purity and newness."[82] There is a moral judgment of the painter that lies just beneath such lines. It informs virtually every statement Su made about Wen Tong's paintings.

A lengthy song by the Tang poet Bo Juyi on a bamboo painting may serve to illustrate the difference between Su's approach and that common in earlier literature. Bo had a friend who was a bamboo painter, just as Su Shi did. But Bo's treatment of Xiao Yue's painting concentrates entirely on the marvelous verisimilitude of the work:

舉頭忽看不似畫	I look up and catch sight of it: it does not look like a painting.
低耳靜聽疑有聲	I bend my ear to listen quietly: it seems to emit sound.
西叢七莖勁而健	The seven stalks to the west stand taut and strong;
省向天竺寺前石上見	I recall seeing them on a rock before Tianzhu Monastery.
東叢八莖疏且寒	The eight stalks to the east are spare and chill;
憶曾湘妃廟裏雨中看	I remember viewing them in the rain inside Xiang Goddess Temple.[83]

Bo Juyi never ventures far beyond such lines. His only references to the painter, contained at the end of his song, lament that fact that Xiao has now grown old and will soon give up painting altogether. The theme Su Shi could not bring himself to avoid whenever he wrote about Wen Tong's bamboos has no place at all in Bo Juyi's poem.

Horse paintings were subjected by Su and his circle to a similar sort of interpretation as the long literary tradition of using the exceptional horse as a metaphor for a man of talent was extended now to painting. Paintings of emaciated horses or steeds lost in the wilds were taken as projections of their painter, who was insufficiently appreciated by the world. Alternately, paintings of powerful steeds were said to capture their artist's grand aspirations. It happened that Li Gonglin (Boshi), the greatest horse painter of the age, was serving as a lowly member of the Secretariat during the early Yuanyou period. Li was befriended by Su and his admirers then, and the literary men added numerous colophons to Li's paintings in which they developed their interpretation of painted horses.

Li Gonglin was a collector as well as a painter, and his collection included a painting of three horses by the Tang artist Han Gan (which Li himself was to paint a copy of). Su Che wrote a poem about this Han Gan painting, comparing it unfavorably with Li's own horse paintings; and several literati, including Huang Tingjian, Liu Bin, and Wang Qinchen, wrote matching poems.[84] Su Shi also contributed a matching piece. A complex piece, Su's poem contrasts Li's paintings with those of the Tang master precisely on the basis of self-revelation in art:

次韻子由書李伯時 所藏韓幹馬	*Matching the Rhymes of Ziyou's* *Inscription on Han Gan's Horse,* *Owned by Li Boshi*
潭潭古屋雲幕垂	In a deep and ancient hall where cloud draperies hang,
省中文書如亂絲	Department documents are strewn like tangled skeins of silk.
忽見伯時畫天馬	Suddenly I watch Boshi paint a divine horse;
朔風胡沙生落錐	Steppe winds and nomad sands spring from the tip of his brush.
天馬西來從西極	The divine horse comes to us from the Western Extremes,
勢與落日爭分馳	Racing east as grandly as the sun proceeds west.
龍膺豹股頭八尺	With dragon chest, leopard haunches, and head eight feet high,

4

8	奮迅不受人間羈	Its frenzied galloping accepts no halter of mankind.
	元狩虎脊聊可友	Tiger Spine of the Yuanshou era would be a fit companion;
	開元玉花何足奇	Jade Flower of Kaiyuan now seems commonplace.
	伯時有道真吏隱	Boshi is a man of the Way, a true recluse in office;
12	飲啄不羨山梁雌	He does not envy the hill-bridge pheasant as it pecks and sips.
	丹青弄筆聊爾耳	Paints and brushwork are but a diversion for him,
	意在萬里誰知之	His intent lies off a thousand miles, but who understands?
	幹惟畫肉不畫骨	Gan painted flesh only, not the bones,
16	而況失實空留皮	He even missed the substance and left nothing but skin.
	煩君巧說腹中事	It took you to explain ingeniously what lay in their bellies,
	妙語欲遣黃泉知	Your marvelous lines should be sent to him in the Yellow Springs.
	君不見	Don't you know?
	韓生自言無所學	Master Han himself said he learned from no one,
20	厩馬萬匹皆吾師	"The myriad horses of the imperial stables are all my teachers."[85]

Lines 9–10. Tiger Spine was a famous horse of Emperor Wudi of the Han, and Jade Flower belonged to Xuanzong of the Tang.

Line 12. The pheasant represents men who have met "their proper time" and enjoy a comfortable life. See *Analects* 10/17.

Li Gonglin's "divine horse" (an ancient phrase for horses imported from Ferghana) is here treated as an embodiment of his creator's noble spirit. It is Li Gonglin whom Su Shi is thinking of in his lines about the creature's untamable majesty. In the case of this painter, it is his ability to retain his exalted values and aspirations (which lie "ten thousand miles distant") while serving in an undistinguished post that attests to his greatness. Hence Su refers to him as one who is not the least bit compromised by his duties or envious of more fortunate men.

It is because Su Shi's interest is in explicating this relationship between Li and his painted horses that he takes so long to address the ostensible subject of the poem, the Han Gan painting that Li owned.

When Su does finally turn to that subject, he has nothing favorable to say. Su describes Han Gan as a painter who concerned himself only with the external appearance of horses. Su is here repeating criticism Du Fu first made of Han Gan, when Du pronounced Han's mentor Cao Ba to be the superior painter;[86] but Su gives it his own twist. Du Fu meant only that Han Gan's horses lacked the aura of vital energy, of inner spirit, that he found in Cao Ba's horses. Su Shi means that Han Gan's horses are not an equine projection of the human spirit, and especially that the crucial link between the painter and his horses is missing in Han Gan's painting. The "you" in line 17 is Su Che, who wrote the first poem on the Han Gan painting, giving it an elaborate and anthropomorphic interpretation.[87] Han Gan's art is inferior because it fails to bring out this sort of significance on its own, and must await Su Che to posit it. In his closing lines Su Shi cleverly turns a boast Han Gan once made into criticism. Han Gan had proudly asserted that he was dependent on no earlier horse painter and that his only model was the real horses in the imperial stables.[88] But since Su Shi does not prize likenesses of real horses as much as he prizes images that embody the personality of the painter, Han Gan's boast means little to him. Su dismisses it and puns on *xue* ("to study, learn from"), implying that Han Gan "had no learning."

Earlier poets had, of course, written often about real or legendary horses as analogues of human traits. Du Fu, for example, regularly treats real horses this way, as when writing of his own long-suffering and sickly mount, or an abandoned imperial horse that he comes across starving in the fields, or the mighty but underutilized steed of the semi-retired General Gao Xianzhi.[89] Du Fu also wrote several poems on paintings of horses, and was, in fact, the first major poet to do so. Du Fu knew the famous Cao Ba, who painted Xuanzong's steeds by imperial commission, and he also was friendly with the horse painter Wei Yan and at least knew of Han Gan (Cao Ba's student). But the poems Du Fu wrote about the paintings by these men do not dwell upon connections between the painted steeds and the inner qualities of the men who created them. Du Fu turns his attention instead to the affinity between the portrait and the real horse, to the superiority of the painting under consideration ("With one stroke he washed away the ordinary horses of all time"), to the present lack of real horses to match those in the painting (a comment on the imperial decline), or to the irony that a man with such painterly skills should be so impoverished.[90] But he does not elaborate on the majesty of the painter's nature as embodied in the painted image of the horse.

Su's method of interpretation was not confined to these two

subjects. He was able to apply the same general manner of interpretation to virtually any landscape or element thereof, though the exact human qualities that are highlighted vary somewhat with each subject. Of Song Fugu (Di) and a landscape he painted of the Xiaoxiang region, Su writes, "How grand is this man's breast: / Hills and rivers coil themselves inside."[91] One of the implications of this is simply that Song, despite his career as a bureaucrat, shows through his painting a lasting affinity for the purer values embodied in nature.

Su Shi's own favorite subjects as a painter seems to have been craggy rocks, bamboo, and withered trees. These are the motifs most frequently mentioned in contemporary references to Su's paintings, and they are also the subjects of the few surviving paintings whose attribution to Su Shi deserves serious consideration (such as the handscroll shown on the endpapers of this book).[92] The human traits that these subjects call to mind are prickliness, contempt for ingratiation, steadfastness amid hardship, and proud aloofness. Su described his impulse to do a painting of rock and bamboo this way:

空腸得酒芒角出	When my empty innards get wine, pointy sprouts appear.
肝肺槎牙生竹石	The forked branches in my liver and lungs produce bamboo and rocks.
森然欲作不可回	Bursting within, I must express them and cannot hold back;
吐向君家雪色壁	I spit them out upon your home's snow-white wall.[93]

The more "extraordinary" or "strange" (*qi, guai*) the style of the rendering, the more remarkable the character of the painter was assumed to be. Mi Fu emphasized this aspect of Su's work: "When Zizhan paints withered trees, the trunk and branches have countless twists and turns; and the *cun* dots in the rocks are also indescribably strange and extraordinary, just like all that is twisted and packed within his breast."[94] Kong Wuzhong (Changfu), another of Su's friends and also a Yuanyou official who was purged during the 1090s, wrote similarly about Su's paintings of strange rocks. Kong first refers to Su's composure in the midst of many frustrations he met in his career, concluding that "everyone knew he was a rare man." Kong continues: "In observing the myriad things, there was nothing he did not like; but he was particularly fond of the rugged aspect of strange rocks. His rocks would rise against the mists and stand in solitude, or they would be arrayed on desolate shores, with such rectitude, power, ugliness, and strangeness that could never be fully described."[95] Such appearances in painting attested to a personality marked by rare qualities.

Pattern, Lodging, Knowledge

There are also times that Su Shi attributes another sort of meaning to painting, one that has to do with the painter's apprehension of the underlying Pattern (*li*) of his subject and his lodging in that subject to release insight and understanding. This mode of describing painting is analogous to Su's writings on calligraphy that link the practice of that art with the attainment of an ideal state of selfless immersion in activity and the replication of natural images, or their "essence," in brushwork. In painting as with calligraphy, it is in connection with the moment of execution that these themes are discussed.[96]

As we would expect, Su writes about the exhilaration of the act of painting, the need to do it quickly and without reflection or painstaking technique, and the advantages of having the complete image, as it will appear when the work is finished, in mind before the first brushstroke is drawn.[97] These themes are similar to his remarks on calligraphic execution, examined above. But Su's thoughts on painting as a mediating activity between the self and the world go beyond what he says on this issue concerning calligraphy. This is probably because the images produced in painting are more obviously modeled on nature than are the brushstrokes in calligraphy. Painting thus lent itself to claims that artistic activity could capture and embody the artist's apprehension of enduring principles of nature. A primary document on this theme is an inscription Su wrote for bamboo paintings by Wen Tong:

> I have said this of painting: men, animals, buildings and furnishings all have a constant form (*changxing*); but as for mountains and rocks, bamboo and trees, water and waves, and mists and clouds, although they do not have a constant form, they do have a constant Pattern (*changli*). If a painter fails to capture a constant form, everyone knows it. But when a constant Pattern is not represented correctly, even connoisseurs of painting may fail to detect it. That is why those painters who would win fame for themselves by fooling the world all choose subjects that have no constant form. Nevertheless, when a constant form is incorrect, the mistake is limited to that one element. One cannot condemn the entire painting because of that single mistake. But if a constant Pattern is wrong, then the entire work must be condemned. If the subject's form is not constant, then the painter cannot but be careful about its Pattern. Among the artisans of the world there are those who capture form down to the

tiniest detail, but as for Pattern only a lofty gentleman or extraordinary talent can distinguish it.[98]

By thus associating Pattern—the organizing principle of things —with painting, Su Shi has made a statement whose significance goes far beyond justifying Wen Tong's bamboos. It was precisely form that had traditionally been the key term in discussions of painting. In the earliest painting criticism the art is defined as "the drawing of forms" (xiexing);[99] and early critics dwell on the correspondence between painted form and reality, remarking frequently on the uncanny power of the painted form to inspire the same feelings in the viewer that the natural object itself inspires. Su was eager, as discussed above, to break free of this preoccupation with form and formal likeness. But here he has gone further than merely to insist upon a higher sort of verisimilitude or liveliness. He has seized upon the term that was just then, in the third quarter of the eleventh century, being developed by philosophically-minded intellectuals into the basis of a new Confucian metaphysics. The Cheng brothers and others wrote about "constant Patterns" as forces that regulated the transformations of the world.[100] Su is suggesting that painting, too, can embody these forces, a suggestion that the philosophers had not bothered to make.

It can hardly escape notice how regularly Su Shi's remarks on Pattern in painting occur in a Buddhist context. That this is so suggests that Su's Pattern was influenced by the concept of the interconnectedness of li and shi ("noumena and phenomena" or "essence and substance") that is emphasized both in currents of Chan and in Huayan thought.[101] What Su calls attention to regarding the painted bamboo is that for all the luxuriant foliage and overlapping growth, each plant retains its own rightness and integrity. The "origin" (yuan) or source of each may yet be discerned. "They exhibit a thousand transformations and ten thousand alterations, and yet they never encroach upon each other and each occupies its proper place."[102] And again:

門前兩叢竹	In the two clusters of bamboo by the gate,
雪節貫霜根	Snowy joints connect to frosty roots.
交柯亂葉動無數	Crisscrossing branches and haphazard leaves are too numerous to count,
一一皆可尋其源	But each one may be traced back to its origin.[103]

Naturally, the monks who presided over the halls in which these paintings hung would be pleased to find that the works could be described in terms so strongly reminiscent of their doctrine that there is no ultimate distinction or duality between worldly appearances and "emptiness" or between false perceptions and underlying truth.

It is interesting to find Su Shi so eager to discuss the role of Pattern in painting, given the misgivings he often expresses over philosophical inquiry into such concepts as Pattern, human nature, and the Way. Yet it must be because there is something tangible under discussion here (those scrolls hanging on the wall) that Su allows himself this exploration. Su may praise Wang Wei's bamboo painting for "capturing that which lies beyond appearances,"[104] but it is almost certainly the conjunction of appearances with what lies beyond them that piques Su's interest.

In fact, the practice of painting came to epitomize for Su one ideal kind of interaction between the mind and the world, even more than calligraphy did. In the second half of the inscription, quoted above, which develops the contrast between form and Pattern, Su says this about Wen Tong and his bamboos: "They accord with the formative forces of Heaven, and satisfy the thoughts of man. They are, indeed, that in which the man of true understanding lodges." What sort of lodging is this?

It is clear, first, that superior painting is dependent upon the artist's losing himself in his subject. Wen Tong "left his body behind" when he painted bamboo; his body and bamboo fused together.[105] Pu Yongsheng, a specialist in water paintings (and also an unrestrained man and a great drinker), allowed "his nature to conjoin with the painting" and so he painted "living water" not "dead water."[106] And why is it, Su asks, that someone who has seen a landscape by Li Gonglin will, if he subsequently visits the site depicted, feel the whole scene to be so familiar that he will swear he has been there before? What enables Li Gonglin to render the likeness of a landscape so perfectly? Su considers the possibility that it is an extraordinarily powerful memory that is at work, that when Li visits a site he takes note of the exact position and appearance of every tree and rock so that he can later reproduce them in his studio. But Su rejects this explanation and offers another in its place: "When this lay Buddhist [Li Gonglin] is in the mountains, he does not allow his mind to abide in any one thing, and so his spirit commingles with the myriad things and his knowledge is the equal of that of the hundred artisans combined."[107] Here, Su's Buddhist ideal of non-abiding is invoked to account for the comprehensive merging of Li's intelligence with countless things in the scene. The lesson is this: if you want your knowledge and skills to equal those of the "hundred artisans" combined, you must be able to set your mind free to merge with the myriad things of the world. On a painting by Wang Shen, Su (appropriating another Buddhist analogy) remarks that the mind of the painter had been emptied so that the myriad passing images of the world could be caught in it just as things are reflected in the surface of a well.[108]

It is because Li Gonglin's painting was a complex scene that Su here emphasizes the capacity of his spirit to involve itself with so many things. But in other places Su takes the position that lodging in a single thing will also suffice to release comprehensive knowledge. This is the opening of his colophon on a tea catalog compiled by Huang Daofu:

> Things have boundaries but Pattern has no special domain. All the insight in the world does not match the Pattern in a single thing. Men of true understanding lodge themselves in a thing to trigger their insight; thus in the transformations of a single thing, one may comprehend all the bamboo that grows on South Mountain.[109]

The South Mountain bamboo here surely represents the myriad things of the world. From lodging (but not abiding) in the one and mastering its Pattern, we gain knowledge of the many. This, moreover, could be said of a tea catalog. Wen Tong's special talent put him considerably closer to a wisdom that plumbed the essence of "South Mountain's bamboo." These statements by Su Shi are reminiscent of Chan notions that Buddha-nature is present in every thing, no matter how humble, and that therefore even commonplace things or utterances may assist in enlightenment.

Painting and Poetry

Su Shi's assertions about on the convertibility of painting and poetry (e.g., "there is painting in his poetry . . . and there is poetry in his painting")[110] are as well known as they are numerous. In the centuries after Su they became part of the essential aesthetic of literati painting in China. Yet the context in which Su's comments were made, and consequently their intent, has often been neglected, as has the question of precisely what it was that he was equating in the two arts.

It was not painting in general or all kinds of painting that Su equated with the more prestigious literary art. We return here to the distinction mentioned earlier that Su drew between "scholars' painting" and that of the "painter craftsmen" (huagong). It was mainly the former that Su singled out for praise. The linking of scholars' painting with poetry did not depend solely on the identity of the persons in question. (It was the scholars who were also poets, whereas the painter-craftsmen were not.) Su maintained that there were traits in the paintings themselves that made scholars' paintings closer to poetry than were the works by painter-craftsmen. What were those traits?

One description of the two divergent approaches to painting is contained in an early poem Su wrote on two murals contained in the Kaiyuan Monastery outside of Fengxiang. The first was by the most celebrated of all Tang figure painters, Wu Daozi. It depicted an elaborate scene of Śākyamuni preaching his final sermon to hordes of the faithful beneath the twin sala trees:

亭亭雙林間	How majestic! Amid Twin Trees,
彩暈扶桑暾	A hued radiance shines like Fusang.
中有至人談寂滅	There the Perfect One lectures on nirvana,
悟者悲涕迷者自捫	The enlightened weep with compassion, the lost clutch their hearts.
蠻君鬼伯千萬萬	Barbarians and demons by the thousand upon thousand
相排競進頭如黿	Push and shove to get closer, their heads like sea-turtles.[111]

In a separate building was a mural by the Tang literatus Wang Wei that presented a much simpler scene of a disciple or disciples in Jetavana Park, the gate to which was flanked by two clumps of bamboo (whose description was quoted earlier):

祇園弟子盡鶴骨	The disciple at Jetavana has the bones of a crane;
心如死灰不復溫	His mind is like dead ashes that cannot be rekindled.
門前兩叢竹	In the two clusters of bamboo by the gate,
雪節貫霜根	Snowy joints connect to frosty roots.

In his closing lines, Su Shi expresses his preference for Wang Wei's mural, which "captures what lies beyond the image" (*dezhi xiangwai*). Wu Daozi, gifted as he was, still ranks, says Su, among the painter-craftsmen. The crucial point is not that Wang Wei's composition was simpler and more spare—though it certainly was that—but that Su detects qualities in Wang Wei's painted forms that serve other ends than simply the delineation of form. Su does not get around to saying so here, but he must consider Wang's images to be a projection of the admirable traits of Wang himself (lack of interest in physical comforts, quieted mind, embodiment of Pattern, etc.). Wang appropriated conventional Buddhist subjects and lodged his nature in them.

Another of Su's poems on paintings helps to clarify his remark about what lies "beyond the image." The subject of this poem is a stone screen, owned by Ouyang Xiu, on which was etched and painted a lone pine tree standing on a mountain peak. (That, at least, is what Su says about the screen. It is also possible that Su imagined he saw a pine in the natural coloration of the rock.) In the opening lines of his poem, which emphasize the solitude and harshness of the setting, Su fancies that the image must have been executed by the Lord of Heaven himself. But immediately Su has another thought, connecting the image on the screen with two Tang painters who were specialists in rocks and pines:

我恐畢宏韋偃死葬 虢山下	When Bi Hong and Wei Yan died, I fear, and were buried below Mt. Guo,
骨可朽爛心難窮	Their bones could rot but their hearts would not die.
神機巧思無所發	Their daimonic devices and clever thoughts, left with no outlet,
化為烟霏淪石中	Transformed into the misty patches concealed within this rock.
古來畫師非俗士	Painters since ancient times have not been common fellows;
摹寫物像畧與詩 人同	They depict the images of things just as poets do.
願公作詩慰不遇	May you, sir, compose a poem to comfort these men born out of their time—
無使二子含憤泣 幽宮	Do not let them harbor anger and weep in the underground palace.[112]

If the hearts of Bi Hong and Wei Yan could reappear on Ouyang's screen, then surely the paintings of rocks and pines that they did when they were alive must likewise have embodied their spirits and thoughts. Therefore, when Su asserts that painters "depict the images of things just as poets do," he does not mean simply that painters, like poets, fill their works with nature imagery, but that they avail themselves of nature imagery to express their intent, just as poets had been doing ever since the *Book of Songs*. (Because these two painters were men "born out of their time," they specialized in images suggesting steadfastness and fortitude.) There is no contradiction in saying that good painters "depict the images of things just as poets do" and that they "capture what lies beyond the image." Both statements affirm that the highest goal of painting is to utilize nature imagery to express aspects of one's values and intent. In yet another formulation of the same idea, on Li Zhiyi's painting of a withered tree, Su says "Painters since ancient times have not been common fellows / Their marvelous thoughts really have the same origin as poetry."[113]

A phrase that occurs several times in Su Shi's discussions of painting and what it shares with poetry is *qingxin* ("purity and newness"). "Poetry and painting have one basic rule, / Divine craft and purity and newness."[114] It will be recalled that it was the same phrase that Su used to describe Wen Tong's bamboo: "His body fused with the bamboo / To express boundless purity and newness." It is clear, moreover, that Su is appropriating traits that belong first to poetry and attributing them now to the best of paintings. (In fact, Du Fu had used the phrase in praise of the poet Yu Xin.)[115] Su says of a landscape by the early-Song painter Yan Su that the brushwork was done in one inspired burst, "and is brilliantly 'new each day.' He has taken leave of the standards and measures of painter-craftsmen and attained to the purity and beauty of poets."[116] The "newness" that Su has in mind is much like the "new meaning" that he looked for in calligraphy. The "purity" that Su demands harks back to his conviction that painting is an embodiment of personality. "Purity" of diction, sentiment, and thought had long been valued in the literary arts, and Su now extends it to painting.

The Question of Motivation

In the foregoing, the issue of Su Shi's motives in developing both calligraphy and painting as fields of literati expression has not been dealt with head on. The issue is difficult, partly because Su himself nowhere addresses it explicitly. The most directly pertinent comments we have are his occasional remarks about the desirable consequences of involvement with these arts. Nevertheless, it is possible to draw inferences both from his voluminous related writings and from his circumstances; and anyone trying to understand Su Shi in his complexity must struggle with the question, since these arts of the brush became such a significant part of his life and legacy.

There is, of course, every reason to assume that we are dealing with a tangle of motives. The subject is so large—the arts themselves are divergent, as are Su's various roles as practitioner, collector, critic, and theorist—that no single motivating factor could possibly account for every aspect of his attraction to calligraphy and painting, much less his active dedication to them. Nor, once we have identified likely factors in Su's motivation, should we expect constancy in the mix over long periods of time (or even from day to day). For purposes of analysis, however, we can single out three distinct ways of thinking that encouraged Su's involvement in these arts and treat them separately.

The first is primarily a literary one, which has to do with Su Shi's sense of his place in the history of literary and artistic expression. The idea here is that Su's awareness of the accomplishments of past poets was so keen that to establish his own identity he felt compelled to branch out into the non-literary arts, thus creating a broader synthesis than had ever been achieved before. A statement that he repeatedly makes about the history of the arts suggests as much. In the opening of a colophon on a painting by the Tang master Wu Daozi, for example, Su writes, "Men of wisdom create things anew, and men of ability transmit them. Nothing is brought to its final and perfect form by a single person. The learning of superior men and the crafts of the various artisans began in the Three Dynasties, continued through the Han, and culminated only in the Tang. So it was that when poetry reached Du Zimei [Fu], prose reached Han Tuizhi [Yu], calligraphy reached Yan Lugong [Zhenqing], and painting reached Wu Daozi, all the transformations of ancient and modern times and all possible excellences in this world were completed."[117] Su goes on to discuss the strengths of Wu Daozi's painting, but his opening is of greater interest and contains, in fact, two remarkable views. The first is his opinion that the practice of each art actually improved through time, reaching its zenith during the Tang. This view is at odds with the traditional habit of crediting the most ancient masters with the highest accomplishments and viewing subsequent developments basically as degeneration, halted only occasionally in later centuries by isolated cases of brilliance. (Thus, in poetry it is the *Book of Songs* and the *Chuci*, or at least the late Han and Wei poets, who are ordinarily considered the finest; in prose it is the other Confucian classics or the early histories; in calligraphy it is Zhong Yao, Zhang Zhi, and the Two Wangs; and in painting it is Gu Kaizhi and Lu Tanwei.) The second is that the culmination of each art form, reached in the Tang, was a synthetic style that drew upon all the stylistic variations developed in earlier times. This same notion is repeated in slightly different language in one of Su's colophons on Yan Zhenqing, quoted above: "All at once [Yan] transformed all earlier models, just as Du Zimei's poetry did. The power of its forms comes directly from Heaven, and it combines in one style the dashing beauty of all the works of the Han, Wei, Jin, Song and later periods. Later calligraphers find it hard even to pick up a brush."[118]

Su Shi's choice for the supreme master in each field seems especially appropriate when we recall that each artist is known for producing an oeuvre that excels in several distinct forms or styles. But if Du Fu had perfected the poetic tradition, what is left for Su Shi to do? In the process of ever broadening synthesis that Su describes, the next logical step is to bring the various arts together in one person. And if each art had been perfected during the Tang, what would be more natural for a man of the succeeding dynasty to attempt? Modesty prevents Su from explicitly laying claim to this next level of achievement, but it is difficult to think that he has not considered it. More than anything else, it is the way Su chooses to represent the past that suggests this. Su and his colleagues were certainly aware that there was no precedent for the diversity of their accomplishments in the arts. Huang Tingjian observes how exceptional it is for Su, as a literary man, to be famous as a calligrapher as well. And Su pointedly remarks that within the field of literature some writers are good at prose but not at poetry, while others (and he names Du Fu) are good at poetry but not at prose.[119] Behind such comments lies an ambition to be good at all the forms of expression, precisely because no one had managed to do so before.

A second motivating factor may be found in the claims Su Shi makes for the connections between active involvement in these arts and knowledge or self-cultivation. If, as we have seen, the execution of calligraphy and painting is associated with an ideal kind of spontaneous interaction with "things," or if it assists in the apprehension of Pattern, or even progress towards the Way, then the individual would seem to have every justification for wanting to immerse himself in these arts. However, as compatible as such claims are with Su's philosophical outlook in general (i.e., his commitment to involvement in the world, his antipathy to abstract speculation), they remain somewhat problematic. They are not, it turns out, a wholly satisfactory explanation of Su Shi's interest in the arts. The subject is a complicated one, as is the related issue of Su's thinking about the value and uses of literature, and will be treated at greater length in the concluding chapter. It may simply be noted here that Su's assertion of such claims about the arts is itself spotty, at best, in his voluminous writings on painting and calligraphy. His most ambitious statements about the value of practicing these arts are not a ringing affirmation that echoes through his inscriptions. On the contrary, they possess a muted and tentative quality, as if in them Su was cautiously exploring uncertain territory. The context of these remarks also raises questions about how they should be taken. With great regularity they are found in writings addressed to personal friends, many of whom did not achieve any great distinction except in the arts (e.g., Wen Tong, Huang Tingjian, Li Gonglin). Surely, when

Su found himself addressing such men, there must have been a strong temptation to maximize the significance of the one field of endeavor in which the person did excel. Equally disturbing is the fact that Su sometimes evinces a tendency to detract from the importance of the arts, that is, to say just the sort of thing we might least expect to hear from him. Calligraphy and painting, he says, are barely superior to commonplace diversions, such as chess.[120] Nothing can so attract a man, but never serve actually to improve him, as these arts of the brush.[121] Wen Tong's paintings are the least important among his achievements and forms of expression.[122] Calligraphy and painting are, after all, "things," and the man of true understanding does not need to take recourse to things at all.[123] We will return to such statements in the final chapter.

We are on surer ground with the third motivating factor, which is rooted in Su's activities outside of the arts. In his writings about calligraphy and painting, Su stresses the link between the personality of the artist and the work he produces, whether it be the link between calligraphic "flavor" and the virtues of the calligrapher or the values projected by the painter onto his representation of bamboo, horses, or rocks and trees. Su also assigns great importance to stylistic innovation: the calligrapher ought to transform old styles, no matter how much admired, to produce new meaning; and the painter strives for "newness" even as he captures the enduring Patterns of things. Together, these two grand themes of Su's views give particular emphasis to the capacity of these arts for self-expression: the practitioner is revealing himself (he is not painstakingly imitating the forms of nature); and in what he reveals, he is proudly idiosyncratic.

We may consider again the particular kind of significance attributed to nature imagery in painting. What is distinctive about Su's interpretations is not the impulse to find some human significance. Du Fu's remarks on paintings of birds of prey, for example, regularly evidence the same general impulse: the image of a valiant and fearsome bird may perhaps be developed by the poet into a lament for the irretrievable glories of Xuanzong's hunting processions (when "cunning hares" could still be properly disposed of) or into expressions of regret that the painted bird (i.e., poet) is so distantly removed from the sovereign it might serve so well.[124] But the kind of connection that Su Shi draws between the valiant image and the painter himself is not a prominent theme in the Tang painting poems. The importance of Su Shi's innovation is that it served to assign new seriousness to the act of painting itself, rather than just to viewing and appreciation. It was now the painter, rather than the poet/interpreter, who endowed the painted image with human and, indeed, self-referential significance.

From many of the sources quoted above, it will already be obvious that Su Shi did not develop his ideas on painting and calligraphy in isolation. Most of writings are either addressed to other literati (his letters and poems), written for them (his inscriptions for studios), or inscribed on the art produced by them (his colophons). It will be useful here to list the persons who are most prominent in Su's voluminous writings on the arts, and give some idea of the chronology of his acquaintance with them. The first group are those he met during his stint in the capital early in the reform era (1069–1071). These included Wen Tong, the calligrapher and painter; the imperial relative Wang Shen, known for his painting; Wang Gong, the poet; and Kong Wenzhong, the essayist (eldest of the "Three Kongs," including Wuzhong and Pingzhong).[125] During the remainder of the 1070s, as Su moved from one provincial post to another, he befriended the four literary figures and calligraphers who came to be known as his "four disciples," Zhang Lei, Chao Buzhi, Qin Guan and Huang Tingjian. When Su was sent into exile at Huangzhou, he was visited by Li Zhiyi, Li Zhi, and Mi Fu, the great connoisseur and calligrapher. Finally, back at the capital in the early Yuanyou years, Su came to know Chen Shidao, the poet; Li Gonglin, the painter; Bi Zhongyou; and Mao Pang.[126]

Although many of these men were closely connected with Su's stance in the political controversies of the day, not all of them were (Mi Fu, for instance, was not). Conversely, not all of Su's political allies were specially interested in the arts of the brush (Lu Tao and Fan Zhen were not). In other words, Su's circle of poets, calligraphers, and painters was not identical with his political cohort, the individuals who came collectively to be known in the Yuanyou era as the Shu (Sichuan) faction or the Su brothers' faction. Nevertheless, the overlap between the two groups is great enough to suggest a link between the two orientations.

Accounts of Song literature and literati aesthetics rightly stress the cohesiveness of "Su's circle." What is sometimes less well appreciated is how thoroughly bound up with Su's political views and fortunes were the official careers of these literati and artists. Wang Gong was, like Su, an early opponent of Wang Anshi's learning and eventually wrote his own commentary on the *Analects* in an effort to refute it.[127] Wen Tong, the painter, was also caught up in the early disputes over the New Policies and lost his position in the Ritual Academy because of his opposition to Wang Anshi.[128] The youthful Chen Shidao found the New Learning so distasteful that, after a promising interview with Zeng Gong, he abandoned plans to sit for the exams or enter officialdom.[129] Wang Shen, Wang Gong, and Huang Tingjian were all among those who were implicated in Su Shi's incrimination in 1079, for having received treasonous writings from Su and failing to report them. The two Wangs were banished as a result, and Huang Tingjian was fined and sent out to a provincial post. It was Su Shi who brought Qin Guan to prominence early in the Yuanyou era by recommending him for the prestigious decree examination. Su was also responsible then for securing a instructorship for Chen Shidao, lifting him from the ranks of the "commoners"; and he helped to get Wang Gong recalled to the capital as well.[130] When Su Shi was subsequently attacked by Zhao Tingzhi, he understood that Zhao's long-standing enmity towards Huang Tingjian was partly to blame. Similarly, when Jia Yi lodged accusations against Su, that censor did so partly through attacks upon Su's protégé Qin Guan.[131] Su Shi was honored as administrator of the *jinshi* examinations in 1088 (Yuanyou 3); and the assistants he took with him into the exam compound, to determine the winners of the coveted degree, included Huang Tingjian, Li Gonglin, Zhang Lei, Chao Buzhi, and Kong Wenzhong. Of course, virtually all of these men were, like Su, sent into distant southern exile soon after the change in rulership in 1093. Huang Tingjian and Chao Buzhi were both accused of falsifying history in their contributions to the *Veritable Records* of Shenzong's reign.

The interests that Su Shi and these associates showed in calligraphy and painting amounted to one of their most distinctive traits. These men were also generally distinguished by their skills as poets and essayists. But nearly everyone at this level of prominence in the bureaucracy had some literary skill. All statesmen were essayists, and several (including, of course, Wang Anshi himself) were respected as poets, too. But Su's group had by far the strongest links to the visual arts.

What Su Shi managed to do, as the most prolific writer on these arts in the group, was nothing less than to promote a new field for literati self-expression. Painting is every bit as valid as poetry, Su kept asserting; but only a small group of literati—his group—subscribed to this belief and explored the new option. In these arts of the brush, which had previously been the domain mostly of specialists, Su and his friends found a new medium in which they could assert their distinctiveness and affirm their moral superiority. Naturally, they made much of the few individuals they could point to as precursors in the endeavor. The effort had begun in the preceding generation, with the promotion of Yan Zhenqing as calligrapher-statesmen by Ouyang Xiu and his colleagues. Su Shi found a similar exemplar in the field of painting, Wang Wei. (We should understand, of course, that Wang Wei was not nearly the precedent that Su claimed he was. If Wang is now often remembered as equally painter and poet, it is largely the result of Su Shi's creation of that image of him. Before Su, Wang Wei's painting was not so insistently equated with his poetry, nor was his painting thought, despite Su's claims to the contrary,[132] to be on a par with that of the greatest Tang artists.) With these precedents in place, and contemporary artists befriended and brought into his embrace, Su proceeded to promote the conception of these arts as revelations of self and to explore the many ramifications of this notion tirelessly.

During the periods that Su and his friends found themselves concentrated together, and at odds with the others, the function that their painting and calligraphy served to set themselves off as separate and superior is especially clear. Such a time was the early Yuanyou era, when Su Shi was under attack from various directions both for his previous history of opposition to the reforms and for his newer disagreements with Sima Guang and Cheng Yi. The comments, contained in poems and colophons, that Su and the others made upon paintings produced by members of the group are filled with images of proud if costly aloofness from ordinary scholars, that is, those who stood against them in Court politics. A landscape painting by Wang Shen owned by Wang Gong prompts Su Shi to remark that "we three are men who know mountains" (alluding to the banishment they suffered upon Su's incrimination in 1079).[133] A painting of a majestic but unappreciated horse by Li Gonglin elicits Su's observation that "It is not only the horse that did not meet its time / The person [i.e., painter] has likewise played the fool [out of contempt for the world] half his life."[134] A painting Su Shi did of a withered tree reminds Huang Tingjian that even as Su drives a wedge through the arrayed forces of Confucians and Mohists (rival schools of statecraft), he still contains "a hill and valley" (i.e., nature) in his breast.[135] To Chao Buzhi, the various paintings that Li Gonglin did in the examination compound were like the enlightened vision acquired in Chan meditation that sees through the false appearances of the world.[136] On a rock and bamboo painting by Su Shi, to which Li Gonglin had added an ox and herdboy, Huang Tingjian inscribed a colophon that closes with the wish that the animal not become involved in a fight lest the bamboo (i.e., Su Shi) get injured, an apparent reference to factional political strife.[137] Such remarks suggest the range of the cultural, moral, and political meanings that were found in paintings done at the time by members of Su's circle.[138]

Actually, the argument can be taken a step further. Not only did painting and calligraphy becomes a means by which Su and his group affirmed their uniqueness, they turned to these arts in part because of the dangers that came to be associated with the more traditional form of self-expression, poetry. This point might seem far-fetched were it not for the fact that Su Shi once nearly lost his life over poetry he had written, and accusations based on his poetry and other writings continued to hound him later in his career. We recall that when Su left the capital in frustration in 1071 for Hangzhou, Wen Tong cautioned him, "West Lake may be beautiful, but do not write any poems."[139] Obviously, Su did not heed this advice, and Wen's words came to seem prescient. Nevertheless, through the decade of the 1070s, and even more so after his arrest at its end, Su began to experiment with developing a language of values that revolved around brush strokes and painted images of nature. Fittingly, Wen Tong's own ink bamboos became a major subject of the discourse.

Su and his friends did not often write explicitly about the prudence of substituting the visual for the literary arts. But occasionally one comes across telling references to that substitution, or at least to hints that they felt obliged now and then to alter the hierarchy of their involvement with the arts. In a note to Wang Gong from Huangzhou, Su thanks his friend for sending recent examples of his verse and comments, "I wanted to write matching poems, but did not want to break my vow so quickly." He goes on to describe his initiation into the farm work at East Slope. The last section of the note concerns calligraphy and painting: "In your recent letters your use of the brush has gradually approached that of the Jin dynasty masters. And does not my own calligraphy also show some small improvement? As for my paintings, they are not all good. But when I have been drinking and paint ten or twenty sheets, sometimes one of them is worth looking at. Usually, however, somebody makes off with it."[140] Su promises to try to put some of his better paintings and calligraphy aside and send them to his friend at a later date. It is evident that Su has none of the apprehension over such efforts that he has over matching Wang's poems.

When the Empress Dowager Xuanren died in 1093 and Su Shi was sent out of the capital to Dingzhou, one of the men he took with him to serve on his staff was Li Zhiyi. Zhiyi (Duanshu) was the younger brother of Li Zhichun, an executive censor who had recently come

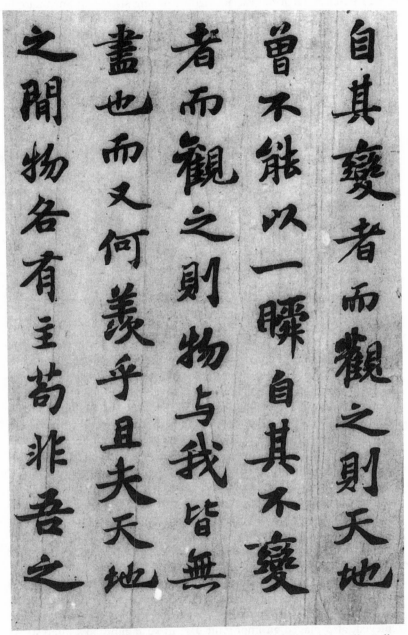

FIGURE 5. Su Shi, "Rhapsody on Red Cliff." Section of a handscroll. Collection of the National Palace Museum, Taiwan, Republic of China.

to Su's defense when he was accused of having slandered Shenzong in the demotion decree of Lü Huiqing he had drafted years before.[141] Zhiyi himself was an accomplished calligrapher, poet, and connoisseur of painting.[142] In Dingzhou, on the eve of the full-scale purge of the Yuanyou officials, Su presented a painting to Zhiyi. It was a work by the Song Taoist Niu Jian and depicted mandarin ducks, bamboo, and rocks. The poem Su wrote to accompany the gift discusses the wisdom of men who stuck to their principles and did not seek to become famous in the world. The solution is not to become a recluse, but simply to rise above all that is contrary in the world. After an insect has metamorphosed and can fly, what need does it have of its cocoon (i.e., hiding-place, protective covering)? Su next addresses the uselessness of books, and offers the painting in their place. The closing lines of the poem read:

此畫聊付君	I present this painting now to you,
幽處得小展	To unroll briefly when you are alone.
新詩勿縱筆	Don't write poems with an unrestrained brush.
羣吠驚邑犬	The pack barks upon hearing one dog in the lane.
時來未可知	What the future holds cannot be known,
妙斲待輪扁	For inspired chopping we await Wheelwright Bian.[143]

Unrestrained literary expression was too risky. It might have provoked a vicious response of the crowd. It was better simply to sit in quietude and view this high-minded image of nature. It should be noted that later in Li Zhiyi's career, the "pack" did indeed bark at him. He was deemed unfit to become a Court official because he had previously been recommended by Su Shi.[144]

The role that fear of political reprisal played in fostering involvement with calligraphy and painting should not be overly emphasized. The suggestion made here is that such apprehension was only one of several factors that encouraged that involvement. While there must have been moments, exampled above, that Su and his friends turned to painting specifically because they felt it to be less politically dangerous than poetry, more often that consideration was probably not uppermost in their minds.

A factor that has not been stressed above is the sheer joy of creative engagement with these arts. Surely, the pleasurableness of doing calligraphy and painting, once technical mastery has been achieved, also played an important part in sustaining Su's interest. As mentioned earlier, in Ouyang Xiu's descriptions of his own engage-

ment with calligraphy, it is the pleasure of the activity that he emphasizes above all else. The spirit of Su Shi's involvement with the art
largely is true to Ouyang's example. The wit and jocularity evident in
so many of Su's colophons (e.g., the caricatures that Su and Huang
Tingjian provided of each other's style) is the most clear-cut indication
of this. Many connoisseurs would also find in the elegant amplitude of
Su's customary running script calligraphy (as exemplified in the Red
Cliff rhapsody scroll [fig. 5]) evidence of the ease and relaxation which
he said that the art brought him.

While the general pleasurableness of practicing these arts may in
some sense be fundamental to Su's unflagging interest in them, the
other factors discussed earlier may ultimately be inseparable components of that same pleasure. With each new painting or calligraphic inscription, as with each new poem, Su and his friends reaffirmed their
distinctiveness from the other literati, statesmen, and philosophers they
held in low esteem; and this reaffirmation, in turn, enhanced the depth
of their enjoyment of the activity. Each new artistic effort by these
eleventh-century literati likewise bolstered their proud claim to be
expressing new meaning (or "not following in the footsteps of the
ancients"), while it also solidified their place in the great literati tradition that stretched back long before their own dynasty. The inquiry
undertaken here suggests, in fact, that the joy that Su and his friends
obviously found or created for themselves in these artistic pursuits was
informed by their preferences on a range of intellectual issues, including
the relationship of the self to the world, ideals of action in the world,
notions of what constituted artistic slavishness or vulgarity, and
theories of knowledge and self-cultivation.

CHAPTER TEN

Washing Away the Silks and Perfumes: Subjectivity in the Song Lyric (Ci)

Everyone acknowledges that Su Shi produced a strikingly new kind of literary song (*ci*). Critics have disagreed about the exact nature of Su's innovations in this genre of poetry and have disputed their value, but no one denies that his way of writing song lyrics was novel. There has also been a persistent, if not necessarily dominant, judgment among scholars that Su's corpus of *ci* is his greatest literary achievement, surpassing even his work in the *shi* form.

Ci was an urban entertainment song that attracted the attention of literati poets during the Five Dynasties and early Northern Song. The music consisted of several hundred standard song tunes. To these tunes poets set their own new lyrics. (There were also literati who wrote both new tunes and new words, but these men were in the minority.) The music, most of which was never transcribed, was lost as the tunes went out of fashion and were gradually replaced by another type of music at the end of the dynasty. What survived were the thousands of lyrics the literati had written, many set to the same tune pattern, which from early on had begun to circulate in written form without any musical transcription.

Actually, the musicality of the *ci* form is itself a knotty problem, in which Su Shi figures prominently. A performance tradition of Five Dynasties *ci* lasted into the Song, but the lyrics were also preserved in book manuscripts that had no musical notation. This meant that Song-dynasty literati were just as likely to pick up a manuscript of earlier *ci* and read it as they were to hear the same *ci* performed. A new way of appreciating, and of perceiving, *ci* thus began to evolve: it could be treated as a literary form. No doubt the spread of printing in the latter part of the eleventh century gave momentum to this trend. Nevertheless, the older way of appreciating *ci*—listening as it was performed—persisted, too. Su Shi's place in the ever widening divergence is distinctly on the literary side. He freely admits that he cannot sing and implies that he has no ear for music.[1] Many of the *ci* he composed depart at places from the tonal or prosodic conventions of the chosen tune, and such violations led to charges early on that Su Shi's *ci* could not be sung and that they were, for this reason and others, untrue to the intrinsic nature of the form (*fei bense*).[2] Yet it is clear from Su Shi's own prefaces to his *ci* and from the anecdotal record that many of his *ci* were sung, often right on the spot as he wrote them.

Even as *ci* grew, through Su's century, somewhat detached from music, it retained the intrinsic characteristics that had been determined by its original setting. Whether performed at the banquets of Court officials or in the wine shops and brothels of Hangzhou's entertainment quarters, *ci* was a sentimental song form that typically treated some aspect of the world of love and romance (and especially love's frustrations), just as entertainment songs have done in countless other times and places. Increased urban affluence, the actual liaisons that often developed between the female singers and their male patrons, and the hostility of elite Confucian values towards romantic impulses may be listed among the factors that helped to make this song form so appealing in Song-dynasty China.

Earlier *ci*, as preserved in the influential anthology *Among the Flowers (Huajian ji)*, compiled in 940, feature depictions of well-to-do ladies alone in their rooms.[3] Evocative descriptions of the lady's dress, hairdo and makeup, and her accoutrements (e.g., mirror, censer, embroidered bedcovers), all hint at the woman's keen sense of ennui, her awareness of time and the loss of her looks, or the lonely vigil she keeps for some word from a departed lover. Such were the images of women conveyed in songs women sang at the banquets attended by the poets featured in this anthology.

By the middle of the eleventh century, *ci* writers had broadened the scope of their compositions. The setting of *ci* was no longer so apt to be confined to the boudoir. It might as well be a garden, a lake, or a house of entertainment. *Ci* began to admit more speech and dialogue (between lovers); even the descriptive language became more colloquial, and writers experimented with narrative and dramatized incident. The themes also gained in breadth. While love in all its aspects remained a primary concern, the related themes of aging, affection for friends, and the passing of the seasons were also regularly treated.

The persona or voice heard in *ci* underwent some changes together with these developments in style. *Ci* in *Among the Flowers* may present an objectified description of a boudoir scene, in which case the poetic persona is that of a detached observer looking in, or the pieces may actually be written in the voice of the person present in the room. Some pieces switch back and forth between the two modes of discourse, alternating third-person description with first-person speech. Whatever the approach, the language used normally makes it abundantly clear that the person who is the focus of the piece, the occupant of the boudoir, is female. We know that virtually all the authors were male, and so we understand that we cannot equate, in any simple sense, the female in the song with the author. (We also know that the singers were female, and this helps to explain the feminine focus and voice in the songs, although it does not establish their authenticity as expressions of feminine experience.)

One of the developments from Five Dynasties to mid-eleventh-century *ci* is the more frequent appearance of songs whose voice is indeterminate with regard to gender. Consider a song such as the following one by Yan Shu (991–1055; in D. C. Lau's translation):

踏莎行	*To the tune, "Treading the Sedge"*
小徑紅稀	On the narrow path a touch of red,
芳郊綠徧	In the fields an expanse of green,
高臺樹色陰陰見	By the tall tower the trees show a darkish hue.
春風不解禁楊花	The spring wind has not the sense to restrain the willow catkins,
濛濛亂撲行人面	Which rush wildly in a drizzle at the faces of passers by.
翠葉藏鶯	The green leaves enfold the oriole,
朱簾隔燕	The red blinds shut out the swallow.
爐香靜逐遊絲轉	The incense from the burner chases the gossamer quietly around.
一場愁夢酒醒時	As I awake from a troubled dream, the wine wearing off,
斜陽卻照深深院	There goes the slanting sun shining on the inner courtyard.[4]

Given the earlier history of the genre, when we read this we might well picture a woman alone in her room. The language itself, however, does not rule out the possibility of a male persona. Certainly, the song hints at loneliness for a lover: the willows suggest a previous parting scene, the mention of the orioles and swallows—common images of spring and its coupling—and especially the drinking alone and the "troubled" dream all leave little doubt about what is on the person's mind. But we still cannot be sure that this is a woman longing for her man rather than a man missing his woman. And if the latter is a possibility, a reader might be tempted to identify the persona with Yan Shu himself. But other readers would insist that the real achievement of such a song is that it is so evocatively detached from any single interpretation or identification, that its effect comes largely from being richly ambiguous.

If songs such as this increased in number by the mid Northern Song, so, too, did those that unambiguously present a male voice. That type of presentation had always been a part of the *ci* tradition, though a very minor one at first. In the songs by Wei Zhuang and Wen Tingyun one can find clear-cut examples of male personas speaking of their longing for women they have known. There was also the special case of Li Yu, the conquered king of the Southern Tang, whose *ci* have always been read autobiographically (though the validity of that practice has recently been challenged).[5]

In Su Shi's time, one *ci* writer became enormously popular and, in literati circles, quite notorious for producing songs that describe the romantic liaisons between men and professional entertainers in surprisingly explicit terms. Moreover, a great many of Liu Yong's *ci* unmistakably feature a male persona, such as the following example (in James R. Hightower's translation):

小鎮西	*To the tune, "West of the Little Market"*
意中有箇人	I'm thinking of someone
芳顏二八	Sweet face, just sixteen
天然俏	Born beautiful—
自來奸點	She has got to be a minx!
最奇絕	Where she is most remarkable
是笑時媚靨深深	Is when she laughs and her dimples show.
百態千嬌	She has a hundred ways and a thousand charms,
再三偎著	And the more you embrace her
再三香滑	The more sweet and slippery she gets.
久離缺	I've neglected her a long time.
夜來魂夢裏	Last night in a dream
尤花殢雪	We made love
分明似舊家時節	Like old times.
正歡悅	Then just when I was happy

313

被鄰鷄喚起	The cock next door woke me up.
一場寂寥	Everything was quiet
無眠向曉	But I could not get back to sleep;
空有半窗殘月	The setting moon outside my window wasted.[6]

Hightower has called attention to the unlikelihood that Liu Yong was chronicling his own love affairs in such songs as this, and concludes that there is no compelling reason to read his songs as autobiographical. Liu Yong was almost certainly drawing upon his own experience of the pleasure quarters when he wrote; but what he wrote, even those pieces cast in a male voice, were still separable from their author. The songs were, after all, written to become part of the fiction of oral performance. That is not to say that every listener might be credited with the ability to keep this distinction, between author and persona, in mind. Liu Yong was a man of low repute among scholars, a man known as dissolute and wanton. Surely, the songs he wrote were themselves largely responsible for this reputation. As for Ouyang Xiu, Liu Yong's contemporary but hardly his associate, political enemies of his seem to have capitalized upon the widespread inability to distinguish persona from author in *ci*. It appears that these enemies, taking advantage of Ouyang's reputation as a *ci* writer, forged some songs in which the male persona is infatuated with a very young girl and circulated them under Ouyang's name, hoping thus to impugn his image as a moral and principled man. It proved difficult for Ouyang to vindicate himself.

A portion of Ouyang's authentic *ci* are in fact quite close stylistically to Su Shi's early work in the genre and may, as Ye Jiaying has pointed out, have influenced Su's first efforts.[7] Ouyang wrote a great many *ci* that describe drinking parties, outings, or farewell banquets, and were no doubt performed at such events that he hosted or attended. A large number of these pieces are written in what sounds like the voice of a male persona, as in the song below:

浪淘沙	*To the tune, "Waves Scour the Sands"*
今日北池遊	Today we come to North Pond for pleasure.
漾漾輕舟	Bobbing in a light boat,
波光激灧柳條柔	The waves shimmer, the willows are supple.
如此春來春又去	So it is that spring arrives and spring departs
白了人頭	Turning a man's hair white.
好妓好歌喉	A lovely singing girl with a lovely voice.
不醉難休	How can we stop before we're drunk?
勸君滿滿酌金甌	Now fill your golden cup to the rim,

| 縱使花時常病酒 | Even if you're sick from wine the whole flower season, |
| 也是風流 | It's still the gallant thing to do.[8] |

The voice in this song might easily be taken for Ouyang's own, but need not be. It is really the voice of any of the party-goers. (The translation is forced to be only slightly more gender-specific than the Chinese: it is quite clear even in the original that *ren* at the end of the first stanza refers to a man or men.) The poem is eminently detachable from its author and was written, of course, so that it could be performed over and over at party after party, whether Ouyang was a participant or not. Its images and themes make it suitable for countless literati gatherings.

In reading chronologically through *The Complete Song Dynasty Ci*, one senses upon reaching Su Shi's section of that vast compilation a dramatic departure. Two traits in particular account for the change: an autobiographical tone and an expansion of subject matter. That the poems are autobiographical is clear from conspicuous subtitles or prefaces (in which Su records the specific occasion on which the piece was written). In the thirteenth century, Yuan Haowen observed that Su was the first writer of *ci* who was not content to use the stock language of the "palace style" tradition but instead wrote of his own "feelings and nature."[9] In his willingness to leave the traditional confines of *ci* subject matter, furthermore, Su is so bold as to make even Li Yu seem narrow by comparison. This was what Hu Yin, a century earlier, was talking about when he observed that Su's *ci* "washed away in one stroke all the colored silks and perfumed oils of earlier compositions."[10] Both traits, moreover, figure in the critical evaluation most commonly given of Su's work: that he wrote *ci* using the methods of *shi* poetry (*yi shi wei ci*).[11] This judgment, naturally, was as often uttered in criticism as in praise.

The *ci* by Su Shi on Red Cliff, quoted in an earlier chapter, already happens to illustrate these innovations. Two more examples are given below to suggest the range of autobiographical experiences Su treated in the genre. The first, from Su's Huangzhou exile, describes his return one night from East Slope to his residence in town. The second commemorates a dream he had of his first wife ten years after she died.

臨江仙	*To the tune, "Immortal by the River"*
夜歸臨皋	*Returning at Night to Lin'gao*
夜飲東坡醒復醉	I drank tonight at East Slope, sobered up, and drank again.

歸來髣髴三更	It must have been midnight before I got home.
家童鼻息已雷鳴	The houseboy was snoring like thunder,
敲門都不應	My pounding on the gate was all in vain,
倚杖聽江聲	I leaned on my staff and listened to the river.

長恨此身非我有	I always regret this body is not mine to control,
何時忘卻營營	When shall I put aside the ambitions of life?
夜闌風靜縠紋平	The night is late, the wind calm, the water rippled.
小舟從此逝	Let me drift off in a tiny boat,
江海寄餘生	Give my remaining years to rivers and lakes.[12]

江城子	*To the tune, "River Town"*
乙卯正月二十日夜	*Recording a Dream on the Night*
記夢	*of the 20th Day of the 1st Month*
	of Yimao [1075]

十年生死兩茫茫	Ten years, the dead and living lie distantly apart.
不思量	I do not try to remember,
自難忘	It is hard to forget.
千里孤墳	The lone grave a thousand miles away,
無處話淒涼	No place to express the heart's chill.
縱使相逢應不識	Even if we met, she would not know me,
塵滿面	Face covered with dust,
鬢如霜	Hair like frost.

夜來幽夢忽還鄉	Last night my lonely dream took me home.
小軒窗	By a small window
正梳妝	She was combing and making up.
相顧無言	We gazed at each other, speechless,
惟有淚千行	Only a thousand rows of tears.
料得年年斷腸處	I picture that place of heartbreak year after year,
明月夜	On moonlit nights,
短松岡	Low pines beside a mound.[13]

Both pieces come with the author's own prefatory note, which ties them to a specific occasion. In this regard the two *ci* are indistinguishable from occasional *shi*. In the body of each piece, moreover, the author cultivates a highly personal voice, and it is a voice that we identify immediately with the historical Su Shi (who frequented East Slope, whose first wife had died ten years before, etc.). Obviously, these *ci* are much more securely linked to their author than those by other writers cited above. As for their content, the two pieces also depart strikingly from the conventional subjects of *ci*. The speaker in the first is alone but not lonely for a lover or friend. His actions (banging on his gate, leaning on his staff) have no place in the stock depictions of *ci*. His desire is reminiscent of the archetypal recluse, Fan Li, and belongs to the tradition of the renunciation of the world in *shi* poetry. Certain elements of the second piece may seem closer to the conventions of *ci* (e.g., loving remembrance, solitary toilette, tears). But these elements are so completely transformed by the substitution of deceased wife for deserted courtesan that their derivation from the vocabulary of *ci* is likely to go unnoticed.

Reasons for a New Style

These examples only begin to suggest the nature of Su Shi's work in the genre, yet it will be useful to ask, even at this early stage in our account, why he effected this change. Why did Su Shi take a form that had, because of its performance tradition, presented fictive personas or, at most, vague and unindividuated voices and transform it into a vehicle for self-expression? The question has rarely been asked, much less satisfactorily answered (short of saying, in effect, that Su Shi was a great literary talent or a strong personality and so naturally his *ci* are distinctive). Most historians of *ci* have concentrated their efforts upon describing Su's achievement rather than probing its causes.

One sympathizes with that approach because, in fact, the answer to the question is not at all obvious. We may contrast the situation with that of Su's innovations in calligraphy and painting. Apart from his practice of those arts, Su expresses his views as a theorist, critic, and connoisseur in hundreds of colophons, poems, and essays. There is, if anything, a surfeit of material written by Su Shi himself that must be sorted through, synthesized, and interpreted by the scholar who would explain his underlying motives and values. The situation is the reverse with *ci*: sources barely exist. Su wrote no essays or poems on the *ci* form. He left no body of critical or theoretical writings on the genre. What survives, in fact, is no more than a few stray remarks he made about *ci*, mostly in notes he sent to friends.

Su Shi's nearly complete silence regarding his and others' work in the genre is a reflection of its low repute during the Northern Song.[14] *Ci* writing was an activity many literati engaged in as a diversion or amusement, but not one to which they wanted to call posterity's attention. *Ci* was for entertainment, not for serious purposes. It was commonly referred to with the pejorative term "little song lyrics" (*xiao ci*). Even the most prolific and accomplished *ci* writers rigorously excluded their work in the genre from their collected literary works. To be known primarily as a composer of *ci* was undesirable—the fate of Liu Yong, rake of the demimonde. At the close of the century, when Yan Jidao neared the end of his life and had nothing to show for himself except a collection of ci, his literati friends considered it awkward and embarrassing. Huang Tingjian tried as best he could to save face for Yan, writing an apologetic and convoluted preface to the collection.[15]

This lack of respect for ci helps explain a crucial difference between Su's handling of the form and his achievements in calligraphy and painting. If the latter arts were, as argued above, a means by which Su Shi and his colleagues set themselves apart from rival factions in the government, it should not be surprising that they labored hard to enhance the prestige of calligraphy and especially painting, so that their involvement could be seen as significant. Ci writing, however, had never enjoyed the stature of calligraphy or painting; and Su Shi did little to augment its standing. Although he composed song lyrics prolifically, Su did not embark upon a campaign to justify his activity. He did not, that is, write about his ci writing. On the contrary, he was conspicuously silent about it. Given the low repute of the form and this absence of a critical effort to elevate it, we must look for the key to Su's motives in changing the song lyric in something less public than its potential for shaping the way he would be perceived by others.

Attention has recently been called to "the problem of the genuine" in ci, and this is a topic that may be relevant to the issue at hand. To put it in the simplest terms, essays by Stephen Owen and Grace Fong have examined the dynamics of the use of personas in song lyrics and suggested that ci writers may themselves have been ambivalent over the apparent requirement of them in this form.[16] Here, the ready adoption in ci of voices that either cannot or need not be identified with the author is contrasted with the shi tradition and its strong assumption of identity between poetic voice and author (as exemplified in the maxim $shi\ yan\ zhi$, "poetry is to express your innermost intent"). Some writers of ci were keenly aware of this disparity between the two poetic traditions, and they produced ci whose themes include a probing of the problem of writing under fictional personas or masks. Thus we find ci in which the genuineness of the speaking voice is itself called into question, or pieces in which masks are created only to be shed before the song ends. In certain writers' hands, this rich interplay of true faces with fabricated masks becomes a stylistic trait and major source of interest.

Is it possible that Su Shi was similarly concerned about the distance between the genuine voice of the poet and standard ci personas, and that he "wrote ci using the methods of shi poetry" because he decided to reject the traditional fictionality of ci? The possibility warrants some attention here. Nowhere does Su Shi say as much, which is hardly surprising since his remarks about his or anyone else's *ci* are so few. However, Su did write about the issue of genuineness (*zhen*) in another context. He associated the value with Tao Qian. Genuineness was, in fact, the essence of Tao's greatness as a poet and a man: "Confucius did not approve of Wei Shenggao, nor did Mencius approve of Ling Zhongzi.[17] Both sages disliked that these men were not true to their feelings. When Tao Yuanming wanted to serve, he served; and he did not consider his quest of office objectionable. When he wanted to withdraw, he withdrew; and he did not consider himself superior for resigning. When he was hungry, he knocked on a stranger's door and begged for food. When he had enough to eat, he set out chicken and millet to entertain his guests. The reason that men in both ancient and modern times have admired him is that they prize his genuineness."[18]

There is a connection with poetry here, because this was written about the great poet and because it was written as part of a colophon on the poetry collection of an acquaintance. It calls to mind Su's statement that he preferred to offend other people by spitting out the words lodged in his mouth rather than offend himself by swallowing them.[19] He himself recalls the statement upon reading one of Tao Qian's drinking poems, which narrates Tao's polite refusal of a friend's advice that he lift himself out of poverty by going back out into the world to join "the muddy game."[20]

It is, admittedly, a long way from such utterances to the proposition that Su was uncomfortable with the assumed persona or masks of *ci*. Yet Su's preferences in diverse forms of expression may be at least loosely connected to a general valuation of genuineness. Certainly, his views on calligraphy and painting stress the importance of the practitioner's personality in his art. Su insists on such a direct link between the inner being of the person and the images he creates. Wen Tong *is* his bamboos, the flavor of the man *is* his calligraphic style. No space is allowed for any pretense, artifice, or craft to intervene between personality and art. Su's emphasis upon rapid and unreflective artistic execution is related to the same general preference. That kind of spontaneity captures the "natural genuineness" (*tianzhen*) of the artist.[21] Painstaking execution ensures that this quality will be lost.

On the other hand, Su Shi does not himself bring *ci* into his discussions of the genuine, and there are times that he seems to sanction or even take delight in the assumed roles that *ci* encouraged. When he was in Hangzhou, once he went to visit the Chan monk Datong (Shanben), of the Jingci Monastery, and took a singing girl along with him on his outing.[22] Datong, predictably enough, was displeased with this antic. In an attempt to mollify the monk by teasing him still further, Su composed a *ci* for the girl to sing. Su speaks in the piece of borrowing the monk's clapper and door-knocker to beat time for the tune, and expresses regret that Maitreya will, if he delays his return to the world too long, not see the girl in the prime of her beauty. The song also contains these lines: "I am just playing as I step upon the stage; / Do not think ill of me."[23] Is Su Shi referring just to his comedy that day or also to the roles assumed in this and most *ci*? And is his apparent acceptance here of the idea of role-playing in *ci* out of the ordinary for him, or do we have to look elsewhere for the cause of his departure from *ci* conventions? The questions are difficult to answer.

It will be useful to pause here to consider a related factor: Su's misgivings about the stock romantic sentimentality of *ci*, especially its preoccupation with emotional dependence, longing, and descriptions of feminine beauty. The stray remarks Su Shi makes about *ci* suggest impatience both with the genre's concentration on a kind of romantic love that may often seem contrived or shallow, given its social realities, and its preoccupation with feminine beauty. (These attitudes anticipate the criticism of Su's own work in the genre as being "deficient in the emotions," a charge that has been disputed as often as it has been lodged.)[24] These would appear to be less exclusively literary issues than the problem of the genuineness of the poetic voice, and may stem from preferences Su held on matters quite unconnected to *ci* writing.

Again, to reach such conclusions we must extrapolate from just a few comments written by Su or attributed to him. Several instances survive in which Su Shi speaks critically of Liu Yong's *ci* and seeks to distance his own efforts in the genre from those of that immensely popular songwriter. From Mizhou, Su Shi included this comment in a letter to a friend: "Recently I have written several little *ci*. They may not have the flavor of Mr. Liu Qi's [Yong's] compositions, but they too represent a style of their own. Ha! A few days ago I went hunting in the countryside and caught quite a few animals. I wrote this *ci* about it. If you have a brawny northeasterner sing it, clapping his hands and stomping his feet, it makes for quite a manly sight! I have copied it out to amuse you."[25] The song this letter accompanies describes Su's hunting experience.[26] It thus departs in its subject, tone, and diction from virtually everything readers normally expected in a *ci*. Su Shi did not continue his experiment with what might be called "martial *ci*," but that at least was one alternative to Liu Yong's style that he attempted.

A clearer notion of precisely what Su Shi objected to in Liu Yong's *ci* is conveyed by the following anecdote that records an exchange between Su and his friend Qin Guan:

When Shaoyou [Qin Guan] returned to the capital from Kuaiji and saw East Slope, East Slope said to him, "I never thought that after we parted you would start writing *ci* in the manner of Liu Qi [Yong]."

"Although I have no learning," Shaoyou replied, "I would not stoop to that."

"'My soul wastes away / Faced with this moment': are these not lines like Liu Qi's?"[27]

The lines that Su quotes are from one of Qin Guan's best-known song lyrics, one in which a male persona describes his sorrow as he parts from the girl he loves, who is a professional entertainer. (A contemporary source says that Qin Guan wrote the piece for a singing girl he was in love with but had to leave.)[28] The lines open the second stanza of a parting song:

銷魂	My souls wastes away
當此際	Faced with this moment;
香囊暗解	A perfume pouch is silently untied,
羅帶輕分	A gauze sash is lightly given.
謾贏得	All I've earned, to no purpose,
青樓薄倖名存	Is fame as a drifter in pleasure houses.
此去何時見也	Leaving now, when will I see her again?
襟袖上	A sleeve is raised uselessly
空惹啼痕	To wipe the stains of tears.[29]

The voice in this *ci* does indeed sound like the remorseful profligate who speaks in many of Liu Yong's songs.

Su Shi was not always negative in his references to Liu Yong. It will be helpful here to take account of some of Liu Yong's writing that Su Shi singles out for praise:

對瀟瀟	I watch the driving storm,
暮雨灑江天	Rains at nightfall splatter the Yangzi sky,
一番洗清秋	Cleansing all at once the pure autumn scene.
漸霜風淒慘	Winds blow sullenly with the coming frost,
關河冷落	Mountain passes and rivers are desolate,
殘照當樓	Fading rays shine on the tall building.
是處紅衰翠減	Blossoms here have faded, leaves are sparse:
苒苒物華休	All flowering and growth has ceased.
惟有長江水	Only the waters of the Yangzi
無語東流	Flow eastward without a word.[30]

The middle lines, Su observed, are in no way inferior to the highest accomplishments of the great Tang poets.[31] The stanza is replete with sentiment, but not with sentiment that is necessarily tied to the world of courtesans and entertainment houses.

Other passages could be adduced in which Su Shi similarly expresses reservations about or pokes fun at male obsession with feminine charms, either inside or outside of *ci*. Su regrets that the world knows the elder scholar Zhang Xian only for his romantic *ci* rather than for his *shi* poetry, which Su considers vastly superior. Is this not another case, Su asks, of the world being more fond of feminine beauty (*se*) than moral virtue?[32] When Li Yu lost his kingdom to the invading armies from the north and was about to be taken from his palace as a prisoner, he wrote a *ci* that described his tearful farewell to the palace women, while parting songs played mournfully. "What was he doing," Su demands, "shedding tears in front of his concubines?" "He should have wailed aloud at the ancestral shrine of the royal clan and admitted his culpability publicly to his people."[33] Huang Tingjian had written a *ci* about the familiar figure of the lone fisherman. When asked what he particularly liked about his piece, Huang recited the opening description of the landscape: "Over Bride Jetty painted eyebrows are sad; / By Maiden Pool watery eyes have the look of autumn," in which images of woman's face, which the poet was encouraged to use by the feminine place names, are used to describe the dark hills and autumnal waters. Su Shi comments: "As soon as he leaves 'Bride Jetty,' he enters 'Maiden Pool.' Isn't this fisherman too much of a philanderer?"[34]

But what of the many *ci* Su Shi himself wrote that dwell upon the romantic relations between literati and singing girls? It is not true, despite how often it is asserted or implied, that Su Shi completely disavowed the traditional interest the genre had in depictions of situations and sentiments that spring from love between courtesans and scholars. Su's best known and most innovative pieces may do so, but not his entire corpus of *ci*.

There are various ways to account for the presence of these seemingly conventional *ci* in Su's collection. One is to acknowledge the weight of the song-lyric tradition and to understand that there were many occasions on which that tradition would prevail over the impulses of even the most innovative writers. Lapses back into powerful and omnipresent conventions hardly require much explanation or defense. Chronology might be another factor. The largest concentration of conventional *ci* in Su's collection is found among his earliest works, especially the pieces that date from his first assignment to Hangzhou. As Su gained experience as a *ci* writer, he moved further away from standard material. Lastly, the argument might also be made that in many, if not all, of the apparently conventional pieces he wrote that dwell upon romantic affections, there is yet some distinctiveness to be discerned.

One important feature is the presence of autobiographical markers in Su's song lyrics (and here we return to the issue of genuineness). Consider a song such as the following:

江城子	*To the tune, "River Town"*
別徐州	*Departing from Xuzhou*

天涯流落思無窮	Adrift at the world's end, with boundless longing.
既相逢	Once we had met
却恖恖	Time rushed faster.
攜手佳人	The beauty who holds my hand
和淚折殘紅	Plucks the fading red blossoms with tears.
為問東風餘幾許	How long, she asks, will the east wind last?
春縱在	Even if spring remains,
與誰同	Who will share it with me?
隋堤三月水溶溶	Sui Canal waters in April stretch afar;
背歸鴻	Against the returning wild geese
去吳中	I set out for Wu
回首彭城	And gaze back toward Pengcheng
清泗與淮通	Where the limpid Si meets the Huai.
欲寄相思千點淚	Though you want to send a thousand love tears,
流不到	They cannot flow all the way
楚江東	To the eastern River in Chu.[35]

It is true that the opening stanza is filled with stock language and is, by itself, quite unremarkable. However, it does not stand by itself. The subtitle or prefatory note has already transformed our understanding of what we are reading. This is not another anonymous love song, detached from its author's life and thus eminently repeatable and adaptable to any parting situation. The subtitle roots the song lyric in a well-known moment of Su Shi's life. The piece, we conclude, must in some sense represent the author's genuine feelings during that occasion. The second stanza confirms the impression given by the subtitle. Through the stanza we follow Su's progress southward toward his new post in Huzhou. The place names all fit. Su sails down the Sui Canal (i.e., the Old Grand Canal) from Xuzhou (Pengcheng), until it meets the Si River, crosses the Huai River, and delivers him to Yangzhou on the Yangzi ("the eastern River in Chu"). He is proceeding into the ancient southeastern region of Wu, just when the migratory geese are flying north in spring. The weight of all these autobiographical details gives an entirely new force to stock lines about the sorrows of parting.

The sentiment itself merits some comment. Even when Su does choose to write about singing girls (the woman in this song could be no one else), he avoids, as Ye Jiaying has pointed out, the popular emphasis on "powder and rouge" or contrived eroticism.[36] That is what Su disapproved of in Liu Yong and Qin Guan. Actually, it is tempting to read the song above as a meditation on the author's predicament (already "adrift at the world's end" and now uprooted again), in which the *jiaren* is just one more object of affection he is forced to relinquish, rather than to understand the piece as a love song written for the woman who has captured his heart. In fact, the piece has been interpreted as a farewell to a dear *friend* in Xuzhou, in which case the *jiaren* is little more than a stock element in the emotional scene (or perhaps even a trope for the friend).[37] This reading is not entirely satisfactory, but the way Su writes about the girl does leave room for such an interpretation. Whichever way this *ci* is taken, Su is certainly striving to write something different from a stock love song. By injecting himself conspicuously into the piece and by linking the parting sorrow on this occasion to the larger restlessness of his life, Su alters the import of the conventional *ci* on lovers' parting.

The issue of chronology in Su's *ci* writing was mentioned above. Chronology points to another factor that must have influenced Su's innovations in the genre. As has often been remarked, Su does not seem to have begun composing *ci* until surprisingly late into middle age. There are no surviving pieces that predate his first tour at Hangzhou, which began when he was thirty-six. This late start is particularly striking given Su's later productivity. No Northern Song writer left more *ci* than Su (over three hundred pieces by him are extant). In the years before his mid thirties, Su Shi could not have been ignorant of *ci* or lacked the opportunity to experiment with it. Rather than to suppose that he was simply busy with other kinds of writing, as is often suggested, it is more likely that he was at first somewhat averse to *ci*, for the reasons that his comments quoted above suggest. However, Su Shi overcame this reluctance in Hangzhou, where he fell under the influence of the great elder *ci* writer Zhang Xian. Su Shi began to compose song lyrics, specializing in farewell songs that were performed at banquets for departing friends.[38] Conventional in some respects, these farewell songs already show Su's preference for explicitly tying his compositions to specific occasions, personalizing them.

Su continued to compose *ci* during his ensuing provincial

assignments. A handful of his most famous pieces date from these years, the remainder of the 1070s, but they are mixed together with a larger number of less remarkable compositions. Su's period of sustained greatness as a *ci* writer did not come until the next stage of his life, his Huangzhou exile. Not only did his productivity in the genre peak during this exile (and the years immediately following), it was then that his new voice in *ci* became firmly established. Huangzhou marked, as leading critics have observed, a new level of achievement for Su in the form.[39]

Could it be just a coincidence that Su's genius as a *ci* writer reached full maturity only during his first exile? What connection might there be between the two events? We know, of course, that Su had been imprisoned and nearly put to death for his literary work immediately before. It was his prose essays, letters, rhapsodies (*fu*), and most of all his *shi* poetry that had landed him in prison. The one genre that goes completely unmentioned in the lengthy indictments against him, which specify dozens of offending pieces, is his *ci*. *Ci* were thought to belong to a much lower order of expression. Su's accusers would naturally pass over them as unworthy of their attention, confident that no writer would have used entertainment songs to express political criticism. In this instance the accusers were correct: there is no political satire or dissent in Su's early *ci*. But Su's enemies did not even bother to trump up charges against him involving his *ci*, as they did with others of his writings. It may also have been that in 1079 there were as yet no printed editions of Su's *ci*, as there were of his writings in other forms (to the great annoyance of Su's prosecutors). This, too, reflects the low status, as well as the oral circulation, of *ci*.

After Su Shi arrived in Huangzhou, he frequently stated in letters to friends that he had given up refined literature (*wen*), by which he meant literary prose and *shi* poetry. He declined to answer poems sent to him or to fulfill requests for prose inscriptions.[40] He was afraid not only for himself but also for the recipients of whatever he might write. His trial had shown how readily such friends could be implicated in his "crimes." Su's family must also have been urging this restraint upon him. (We recall his wife's outburst, denouncing his incessant writing, when her boat was boarded by soldiers looking for more incriminating evidence in 1079.) We know, of course, that Su did not give up the more prestigious forms altogether, no matter how many times he announced his intention to do so. But his productivity in the *shi* form did decline, by 50 to 75 percent, while his output of *ci* actually increased during the same period.[41] On at least one occasion Su specifically identified his different attitudes towards the two forms.

Writing to a friend from Huangzhou, Su enclosed a copy of a newly written *ci* and explained, "Although recently I no longer write *shi* poetry, I have no such constraint when it comes to little song lyrics."[42] In another note, his excitement over the heightened interest he now took in *ci* is evident: "Recently I have composed several new musical verses, and each one is extraordinary."[43]

It appears that Su Shi was less apt to avoid writing *ci* than *shi* at Huangzhou because he felt *ci* to be less risky. This helps to explain the quantitative shift in his output: he wrote more *ci* and appreciably fewer *shi* than before. The qualitative change in his *ci* from Huangzhou—the final emergence of the intensely personal style as the dominant mode in his work in the genre—must be a related development. As he turned increasingly to *ci*, he invested it more thoroughly than he had ever done before with the autobiographical voice of the *shi* tradition. It must be remembered that Su Shi had not grown disillusioned or tired of *shi*. It was external constraints that caused him to curtail his efforts in the more established form. Now he found a new outlet for personal expression. But for *ci* to serve as that outlet, Su's earlier experiments— encouraged, it seems, by his low regard for stock depictions of romantic longing—had to be given full rein. In Huangzhou there were finally reasons for doing so.

There is one last factor that warrants mention. In *shi* poetry, as we have seen, the expression of certain sentiments was a problem with which Su Shi struggled. As full of feeling as many of his *shi* poems may be—with fond longing for his brother or friends, nostalgia for Meishan, or muted delight in monastery scenes—there often remains some unease with the self-centeredness of sentiment; and, consequently, some effort to objectify the emotion and viewpoint is evident. The expression of frustration over lack of worldly advancement or exile was particularly problematic, for it contradicted the ideal of remaining unaffected by life's vicissitudes.

An apparent contradiction surfaces here. If it is true that in the *shi* form Su Shi strove to transcend self-centeredness, why is his *ci* poetry famous for cultivating a highly personal voice that can only be identified with the author himself? Do not the two innovations run directly against each other? The contradiction is real but becomes less troubling when each genre is examined in its peculiar niche in the hierarchy of expressive forms.

Because *ci* was considered less weighty and more frivolous than *shi*, the problem of the emotions (*qing*) did not apply with nearly so much urgency. Su Shi indulged himself more freely with *ci* than with the more prestigious form. *Ci* had always been the supremely sen-

timental form. But *qing* in the context of *ci* had normally been restricted to those emotions associated with stock romantic situations. If
Su turned to *ci* in part because its low stature liberated it from the constraints under which he wrote *shi*, naturally he would not be content
simply to mimic the public voices of entertainment songs. The recourse
to *ci* as a form in which *qing* need not be inhibited by the desire to
appear morally cultivated made sense only if the feelings expressed
could be personalized, tailored to the life of the author.

It would be easy to overstate the argument, exaggerating the
difference in the scope given to emotions in the two forms. Nevertheless, there is some emotional latitude or release evident in Su's *ci* when
they are read against his *shi* poetry. We might consider the occasion of
Su's departure from his post as prefect of Xuzhou in 1079. One of the
shi poems he wrote then was translated in an earlier chapter. "Don't let
the people hold me back," the poem opens, "Don't let the singers and
pipes play mournfully." Su seeks to transcend whatever regrets he has
upon leaving. He goes on to reflect upon all the similar departures that
the stone statues at the roadside have witnessed, setting his departure
in the larger historical context.

The *ci* that Su wrote on the same occasion treat much more
openly, and with less denial, the sorrow of the farewell. The *ci* also
show less resolve to conceptualize the event in objective terms
(whether spatial, historical, or psychological). One of the two *ci* Su
wrote at the time was translated above. It dwells on a woman Su leaves
behind in Xuzhou, her loneliness, and her tears (which cannot flow in
the river as far as Su's new location). The woman embodies the sorrow of the moment; she, like the author, is consumed by "endless
longings." A second *ci* explicitly broaches the ideal Su holds to in *shi*
poetry, and then admits that, in this form at least, it cannot be maintained. This is the opening verse:

玉觴無味	The jade goblet has no flavor,
中有佳人千點淚	Containing a thousand of her tears.
學道忘憂	We study the Way and overcome vexations,
一念還成不自由	But all at once they return, taking control.[44]

Su Shi was less apt to allow his emotions to have the upper hand when
writing *shi*.

A similar sort of divergence may be seen on other occasions and
topics as well. (Actually, the observations made earlier about the differences between Su Shi's *ci* on Red Cliff and his first rhapsody on the
same theme already anticipate this point.) There are, for example,

intensely emotional occasions on which Su opted for *ci* instead of *shi*, and his choice must have been influenced by his relative comfort with strong feelings in the junior form. The *ci* he wrote on the tenth anniversary of his first wife's death was quoted above. There is no comparable *shi* on the subject. Likewise, when Su visited Ouyang Xiu's Pingshan Hall in Yangzhou nearly ten years after Ouyang had died, it was a *ci* rather than a *shi* that Su chose to write to remember Ouyang and lament his passing.[45]

There is also at least one death that Su Shi treated in both poetic forms, and the difference between the pieces is telling. After his concubine Zhaoyun died in Huizhou, Su composed this *shi*:

悼朝雲	*Mourning Zhaoyun*
苗而不秀豈其天	To sprout but not mature, could this have been his fate?
不使童烏與我玄	Tongwu never got to discuss the Great Mystery with me.
駐景恨無千歲藥	To halt time we had no thousand-year elixir,
贈行惟有小乘禪	For her departure I can only present Chan of the lowest kind.
傷心一念償前債	A moment of grief repays my debt from a former life;
彈指三生斷後緣	The three existences are an instant, I sever all karmic bonds.
歸臥竹根無遠近	Reclining on bamboo roots, there is no near or far;
夜燈勤禮塔中仙	By a night lamp I earnestly worship the pagoda god.[46]

The opening couplet refers by way of a literary allusion to the son, Dun, that Zhaoyun bore years before.[47] He died in infancy and thus never had a chance to show intellectual precociousness.[48] Zhaoyun, as Su explains in a long preface to the poem, had considerable knowledge of Buddhism, having been tutored by a nun. The remainder of the poem is full of references to the couple's shared Buddhist faith. The third couplet concerns Su Shi's own attempt to cope with the death. He allows himself a brief outpouring of sorrow but then seeks to overcome his grief (so as not to incur any more karmic debts for the future) with reflections on life's brevity. The penultimate line refers indirectly to the couple's distant remove from familiar lands,[49] Su suggesting that in death that remoteness no longer matters, and leads into the poem's concluding image of religious devotion.

The *ci* that Su wrote after Zhaoyun's death does not mention her at all. Ostensibly, the subject of the song lyric is the flowering plum Su finds in Huizhou. There are many indications in the song itself, however, that Su is using the plum as a trope for his deceased lover, and this interpretation is confirmed by several contemporary sources.[50]

西江月	*To the tune, "Moon on the West River"*
玉骨那愁瘴霧	Jade bones did not mind malarial mists;
冰姿自有仙風	The icy face had its own divine manner.
海仙時遣探芳叢	The ocean god sent it to explore fragrant grasses,
倒挂綠毛幺鳳	A green-feathered little phoenix, hanging upside down.
素面常嫌粉涴	The white face disdained powdery rinse;
洗妝不褪唇紅	Cleansed of makeup, the lips still shone red.
高情已逐曉雲空	But lofty feelings vanished with the morning cloud,
不與梨花同夢	Not the same dream as pear blossoms.[51]

The song treats the plum, and by extension Zhaoyun herself, as an inhabitant of divine precincts who was sent temporarily to this world. The opening lines refer to Zhaoyun's self-sufficiency and contentment even in Huizhou. The end of the first stanza describes the exquisite colorfulness of the Lingnan plum blossom by likening it to a kind of southern parrot (with green feathers and red beak) that is said to hang inverted from its branch. The second stanza stresses Zhaoyun's natural beauty, which did not rely upon powder or paint, and then alludes to her death (her name, literally "dawn cloud," is synonymous with "morning cloud").

Unlike Su Shi's *ci* on the tenth anniversary of his wife's death, there is no direct mention of emotion in this piece at all. There are no tears streaming down, no memory of a lonely grave. Overt emotion is hidden beneath the pretense of nature description. And yet, every line of this *ci* testifies to Su's affection for his long-time companion. There is nothing but loving description here, which builds toward a sense of irreplaceable loss at the end. Unlike the *shi* lament for Zhaoyun, there is no recourse in this *ci* to consoling philosophy or faith. Nor is there reference to anything else in the couple's life (e.g., the tragic loss of the infant son). The song gives unwavering attention to the beauty of its subject and to the speaker's fond and meticulous observation. Zhaoyun's name was taken from a famous Tang song about a romantic dream. It is fitting, then, that Su's *ci* concludes with a reference to the uniqueness of *his* dream.

It will surprise no one who is familiar with Song-dynasty *ci* that when Su's *shi* and *ci* on the very same topic are compared, the *shi* has the greater burden of intellectual content and the wider perspective, while the *ci* features minutely focused physical description that has strong emotive connotations. (The criticism that Su's *ci* are deficient in emotion would seem especially bizarre now if we did not realize that the criticism was made with a very specific type of emotion in mind.) What is more remarkable is that this particular comparison is possible at all: earlier *ci* writers did not regularly use the form to lament a death. The point here is not that Su's *ci* tend to be more "sentimental" than his *shi*, but that Su's interest in *ci* is partly explained by the potential he saw in it for relatively unconstrained expression of emotions. Once this appeal is recognized, Su's transformation of *ci* conventions—broadening them to include autobiographical subjects— is easier to understand.

Xiaoling: Abroad in the World

Motives aside, Su's achievement in the *ci* form deserves to be more fully described. His main innovations have been referred to above, but only in the simplest terms. What kind of autobiographical presence did he cultivate in *ci*; and as he turned away from the stock romantic themes, with what did he replace them? It will be convenient to discuss the two forms of *ci*, *xiaoling* and *manci*, separately. Related as Su's work in the two may be, he used them for rather different purposes. Whatever musical features originally differentiated the two forms, for us today the two are distinguished primarily by length: *xiaoling* is the shorter form, usually with only three to six lines in each of its two stanzas. The *man* is roughly twice as long, and some *man* tunes are even longer. Also, the prosody of the *man* is marked by extreme variation of line length (lines as short as two syllables or as long as ten are not unusual), whereas *xiaoling* lines tend to vary through a much narrower range (five to seven syllables). Strophic units (rhyme units) are also shorter and more regular in *xiaoling*. There the standard is the two-line unit, but in the *man* the size of strophic units is more unpredictable. These several features make the prosodic structure of *xiaoling* reminiscent of that of Regulated Poetry (*lüshi*), whereas the *man* presents a radically different appearance.[52] The consequences these formal differences have upon the literary effect of the forms will be considered below.

The topic of the autobiographical voice in Su's *ci* may be resumed here, now with particular reference to his *xiaoling*. The *xiaoling* translated below are from a series of five pieces Su wrote in 1078 while touring the outlying counties of Xuzhou, where he was prefect, to give thanks for recent rains.

浣溪沙   *To the tune, "Sands of the Washing Stream"*
No. 2

旋抹紅妝看使君	Rouge smeared on, they stare at the official,
三三五五棘籬門	Standing in threes and fives by bramble gates.
相排踏破蒨羅裙	Pushing and shoving, a madder-dyed skirt is torn underfoot.
老幼扶攜收麥社	Young and old crowd to the millet harvest altar;
烏鳶翔舞賽神村	Crows and kites dance over the sacrificing town.
道逢醉叟臥黃昏	A drunken old man dozes beside the road at sunset.

No. 3

簌簌衣巾落棗花	Fallen date blossoms cling to kerchief and robe.
村南村北響繰車	North and south of the village, the rattling of silk-reeling treadles.
半依古柳賣黃瓜	Propped against an old willow, a man sells cucumbers.
酒困路長惟欲睡	Weary with wine, the road long, all I want is to nap.
日高人渴漫思茶	The sun is high, thirst sets in, I yearn for tea.
敲門試問野人家	I knock on doors, asking peasant families.[53]

When Su had started to write *xiaoling* in Hangzhou, he concentrated on farewell pieces. The language and tone of many of his earliest works, as well as their occasion, fell well within the conventions of the form. The most significant early change that Su introduced was the addition of prefatory notes. These notes rooted their pieces in unique occasions: this piece, Su declared, was written for the departure of Chen Shugu; this one was composed at a farewell banquet for Yang Yuansu; and this one I wrote as I myself was leaving Hangzhou. The prefaces altered the way the pieces would be read, even while their content remained largely traditional.

In these early farewell songs, however, Su still had not fully discovered his own voice as a *ci* writer. In the later 1070s he attempted, from time to time, more radical breaks with convention. The most famous of these is the hunting *ci*, mentioned above. "Now let an old man be wild as a youngster,"[54] the piece begins, and goes on to describe his adventure on the plain. Su would boast to a friend, as we have seen, that he had finally written a song lyric that bore no resemblance to Liu Yong's romantic style.

Though not as virile (*zhuang*) as the hunting *ci*, the series of pieces on countryside scenes outside Xuzhou is equally striking and, in fact, better anticipates a style of *xiaoling* Su would later settle on. The series presents his impressions of the rural villages. Su makes an effort to include concrete details of peasant life (e.g., the madder-dyed skirt, the silk-reeling machine)[55] to render his descriptions convincing. The abundance of such images together with the relative lack of intellectual reflection by the author gives the works a strong flavor of immediacy. These are vivid portraits of rural life (idealized to some degree, no doubt), with a minimum of interpretation. Still, Su is not completely self-effacing. He remains a discernible presence, now a spectacle for the village women to gawk at, and later a thirsty wayfarer on an unlikely quest for tea. The incongruousness of the presence of the high official in these humble surroundings is a theme that runs throughout the series. The very last line of the last poem brings the theme to its culmination: "This official, actually, is a native of this place." The claim is patently false but explicitly and aptly conveys, at last, Su's fondness for the land and life he has been describing.

The importance of the outdoors setting should be recognized. As different as these song lyrics are from the Mizhou hunting piece, what the works have in common is that they take place outside. A large percentage of Su's famous later *xiaoling* share this feature, but it is not a mark of his earliest work in the genre (the Hangzhou parting songs). Historically, *ci* had been a poetry kept indoors, and especially in women's bedrooms. The genre had moved out into more open settings in the mid eleventh century, with the works of Zhang Xian, Yan Shu, and Ouyang Xiu. Still, "outdoors" in mid-century usually meant a garden or at least some highly refined and cultured setting. Ouyang Xiu, for example, wrote a series of *ci* celebrating the beauty of West Lake in Yingzhou (where he retired). The pieces describe carefree drinking and entertainment on boats that floated across the lake. These works remain much within the tradition of the banquet song. Another kind of outdoor setting is found in songs Ouyang and Yan Shu wrote about the stock figure of the lotus-picking girl (*cailian nü*). But the lotus patch is a very special kind of natural setting, a highly romanticized or erotic one, because of the feminine associations of the plant, and one that is really little more than an outdoor version on the boudoir.

For a man to be alone outdoors and in a setting that is neither refined nor filled with reminders of romance, as Su Shi is in his rustic Xuzhou songs, was a very different matter. Of course, Su was experimenting, and he must have been curious to see what the effect would be of investing the urban song lyric with a "crude" setting. Yet it is also tempting to see this, and Su's hunting *ci* as well, as something more than whimsical experiment. To help to rid himself of what might be perceived as the cloying or contrived romanticism of conventional *ci*, Su took a very large stride outside its normal setting. That stride landed him in the uncultivated outdoors, and it was there that he began writing *ci* all over again.

When he was exiled to Huangzhou, Su's efforts at *ci* writing, as mentioned above, acquired new impetus. There were not nearly the constraints or dangers regarding involvement with *ci* that there were for *shi*. Furthermore, the *ci* form seems to have been especially well suited to a type of literary expression that became one of Su's favorites in Huangzhou, the spontaneous affirmation of joy or contentment in one's surroundings. A piece that Su wrote for Wang Gong may serve to introduce the topic. Wang Gong, it will be recalled, had been implicated in the charges brought against Su in 1079 and had been exiled to Binzhou (in Guangxi) as a result. Wang was pardoned in 1083 and, on his return to the north, visited Su in Huangzhou. Wang had a concubine named Rounu, who was a skilled singer. When Su greeted her, he asked her if she had not found the distant south an unpleasant place to be confined. "Wherever my heart is at peace," she answered, "is my homeland." Su was so taken with this response that he wrote a *ci* about Rounu and her recent experience, making her words the concluding line:

萬里歸來年愈少	Returning a thousand miles she looked even younger.
微笑	Her subtle smile
笑時猶帶嶺梅香	Still carried the fragrance of the Lingnan plum.
試問嶺南應不好	I asked, "Wasn't Lingnan unpleasant?"
卻道	She responded,
此心安處是吾鄉	"Wherever my heart is at peace is my homeland."[56]

It does not surprise us that Su Shi was so impressed by this woman and her answer. Her reaction to exile was precisely the one that Su strove to cultivate in himself. Yet the song lyrics he wrote that best exemplify this reaction, which are quite unlike anything he wrote before Huangzhou, contain no such explicit statement of the problem or its resolution. Su Shi is a lone presence in them (whether or not friends accompany him), he is outdoors, and he seems quite unaware of anything except the natural setting. Two examples are translated below:

西江月   *To the tune, "Moon on the West River"*

頃在黃州春夜行蘄
水山中過酒家飲酒
醉乘月至一溪橋上
解鞍曲肱醉臥少休
及覺已曉亂山攢擁
流水鏘然疑非塵世
也書此詞橋柱上

When I was at Huangzhou, I rode out one spring night along Qi River. I stopped on the way at a wine shop and drank. I continued on in the moonlight to a bridge over the river where I untied my saddle and lay my head on my arm, intending to rest a while in my drunkenness. When I awoke, it was already dawn. Towering mountain peaks rose haphazardly all around me and the stream flowed with a clear ringing sound. I half suspected I was no longer in the dusty world. I wrote this song on one of the bridge's pillars.

照野瀰瀰淺浪
橫空隱隱層霄
障泥未解玉驄驕
我欲醉眠芳草

Illuminating the wilds, a band of shallow waves,
Layered clouds lie dimly across the sky.
My horse is proud, still wearing a dust blanket;
I long to nap drunkenly in fragrant grasses.

可惜一溪明月
莫教蹋碎瓊瑤
解鞍敧枕綠楊橋

How lovely, the stream in the bright moon!
Don't let hoofs trample those jades and jaspers.
My saddle becomes a pillow on the green willow bridge.

杜宇一聲春曉

One oriole call—spring dawn![57]

定風波   *To the tune, "Stilling Wind and Waves"*

三月七日沙湖道中
遇雨雨具先去同行
皆狼狽余獨不覺已
而遂晴故作此

On the seventh day of the third month, while we were on the way to Sandy Lake, we encountered rain. Our rain gear had been sent ahead, and so my companions balked at continuing on. I alone took no notice. After a while the sky cleared and I composed this song.

莫聽穿林打葉聲
何妨吟嘯且徐行
竹杖芒鞋輕勝馬

Don't listen to rain pelting the forest's leaves—
Why should that stop our singing, strolling along?
Bamboo staffs and sandals are less trouble than horses.

誰怕
一蓑煙雨任平生

Who minds?
One reed coat full of rain, all my life!

料峭春風吹酒醒
微冷

A nipping spring breeze sobers me up
As it grows chilly.

山頭斜照卻相迎	Slanting rays above the peak come to greet us,
回首向來蕭瑟處	I look back along our rain-soaked path.
歸去	On our way home
也無風雨也無晴	There'll be neither storms nor fair skies.[58]

Obviously, it is not adequate simply to say that Su Shi is outdoors in these pieces. He is insistent about his self-sufficiency outdoors. He prides himself on being able to spend the night without shelter and upon being unaffected by adverse weather. Su is demonstrating here quite complete self-abandonment into the natural setting of his confinement.

These *ci* are, in effect, glossed by a short prose piece Su wrote during his subsequent Huizhou exile.

A Record of an Outing near Pine Winds Pavilion

Once when I was staying temporarily in the Jiayou Monastery in Huizhou, I went out walking beneath Pine Winds Pavilion. Soon I had exhausted all the strength in my legs and I longed to stretch out on a bed and rest. Looking up to the pavilion, which stood at the tips of the trees, I wondered how I would ever climb back to it. After some time, suddenly I thought to myself, "What is there to prevent me from resting right here?" My heart was like a fish that had been hooked and all at once swam free. If a person really understands this, then even in the midst of battle, when the war drums are beating like thunder, and when to advance means death at the enemy's hands and to retreat means death for desertion, even at such a moment he will be able to relax and rest.[59]

It has recently been suggested that this piece was written after Su had been forced by hostile officials to move out of the government quarters in Huizhou and to return a second time to lodge in the Jiayou Monastery out of town.[60] This prose account of an outing was partly intended, according to this interpretation, to show that no such removal could discomfit him. A similar intent must have some bearing upon the Huangzhou *ci* under discussion.

These Huangzhou *ci* are quite distinct from anything else found in Su's *shi* corpus from the period. This is not really the farmer of East Slope speaking in these *ci*. There is, first of all, no obvious precursor or precedent to the voice we hear. The relationship of the speaker to nature is not that of Tao Qian or any other gentleman farmer. Tao Qian does not sleep outdoors and he does not boast of being undeterred by rainstorms. There is also less thought in these pieces. The farmer of East Slope may keep his poetic attention focused mainly upon his chores, but still he pauses from these long enough to reflect upon his new life (e.g., "For years I've eaten from the government granary / Reddish rotting rice no better than dirt" and "Now I regret a lifetime of laziness; / Heaven is right to make me farm in old age."[61] There is less reflection in the ci, less distance put between the particulars of the moment and the lines of the song.

Generally, the ci form lends itself to the illusion of spontaneous thought or expression. Its lines of unequal lengths and prosodically irregular rhyme contribute to its aura of unpredictability. Both features stand in marked contrast to the regular rhythm and rhyme of the shi form. Su Shi took full advantage of the inherent features of the form to produce ci that project an image of himself that suited his ideals in exile. Su wanted to show that he could find contentment even in an obscure and remote Yangzi town. He wanted to demonstrate that he could rise above all the worries (about his future) and frustrations (over his past) that we would expect to consume his thinking. He resolved to be "free from worries" ($wuyou$); and this meant that now, even more than before, he should be "free from thoughts" ($wusi$) and should react in a spontaneous and accommodating manner to whatever he encountered ($yingwu$). The ci form was particularly suited to dramatized presentations of this attitude. In it Su could depict himself deciding without premeditation to doze beside a moonlit stream, or leading his companions on through a rainstorm.

Su also continued, however, to write ci that evoke more tangibly some sense of what their author had been through, even as they describe sights in the Huangzhou countryside or depict Su out enjoying it. These are pieces that fit Ye Jiaying's characterization of Su's ci as concealing, under a dominant tone of transcendence of worldly worries, a note of frustration and haplessness.[62] An example follows:

鷓鴣天	*To the tune, "Partridge Sky"*
林斷山明竹隱墻	Where trees end and the mountain emerges, bamboo conceals a wall.
亂蟬衰草小池塘	Random cicadas, fading grasses, a small pool.
翻空白鳥時時見	White birds against the sky appear now and then;
照水紅蕖細細香	Red blossoms reflected in the water give a delicate scent.
村舍外	Outside the village,
古城旁	By an old city wall,
杖藜徐步轉斜陽	I stroll with a staff, turning in the setting sun.
殷勤昨夜三更雨	How considerate the rains at midnight were—
又得浮生一日涼	I enjoy one more cool day in this floating life.[63]

It is midsummer, and Su is out walking, for no apparent purpose. The first stanza presents a selective list of images in the scene, evidencing Su's observation and appreciation of his surroundings. The second stanza allows us to visualize Su more concretely in the setting. The closing lines transform all that has preceded. By attributing a particular act of kindliness to nature, which has brought one more pleasant day, and by using the phrase "floating life," Su hints at the rarity of such moments as these. No more needs to be said. The image of Su Shi out walking aimlessly amid ruins, eager not to let a pleasurable few hours slip by, will be sufficiently poignant for most readers.

Su goes even further towards evoking his own sense of rootlessness in the following Huangzhou *ci*:

卜算子 黃州定慧院寓居作	*To the tune, "The Fortuneteller"* *Composed while Lodging at* *Dinghui Monastery in Huangzhou*
缺月挂疏桐	A crescent moon hangs in the thinning phoenix tree;
漏斷人初靜	The water-clock silent, people no longer stir.
誰見幽人獨往來	Who sees the movements of the solitary man?
縹緲孤鴻影	High above, the silhouette of a lone goose.
驚起却回頭	Startled into flight, it gazes back
有恨無人省	With grievances no one notices.
揀盡寒枝不肯棲	It has tried every cold branch but will not roost,
寂寞沙洲冷	Isolated there in the sandspit's chill.[64]

The opening stanza suggests a relationship, or at least an analogy, between the lone goose and the solitary man. Therefore it becomes quite natural to read the description of the bird that develops in the second stanza as having some reference back to the poet-in-exile.[65] Huang Tingjian singled this *ci* out for praise, commenting: "The meaning of the words is lofty and marvelous, as if not written by someone who eats the food of mortal men. If he did not have ten thousand scrolls in his breast and a brush tip free from even a single drop of vulgarity, how could he have written this?"[66] Huang is alluding, I believe, equally to the purity of the nighttime scene, the suggestiveness of the link between the bird and its observer, and Su's restraint in not broaching his own grievances openly.

Su Shi became, in fact, a master at devising lines that subtly evoked some quiet sense of the forlorn in the midst of beauty or the determination to take pleasure. One noted couplet from a later *ci* comes at the end of a stanza devoted entirely to a description of a late spring scene. The couplet reads: "Willow-fluff on the branches diminishes with each gust of wind. / To the ends of the earth where are there no fragrant grasses?"[67] In the second line it is the juxtaposing of "fragrant grasses" with "ends of the earth" that makes the line effective. The line is memorable enough by itself, but it happened that the events of Su's life conspired to lend it particular force (if we can believe a story told about this *ci*). When Su was in Huizhou one autumn day, he asked Zhaoyun to sing this spring piece to relieve the dismal mood of the season. When she got to this particular couplet she broke off her song. Now that the two of them found themselves actually living in what they and most others considered "the ends of the earth," the lines took on added meaning and she could no longer bear to repeat them.[68]

Manci: Fading Visions, Fleeting Thoughts

Before Su Shi, the *manci* was the domain really of only one major *ci* writer, Liu Yong. This means that the *manci* was associated more with the popular tradition of performance *ci* than with the literary elevation of the same. Zhang Xian, Yan Shu, and Ouyang Xiu were known overwhelmingly for *xiaoling* rather than *manci*. It was Liu Yong, the songwriter whom the scholars (including Su Shi) often derided, who explored the potential of the longer form. Actually, Liu Yong developed the *man* to the point where it became, for later writers like Zhou Bangyan, fully as attractive as *xiaoling*.

Liu Yong's fondness for putting his *ci* in the voice of a male was mentioned earlier, and the song lyric of his quoted above is an example of the male voice in the *manci* form. Another example is given below (also in Hightower's translation), in which the speaker contrasts the gaiety of years past with his present situation. The extended description of both the lonely hostel and the former joys are facilitated by the length of the form.

宣清	To the tune, "Xuan Qing"
殘月朦朧	The setting moon was dim
小宴闌珊	The little party over.
歸來輕寒凛凛	At home I shivered with the chill,
背銀缸	Covered the silver lamp
孤館乍眠	And prepared to go to sleep in the lonely hostel.
擁重衾	Wrapped in double covers

醉魄猶噤	My drunken soul still clenched teeth against the cold.
永漏頻傳	The eternal clock kept announcing
前歡已去	The old joys are gone.
離愁一枕	Sorrow of separation, on a single pillow
暗尋思舊追遊	Silently recalling the old outings,
神京風物如錦	The capital city like brocade.
念擲果朋儕	I remember when the girls chased after us,
絕纓宴會	The wild parties:
當時曾痛飲	I drank a lot in those days.
命舞燕翩翩	We got them to dance—swallows swooping,
歌珠貫串	To sing—strung pearl notes—
向玳筵前盡是神仙流品	At our banquet they were all first-class goddesses.
至更闌疏狂轉甚	When it grew late, we were ever wilder
更相將鳳幃鴛寢	And led them to bed inside phoenix curtains.
玉釵亂橫	Jade hairpins fallen askew,
任散盡高陽	The drinking companions gone their way.
這歡娛甚時重恁	When will there ever be such joys again?[69]

Su Shi was certainly aware of such songs by Liu Yong. One of Su's early *manci* shows both the influence of Liu's use of the form and Su's own transformation of the current style. This piece was written at a historical site in Xuzhou (Pengcheng). Swallow Pavilion was a residence in which the ninth-century military governor, Zhang Jian-feng, had lived with the courtesan and singer Panpan. After Zhang died, Panpan secluded herself inside Swallow Pavilion for ten years, choosing to remain faithful to Zhang's memory rather than to remarry. While prefect of Xuzhou, Su went once to visit the pavilion:

永遇樂	*To the tune, "Always Having Fun"*
徐州夜夢覺此登燕子樓作	*Awaking from a Dream at Xuzhou One Night, Written at Swallow Pavilion*
明月如霜	Bright moonlight like frost,
好風如水	Gentle breeze like a stream,
清景無限	The clear view is endless!
曲港跳魚	Fish jump in the winding pond,
圓荷瀉露	Curled lotuses secrete dew,
寂寞無人見	In the quiet, no one notices.
紞如三鼓	The third watch sounds,
鏗然一葉	A leaf rustles,
黯黯夢雲驚斷	Darkly, the dream of clouds is interrupted.

339

夜茫茫	The night stretches afar,
重尋無處	There is nowhere to look.
覺來小園行徧	Awaking, I pace about the small garden.
天涯倦客	A weary traveller at the world's edge.
山中歸路	To the homeward road over mountains,
望斷故園心眼	The eyes of my homeland heart gaze in vain.
燕子樓空	Swallow Pavilion is empty—
佳人何在	Where is the fair one now?
空鎖樓中燕	Swallows are locked emptily inside.
古今如夢	Past and present are like a dream—
何曾夢覺	When shall we awake?
但有舊歡新怨	There are only former joys and new distress.
異時對	Someday, viewing
黃樓夜景	A night scene at Yellow Pavilion,
為余浩歎	May someone sigh for me![70]

The isolation Liu Yong's speaker feels prompts him to remember happier times, the raucousness and abandon of the youthful years he spent in the company of "first-class goddesses." Su Shi also dreams of a beautiful woman and wakes to the reality of his loneliness and isolation. But Su Shi's amorous fancy ("dream of clouds") focuses on a woman he knows only through historical legend, and this fact allows Su's composition to develop meanings that have no place in Liu Yong's piece. Su's transformation of the convention of brooding over a lost lover, an irrecoverable "fair one," is as complete in this piece as in his *ci* cited earlier on his deceased wife. There may still be romantic nostalgia and even a hint of eroticism in Su's reminiscences—intrinsic conventions of the genre encouraged this—but Su steers them in new directions.

The challenge this *manci* presents is to understand how the multiple themes, which give way one to the other with remarkable swiftness, hold together. What meaning, in other words, do they collectively point to? (We shall see that this is a question that surfaces often in reading Su's *manci*.) There is the infatuation with Panpan (the dream), the longing for home, reflections on the "emptiness" of the pavilion (Panpan's mortality), and thoughts about the author's own fleeting life as imagined from some future moment. We may allow that it is somehow appropriate that these various themes are "intermingled" in this poem, but is there not some more coherent reading to be untangled here?[71]

The poem begins (in its preface) with Panpan, develops into a lament for her disappearance, and ends with sorrow over Su's own imminent vanishing. Su is not just fantasizing about romantic dalliance with the famous beauty, he is identifying himself with her. The nostalgia he now feels for her, experienced at *her* Xuzhou building, is analogous to the sentiment others will in the future feel for the deceased Su Shi at *his* Xuzhou building (the Yellow Tower Su had constructed to commemorate the city's survival of the flood). What is the basis of this identification of the Song-dynasty prefect with the Tang courtesan? This, I suspect, is where the theme of separation from home is relevant. Out of a sense of loyalty to her lover, Panpan did not return home (or choose a new one—a new lover) after Zhang's death but imposed solitude and loneliness upon herself for the next decade. That choice was what she was famous for. Su Shi's separation from his home was caused, of course, by his decision to embark upon an official career; and it was precisely that career, advantageous as it might have been, that kept him from ever returning home and kept him, at the time he wrote this piece, confined in Xuzhou. Loyalty of a related kind (to emperor and dynasty) figured in Su's isolation. The conventional trope of loyal minister as dutiful female has a dim presence in this poem, even though, with all the vivid details of the scene and the complicating factor of historical time, it is entirely possible to read and appreciate the piece without being conscious of it.

On the rapid movement from one theme to another, and the economy of statement that goes with it, an exchange between Su Shi and Qin Guan may be cited. It is recorded that Su once asked Qin what new *ci* lines he had recently composed. Qin quoted the opening couplet of a piece about parting: "A short pavilion and garden floats in the sky / Looking down upon colored wheels and carved saddle."[72] "Thirteen characters," Su replied, "and all you've said is that there is a man riding a horse in front of the pavilion." Then Qin Guan asked Su about his recent *ci*, whereupon Su quoted this passage from the piece above: "Swallow Pavilion is empty, / Where is the fair one now? / Swallows are locked emptily inside." Chao Buzhi remarked that in a mere three lines Su had said all there was to say about Zhang Jianfeng and his pavilion.[73] The lines are indeed dense with meaning and hinge upon two clever repetitions. The pavilion is *empty*; and the birds, for which the pavilion is named, are now locked *emptily* (i.e., pointlessly) inside. Panpan was the occupant who had previously been kept inside, first with her lover and later sorrowfully without him. Today the pairs of swallows, which are conventional reminders of romance between humans, are still there; but their presence has no meaning without even the solitary Panpan to observe them.

We have already seen two instances in Su's *manci* of dreams: his dream of his first wife and his dream of Panpan. As different as the two dreams are, both take the speaker back in time and offer him a vision from the past (his deceased wife combing her hair, Panpan residing at Swallow Pavilion). Both visions eventually dissipate, so that each song ends with Su pondering the disparity between the vision from the past and the present reality.

Another instance of a dream of the past may be presented here, this one of a male friend rather than a woman. Lüqiu Xiaozhong had years before served as prefect of Huangzhou. Su knew Lüqiu from the time he visited him in retirement in Suzhou in 1074.[74] Now, Su dreamed about Lüqiu returning to his former place of office:

水龍吟   *To the tune, "The Water Dragon Song"*

閭丘大夫孝終公顯 嘗守黃州作棲霞樓 為郡中絕勝元豐五 年余謫居黃州正月十 七日夢扁舟渡江中 流回望樓中歌樂雜 作舟中人言公顯方 會客也覺而異之乃 作此曲蓋越調鼓笛 慢公顯時已致仕在 蘇州	When Grand Master Lüqiu Xiaozhong (Gongxian) served as prefect of Huangzhou, he built Cloud Perch Pavilion, which was the most extraordinary in the entire prefecture. In the fifth year of Yuan-feng [1082] I was living in exile in Huang. On the seventeenth day of the first month, I dreamed of crossing the Yangzi in a small boat. Midway I looked back: music and song were being performed in the pavilion. Someone in the boat said that Gongxian was just then entertaining guests. When I awoke, I was intrigued by my dream and wrote this song about it, using the Yue tune pattern, "Drum and Flute *Man*." At the time Gongxian had already retired and was living in Suzhou.

	小舟橫截春江	My small boat slices across the spring river,
	臥看翠壁紅樓起	Reclining, I gaze at the green walls and crimson tower.
	雲間笑語	Laughter and talk amid the clouds,
4	使君高會	At the prefect's elegant banquet
	佳人半醉	The beautiful lady is half drunk.
	危柱哀絃	From high frets and mournful strings
	豔歌餘響	Come lingering echoes of romantic songs
8	繞雲縈水	Encircling the clouds and bending around the river.
	念故人老大	I realize my friend, though old,
	風流未減	Is as high-spirited as before.
	空回首	In vain I look back
12	煙波裏	Amid mist and waves.

	推枕惘然不見	I rise from my pillow in a daze, the vision gone.
	但空江	There is only the empty river,
	月明千里	Moonlight stretching a thousand miles.
16	五湖聞道	He heard the Way on Five Lakes,
	扁舟歸去	Sailed off in a small boat,
	仍攜西子	Holding Xi Shi by the hand.
	雲夢南州	The prefecture south of Yunmeng,
20	武昌東岸	The bank east of Wuchang,
	昔遊應記	He must remember his former outings there.
	料多情夢裏	Probably, in sentimental dreams,
	端來見我	He came deliberately to visit me:
20	也參差是	All was more or less the same.[75]

Preface. "Drum and Flute *Man*" is an alternate name of the tune "The Water Dragon Song."

Lines 16–18. These lines allude to the ancient minister Fan Li. In one version of his life, after he helped his native Yue conquer Wu, Fan Li took the famous beauty Xi Shi, who had facilitated the demise of Wu, with him when he disappeared to the Five Lakes.[76]

Lines 19–20. "South of Yunmeng" and "east of Wuchang" both designate Huangzhou.

It was Su Shi who dreamed of Lüqiu, but at the end of the song Su fancies that it was Lüqiu who decided to come visit Su and his former residence in a dream. To say that Lüqiu found everything "more or less" the same emphasizes, if anything, how different everything is now. Lüqiu is no longer the ebullient prefect, famed for the banquets he hosted at Cloud Perch Pavilion. Su's own situation has changed even more. When the two friends last saw each other, it was Su who took the initiative to go find Lüqiu in retirement. Now, Su the banished official is no longer free to move about, and so Lüqiu comes solicitously to visit him in his dreams.

One more example of a similar type of vision in Su's *manci* might be adduced. It occurs not in a dream but in a vivid recollection, specifically, the images of Zhou Yu (Gongjin) and the Red Cliff battle presented in Su's most famous *ci*:

遙想公瑾當年	Dimly I picture Gongjin then:
小喬初嫁了	He had just married Little Qiao,
雄姿英發	Valor shone everywhere in his bearing.
羽扇綸巾	His fan of plumes, kerchief of silk—
笑談間	As he chatted and laughed,
墙艢灰飛煙滅	Masts and hulls became flying ashes and smoke.[77]

So, too, does Su Shi's vision of the battle gradually fade, leaving his soul to wander among the battlement ruins. This entire piece is, of course, primarily concerned with the vanishing glories of the past ("waves scour away / the dashing heroes of a thousand ages") and Su's effort to confront the ramifications that has for his own mortality.

Images from the past, whether recent and personal or distant and historical, come in and out of focus in these *manci*. The pieces all contain some description of Su's immediate situation, some intrusion of an image from the past, and some reflection on its eventual passing; but the ordering of these elements and the amount of space devoted to them are quite unpredictable. The remembered image (the dream image) may appear either in the first or second stanza. About the only generalization that can be made concerning the structure of these pieces is that Su uses the stanza break to emphasize the disjuncture of past and present. The present is suddenly eclipsed by the past, or a vision of the past abruptly dissolves. The poems thus represent in dramatized form the transience of experience that is their theme.

Dramatization is a mark of all these *manci*. Whether inside or outside the glimpse of the past, the emphasis is on temporality and action: "As he chatted and laughed," "By a small window / She was combing and making up," "The third watch sounds, / A leaf rustles," "I rise from my pillow in a daze, the vision gone." In *shi* poems on historical sites or themes, even Su Shi's, we do not find such thoroughgoing dramatization of past, present, or the intermingling of the two. Perhaps this is because the expectation of statement weighs heavier in the *shi* form or because historical themes had already become highly conventionalized in *shi*. There was little precedent in *ci* for such representations of the past as Su explored, and he takes obvious delight in treating them with as much immediacy as he can.

As distinctive as each piece is, the reader begins to suspect that over the years Su Shi kept returning to a core of fairly stable elements, reworking them again and again. A quiet night, a fleeting vision of the past, mulling over the gulf between then and now. The crucial point is not that the *manci* that contain these elements, in one variation or another, are so numerous, but that they have always been considered to be among Su Shi's finest achievements in the genre.

The core elements might also include the moon and other astral phenomena. Often it is moonlight that steals into the speaker's room and prevents him or her from sleeping. The moon may also remind the person of distant loved ones (this is the conventional association). Then, too, the waxing and waning of the moon, or the rotation of astral forms, may trigger thoughts about the passage of time. In fact, observation of the subtle changes in the nighttime sky may replace the dream vision of the past, calling forth much the same awareness of mortality.

Su recreated one *manci* out of a snippet of a Five Dynasties piece he had once heard but then forgot (here, a *ci* itself is a fading presence). An elderly Buddhist nun had recited the work, by Meng Chang, ruler of the Later Shu, to Su when he was a boy of seven. Forty years later, however, Su could remember only the opening two lines: "Flesh of ice and bones of jade / Remain cool by themselves and do not perspire."[78] These lines presented Su with a female persona (and with the season of summer). He could not write in a male voice, his forte. However, the *ci* he did develop even out of this beginning bears a strong resemblance to those examined above. The first stanza describes the woman alone in her room. A streak of moonlight peeks in through her window. She cannot sleep and rests fitfully in bed. The second stanza continues:

8	起來攜素手	She arises and takes a white arm.
	庭戶無聲	The courtyard is silent,
	時見疏星渡河漢	Lone stars drift now and then across Heaven's river:
	試問夜如何	She asks about the night.
12	夜已三更	It is the third watch already.
	金波淡	The golden waves grow faint,
	玉繩低轉	The jade cord descends and turns.
	但屈指	She counts on her fingers,
16	西風幾時來	When will the west winds arrive?
	又不道流年	Not mentioning
	暗中偷換	Drifting years being stolen secretly away.

Line 8. The arm of her maid or female companion.
Line 10. "Heaven's river" is the Milky Way.
Line 13. "Golden waves" are the moonlight on the ground.
Line 14. "Jade cord" is a portion of the handle of the Northern Dipper, said to pivot as dawn approaches.
Line 16. The winds of autumn.

Su's best known moonlight *ci* is the midautumn moon festival song he wrote for his brother.

水調歌頭	*To the tune, "Water Melody"*
丙辰中秋歡飲達旦 大醉作此篇兼懷子 由	On the midautumn festival of *bingchen* [1076] I drank and amused myself all night until dawn. Completely drunk, I composed this piece, intending it also to express my longing for Ziyou.

明月幾時有	How long has the bright moon existed?
把酒問青天	I lift my cup to ask azure Heaven.
不知天上宮闕	In those Heavenly palaces, I wonder,
今夕是何年	What year it is tonight?
我欲乘風歸去	I long to mount the wind and return there
惟恐瓊樓玉宇	But fear those jeweled balconies and jade roofs
高處不勝寒	So high aloft will be too cold.
起舞弄清影	I stand up to dance with my clear shadow,
何似在人間	How could this be the world of men!
轉朱閣	It comes round the crimson hall,
低綺戶	Dips to my painted doorway,
照無眠	And shines on the sleepless one.
不應有恨	I should not resent it,
何事長向別時圓	But why is it always full when we're apart?
人有悲歡離合	Men have sorrow and joy, partings and reunions,
月有陰晴圓缺	The moon is obscured or clear, waxing or waning.
此事古難全	Such things have never been perfect.
但願人長久	We can only hope through long lives
千里共嬋娟	To share her charms across a thousand miles.[79]

The final line alludes to the belief that the woman Chang E lives as an immortal in the moon.

There are several elements in this piece that we have encountered before: the still night, the moonlight interfering with sleep, the lingering concern about time. The piece also has its more novel features, including the speculations about the moon, the distinct echo at the end of the first stanza of Li Bo's cavorting with his shadow, and the consoling philosophy of stanza 2. This last element is very conspicuous (and anticipates, in fact, the philosophizing in the first Red Cliff rhapsody). It is unusual to find such an extended passage of abstract thought in Su's *ci*.

The feature to which I would call particular attention is a different order of "thought," contained in the opening stanza. The piece is so well known—being widely anthologized and often reread—that it is easy to overlook how swiftly the thinking moves in this stanza. Su begins by wondering about the age of the moon, and this leads to a query about how time is counted on the moon. The moon had always been associated with the quest for immortality in China. (Chang E, with whom the song concludes, fled to the moon after she stole her husband's immortality potion.) The implication is that in those lunar palaces time is counted very differently indeed. Perhaps it does not exist at all. So Su longs to ascend to that refuge from mortality. But immediately his desire gives way to doubts. What if the moon is too inhospitable, too cold? Then Su arises and begins to dance with the "partner" he finds with him there, courtesy of the moon.

The final line of the stanza is grammatically ambiguous and has been interpreted in at least three ways: 1) How could anything compare to life here on earth? That is, the idea of ascending to the moon has been abandoned and Su expresses his satisfaction with the mortal world. 2) How unlike the mortal world this is! That is, I feel I am among the celestial immortals and have no sense of remaining in the world. 3) It does not even seem that I am still in the mortal world. That is, I have found such joys here that without taking leave of this world, I have transcended ordinary life—the meaning intended in my translation above. The second and third interpretations are close, but there is a difference in emphasis. Arguments have been advanced for each of these three readings by distinguished scholars of *ci*.[80] The difficulty of the line stems from more than grammatical uncertainty. The real problem here is that, grammar aside, it is hard to guess what Su intends to say at this point. The thinking throughout the stanza is whimsical and unpredictable. It is difficult to anticipate his next utterance or to gauge the relative likelihood of the various interpretations.

Passages in which similarly abrupt leaps occur can be found in others of Su's *manci*. Among those already cited, for instance, were the lines on Swallow Pavilion ("Swallow Pavilion is empty, / Where is the fair one now? / Swallows are locked emptily inside"). In the famous Red Cliff piece there come these lines:

故國神遊	My soul wanders the ancient realm,
多情應笑我	So full of feeling, others will laugh at me;
早生華髮	My hair turns grey prematurely.
人生如夢	Life is like a dream,
一樽還酹江月	Let me pour a libation to the river moon.[81]

Even as Su indulges in historical nostalgia, he is aware that other people would consider him slightly ridiculous. Yet still his weakness ages him prematurely. Precisely what does Su mean when he uses the cliché, "Life is like a dream"? And for what reasons does he make an offering to the moon? Readers might well have variant responses.

There is a rapidity of thought in such lines, an agile jumping from one notion to the next, without alighting too long to explain or develop. Critics have commented on this stylistic trait. Kang-i Sun Chang has remarked on the "lyrical density" of Su's *ci*, contrasting the technique of presenting no more than a selective, summary statement with the more leisurely and expansive style found in his *shi*.[82] Likewise, Ye Jiaying has called attention to the habit Su's "*ci* brush" has of making abrupt turns and changes of direction in its method of exposition.[83] Obviously, this aspect of Su's style is related to the fondness for dramatization and a highly cultivated sense of immediacy that were mentioned earlier, but here it is the intellectual content of Su's *ci* rather than imagery and actions that is our focus.

Even in *manci* that are exceptional in Su's corpus, the same trait is evident. The *ci* translated below is on willow catkins and is thus in subject and tone closer to the *Among the Flowers* tradition of *ci* on feminine themes than most of Su's works. Here, too, however, Su's distinctive manner of exposition is retained. The leading late-Qing critic Wang Guowei called this piece the finest "*ci* on an object" (*yongwu ci*) ever written.[84] Many others have also praised it and commented specifically on the many transformations in its exposition:[85]

水龍吟	To the tune, "Water Dragon Song"
次韻章質夫楊花詞	Matching the Rhymes of Zhang Zhifu's
	Ci on Willow Catkins

似花還似非花	They resemble a flower but do not,
也無人惜從教墜	And no one regrets their falling.
拋家傍路	Abandoning home, they lie beside the road,
思量卻是	Seeming, after all,
無情有思	To have memory though no feelings.
縈損柔腸	A tender heart, twisted with longing,
困酣嬌眼	Pretty eyes, weary with wine,
欲開還閉	When almost open they close again.
夢隨風萬里	Dreaming a thousand miles on the wind,
尋郎去處	They pursue him as he leaves,
又還被	Only to be awakened
鶯呼起	By the oriole's song.
不恨此花飛盡	Let the catkins fly away,
恨西園	What I regret, in the west garden,
落紅難綴	Is fallen red blossoms that cannot be restored.
曉來雨過	As morning comes and the storm passes,
遺蹤何在	Where are their traces now?
一池萍碎	The whole pond of duckweed is shattered.
春色三分	Of the three parts of the signs of spring,
二分塵土	Two lie in the dirt,
一分流水	One flows away with the river.
細看來	Looking closely I see
不是楊花	They are not willow catkins at all,
點點是	Dot after dot they are
離人淚	A parted lover's tears.[86]

Line 1. This echoes the opening of Bo Juyi's famous love' song: "Flowers are not flowers, the mist is not mist."[87]

Lines 4–5. This contradicts Han Yu's statement that willow catkins have neither ability nor memory (since they know only to fly away).[88] *Si* ("memory," here) is also a pun on *si* "thread," the fluff or fibers of the catkin.

Line 6. The aptness of this line is lost in the translation, for the original says "intestines" (the seat of the emotions in Chinese) rather than "heart," suggesting an analogy with the curved line of the catkin's shape (as in the following line).

Lines 9–12. This alludes to the Tang poem by Jin Changxu, in which a woman's dream of her distant lover is interrupted by an oriole's song.[89]

Line 18. Su's own note on this line refers to the widespread belief that when willow catkins blow into the water, they turn into duckweed floating on the surface, a belief Su credits.

The reader must be aware of three common associations of the willow: that the growth and shedding of its catkins is one of the most widely evoked signs of the arrival and transience of spring, that it is preeminently the plant of human farewells and loneliness for a departed love, and that its gender associations are distinctly feminine (e.g., the swaying of its branches are said to resemble female dancers). Su Shi draws upon all these meanings, weaving them together.

Su's dominant trope is that of the willow catkin as woman, but he does not settle on any single metaphor or equivalence. At first the catkins are vaguely suggested to be a most unusual kind of woman: they resemble flowers (an even less ambiguous metaphor for women) but are not flowers. They abandon their own homes, but linger outside by the road, showing that while they may be unfeeling, at least they have memories. All at once the catkins are likened to parts of female anatomy: intestines contorted with emotion and then languorous eyes. These drowsy eyes anticipate the dream with which the stanza concludes. Now, the catkins are fully a woman again, but this time one who *remains* at home while her lover ventures distantly away. The literary allusion in these lines (concerning a woman, not a willow) adds another level of meaning.

A new voice is introduced at the start of the second stanza: now there is a human persona who acts as an intermediary in the poem. The reader's relation to the subject has changed. First, this new voice harks back to the issue of catkins versus real flowers, insisting that the former are only of incidental importance. But the focus on flowers is dropped abruptly, as the persona observes the effect of the storm on the waterborne catkins. Behind the unusual mathematical formulation in the following lines lies a new conviction: that willows are all that matters about spring. The closing lines revert back to the trope of catkin as woman, resuming, in effect, the image that ended the first stanza, but now offering a close-up image of tears on the woman's face. How could one ever produce a *ci*, the critic Zhang Yan asked, in which every single line is skillful and effective? Zhang cites this piece as one that lives up to that nearly impossible ideal. The critic calls attention to the "simplicity" of several lines (the opening couplet, those on the "parts" of spring).[90] But if there was not such constant shifting of image, analogy, voice, and literary allusion the seemingly simple lines, when aligned, would not be so effective.

At the start of this chapter the question of why Su Shi embarked upon his famous innovations in *ci* was raised. Several possible influences and motivating factors were discussed, including his uneasiness over the contrived romantic sentimentality of conventional *ci*, the virtue he made of "genuineness" in literature, his exile to Huang-zhou and consequent turning to a less prestigious poetic form, and the relative lack of constraint concerning the expression of emotions in *ci*. Now, in the course of describing the nature of Su's work in the two types of *ci*, *xiaoling* and *manci*, we have in effect uncovered yet another possible explanation of Su's interest in the form and peculiar approach to it. In *ci* Su Shi discovered a literary genre that was aptly suited to his philosophy of spontaneity, thoughtlessness, and ever-changing adaptability. But Su did not stop with the inherent features of the form that encouraged this mode of expression (the irregular prosody and rhyme, the relatively low expectation of propositional language). On top of these he actively cultivated a quick and unpredictable style of presentation, in *xiaoling* depicting himself acting whimsically and in *manci* dramatizing short-lived visions, himself *thinking* whimsically, and otherwise favoring expositions with multiple and impromptu shifts.

The most frequently quoted description Su Shi ever gave of his own writing (in general) is an account of its spontaneity:

> My writing is life a ten-thousand-gallon underground spring. It is liable to spurt forth randomly at any given place. On level ground it streams gurgling forward and can easily travel a thousand miles a day. When it flows up against hills, rocks, or other obstacles, it adapts its course to the shape of the object in ways that defy comprehension. All that can be known is that it always goes where it should go and always stops when it has to stop. That is simply the way it behaves. As for the rest, I myself do not understand anything more about it.[91]

This short entry, whose date is unknown, is valuable primarily as a description of how Su Shi wanted people to think of the way he wrote. Su's writing in most forms evidences too much calculation and careful arrangement of thought and word for this to be a credible account of how the writing was composed. (A rare manuscript of the draft of a *shi* poem supports this impression, for it shows that Su revised the piece extensively and painstakingly.)[92] His statement does, however, seem to have special relevance to the stylistic traits we have been noticing in his *ci*. Even in that form, of course, the appearance of spontaneous creativity may itself result from painstaking effort and deliberation. We do not know that Su was any more or less spontaneous when writing *ci* than when writing in other forms. Still, as for appearances alone, those regularly evinced by Su's *ci* remind one of this famous self-description of his writing. Thus, not only are these traits an important mark of his *ci* style, in special combination with his distinctive autobiographical tone, they also help to explain why he was drawn to the form and found it so congenial.

CHAPTER II

CONCLUSIONS

Early Appraisals

It remains to offer some observations on Su Shi's posthumous reputation, and to address directly the related matter of the balance between literary pursuits and other activities in his life. It will be useful to begin with evaluations of his life that were made by his closest friends, and then to consider Zhu Xi's different appraisal. Certain of Su's most devoted followers either predeceased him (e.g., Qin Guan) or died soon after he did (e.g., Chen Shidao). But others had the opportunity, despite the risks involved, to reflect in writing upon the meaning of Su's life. A poem Huang Tingjian composed about Su and a strange-shaped rock he had written about, which subsequently disappeared, broaches the key elements of Huang's evaluation of this life:

追和東坡壺中九華 并序	*Posthumously Matching the Rhymes of East Slope's "Nine-Flower Mountain in the Jug."*
湖口人李正臣蓄異石九峯東坡先生名曰壺中九華并為作詩後八年自海外歸湖口石已為好事者所取乃和前篇以為笑實建中靖國元年四月十六日明年當	A Hukou resident, Li Zhengchen, possessed a strange rock with nine peaks, which the Master of East Slope called "Nine-Flower Mountain in a Jug" and commemorated with a poem. Eight years later, when he returned from beyond the seas, the Hukou rock had been taken off by some collector, and East Slope wrote a second, matching poem simply as material for amusement. That was on the

352

崇寧之元五月二十日庭堅繫舟湖口李正臣持此詩來石既不可復見東坡亦下世矣感歎不足因次前韻

sixteenth day of the fourth month of the first year of the Jianzhong jingguo period [1101]. The following year, on the twentieth day of the fifth month of the Chongning period, I moored my boat at Hukou, and Li Zhengchen brought the second poem to show me. The rock is no longer here to be viewed, and East Slope has likewise departed this world. Not satisfied merely to sigh over these events, I wrote this poem, using the same rhymes.

有人夜半持山去
Someone at midnight
carried the mountain off,

頓覺浮嵐暖翠空
Suddenly the hovering mists and
sunlit greens seemed empty.

試問安排華屋處
How could being kept
in an ornate room

何如零落亂雲中
Compare with abandonment
amid unsettled clouds?

能回趙璧人安在
Where is the man who could return
the jade disk to Zhao?

已入南柯夢不通
He has entered Southern Bough
where even dreams cannot go.

賴有霜鐘難席卷
Luckily the frosty bell
is hard to roll up and take away.

袖椎來聽響玲瓏
A clapper in my sleeves, I come to hear
the pure jingling notes.[1]

Lines 5–6. It was the shrewd retainer Lin Xiangru who saw through the deceit of the king of Qin and safely returned the priceless He clan jade to his native state of Zhao.[2] Here, the jade is analogous to the missing rock. Southern Bough is the name of an imaginary prefecture in the famous Tang dream story, used here to evoke an inaccessible realm (that Su entered upon his death) to which even dreams do not reach.[3]

Su Shi had named the rock he was shown after a real mountain (Jiuhua shan), making it a miniature of a larger reality. To Huang Tingjian, Su Shi himself is a mountain, and his disappearance leaves a gaping emptiness in the landscape. The opening couplet contains an echo of a well-known passage in *Zhuangzi*: "We store our boat in the ravine, our fishnet in the marsh, and say it's safe there; but at midnight someone stronger carries it away on his back, and the dull ones do not know it."[4] In Huang's version what the thief has spirited away is the central element in the landscape itself.

The subject of the second couplet is Su's life rather than his death. There were periods when Su found himself on display, as it were, in luxurious surroundings, as when he was at Court as a Hanlin academician or drafting official. But ultimately such favor did not rest well with him; and he, like the rock, was better suited to "abandonment" in remote landscape. The couplet evokes Su's lifelong unwillingness to make the compromises necessary to remain in the capital as well as the irony that he found his greatest contentment amid obscurity and exile.[5]

The final couplet alludes to a prose inscription Su Shi had written about Stone Bell Mountain (Shizhong shan), also located in Hukou, at the mouth of Boyang Lake.[6] Su had not been satisfied with traditional explanations of the origin of the mountain's name, which were vague and imprecise. When he passed by the mountain in 1084, he took the opportunity to investigate for himself. A local monk believed that the name derived from special properties of the mountain's rocks, and he struck them with a stick to show Su how much like a bell they sounded (Huang's final line recalls this event). To Su this demonstration was ridiculous and he remained unconvinced. Later, on a moonlit night Su and his son hired a small fishing boat to explore around the base of the mountain. They eventually came upon a huge cave in the cliff at sea level. As each wave surged into the cave, air came rushing out and a deep roar resounded from the hidden recesses of the cavern. Su felt he had found a more plausible explanation of the mountain's name. In the conclusion of his inscription, Su comments on the folly of those who dreamed up erroneous explanations without bothering to investigate with their own eyes and ears; and he adds this thought: "The fact is, scholars have not been willing to float on a small boat at night beneath sheer cliffs and so none could discover the truth, while fishermen and boatmen, who did know, could not express themselves in writing."

The miniature mountain that Su enjoyed had, like Su himself, been wrest away. But the landscape through which Su had roamed remained, and Huang consoles himself by thinking that he might retrace Su's steps nostalgically. Now the "pure jingling notes" that Huang anticipates hearing take on a secondary and quite different meaning: they recall Su's writings, in which with his special boldness he clarified the true nature of things and dispelled hearsay and error.[7] (It befits Su Shi that the truth he uncovered about this huge rock had to do with water.)

Other descriptions of Su that Huang Tingjian left confirm the impression given by the second couplet here that, for this colleague, the tension between high officialdom and "abandonment," with all the contradictions it entailed (both in the bureaucracy's treatment of Su and in Su's attitudes toward service) were of central importance to Su's life. When writing about Su, Huang cannot long forget the tragedy, as he viewed it, of talent that went underutilized or even was abused by those in power. "If Jade Hall [the Hanlin Academy] wants a real man of learning, / It will have to recruit the bald old fellow of Danzhou."[8] The lines disparage the government for banishing its finest talent to its most wretched extremity (Hainan Island). A similar consciousness of wasted potential and oppression informs another of Huang's appreciations. "When Zizhan [Su Shi] was banished to Lingnan, / The grand councilors wanted to kill him."[9] One could not be more candid than that. But despite the persecution, Huang continues, Su enjoyed himself, "eating to the full on Huizhou rice" and painstakingly matching Tao Qian's poems. In his concluding lines Huang is thinking as much about the separate paths taken by Su and Tao as the apparent similarity of their verse: "Although they differed in their choice of whether to serve or withdraw, / In their style and flavor they remained much the same." Actually, this remark seems to anticipate Li Zehou's comment that although Su never did withdraw from the world, no earlier poet was as disillusioned with it (that is, in the manner of a recluse) as he was. Key to both observations is the inseparability of worldly ambition, frustration, and transcendence in Su's life and art.

For a fuller summation of Su Shi's life one may turn to a series of fifteen poems written by Canliao, Su's longtime monk friend.[10] The poems are entitled "dirges" (or "bearer's songs," *wanci*) for the Master of East Slope and comment unsystematically on a wide variety of events and issues. A small number of central themes emerge, however, as Canliao turns from one to another aspect of Su's life.

One of Canliao's persistent concerns in these poems is to equate Su with some famous historical figure, that is, to praise him by likening him to a great man everyone knows of. But Canliao struggles with this task, as it is not easy to find a precedent for Su Shi's particular breadth and distribution of achievements. Canliao resorts to multiple pairings (e.g., in this field he was like so-and-so, in that he was another X), which is itself a familiar device and one encouraged by the couplet form. Still, Canliao keeps altering his analogies as he evidently continues to think of new ways Su might be viewed. These are his statements: in governance Su was on a par with the ancient advisors Yi Yin and Lü Shang, while in letters he surpassed the great Han writers Ban Gu and Yang Xiong, referred to here as essayists and rhapsodists (poem no. 1). This is the most clichéd of the comparisons and reveals little except Canliao's feeling that both politics and letters were fundamental to Su's accomplishments. Subsequently, Canliao says that in his "capacity for tolerance" (*yaliang*) Su rivaled Xie An, the fourth-century aristocrat and mountain-climber, who was Wang Xizhi's friend and a guest at the famous Orchid Pavilion gathering, while in his talent (*cai*) he resembled Zhuge Liang (no. 2). The comparison with Zhuge is one, of course, that Su himself had suggested. That with Xie An is more unexpected, as is the category of *yaliang*, which anticipates another of Canliao's themes (Su's *fengliu*) that we will come to presently. Finally, the monk observes that for powerful rhetoric and argumentation (*xiongbian*) Su did not bow before Zigong, the disciple of Confucius known for speaking well, while for his inscriptions and evaluations he was not inferior to Guo Tai (2nd c.), famed for his insightfulness in judging and ranking men according to their ability (no. 5). This last statement must refer to Su's colophons on history, literature, and art.

We might expect more attention to Su's practice of poetry, calligraphy, and painting. Certainly a modern scholar who sought to mimic Canliao's method of praise would not omit these categories from anything that purported to be a comprehensive evaluation of Su, nor would many scholars from the later imperial period. Is it entirely the formality of the occasion that accounts for this conspicuous deemphasis of aesthetic pursuits, or are there other factors also involved? In any case, as varied as Canliao's parallels are, cumulatively they have a definite thrust or direction, which is to emphasize Su's talent for statecraft, persuasion (even the Han rhapsody had, of course, its rhetorical dimension), and intellectual discrimination.

Su's record of conscientiousness and compassion as an official also figures in several of Canliao's poems. An entire piece is devoted to Su's heroics during the Xuzhou floods (no. 11), and we are told, in the final poem, that the legacy of his virtuous acts fills the land (no. 15). Su's loyal opposition to the New Policies is also described as being rooted in his devotion to the interests of the common people (no. 3). (In the Southern Song, it was precisely these that became the dominant themes of Lu You's writings about Su.)[11]

Canliao's poems really distinguish themselves, however, with the prominence they give to Su's affability, large-mindedness, and *fengliu* ("charm"). This is the theme that will strike many readers as quite plainly congruent with the way Su would have liked to be remembered. It is also this element that sets Canliao's poems apart from another important early account of this life—Su Che's grave inscription for his brother, where the formal tone and the obligation to chronicle events mitigate against such a focus. (Su Che's emphasis is on Su's loyal opposition in national politics and his outstanding record as a prefect.) Here is a sampling of the relevant lines from Canliao's poems: "Even when caught up in momentous affairs, he was able to chat and laugh" (no. 9); "Deprived of merit and fame [in national politics], he remained at ease" (no. 7); "Were the malarial rains and aboriginal mists [of Hainan Island] easy to endure? / . . . He befriended Dan tribesmen, his joy undiminished" (no. 6); and "The cultured charm of the Lotus Society [headed by Su's monk friend Foyin at Lu Mountain] has declined [i.e., without Su]" (no. 8). Similarly, one of the poems (no. 10) describes how awe-inspiring Su was when, clothed in official dress, he held forth on matters of national policy at the Court, and then notes that he was equally in his element when he returned home and went out strolling ("with walking stick and sandals").

Lastly, Canliao makes it clear that he, like Huang Tingjian, considers Su's capacity to serve his nation to have gone largely unused. "Su's portrait has not yet been hung in the Lingyan Pavilion" (where Tang Taizong hung paintings of his meritorious ministers), though it surely would have been if he had been properly employed (no. 15). There is a tragic wastefulness to this lost opportunity; and it occasioned in Su Shi a sense of profound disappointment which, his affability notwithstanding, lasted all his days. "His lifelong ambition of meritorious service / Lingers in pent-up frustration at his grave" (no. 2). The unfairness of it all makes one want to question Heaven itself, but Heaven remains impassive and silent (no. 1).

Canliao and Huang Tingjian were two of Su Shi's closest friends and admirers. We can hardly expect them to be objective or unbiased in their poetic treatments of Su's life, especially in the laments they wrote shortly after his death. Still, what they do say about Su and the emphases they choose are revealing in their own way. Canliao and Huang possessed, after all, intimate knowledge of their subject. It is likely that they had a good sense of how Su would have wanted his life to be represented for posterity, and it is unthinkable that they would have strayed far from that sense in writing their poems.

It will be worthwhile to introduce a contrast here, a much less sympathetic or favorable evaluation of Su Shi's life and thought. This is the evaluation that comes from Zhu Xi, roughly a century after Su's death. Not only do Zhu's views of Su provide an interesting alternative to those of his close friends, they must also have had tremendous impact, as virtually everything that Zhu Xi said had during his life and even more so in the centuries afterward.[12]

If we think of Zhu Xi as the inheritor of Cheng Yi's orientations on many key intellectual issues, we acquire a good initial sense of his view of Su Shi. "If you only look," Zhu Xi said, "at what East

Slope wrote [about Cheng Yi]—'When will I get to smash to pieces that word "reverence" (*jing*) of his?'—you will see that what he longed to do was flail his fists, roll up his sleeves, and indulge his most wanton impulses, with no limits at all on what he might do."[13] To Zhu Xi, because Su Shi epitomized self-indulgence and lack of restraint, naturally Su could not abide Cheng Yi's notion of the importance of mental discipline.

On philosophical issues, Zhu Xi's quarrel with Su Shi revolved around the question of the relation between writing, especially literary composition (*wen*), and the Way. Zhu Xi attributed to Su the claim that literary work may be, at its best, nothing less than the manifestation of the Way (a claim we do not have from Su himself). To Zhu this was a grave error, for it amounted to viewing writing as separate and equal to the Way, rather than merely a vehicle to express the Way and always thus of subordinate importance. Here is a representative passage from Zhu's *Classified Savings*:

> East Slope said, "What I consider writing coexists with the Way." In that case, writing stands on its own and so does the Way. When he writes, he goes off in search of the Way to insert it into his writing. That is his great error. His writing is always ornate and marvelous. He wraps it up and carries it off with him as he goes, not realizing that it is empty inside. If one were to identify his fundamental error, it is simply that he begins with writing and seeks thereby to gradually work up to the Way. He does not try to understand the Way before he proceeds to write. That is why he is wrong from the start. Ouyang Xiu's writing was somewhat closer to the Way, for he did not compose empty words. As he said in the "Treatise on Ritual and Music" in his Tang history: "Before the Three Dynasties, order derived from the One [ritual]. After the Three Dynasties, order derived from Two [ritual and the Qin institutions]."[14] This view is excellent, and it shows he still knew that there should be only one basis. As for East Slope's doctrine, it creates two bases rather than one.[15]

If Su Shi had simply expressed his views in philosophical writings, Zhu Xi could have refuted them once and been done with it. Instead, in his recorded remarks and essays Zhu keeps returning to the problem of Su Shi. He does so because he knows that Su was not just a philosopher. In fact, Zhu Xi is keenly aware of the great appeal Su Shi's literary work holds for his contemporaries. Zhu himself freely admits, as we see in the passage above, that Su's writing has its power and beauty. It is because of this appeal that Zhu felt impelled to keep arguing against it, to keep warning others about the mistaken priorities it embodies and the great potential it has for corrupting those who come under its influence.

Despite his own literary abilities, or perhaps because of them, Zhu Xi insisted that the literary excellences of Su's writing not be divorced from any general evaluation of the man and his thought, both of which Zhu found objectionable. Zhu's apprehensions make him sound, at times, more than a bit extreme on the subject. The passage below comes from a letter Zhu wrote to Lü Zuqian. Lü and others had suggested to Zhu that it was quite unnecessary for him to keep attacking Su as if he were a Mozi or Yang Zhu (Mencius's arch-rivals). Su might be looked upon merely as a Tang Le or Jing Cha, that is, a minor poet in the Chu song tradition, whom Mencius had not bothered to criticize. Zhu was not pleased by this idea, and he took the occasion to lecture his friend on the Way. If the Way did not encompass all things, then it would have been permissible to compose literary work that was self-indulgent and irresponsible. Lying outside the Way, such writing would not do any serious harm. However, since the Way in fact is all-encompassing, any words at all that do not accord with it are potentially harmful to it. Su's writings cannot be enjoyed merely as literature nor can their errors be overlooked. Zhu continues:

> I myself used to enjoy reading the literary compositions of Qu Yuan, Song Yu, Tang Le, and Jing Cha [the Chu poets]. But later I thought about it and realized that although their words are profuse, their substance comes down to two themes: sorrow and self-abandonment. If someone were to recite these works daily and be transformed by them, would he not do great injury to his mind? After this I put them aside and did not dare to look at them again. Today, because of what my colleagues have said, I would add the following: these poetic works, which were composed at one time in the Chu region, were not necessarily ever heard by Mencius. If they had circulated to all quarters of the empire so that scholars passed them down from one generation to the next and everyone recited them, as is now done with the words of Mr. Su, Mencius would not have failed to denounce them. To make it worse, the learning of Mr. Su includes, on the one hand, talk about human nature and Heaven's decree and, one the other, discussions of governance. His words are not confined to the poetic tradition of Qu, Song, Tang, and Jing. Students are at first delighted by his literary work and study it, hoping to reap some ready benefit [i.e., on the examinations]. But after some time his writings seep into the marrow of their bones, until it is impossible to be free of them. The damage that is thus done to individual ability and to social customs is not inconsiderable.[16]

Elsewhere, Zhu Xi criticized Su Shi on many particulars. He found Su to be inconsistent on the issue of institutional reforms; he considered Su's thinking to be heavily tainted with Buddhist and Taoist doctrines; and he found Su's judgment of men to be seriously flawed.[17] So strongly did Zhu object to two men whom Su had sponsored, Qin Guan and Huang Tingjian, that he surmised that if Su Shi had ever become grand councilor, he would have been even worse for the country than Wang Anshi had been. This was an observation that Zhu Xi repeated often, with apparent relish.[18] Zhu also picked apart Su's commentary on the *Book of Changes*, using it as evidence of Su's misunderstanding of basic Confucian values.[19]

Despite all of these disagreements, it is Zhu Xi's conception of Su Shi as an aesthete, in the worst sense of the word, that seems to be at the root of his disapproval. Zhu's attitude is best exemplified by the following exchange, in which Ouyang Xiu is also dealt with harshly:

> Someone asked, "How does East Slope compare with Master Han [Han Yu]"?
>
> Zhu Xi replied, "In rectitude he does not measure up to Han."
>
> "What about Master Ou?"
>
> "He is shallow."
>
> After some time, Zhu Xi added, "Such persons [i.e., Su and Ouyang] sought to establish themselves as men of letters (*wenren*). When they studied, all they investigated was the causes of the rise and fall of dynasties in ancient and modern times. They wrote but never exerted any effort at cultivating their own person. They spent their days doing nothing more than reciting poetry, drinking wine, and telling jokes."[20]

Zhu Xi's conviction about the frivolousness of Su and his circle comes through even in his opinion of their brushwork, which he faults for its idiosyncrasies: "Calligraphy has been thrown into turmoil and ruined by Su and Huang. Recently, I saw an example of Cai Junmo's writing. Every character has the correct standard. It is just like a principled man or upright scholar. Now, that is calligraphy!"[21]

These comments by Zhu Xi, especially the one about how Su and his friends spent their days ("reciting poetry, drinking wine, and telling jokes"), call to mind the famous painting of the group at leisure on the grounds of a nobleman's estate. Although "The Elegant Gathering in the Western Garden" (*Xiyuan yaji tu*) was painted to celebrate the cultural refinements of its subjects, rather than to belittle them as Zhu Xi does, still the image it presents of these men seems to have much in common with that conveyed by Zhu's remarks. The provenance of the painting, which was reputedly first done by Li Gonglin, is uncertain. Yet the scene was copied or redrawn so frequently in subsequent centuries that it became one of the classic scenes of Chinese figure painting and must have had a powerful influence upon common conceptions of Su Shi and his circle. (Ellen Johnston Laing has counted forty-one extant versions of the painting and references in written sources to forty-seven more.)[22]

The painting, in a version attributed to Zhao Mengfu (in the National Palace Museum in Taipei), depicts sixteen gentlemen amusing themselves with various literati pursuits in the garden party.[23] The men are all identified in various written descriptions of the painting, and the party itself is endowed with historicity: it is said to have occurred at the estate of Wang Shen, the art connoisseur and imperial in-law, in the capital in the second year of the Yuanyou period (1087). In the lower foreground Su Shi is seated at a table and engaged in writing out an inscription. Seated around him are Wang Shen, his host, together with Cai Zhao and Li Zhiyi, who watch respectfully as Su does the calligraphy. Two of Wang Shen's concubines also look on from behind. In the middle ground Li Gonglin himself is the process of painting his illustration of Tao Qian's poem "The Return." Li is being observed by Su Che, Huang Tingjian, Chao Buzhi, Zhang Lei, and Zheng Jinglao. Further back, beneath a twisted pine, Qin Guan sits on the ground listening to Chen Jingyuan play the *qin*, while to their left Mi Fu is in the process of writing an inscription upon a huge rock (like those he called "friend"), as Wang Qinchen looks on. Secluded inside a bamboo thicket in the upper left, the monk Faxiu lectures Liu Jing on the doctrine of non-arising (*wusheng lun*). "For pure and elevated happiness," observes a colophon, "nothing in the world of men could surpass this scene."[24]

As intriguing as this scene has unquestionably been to centuries of viewers, seeming to capture a virtually unmatched concentration of literati talent, it is evidently an idealized vision of Yuanyou elegance. It is most unlikely that any such gathering ever took place, as Wang Shizhen first realized in the sixteenth century.[25] Contemporary sources are conspicuously silent about it.[26] The earliest paintings of such a gathering seem to date from nearly 150 years later (if then), as do the first reliable references to a Li Gonglin painting of the event. It is not until the fourteenth and fifteenth centuries that descriptions of the event and Li Gonglin's painting (both full of discrepancies) become widespread. Probably, the legend about such a gathering and a painting commemorating it began during the Southern Song, when many scholars looked back fondly upon the supposedly enlightened period of Yuanyou rule.[27]

Imaginary representations may, of course, have their own validity or convey a sense of "rightness" that surpasses that of any historical event. Or they may be misleading. Or, more probably, they may permit a range of interpretations, depending upon the knowledge and sympathies of the viewer. The intriguing question of what the first painter of the "Elegant Gathering" thought of these Yuanyou gentlemen cannot now be answered. Did he admire these men simply for their devotion to the high-minded cultural pursuits, or did he think of those pursuits as inseparable from the fractious reality of their lives (and all the more meaningful because of it) and assume that viewers of the painting would think likewise? Regardless of the original intent, in later centuries, as biographical knowledge dimmed and dynastic nostalgia was no longer relevant, the painting must often have been viewed merely as a vision of cultured elegance. In that interpretation, the painting has much in common with with Zhu Xi's remarks about Su and his circle, even though the implicit judgment differs. Both accounts dwell, or seem to dwell, upon Su's aesthetic activities. Thus they depart from the appraisal of Su found in the poetic laments written by Huang Tingjian and Canliao. It is not that the two images of Su have nothing in common. Yet their emphases are different, especially in the role they attribute to aesthetic pursuits. It is a question, to use Su's own terminology, of *ben* and *mo*, "basis and extremity." Zhu Xi thinks of Su Shi as someone who "sought to establish himself" on the strength of his literary skills, and he faults him for it. Huang and Canliao present a more rounded picture of the basis of Su's talent and accomplishments. Qin Guan has sharp criticism for an admirer who singles out Su's literary skill for praise. "You intend to exalt Mr. Su, but in fact you belittle him."[28] Qin explains that Su's literary talent, while real, is "the most crude" of his many talents and ways of interacting with the world, in other words, his *mo*. According to Qin, the traits that Su ought to be admired for are, first, his wisdom concerning human nature and, second, his capacity for service to his realm and his general understanding of human affairs. Literary work ranks behind all these. Even Canliao's notion of Su's *fengliu* or his "capacity for tolerance" differs importantly from Zhu Xi's image of Su as a frivolous man of letters. Canliao is careful always to set Su's affability and charm in a context that prevents it from being perceived as "shallow" (to use Zhu Xi's word). Su is able to chat and laugh even when caught up in momentous events, or he enjoys the company of rustic men in his exile. Zhu Xi's impression of Su's gaiety has no such resonating context or depth. Zhu seems to fasten on some such conception of Su as came to be pictured in the "Elegant Gathering" tradition, and, interpreting it as narrowly and unfavorably as possible, takes it to epitomize Su's life.

Zhu Xi's view on how Su spent his days does not warrant a serious rebuttal. That does not mean that we ought to accept unquestioningly the representation of Su transmitted by his admirers. For example, Qin Guan's account of "the basis and the extremity" in Su's life may be facile in its own way. Yet can we afford to dismiss it out of hand? On what basis would we do so? We might be tempted to disregard it because it does not fit with the image of Su conveyed by so much modern literary scholarship, which, naturally, stresses his achievement in poetry. But once we begin to treat the historical sources selectively in this way, giving attention only to those historical statements that match our modern perspectives, we will never find anything but our own values in the past. Another viewpoint would be that the potential value of such statements as Qin's lies precisely in its departure from modern opinion, of which it may effect a critical reconsideration, whether or not we adopt it in the end. Today we approach Su Shi primarily as a poet and are convinced, rightly so, of the deep significance that literary expression held in his life. It is, actually, difficult for us to hold any other assessment of him in mind, so comfortable are we with our modern categories, and consequently we are apt to be dismissive of other evaluations or to discount them as mere bows to conventional valuations of conduct and moral cultivation over literary achievement. At the very least, however, there is some circularity in our modern perspective of Su, loath as we may be to admit it, since it is usually formed on the basis of his output as a poet. Su's friends and associates knew him differently from the way we do, and differently also from Zhu Xi. While acknowledging at the outset the absolutely essential role of literary work in Su's life—amply evidenced in preceding chapters—we may also acknowledge the likelihood that no simple biographical tag or single level of interpretation will ever do justice to this complex life and personality (much as we would not be satisfied with any such interpretation imposed upon our own lives). In any case, the fact that even in the Song dynasty there was such disagreement as we find between Su's immediate followers and Zhu Xi about the significance and distribution of his various activities underscores the need to consider anew their meaning and balance.

Ambivalence over Aesthetic Pursuits

There are times when Su appears to be making very ambitious claims for the meaning of aesthetic endeavors. We have seen several of these occasions in the preceding chapters, as for example when, in comments addressed to the monk Sicong and to Qin Guan, Su implies that mastery of calligraphy or *qin* playing is inseparable from mastery of the Way for, after all, none of the ancients who approached this ultimate wisdom did so "through emptiness and vacuity." The idea seems to be that supreme knowledge of the world, which is innate but latent in the mind, can only be "triggered" (*fa*) through active contact with things (*wu*). We are reminded of Su's enthusiasm for images found in the

Book of Changes of contact between the sage ruler and "things." Now we understand that artistic involvement may also be an enlightening thing or activity.

Especially in his remarks on painting, Su is likewise apt to speak of art as an embodiment of the Pattern (*li*) of the universe. This theme is part of his desire to deemphasize the value of sterile verisimilitude and of training that stresses, whether in painting or calligraphy, technical control and the imitation of past styles. Su's preference leads him to dwell on the artist's apprehension of underlying truths, rather than preoccupation with formal appearances, and his descriptions of this suggest a profound union between artist and the world. To Su, Wen Tong captures the Pattern of bamboo, he leaves his body behind, he and the bamboo are fused together. And in the calligraphy of Huaisu, Su sees embodied the workings of a mind that remains unmoved amid a furious flurry of activity: is this not, Su asks, just like the enlightened man?

Regarding poetry Su makes similarly comprehensive claims. He tends to emphasize its ability to admit or represent all the myriad phenomena of the world. The comparison is that of a mirror or pool that is capable of reflecting all things. Such "capacity" implies wisdom concerning those things. The poet Su evokes sounds like a sage who has mastered the art of emptying his own mind so that he can comprehend, and relate the truth about, everything around him.

On writing in general, one of Su's most grandiose and often quoted statements is the following, from a letter to Xie Minshi, in which Su considers two apparently contradictory statements Confucius had made about words or writing and provides his own novel interpretation:

> Confucius said, "If words are not elegant, they will not travel far."[29] He also said, "Words should communicate, and that is all."[30] Now, if words should do nothing more than communicate their author's intent, they would seem not to need to be elegant. But that is not what he meant at all. To capture the marvelous essence of things is as difficult as harnessing the wind or catching a shadow. Not one man in a million can fully comprehend the nature of things in his mind, much less express that understanding with his mouth or hands. That is what is meant by "words communicating." If words can really attain to that kind of communication, then the usefulness of writing can never be exhausted.[31]

Such a strained interpretation of Confucius's utterance naturally makes us suppose that it was particularly important to Su that he articulate this account of the power of words.

Complementing such statements are remarks Su makes about

the weighty responsibilities that he and his literary colleagues feel they have to preserve the cultural heritage, and its standards of right and wrong, in the face of hostile forces. In a letter of 1085 to Zhang Lei, Su writes, "I am old now. If the younger generation is to see the great fullness of the ancients, it will depend upon Huang Luzhi, Qin Shaoyou, Chao Wujiu [Buzhi], Chen Lüchang [Shidao], and yourself."[32] One of Su's followers even states that Su once spoke of a pact or alliance (*meng*) formed by the leading men of letters, and broached, as above, the notion of leadership within this alliance and its weighty responsibilities.

> East Slope once said, "The responsibility for letters lay with the famous scholars of the age. If they take their turn leading the alliance (*zhumeng*), the proper Way of letters will not be lost. At present, we live at the height of a peaceful era. Consequently, scholars of letters are numerous, and it is necessary that writing have an acknowledged leader in charge. Formerly, Ouyang Wenzhong [Xiu] passed this responsibility on to me, and I did not dare to take it lightly. In the future the leadership of the alliance of letters should be bequeathed to these gentlemen [Su's followers], just as Ouyang passed it on to me."[33]

Combining such remarks with those Su occasionally makes about the profound meaningfulness of aesthetic pursuits, it would be easy, particularly if we lump all those pursuits together as one, to conclude that Su had developed a political and intellectual agenda based upon writing and associated cultural activities that he championed in opposition to the New Learning, which was ascendant through much of his life. Actually, this interpretation of Su Shi has much in common with that propagated by Zhu Xi, except that it is not negative. Here again we have Su defining himself primarily as a literatus. Literary and artistic expression is his basis (we have seen how Qin Guan would disagree), but now it is no longer thought of as frivolous. Because of the claims Su himself sometimes made for the deep significance of these activities, and his apparent self-consciousness as the leader of the besieged literary alliance, serious purposes are imputed to all of Su's efforts as writer, poet, calligrapher, and painter; for they are understood to lie at the heart of his self-image and ambitions.

This evaluation of Su Shi shows itself in much of modern scholarship, especially in that which seeks to explore Su's contributions to thinking about the arts and thus stresses, understandably, his most far-reaching claims. Naturally, the striking independence of so much of modern literary scholarship from the other disciplines has lent support to this evaluation. Literary critics find in Su's many affirmations of the importance of writing implicit validation for their focus on this aspect of his life. Native premodern developments also contributed to this conception of Su. The vogue of the *wenren* in Yuan and subsequent dynasties, brought on by circumstances unknown in the Song, caused a rethinking of Su Shi's life, as later values were imputed anachronistically to him. Yoshikawa Kōjirō has discussed the crucial differences between these later *wenren*, who devoted themselves solely to literature, and the eleventh-century exemplars they claimed; but his point has not been widely appreciated.[34] Moreover, even during the Song dynasty itself there were, as we have seen, intellectuals who insisted that poetry was everything to Su, intending thus to discredit him.

Needless to say, this image of Su does not begin to do justice to his activism in national or, especially, local administration, as described earlier in this volume. But there are less obvious problems with it as well, which threaten our understanding even of Su's literary work. It is not that there is no validity to this notion of the importance of aesthetic expression in Su's life and thought. The difficulty lies in seeing how to evaluate certain of his remarks in light of the entire body of his writings on the arts, in understanding the difference between our apprehension of his legacy (which is based upon his literary work) and his own self-image, and in appreciating the implications of the distinction he drew between art as formal beauty and art as embodiment of personality.

To begin with, Su's most ambitious statements about the significance of aesthetic pursuits are extreme and exceptional. In fact, he retreats from his most advanced claims on numerous occasions, both before and after he makes them. It is a distortion, then, to seize upon these extreme statements (one does this, of course, because they are so interesting) and to let them alone represent his views. Consider the issue of how to interpret Confucius's famous pronouncement that "words should communicate and that is all" (*ci da eryi yi*). Su's treatment of this in his letter to Xie Minshi, quoted above, is a strong affirmation of the value and potentials of literary expression. Words, he tells us, are capable of capturing the "marvelous essence" of things. And he makes it sound like there can never be too much good writing (its usefulness "can never be exhausted"), since it can accomplish so much. Because these comments were made upon reading Xie's poetry, rhapsodies, and prose, critics are tempted to discern in them justification for Su's own lifelong productivity as a poet.

What are we to make, then, of a radically different interpretation Su gave (from the same, late period of his life) of the very same Confucian utterance? When another young man, Wang Xiang, wrote to Su, sending copies of his writings, Su wrote back: "Confucius said,

'Words should communicate and that is all.' Once words succeed in communicating they should stop. Nothing more ought to be added to them."[35] This amounts to a rejection of the whole notion of elegant, polished, or literary expression, that is, of *wen*, which is always the alternative to "communicate and that is all." The remainder of the letter confirms this position, as Su decries literary exercises that serve no pragmatic purpose (including his own essays on historical figures). "The great defect among scholars," he lectures Wang, "is that they produce many empty writings (*kongwen*) with few practical uses." He goes on praise Jia Yi and Lu Zhi (known for their pragmatic memorials on statecraft) as having represented the highest form of learning and, hence, writing, and to lament the decline of the tradition they exemplify. If one assumed that one had found, in Su's letter to Xie Minshi, an affirmation of Su's belief in the extraordinary potentials of *wen*, what of his letter to Wang? Nor does the statement to Wang Xiang stand alone: many others might be adduced that complement it in a variety of ways. His own father, Su tells us, had admonished him on the dangers of elegant literary expression (*wenzhang*) that neglects the Way, and of ornamentation that lacks substance. (Zhu Xi would have appreciated this.) "My father's poetry and prose," Su wrote, "was all written to accomplish something (*youwei er zuo*): its tone is forceful and insistent, and its words invariably assail the excesses of the day."[36] This is a conservative and much narrower view of literary work. It is a far cry from the generalization often drawn from the claim about writing capturing the marvelous essence of things.

It is evident that Su Shi had, at least in certain contexts, a clear-cut sense of hierarchy among forms of expression and their relation to personality (much as Qin Guan did on Su's behalf). This is brought out in his colophon on an ink-bamboo painting by Wen Tong (Yuke):

> Yuke's prose writings are just the dregs and lees of his virtuous character (*de*), and his poetry is just the hairtip of his prose. Whatever remains unexpressed by his poetry spills out of him as calligraphy, or is transformed into painting: these arts are both just the overflow of his poetry. Now, those who admire his poetry and prose are progressively few, so is there likely to be anyone at all who admires his virtuous character as much as they admire his painting? What a pity it is![37]

Here Su's formulation is particularly detailed and clear. But similar notions about the subordinate role of outer expression to inner virtue are of course a major theme of Su's views on calligraphy and painting. How, Su asks, could it be the brushwork that makes Ouyang Xiu's calligraphy so valuable?[38] This manner of thinking led to an apparent contradiction: on the one hand, it validated thoroughgoing involvement with the arts and supported the prodigious and wide-ranging output we associate with Su Shi and his followers. On the other, it meant that the products of this abundant activity tended to be referred back to the personalities of those who created them. The art form is merely a receptacle in which the artist "lodges" his inner qualities. The poems and calligraphic inscriptions were less important in their own right than they were as manifestations of the artist's character.

Su Shi is best remembered for his literary work, but it is worth noting that the literary enterprise does not bulk large in his own thought as articulated at the most formal level. Justification for literary and aesthetic pursuits, though ample, is confined to Su's relatively informal writings: letters to friends, colophons, poems, studio inscriptions, and poetry itself. The importance of these writings and views to Su is undeniable—as is that of poetry in his life—but their place in Su's entire corpus should also be taken into account.

The themes that are central to Su's thought as it is represented in such formal writings as his commentaries on the classics, his examinations portfolio, and essays (*lun*), are those that have come up repeatedly and in many different guises in the preceding chapters. They include a deep antipathy to self-centered thinking and conduct, the ability to accommodate oneself to changing worldly circumstances, a commitment to thoroughgoing involvement with the world (rather than introspective aloofness from it), and inner constancy that is unaffected by one's misfortunes in life, especially political disfavor and its consequences. Collectively, these ideals amount to Su's own conception of sagehood. Many of these notions have a strong affinity with currents of Chan and Pure Land thought, and Su's exposure to Buddhism certainly reinforced them, if it was not the source for them originally. Su's beliefs that apply specifically to governance, and official service, include the conviction that the imperial bureaucracy's primary responsibility is to improve the lot of the common people, that policy should respond intimately to ever-changing popular need, and that loyal dissent by ministers is absolutely essential and must be protected.

The argument here is not that this body of thought, expressed in Su's formal essays and commentaries, is ultimately more valid or fundamental than that he expressed in other contexts or which might be extrapolated from his lifelong practice as a poet. I do not question that, in the larger literati tradition, lyrical expression had its own profound validation and ethical standing. Nor would I deny that literary and other aesthetic pursuits often became in Su's life an indispensable and central act of self-definition, as we have seen. The point is simply to take account of this other level of conceptualization in Su's thinking and to begin to explore the ramifications of its existence. A similar point has recently been made by Xue Ruisheng, who narrows the key themes of Su's "learning" down to just a few precepts, none of which mentions literary expression, though in practice they may involve it as a method or means. Xue argues against equating the central component of Su's fame (his literary work) with that of his "learning," insisting that the latter is rooted in concepts of how the individual should react to his worldly fortunes and how the rulers should rule.[39]

The discrepancies discussed here, as well as the differences between separate forms of Su's writings, raises a key interpretative issue. In our effort to understand this protean eleventh-century figure, shall we feel bound to discover a simple commonality that runs through all the facets of his life, a unity that pervades whatever he undertakes? Or shall we not instead be willing to hold in our purview and take seriously each of the divergent aspects of his pronouncements and practice, thus according to this man some degree of the complexity, multidimensionality, or even contradictoriness that we readily accept in our own lives?

The Meanings of *Wen*

The problem of the meaning and range of the term *wen* must be considered here because of its bearing upon our perceptions of the place of aesthetic expression in Su's life. There is a temptation to group all of Su's literary and artistic work together, and to think that jointly it constitutes what he would have called his *wen* (in the sense of aesthetic, refined, or *cultured* expression). Encouragement to do this comes from the later history of the word and its compounds (e.g., *wenhua*, "culture"; *wenyi*, "the arts"), as well as from the ubiquitous presence of the *wenren* ("gentleman of culture") in later imperial China, denoting a man who considered himself an "independent [free] artist" (as Yoshikawa renders the term), and who often looked back to Su Shi as his model. The problem is that Su almost never uses *wen* in a way that will permit such a broad or blanket interpretation. The point is significant in that it affects our understanding of Su's conception of the cultural activities in which he participated and the relationship between them.

It is frequently assumed that *wen*, in Su's usage, denotes all forms of learned or polite expression. If one does not trouble to identify the word's specific referent each time Su employs it, Su does indeed begin to sound like a champion of "culture": "When I was young, I heard my father discuss *wen* and explain that sages in antiquity engaged in it because they could not keep themselves from doing so."⁴⁰ "Formerly, from the Five Dynasties on, the tradition of *wen* declined and customs became degenerate."⁴¹ "My own *wen* is like a ten-thousand-gallon underground spring . . ."⁴²

Actually, most often Su uses *wen* simply to mean prose writings, as in the description of Wen Tong quoted above: "Yuke's *wen* [prose writings] are just the dregs and lees of his virtuous character (*de*), and his poetry is just the hairtip of his prose." It is frequently the case, as here, that *wen* is used in distinction to *shi* "poetry." Another example is found in Su's preface to Shao Ying's poetry collection: "[Shao Ying's] *wen* (prose writings) are pure, harmonious, and decorous, just like those produced by Jin and Song dynasty writers [265–478]. However, his *shi* is even more attractive. As one chews on it, the flavor endures, while occasionally he blends in the style of Southern Dynasties and Tang poets."⁴³ Another example of this usage, translated earlier, is Su's account of the culmination of each form of expression in the Tang dynasty: *shi* culminated with Du Fu, *wen* ("prose") with Han Yu, calligraphy with Yan Zhenqing, and painting with Wu Daozi. In each passage, Su uses the term *wen* to distinguish one form of expression (prose) from others rather than to refer jointly to all of them.

Another use of the term by Su designates literary prose together with *shi* poetry and the *fu* ("rhapsody"). This usage derives from the ancient distinction between *wen* and *bi*, that is between literary and euphonic writing, on the one hand, and "plain" and more pedestrian prose, on the other. In this meaning *wen* may be understood as shorthand for the compound *wenzhang*, in the sense of "refined literature" or "belles lettres." Su uses both *wen* and *wenzhang* in this sense, referring collectively to all the literary forms.⁴⁴ Although *wen* in this broader meaning does cover more than "prose," it is still wrong to think that it applies also to other "cultured" pursuits, such as calligraphy and painting. Su does not use the term *wen* to refer comprehensively to cultured pursuits. In other words, as fond as Su was of associating the arts of the brush with the literary forms, and as often as he stressed the convertibility of, especially, painting and poetry, he did not place the different media together as equals or joint components of an overarching construct called *wen*. The arts of the brush are described, as we have seen, as just the tip of the tip of the expression of personality. Actually, even in the broader sense of "refined literature" *wen* did not include all literary work. The *ci* form was not generally considered part of *wen*, which is why it was excluded from *wenji* "literary collections." Here we must face the irony that the portion of Su's work as a poet that many modern readers consider to be his greatest achievement and to best exemplify his talent in "literature" (*wenxue*) was not in his day a fully reputable literary form.

Another use of *wen* by Su is in the compound *wenzi* "writing," which he uses particularly to designate the most public and visible kind of writing composed in his time: documentary and expository prose as produced in the examinations halls and at the Court. Although sometimes this public writing, too, is referred to as *wenzhang*, usually *wenzhang* is reserved for the more private and literary expression that makes up the bulk of individuals' "literary collections." In Su's usage a distinction is regularly (though not exhaustively) maintained between *wenzi* and *wenzhang*. It was, of course, *wenzi* (not *wenzhang*) that lay at the heart of the operation of the bureaucracy, especially the one that Su knew. His was a dynasty, after all, that prided itself on its empowerment of civil rather than military officials, that gave special place to its institutions of policy review and criticism, and that relied far more heavily than had any previous dynasty on written examinations for the recruitment of officials.

In Su Shi's view, *wenzi* had undergone two crises since the founding of the dynasty. The first was the threat posed in the first half of the eleventh century by the euphuistic style of parallel prose.[45] This manner of writing, which was perfected first by Yang Yi (972–1020) and his colleagues, had become conventional on the examinations and in the bureaucracy. Known as the "current style" (*shiwen*), it was composed in "couplets" of grammatically parallel lines (for euphonic effect) and it relied upon learned and allusive diction. Its critics condemned it for hobbling thought and directing the writer's attention to superficial ornamentation. Ouyang Xiu became a staunch opponent of this "current style"; and he dealt it a serious blow when, as administrator of the examinations in 1057 (the year Su Shi placed second), he gave highest grades to those candidates who wrote in the so-called "ancient prose" (*guwen*) style, the alternative to parallel prose that he promoted.

The second threat to *wenzi* was brought on by Wang Anshi and his reformed examinations, a threat that recurred throughout Su's official life. This time the problem was the stultifying uniformity of thought that was imposed (by the narrowing of fields and by the requirement that the few classics examined be explicated according to the New Learning commentaries), as well as the new vogue of vapid speculation, as Su considered it, about human nature and Heaven's decree. "The decline of writing (*wenzi*)," Su says to Zhang Lei at the start of the Yuanyou era, "has never been as extreme as it is today. The cause may be traced to Mr. Wang. Wang's own writing is not necessarily bad. The problem is that he wants to make everyone be the same as he."[46] Su goes on to mention how he had heard that the late emperor (Shenzong) had grown disillusioned with the reformed exams and had wanted to revert to the pre-reform regulations. Elsewhere, Su comments, "Today, in the writing (*wenzi*) done on the examinations a thousand men all sound exactly alike. The examiners themselves are fed up with it."[47]

It is necessary to distinguish these different meanings and referents of *wen* in Su's works. Failure to do so leads to an impression of unity in the conception of *wen* that conflates Su's usage. The general principle that "the character (*zi*) may be the same but the meaning varies" is one whose validity has long been acknowledged in Chinese letters. Su Shi himself cautioned scholars against the practice of "interpreting a given character the same way every time," thus introducing distortions under the guise of maintaining consistency; and recently Qian Zhongshu has written persuasively on the same point.[48] Although obviously the many meanings of *wen* and its compounds are related and sometimes cannot be neatly separated, it is rare that one cannot identify a quite specific and restricted denotation. The distinction between refined literature (*wenzhang*) and writing in the public sphere (*wenzi*) is particularly significant. It is clear, for example, that *wenzi* rather than *wenzhang* is the context Su ordinarily has in mind when he uses many related compounds, such as *wenshi* (lit., "scholar of *wen*"), *wenren*, *wenjiao* (the teaching or tradition of *wen*), and *siwen* (our [collective] *wen*).

With these distinctions in mind, we may reconsider what Su really means when he refers to the weighty role that will pass to his literary followers, saying that they are the ones who will transmit the "great fullness" of the ancients to the next generation. Does this really signify all that is often claimed for it regarding Su's valuation of literary work? Su's remarks are part of the complaint he voices to Zhang Lei about the decline of *wenzi* brought about by the reformed examinations. "I have heard," Su concludes his letter, "that you may be appointed erudite in the Imperial Academy, and so I have written this to encourage you to exert yourself at the task." It was just then, as the Yuanyou administration was forming, that Su was instrumental in securing such appointments for the men he singles out in this passage: Huang Tingjian and Chao Buzhi were charged with compiling the *Veritable Records* of the preceding reign, and Qin Guan became an instructor in the Imperial Academy, as did Zhang Lei. Su even managed to secure a teaching post for Chen Shidao (who had never passed the *jinshi*). Su took pains to ensure that these men were placed in positions in which they might have great influence over the state of writing (and thinking and policy formulation) in the public sphere. His actions suggest that the expectations he had for them as transmitters of ancient values did not depend solely, or even primarily, upon whatever literary works they might produce in their private lives. The same must be true for the context of the comment Su is reputed to have made about leadership of the "alliance of letters."[49]

The case of Qin Guan is especially instructive. Qin Guan is remembered today exclusively as a poet, and his accomplishment in the *ci* form is considered his greatest legacy. Naturally, then, we tend to think that it is Qin's skills as a poet that Su has in mind when he refers to him as a leader among *wenren*. But the contemporary sources provide a rather different picture of Qin Guan and his skills. Among Su's followers, Qin Guan (together with Chao Buzhi) were known especially for their expository prose (*yilun*).[50] Su Shi must have appreciated this aspect of Qin's talent; for at the start of the Yuanyou era he recommended Qin to take the decree examination, the same exam Su had taken years before. The portfolio of fifty essays that Qin composed for this exam (again, like Su, twenty-five policy essays and twenty-five treatments of historical figures) survives in his collected works; and these, together with the other examples of Qin's documentary prose, have been praised as belonging to the highest tradition of policy criticism.[51] Now, there is no question that Su Shi also thought highly of Qin's *shi* poetry and his *ci*, even if he sometimes joked with him about the latter. Yet his esteem was certainly not limited to these two genres. A remark that Su made to a friend soon after Qin's death suggests, moreover, that the relative weight, in Su's mind, of Qin's various accomplishments was the opposite of what one might today suppose it to have been: "Even among the finest of today's *wenren*, how could his equal ever be found? When such a man as he is born into the world, he should certainly be given great responsibilities in the realm. And if he is not given such responsibilities, he is bound to produce discursive writings (*bi you suo lunzhu*) to instruct men of future generations. That which [Qin] already wrote ensures that his name will live on, but he had not completed all that he planned to do."[52] Su is thinking first of the tragedy of the waste of Qin's unused talents for official service and second of Qin as an essayist and commentator on statecraft. Qin's gift for poetry is not uppermost in Su's mind.

We must reconstruct our understanding of *wenren* if we are to appreciate what Su means by it and related terms. We might ask, for example, who in Su's eyes was the greatest *wenren* of recent centuries?

One might expect it to be Du Fu, Wang Wei, or at least Han Yu. But Su passes over all these men in favor of their contemporary Lu Zhi, the Hanlin academician and memorialist.

> The ascendancy of *wenren* has been greater in recent times than ever before. I myself, however, have esteem for one of them and one only, Lu Xuangong [Lu Zhi]. My family owns a rare copy of his collected memorials. Not long ago, when I served as academician reader-in-waiting, I copied it over and presented it to the throne.[53] I thought to myself that the loyalty I thus showed, although of no consequence, might approximate the loyalty that Mencius showed for his ruler. I hoped, moreover, to spread the thought and example of Lu Zhi throughout the empire, causing every household to possess this prescription and every person to hold this medicine, to use to treat whatever ills the world developed. Is this not the most fundamental desire of every humane person and worthy man? When we look today at what Lu Zhi's essays, particularly the ten pieces that begin with the Eastern Han, his intent is entirely to draw upon the past to guide the present.[54] His interest is in applications to improve the world, and he does not seek to offer pleasing appearances to the eye and ear. This is precisely what I have looked for all my life in friends and all other worthy men who devote themselves to the Way.[55]

Su Shi's description of Lu Zhi certainly does not coincide with Zhu Xi's notion of a *wenren*, nor does it sound remotely like the independent artists of the later imperial dynasties.

The Utility of a Multidimensional View

Su's usage of the difficult term *wen* and its many compounds holds, then, these several surprises. *Wen* does not have the same meaning every time it is used. *Wenren* means something different to Su from what it came to mean in later times. Even in the sense of "refined literature" (*wenzhang*), the term does not include other "cultural" pursuits such as the arts of the brush; and "literature" itself excludes one important literary form (*ci*). It would be wrong to equate *wen* in each occurrence with *siwen* "our culture" (as used in the *Analects*), and *siwen* itself is not as all-inclusive as we might suppose. Su Shi's thought, as articulated at the most formal level, does not give much attention or importance to *wen*, and certainly not to "refined literature." Moreover, in several of the most exalted statements Su makes about the function of *wen*, it is clear that he is referring primarily to *wenzi*, documentary and utilitarian writing done in service of the state. As for *wenzhang*, it is worth remembering that Su and his circle had no monopoly upon interest or talent in that field, as shown by the accomplishment in poetry by none other than Su's great antagonist, Wang Anshi, who is rightly considered a major Northern Song poet.

These qualifications regarding the place and meaning of *wen* in Su's thought are consistent with his repeated statements about refined literature being a *mo* ("extremity"), and related aesthetic pursuits being even less significant. The attitude is also consistent with Su's occasional dismissal of his own poetry as being like the chirping of birds or insects ("now they sing out and now they stop—what difference does it all make?"),[56] and his *wen* as being something that is entirely devoid of substance and, in fact, nothing more than the manifestation of a flaw (*bing*) in his character.[57] One recalls Su's exasperation with those who took Ouyang Xiu's "Old Tippler's Pavilion" too seriously (a viewpoint we ourselves would do well to bear in mind).[58] A similar attitude may be seen in remarks Su commonly made about calligraphy being just a harmless diversion analogous to chess, and his concurrence with Wen Tong that a fondness for engaging in painting betrays a *shortfall* in one's moral cultivation.[59] Disparaging remarks Su makes about his and his friends' "little *ci*," and the error the world makes by neglecting a man's more consequential writings, are obviously of like import.[60]

One might ask how such views can be reconciled with the assertions Su makes elsewhere that stress the significance of literary and artistic expression? It is evident that Su was working towards some very ambitious claims for the meaning of aesthetic endeavors. That is the most that can be said, at least in the realm of aesthetic theory. Su broaches these claims in casual writings addressed to like-minded friends. Substituting the poet and calligrapher for *Zhuangzi*'s craftsmen who attained the Way through the execution of their craft, Su suggests that literary or artistic activity may trigger insight into the nature of "things." Beginning as Su did with the unshakable conviction that the Way could not be directly approached or apprehended, the arts came to be viewed as one kind of mediating activity to lead one forward in the quest. Thus the arts could, as could the other worldly pursuits into which Su threw himself (including everything from famine relief to alchemy), be a realization of the ideal of remaining in intimate and ever responsive "contact with things" (the alternative to vacuous introspection). Poetry could, like a mirror, contain all of the phenomena of the world; calligraphy could mimic its organizing forces; and painting could capture the underlying Patterns. Each form, moreover, also embodied the values and character of its creator, and the uniqueness of a personal style (reflecting each man's distinctive personality) became a highly prized achievement. As significant as these claims about the arts are, however, for understanding both Su's life and his contributions to Song thinking about aesthetics, it is important to recognize that Su does not consistently sustain them. He regularly backs away from them, especially in moments of formal discourse, and withdraws to much more traditional and unambitious positions: the greatest man of letters is one who did not venture outside of utilitarian prose (Lu Zhi), a person of the highest wisdom would not need to avail himself of the arts at all.[61] For all Su's greatness as a poet and boldness as a critic, something of the age-old ambivalence about the ultimate value of the arts and how to reconcile them with commitment to moral cultivation and the nation lived on in him.

There are several advantages of acknowledging this equivocation in Su's pronouncements and the divergences between his practice as a poet and his other activities. Much of the time, poetry, calligraphy, and painting represented to Su a great alternative to his ambition to serve the state as a leading member of the Court. Aesthetic expression was in this sense a turning away from these other duties and aspirations. To look exclusively at the boldest claims Su makes about the arts is to fail to place them in the context of his life and to miss this meaning that they held for him. An amusing anecdote is told about a question Su once put to Zhaoyun and two other concubines:

> One day when East Slope returned from the Court, after he finished eating he strolled outside, patting his stomach. He turned to his female attendants and asked, "Come, tell me what it is I have in here [pointing to his stomach]."
> One maid answered right away, "It is filled with refined literature (*wenzhang*)."
> East Slope did not agree.
> Another maid said, "It is full of cleverness and wit."
> East Slope still did not agree.
> Zhaoyun said, "Sir, your stomach is full of inability to accord with the times."
> East Slope held his stomach and laughed long and hard.[62]

The story is intended to show how much better Zhaoyun understood Su than any other of his attendants. Its historicity is open to question; but its gist is anticipated in Su's own writings, as for example in lines he wrote to Li Zhaoji: "I always think of how deprived and entrapped is my position in the world. In whichever direction I go, I run up against a wall or a ravine. Consequently, my aims have not once been fulfilled."[63] Su goes on to explain that his only pleasure in life has been his friendship with his literary friends (Huang Tingjian, Qin Guan, etc.), men who are completely unknown in the world. Elsewhere, Su confides to a friend, "All my life the only source of delight and relief I have had is literary composition."[64] Yet even while this remark attests to the unflagging appeal that literary work held for Su, it also suggests that there is a larger context in which that work should properly be considered.

To say that literary pursuits represented a great "other" or alternative in Su's life is not to say they were unimportant. It is simply to put them in perspective in a life that was, after all, marked by extraordinary early fame and expectations of distinguished service, the impact of which remained with Su all his days. On the periphery of Su's circle there was one man for whom aesthetic expression seems to have been more central, perhaps even consistently conceived of as a *ben*, "basis." That man was Mi Fu, whose unique devotion to calligraphy and connoisseurship is well attested by his own writings, and whose reputation for eccentricity and "madness" because of that devotion is reflected everywhere in the anecdotal record. Su Shi is no Mi Fu. Mi makes claims about the significance of the arts that Su Shi never would have made, and Mi acted on his beliefs in ways that Su criticized.[65] As much as Su may have admired Mi Fu's brushwork, it is not fair to either man to deny the gulf between them. In fact, Mi Fu anticipates far more satisfactorily than does Su the values of the *wenren* of subsequent centuries.

Su Shi says that his commentaries on the classics, which resulted from his dispute with the New Learning, are what makes him think that perhaps his life has not been lived in vain.[66] Posterity has paid virtually no attention to those commentaries and has always celebrated Su primarily as a poet. This is a common enough disparity in literary history. The point of mentioning it is not to attempt to reverse perceptions of Su's greatness, which would be ill advised. For later ages Su's poetry *is* his primary achievement. No doubt he also intended posterity to know him by his poetry. Yet the significance he attached to his commentaries on the classics and other activities cannot be lightly dismissed. Certainly, the effort that went into them was not slight. Moreover, the comparisons that are inevitably made in literary history between Su Shi and earlier poets (e.g., Tao Qian, Du Fu, Li Bo), valid as they may be in literary terms, are flawed if they give no attention to the ramifications that these other aspects of Su's life and expression have for his literary work. It is, after all, Su's breadth of accomplishment outside of literature as well as his political prominence and activism that distinguishes him so immediately and sharply from many of the great earlier poets.

Naturally, in the course of Su's engagement with poetry, and perhaps even with the other arts as well, there is also a sense in which the manifestation of personality this engagement affords becomes itself a completely self-sufficient and self-justifying act. Here we see the reversal of the formally articulated hierarchy of *ben* and *mo*, as poetry and the other arts emerge as key elements in Su's self-image. This reversal corresponds in the realm of praxis to the divergent tendencies in Su's theoretical statements, discussed above. Thus there are the many times that Su calls himself "poet" (*shiren*) and his apparent inability to turn away from literary work despite the risks involved. Certainly, there was ample precedent within the literati tradition for the idea that nothing reveals the inner character so faithfully as *shi* poetry, as well as recognition of the ethical grounding of this act of lyrical revelation. (We have discussed how Su helped to spread similar understandings of calligraphy and painting.) More specifically, we have seen how in countless situations Su relied upon *shi* and, unexpectedly, even *ci* to capture, explore, or give meaning to his experience of the world. All of this is beyond dispute. Nevertheless, the importance of this activity in Su's life still does not justify studious disregard of his statements that point to a contrary assessment of the arts, neglect of what he says about his classical commentaries, or dismissal of the emphasis his closest friends placed posthumously upon his career and deeds. Su's values and activities may be referred to more than one level of analysis. Modern literary history, owing to its own values and goals, tends to present Su simply as the Song-dynasty counterpart of his poetic heroes, Tao Qian and Du Fu, or as the precursor of the "independent artists" of the Yuan and later periods. This is a representation that ought to be historicized and criticially examined.

Acknowledgment of Su's ambivalence about the arts better prepares us to appreciate the whimsy and humor that runs through his work. If one focuses only upon Su's statements that broach the serious and profound meaning of artistic expression, it will be easy to neglect the playful and self-mocking tone of so much of his work. Among the Song-dynasty poets, and most of those who came before, no one delights so abundantly in play (*xi*) as Su Shi. Aesthetic expression was indeed often a "flaw," a madness, an obsession, a useless indulgence. And so Su loved to amuse himself at it. "Once I joked with Junmo [Cai Xiang]," Su writes, "telling him that practicing calligraphy is just like trying to go upstream against a swift current. You use up all your energy, and your boat hasn't moved an inch."[67] But these profitless pursuits had the ability to unburden the mind and to relieve it from life's cares. When Su sent some of his new *ci* to Cheng Zhengfu, who was in mourning, he counseled him, "We are old men now and should not allow ourselves to remain too long in grief. Amuse yourself from time to time with poetry and wine—that's the best plan."[68]

Play need not be frivolous. The notion was widespread in the Song that it is in unguarded moments of levity that a man reveals his true nature. Likewise, whether in the painter's "ink-plays" or the poet's "jesting verses," wit and humor had a key role in affirming the special bond of intimacy that developed among Su and his followers. These are, to be sure, serious matters, but they are hardly in the forefront of so much of the expression itself. There is, then, some distinction between the playful poet, who sometimes did even produce frivolous verse, and the critic who would explore new horizons of meaning for the arts, which is another of Su's faces. Modern literary history, with all of its accustomed gravity, is apt to overlook this distinction.

The last reason to take account of the range of Su's thinking about aesthetic pursuits is that it reminds us how complex and uneven were his motives. To think that everything he produced sprang from one grand vision or calling that he embraced is a simplification. In each field he set himself a different challenge and grappled with distinct issues. Occasionally, his efforts seem contradictory. For example, in *shi* poetry he moved towards a kind of large-mindedness that rises above the traditional "self" of the lyric poet, whereas in *ci* he is famed for cultivating a highly autobiographical voice, thus departing from generic convention. Such an apparent contradiction can be explained only by understanding the separate sets of issues and choices operative in each form. Similarly, Su's contributions to thinking about calligraphy and painting were formulated in response to the very different positions each art held in the mid eleventh century. The two did not stand wholly in the same sphere. Current standards in calligraphy were to Su's mind a public issue because they were imposed upon an entire class of people. Painting was an entirely different matter, and Su's interest in it was rooted in other personal needs. Only two forms of expression, painting and *shi*, are occasionally viewed by Su as mutually convertible or based upon the same principles, and then it is clear that he makes such assertions as part of an effort to enhance the repute of painting among literati. Regarding the different script types in calligraphy, Su Shi maintains that there is a single underlying principle or idea (*yi*) and that once it has been mastered, the writer will excel at all the script types: regular, running draft, clerical, and even "flying white."[69] Su stops short of making any such explicit claim that ties together all the literary and visual forms.

We have seen that the reasons for Su's activity as poet and as critic on the arts were several. There was no single agenda or plan.

Sometimes he wrote for the sheer fun of it. He also wrote, in a very different mood, to correct the errors of the age (e.g., his satirical verse on the New Policies). As the years passed and his frustrations and sense of injustice increased, another motive surfaced: he began to write because he would not be silenced. Writing itself, even when the product was quite innocuous, became an act of quiet defiance. In the meantime, Su had discovered other uses for self-expression. Through willed assertion, contentment could be found in disagreeable circumstances. This was not simply self-delusion, as his exile periods show. *Shi* poetry became Su's vehicle for reflecting upon the events that had befallen him and especially for trying to rise above self-pity and locate the self in the larger social and historical context. This literary accomplishment clearly has some relation to Su's extraordinary capacity for commiseration towards others and his impressive record of humane initiatives both in and out of office. The *ci* Su wrote at the same time are very different from the *shi* because he approached *ci* with fewer constraints and developed its intrinsic qualities in new directions that suited his needs so well. Ironically, this less prestigious poetic form, these "little songs," which Su had previously neglected, proved to be wonderfully adapted, once certain conventions of the form were transformed in his hands, to the light wistfulness and spontaneity that he wanted now to evoke and explore. There will always be readers who prize his limited output in this form above all others.

Su's views on the arts also arose from diverse circumstances. Among the close circle of his political and social confidants, the old notion that aesthetic expression embodies character traits was put to new use. When the idea was extended beyond poetry to calligraphy and painting, the arts became a means of affirming common values (including esteem for eccentricity) and the group's sense of itself as a distinct and morally superior though politically disenfranchised unit. The obliqueness of artistic expression proved useful not only in conveying admirable personality traits that defy prosaic description ("the style of the man"), but also as a safeguard against recriminations in such contentious times. Artistic expression thus became a constant activity, an ongoing process of revelation and self-definition. Finally, in response partly to contemporary intellectual trends that he considered naive, Su began to develop the idea that engagement in literature or the arts could be a means to knowledge in that it brought the individual into intimate contact with things. This was yet another sign of Su's disapproval of aloofness from the world and of introspection as a means to wisdom. Yet it was also a valuation of the arts with which Su was not entirely comfortable (because it might lead to the neglect of social responsibilities) and from which he often withdrew.

All of these meanings and motives were equally part of Su's achievement in the various fields. They are most of them all bound up with frustrations and disputes outside of the arts and literature, which in Su's case spurred him on to more and greater work as poet, critic, and connoisseur. These motivating factors are of a different order from any abstract commitment to "literature" or "culture" that may be attributed to him. The richness of his work reflects how varied were the reasons Su Shi picked up the brush to write and how dissimilar were the challenges that each form, whether literary or visual, posed each time he did so.

Abbreviations Used in the Notes

Dongpo shuzhuan	Su Shi, *Dongpo shuzhuan*
Jishi benmo	*Songshi jishi benmo*, compiled by Chen Bangzhan
Su Shi shiji	Su Shi, *Su Shi shiji*
Su Shi yizhuan	Su Shi, *Su Shi yizhuan*
Wenji	Su Shi, *Su Shi wenji*
Xu changbian	Li Tao, *Xu zizhi tongjian changbian*
Zongan	Wang Wen'gao, *Su Wenzhonggong shi bianzhu jicheng zongan*

Notes

Note: The citation of a premodern source previously in secondary scholarship is indicated by the scholar's name and page number in parentheses after the reference to the premodern work.

CHAPTER ONE

1. Zhang Fangping, "Wenan xiansheng mubiao," *Lequan ji* 39.57b–58a; and Ye Mengde, *Bishu luhua* B.5b–6a. Cf. Zeng Zaozhuang, *Su Xun pingzhuan*; see esp. pp. 58–63, 210–212.

2. Su Xun, "Shang Ouyang Neihan diyi shu," *Jiayou ji* 11.107–109.

3. Ouyang Xiu, "Jian buyi Su Xun zhuang," *Zouyi ji* 14.10–11; and Ouyang Xiu, "Gu Bazhou Wenan xian zhubo Su Jun muzhiming," *Jushi ji* 34.84–86 (Zeng, *Su Xun*, pp. 213–214).

4. Ye Mengde, *Shilin shihua* C.430.

5. Ye Mengde, *Bishu luhua* A.29a–b (Zeng, *Su Xun*, pp. 215, 216).

6. Su Che, "Wangxiong Zizhan Duanming muzhiming," *Luancheng ji,* "houji," 22.1411.

7. Su Shi's essay is "(Shengshi) Xingshang zhonghou zhi zhi," *Wenji* 2.33–34. The theme comes from the commentary attributed to Kong Anguo in the chapter in the *Book of Documents* translated by James Legge as "The Counsels of the Great Yü" in *The Chinese Classics* 3:59; see *Shangshu zhushu* 4.7a.

8. See the comments of the Ming critics Yang Shen (Shengan) and Wang Shizhen (Fengzhou) in Yang's (*Bai sanshier jia pingzhu pingzhu*) *San Su wenfan* 5.1b.

9. Yang Wanli, *Chengzai shihua*, pp. 148–149 (*Songren yishi huibian*

12.591); Lu You, *Laoxue an biji* 8.102; and Ye Mengde, *Shilin yanyu* 8.115.

10. Ouyang Xiu, "Yu Mei Shengyu shujian," no. 31, *Shujian* 6.46.

11. On the decree examination, see the monograph by Wang Deyi, *Songdai xianliang fangzheng ke kao.* Cf. E. A. Kracke, Jr., *Civil Service in Early Sung China, 960–1067,* pp. 71–72, 95–97. On the number of *jinshi* degrees, see John W. Chaffee, *The Thorny Gates of Sung Learning,* table 21, p. 133, and appendix 2, pp. 192–195.

12. The original grouping of the essays is preserved in Lang Ye's selection of Su Shi's prose, *Jingjin Dongpo wenji shilüe,* juan 4–8, 15–19. Unfortunately, the original grouping is not evident in Kong Fanli's edition of Su Shi's complete prose (*Wenji*), arranged by genre, to which references are given here.

13. "Da Li Duanshu shu," *Wenji* 49.1432.

14. "Zhongyong," no. 2, *Wenji* 2.62. Cf. *Zhongyong,* in *Liji zhushu* 52.7a. Su's essays on *Zhongyong* have been analyzed by Christian Murck, "Su Shih's Reading of the *Chung yung,*" in *Theories of the Arts in China,* ed. Susan Bush and Christian Murck, pp. 267–292.

15. This paragraph is based on concepts discussed in Su's essay "Li yi yangren wen ben lun," also written for the decree examination of 1061, *Wenji* 2.49. For the account of *li* in the *Classic of Rites,* see *Liji zhushu,* "Fangji" 51.8b; cf. James Legge, *The Li Ki* 2:284.

16. "Zhongyong lun," no. 2, *Wenji* 2.62, correcting *tianzi* to *tianxia* in the final sentence.

17. "Yang Xiong lun," *Wenji* 4.111.

18. "Han Fei lun," *Wenji* 4.102.

19. Li Ao, "Fu xing shu," *Li Wengong chi* 2.1a–9b.

20. Su probably knew Han Yu's views on human nature best from his famous essay, "Yuanxing," *Han Changli ji* 11.64–65. Cf. Charles Hartman's discussion of other sources for Han Yu's views, *Han Yü and the Search for T'ang Unity,* pp. 204–210.

21. "Han Yu lun," *Wenji* 4.114–115.

22. Han Yu, "Yuanxing," *Han Changli ji* 11.65.

23. "Yang Xiong lun," *Wenji* 4.110–111.

24. "Cebie: an wanmin," no. 3, *Wenji* 8.259–260.

25. "Cebie: ke baiguan," no. 3, *Wenji* 8.246.

26. "Celüe," no. 4, *Wenji* 8.236.

27. "Cebie: ke baiguan," no. 3, *Wenji* 8.246.

28. The passage is found in "Yang Xiong lun," *Wenji* 4.111. A similar analysis of its significance is given by Jin Zheng, "Lun Su Shi yu lixue zhi zheng," *Xueshu yuekan* 1985.2:64.

29. "Celüe," no. 3, *Wenji* 8.232.

30. "Ying zhiju shang liangzhi shu," *Wenji* 48.1391.

31. "Cebie: ke baiguan," no. 5, *Wenji* 8.250.

32. "Cebie: ke baiguan," no. 2, *Wenji* 8.243–245.

33. "Cebie: ke baiguan," no. 6, *Wenji* 8.252–253. The quotation is found on the first page.

34. "Yue Yi lun," *Wenji* 4.100.

35. Shao Bo, *Shaoshi wenjian houlu* 14.111.

36. "Yi Yin lun," and "Huo Guang lun," *Wenji* 3.84–85 and 4.108–109.

37. "Liu hou lun," *Wenji* 4.103–104.

38. "Chia Yi lun," *Wenji* 4.105–106.

39. "Celüe," no. 4, *Wenji* 8.236.

40. "Celüe," no. 1, and "Cebie: an wanmin," *Wenji* 8.227 and 8.263–264.

41. "Celüe," no. 3, *Wenji* 8.233–234.

42. Throughout, I translate *li* (normally, "principle") as "Pattern" or "inherent Pattern." See Michael A. Fuller's argument in favor of this rendering, *The Road to East Slope*, pp. 82–89.

43. "Celüe," no. 4, *Wenji* 8.236.

44. *Mencius* 7B/27; trans. D. C. Lau, pp. 202–204.

45. "Zhongyong lun," no. 3, *Wenji* 2.63. Cf. *Zhongyong, Liji zhushu* 52.3a.

46. "Bian shiguan zhi cewen," no. 2, *Wenji* 27.790.

47. Cheng Yi, "Yanzi suhao he xue lun," *Henan Chengshi wenji* 8.577–578.

48. "Qianzhou xue ji," *Wang Linchuan ji* 82.91. For the date of this piece, see Cai Shangxiang, *Wang Jinggong nienpu kaolue* 11.164.

49. "Ying zhiju shang liangzhih shu," *Wenji* 48.1392.

50. See Ouyang's two letters to Li Xu in Ouyang Xiu, *Jushi ji* 47.2–4.

51. *Shiji* 55.2034–2035. The entire biography of Zhang Liang is translated by Burton Watson, *Records of the Grand Historian of China* 1:134–151.

52. Meng Ben and Xia Yu, brave and mighty warriors of antiquity: see Wang Chong, *Lunheng*, "Yu zeng," 7.339.

53. The principal advisors to the founders of the ancient Shang and Zhou dynasties.

54. Jing Ke attempted to assassinate the first Qin emperor. Nie Zheng did assassinate a minister of the ancient state of Hann.

55. *Zuozhuan* 195/Xuan 12/2; cf. Legge, *The Chinese Classics* 5:316.

56. After Goujian, King of Yue, was captured by the rival state of Wu, he toiled as a servant for three years in Wu before being allowed to return to Yue. Subsequently, he avenged himself by leading troops to conquer Wu. Su Shi appears to be following the *Guoyu* version of the story, *Guoyu*, "Yue yu xia," 21.643–645.

57. Han Xin, one of Han Gaozu's most important generals, balked at coming to Gaozu's aid once because Gaozu had never rewarded him with an enfeoffment. When he first learned of Han Xin's reluctance, Gaozu became furious; but Zhang Liang intervened and arranged to have Han Xin properly rewarded, winning his loyalty. *Shiji* 92.2621.

58. *Shiji* 55.2049.

59. "Liu hou lun," *Wenji* 4.103–104.

60. The assertion that the old man was a "ghost" is first made in Wang Chong's *Lunheng*, "Ziran," 18.779.
61. *Shiji* 55.2044 and 2048.
62. For these claims and self-images, see Su Shi's *ci*, "Xinyuan chun," no. 51 in his *Su Dongpo ci*, ed. by Cao Shuming (see also, Long Muxun, ed., *Dongpo yuefu jian* 1.29b and *Quan Songci* 1:282).

CHAPTER TWO

1. My summary of the fiscal and military situation in this paragraph is informed by Paul J. Smith's study, "State Power and Economic Activism During the New Policies, 1068–1085," prepared for the Conference on Sung Dynasty Statecraft in Thought and Action, Scottsdale, Arizona, 1986; and his *Taxing Heaven's Storehouse*, esp. pp. 111–118.
2. Shiba Yoshinobu, "Sōdai shiteiki seido no enkaku," in *Aoyama hakushi koki kinen: Sōdaishi ronsō*, ed. Aoyama hakushi koki kinen kankokai, p. 128 (Smith, "State Power," p. 5).
3. Sogabe Shizuo, *Sōdai zaiseishi*, p. 3 (Smith, "State Power," p. 5).
4. Cheng Minsheng, "Lun Bei Song caizheng de tedian yu chengpin de jiaxiang," *Zhongguo shi yanjiu* 1984.3:27–40 (Smith, "State Power," p. 6).
5. *Jishi benmo* 40.385–387.
6. See *Xu changbian*, "shibu," 3A.14b–15a, and Ma Duanlin, *Wenxian tongkao* 24.232c (Smith, p. 8). Cf. Sima Guang, "Cimian caijian guoyong chazi," *Sima Wenzhenggong chuanjia ji* 42.533–534.
7. See James T. C. Liu, *Reform in Sung China*; and John Meskill, ed., *Wang An-shih*. More recent studies include the works by Paul J. Smith, cited above, as well as Peter K. Bol's "Rulership and Sagehood, Bureaucracy and Society: An Historical Inquiry into the Political Visions of Ssu-ma Kuang (1019–1086) and Wang An-shih (1021–1086)," in *Jinian Sima Guang Wang Anshi shishi jiubai zhounian xueshu yantao hui lunwen ji*, ed. Guojia wenyi jijin hui, pp. 5–107; and Bol's "*This Culture of Ours*," pp. 212–253. Recent Chinese studies of Wang and his reforms include Qi Xia, *Wang Anshi bianfa*; and Deng Guangming, *Wang Anshi*.
8. Wang Anshi, "Da Zeng Gong li shu," *Wang Linchuan ji* 73.13 (Smith, "State Power," p. 7).
9. Wang Anshi, "Shang Renzong huangdi yanshi shu," *Wang Linchuan ji* 39.86.
10. *Jishi benmo* 37.326. Variant versions of this debate appear in *Xu changbian*, "shibu," 3.3b–4a, and Sima Guang, *Sima Wenzhenggong chuanjia ji* 42.543–545.
11. John Chaffee, table 4, p. 27 (Smith, p. 11).
12. *Xu changbian* 250.6095.
13. See Smith's two studies, cited above.
14. The description of Wang's entrepreneurial bureaucracy given here is derived from Smith, "State Power," esp. pp. 11–14.

15. *Xu changbian* 221.5370.
16. See, for example, Fan Cunyan's criticism in *Xu changbian*, "shibu," 5.10b–12a; *Jishi benmo* 37.330; cf. Cheng Hao's criticism, *Jishi benmo* 37.340.
17. See Han Qi's memorial in *Xu changbian*, "shibu," 7.3b–6b; *Jishi benmo* 37.337; cf. Sima Guang's in *Jishi benmo* 37.338–339.
18. Errors in the traditional dating of these memorials have recently been corrected by Huang Renke, "Su Shi lun xinfa wenzi liupian nianyue kaobian," in *Su Shi yanjiu zhuanji*, pp. 103–110. The memorials and their dates are as follows: "Yi xuexiao gongju zhuang," 1069.2, *Wenji* 25.723–726; "Guoxue qiushi cewen," 1069.8, *Wenji* 7.208–210; "Jian mai Zhe deng zhuang," 1069.12, *Wenji* 25.726–729; "Shang Shenzong huangdi shu," 1069.12, *Wenji* 25.729–748; "Zai shang huangdi shu," 1070.2, *Wenji* 25.748–752; and "Ni jinshi dui yushi ce," 1070.3, *Wenji* 9.301–309.
19. This memorial is the fourth listed above. In Lang Ye's selection of Su Shi's prose it is actually called "Ten Thousand Word Memorial": Lang Ye, *Jingjin Dongpo wenji shilue* 24.369.
20. *Zongan* 6.3b and *Xu changbian* 216.5263.
21. *Xu changbian*, "shibu," 6.3a–b.
22. *Xu changbian* 214.5201–5202, 5207, and 216.5263.
23. "Shang Shenzong huangdi shu," *Wenji* 25.736.
24. "Yi xuexiao gongju zhuang," *Wenji* 25.724.
25. James T. C. Liu, *Reform in Sung China*, pp. 40–58.
26. I am aware that at the end of his "Ten Thousand Word Memorial" Su Shi acknowledges the usefulness of certain of the changes Wang advocates (e.g., restricting the *yin* ["hereditary privilege"] route into office, improving the readiness of the army). But these are minor points of Wang's reforms, and are probably referred to by Su mainly for rhetorical effect. Recently, Gong Yanming has argued that Su Shi's dissatisfaction with the New Policies was not categorical, but many of his examples come from Su's later years (when his stance altered): see Gong Yanming, "Lüe lun Su Shi fandui Wang Anshi bianfa de xingzhi," *Su Shi yanjiu zhuanji*, esp. pp. 85–89.
27. Zhu Xi, *Zhuzi yulei* 130.3112; and Luo Siding, "Cong Wang Anshi bianfa kan Ru Fa lunzhan de yanbian," *Hungqi* 1974.2:26.
28. Kracke, pp. 33–37.
29. *Lunyu* 13/23.
30. *Zuozhuan* 403/Zhao 20/1–10; trans. Legge, *The Chinese Classics* 5:684b.
31. *Hanshu* 77.3263.
32. "Shang Shenzong huangdi shu," *Wenji* 25.740–741.
33. For a summary of arguments against the attribution to Su Xun, see Liu Naichang, "Su Shi tong Wang Anshi de jiaowang," *Su Shi wenxue lunji*, pp. 217–222.
34. Zhang Fangping, "Wenan xiansheng mubiao," *Lequan ji* 39.60a–61b;

and Su Shi, "Xie Zhang Taibao zhuan xianren mubiao," *Wenji* 49.1426. Other early sources that attest Su Xun's authorship include Fang Shao's *Bozhai bian* A.65–66, Shao Bo's *Shaoshi wenjian houlu* 12.130–131, and Ye Mengde's *Bishu luhua* A.28b–29b. Modern scholars who have argued for acceptance of the attribution to Su Xun include Zhang Peiheng, "'Bianjian lun' fei Shao Bowen weizuo," in *Gudian wenxue luncong*, pp. 138–183; and Zeng Zaozhuang, *Su Xun pingzhuan*, pp. 102–115. Cf. Zheng's "Su Xun 'Bianjian lun' zhenwei kao," *Sichuan daxue xuebao congkan* 15:109–116 (1982).

35. Miyazaki Ichisada has recently suggested that the "treacherous one" being criticized was originally not even Wang Anshi. See his "Ben kan ron no kan o benzu," in *Liu Zijian boshi songshou jinian Songshi yanjiu lunji*, ed. Kinugawa Tsuyoshi, pp. 317–326.

36. See, for example, Fan Zhen's criticisms of the suppression of dissent by Wang and his subordinates, *Xu changbian* 216.5263–5265.

37. "Shang Shenzong huangdi shu," *Wenji* 25.731.

38. "Qijun chazi," *Wenji* 29.829.

39. For references to this printing in the indictments against Su filed by He Dazheng and Shu Dan, see *Wutai shian* 1b and 2b. Cf. Li Ding's statements about the widespread dissemination and injurious influence of Su's poems, *Wutai shian*, p. 5a.

40. Su Shi, "Shan cun wujue," no. 4, *Su Shi shiji* 9.439. I have profited from the translation and annotations in Ogawa and Yamamoto, *So Tōba shishū* 2:509–510.

41. See Su's explication of the poem in *Wutai shian*, p. 10b.

42. "Qi bujisan qingmiao qianhu zhuang," *Wenji* 27.784.

43. "Shan cun wujue," no. 3, *Su Shi shiji* 9.438–439. For the meaning of *cankui* in line 2, see Zhang Xiang, *Shi ci qu yuci huishi* 6.773.

44. *Lunyu* 7/14.

45. "Xii Ziyu," *Su Shi shiji* 7.324–326; Ogawa and Yamamoto, *So Tōba shishū* 2:215–220.

46. *Hanshu* 65.2843.

47. For Jester Zhan, see *Shiji* 126.3202. For Su's own explanation of this couplet of the poem, see *Wutai shian*, p. 9a–b.

48. *Wutai shian*, p. 9b.

49. *Lunyu* 17/1.

50. "Shang Han chengxiang lun zaishang shoushi shu," *Wenji* 48.1397. Cf. "Shang Wen Shizhong lun queyan shu," *Wenji* 48.1401.

51. "Mobao tang ji," *Wenji* 11.358.

52. "He Liu Daoyuan ji Zhang Shimin," *Su Shi shiji* 7.333–334; Ogawa and Yamamoto, *So Tōba shishū* 2:244–246.

53. Apparently one of the lost odes. Zhuangzi quotes it in an attack upon Confucians: "The Confucians rob graves in accordance with the *Odes* and ritual . . . Just as the Ode says: " 'Green, green the grain / Growing on the grave mound slopes; / If in life you gave no alms / In death how do you deserve a pearl?' " The passage sounds like a commoners' jus-

tification for robbing the ritual mouth jade out of corpse of a nobleman. *Zhuangzi* 74/26/16–17; trans. Watson, *Chuang Tzu*, pp. 296–297.

54. *Zhuangzi* 45/17/85–88.

55. *Wutai shian*, p. 36a.

56. "He Qian Andao ji hui Jian cha," *Su Shi shiji* 11.530-531; Ogawa and Yamamoto, *So Tōba shishū* 3:197–204.

57. *Wutai shian*, p. 40b.

58. "He Shugu dongri mudan," no. 1, *Su Shi shiji* 11.525–526; Ogawa and Yamamoto, *So Tōba shishū* 3:173–174. The odd use of *cui* in the first line ("bright") is explained as a Shu dialect meaning of the word.

59. *Wutai shian*, pp. 32b–33a.

60. Ye Mengde, *Shilin shihua* B.417, quoted in Hu Zi, *Tiaoxi yuyin conghua*, "qianji," 39.263–264.

61. Huang Tingjian, "Yu Hong Jufu shu," no. 2, *Yuzhang Huang xiansheng wenji* 19.23a. Huang's assessment must have been well known. It is quoted by Chen Shan (d. c. 1160) in his *Menshi xinhua* A1.4b.

62. Yuan Haowen, "Lunshi sanshi shou," nos. 23 and 25, *Yishan xiansheng wenji* 11.5b–6a; and see the discussion of these poems by John Timothy Wixted, *Poems on Poetry: Literary Criticism by Yuan Haowen (1190–1257)*, pp. 173, 179–181, and 190–194; and Wang Fuzhi, *Jiangzhai shihua* B.18 (Tao Daoshu, "Wutai shian xinkan," *Wenxue yichan zengkan* 14:305 [1982]). For another evaluation by one of Su's contemporaries, see Yang Shi, *Guishan yulu* 2.2b (Zhou Zhizhi, *Shiyan*, pp. 2b–3a).

63. "Mizhou tongban ting ti ming ji," *Wenji* 11.376.

64. "Lu Tao Yuanming shi," *Wenji* 67.2111.

65. Zheng Xia's experiences are narrated in *Jishi benmo* 37.359–360, 363.

66. "Huzhou xie shang biao," *Wenji* 23.654.

67. *Wutai shian*, p. 1b.

68. On the legal aspects of the case brought against Su, see Charles Hartman, "Poetry and Politics in 1079: The Crow Terrace Poetry Case of Su Shih," *Chinese Literature: Essays, Articles, Reviews* 12:18–22 (1990).

69. For Shu Dan's indictment, see *Wutai shian*, p. 2b. For Li Ding's, see ibid., pp. 5a–b.

70. "Hangzhou zhaohuan qijun zhuang," *Wenji* 32.912.

71. Ibid.

72. "Huangzhou shang Wen Lugong shu," *Wenji* 48.1380.

73. See Su's note on his poem, "Hangzhou guren xin zhi Qian," *Su Shi shiji* 21.1091.

74. Several of the entries on specific poems in *Wutai shian* are dated or refer to previous interrogations, mostly in the eighth or ninth month, during which Su Shi failed to confess fully to the charge against him.

75. *Wutai shian*, pp. 43a–b.

76. See the poem title, "Yu yi shi xi yushi taiyu . . . ," *Su Shi shiji* 19.998. The fellow prisoner was Su Song (no relation, and not jailed for the same reason). See Zhou Bida, "Ji Dongpo Wutai shian," *Erlao tang shi-*

hua, pp. 667–668. Cf. other poems that Su Song wrote on the occasion to commiserate with Su Shi's plight, "Jiwei jiuyue yu fuju Yushi . . . ," *Su Weigong wenji* 10.129–130.

77. *Wutai shian*. The present text is said to reproduce the trial affidavits and testimony, the original of which were examined and verified as authentic by Zhou Bida in the early Southern Song; see his "Ji Dongpo Wutai shian," *Erlao tang shihua*, pp. 667–668. A certain Peng Jiuwan is said to have compiled the work; but it is evident that various recensions (of different lengths) circulated in the Southern Song, and the exact filiation or relation between them and Peng's compilation is unknown. See *Siku quanshu zongmu tiyao*, p. 1396. Though not as complete, Zhou Zizhi's compilation, *Shiyan*, is also useful and reproduces the complete text of the poems by Su under consideration.

For more information on the textual history of the documents relating to Su's trial, as well as the legal and literary issues raised by the event, see Hartman, "Poetry and Politics in 1079," pp. 15–44. Two other useful modern studies of the trial are: Tao Daoshu, "*Wutai shian* xinkan," *Wenxue yichan zengkan* 14:290–317 (1982); and Wang Xuetai, "Cong *Wutai shian* kan fengjian zhuanzhi zhuyi dui Songdai shige chuangzuo de yingxiang," *Wenxue yichan zengkan* 16:198–220 (1983). On Su's poetry of political protest generally, see Yokoyama Iseo, "So Shoku no seiji hihan no shi ni tsuite," *Kambun gakkai kaihō* 31:26–39 (1972).

78. "Lingbe Zhangshi yuanting ji," *Wenji* 11.369.

79. *Wutai shian*, pp. 4a–b.

80. "Wang Fu xiucai suoju shuang kuai," no. 2, *Su Shi shiji* 8.413; Ogawa and Yamamoto, *So Tōba shishū* 2:453.

81. Ye Mengde, *Shilin shihua* A.410; and quoted from there in Hu Zi, *Tiaoxi yuyin conghua*, "qianji," 46.312. See also *Yupi zizhi tongjian gangmu xubian* 7.46b. Cf. another anecdote based on the accusation concerning this poem in Hu Zi, *Tiaoxi yuyin conghua*, "houji," 30.223.

82. "Ji Liu Xiaoshu," *Su Shi shiji* 13.633–637 (*Wutai shian*, p. 18a); and "Da Huang Luzhi," no. 1, *Wenji* 52.1531–1532 (*Wutai shian*, p. 22a).

83. *Wutai shian*, p. 25b.

84. See the poems, "Song Zeng Zigu zu Yue de yan zi," and "Zhang Andao xianshi jin shi," *Su Shi shiji* 6.246 and 17.874, on cicadas and frogs (*Wutai shian*, pp. 33a–34a, 27b–28a); "Song Qian Zao zhu shou Wuzhou de ying zi," *Su Shi shiji* 6.242, on beatings (*Wutai shian*, p. 25b); and "Ciyun Liu Gongfu Li Gongze jian ji," no. 2, *Su Shi shiji* 13.647, on corpses (*Wutai shian*, pp. 28a–b).

85. He Zhengchen was another censor who was active in prosecuting Su in 1079 (not be to confused with He Dazheng, referred to above).

86. "Qi jun chazi," *Wenji* 29.829.

87. See Ouyang Xiu, "Yu Gao sijian shu," *Jushi waiji* 17.58.

88. Zhao Yi, *Oubei shihua* 5.64–65.

89. Zhang Fangping, "Lun Su Neihan," *Lequan ji* 26.16a–18a. Fan Zhen's memorial is mentioned in *Xu changbian* 301.7334, where Zhang's memorial is quoted.

90. Su Che, "Wei xiong Shi xia yu shang shu," *Luancheng ji* 35.778.
91. *Xu changbian* 301.7336; and Lü Xizhe, *Lüshi zaji* (Yan Zhongqi, *Su Dongpo yishi huipian*, pp. 59–60, although I have been unable to find this passage in the *Siku quanshu zhenben* edition of *Lüshi zaji*).
92. *Songshi* 242.8622.
93. "Shu *Nanshi* Lu Du zhuan," *Wenji* 66.2048.
94. "Chen Jichang suoxu Zhuchen cun jiaqu tu," no. 2, *Su Shi shiji* 20.1030–1031.

CHAPTER THREE

1. *Sunzi* 11.83.
2. *Lunyu* 19/7.
3. "Ri yu," *Wenji* 64.1980–1981.
4. "Yanguan dabei ge ji," *Wenji* 12.387.
5. Wang Anshi, "Li yue lun," *Wang Linchuan ji* 66.42.
6. Two important analyses, upon which I have drawn, are those by Hou Wailu, *Zhongguo sixiang tongshi* 4.1: 420–469; and Ma Zhenfeng, *Zhengzhi gaigejia Wang Anshi de zhexue sixiang*, esp. pp. 90–163. The older study by Ke Changyi is also still useful, *Wang Anshi pingzhuan*, pp. 193–238; as are Winston W. Lo, "Wang An-shih and the Confucian ideal of "inner sageliness," *Philosophy East and West* 26.1:42–53 (1976); Fumoto Yasutaka, *Hakusō ni okeru jugaku no tenkai*, pp. 351–428; Qi Xia, pp. 70–93; and Peter K. Bol's chapter on Wang in *"This Culture of Ours,"* pp. 212–253.
7. For a list of Wang's writing, both those extant and those lost, see Hou Wailu, pp. 441–448.
8. Many of the essays are translated in H. R. Williamson, *Wang An-shih*, 2 vols.
9. Wang Anshi, "Da Cai Tianqi," *Wang Linchuan ji* 73.16 (Ma Zhenfeng, p. 154).
10. Wang Anshi, "Shang Zhongyong," *Wang Linchuan ji* 71.90.
11. *Lunyu* 12/1; and Wang Anshi, "Li yue lun," *Wang Linchuan ji* 66.42.
12. Wang Anshi, "Li yue lun," *Wang Linchuan ji* 66.42.
13. Ibid., 66.41. Throughout I follow A. C. Graham's rendering of *shen* as daimon or daimonic, referring both to the power and intelligence in the cosmos that is higher than man and to man's innate capacity to partake of that power. See A. C. Graham, *Chuang-tzu*, p. 35, n. 72.
14. From Wang Anshi's commentary on *Laozi* (Book 48): see *Wang Anshi Laozi zhu jiben*, p. 43 (Ma Zhenfeng, p. 161).
15. Wang Anshi, "Hongfan zhuan," *Wang Linchuan ji* 66.25–26.
16. See the three essay: Wang Anshi, "Xingqing," "Yuanxing," and "Xing-shuo," *Wang Linchuan ji* 67.53–54 and 68.64–66.
17. This point is made by Xia Changpu, "Wang Anshi sixiang yu Mengzi de guanxi," in *Jinian Sima Guang Wang Anshi shishi jiubai nian xueshu*

yantao hui lunwenji, pp. 315–317, who refers to an essay, "Xing lun," that is contained only in a supplement to Wang's literary collection (see "Buyi," in Wang Anshi, *Linchuan xiansheng wenji,* pp. 1064–1065). Xia speculates that Wang wrote this essay, changing his earlier views, after his retirement in 1076.

18. Wang Anshi, "Li yue lun," *Wang Linchuan ji* 66.42.

19. Ibid., 66.43.

20. *Xu changbian* 220.5334; cf. *Jishi benmo* 38.372–373.

21. *Jishi benmo* 38.371. On Wang's opinion of the *Chunqiu,* and the question of whether or not he actually so described the work, see James T. C. Liu, *Reform,* pp. 30–33.

22. *Jishi benmo* 38.372.

23. Wang Anshi, "Da Wang Shenfu shu," no. 2, *Wang Linchuan ji* 72.8.

24. *Xu changbian* 243.5917.

25. Wang Anshi, "Chu zuopu she xian biao," *Wang Linchuan ji* 57.65.

26. Wang Anshi, "Jin zishuo biao," and "Xining zishuo," *Wang Linchuan ji* 56.55–56 and 84.12. Cf. Hou Wailu, 4.1:445–446.

27. Lo, "Wang An-shih and 'inner sageliness,'" pp. 48–49.

28. These and other examples are reproduced from various sources in Ke Changyi's *Wang Anshi pingzhuan,* pp. 241–247.

29. Chao Gongwu, *Qunzhai dushu zhi* 1B.90.

30. Zhao Bingwen, "Xingdao jiaoshuo," *Xianxian laoren fushui wenji* 1.4b (Xu Yuanhe, *Luoxue yuanliu,* pp. 33–34).

31. "Lishi shanfang cangshu ji," *Wenji* 11.359.

32. "Songren xu," *Wenji* 10.325.

33. "Da Zhang Wenqian xiansheng shu," *Wenji* 49.1427.

34. Chao Yuezhi, "Ruyan," *Songshan wenji* 13.27a–b and 36b–37a.

35. For Wang Jin and his Buddhism, see Michael T. Dalby, "Court Politics in Late T'ang Times," in Denis Twitchett, ed., *The Cambridge History of China* 3:578–579.

36. *Lunyu* 5/13.

37. "Yi xuexiao gongju zhuang," *Wenji* 25.725.

38. See Su's testimony concerning statements he made in a poem of 1078: *Wutai shian,* p. 28a. Cf. the same criticism as voiced by Zhao Bingwen, "Xingdao jiaoshuo," *Xianxian laoren fushui wenji* 1.4b.

39. Chao Gongwu, *Qunzhai dushu zhi* 1B.90; Chen Shan, *Menshi xinhua* 3.6b–7a; Ye Mengde, *Yanxia fangyan* A.13a–b (Fumoto Yasutaka, p. 406); and Zhu Xi, *Zhu Wengong wenji* 70.8a–b.

40. Fragments of Wang's commentary on the *Laozi* have been gathered together by Rong Zhaozu in his *Wang Anshi Laozi zhu jiben.*

41. "Ba Wangshi huayan jing jie," *Wenji* 66.2060.

42. *Lunyu* 19/5.

43. *Lunyu* 15/31.

44. "Yanguan dabei ge ji," *Wenji* 12.386–387.

45. "Sitang ji," *Wenji* 11.363.

46. "Da Su Bogu," no. 3, *Wenji* 57.1741.

47. "Shu Hepu zhou xing," *Wenji* 71.2277. Cf. Su's statement that when he browsed through his three commentaries, he felt that his life "had not been passed in vain": "Da Su Bugu," no. 3, *Wenji* 57.1741.

48. "Yu Zhu Zhen," no. 1, *Wenji* 58.1767.

49. See, for example, "He Tao zashi," nos. 9 and 10, and "He Tao zeng Yang changshi," *Su Shi shiji* 41.2277–2278 and 41.2281–2283.

50. "Da Li Duanshu," no. 3 and "Da Su Bogu," no. 3, *Wenji* 52.1540 and 57.1741.

51. See Su Che's grave inscription, "Wangxiong Zizhan Duanming muzhiming," *Luancheng ji*, "houji," 22.1422; and Su Shi's letter, "Huangzhou shang Wenlu gong," *Wenji* 48.1380.

52. "Da Li Duanshu," no. 3, "Da Su Bogu," no. 3, and "Ti suozuo shu yi zhuan lunyu shuo," *Wenji* 52.1540, 57.1741, and 66.2073.

53. For previous discussions of Su's commentary on the *Documents*, see George Hatch's notice on *Dongpo shuzhuan* in *A Sung Bibliography*, pp. 13–19; and Peter K. Bol's "*This Culture of Ours*," pp. 282–293.

54. *Dongpo shuzhuan* 9.12a–13a. The passage in question from the *Documents* is found in Legge, *The Chinese Classics* 3:316.

55. *Dongpo shuzhuan* 6.9b–10a; trans. Legge, *The Chinese Classics* 3:169.

56. *Dongpo shuzhuan* 8.2b (emphasis added); trans. Legge, *The Chinese Classics* 3:223–224.

57. *Dongpo shuzhuan* 8.3b.

58. Previous studies of Su Shi's commentary on the *Book of Changes* include: Zeng Zaozhuang, "Cong *Piling Yizhuan* kan Su Shi de shijie guan," *Su Shi yanjiu zhuanji*, pp. 59–66; Kong Fan, "Su Shi *Piling yichuan* de zhexue sixiang," *Zhongguo zhexue* 9:221–239 (1983); Peter K. Bol, "Su Shih and Culture," in *Sung Dynasty Uses of the I Ching*, Kidder Smith, Jr., Peter K. Bol, Joseph A. Adler, and Don J. Wyatt, pp. 56–99; and Bol's "*This Culture of Ours*," pp. 282–293. See also Wang Yu, "Su Shi de zhexue yu zongjiao," in *Tang Song shi yanjiu*, ed. Lin Tienwai and Joseph Wong, pp. 197–215; and Zeng Zaozhuang, *Su Shi pingzhuan*, rev. ed., pp. 230–246.

59. *Sushi yizhuan* 8.174.

60. Ibid., 6.138.

61. Ibid., 4.98.

62. Ibid., 4.95.

63. *Zhouyi* 24/38/*tuan*; trans. James Legge, *The Text of the Yi King*, ed. Z. D. Sung, p. 164.

64. *Sushi yizhuan* 4.90.

65. Ibid., 9.190.

66. *Laozi: Daode jing* A/8/8a; cf. D. C. Lau, *Tao te ching*, p. 64.

67. *Sushi yizhuan* 7.159.

68. Ibid., 7.153–154.

69. Ibid., 7.168.

70. Ibid., 5.124.
71. Ibid., 6.137.
72. *Zhouyi Chengshi zhuan* 3:968.
73. I am aware that the preface to Cheng Yi's commentary on the *Changes* has a very late date (1099) and that the commentary itself did not assume its present form until after Su Shi's (and even Cheng Yi's) death. But it is also known that Cheng Yi worked on his commentary for decades and lectured on it to his students, so that it is at least chronologically possible that Su Shi was aware of Cheng's interpretations.
74. *Dongpo shuzhuan* 6.4a and 7.1a.
75. Ibid., 7.1a–b.
76. Hou Wailu, 4.1:461–462.
77. *Wang Anshi Laozi zhu jiben*, p. 30.
78. Ibid., p. 8.
79. Ibid., p. 22. This and the preceding two quotations are cited by Hou Wailu, 4.1:461.
80. *Laozi: Daode jing* A/5/5b6a; cf. D. C. Lau, *Tao te ching*, p. 61.
81. *Wang Anshi Laozi zhu jiben*, p. 11. See Rong Zhaozu's comments on the attribution of this entry to Wang Anshi. Further support comes from the similarity between this passage and the others reproduced by Rong on the preceding portions of Wang's commentary on the same *Laozi* chapter, see pp. 9–10.
82. Wang Anshi, "Zhiyi lun," *Wang Linchuan ji* 66.46.
83. The ideal described in "Explanations of the Hexagrams," appended to the *Changes*, see *Zhouyi* 49/Shuo/1; cf. Legge, *Yi King*, pp. 338–339.
84. *Sushi yizhuan* 8.177.
85. Ibid., 3.69.
86. See the openings lines of Sima Qian's account of Taoism in *Shiji* 130.3292; cf. *Laozi: Daode jing* A/27/31a–b and B/49/15a and Wang Bi's commentary on these passages (Qian Zhongshu, 1:311–312).
87. *Dongpo shuzhuan* 10.12b–13a.
88. *Sushi yizhuan* 8.181, on the classic's statement that the well is where virtue dwells.
89. *Sushi yizhuan* 1.9.
90. Ibid., 6.142.
91. Ibid., 7.155.
92. Ibid., 4.75.
93. Ibid., 8.178.
94. *Dongpo shuzhuan* 7.19b; cf. Legge, *The Chinese Classics* 3:217–218.
95. George Hatch and Michael Fuller both understand Su to say in this passage of the commentary that the emotions are external things, but this runs contrary to his beliefs about the inseparable closeness of emotions to human nature. Cf. *Dongpo shuzhuan* 3.7b. See *A Sung Bibliography*, p. 15; and Fuller, p. 86.
96. *Sushi yizhuan* 1.26.

CHAPTER FOUR

1. "Qi buji san qingmiao qiehu zhuang," *Wenji* 27.783–785.
2. "Lü Huiqing zeshou Jianning jun jiedu fushi," *Wenji* 39.1100.
3. This point is made by Wang Shuizhao, "Guanyu Shi Shi 'Yu Teng Dadao shu' de xinian he zhuzhi wenti," *Wenxue pinglun* 1981.1:63.
4. *Xu changbian* 364.31b and 378.12b.
5. Ibid., 376.6b–8a.
6. Zhu Xi, *Sanchao mingchen yanxing lu* 6.26a–b (Wang Shuizhao, "'Teng Dadao shu,'" p. 63).
7. "Lun jitian muyi zhuang," *Wenji* 26.768.
8. Su's experience on the commission is described in his four memorials, see *Wenji* 27.778, 781–782.
9. "Yu Teng Dadao," no. 8, *Wenji* 51.1478.
10. See Wang Shuizhao, "'Teng Dadao shu,'" pp. 58–64. Zeng Zaozhuang prefers to date the letter to 1083 (Yuanfeng 6) because we know that Teng made a trip to the capital that year; see his *Su Shi pingzhuan*, pp. 328–343.
11. It should be mentioned that one Su Shi authority, Zeng Zaozhuang, has argued that Su's letter to Teng does not indicate any change in Su's politics and that Su is merely trying to warn Teng against being overly contentious in his opposition to the reforms. (See his *Su Shi pingzhuan*, pp. 315–327.) Zeng's interpretation of the letter stems from his commitment to the idea that Su Shi's politics were consistent and unwavering through the years. This reading of the letter seems strained, however, and has been disputed by other scholars. (See Wang Shuizhao, "'Teng Dadao shu,'" pp. 58–62; and Zhu Jinghua, *Su Shi xinlun*, pp. 34–35.)
12. The poems exchanged by Su and Wang have been analyzed by Zhang Zhilie, "Su Wang changhe guankui," *Su Shi yanjiu zhuanji*, pp. 96–101.
13. "Xuehou shu beitai bi ershou," *Su Shi shiji* 12.602–605. The poems are discussed by Zhang Zhilie, pp. 96–97. See also Wang Shuizhao, *Su Shi xuanji*, pp. 83–87.
14. According to a statement by Zhao Cigong quoted in the Wang Shipeng commentary to Su's poems; see *Su Shi shiji* 12.605.
15. See Wang Anshi, "Du Meishan ji ciyun xueshi wushou," and "Du Meishan ji ai qi xueshi neng yongyun fu ciyun yishou," *Wang Linchuan ji* 18.23–24.
16. "Xieren jianhe qianpian ershou," *Su Shi shiji* 12.605–607.
17. This is the interpretation of Zhang Zhilie, p. 98.
18. See Zhou Zizhi's postscript to his account of Su Shi's trial, *Shiyan*, p. 17b.
19. "Yu Teng Dadao," no. 38, *Wenji* 51.1487.
20. "Ci Jinggong yun sijue," no. 3, *Su Shi shiji* 24.1252.
21. "Yu Wang Jinggong," no. 2, *Wenji* 50.1444.
22. "Yu Wang Jinggong," no. 1, *Wenji* 50.1444.

23. Shao Bowen, *Shaoshi wenjian lu* 12.127–128. Zhang Zhilie (p. 100) discusses this story and makes a case for its reliability.

24. "Lun Zhou Zhong shanyi peixiang zihe chazi," nos. 1 and 2, *Wenji* 29.832 and 834.

25. These later condemnations of Wang Anshi are ignored by Zhang Zhilie ("Su Wang changhe guankui"), who makes too much, I believe, of the private expressions of mutual admiration referred to above.

26. On the general divergence in outlook between Su Shi and Sima Guang, as well as certain similarities between Su and Wang Anshi, see the useful discussion by Zhu Jinghua, pp. 27–41.

27. "Qijun chazi," *Wenji* 29.827.

28. "Bian shiguan zhi cewen chazi," no. 2, *Wenji* 27.792.

29. "Yu Yang Yuansu," no. 17, *Wenji* 55.1655–1656.

30. Sima Guang, "Yu Lü Gongzhu tongju Cheng Yi chazi," *Sima Wenzhenggong chuanjia ji* 48.616.

31. The most convenient, if uncritical, source for many of these, as well as for a general account of the rivalry between Su Shi and Cheng Yi, is the chapter in *Jishi benmo* devoted to the subject, *juan* 45.

32. Shao Bo, *Shaoshi wenjian houlu* 12.159–160. There are many different versions of this anecdote (which are conveniently collected together by Yan Zhongqi, *Su Dongpo yishi huibian*, pp. 109–110, 112). In some of them the quip is uttered by an unidentified "guest," but Su Shi still leads everyone else in laughing at Cheng Yi.

33. See the two versions of this anecdote quoted in Zhu Xi's chronology of Cheng Yi, "Yichuan xiansheng nianpu," *Er Cheng ji* 1:343.

34. Cheng Yi, *Henan Chengshi cuiyan* 1.1170–1171. Quoted in Xu Yuanhe's useful discussion of the Cheng brothers' concepts of Pattern and desire, *Luoxue yuanliu*, p. 149. I have also benefited from the analysis of Cheng Yi's thought, and its similarities to Wang Anshi's, in Jin Zheng, pp. 61–67. See also see Peter K. Bol, "*This Culture of Ours*," pp. 300–342; and Kusumoto Bun'yū, *Sōdai jugaku no zen shisō kenkyū*, pp. 196–245. On the Cheng brothers' thought generally, see A. C. Graham, *Two Chinese Philosophers*.

35. Cheng Yi, *Henan Chengshi yishu* 25.319.

36. Ibid.

37. Cheng Yi, *Henan Chengshi waishu* 12.433 and *Henan Chengshi cuiyan* 1.1179. (Xu Yuanhe, p. 153).

38. Cheng Yi, *Henan Chengshi yishu* 15.149 (Xu Yuanhe, p. 153).

39. Ibid., 18.239.

40. Cheng Yi, *Henan Chengshi waishu* 12.443.

41. "Hangzhou zhaohuan qijun zhuang" and "Zai qijun chazi," *Wenji* 32.913 and 33.930.

42. Zhu Xi, "Yichuan xiansheng nianpu," p. 343.

43. Ibid., p. 344, quoting Fan Zuyu.

44. Ibid., p. 340.

45. See *Xu changbian* 397.5a–9a; Cheng Yi, "You shang taihuang taihou shu," *Henan Chengshi wenji* 6.549–552.

46. For this and the others of Cheng Yi's requests listed in this paragraph, see his memorial "Shang taihuang taihou shu," *Henan Chengshi wenji* 6.541–546; and Zhu Xi's narrative in "Yichuan xiansheng nianpu," pp. 340–341.

47. Cheng Yi, "Shang taihuang taihou shu," *Henan Chengshi wenji* 6.544.

48. Zhu Xi, "Yichuan xiansheng nianpu," p. 341.

49. Ibid., p. 343.

50. Ibid., p. 343; and *Xu changbian* 404.1b–4a.

51. The most thorough description of the factional strife in which Su Shi became embroiled during the Yuanyou period is Nishino Teiji, "So Shoku to Genyū tō sōka naka no hitobito," *Jimbun kenkyū* 23.3200–3214 (1972). The study is not analytic, however, nor does it cite documentary sources.

52. "Shi guan zhi cewen," no. 1, *Wenji* 7.210.

53. *Xu changbian* 393.13a–18a.

54. *Zongan* 27.18a–b.

55. On the friction between Su and the commissioners, see "Zai qi ba xiangding yifa zhuang," "Shensheng qi pu dingduo yifa yizhuang," and "Bian shiguan zhi cewen chazi," no. 2, *Wenji* 27.781, 27.782, and 27.792.

56. "Bian shiguan zhi cewen chazi," no. 2, *Wenji* 27.791.

57. Ibid., pp. 790 and 789.

58. Wang Cheng, *Dongdu shilüe* 94.2a–b (*Zongan* 27.18a).

59. "Qi ba xueshi chu xianman chaiqian chazi," *Wenji* 28.816–817.

60. "Qijun chazi," *Wenji* 29.827–830.

61. "Qijun chazi" and "Chu Lü Tafang te shou taizhong dafu . . . ," *Wenji* 29.828 and 38.1095. See *Shijing*, no. 253.1: "The people are heavily burdened."

62. "Qijun chazi," *Wenji* 29.829.

63. See the second of Su's memorials of self-defense, "Lun Zhou Zhong shanyi peixiang zihe chazi," no. 2, *Wenji* 29.834.

64. "Hangzhou zhaohuan qijun zhuang," *Wenji* 32.911–914.

65. "Zai qijun chazi," *Wenji* 33.930.

66. "Qi buwai huibi Jia Yi chazi," *Wenji* 33.934–935.

67. "Bian Jia Yi tan zou daizui chazi," *Wenji* 33.935–937.

68. "Gui Yixing liuti Zhuxi si," no. 3, *Su Shi shiji* 25.1348.

69. "Bian tishi chazi," *Wenji* 33.937.

70. *Songshi* 471.13708. The decree is "Lü Huiqing ze shou Jianning jun . . . ," *Wenji* 39.1100.

71. "Bian Huang Qingji tan he chazi," *Wenji* 36.1015.

72. *Jishi benmo* 44.431–432 and 46.443.

73. "Zhao ci fu Dingzhou lunshi zhuang," *Wenji* 36.1018–1020. Cf. *Jishi benmo* 46.445.

74. *Jishi benmo* 46.446–447.
75. *Xu changbian*, "shibu," 10.17a–19b.
76. *Jishi benmo* 49.482–484; cf. *Xu changpian*, "shibu," 20.9a–14b, and 21.9b.
77. *Zuozhuan* 403/Zhao 20/6; trans. Legge, *The Chinese Classics* 5:684b.
78. Derived from *Lunyu* 13/15.
79. "Bian shiguan zhi cewen," no. 2, *Wenji* 27.790.

CHAPTER FIVE

1. "Yu Mo tongnian yuzhong yin hushang," *Su Shi shiji* 31.1647.
2. These relief measures are the subject of an article by Kondō Kazunari, "Chi Kōshū So Shoku no kyūkōsaku—Sōdai bunjin kanryō seisaku kō," *Sōdai no shakai to bunka*, ed. Sōdai kenkyūkai, pp. 139–168; an English translation has appeared under the title, "Su Shih's Relief Measures as Prefect of Hangzhou—A Case Study of the Policies Adopted by Sung Scholar-Officials," *Acta Asiatica* 50:31–53 (1986). Although Kondō's interest is in the workings of the Song bureaucracy, rather than in Su Shi himself, his study has benefited my own understanding of this episode in Su's life considerably.
3. "Qi zhenji Zhexi qizhou zhuang," *Wenji* 30.849–851.
4. The phrase "half the population" comes from "Qi zhenji Zhexi qizhou zhuang," *Wenji* 30.851; and the 500,000 figure comes from "Zou Zhexi zaishang diyi zhuang," *Wenji* 31.883.
5. See, in addition to Kondō Kazunari's article cited above, Wang Deyi, *Songdai zaihuang de jiuji zhengce*; Yoshida Tora, "*Kyūkō katsumin sho to Sōdai no kyūkō seisaku*," in *Aoyama hakushi koki kinen: Sōdaishi ronsō*, pp. 447–475; and Robert P. Hymes, "Moral Duty and Self-Regulating Process: Tung Wei's *Book for Relieving Famine and Reviving the People* and Southern Sung Views on Famine Relief" (paper presented at the Conference on Sung Dynasty Statecraft in Thought and Action, Scottsdale, Arizona, 1986).
6. See Su's memorial of 1090, "Xiangdu zhunbei zhenji disi zhuang," *Wenji* 31.899–900. On the transport tax, known as *wugu lisheng qian*, see "Zou Zhexi zaishang diyi zhuang" and "Qi mian wuku lisheng shuiqian," *Wenji* 31.886 and 35.990–991.
7. Dong Wei, *Jiuhuang huomin shu* 1.15. Cf. 2.26, where Dong qualifies his praise by noting that Su's methods would be advantageous for cities but not for residents of the countryside.
8. "Shen sansheng qiqing kaihu liutiao zhuang," *Wenji* 30.870, in Su's own note.
9. At first the Court was prepared to reduce the quota of rice to be delivered to the capital by only 200,000 piculs, or one-eighth of the original quota. Later, it augmented the reduction to the one-third Su had mentioned. See "Shang zhizheng qi dudie jizhen yin xiu xieyu shu" and "Zou Zhexi zaishang diyi zhuang," *Wenji* 48.1408 and 31.883.

10. "Zou Zhexi zaishang diyi zhuang," *Wenji* 31.883.

11. "Qi qiang dudie chaoren ruzhong hudou chutiao jiji deng zhuang" and "Shang zhizheng qi dudie zhenji yin xiu xieyu shu," *Wenji* 30.859–860 and 48.1407–1408.

12. For a history of the use of ordination certificates, see Chikusa Masaaki, "Sōdai bai chōkō," in his *Chōgoku bukkyō shakaishi kenkyū*, pp. 17–82.

13. "Shang zhizheng qi dudie zhenji yin xiu xieyu shu" and "Qi qiang dudie chaoren ruzhong doudou chutiao jiji deng zhuang," *Wenji* 48.1406–1408 and 30.859–860.

14. "Lun Ye Wensou fenbo dudie bugong zhuang," *Wenji* 30.860–863.

15. Ye Mengde, *Bishu luhua* B.10a–b. It is also here that we read of a prior history of friction between Su and Ye Wensou.

16. Su Che, "Wangxiong Zizhan Duanming muzhiming," *Luancheng ji*, "houji," 22.1417.

17. "Hangzhou qi dudie kai Xihu zhuang," *Wenji* 30.863–866.

18. "Shen sansheng qiqing kaihu liutiao zhuang," *Wenji* 30.866–872.

19. "Hangzhou qi dudie kai Xihu zhuang," *Wenji* 30.865.

20. "Zou hubu jushou dudie zhuang," *Wenji* 30.873–874.

21. "Shang zhizheng qi dudie zhenji yin xiu xieyu shu," *Wenji* 48.1407.

22. "Zou hubu jushou dudie zhuang," *Wenji* 30.873.

23. *Xu changbian* 442.13a. We know that the recall of certificates never went through from numerous references Su subsequently makes to their beneficial effect.

24. See the note Su wrote on his "Shen sansheng qiqing kaihu liutiao zhuang," *Wenji* 30.870. See also "Hangzhou qi dudie kai Xihu zhuang" and "Zou hubu jushou dudie zhuang," *Wenji* 30.865 and 30.873.

25. "Zou Zhexi zaishang diyi zhuang," *Wenji* 31.884.

26. Ibid., p. 886.

27. "Xiangdu zhunbei zhenji dier zhuang," *Wenji* 31.894–895.

28. "Xiangdu zhunbei zhenji disan zhuang," *Wenji* 31.898.

29. Ibid.

30. Ibid.

31. "Zai qi fayun si yingfu Zhexi mi zhuang," *Wenji* 32.909–911.

32. Ibid., p. 910.

33. "Jin Shan E Wuzhong shuili shu zhuang" and "Lujin Shan E Wuzhong shuili shu," *Wenji* 32.915–917 and 917–927.

34. "Qi jiang shanggong fengzhuang hudou yingfu Zhexi zhujun jiexu tiaomi chazi," *Wenji* 33.931–933.

35. *Xu changbian* 462.2b.

36. Ibid., 462.3b.

37. "Hangzhou zhaohuan qijun chazi," *Wenji* 32.913.

38. "Zai qijun chazi," *Wenji* 33.930.

39. *Jishi benmo* 45.440.

40. Fan Zuyu, "Fenghuan chenliao lun Zhexi zhenji shi zhuang," *Fan Taishi ji* 20.9a–16b. Excerpted in *Xu changbian* 462.6b–8a.

41. "Xiangdu zhunbei zhenji dier zhuang," *Wenji* 31.895.

42. For Ma Sheng, see Kong Fanli's commentary on Su Shi's note, "Yu Ma Zhongyu," *Wenji*, "Yiwen huibian," 3.2485.

43. Zigong is Fan Bailu, who had been appointed Hanlin Academician earlier in the year and presumably was sent as a special commissioner to the Zhexi region that fall.

44. For this use of the phrase *shushe*, see Su's "Yu Chiweng," *Wenji* "Yiwen huibian," 3.2497.

45. "Yu Qian Mufu," no. 11, *Wenji* 51.1505.

46. *Song huiyao jiben* 15239.10a.

47. "Qi ci dudie di hudou zhunbei zhenji Huai Zhe liumin zhuang," *Wenji* 33.947.

48. "Zailun jiqian liushi sishi chazi," *Wenji* 34.971.

49. *Xu changbian* 483.2a–b.

50. "Lun jiqian liushi bing qi jianhui yingzhao solun sishi yichu xingxia zhuang," *Wenji* 34.959.

51. "Yingzhao lun sishi zhuang," *Wenji* 31.879–880.

52. Ibid., 31.881.

53. Ibid., 31.877–878.

54. "Lun jiqian liushi bing qi jianhui yingzhao suolun sishi yichu xingxia zhuang," *Wenji* 34.959.

55. *Xu changbian* 474.1a.

56. The sources for the project are Su's "Jiang yu chi ji," *Wenji* 11.380–381, supplemented by "Yu Liu Gongfu," nos. 2 and 4, "Yu Ouyang Zhong-chun," nos. 1 and 2, and "Da Fan Jingshan," *Wenji* 50.1464, 1465–1466, 53.1560–1561, and 59.1794. Cf. Su Che's "Huanglou fu xu," *Luan-cheng ji* 17.417–418.

57. "Qi jiang dudie Dingzhou jinjun yingfang zhuang," *Wenji* 36.1022.

58. "Qi yiliao bingqiu zhuang," *Wenji* 26.763–766.

59. "Yu Zhang Jiafu," no. 3, *Wenji* 53.1563.

60. Wang Deyi, *Songdai zaihuang de jiuji zhengce*, pp. 124–129.

61. Qian Shuoyou, *Xianchun Lin'an zhi* 8 (Wang Deyi, *Songdai zaihuang*, pp. 129–130, although the passage is not found in the *Siku quanshu zhenben* edition of *Xianchun Lin'an zhi*).

62. Su Che, "Wangxiong Zizhan Duanming muzhiming," *Luancheng ji*, "houji," 22.1416; Zhou Hui, *Qingbo biezhi* A.127; and Su Shi, "Yu mou Xuande shu," *Wenji*, "Yiwen huibian," 2.2447. See also the passage in *Xianchun Lin'an zhi* cited in the preceding note.

63. "Yu mou Xuande shu," *Wenji* "Yiwen huibian" 2.2447. This letter specifies a larger amount of gold (one hundred and fifty *liang*) than Su Che refers to. I suspect that the "one hundred" has either been interpolated into the letter or inadvertently dropped out of Su Che's text. The letter is translated in my "Su Shih's 'Notes' as a Historical and Literary Source," *Harvard Journal of Asiatic Studies* 50.2:568 (1990).

64. Zhou Hui, *Qingbo biezhi* A.127.
65. "Yu Luo mijiao," no. 1, *Wenji* 58.1769.
66. Fei Gun, *Liangxi manzhi* 4.3b–4b; Liu Naichang, "Dongpo Lingnan shi de chengjiu he fengge," *Lun Su Shi Lingnan shi ji qita*, ed. Su Shi yanjiu xuehui, pp. 81–82; and Su Huanzhong, "Qianlun Su Shi Lingnan shi," *Lun Su Shi Lingnan shi ji qita*, pp. 98–100, and 106–107.
67. "Yu Zhu Ezhou shu," *Wenji* 49.1416–1417.
68. "Huang E zhi feng," *Wenji* 72.2316.
69. "Liangqiao shi," *Su Shi shiji* 40.2199–2201.
70. "Yu Cheng Zhengfu," no. 36, *Wenji* 54.1604–1605. Cf. also nos. 27 and 30, *Wenji* 54.1599 and 1600.
71. "Yu Cheng Zhengfu," no. 60, *Wenji* 54.1616.
72. See "Ciyun Ding Huiqin changlao jianji," no. 6, *Su Shi shiji* 39.2117; "Yu Cheng Zhengfu," no. 60, "Zang kugu shu," and "Huizhou ji kugu wen," *Wenji* 54.1616, 62.1911 and 63.1961.
73. "Yu Cheng Zhengfu," no. 30, *Wenji* 1600–1602.
74. Ibid., nos. 47 and 49, *Wenji* 54.1608–1609 and 1609–1612.
75. Ibid., no. 18, *Wenji* 54.1595–1596.
76. "Yu Wang Minzhong," no. 11, *Wenji* 56.1692–1693.
77. Ibid., no. 15, *Wenji* 56.1695.
78. "Yu Cheng Zhengfu," no. 47, *Wenji* 54.1608.
79. Ibid., no. 30, *Wenji* 54.1600.
80. Ibid., no. 36, *Wenji* 54.1605.
81. "Yu Wang Minzhong," no. 11, *Wenji* 56.1693.
82. Fei Gun, *Liangxi manzhi* 4.4b–5a.

CHAPTER SIX

1. The standard treatment of Su Shi's developing interest in Budddhism is Chikusa Masaaki's "So Shoku to bukkyō," *Tōhō gakuhō* 36:457–480 (1964). See also Beata Grant, *Mount Lu Revisited: Buddhism in the Life and Writings of Su Shi*, forthcoming; and the relevant sections of Abe Chōichi's work, *Chūgoku zenshūshi no kenkyū*, cited below. Less extensive treatments, of which there are many, include Liu Naichang, "Lun fo lao sixiang dui Su Shi wenxue de yingxing," in his *Su Shi wenxue lunji*, pp. 188–201; and Cao Shuming, "Su Dongpo yu dao fo zhi guanxi," *Guoli zhongyang tushuguan guankan* 3.2:7–21 (1970) and 3.3–4:34–55 (1970).
2. "Ciyun Dinghui Qin Zhanglao jianji," no. 7, *Su Shi shiji* 39.2117.
3. "Yu Nanhua Bianlao," no. 12, *Wenji* 61.1875.
4. Paraphrasing "Ciyun Dinghui Qin Zhanglao jianji," no. 6, *Su Shi shiji* 39.2117.
5. "Yu Quanlao," *Wenji* 61.1892.
6. See the first of the two poems entitled "Liangqiao shi," *Su Shi shiji* 40.2199–2200.

7. "Yu Wang Minzhong," no. 11, *Wenji* 56.1692.
8. "Shu Nanshi Lu Du zhuan," *Wenji* 66.2048.
9. "Shu zeng Chen Jichang shi," *Wenji* 68.2133.
10. "Shu Liu Zihou niufu hou," *Wenji* 66.2058.
11. Liu Zongyuan "Niufu," *Liu Hedong ji* 2.30.
12. Yuan Hong, *Hou Hanji* 10.276. Su may have read the passage in the better known *Hou Hanshu*, by Fan Ye, where it is quoted in the Tang commentary by Li Xian; see *Hou Hanshu* 42.1429. There are minor textual differences between Yuan Hong's text as it is preserved today and Su's reproduction of it. I have followed Su's version.
13. "Ji Yuan Hong lunfo," *Wenji* 66.2083.
14. *Lengjia jing* 1.480a.
15. Huihong, *Lengzhai yehua* 7.3b.
16. "Shu Lengjia jinghou," *Wenji* 66.2085.
17. For Wen Yanbo, see below. For Fu Bi and Han Qi (as well as for many other less prominent statesmen), see Chi-chiang Huang, "Experiment in Syncretism: Ch'i-sung (1007–1072) and Eleventh-Century Chinese Buddhism," Ph.D. diss., pp. 71–101, 112–115, and 158–164.
18. See *Liangshu* 18.291–292.
19. "Ba Liu Xianlin muzhi," *Wenji* 66.2071.
20. See Hattori Eijun, *Jōdokyō shisō ron*, pp. 163–204, as well as the Ph.D. dissertation by Shih Heng-ch'ing, "The Ch'an-Pure Land Syncretism in China: With Special Reference to Yung-ming Yen-shou," University of Wisconsin-Madison, 1984.
21. Zongxiao, *Lebang wenlei* 4.207.
22. Abe Chōichi, pp. 222–227, 269 and 389–403. On the associations generally, see also Suzuki Chūsei, "Sōdai ni okeru bukkyō kessha no kakudai to sono seikaku," in his *Chōgoku shi ni okeru kakumei to shūkyō*, pp. 48–65.
23. Zongjian, *Shimen zhengtong* 8.15b (p. 900) (Abe Chōichi, p. 401).
24. Nianchang, *Fozu lidai tongzai* 19.679c (Abe Chōichi, p. 395).
25. Abe Chōichi, pp. 234–235, 385, and 401. Cf. Stephen F. Teiser, *The Ghost Festival in Medieval China*, p. 108.
26. Wang Rixiu, *Longshu zengguang jingtu wen* 2.258.
27. Ibid., 6.269–270.
28. Ibid., p. 270.
29. Ibid., 2.258.
30. Ibid.
31. "Zhonghe shengxiang yuan ji" and "Si pusa ge ji," *Wenji* 12.384–385 and 385–386; cf. Chikusa Masaaki, "So Shoku to bukkyō," pp. 458–460.
32. Chikusa Masaaki, "So Shoku to bukkyō," pp. 464–475; and Huang Chi-chiang, pp. 124–130 (on Huailian) and 171–176 (on Qisong).
33. "Ami tafo song," *Wenji* 20.585.
34. "Ami tafo zan," *Wenji* 21.619.

35. Su Che, "Wangxiong Zizhan Duanming muzhiming," *Luancheng ji* "houji," 22.1416.

36. "Shuilu faxiang zan," *Wenji* 22.631.

37. *Jinguang mingjing* 4.352b–354c.

38. "Shu Jinguang ming jing," *Wenji* 66.2086–2087.

39. Trans. Leon Hurvitz, *Scripture of the lotus blossom of the fine dharma*, p. 317; cf. *Miaofa lienhua jing* 7.25.57c–58a.

40. "Gai Guanyin jing," *Wenji* 66.2082.

41. "Guanshiyin pusa song," *Wenji* 20.586.

42. "Yingmeng Guanyin zan," *Wenji* 21.620.

43. Chikusa Masaaki, "Fukken no ji-in to shakai," in *Chūgoku bukkyō shakaishi kenkyū*, pp. 145–198.

44. Abe Chōichi, pp. 231–247 (esp. p. 235); cf. pp. 325–329.

45. See "Si pusa ge ji" and "Ami tafo song," *Wenji* 12.385–386 and 20.585.

46. For a discussion of Qisong's critique of Han Yu, see Huang Chichiang, pp. 250–267 (pp. 263–264 on human nature); and on Qisong's contact with Zhang Fangping, see pp. 151–158 of the same work.

47. "Chengdu dabei ge ji," *Wenji* 12.394–395.

48. Trans. Thomas Cleary, *The Flower Ornament Sutra* 1:308; cf. *Huayan jing* 13.68b

49. *Jinguang mingjing* 2.344b.

50. See Robert E. Buswell, Jr., for a concise discussion of the concept: "The 'Short-cut' Approach of *K'an-hua* Meditation: The Evolution of a Practical Subitism in Chinese Ch'an Buddhism," in *Sudden and Gradual: Approaches to Enlightenment in Chinese Thought*, ed. Peter N. Gregory, pp. 331–334.

51. Trans. Philip B. Yamplosky, *The Platform Sutra of the Sixth Patriarch*, pp. 138, 153; Chinese text, pp. 7, 14.

52. Pei Xiu, *Chuanxin fayao*, p. 383c.

53. The text is quoted and discussed by He Guoquan, *Zhongguo chanxue sixiang yanjiu*, p. 158.

54. Quoted in ibid., p. 158.

55. Yanshou, *Zongjing lu* 45.680b–c.

56. Ibid., p 681a.

57. Canliao, *Canliaozi ji* 7.4a.

58. Huihong, "Chantan sishier bi Guanyin zan," *Shimen wenzi chan* 18.3a.

59. George Hatch in *A Sung Bibliography*, p. 8.

60. "Donglin diyi dai Guanghui chanshi zhenzan," *Wenji* 22.623.

61. "Haiyue Biangong zhenzan," *Wenji* 22.638.

62. "Yu Wang kunzhong ji erzi Mai . . . ," no. 4, *Su Shi shiji* 19.986.

63. Yampolsky, p. 138; Chinese text, p. 7.

64. See Yampolsky, p. 133, n. 4.

65. Trans. Charles Luk, *The Śūrangama Sutra*, p. 169; cf. *Lengyan jing* 8.124b.

66. *Liezi jishi*, "Zhongni shuo," 4.73.
67. Wang Rixiu, *Longshu zengguang jingtu wen* 10.282.
68. "Baohui tang ji," *Wenji* 11.356.
69. "Ji Wu Deren jian jian Chen Jichang," *Su Shi shiji* 25.1341.
70. "Qingfeng ge ji," *Wenji* 12.383.
71. The problem surfaces in Ouyang's autobiographical piece, "Liuyi jushi zhuan," *Jushi ji* 44.78–79; trans. in my *The Literary Works of Ouyang Hsiu*, pp. 223–224.
72. "Shu Liuyi jushi zhuan hou," *Wenji* 66.2048–2049.
73. "Chaoren tai ji," *Wenji* 11.351.
74. Su Che, "Chaoren tai fu," *Luancheng ji* 17.413–414.
75. This point is made by Fuller, p. 212.
76. Su Shi, *Sushi yizhuan* 6.137: "To be transcendent and outside [things], and thus to be unencumbered by things, this is merely the inferior person's way of being joyful by having no desires." Cf. 5.124, on the *tuan* lines.
77. "Da Zhou Xunzhou," *Su Shi shiji* 39.2151.
78. "Ciyun Ziyou guba," *Su Shi shiji* 42.2303.
79. "Zi Puzhao you eran," *Su Shi shiji* 9.434.
80. "Yanguan dabei ge ji," *Wenji* 12.386–388.
81. *Wutai shian*, pp. 32a and 44a.
82. Robert M. Gimello, "Mārga and Culture: Learning, Letters, and Liberation in Northern Song Ch'an," in *Paths to Liberation: The Mārga and Its Transformations in Buddhist Thought*, ed. Robert E. Buswell, Jr., and Robert M. Gimello, pp. 374–384.
83. Deleting the words "to drink and eat" before "dragon meat," which contradict the sense of the following sentences.
84. "Yu Bi Zhongju," no. 1, *Wenji* 56.1671–1672.
85. "Huangzhou Anguo si ji," *Wenji* 12.391.
86. "Yanguan dabei ge ji," *Wenji* 12.387.
87. "Yu Ziyou di," no. 3, *Wenji* 60.1834.
88. Su is referring here to an elaboration of the five-phases theory that credits the earth with complementing or filling out Heaven's five initial creations with five of its own. See Kong Yingda's commentary on the "Hongfan" chapter of *Shangshu zhushu* 12.6a (Yan Zhongqi, *Su Shi lun wenyi*, pp. 137–138).
89. Quoted from *Zongyong*, in *Liji zhushu* 53.2b. Zisi is the reputed author of the work.
90. "Song Qiantang seng Sicong gui Gushan xu," *Wenji* 10.325.
91. Referring to two of Zhuangzi's illustrations of acting according to knack, see *Zhuangzi* 36/13/69–74 and 48/19/17–21.

CHAPTER SEVEN

1. For a detailed chronological account of Su's development as a *shi* poet down through the Huangzhou exile, see Fuller, *The Road to East*

NOTES TO PP. 169–176

Slope. On the problem of periodizing Su's *shi* collection, see Xie Taofang, "Su shi fenqi pingyi," and Zeng Zaozhuang, "'Su shi fenqi pingyi' de pingyi," in *Lun Su Shi Lingnan shi ji qita*, ed. Su Shi yanjiu xuehui, pp. 6–23 and 24–41. Cf. Wang Shuizhao, "Lun Su Shi chuangzuo de fazhan jieduan," *Shehui kexue zhanxian* 1984.1:259–269.

2. Ye Mengde, *Yanxia fangyan* A.4b–5a; and Chen Shan, *Menshi xinhua* A1.4b–5b. Modern studies of the subject include those by Pierre Daudin, "Les récréations intellectuelles de Sou Tong-p'o et Tshou Hi," *Bulletin de la Société des Etudes Indochinoises* 45.4:1–38 (1970); and Nishino Teiji, "So Shoku to sono monka no gesaku shi," *Jimbun kenkyū* 16.5:34–50 (1965).

3. Huang Tingjian, "Shuangjing cha song Zizhan," *Shan'gu shizhu*, "neiji," 6.99.

4. Cai Xiang, *Chalu*, pp. 1–2; Ouyang Xiu, *Guitian lu* 1.85. Cf. Aoki Masaru, *Chūka chasho*, pp. 5–6 and 8–10.

5. *Guoyu* 21.659.

6. "Huang Luzhi yi shi kui shangjing cha ciyun wei xie," *Su Shi shiji* 28.1482.

7. Ouyang Xiu, *Guitian lu* 1.85.

8. Huang Tingjian, "Heda Zizhan," *Shan'gu shizhu*, "neiji," 6.99–100.

9. "Ciyun Huang Luzhi chimu," *Su Shi shiji* 27.1457. In Wang Wengao's edition this poem appears before the poem by Su translated earlier, but it is obvious that that order is incorrect (because of Huang's reference to Su's line about the southeast). See Nishino Teiji, "So Shoku to sono monka no gesaku shi," *Jimbun kenkyū* 16.5:36–38 (1965).

10. For Zixia see *Liji zhushu*, "Tangong shang," 7.8b. The tradition about Qiuming is mentioned in Sima Qian's famous letter, "Bao Ren Shaoqing shu," *Wenxuan* 41.16b, although there the history he is credited with is *Guoyu*.

11. *Xin Tangshu* 196.5607 (Wang Shipeng).

12. Huang Tingjian, "Zizhan yi Zixia Qiuming jianxi liao fu xida," *Shan'gu shizhu*, "neiji," 6.100.

13. *Zhuangzi* 6/2/76–77; trans. A. C. Graham, *Chuang-tzu*, p. 59.

14. "Xishu Li Boshi hua yuma haotou chi," *Su Shi shiji* 30.1590–1591. The poem is discussed by Nishino, "Gesaku shi," p. 49, where he makes the point reiterated in this paragraph.

15. Huang Tingjian, "Yi Shuangjing cha song Kong Changfu," *Shan'gu shizhu*, "neiji," 6.101–102.

16. Yamamoto Kazuyoshi, "Zōbetsu no shosō—So shi satsuki," *Nanzan kokubun ronshū* 5:7–11 (1981).

17. "Cao ji jianhe fu ciyun," *Su Shi shiji* 21.1133.

18. "Ciyun Wang Lang Zili fengyu yougan," *Su Shi shiji* 30.1595.

19. "Zeng Liang daoren," *Su Shi shiji* 24.1294.

20. "Cao ji jiaohe fu ciyun," *Su Shi shiji* 21.1133.

21. "He ren jiashan," *Su Shi shiji* 27.1435.

22. "Lamei yishou zeng Zhao Jingkuang," *Su Shi shiji* 34.1828.

23. See the article on this theme in Su's poetry by Yokoyama Iseo, "Shijin

407

ni okeru 'kyō' ni tsuite—So Shoku no baai," *Kambun gakkai kaihō* 34:1–12 (1975), which quotes the two poems cited below.

24. "Huai Xihu ji Chao Meishu tongnian," *Su Shi shiji* 13.644.
25. "Song Cen zhuzuo," *Su Shi shiji* 7.329–330.
26. On the tradition of such madmen and political dissent, see Laurence A. Schneider, *A Madman of Ch'u: The Chinese Myth of Loyalty and Dissent*, pp. 17–86.
27. Du Fu, "Kuangfu," *Dushi xiangzhu* 9.743 (Yokoyama, "Shijin ni okeru 'kyō,'" p. 1).
28. "Deng Yunlong shan," *Su Shi shiji* 17.877.
29. Li Zehou, *Meixue zhesi ren*, p. 171.
30. See Yoshikawa Kōjirō, *An Introduction to Sung Poetry*, trans. Burton Watson, pp. 104–118; Hong Bozhao, "Shi lun Su shi de yilunhua he sanwenhua," in *Dongpo yanjiu luncong*, ed. Su Shi yanjiu xuehui, pp. 32–45; Wang Wenlong, "Shi lun Su shi de zheli xing," in *Dongpo yanjiu luncong*, ed. Su Shi yanjiu xuehui, pp. 64–78.
31. Zhang Jie, *Suihan tang shihua* A.455 (Hong Bozhao, "Shi lun Su shi de yilunhua," p. 33); Yan Yu, *Canglang shihua*, "Shi bian," p. 688; and Zhao Yi, *Oubei shihua* 5.56. The observation about fashioning poetry out of prose was first applied to Han Yu but was later extended, by Zhao Yi and others, to Su Shi.
32. The second and third couplets echo lines about similar circumstances in a poem by Mei Yaochen, "Longnü ci qi shunfeng," *Mei Yaochen ji biannian jiaozhu* 23.709 (Wang Wen'gao).
33. This couplet is anticipated by a passage in Liu Yuxi's "Hu bu fu," *Liu Yuxi ji* 1.9 (Shi Yuanzhi).
34. "Sizhou Sengjia ta," *Su Shi shiji* 6.289–291.
35. Han Yu, "Song seng Chengguan," *Han Changli shi xinian jishi* 1.127–128.
36. "Mobao tang ji," *Wenji* 11.357–358.
37. "Dengzhou haishi bing xu," *Su Shi shiji* 26.1389.
38. Su explains the circumstances under which the poem was written in a preface/title written during his second Hangzhou tour some twenty years later, "Xining zhong Shi tongshou cijun . . . ," *Su Shi shiji* 32.1722–1724.
39. "Shang Wen Shizhong lun queyan shu," *Wenji* 48.1400; cf. "Shang Han Chengxiang lun zaishang shoushi fa," *Wenji* 48.1397.
40. Wang Wen'gao cites several instances of this.
41. "Ba Xuzhou wang Nanjing mashang zoubi ji Ziyou," no. 1, *Su Shi shiji* 18.936.
42. Wang Renyu, *Kaiyuan tianbao yishi* A.66 (Shi Yuanzhi).
43. *Shiji* 126.3198 (Wang Shipeng).
44. "Fahui si Hengcui ge," *Su Shi shiji* 9.426.
45. "Ti Xilin bi," *Su Shi shiji* 23.1219.
46. "Li Sixun hua Changjiang juedao tu," "Liu yue ershiqi ri Wanghu lou

zuishu," no. 2, and "Chu Yingkou chujian Huaishan . . . ," *Su Shi shiji* 6.283, 7.320, and 17.873.

47. "Lianri yu Wang Zhongyu . . . ," *Su Shi shiji* 32.1682.

48. "Shu Wang Dingguo suocang Wang Jinqing hua zhuose shan," no. 1, *Su Shi shiji* 31.1639.

49. "Ciyun Wu Chuanzheng kumu ge," *Su Shi shiji* 36.1962.

50. "Song Canliao shi," *Su Shi shiji* 17.906. The poem is translated and discussed below.

51. Adopting the variant *zu* for *cheng* since an allusion to the legendary Pengzu makes this line a better match with the next.

52. "Song Zheng hucao," *Su Shi shiji* 16.833–834.

53. Wang Shipeng, cf. *Jiu Tangshu* 110.3311.

54. See "Fahui si hengcui ge," *Su Shi shiji* 9.426 and the *ci* on Swallow Pavilion (to the tune "Always Having Fun") discussed in the *ci* chapter below.

55. Some commentators understand the second half of the line as "the cold crawlers murmur," where the sound is a metaphor for the quiet lapping of the tide. See Wang Shuizhao, *Su Shi xuanji*, p. 122.

56. "Zhouzhong yeqi," *Su Shi shiji* 18.942.

57. Cf. "Ji Chengtian yeyou," *Wenji* 71.2260; see also Michael Fuller's discussion (pp. 234–245) of "pure, moonlit scenes" in Su's Xuzhou poems (including this one).

58. See "Nanxing qianji xu," *Wenji* 10.323.

59. "Lari you Gushan fang Huiqin Huisi erseng," *Su Shi shiji* 7.316–319.

60. "Liuyi quanming," *Wenji* 19.565.

61. Ogawa and Yamamoto, *So Tōba shishū* 2:201.

62. "Dengzhou haishi bing xu," *Su Shi shiji* 26.1389.

63. Wang Wen'gao's commentary, in *Su Shi shiji* 26.1389.

64. For Song observations, see the comments of Han Ju quoted in Wei Qingzhi, *Shiren yuxie* 17.383; and those of Hong Mai, *Rongzhai suibi*, "sanbi," 6.489–490. Modern scholars who have remarked on this aspect of Su's verse include Liu Naichang, "Tan Su Shi de yishu gexing," in his *Su Shi wenxue lunji*, pp. 92–94; and Shou Min, "Qiantan Su shi fengge ti duoyanghua," *Dongpo shi luncong*, ed. Su Shi yanjiu xuehui, pp. 48–49. For specialized studies, see Ogawa Tamaki, "Shi ni okeru hikaku no kōsetsu no gazoku: So Tōba no baai," *Chūgoku bungaku hō* 2:1–17 (1955) (rpt. in Ogawa, *Kaze to kumo: Chūgoku bungaku ronshū*, pp. 145–167); Arai Ken, "So Tōba ron," *Chūgoku bungaku ronshū*, ed. Yoshikawa Kōjirō, pp. 237–246; and Xiang Chu, "Su shi biyu suotan," in *Su Shi yanjiu zhuanji*, pp. 26–35.

65. "Jiangshang zhixue . . . ," *Su Shi shiji* 1.20.

66. "Sun Xinlao qiu Momiao ting shi," *Su Shi shiji* 8.372.

67. "Yu yishi xi yushi taiyu . . . ," *Su Shi shiji* 19.999.

68. "Wendeng Penglai ge xia . . . ," *Su Shi shiji* 31.1652.

69. Joseph Needham's term for the device is "square-pallet chain-pump"; see Needham and Wang, *Mechanical Engineering*, pp. 339–352.

70. "Wuxi daozhong fu shuiche," *Su Shi shiji* 11.558.
71. "Du Meng Jiao shi," no. 1, *Su Shi shiji* 16.796–797.
72. "Suiwan xiangyu kuiwen . . . ," no. 3 ("Shousui"), *Su Shi shiji* 4.161.
73. "Yu Hu Sibu you Fahua shan," *Su Shi shiji* 19.989.
74. "He Ziyou Mianchi huaijiu," *Su Shi shiji* 3.97.
75. "Xincheng daozhong," no. 1, *Su Shi shiji* 9.436.
76. "Qianju Lin'gao ting," *Su Shi shiji* 20.1053.
77. "You Jinshan si," *Su Shi shiji* 7.308.
78. "Youshu Wang Jinqing hua," no. 4, *Su Shi shiji* 33.1774.
79. See the comments of Fang Hui and Ji Yun on the second couplet on Su's "Xincheng daozhong," no. 1, in Fang's *Yingkui lüsui* 14.15a; and Ji's *Su Wenzhonggong shiji* 9.5a (quoted and discussed by Ogawa Tamaki, "Shi ni okeru hikaku no kōsetsu to gazoku," pp. 6–14). Cf. Qian Zhongshu's comments on the same couplet as an example of the diminishing or domesticating metaphor, *Guanzhui bian* 2:748–750.
80. Du Fu, "Luye shuhuai," *Dushi xiangzhu* 14.1229.
81. Zhang Sanxi, "Lun Su shi zhong de kongjian gan," *Wenxue yichan* 1982.2:87–96; and Beata Grant, who draws and expands upon Zhang, in *Mount Lu Revisited: Buddhism in the Life and Writings of Su Shi*, forthcoming.
82. "Yu Wang Lang kunzhong ji erzi Mai . . . ," *Su Shi shiji* 19.985.
83. "Yingzhou chubie Ziyou," no. 2, *Su Shi shiji* 6.280.
84. Luk, p. 38; cf. *Lengyan jing*, 2.111c.
85. Luk, pp. 106–107; cf. *Lengyan jing* 4.122c.
86. Trans. Robert A. F. Thurman, *The Holy Teaching of Vimalakīrti*, pp. 52–53; cf. *Weimojie suoshuo jing* B.6.546b–c.
87. See Thurman, p. 51; cf. *Weimojie suoshuo jing* B.6.546b.
88. "Mona zan," *Wenji* 22.635–636.
89. Han Yu, "Song Gaoxian shangren xu," *Han Changli ji* 21.28–29; trans. Hartman, pp. 222–223.
90. "Song Canliao shi," *Su Shi shiji* 17.905–907.
91. See my *Ou-yang Hsiu*, pp. 93–99.
92. "Ciyun Liu Dajing," *Su Shi shiji* 16.820.
93. "Zhongqiu yue ji Ziyou," no. 2, *Su Shi shiji* 17.860–861.
94. Su Che, "Shuidiao getou," *Quan Songci* 1:355.
95. Liu Yuxi, "Dongting qiuyue xing," *Quan Tangshi* 356.3995 (Wang Shipeng); and Shen Quanqi, "He Luozhou Kang Shicao Tingzhi wangyue youhuai," *Quan Tangshi* 96.1033 (Feng Yingliu).
96. The phenomenon has been discussed by Chikusa Masaaki, "Hoku Sō shitaifu no shikyo to baiden—omo ni Tōba sekitoku o shiryō to site," *Shilin* 54.2:28–52 (1971).
97. "Liu yue ershiqi ri Wanghu lou zuishu," no. 5, *Su Shi shiji* 7.341.
98. See Chikusa, "Hoku Sō shitaifu," pp. 33–37.
99. "Chuqiu ji Ziyou," *Su Shi shiji* 22.1169.

100. "Canliaozi zhenzan," *Wenji* 22.639.
101. "Zai he Qianshi," *Su Shi shiji* 22.1186.
102. *Liezi jishi*, "Huangdi," 2.45; trans. A. C. Graham, *The Book of Lieh Tzu*, p. 48.
103. Yamamoto Kazuyoshi, "So Shoku shi ronkō," *Chūgoku bungaku hō* 13:80–85 (1961).
104. "Gushi shijiu shou," no. 12, *Wenxuan* 29.6b.
105. Cao Zhi, "Fou ping pian," *Xian Qin Han Wei Jin Nanbeichao shi* A.424.
106. "He Wang Jinqing," *Su Shi shiji* 27.1423.
107. "Zi Puzhao you eran," *Su Shi shiji* 9.434.
108. "Fan Ying," *Su Shi shiji* 34.1794–1795.

CHAPTER EIGHT

1. Su's literary responses to exile, in all their range and complexity, are the subject of the excellent recent study by Kathleen M. Tomlonovic, "Poetry of Exile and Return: A Study of Su Shi (1037–1101)," Ph.D. diss., University of Washington, 1989. Tomlonovic's study, which is far lengthier and more detailed than this chapter, parallels my own analysis of Su's exile literature at several points, while the themes emphasized and the interpretations of certain pieces differ.
2. "Da Qin Taixu," no. 4, *Wenji* 52.1536.
3. "Yu Zhang Zihou cangzheng shu," and "Yu Wang Dingguo," no. 5, *Wenji* 49.1412 and 52.1515.
4. "Yu Li Gongze," *Wenji* 51.1499.
5. "Da Bi Zhongju," no. 1, *Wenji* 56.1671.
6. See Wang Wen'gao's commentary on Su's South Hall poems, *Su Shi shiji* 22.1166.
7. "Da Li Sicheng," no. 2, *Wenji* 60.1825.
8. In "Yu Yang Yuansu," no. 9, *Wenji* 55.1653, Su says he still has 200,000 cash. Cf. his mention of being able to raise as much as 800,000 from the sale of his capital residence, "Da Fan Shugong," no. 3, *Wenji* 50.1446–1447. Chikusa Masaaki suggests that the capital residence may have been inherited from Su Shi's father; see "Hoku Sō shitaifu," p. 33.
9. See the detailed study of this matter in the article by Chikusa Masaaki cited in the previous note as well as the earlier article by Nishino Teiji, "Tōba shi no baiden no go ni tsuite," *Jimbun kenkyū* 19.10:757–763 (1968).
10. "Yu Chen Jichang," no. 3, *Wenji* 53.1565.
11. "Yu Yang Yuansu," no. 9, *Wenji* 55.1653.
12. "Yu Yang Yuansu," nos. 5 and 9, *Wenji* 55.1651 and 1653.
13. "Shu tian," *Wenji* 71.2259.

14. Zhou Bida, *Yigong tiba* 12.16b (Chikusa, "Hoku Sō shitaifu," pp. 35–36).

15. For this information see, in addition to the East Slope poems translated below, "Yu Li Gongze," no. 9, and "Yu Wang Dingguo," no. 13, *Wenji* 51.1499 and 52.1520–1521.

16. "Yu Wang Dingguo," no. 13, *Wenji* 52.1520–1521. Cf. "Yu Zhang Zihou," no. 1, *Wenji* 55.1639.

17. See, for example, "Yu Wang Dingguo," nos. 2 and 5, *Wenji* 52.1513 and 1515.

18. "Yu Teng Dadao," no. 15, *Wenji* 51.1480.

19. For example, "Yu Li Gongze," no. 12, *Wenji* 51.1500.

20. "Yu Wang Dingguo," no. 8, and "Yu Qin Taixu," no. 4, *Wenji* 52.1517 and 52.1535.

21. "Huangzhou Anguo si ji," *Wenji* 12.391–392.

22. "Da Li Duanshu shu," *Wenji* 49.1432.

23. "Yu Canliaozi," no. 13, *Wenji* 61.1863.

24. "Fu Yingzhou qi chuanxing zhuang," *Wenji* 37.1042–1043.

25. "Shu liufu hou," *Wenji* 66.2072.

26. Wu Shiduan, "Dongpo zai Huizhou zheju shenghuo tan," *Lun Su Shi Lingnan shi ji qita*, ed. Su Shi yanjiu xuehui, pp. 222–239.

27. "Wen Zhengfu biaoxiong jiangzhi yishi yingzhi," *Su Shi shiji* 39.2143, and "Yu Cheng Zhengfu," no. 63, *Wenji* 54.1619.

28. On this bond, see "Yu Wang Minzhong," nos. 8 and 12, *Wenji* 56.1691 and 56.1694; cf. the comments of Wang Wen'gao, *Zongan* 40.12a and 41.1b.

29. See the poems "Huizhou Zhanjun jianhe fu ciyun," and "Da Zhou Xunzhou," *Su Shi shiji* 38.2078 and 39.2151; and the comments by Wu Shiduan, pp. 237–238. Cf. a poem in which the reference to such a gift is straightforward: "Xie Dushi hui mi," *Su Shi shiji* 50.2761.

30. "Yu Cheng Zhengfu," no. 13, and "Yu Wang Minzhong," no. 6, *Wenji* 54.1593 and 56.1691. On Chang Dun's attempt to have the exiles made permanent, see *Jishi benmo* 46.452 and *Zongan* 39.16b.

31. See the note to Wang Minzhong cited immediately above, as well as "Yu Fan Chunfu," no. 11, *Wenji* 50.1457, and Su's colophon on his poem "Ciyun Hui Xun ershou xianghui," *Su Shi shiji* 40.2220.

32. "Yu Cheng Zhengfu," no. 16, *Wenji* 54.1594.

33. Luo Dajing, *Helin yulu*, "bingji," 5.315. A similar passage is quoted by Yan Zhongqi, *Yishi huibian*, p. 214, and attributed to Lu You's *Laoxue an biji*; but I have been unable to locate the passage in that work.

34. "Yu Wang Minzhong," no. 16, *Wenji* 56.1695.

35. See Shi Yuanzhi's commentary on "Xinju," *Su Shi shiji* 42.2312, and *Xu changbian* 508.5a. Cf. *Zongan* 42.4a. The incident is also alluded to in Su Che's grave inscription for his brother, "Wangxiong Zizhan Duanming muzhiming," *Luancheng ji*, "houji," 22.1421.

36. "Xinju," *Su Shi shiji* 42.2312. In a note to Cheng Jie, Su gives more particulars, see "Yu Cheng Quanfu," no. 9, *Wenji* 55.1626.
37. "Yu Cheng Xiucai," no. 1, *Wenji* 55.1628.
38. "Yu Wang Minzhong," no. 13, *Wenji* 56.1695.
39. "Yu Cheng Quanfu," no. 12, *Wenji* 55.1627.
40. "Yu Zhisun Yuanlao," no. 1, *Wenji* 60.1841.
41. See "Yu Jiang Tangzuo xiucai," nos. 1–6, *Wenji* 57.1739–1740; and "Qusui yu Wu Ziye you Xiaoyao tang . . ." and "Zeng Zheng Qingshou xiucai," *Su Shi shiji* 42.2309–2310 and 2321–2322.
42. "Yu Zhu Xingzhong," nos. 5, 7, 8, 10, and "Da Su Bogu," no. 2, *Wenji* 58.1771–1773 and 57.1741.
43. "Yu Qian Jiming," no. 10, *Wenji* 53.1554.
44. "Yu Ziyou di," no. 8, *Wenji* 60.1837.
45. Su Che, "Zai ji wangxiong Duanming wen," *Luancheng ji*, "hou," 20.1390.
46. "Yu Li Gongze," no. 12, *Wenji* 51.1500.
47. See "Yu Fan Zifeng," no. 7, and "Ji Chibi," *Wenji* 50.1452–1453 and 71.2255.
48. All twenty-three of Su's rhapsodies are translated by Cyril Drummond Le Gros Clark, *The Prose-Poetry of Su Tung-p'o*. For Ouyang Xiu's rhapsodies, see my *Ou-yang Hsiu*, pp. 123–132.
49. Poems from the *Shijing*, nos. 143 and 1.
50. The lines are from Cao Cao, "Duange xing," *Wenxuan* 27.17b–18a.
51. "Chibi fu," *Wenji* 1.5–7. In addition to Le Gros Clark's translation, the rhapsody has also been translated by A. C. Graham in *Anthology of Chinese Literature*, ed. Cyril Birch, pp. 381–382; Burton Watson, *Su Tung-p'o: Selections from a Sung Dynasty Poet*, pp. 87–90; and Yu-shih Chen, *Images and Ideas in Chinese Classical Prose*, pp. 143–144.
52. On this treatment of "change" in the *Book of Changes*, see Qian Zhongshu, 1:6–8 (where Su's rhapsody is included in the references). For a similar explanation of the Buddhist concept of the permanence of the true nature (as opposed to the body), see *Lengyan jing* 2.110a–c; trans. Luk, pp. 24–27. The Ming painter Dong Qichang, in his *Huachan shi suibi* 3.5a, has suggested that Su was influenced by the fourth-century Buddhist Sengzhao, in his essay on non-transference in *Zhaolun*, p. 151a–b: "There is rest with motion going on; therefore, though (things) move they are forever at rest . . . The Yangzi and Yellow River flow along but do not move" (Wang Shuizhao, *Su Shi xuanji*, p. 386).
53. "Nian nu jiao" (*Dajiang dongqu*), *Su Dongpo ci*, no. 130 (see also Long Muxun, ed., *Dongpo yuefu jian* 2.9b; and *Quan Songci* 1:282). There are several variants in the text of this song. I have followed Cao Shuming's version of the text in *Su Dongpo ci* (except for the parsing of lines 8–9 in the second stanza), which is also the version given by Hu Yunyi, *Songci xuan*, , pp. 75–76. See arguments put forth for the more important of the choices by Wang Shoumei, "Su Shi 'Nian nu

jiao: Chibi huaigu' yiwen bianxi," *Sichuan daxue xuebao congkan* 15:90–92 (1982).

54. Both comments are quoted by Wang Shuizhao, *Su Shi xuanji*, p. 294. See Yuan Haowen, "Ti Xianxian shu 'Chibi fu' hou," *Yishan xiansheng wenji* 40.16b. I have been unable to identify Huang Liaoyuan or his *Liaoyuan cixuan*.

55. "Han shih yu," no. 2, *Su Shi shiji* 21.1113.

56. "Dongpo bashou," *Su Shi shiji* 21.1079–1084. For translations and discussions of the complete series of eight poems, see Alice Wen-chuen Cheang, "Poetry, Politics, Philosophy: Su Shih as the Man of the Eastern Slope," *Harvard Journal of Asiatic Studies* 53.2:325–387 (1993); and Fuller, pp. 271–284.

57. See Zhao Cigong's comment, quoted in Wang Wen'gao's commentary, *Su Shi shiji* 21.1084; for a modern opinion, see Wang Shuizhao, *Su Shi xuanji*, "Preface," pp. 13–14.

58. See "Yu Wang Dingguo," no. 13, *Wenji* 52.1521; and also Su's "Jiang chengzi," *Su Dongpo ci*, no. 119 (see also Long Muxun, ed., *Dongpo yuefu jian* 2.2a; and *Quan Songci* 1:298, under the title "Jiang shenzi, no. 1).

59. Tao Qian, "Gui yuantian ju," no. 2, *Tao Yuanming ji jiaojian*, ed. Yang Yong, 2.59; trans. James R. Hightower, *The Poetry of T'ao Ch'ien*, p. 51.

60. See Su's remarks, quoted by Su Che, "Zizhan he Tao Yuanming shiji yin," *Luancheng ji*, "houji," 21.1401–1402. There are some twenty poems by Tao Qian for which no matching poem by Su survives. See A. R. Davis's suggestion that Su never wrote these poems because they did not fit his circumstances, "Su Shih's 'Following the Rhymes of T'ao Yuan-ming' Poems: A Literary or a Psychological Phenomenon?," *Journal of the Oriental Society of Australia* 10:93–108 (1974).

61. Tao Qian, "Yuzi Yandeng shu," *Tao Yuanming ji jiaojian* 7.301; trans. Hightower, *T'ao Ch'ien*, p. 5.

62. Quoted by Su Che, "Zizhan he Tao Yuanming shiji yin," *Luancheng ji*, "houji," 21.1401–1402.

63. For Su's new views on the supremacy of Tao Qian, see his statement quoted by Su Che, "Zizhan he Tao Yuanming shiji yin," *Luancheng ji*, "houji," 21.1402. For Su's previous assertions of Du Fu's supremacy, see "Wang Dingguo shiji xu," "Shu Wu Daozi huahou," and "Shu Huang Zisi shiji hou," *Wenji* 10.318, 67.2124, and 70.2210. The point about the change in Su's views during his Lingnan exile is also made by Chen Huachang, "Xinling wei Tao Yuanming suo xiyin—lun Su Shi wannian de sixiang bianhua," in *Lun Su Shi Lingnan shi ji qita*, ed. Su Shi yanjiu xuehui, pp. 216–222.

64. Su Che, "Zizhan he Tao Yuanming shiji yin," *Luancheng ji*, "houji," 21.1402.

65. The only full-length study of Su's matching poems is Song Qiulong, *Su Dongpo he Tao Yuanming shi zhi bijiao yanjiu* (1985). There are also useful articles by A. R. Davis and Chen Huachang (cited above nn. 60 and 63). Two recent articles deserve special note for their sensi-

tivity to the divergences between Su's and Tao's circumstances, and the effect these divergences have upon Su's claim to be a latterday Tao Qian (a theme of my discussion here): Tang Lingling, "Lun Su Shi de he Tao shi," and Wang Yunsheng, "Su Dongpo zai Huizhou he Tao shi de sixiang qingxiang," in *Lun Su Shi Lingnan shi ji qita*, ed. Su Shi yanjiu xuehui, pp. 166–184 and 185–196.

66. "He Tao gui yuantian ju," no. 2, *Su Shi shiji* 39.2104–2105.
67. Tao Qian, "Gui yuantian ju," nos. 1 and 2, *Tao Yuanming ji jiaojian* 2.57 and 59; trans. Hightower, *T'ao Ch'ien*, pp. 50 and 51. The others of Tao's lines referred to in this paragraph are also given in Hightower's translation.
68. Tao Qian, "Yong pinshi," no. 4, *Tao Yuanming ji jiaojian* 4.220; trans. Hightower, *T'ao Ch'ien*, p. 208.
69. Tao Qian, "Yong pinshi," no. 2, *Tao Yuanming ji jiaojian* 4.217; trans. Hightower, *T'ao Ch'ien*, p. 205. "Crisis in Chen" refers to Confucius's hardship in that state, when he and his followers were in danger of starving; see *Lunyu* 15/2.
70. "He Tao pinshi," no. 3, *Su Shi shiji* 39.2138.
71. See poem no. 7, the last in the series.
72. Tao Qian, "Yuanshi Chu diao," *Tao Yuanming ji jiaojian* 2.74; trans. Hightower, *T'ao Ch'ien*, pp. 64–65.
73. "He Tao yuan shi shi Pang Deng," *Su Shi shiji* 41.2271–2272.
74. "Liuyue ershi ri ye duhai," *Su Shi shiji* 43.2366–2367.
75. "Wu che Hainan Ziyou Leizhou . . ." and "Bie Hainan limin biao," *Su Shi shiji* 41.2245 and 43.2363.
76. "Yu ju Hejiang lou," "He Tao Taohua yuan," and "Xing Qiong Dan jian . . . ," *Su Shi shiji* 38.2072, 40.2196–2198, and 41.2246–2248.
77. "Shibi zishu," *Wenji* "Yiwen huibian" 5.2549.
78. "Xue tang ji," *Wenji* 12.410.
79. Ibid., p. 412.
80. Ibid.
81. Ibid.
82. "Yu Cheng Zhengfu," no. 55, *Wenji* 54.1615. Cf. a similar statement in a Huangzhou period letter to Wang Gong, "Yu Wang Dingguo," no. 7, *Wenji* 52.1517.
83. Both of the letters cited immediately above contain such requests.
84. Huihong, "Ba Dongpo chenchi lu," *Shimen wenzi chan* 27.6b–7b.
85. "Longhu yangong shuo," *Wenji* 73.2332.
86. See Isabelle Robinet, "Original Contributions of *Neidan* to Taoism and Chinese Thought," in *Taoist Meditation and Longevity Techniques*, ed. Livia Kohn, pp. 297–330.
87. "Da Zhang Wenqian," no. 2, and "Yu Lu Zihou," *Wenji* 52.1539 and 60.1853–1854.
88. "Chen Taichu shijie," *Wenji* 72.2322–2323.
89. "Longhu yangong shuo," *Wenji* 73.2331.

90. "Yangshenjue," "Ji Ziyou sanfa," no 3, and "Xue guixi fa," *Wenji* 73.2336, 2339, and 2339.

91. "Cang dansha fa," *Wenji* 73.2339.

92. "Yiren youwu," *Wenji* 73.2327.

93. *Hanshu* 45.2167.

94. "Anqi Sheng," *Su Shi shiji* 43.2349.

95. Huang Tingjian, "Ti Dongpo shu daoshu hou," *Yuzhang Huang xiansheng wenji* 25.10b.

96. "Tong Zhengfu biaoxiong you Baishui shan," *Su Shi shiji* 39.2147–2148, as well as the poem immediately following it.

97. "He Tao du Shanhai jing," no. 1, *Su Shi shiji* 39.2130.

98. *Liezi jishi* 5.100; trans. Graham, *The Book of Lieh-tzu*, p. 100.

99. See poem no. 12 in the series, *Su Shi shiji* 39.2135–2136.

100. "He Tao zashi," no. 6, *Su Shi shiji* 41.2275.

101. For the special properties of sweet flag (*changpu*), see Su's poem, "He Ziyou ji yuanzhong caomu," no. 9, *Su Shi shiji* 5.207, and Wang Wengao's commentary. For the plant's association with Zhuming Grotto, see "Ciyun Chengfu tong you Baishiu shan," *Su Shi shiji* 39.2149.

102. "He Tao shenshi," *Su Shi shiji* 42.2307.

103. The tigers and leopards here must be rocks whose shape reminds the poet of those animals, and the scaly dragon a tree.

104. Lin'gao is the site of Su's house. Some texts read "two Taoists." In preferring a single priest, to match the single crane, I am following Kong Fanli, *Wenji* 1.8 (as well as an early note by Zhu Xi, see *Zhuzi yulei* 130.3115–3116). For arguments in favor of the other reading, see Yu-shih Chen, *Images and Ideas*, pp. 148–153.

105. "Hou Chibi fu," *Wenji* 1.8. Cf. other translations by A. C. Graham in *Anthology of Chinese Literature*, ed. Cyril Birch, pp. 383–384; and Chen Yu-shih, *Images and Ideas*, pp. 144–146.

106. These critical comments and many others are conveniently gathered together in Wang Shuizhao, *Su Shi xuanji*, pp. 393–394. Yuan Hongdao's comment is taken from Zheng Zhihui and Ling Qikang, *Su Changgong hezuo*, juan 1; Wang Wenru's from his *Pingjian yinzhu guwen ci leizuan*, juan 71; and Jin Shengtan's from his *Tianxia caizi bidu shu* 15.363.

107. See "Yu Fan Zifeng," no. 7, and "Ji Chibi," *Wenji* 50.1452–1453 and 71.2255.

108. Li Bo, "You Taishan," no. 1, *Li Taibo quanji* 20.922; trans. and discussed by Paul Kroll, "Verses from on High: The Ascent of T'ai Shan," *The Vitality of the Lyric Voice*, ed. Shuen-lin Fu and Stephen Owen, pp. 199–203; see esp. p. 201 and n. 96. On the history and significance of whistling, see Aoki Masaru, "Shō no rekishi to jigi no hensen," *Aoki Masaru zenshū* 8:161–168 (Kroll).

109. From Su's "Ciyun Wang Dingguo de Ying zu," no. 1, *Su Shi shiji* 26.1394, describing Wang Shen. The poem is quoted in the helpful study of whistling in Su's works, including the second Red Cliff rhap-

sody, by Yamamoto Kazuyoshi, "Shijin no chō shō—So shi satsuki," *Nanzan kokubun ronshū* 4:38 (1979).

110. Liu Yiqing, *Shishuo xinyu jianshu*, "Qiyi," 18.648; trans. Richard B. Mather, *Shih-shuo Hsin-yü*, p. 332. This anecdote is also referred to in Yamamoto's study, cited above.

111. Su Shi, "Shuidiao getou," *Su Dongpo ci*, no. 65 (see also Long Muxun, ed., *Dongpo yuefu jian* 1.40b and *Quan songci* 1:280).

112. "Wen Zhengfu biaoxiong jiangzhi yishi yingzhi," *Su Shi shiji* 39:2144.

113. "Xi'er xizuo," *Su Shi shiji* 47.2535

114. "Yuju Dinghui yuan zhi dong . . . ," *Su Shi shiji* 20.1037.

115. Moreover, the image of the soaring goose is a fitting compliment to the memory of his father. It is Xu Xu who proposes this reading of the line in his *Su Shi shixuan*, p. 122.

116. "Meihua," no. 1, *Su Shi shiji* 20.1026.

117. "Zhengyue ershi ri wang Qiting . . . ," *Su Shi shiji* 21.1078.

118. "Hanshi yu," no. 1, *Su Shi shiji* 21.1112.

119. "Shiyi yue ershiliu ri Songfeng ting xia meihua shengkai," *Su Shi shiji* 38.2075–2076.

120. "Zongbi," *Su Shi shiji* 40.2203. The crucial last couplet of the quatrain also appears as verses in a prose work Su wrote at the time, "Baihe xinju shang liang wen," *Wenji* 64.1989.

121. Zeng Jili, *Tingzhai shihua*, p. 310, where it is the occurrence of the couplet in the prose piece cited above, rather than in the quatrain, that is mentioned. Wang Wen'gao (*Zongan* 41.1a), and several modern scholars after him, quotes a similar passage from the early-twelfth-century work *Yudi guangji*, by Ouyang Min, but I do not find the passage (or anthing remotely like it) in that work. Did Wang, or some earlier commentary he was relying on, have a different version of *Yudi guangji*?

122. "Zongbi sanshou," no. 1, *Su Shi shiji* 42.2327–2328.

123. See Wang Shuizhao's comment on the line, *Su Shi xuanji*, p. 238; and the remarks of Zhou Xianshen, "Manshuo Su Shi zongbi shi: jiantan shiren zai Hui Dan shiqi de chuangzuo xintai shenghuo sixiang," *Beijing daxue xuebao* 1988.5:50.

124. "He Tao yong sanliang," *Su Shi shiji* 40.2184–2185.

125. Tao Qian's poem is "He sanliang," *Tao Yuanming jiaojian* 4.228; trans. Hightower, *Tao Ch'ien*, pp. 219–220. Su Shi's earlier treatment is "Qin Mugong mu," *Su Shi shiji* 3.118–119.

126. "Gengchen sui renri zuo . . . ," *Su Shi shiji* 43.2343.

127. "Zongbi sanshou," no. 2, *Su Shi shiji* 42.2328.

128. "Beijiu duxing pianzhi Ziyun Wei Hui Xianjue si Li zhi she," no. 1, *Su Shi shiji* 42.2322–2323.

129. Ji Yun, *Su Wenzhonggong shiji* 42.10a (Wang Shuizhao, *Su Shi xuanji*, p. 237). In his commentary on the poem Wang Wen'gao defends Su against Ji Yun's criticism.

CHAPTER NINE

1. Valuable discussions of Su's views on painting are contained in Susan Bush, *The Chinese Literati on Painting*, pp. 29–51; and Susan Bush and Hsio-yen Shih, *Early Chinese Texts on Painting*, pp. 191–240 (both of which include numerous translations of key writings by Su and critics associated with him). See also Yan Zhongqi, *Su Shi lun wenyi*, pp. 19–24; Huang Mingfen, *Lun Su Shi de wenyi xinli guan*, esp. chapters 1, 2, and 6; Tao Wenpeng, "Shi lun Su Shi de shihua tongyi shuo," *Wenxue pinglun congkan* 13:15–37 (1983); and my article, "Poems on Paintings: Su Shih and Huang T'ing-chien," *Harvard Journal of Asiatic Studies* 43.2:413–451 (1983); as well as that by Stuart Sargent, "Colophons in Countermotion: Poems by Su Shih and Huang T'ing-chien on Paintings," *Harvard Journal of Asiatic Studies* 52.1:263–302 (1992).

   On Su's views on calligraphy, see Yan Zhongqi, *Su Shi lun wenyi* 24–34; Amy McNair, "Su Shih's Copy of the *Letter on the Controversy over Seating Protocol*," *Archives of Asian Art* 43:38–48 (1990); Nakata Yūjirō, "So Tōba no sho to shoron," in his *Chūgoku shoron shū*; and my study, "Ou-yang Hsiu and Su Shih on Calligraphy," *Harvard Journal of Asiatic Studies* 49.2:365–419 (1989). The Ph.D. diss. by Shen C. Y. Fu, "Huang T'ing-chien's Calligraphy and His *Scroll for Chang Ta-t'ung*: A Masterpiece Written in Exile," contains much relevant discussion of contemporary issues in calligraphy, esp. chapter 6.

2. Li Fushun, *Su Shi lun shuhua shiliao*. The first section of Li's compilation, pp. 29–169, reproduces Su's writings on the two arts.

3. Egan, "Ou-yang Hsiu and Su Shih on Calligraphy," pp. 365–419.

4. Ouyang Xiu, "Xueshu zichengjia shuo," *Shibi*, p. 123.

5. Ouyang Xiu, "Tang Yan Zhenqing Mogu tan ji," *Jigu lu* 7.3.

6. McNair, "Su Shih's *Letter*," p. 39. Cf. Liu Chang's preface, reproduced in a later recension of Yan's collected works, *Wenzhong ji*, p. i.

7. My description of Yan's style has benefited from Amy McNair's analysis, as found in her "Su Shih's *Letter*" and in her paper, "Ouyang Xiu and Literati Taste in Calligraphy in the Northern Song Period," presented at the 1990 annual meeting of the Association for Asian Studies in Chicago.

8. "Ba suoshu Qingxu tang ji," *Wenji* 69.2186–2187; and "Shi Cangshu Zuimo tang," *Su Shi shiji* 6.236, lines 19–20.

9. "Ba Dongpo shutie hou," *Yuzhang Huang xiansheng wenji* 29.8b.

10. "Ji Pan Yanzhi ping yu shu," *Wenji* 69.2189; and "Ciyun Ziyou lunshu," *Su Shi shiji* 5.210, line 2.

11. The Ming edition is Mao Wei's *Su Wenzhonggong quanji* (the text on which Kong Fanli's *Su Shi wenji* is based). On Mao's various sources for his six *juan* of Su's colophons (one of which contains the colophons on calligraphy), see Kong Fanli's preface, *Wenji*, p. iv. Subsequently, the seventeenth-century scholar Mao Jin reprinted Mao's edition of the colophons separately under the title *Dongpo tiba*, a work

that was republished several times and became widely available. Cf. George Hatch's notice on *Dongpo tiba* in *A Sung Biography*, p. 264.

12. "Ba Junmo feibai," "Ba Junmo shufu," and "Ba Chen Yinju shu," *Wenji* 69.2181, 2182, and 2184.

13. "Ba Junmo feibai," *Wenji* 69.2181.

14. "Ba Du Qigong shu," "Ping Yangshi suo cang Ou Cai shu," and "Shu Tangshi liujia shu hou," *Wenji* 69.2184, 2187, and 2206.

15. *Liezi jishi*, "Shuotu," 8.173–174; trans. Graham, *Lieh-tzu*, p. 180.

16. From Du Fu, "Li Chao bafen xiaozhuan gu," *Dushi xiangzhu* 18.1550.

17. *Jiu Tangshu* 165.4310.

18. "Shu Tangshi liujia shu hou," *Wenji* 69.2206–2207.

19. Yan Zhenqing's admonition of Grand Councilor Lu Qi and his ringing denunciation of the usurper Li Xilie are both recorded in Yan's biography in *Jiu Tangshu* 128.3595–3596.

20. "Ti Lugong tie," *Wenji* 69.2177.

21. "Ti Zijing shu," *Wenji* 69.2173. Xie An had hinted to Wang Xianzhi that he might grace Xie's new palace with an inscription, but Wang rebuffed him so firmly that Xie never dared to ask him directly; see *Jinshu* 80.2105.

22. Ouyang Xiu, "Tang Bianfa shi bei," *Jigu lu* 5.150.

23. Han Yu, "Shigu ge," *Quan Tangshi* 340.3810–3811.

24. Ouyang Xiu, "Song Wendi shendao bei," *Jigu lu* 4.128.

25. "Sun Xinlao qiu Momiao ting shi," *Su Shi shiji* 8.372.

26. See Huang Tingjian's reference to them towards the end of his poem, "Ciyun Zizhan he Ziyou guan Han Gan ma yinlun Boshi hua tianma," *Shan'gu shizhu* 7.122.

27. "Ciyun Ziyou lunshu," *Su Shi shiji* 5.210.

28. Ibid., p. 211. There are useful annotation of these difficult lines in Yan Zhongqi, *Su Shi lun wenyi*, pp. 244–245.

29. "Ji Ouyang lun babi," *Wenji* 70.2234. There is a rare punctuation error in the *Wenji* text; cf. Yan Zhongqi, *Su Shi lun wenyi*, p. 270.

30. "Yongbi zhi fa," *Shibi*, pp. 129–130.

31. "Ba Dongpo shuilu zan," *Yuzhang Huang xiansheng wenji* 29.4a–5a. The colophon is translated and discussed in my article, "Su Shih and Huang T'ing-chien on Calligraphy," pp. 414–415.

32. McNair, "Su Shih's *Letter*," pp. 38–48.

33. "Ping caoshu," *Wenji* 69.2189.

34. "Ti Ouyang tie," *Wenji* 69.2197.

35. See my discussion in "Ou-yang Hsiu and Su Shih on Calligraphy," pp. 385–388.

36. Su Shi's calligraphy in the *kai* and *xing* styles was commonly said to derive from that of Xu Hao (703–782). The metaphorical language here is lifted from earlier celebrations of Xu Hao's style; see *Xin Tangshu* 160.4966.

37. This was the response that Du Zhou, a Former Han official, gave to someone who accused him of manipulating laws to incriminate only those people whom the emperor wanted incriminated; see *Shiji* 122.3153.

38. A reference to the controversy surrounding Han Yu's "Ping Huaixi bei" for its alleged biases; see Hartman, *Han Yü*, pp. 83-84, 261-262.

39. "This lad's another case of someone 'peeping at a leopard through a tube'; every now and then he sees a spot." Liu Yiqing, *Shishuo xinyu jiansha* 5.334; trans. from Mather, *Shih-shuo Hsin-yü*, p. 176.

40. A syncophantic Sui and early-Tang minister who was intolerant of those whose views differed from his own; see *Jiu Tangshu* 63.2396.

41. Huang Tingjian, "Ba Dongpo shiulu zan," *Yuzhang Huang xiansheng wenji* 29.4a–5a.

42. See as well Huang's other colophons, "Ti Ouyang Tianfu suoshou Dongpo dazi juan wei," "Ba Dongpo lunbi," and "Ba Dongpo shu Yuanjing lou fu hou," *Yuzhang Huang xiansheng wenji* 29.6b–7a.

43. Cf. Su's "Ti Yan gong shuhua zan," *Wenji* 69.2177.

44. See Fu, pp. 223–233.

45. "Ciyun Mi Fu er Wang shu bawei ershou," *Su Shi shiji* 29.1536–1538.

46. "Ba Ye Zhiyuan suocang Yong Chanshi qianwen," *Wenji* 69.2204.

47. "Shu Tangshi liujia shu hou," *Wenji* 69.2204. Cf. a similar statement in "Ji Pan Yanzhi ping yu shu," *Wenji* 69.2189.

48. "Ji Pan Yanzhi ping yu shu," *Wenji* 69.2189.

49. See, for example, Huaisu's claim of apprenticeship to summer clouds, quoted in Lu Yu's biography of him, "Seng Huaisu zhuan," *Quan Tangwen* 433.16a.

50. "Shu Zhang Shaogong panzhuang" and "Ba Wen Yuke lun caoshu hou," *Wenji* 69.2178 and 2191.

51. In addition to the Dou Ji poem cited above, see Lu Shou's "Huaisu shangren caoshu ke," *Quan Tangshi* 204.2135.

52. "Ping caoshu," *Wenji* 69.2183.

53. "Ba Shan'gu caoshu," *Wenji* 69.2202–2203. Su's praise is actually a quotation of a boast made by Zhang Rong (5th c.); see *Nanshi* 32.835.

54. "Ba Luzhi wei Wang Jinching xiaoshu Erya," *Wenji* 69.2195.

55. Zeng Minxing, *Duxing zazhi* 3.4a.

56. These first two stories are told about Zhang Zhi (2nd. c.); see *Hou Hanshu* 65.2144.

57. Said to have been done by the monk Zhiyong (6th c.); see He Yanzhi, "Lanting shimo ji," *Quan Tangwen* 301.17a; see also *Xuanhe shupu* 17.389–390.

58. Zhong Yao had his rival Wei Dan's tomb robbed of the sample of Cai Yong's calligraphy that Wei had refused to give him while he was alive; see Wei Xu, *Mosou* 8.27.

59. "Ti bizhen tu," *Wenji* 69.2170.

60. "Shi Cangshu zuimo tang," *Su Shi shiji* 6.236.

61. See the passages he wrote translated in my "Ou-yang Hsiu and Su Shih on Calligraphy," pp. 378–379.
62. "Shu suozuo zi hou," *Wenji* 69.2180.
63. "Shu zhouzhong zuozi," *Wenji* 69.2203.
64. "Ba Wen Yuke caoshu," *Wenji* 69.2183.
65. "Xianzhuan Panruo xinjing zan," *Wenji* 21.618.
66. "Ti Lugong shucao," *Wenji* 69.2178. The saying quoted is from *Zhuangzi* 49/19/25–26. The calligraphy was Yan's *Letter on the Controversy over Seating Protocol* referred to above.
67. "Ping caoshu," *Wenji* 69.2183.
68. "Ba Qin Shaoyou shu," *Wenji* 69.2194.
69. "Song Qiantang seng Sicong gui Gushan xu," *Wenji* 10.326.
70. "Ba Wang Gong suoshou Cangzhen shu," *Wenji* 69.2177.
71. "Wen Yuke feibai zan," *Wenji* 21.614. Cf. Su's comment that Liang Wudi and Huaisu excelled at likening calligraphy to "images of things," in "Ba Wang Gong suoshou Cangzhen shu," *Wenji* 69.2177.
72. "Song Qiantang seng Sicong gui Gushan xu," *Wenji* 10.326.
73. "Shu Yanling Wang zhubo suohua zhezhi," no. 1, *Su Shi shiji* 29.1525.
74. "Shu Chen Huaili chuanshen," *Wenji* 70.2214–2215.
75. "You ba Hanjian huashan," no. 2, *Wenji* 70.2216.
76. Ouyang Xiu, "Jianhua," *Shibi*, p. 128, discussed in my *Ou-yang Hsiu*, pp. 197–199.
77. "Shu Dai Song huaniu," *Wenji* 70.2213–2214.
78. "Shu Huang Quan huaque," *Wenji* 70.2213.
79. For examples of these, see my article, "Poems on Paintings," pp. 431–443.
80. The literary works Su addressed to or wrote about Wen Tong are conveniently gathered together in the appendix to Wen's literary collection, *Danyuan ji*, "fu-lu," pp. 2b–25a. See also the additional letters in Su's *Wenji* 51.1511–1512 and *Wenji*, "Yiwen huibian," 2.2440–2446.
81. "Mojun tang ji," *Wenji* 11.355–356.
82. "Shu Chao Buzhi suocang Yuke huazhu," nos. 3 and 2, *Su Shi shiji* 29.1523 and 1522.
83. Bo Juyi, "Huazhu ge," *Quan Tangshi* 435.4816.
84. The matching poems are quoted in Wang Wen'gao's commentary in *Su Shi shiji*. Su Song later wrote a match to Su Shi's poem: "Ciyun Su Zizhan ti Li Gonglin huama tu," *Su Weigong wenji* 5.48.
85. "Ciyun Ziyou shu Li Boshi suocang Han Gan ma," *Su Shi shiji* 28.1502–1505.
86. Du Fu, "Danqing yin," *Dushi xiangzhu* 13.1150.
87. This understanding of "you" is from Ji Yun, quoted in Wang Wen-gao's commentary in *Su Shi shiji*.
88. *Xuanhe huapu* 13.360.
89. "Bingma," "Shouma xing," and "Gao Tuhu congma xing," *Dushi xiangzhu* 8.621–622, 6.472–474, and 2.86–89.

90. These themes are contained in the following poems: Du Fu, "Tianyu piao tu ge," "Ti bishang Wei Yan huama ge," "Danqing yin," and "Wei Fenglu zhai guan Cao Jiangju huama tu ge," *Dushi xiangzhu* 4.253–255, 9.753–754, 13.1147–1151, and 13.1152–1156.

91. "Song Fugu hua Xiaoxiang wanjing tu," no. 2, *Su Shi shiji* 17.900.

92. For this and other paintings attributed to Su Shi, see James Cahill, *An Index to Early Chinese Paintings*, pp. 176–177.

93. "Guo Xiangzheng zhia zuihua zhushi bishang . . . ," *Su Shi shiji* 23.1234.

94. Mi Fu, *Huashi*, p. 21a. I have dropped the word *ying* ("hard") after "*cun* dots" because it does not make sense and ruins the parallelism with the preceding unit.

95. Kong Wuzhong, "Dongpo jushi hua guaishi fu," *Qingjiang san Kong ji* 3.7b–8a (Huang Mingfen, *Su Shi lun shuhua shiliao*, p. 203).

96. The themes examined in the following pages are also discussed by Huang Mingfen, *Lun Su Shi de wenyi xinli guan*, especially pp. 7–14, 39–47, and 221–237.

97. "Wen Yuke hua Yandang gu yanzhu ji," and "Huashui ji," *Wenji* 11.365–366 and 12.408–409.

98. "Jingyin yuan hua ji," *Wenji* 11.367.

99. See the statement attributed to Yan Zhitui by Zhang Yanyuan, *Lidai minghua ji* 1.9.

100. See Graham, *Two Chinese Philosophers*, pp. 8–22.

101. See Kusumoto Bun'yū's discussion of the Chan and Huayan origins of the Cheng brother's notion that *shi* and *li* are inseparable, pp. 224–226, 227–228, n. 3, and 367–368. Michael Fuller has also called attention to Buddhist influences upon Su's understanding of Pattern; see *The Road to East Slope*, pp. 89–91.

102. "Jingyin yuan huaji, *Wenji* 11.367.

103. "Wang Wei Wu Daozi hua," *Su Shi shiji* 3.109.

104. Ibid.

105. "Shu Chao Buzhi suocang Yuke huazhu," no. 1, *Su Shi shiji* 29.1522.

106. "Huashui ji," *Wenji* 12.408–409.

107. "Shu Li Boshi shanzhuang tu hou," *Wenji* 70.2211.

108. "Shu Wang Dingguo suocang Wang Jinqing hua zhuose shan," no. 1, *Su Shi shiji* 31.1639.

109. "Shu Huang Daofu pincha yaolu hou," *Wenji* 66.2067.

110. "Shu Mojian Lantian yanyu tu," *Wenji* 70.2209.

111. "Wang Wei Wu Daozi hua," *Su Shi shiji* 3.108–110.

112. "Ouyang Shaoshi lin fu suocang shiping," *Su Shi shiji* 6.277–278.

113. "Ciyun Wu Chuanzheng kumu ge," *Su Shi shiji* 36.1962.

114. "Shu Yanling Wang Zhubo suohua zhezhi," no. 1, *Su Shi shiji* 29.1525–1526. See Huang Mingfen's discussion of these terms in Su's painting criticism, *Lun Su Shi de wenyi xinli guan*, pp. 214–220.

115. Du Fu, "Chunri yi Li Bo," *Dushi xiangzhu* 1.52.

116. "Ba Pu Chuanzheng Yangong shanshui," *Wenji* 70.2212.

117. "Shu Wu Daozi hua hou," *Wenji* 70.2210.

118. "Shu Tangshi liujia shu hou," *Wenji* 69.2206.

119. Yan Youyi, *Yiyuan cihuang*, p. 193.

120. "Ti bizhen tu," *Wenji* 69.2170.

121. "Baohui tang ji," *Wenji* 11.356, beginning of second paragraph. My understanding of the crucial term *yi* ("to improve") assumes that Su is using it as it is used in *Mencius* 7A/36: "A man's surroundings may improve his air just as the food he eats nourishes his body."

122. "Wen Yuke hua mozhu pingfeng zan," *Wenji* 21.614.

123. "Ti bizhen tu," *Wenji* 69.2170.

124. Du Fu, "Yang Jian you chu huayan shier shan" and "Jiang Chugong hua jiayan ge," *Dushi xiangzhu* 15.1340–1342 and 11.924–925; cf. "Huayan," *Dushi xiangzhu* 1.19–20.

125. For Su's friendship with Wang Shen, see the study by Weng Tongwen, "Wang Shen shengping kaolüe," *Songshi yanjiu ji* 5:135–168.

126. A fuller list of these associates is provided by Gōyama Kiwamu, "So Shoku no bunjin katsudō to sono yōin," *Kyūshū Chūgoku gakkai hō* 15:73 (1968).

127. Qin Guan, "Wang Dingguo zhu Lunyu xu," *Huaihai ji* 39.7b–8a.

128. Fan Bailu, "Wen gong muzhiming," in Wen Tong, *Danyuan ji*, p. iib; cf. *Xu changbian* 213.5185; and Su Shi's "Song Wen Yuke chu shou Lingzhou," *Su Shi shiji* 6.251.

129. *Songshi* 444.13115.

130. "Jian bupi Chen Shidao zhuang" and "Bian ju Wang Gong chazi," *Wenji* 27.795. Cf. Su Che, "Ju Wang Gong qi wairen chazi," *Luancheng ji*, "houji," 16.1338–1340.

131. For Zhao Tingzhi, see Su's "Qijun chazi," *Wenji* 29.827–828. For Jia Yi, see Su's "Bian Jia Yi tanzou daizui chazi," *Wenji* 33.935–937.

132. See lines 5–6 of "Wang Wei Wu Daozi hua," *Su Shi shiji* 3.108.

133. "Shu Wang Dingguo suocang Wang Jinqing hua zhuose shan," no. 2, *Su Shi shiji* 31.1639.

134. "He Wang Jinqing ti Boshi huama," *Wenji* 30.1588–1589.

135. Huang Tingjian, "Ti Zizhan kumu," *Shan'gu shizhu* 9.172–173.

136. Chao Buzhi, "Ciyun Luzhi shiyuan zeng fengyi Li Boshi huama," *Jilei ji* 12.10b–11a.

137. Huang Tingjian, "Ti zhuzhi muniu," *Shan'gu shizhu* 9.174–175. For this interpretation, see Chen Yongzheng, *Huang Tingjian shixuan*, p. 171.

138. The general point I am making here about the connection between aesthetic expression and the politics of Su's group has been made by Gōyama Kiwamu, "So Shoku no bunjin katsodō to sono yōin," pp. 73–77.

139. Ye Mengde, *Shilin shihua* B.417.

140. "Yu Wang Dingguo," no. 13, *Wenji* 52.1520–1521.

141. *Xu changbian* 484.12a–b.
142. On his calligraphy, see the remark attributed to Su Shi in *Songshi* 344.10941. A balanced judgment of Li's poetry is contained in the *Siku quanshu zongmu tiyao* notice on his literary collection (*Guxi jushi quanji*), 4:3257.
143. "Ciyun Li Duansu xie song Niu Jian yuanyang zhushi tu," *Su Shi shiji* 37.2018–2019.
144. *Songshi* 344.10941.

CHAPTER TEN

Note: References to Su Shi's *ci* are given in the following form: tune title, piece number in Cao Shuming's edition (*Su Dongpo ci*), *juan* and page number in Long Muxun's edition (*Dongpo yuefu jian*), and page number in *Quan Songci*. I follow the text and the line breaks in Cao's edition, except where noted otherwise.

1. "Yu Ziming xiong," *Wenji* 60.1832.
2. See Chao Buzhi's and Li Qingzhao's comments as quoted in Hu Zi, *Tiaoxi yuyin conghua*, "houji," 33.253–254; see also Chen Shidao, *Houshan shihua*, p. 309. Cf. Ye Jiaying's discussion of the point, "Lun Su Shi ci," *Lingxi cishuo*, p. 221.
3. The anthology has been translated by Lois Fusek, *Among the Flowers*.
4. Yan Shu, "Ta suo xing," *Quan Songci* 1:99; trans. D. C. Lau, "Twenty Selected Lyrics," *Renditions* 11–12:8 (1979).
5. See Daniel Bryant, *Lyric Poets of the Southern Tang*, pp. xxiv–xxx.
6. "Xiao zhen xi," *Quan Songci* 1:43; trans. James R. Hightower, "The Songwriter Liu Yong: Part I," *Harvard Journal of Asiatic Studies* 41.2:350–351 (1981).
7. Ye Jiaying, "Lun Su Shi ci," pp. 196–197.
8. "Lang tao sha," *Quan Songci* 1:141.
9. Yuan Haowen, "Xinxuan yuefu yin," *Yishan xiansheng wenji* 35.19a–b. Yuan Haowen's comment is quoted and glossed in Huang Haipeng, "Zhi you minghua ku you du—Su ci de gexing hua xiaoyi," *Dongpo ci luncong*, p. 121.
10. Hu Yin, "Jiubian ci xu," *Jiubian ci*, p. i.
11. The evaluation was originally given by Su's associate, Chen Shidao, p. 309.
12. "Lin jiang xian," no. 133, 2.12a, 1:287.
13. "Jiang chengzi," no. 54, 1.32b–33a ("Jiang shenzi"), 1:300.
14. A fuller treatment of this subject, and its influence upon Su Shi's *ci* writing, may be found in my paper, "The Problem of the Repute of *Tz'u* During the Northern Sung," in *Voices in the Song Lyric in China*, ed. Pauline Yu, pp. 191–225.
15. Huang Tingjian, "Xiaoshan ji xu," *Yuzhang Huang xiansheng wenji* 16.24a–25a.
16. Stephen Owen, "Meaning the Words: The Genuine as a Value in the

Tradition of the Song Lyric," in *Voices in the Song Lyric in China*, ed. Pauline Yu, pp. 30–69 and Grace Fong, "Persona and Mask in the Song Lyric (*Ci*)," *Harvard Journal of Asiatic Studies* 50.2:459–484 (1990).

17. Wei Shenggao had a reputation for uprightness; but once when someone asked for some vinegar, Wei got some from his neighbor and then represented it as his own gift. See *Lunyu* 5/24. Chen Zhongzi ("Ling" must be a mistake for "Chen") was known for his scrupulousness, but he carried it to the point of neglecting his obligations to his family (e.g., refusing to live with his brother and mother, because he considered his brother's house ill-gotten). See *Mencius* 3B/10.

18. "Shu Li Jianfu shiji hou," *Wenji* 68.2148.

19. See "Lu Tao Yuanming shi," *Wenji* 67.2111; and the full quotation above, p. 47.

20. Tao Qian, "Yin jiu," no. 9, *Tao Yuanming ji jiaojian* 3.151.

21. "Shu Zhang changshi caoshu," *Wenji* 69.2178–2179.

22. In a note found in Zeng Zao's compilation of Su Shi's *ci* (1151, reproduced in *Quan Songci* 1:293), the source for this story is identified as Huihong's *Lengzhai yehua*; and Hu Zi's *Tiaoxi yuyin conghua*, "qianji," 57.393 cites the same source. In fact, the story is not contained in the extant version of Huihong's work (in *Yinli zaisi tang congshu*). An alternative tradition is reflected in an early note on a matching *ci* by Huang Tingjian, which holds that Su Shi wrote his song when visiting a Chan monk in Chuzhou. See *Quan Songci* 1:399.

23. "Nan gezi," no. 279, 3.31a, 1:293.

24. The criticism was first uttered by Chao Buzhi and was disputed immediately by Chen Shidao, but the controversy persisted through the centuries. See Wang Ruoxu, *Hunan shihua* B.70. For recent discussions of the issue, see Zhang Jie, "Dongpo ci mantan," in *Dongpo ci luncong*, ed. Su Shi yanjiu xuehui, pp. 231–237; and Ye Jiaying, pp. 205–208.

25. "Yu Xianyu Zijun," no. 2, *Wenji* 53.1560.

26. "Jiang chengzi," no. 56, 1.34a, ("Jiang shenzi") 1:299.

27. Zeng Zao, *Gaozhai shihua*, p. 137 (Long Muxun, *Huaihai jushi changduan ju*, p. 82).

28. Yan Youyi, *Yiyuan cihuang*, pp. 226–227 (Hu Zi, *Tiaoxi yuyin conghua*, "houji," 33.248).

29. Qin Guan, "Man ting fang," no. 1, *Quan Songci* 1:458.

30. Liu Yong, "Basheng Ganzhou," *Quan songci* 1:43.

31. Zhao Lingzhi, *Houzheng lu* 7.11a; cf. Wu Zeng, *Nenggai zhai manlu* 16.469, where the praise for Liu Yong is attributed to Chao Buzhi.

32. "Ti Zhang Ziye shiji hou," *Wenji* 68.2146.

33. "Shu Li zhu ci," *Wenji* 68.2151–2152. Li Yu's *ci* is "Pozhen zi," *Quan Tang Wudai ci* 1:231–232.

34. "Ba Qianan jushi 'Yufu ci,'" *Wenji* 68.2157. Huang's *ci* is "Wan xi sha," *Quan songci* 1:398–399.

35. "Jiang chengzi," no. 91, 1.55a, ("Jiang shenzi") 1:299.

36. Ye Jiaying, p. 206; cf. 199.

37. Huang Liaoyuan, *Liaoyuan cixuan* (quoted by Wang Shuizhao, *Su Shi xuanji*, pp. 272–273).

38. On Zhang Xian's contact with Su Shi, their *ci* writing together, and Su's many Hangzhou farewell *ci*, see Nishi Noriaki, "Tōba no shoki no sōbetsu-shi," *Chūgoku chūsei bungaku kenkyū* 7:64–73 (1968); trans. Sun Kangyi, "Su Shi chuqi de songbie ci," *Zhongwai wenxue* 7:64–77 (Oct. 1978).

39. Wang Shuizhao, "Lun Su Shi chuangzuo de fazhan jieduan," pp. 263–264. Long Muxun has much the same opinion, although he includes the three years before Huangzhou, starting with Su's appointment to Xuzhou, in this stage. See Long Muxun, "Dongpo yuefu zonglun," *Cixue jikan* 2.3:6–7 (1935) (Ogawa Tamaki, *Kaze to kumo*, p. 114).

40. "Yu Teng Dadao," no. 15, "Da Qin Taixu," no. 4, "Yu Shen Ruida," no. 2, and "Yu Cheng Yizhong," no. 6, *Wenji* 51.1480, 52.1536, 58.1745, and 58.1752.

41. The numbers of Su Shi's *shi* poems that survive from his four years in Huangzhou are, by year, 57, 47, 39, and 34. In the two years before his exile he produced 114 and 82 poems, respectively (the latter number must have been affected by his incarceration during the final months of 1079), and in the year after he was allowed to leave Huangzhou he wrote 111. While his *shi* output in Huangzhou was in decline, his activity as a *ci* writer increased. The quantity of Su's datable *ci* from the four years at Huangzhou is 61, while it is only 42 for the preceding four years. (The *shi* figures are taken from Kong Fanli's edition of Su's complete *shi*, while the *ci* figures come from Cao Shuming's edition of his song lyrics, *Su Dongpo ci*.) The huge discrepancy in Su's lifetime totals for the two genres must be borne in mind to understand the significance of these figures: in all, Su left over 2,400 *shi* but only just over 300 *ci*.

42. "Yu Chen Dafu," no. 3, *Wenji* 56.1698.

43. "Yu Chen Jichang," no. 9, *Wenji* 53.1567.

44. "Jianzi mulan hua," no. 92, 1.55b, 1:312.

45. "Xijiang yue," no. 93, 1.56a, 1:285.

46. "Dao Zhaoyun," *Su Shi shiji* 40.2202–2203.

47. Tongwu was Yang Xiong's precocious son, who discussed the Great Mystery with his father at age nine. See Yang Xiong, *Fayan* 4.14.

48. The *shi* poems Su wrote upon the death of Dun lend further support to the argument made in these pages about the recourse to philosophy Su tends to take in that genre; see *Su Shi shiji* 23.1239–1240.

49. Zeng Zaozhuang has a different interpretation of the line, suggesting that Su means to imply that his own death, when he will join Zhaoyun "reclining on bamboo roots," does not lie far off. See his "Dongpo cizhong de Zhaoyun," in *Dongpo ci luncong*, ed. Su Shi yanjiu xuehui, pp. 225.

50. Huihong, *Lengzhai yehua* 1.2b–3a; Chen Gu, *Xitang ji qijiu xuwen* 2.1a–b (quoting Su's friend, Chao Yuezhi); and Yuan Wen, *Wengyou*

xianping 5.10a–b (all quoted by Wang Shuizhao, *Su Shi xuanji*, p. 325). See also Zeng Zaozhuang's discussion of this *ci*, "Dongpo cizhong de Zhaoyun," pp. 224–225.

51. "Xijiang yue," no. 246, 2.69a, 1:284.

52. A fuller discussion of the prosodic features of each form, and their consequences, may be found in Shuen-fu Lin, *The Transformation of the Chinese Lyrical Traditon*, pp. 98–141.

53. "Wan xi sha," nos. 80 and 82, 1.50a and 1.51a, 1:316.

54. "Jiang chengzi," no. 56, 1.34a, ("Jiang shenzi") 1:299.

55. For which, see Dieter Kuhn, *Reeling and Spinning*, vol. 5, pt. 9 of *Science and Civilisation in China*, gen. ed. Needham pp. 354–364.

56. "Ding fengbo," no. 149, 2.23a–b, 1:290.

57. "Xijiang yue," no. 123, 2.4a–b, 1:284–285.

58. "Ding fengbo," no. 121, 2.2b–3a, 1:288.

59. "Ji you Songfeng ting," *Wenji* 71.2271.

60. Wu Shiduan, "Dongpo zai Huizhou zheju shenghuo tan," pp. 231–233.

61. The first couplet comes from the fourth of the East Slope poems, translated earlier. The second comes from "Ciyun Kong Yifu jiu han yi er shen yu," no. 2, *Su Shi shiji* 21.1123.

62. Ye Jiaying, p. 211.

63. "Zhegu tian," no. 150, 2.24a, 1:288.

64. "Busuan zi" no. 142, 2.17b, 1:295.

65. This is the way the *ci* has been read by Huang Liaoyuan and Wang Shuizhao; see Wang, *Su Shi xuanji*, p. 278. See the immediately preceding pages of Wang's compilation for summaries of other less plausible interpretations of the song, including those that explain the bird as a metaphor for one or another woman who had resisted Su's offer of marriage (for himself or a son) and later died.

66. Huang Tingjian, "Ba Dongpo yuefu," *Yuzhang Huang xiansheng wenji* 26.7a.

67. "Die luanhua," no. 285, 3.36a, 1:300.

68. Yi Shizhen, *Langhuan ji* B.6a–b, quoting a work not preserved except in fragments, *Linxia citan* (Wang Shuizhao, *Su Shi xuanji*; p. 323).

69. Trans. Hightower, "Liu Yung: Part I," pp. 363–364; translating *Quan Songci* 1:29.

70. "Yong yu le," no. 86, 1.52b, 1:302.

71. "Intermingled" comes from James J. Y. Liu's discussion of this poem; see his *Major Lyricists of the Northern Sung A.D. 960–1226*, p. 71.

72. "Shuilong yin," *Quan Songci* 1:455. Reading the textual variant *yuan* ("garden") for *yuan* ("distant") as in the *Gaozhai shihua* quotation, see below.

73. Zeng Zao, *Gaozhai shihua*, p. 137 (Wang Shuizhao, p. 270).

74. "Suzhou Lüqiu Jiangjun er jia yuzhong yinjiu ershou," *Su Shi shiji* 11.561–563.

75. "Shuilong yin," no. 117, 2.1a, 1:278.

76. On Su's use of the Fan Li story, see Wang Shuizhao, *Su Shi xuanji*, p. 64.
77. "Nian nu jiao," no. 130, 2.9b, 1:282.
78. "Dongxian ge," no. 129, 2.8a–b, 1:297. A very similar *ci* is now attributed to Meng Chang and found in his collection (see *Quan Tang Wudai ci* 5.96). That *ci* differs mostly just in prosody from the one Su wrote (it is set to a different tune pattern). It must, as Wang Shuizhao argues, be the result of later tampering. Based upon Su's preface, someone reworked Su's piece and inserted it back into Meng's collection. See Wang Shuizhao, *Su Shi xuanji*, pp. 287–291.
79. "Shuidiao getou," no. 65, 1.40b, 1:280.
80. For the first, see Hu Yunyi, p. 64. For the second, see Miao Yue, "Lun Su Xin ci yu Zhuang Sao," *Lingxi cishuo*, p. 235, appended note; and Wu Xiaoru in Wang Siyu, ed., *Su Shi ci shangxi ji*, pp. 105–106. For the third, see James J. Y. Liu, *Major Lyricists*, p. 128.
81. "Nian nu jiao," no. 130, 2.9b, 1:282. For the text end parsing, see the translation of the entire song in chapter 8.
82. Kang-i Sun Chang, *The Evolution of Chinese Tz'u Poetry*, pp. 169–184, see esp. p. 175.
83. Ye Jiaying, p. 213.
84. Wang Guowei, *Renjian cihua*, p. 19 (para. no. 38).
85. See, for example, Huang Liaoyuan's comments in *Liaoyuan cihua*, quoted by Wang Shuizhao, *Su Si xuanzhu*, p. 312.
86. "Shuilong yin," no. 188, 2.41a, 1:277.
87. Bo Juyi, "Hua fei hua," *Quan Tangshi* 425.12.4822 (Long Muxun).
88. Han Yu, "You chengnan," no. 3, *Quan Tangshi* 343.3850 (Hu Yunyi, *Songci xuan*, p. 85).
89. Jin Changxu, "Chun yuan," *Quan Tangshi* 768.8724 (Long Muxun).
90. Zhang Yan, *Ciyuan* B.3b (Wang Shuizhao, *Su Shi xuanji*, p. 311).
91. "Zi ping wen," *Wenji* 66.2069.
92. See Liu Zhengcheng, ed., *Su Shi* 1, vol. 33 of *Zhongguo shufa quanji*, Liu Zhengcheng, gen. ed., pl. 48. The poem is Su's "Dinghui yuan yueye ouchu," *Su Shi shiji* 20.1032–1033.

CHAPTER ELEVEN

1. Huang Tingjian, "Zhuihe Dongpo huzhong jiuhua," *Shan'gu shizhu*, "neiji," 17.307–308.
2. *Shiji* 81.2439–2441.
3. Li Gongzuo, "Chunyu Fen" (or "Nanke taishou zhuan"), *Taiping guangji*, comp. Li Fang, 475.3910–3915.
4. *Zhuangzi* 16/6/25; trans. Graham, *Chuang-tzu*, p. 86.
5. I am following the interpretation of this couplet given by Chen Yongzheng, p. 255.
6. "Shizhong shan ji," *Wenji* 11.370–371.

7. But compare the later tradition, which developed as an alternative to Su's, that the mountain's name derived from the shape of its towering caverns, which looked like the inside of a bell and could be entered and explored when the water level of the lake fell. See the passages quoted by Wang Shuizhao, *Su Shi xuanji*, pp. 400–401. Su added a colophon to his inscription, affirming his explanation of the name, the year before he died; see "Pa Shizhong shan ji," *Wenji* 66.2074.

8. Huang Tingjian, "Bingqi Jingjiang ting jishi," no. 7, *Shan'gu shizhu*, "neiji," 14.265–266.

9. Huang Tingjian, "Ba Zizhan he Tao shi," *Shan'gu shizhu*, "neiji," 17.312.

10. Canliao, "Dongpo xiansheng wanci," *Canliaozi ji* 11.6a–8a.

11. See Lu You, "Ba Dongpo ji Chen Ling juwen," "Ba Dongpo tie," "Ba Dongpo jianshe cao," *Weinan wenji* 28.2251, 29.2261 and 29.2262.

12. On the subject of Zhu Xi's opinions of Su Shi, see Gōyama Kiwamu, "Shi Ki no So-gaku hihan josetsu," *Chūgoku bungaku ronshū* 3:29–36 (1972); and Peter K. Bol, "Chu Hsi's Redefinition of Literati Learning," *Neo-Confucian Education*, ed. Wm. Theodore de Bary and John W. Chaffee, pp. 151–185.

13. Zhu Xi, *Zhuzi yulei* 130.3110, par. 1.

14. *Xin Tangshu* 11.307.

15. Zhu Xi, *Zhuzi yulei* 139.3319, par. 2.

16. Zhu Xi, "Da Lü Bogong," *Zhu Wengong wenji* 33.516.

17. Zhu Xi, *Zhuzi yulei* 130.3111, par. 1, and 3112, pars. 1–2; and "Da Cheng Yunfu," *Zhu Wengong wenji* 41.11a–b.

18. In addition to the *yulei* passages cited above, see Zhu Xi, *Zhuzi yulei* 130.3109, par. 2, and 3116, par. 4.

19. Zhu Xi, "Sushi Yijie," in "Zaxue bian," *Zhu Wengong wenji* 72.17b–25b.

20. Zhu Xi, *Zhuzi yulei* 130.3113, par. 8.

21. Ibid., 140.3336, par. 12.

22. Ellen Johnston Laing, "Real or Ideal: The Problem of the 'Elegant Gathering in the Western Garden' in Chinese Historical and Art Historical Records," *Journal of the American Oriental Society* 88:419–435 (1968).

23. The painting is reproduced in vol. 4 of *Gugong shuhua tulu*, p. 67; in Maggie Keswick, *The Chinese Garden*, pl. 94 (p. 103), and in Gimello, fig. 1. Gimello (pp. 384–409) discusses the painting and its depiction of the monk Faxiu as a visual allegory of the place of Ch'an Buddhism in eleventh-century literati life.

24. Mi Fu, *Baojin yingguang ji*, "buyi," p. 76. In my description of the painting I am following this well-known account, which is, however, of dubious origin and not referred to before the late sixteenth century; see below.

25. Wang Shizhen, "Ming Qiu Ying lin Xiyuan yaji tu," in Su Yueban, comp., *Peiwen zhai shuhua pu* 87.38a–b (Laing, p. 428).

26. See Laing, p. 429, on the unreliability of the account attributed to Mi Fu (cited above), the only reputedly contemporary record.
27. This is Ellen Johnston Laing's conclusion.
28. Qin Guan, "Ta Fu Binlao jian," *Huaihai ji* 30.1b.
29. *Zuozhuan* 307/Xiang 25/fu 2/line 12.
30. *Lunyu* 15/41.
31. "Yu Xie Minshi tuiguan shu," *Wenji* 49.1418.
32. "Da Zhang Wenqian xiancheng shu," *Wenji* 49.1427.
33. Li Zhi, *Shiyou tanji* 20.
34. See Yoshkawa Kōjirō, *Five Hundred Years of Chinese Poetry, 1150–1650*, trans. John Timothy Wixted, pp. 84–89.
35. "Yu Wang Xiang shu," *Wenji* 49.1422.
36. "Fuyi xiansheng shiji xu," *Wenji* 10.313.
37. "Wen Yuke hua mozhu pingfeng zan," *Wenji* 21.614.
38. "Ti Ouyang tie," *Wenji* 69.2197–2198.
39. Xue Ruisheng, "Sumen Suxue yu Suti: Jianlun Beisong de dangzheng yu wenxue," *Wenxue yichan* 1988.5:60–68 (esp. pp. 60–62 and 63–64).
40. "Nanxing qianji xu," *Wenji* 10.323.
41. "Xie Ouyang neihan shu," *Wenji* 49.1423.
42. "Ziping wen," *Wenji* 66:2069.
43. "Shao Moucheng shiji xu," *Wenji* 10.320.
44. "Da Huang Luzhi shu," and "Da Mao Zemin," no. 1, *Wenji* 52.1531–1532 and 53.1571.
45. See two of Su's descriptions of Ouyang Xiu and his achievement, "Xie Ouyang neihan wen" and "Liuyi jushi ji xu," *Wenji* 49.1423 and 10.315–316.
46. "Da Zhang Wenqian xiancheng shu," *Wenji* 49.1427.
47. "Yu Wang Xiang shu," *Wenji* 49.1422.
48. "Shu 'Zhuansui' hou," *Wenji* 69.2205. Cf. Qian Zhongshu, *Guanzhui bian* 1:169–172.
49. Actually, in Su's own writings no such language is used, except for a remark addressed to Cai Xiang about leadership in the field of calligraphy, where the tone is mock-heroic; see "Ji yu Junmo lunshu," *Wenji* 69.2193. The second part of this colophon is translated below.
50. See the iterations of this point in Wu Zeng, *Nenggai zhai manlu* 11.313.
51. See Zhang Yan's preface to Qin's collection (1539), *Huaihai ji*, p. 1b.
52. "Yu Ouyang Yuanlao," *Wenji* 58.1756.
53. Su is referring to the collection of Lu Zhi's memorials traditionally known as *Lu Xuangong Hanyuan ji* or *Lu Xuangong zouyi*. The memorial Su wrote to accompany the edited copy of the work he presented to the throne is "Qi jianzheng Lu Zhi zouyi shangjin chazi," *Wenji* 36.1012–1013.
54. Lu Zhi's memorials exist today in several recensions, and it is unlikely that any of them are the same as the collection Su possessed. It is not

clear which essays Su is referring to here, since in its present form the collection does not include essays on historical topics.

55. "Da Qian cui Yu Kuo," *Wenji* 59.1793.

56. "Yu Cheng Zhengfu," no. 54, *Wenji* 54.1614.

57. "Da Li Duanshu shu," *Wenji* 49.1432–1433.

58. "Ji Ouyang lun Tuizhi wen," *Wenji* 66.2055.

59. "Ba Wen Yuke mozhu," *Wenji* 70.2209–2210.

60. "Ti Zhang Ziye shiji hou," *Wenji* 68.2146.

61. Said specifically of calligraphy; see "Ti bizhen tu," *Wenji* 69.2170. Cf. "Ba Wen Yuke mozhu," *Wenji* 70.2209, where Su approvingly quotes Wen Tong saying much the same about painting.

62. Mao Jin, *Dongpo biji* (Zeng Zaozhuang, "Dongpo cizhong de Zhao-yun," pp. 215–216). Mao Jin's compilation, which is not his *Dongpo tiba*, is unavailable and otherwise unknown to me.

63. "Da Li Zhaoji shu," *Wenji* 49.1439.

64. He Yuan, *Chunzhu jiwen* 6.84.

65. See the preface to Mi Fu's *Huashi*, pp. 1a–2a, for his astonishingly bold assertion of the importance of artistic work, and Su's poems "Ciyun Mi Fu er Wang shu bawei," nos. 1–2, *Su Shi shiji* 29.1536–1538 for Su's criticisms of what he considered Mi Fu's overzealousness. My understanding of Mi Fu's position on these issues derives in large part from Peter Sturman's analysis in "Mi Youren and the Inherited Literati Tradition: Dimensions of Ink-Play," Ph.D. diss.; see esp. pp. 29–47 (the preface to Mi Fu's *Huashi* is translated on p. 44).

66. "Da Su Bogu," no. 3, *Wenji* 57.1741; and see also the passage summarized on pp. 68–69 above.

67. "Ji yu Junmo lunshu," *Wenji* 69.2191.

68. "Yu Cheng Zhengfu," no. 59, *Wenji* 54.1616.

69. "Ba Junmo feibai," *Wenji* 69.2181.

List of Works Cited

Note: Dates are given for premodern authors.

Abe Chōichi 阿部肇一. *Chūogoku zenshūshi no kenkyū* 中國禪教史の研究. Tokyo: Seishin Shobō, 1963.

Anthology of Chinese Literature: From Early Times to the Fourteenth Century, edited by Cyril Birch. New York: Grove Press, 1965.

Aoki Masaru 青木正兒. *Chūka chasho* 中華茶屋. Tokyo: Shunshūsha, 1962.

———. "Shō no rekishi to jigi no hensen" "嘯"の歷史と字義の變遷. In *Aoki Masaru zenshū* 青木正兒全集, 8:161–168. Tokyo: Shunjūsha, 1971.

Aoyama hakushi koki kinen: Sōdaishi ronsō 青山博士古稀紀念宋代史論叢, edited by Aoyama hakushi koki kinen kankokai. Tokyo: Seishin shobō, 1974.

Arai Ken 荒井健. "So Tōba ron" 蘇東坡論. In *Chūgoku bungaku ronshū* 中國文學論集, edited by Yoshikawa Kōjirō 吉川幸次郎, 217–248. Tokyo: Shinchōsha, 1966.

Baibu congshu jicheng 百部叢書集成. Taipei: Yiwen yinshuguan, 1965–1969.

Bol, Peter K. "Chu Hsi's Redefinition of Literati Learning." In *Neo-Confucian Education: The Formative Stage*, edited by Wm. Theodore de Bary and John W. Chaffee, 151–185. Berkeley: University of California Press, 1989.

———. *"This Culture of Ours": Intellectual Transitions in T'ang and Sung China*. Stanford: Stanford University Press, 1992.

———. "Rulership and Sagehood, Bureaucracy and Society: An Historical Inquiry into the Political Visions of Ssu-ma Kuang (1019–1086) and Wang An-shih (1021–1086)." In *Jinian Sima Guang Wang Anshi shishi jiubai zhounian xueshu yantao hui lunwen ji* (q.v.), 5–107.

————. "Su Shih and Culture." In *Sung Dynasty Uses of the I ching*, by Kidder Smith, Jr., Peter K. Bol, Joseph A. Adler, and Don J. Wyatt, 56–99. Princeton: Princeton University Press, 1990.

Bryant, Daniel. *Lyric Poets of the Southern Tang: Feng Yen-ssu, 903–960, and Li Yü, 937–978*. Vancouver: University of British Columbia Press, 1982.

Bush, Susan. *The Chinese Literati on Painting: Su Shih (1037–1101) to Tung Ch'i-ch'ang (1555–1636)*. Harvard-Yenching Institute Studies, no. 27. Cambridge: Harvard University Press, 1971.

———— and Hsio-yen Shi. *Early Chinese Texts on Painting*. Cambridge, Harvard University Press for the Harvard-Yenching Institute, 1985.

Buswell, Robert E., Jr. "The 'Short-cut' Approach of *K'an-hua* Meditation: The Evolution of a Practical Subitism in Chinese Ch'an Buddhism." In *Sudden and Gradual: Approaches to Enlightenment in Chinese Thought*, edited by Peter N. Gregory, 321–380. Kuroda Institute Studies in East Asian Buddhism, no. 5. Honolulu: University of Hawaii Press, 1987.

Cahill, James. *An Index to Early Chinese Paintings*. Berkeley: University of California Press, 1980.

Cai Shangxiang 蔡上翔 (fl. 1804). *Wang Jinggong nianpu kaolue* 王荆公年譜考略. Shanghai: Renmin chubanshe, 1959.

Cai Xiang 蔡襄 (1012–1067). *Chalu* 茶録. In *Congshu jicheng* (q.v.).

————. *Duanming ji* 端明集. In *Siku quanshu* (q.v.)

Canliao 參寥 (Daoqian 道潛; 1043–ca. 1116). *Canliaozi ji* 參寥子集. In *Siku quanshu* (q.v.).

Cao Shuming 曹樹名. "Su Dongpo yu dao fo zhi guanxi" 蘇東坡與道佛之關係. *Guoli zhongyang tushuguan guankan* 國立中央圖書館館刊 3.2:7–21 (1970) and 3.3–4:34–55 (1970).

Chaffee, John W. *The Thorny Gates of Sung Learning: A Social History of Examinations*. Cambridge: Cambridge University Press, 1985.

Chang, Kang-i Sun. *The Evolution of Chinese Tz'u Poetry: From Late Tang to Northern Sung*. Princeton: Princeton University Press, 1980.

Chao Buzhi 晁補之 (1053–1110). *Jilei ji* 雞肋集. In *Sibu congkan* (q.v.).

Chao Gongwu 晁公武 (d. 1171). *Qunzhai dushu zhi* 郡齋讀書志. In *Guoxue jiben congshu* (q.v.).

Cheang, Alice Wen-chuen. "Poetry, Politics, and Philosophy: Su Shih as the Man of Eastern Slope." *Harvard Journal of Asiatic Studies* 53.2:325–387 (1993).

————. "The Way and the Self in the Poetry of Su Shih." Ph.D. diss., Harvard University, 1991.

Chen Gu 陳鵠 (early 13th c.). *Xitang ji qijiu xuwen* 西唐集耆舊續聞. *Zhibuzu zhai congshu* (q.v.).

Chen Huachang 陳華昌. "Xinling wei Tao Yuanming suo xiyin—lun Su Shi wannian de sixiang bianhua" 心靈為陶淵明所吸引:論蘇軾晚年的思想變化. In *Lun Su Shi Lingnan shi ji qita* (q.v.), 216–222.

Chen Shan 陳善 (d. ca. 1160). *Menshi xinhua* 押蝨新話. In *Ruxue jingwu congshu* 儒學警悟叢書, in *Baibu congshu jicheng* (q.v.).

Chen Shidao 陳師道 (1053–1101). *Houshan shihua* 後山詩話. In *Lidai shihua* (q.v.) 1:302–315.

Chen Yingji 陳英姬 (Chin Yong-hui). "Su Dongpo de zhengzhi shengya yu wenxue de guanxi" 蘇東坡的政治生涯與文學的關係. Ph.D. diss., Guoli Taiwan shifan daxue (National Taiwan Normal University, Taipei), 1989.

Chen Yongzheng 陳永正. *Huang Tingjian shixuan* 黃庭堅詩選. Hong Kong: Sanlian shudian, 1980.

Chen, Yu-shih. *Images and Ideas in Chinese Classical Prose: Studies of Four Masters.* Stanford: Stanford University Press, 1988.

Cheng Minsheng 程民生. "Lun Bei Song caizheng de tedian yu chengpin de jiaxiang" 論北宋財政的特點與積貧的假象. *Zhongguo shi yanjiu* 1984.3:27–40.

Cheng Yi 程頤 (1033–1107). *Henan Chengshi cuiyan* 河南程氏粹言. In Cheng Yi and Cheng Hao (q.v.), 4:1167–1272.

———. *Henan Chengshi waishu* 河南程氏外書. In Cheng Yi and Cheng Hao (q.v.), 2:351–446.

———. *Henan Chengshi wenji* 河南程氏文集. In Cheng Yi and Cheng Hao (q.v.), 2:447–688.

———. *Henan Chengshi yishu* 河南程氏遺書. In Cheng Yi and Cheng Hao (q.v.), 1:1–349.

———. *Zhouyi Chengshi zhuan* 周易程氏傳. In Cheng Yi and Cheng Hao (q.v.), 3:687–1026.

——— and Cheng Hao 程顥 (1032–1085). *Er Cheng ji* 二程集, edited by Wang Xiaoyu 王孝魚, 4 vols. Beijing: Zhonghua shuju, 1981.

Chikusa Masaaki 竺沙雅章. *Chūgoku bukkyō shakaishi kenkyū* 中國佛教社會史. Kyoto: Doshosha, 1982.

———. "Fukken no ji-in to shakai" 福建の寺院と社會. In his *Chūgoku bukkyō shakaishi kenkyū* (q.v.), 145–198.

———. "Hoku Sō shitaifu no shikyo to baiden—omo ni Tōba sekitoku o shiryō to site" 北宋士大夫の徙居と買田—主に東坡尺牘を資料として. *Shilin* 54.2:28–52 (1971).

———. "So Shoku to bukkyō" 蘇軾と佛教. *Tōhō gakuhō* 36:457–480 (1964).

———. "Sōdai bai chōkō" 宋代賣牒考. In his *Chūgoku bukkyō shakaishi kenkyū*, 17–82.

Clark, Cyril Drummond Le Gros. *The Prose-Poetry of Su Tung-p'o.* 2nd ed. New York: Paragon Books, 1964.

Cleary, Thomas, trans. *The Flower Ornament Sutra: A Translation of the Avataṁsaka Sutra*, vol. 1. Boulder: Shambhala, 1984.

Congshu jicheng 叢書集成. Shanghai: Commercial Press, 1935.

Dalby, Michael T. "Court politics in late T'ang times," in *The Cambridge History of China*, vol. 3: *Sui and T'ang China, 589–906, Part I*, edited by Denis Twitchett. Cambridge: Cambridge University Press, 1979.

Daudin, Pierre. "Les récréations intellectuelles de Sou Tong-p'o et Tchou Hi." *Bulletin de la Société des Etudes Indochinoises* 45.4:1–38 (1970).

Davis, A. R. "Su Shih's 'Following the Rhymes of T'ao Yuan-ming's Poems: A Literary or a Psychological Phenomenon?" *Journal of the Oriental Society of Australia* 10:93–108 (1974).

Deng Guangming 鄧廣銘. *Wang Anshi: Zhongguo shiyi shiji shi de gaigejia* 王安石:中國十一世紀時的改革家. Beijing: Renmin chubanshe, 1981.

Dong Qichang 董其昌 (1555–1636). *Huachan shi suibi* 畫禪室隨筆. In *Siku quanshu* (q.v.).

Dong Wei 董煟 (*jinshi* 1194). *Jiuhuang huomin shu* 救荒活民書. In *Congshu jicheng* (q.v.).

Dongpo ci luncong 東坡詞論叢, edited by Su Shi yanjiu xuehui 蘇軾研究學會. Chengdu: Sichuan renmin chubanshe, 1982.

Dongpo shi luncong 東坡詩論叢, edited by Su Shi yanjiu xuehui. Chengdu: Sichuan renmin chubanshe, 1983.

Dongpo yanjiu luncong 東坡研究論叢, edited by Su Shi yanjiu xuehui. Chengdu: Sichuan wenyi chubanshe, 1986.

Du Fu 杜甫 (712–770). *Dushi xiangzhu* 杜詩詳註, edited by Qiu Zhaoao 仇兆鰲 (1638–1717). Beijing: Zhonghua shuju, 1979.

Egan, Ronald C. *The Literary Works of Ou-yang Hsiu (1007–72)*. Cambridge: Cambridge University Press, 1984.

———. "Ou-yang Hsiu and Su Shih on Calligraphy." *Harvard Journal of Asiatic Studies* 49.2:365–419 (1989).

———. "Poems on Paintings: Su Shih and Huang T'ing-chien." *Harvard Journal of Asiatic Studies* 43.2:413–451 (1983)

———. "The Problem of the Repute of *Tz'u* during the Northern Sung." In *Voices in the Song Lyric in China*, edited by Pauline Yu, 191–225. Berkeley: University of California Press, 1994.

———. "Su Shih's 'Notes' as a Historical and Literary Source." *Harvard Journal of Asiatic Studies* 50.2:561–588 (1990).

Fan Bailu 范百祿 (1030–1094). "Wen gong muzhiming" 文公墓誌銘. Contained in the Prefatory material to Wen Tong, *Danyuan ji* (q.v.).

Fan Ning 范寧. "Cong Bei Song houqi wentan kan wenxue chuangzuo he zhengzhi douzheng de guanxi" 從北宋後期文壇看文學創作和政治鬥爭的關係. *Dongbei shida xuebao* 1982.1:1–12.

Fan Zuyu 范祖禹 (1041–1098). *Fan Taishi ji* 范太史集. In *Siku quanshu* (q.v.).

Fang Hui 方回 (1227–1307). *Yingkui lüsui* 瀛奎律髓. In *Siku quanshu* (q.v.).

Fang Shao 方勺 (b. 1066). *Bozhai bian* 泊宅編, 3 *juan* recension. Beijing: Zhonghua shuju, 1983.

Fei Gun 費袞 (fl. c. 1192). *Liangxi manzhi* 梁溪漫志. In *Zhibuzu zhai congshu* (q.v.).

Feng Yingliu 馮應榴 (1740–1800), comm. *Su Wenzhonggong shi hezhu* 蘇文忠公詩合註. 1793. Endnote references are to Feng's commentary as quoted in Wang Wen'gao's commentary in *Su Shi shiji*.

Fong, Grace. "Persona and Mask in the Song Lyric (*Ci*)." *Harvard Journal of Asiatic Studies* 50.2:459–484 (1990).

Fu, Shen C. Y. "Huang T'ing-chien's Calligraphy and His *Scroll for Chang Ta-t'ung*." Ph.D. diss., Princeton University, 1976.

Fuller, Michael A. *The Road to East Slope: The Development of Su Shi's Poetic Voice*. Stanford: Stanford University Press, 1990.

Fumoto Yasutaka 麓保孝. *Hakusō ni okeru jugaku no tenkai* 北宋に於ける儒學の展開. Tokyo: Shoseki bumbutsu ryūtsūkai, 1967.

Fusek, Lois. *Among the Flowers: The* Hua-chien chi. New York: Columbia University Press, 1982.

Gimello, Robert M. "Mārga and Culture: Learning, Letters, and Liberation in Northern Sung Ch'an." In *Paths to Liberation: The Mārga and Its Transformations in Buddhist Thought*, edited by Robert E. Buswell, Jr., and Robert M. Gimello, 371–437. A Kuroda Institute Book. Honolulu: University of Hawaii Press, 1992.

Ginsberg, Stanley Mervyn. "Alienation and Reconciliation of a Chinese Poet: The Huangzhou Exile of Su Shi." Ph.D. diss., University of Wisconsin, 1974.

Gong Yanming 龔延明. "Lüe lun Su Shi fandui Wang Anshi bianfa de xingzhi" 略論蘇軾反對王安石變法的性質. *Su Shi yanjiu zhuanji* (q.v.), 83–92.

Gōyama Kiwamu 合山究. "Shi Ki no So-gaku hihan josetsu" 朱熹の蘇學批判序說. *Chūogoku bungaku ronshū* 3:29–36 (Kyūshū daigaku, 1972).

———. "So Shoku no bunjin katsudō to sono yōin" 蘇軾の文人活動とその要因. *Kyūshū Chūgoku gakkai hō* 15:63–77 (1968).

———. "So Tōba no shizenkan" 蘇東坡の自然觀. In *Chūgoku bungaku ronshū: Mekada Makoto hakushi koki kinen* 中國文學論集：目加田誠博士古稀紀念, edited by Mekada Makoto hakushi koki kinen Chūgoku bungaku ronshū henshū i-inkai, 363–386. Tokyo: Ryūkei Shosha, 1974.

Graham, A. C. *The Book of Lieh-tzu*. London: John Murry, 1973.

———. *Chuang-tzu: The Seven Inner Chapters and other writings from the book Chuang-tzu*. London: Allen and Unwin, 1981.

———. *Two Chinese Philosophers: Ch'eng Ming-tao and Ch'eng Yi-ch'uan*. London: Lund Humphries, 1958.

Grant, Beata. *Mount Lu Revisited: Buddhism in the Life and Writings of Su Shih*. Honolulu: University of Hawaii Press, forthcoming.

Gugong shuhua tulu 故宮書畫圖録, vol. 4. Taipei: Guoli gugong bowuguan, 1990.

Guo Shaoyu 郭紹虞, comp. *Song shihua jiyi* 宋詩話輯佚. 2 vols. *Yenjing xuebao, zhuanhao* nos. 13–14. Beijing: Harvard-Yenching Institute, 1937.

Guoxue jiben congshu 國學基本叢書. Taipei: Commercial Press, 1968.

Guoyu 國語. Shanghai: Shanghai guji chubanshe, 1978.

Han Yu 韓愈 (788–824). *Han Changli ji* 韓昌黎集. In *Guoxue jiben congshu* (q.v.).

———. *Hong Changli shi xinian jishi* 韓昌黎詩繫年集釋, edited by Qian Zhonglian 錢仲聯. Shanghai: Shanghai guji chubanshe, 1984.

Hanshu 漢書. Beijing: Zhonghua shuju, 1962.

Hartman, Charles. *Han Yü and the Search for T'ang Unity*. Princeton: Princeton University Press, 1986.

————. "Poetry and Politics in 1079: The Crow Terrace Poetry Case of Su Shih." *Chinese Literature: Essays, Articles, Reviews* 12:15–44 (1990).

Hatch, George C., Jr. "Su Shih." In *Sung Biographies* (q.v.), 900–968.

————. Notices on *Sushi yizhuan, Dongpo shuzhuan, Dongpo tiba, Dongpo zhilin, Chouchi biji, Dongpo qiji*, and *Dongpo yuefu*. In *A Sung Bibliography* (q.v.), 4–9, 13–19, 264–268, 280–288, 330–332, 396–398, and 459–461.

Hattori Eijun 服部英淳. *Jōdokyō shisō ron* 淨土教思想論. Tokyo: Sankibō bushhorin, 1974.

He Guoquan 何國銓. *Zhongguo chanxue sixiang yanjiu* 中國禪學思想研究. Taipei: Wenjin chubanshe, 1987.

He Yuan 何薳 (1077–1145). *Chunzhu jiwen* 春渚紀聞. Beijing: Zhonghua shuju, 1983.

Hightower, James R. *The Poetry of T'ao Ch'ien*. Oxford: Clarendon Press, 1970.

————. "The Songwriter Liu Yong: Part I." *Harvard Journal of Asiatic Studies* 41.2:323–376 (1981).

Hong Bozhao 洪柏昭. "Shi lun Su shi de yilunhua he sanwenhua" 試論蘇詩的議論化和散文化. *Dongpo yanjiu luncong* (q.v.), 32–50.

Hong Mai 洪邁 (1123–1202). *Rongzhai suibi* 容齋隨筆. Shanghai: Shanghai guji chubanshe, 1978.

Hou Hanshu 後漢書, by Fan Ye 范曄 (398–446). Beijing: Zhonghua shuju, 1965.

Hou Wailu 侯外廬. *Zhongguo sixiang tongshi* 中國思想通史, vol. 4, part 1. Beijing: Renmin chubanshe, 1959.

Hu Yin 胡寅 (1098–1156). "Jiubian ci xu" 酒邊詞序. In *Jiubian ci*, by Xiang Ziyin 向子諲, i. In *Song liushi mingjia ci* 宋六十名家詞, edited by Mao Jin 毛晉 (1598–1659). In *Guoxue jiben congshu* (q.v.).

Hu Yunyi 胡雲翼. *Songci xuan* 宋詞選. Hong Kong: Zhonghua shuju, 1986.

Hu Zi 胡仔 (1082–1143). *Tiaoxi yuyin conghua* 苕溪漁隱叢話. Beijing: Renmin chubanshe, 1962.

Huang, Chi-chiang. "Experiment in Syncretism: Ch'i-sung (1007–1072) and Eleventh-Century Chinese Buddhism." Ph.D. diss., University of Arizona, 1986.

Huang Haipeng 黃海鵬. "Zhi you minghua ku you du—Su ci de gexing hua xiaoyi" 只有名花苦幽獨—蘇詞的個性化小議. In *Dongpo ci luncong* (q.v.), 120–126.

Huang Liaoyuan 黃蓼園. *Liaoyuan cixuan* 蓼園詞選. Quoted by Wang Shuizhao, *Su Shi xuanji* (q.v.).

Huang Mingfen 黃鳴奮. *Lun Su Shi de wenyi xinli guan* 論蘇軾的文藝心理觀. Fuzhou: Haixia wenyi chubanshe, 1987.

Huang Renke 黃任軻. "Su Shi lun xinfa wenzi liupian nianyue kaobian" 蘇軾論新法文字六篇年月考辨. *Su Shi yanjiu zhuanji* (q.v.), 103–110.

Huang Tingjian 黃庭堅 (1045-1105). *Shan'gu shizhu* 山谷詩注, edited by Ren Yuan 任淵 (d. after 1144) et al. In *Guoxue jiben congshu* (q.v.).

——. *Yuzhang Huang xiansheng wenji* 豫章黃先生文集. In *Sibu congkan* (q.v.).

Huayan jing. Dafang guangfo huayan jing 大方廣佛華嚴經. In *Taishō Tripitaka* (q.v.), no. 279, 10:1-444.

Huihong 慧(惠)洪 (1071-1128). *Lengzhai yehua* 冷齋夜話. In *Yinli zaisi tang congshu* 殷禮在斯堂叢書. Taipei: Yiwen yinshuguan, 1970.

——. *Shimen wenzi chan* 石門文字禪. In *Sibu congkan* (q.v.).

Hurvitz, Leon, trans. *Scripture of the lotus blossom of the fine dharma*. New York: Columbia University Press, 1976.

Hymes, Robert P. "Moral Duty and Self-Regulating Process: Tung Wei's *Book for Relieving Famine and Reviving the People* and Southern Sung Views on Famine Relief." Presented at the Conference on Sung Dynasty Statecraft in Thought and Action, Scottsdale, Arizona, 1986.

Ji Yun 紀昀 (1724-1805). *Su Wenzhonggong shiji* 蘇文忠公詩集. 1869.

Jin Shengtan 金聖嘆 (1608-1661). *Tianxia caizi bidu shu* 天下才子必讀書. In *Jin Shengtan xuanpi caizi bidu shu xinzhu* 金聖嘆選批才子必讀新註, 2 vols. Hefei: Anhui wenyi chubanshe, 1988.

Jin Zheng 金諍. "Lun Su Shi yu lixue zhi zheng" 論蘇軾與理學之爭. *Xueshu yuekan* 1985.2:61-67.

Jindai bishu 津逮祕書. In *Baibu conshu jicheng* (q.v.).

Jinguang mingjing 金光明經. In *Taishō Tripitaka* (q.v.), no. 663, 16:335-359.

Jinian Sima Guang Wang Anshi shishi jiubai zhounian xueshe yantao hui lunwen ji 紀念司馬光王安石逝世九百周年學術研討會論文集, edited by Guojia wenyi jijin hui 國家文藝基金會. Taipei: Wen shi zhe chubanshe, 1986.

Jinshu 晉書. Beijing: Zhonghuan shuju, 1974.

Jiu Tangshu 舊唐書. Beijing: Zhonghua shuju, 1975.

Ke Changyi 柯昌頤. *Wang Anshi pingzhuan* 王安石評傳. Shanghai: Commercial Press, 1947.

Keswick, Maggie. *The Chinese Garden: History, Art and Architecture*. New York: Rizzoli, 1978.

Kinugawa Tsuyoshi 衣川強, ed. *Liu Zijian boshi songshou jinian Songshi yanjiu lunji* 劉子健博士頌壽紀念宋史研究論集. Tokyo: Dohōsha, 1989.

Kondō Kazunari 近藤一成. "Chi Kōshū So Shoku no kyūkōsaku—Sōdai bunjin kanryō seisaku kō" 知杭州蘇軾の救荒策—宋代文人官僚政策考. In *Sōdai no shakai to bunka* 宋代の社會と文化, edited by Sōdai kenkyūkai, 139-168. Tokyo: Kūko shoten, 1983. Translated as: "Su Shih's Relief Measures as Prefect of Hang-chou—A Case Study of the Policies Adopted by Sung Scholar-Officials." *Acta Asiatica* 50:31-53 (1986).

Kong Fan 孔繁. "Su Shi *Piling yichuan* de zhexue sixiang" 蘇軾《毗陵易傳》的哲學思想. *Zhongguo zhexue* 9:221-239 (1983).

Kong Wuzhong 孔武仲 (*jinshi* 1063). *Qinjiang san Kong ji* 清江三孔集. In *Siku quanshu* (q.v.).

Kracke, E. A. Jr. *Civil Service in Early Sung China, 960–1067.* Harvard-Yenching Institute Monograph Series, no. 13. Cambridge: Harvard-Yenching Institute, 1953.

Kroll, Paul. "Verses from on High: The Ascent of T'ai Shan." In *The Vitality of the Lyric Voice*, edited by Shuen-lin Fu and Stephen Owen, 167–216. Princeton: Princeton University Press, 1986.

Kuhn, Dieter. *Reeling and Spinning*, pt. 9 of *Chemistry and Chemical Technology*, vol. 5 of *Science and Civilisation in China*, edited by Joseph Needham, gen. ed. Cambridge: Cambridge University Press, 1988.

Kusumoto Bun'yū 久須木文雄. *Sōdai jugaku no zen shisō kenkyū* 宋代儒學の禪思想研究. Tokyo: Nisshindō shoten, 1980.

Laing, Ellen Johnston. "Real or Ideal: The Problem of the 'Elegant Gathering in the Western Garden' in Chinese Historical and Art Historical Records." *Journal of the American Oriental Society* 88:419–435 (1968).

Lang Ye 郎曄 (fl. 1229). *Jingjin Dongpo wenji shilüe* 經進東坡文集事略. Hong Kong: Zhonghua shuju, 1979.

Laozi: Daode jing 老子道德經, commentary by Wang Bi 王弼 (226–249). In *Siku quanshu* (q.v.).

Lau, D. C. *Lao Tzu: Tao te ching.* Harmondsworth: Penguin Books, 1963.

———. "Twenty Selected Lyrics." *Renditions* 11–12:5–24 (1979).

———. *Mencius.* Harmondsworth: Penguin Books, 1970.

Legge, James. *The Chinese Classics.* 5 vols. Hong Kong: Hong Kong University Press, 1960.

———. *The Li Ki.* 2 vols. In *The Sacred Books of the East*, edited by F. Max Müller. Oxford: Clarendon Press, 1885.

———. *The Text of the Yi King*, edited by Z. D. Sung. Shanghai: The Chinese Modern Education Co., 1935.

Lengjia jing 楞伽經. *Lengjia aba duoluo baojing* 楞伽阿跋多羅寶經. In *Taishō Tripitaka* (q.v.), no. 670, 16:479–514.

Lengyan jing 楞嚴經. *Dafoding rulai miyin xiuzheng liaoyi zhupusa wanxing shou lengyan jing* 大佛頂如來密因修證了義諸菩薩萬行首楞嚴經. In *Taishō Tripitaka* (q.v.), no. 945, 19:105–155.

Li Ao 李翱 (772–841). *Li Wengong ji* 李文公集. In *Sibu congkan* (q.v.).

Li Bo 李白 (701–762). *Li Taibo quanji* 李太白全集. Beijing: Zhonghua shuju, 1977.

Li Fushun 李福順. *Su Shi lun shuhua shiliao* 蘇軾論書畫史料. Shanghai: Renmin meishu chubanshe, 1988.

Li Tao 李燾 (1114–1183). *Xu zizhi tongjian changbian* 續資治通鑑長編 (abbreviated *Xu changbian*). Beijing: Zhonghua shuju, 1986– . This punctuated but as yet incomplete editions is used for all references through *juan* 363 (Yuanfeng 8). References beyond *juan* 363 are to the older, unpunctuated edition: Taipei: Shijie shuju, 1961. (Note: *Juan* 8–14 of the supplementary "Shibu" section are found between *juan* 484 and 485.)

Li Zehou 李澤厚. *Meixue zhesi ren* 美學 · 哲思 · 人. Taipei: Fengyun shidai chubanshe, 1989.

Li Zhi 李廌 (1059–1109). *Shiyou tanji* 師友談記. In *Congshu jicheng* (q.v.).

Li Zhiyi 李之儀 (*jinshi* ca. 1080). *Guxi jushi quanji* 姑溪居士全集. In *Congshu jicheng* (q.v.).

Liangshu 梁書. Beijing: Zhonghua shuju, 1973.

Liezi jishi 列子集釋, edited by Yang Bojun 楊伯峻. Hong Kong: Taiping shuju, 1965.

Lidai shihua 歷代詩話, comp. by He Wenhuan 何文煥 (fl. 1770). 2 vols. Beijing: Zhonghua shuju, 1981.

Lidai shihua xubian 歷代詩話續編, comp. by Ding Fubao 丁福保. 3 vols. Beijing: Zhonghua shuju, 1983.

Liji zhushu 禮記注疏. In *Shisan jing zhushu fu jiaokan ji* (q.v.).

Lin Guanqun 林冠群. "Su Shi Lingnan shizuo de sixiang pinge" 蘇軾嶺南詩作的思想品格. In *Lun Su Shi Lingnan shi ji qita* (q.v.), 109–124.

Lin, Shuen-fu. *The Transformation of the Chinese Lyrical Tradition: Chiang K'uei and Southern Sung Tz'u Poetry*. Princeton: Princeton University Press, 1978.

Lin, Yutang. *The Gay Genius: The Life and Times of Su Tungpo*. New York: The John Day Company, 1947.

Liu, James J. Y. *Major Lyricists of the Northern Sung A.D. 960–1126*. Princeton: Princeton University Press, 1974.

Liu, James T. C. *Reform in Sung China: Wang Au-shih (1021–1086) and his New Policies*. Cambridge: Harvard University Press, 1959.

Liu Naichang. 劉乃昌. "Dongpo Lingnan shi de chengjiu he fengge" 東坡嶺南詩的成就和風格. In *Lun Su Shi Lingnan shi ji qia* (q.v.), 80–91.

———. "Lun fo lao sixiang dui Su Shi wenxue de yingxiang" 論佛老思想對蘇軾文學的影響. In his *Su Shi wenxue lunji* (q.v.), 188–201.

———. "Su Shi tong Wang Anshi de jiaowang" 蘇軾同王安石的交往. In his *Su Shi wenxue lunji* (q.v.), 217–232.

———. *Su Shi wenxue lunji* 蘇軾文學論集. Jinan: Qilu shushe, 1982.

———. "Tan Su Shi de yishu gexing" 談蘇軾的藝術個性. In his *Su Shi wenxue lunji* (q.v.), 75–94.

Liu Shangrong 劉尙榮. *Su Shi zhuzuo banben luncong* 蘇軾著作版本論叢. Chengdu: Bashu shushe, 1988.

Liu Yiqing 劉義慶 (403–444). *Shishuo xinyu jianshu* 世說新語箋疏, edited by Yu Jiaxi 余嘉錫. Beijing: Zhonghua shuju, 1983.

Liu Yuxi 劉禹錫 (772–842). *Liu Yuxi ji* 劉禹錫集. Shanghai: Rennmin chubanshe, 1975.

Liu Zhengcheng 劉正成, ed. *Su Shi* 蘇軾. 2 vols. Vols. 33–34 of *Zhongguo shufa quanji* 中國書法全集, Liu Zhengcheng, gen. ed. Beijing: Rongbao zhai, 1991.

Liu Zongyuan 柳宗元 (773–814). *Liu Hedong ji* 柳河東集. Shanghai: Renmin chubanshe, 1974.

Lo, Winston W. "Wang An-shih and the Confucian ideal of "inner sageliness." *Philosophy East and West* 26.1:42–53 (1976).

Long Muxun 龍沐勛, ed. *Dongpo yuefu jian* 東坡樂府箋. Shanghai: Commercial Press, 1936.

————. "Dongpo yuefu zonglun" 東坡樂府綜論. *Cixue jikan* 2.3:1–11 (1935).

————. *Huaihai jushi changduan ju* 淮海居士長短句. In his *Sumen si xueshi ci* 蘇門四學士詞. Beijing: Zhonghua shuju, 1957.

Lu You 陸游 (1125–1210), *Laoxue an biji* 老學庵筆記. Beijing: Zhonghua shuju, 1979.

————. *Weinan wenji* 渭南文集. In *Lu You ji* 陸游集. 5 vols. Beijing: Zhonghua shuju, 1976.

Lu Zhi 陸贄 (754–805). *Lu Xuangong ji* 陸宣公集. Hangzhou: Zhejiang guji chubanshe, 1988.

Lü Xizhe 呂希哲 (1036–1114). *Lüshi zaji* 呂氏雜記. In *Siku quanshe* (q.v.).

Luk, Charles (Lu K'uan Yü). *The Sūraṅgama Sūtra (Leng Yen Ching)*. London: Rider and Company, 1966.

Lun Su Shi Lingnan shi ji qita 論蘇軾嶺南詩及其他, edited by Su Shi yanjiu xuehui. Guangdong: Renmin chubanshe, 1986.

Lunyu 論語. Standard book and paragraph divisions.

Luo Dajing 羅大經 (*jinshi* 1226). *Helin yulu* 鶴林玉露. Beijing: Zhonghua shuju, 1983.

Luo Siding 羅思鼎. "Cong Wang Anshi bianfa kan Ru Fa lunzhan de yanbian" 從王安石變法看儒法論戰的演變. *Hongqi* 1974.2:24–31.

Ma Duanlin 馬端臨 (1254–1325). *Wenxian tongkao* 文獻通考. In *Shitong* 十通. Shanghai: Commercial Press, 1936.

Ma Zhenfeng 馬振鋒. *Zhengzhi gaigejia Wang Anshi de zhexue sixiang* 政治改革家王安石的哲學思想. Hebei: Renmin chubanshe, 1984.

Mao Jin 毛晉 (1599–1659). *Dongpo tiba* 東坡題跋. In *Congshu jicheng* (q.v.).

Mao Wei 茅維 (early 17th c.). *Su Wenzhonggong quanji* 蘇文忠公全集. 75 *juan*.

Mather, Richard B. *Shih-shuo Hsin-yü: A New Account of Tales of the World*. Minneapolis: University of Minnesota Press, 1976.

McNair, Amy. "Ouyang Xiu and Literati Taste in Calligraphy in the Northern Song Period." Paper presented at the 1990 annual meeting of the Association for Asian Studies in Chicago.

————. "Su Shih's Copy of the *Letter on the Controversy over Seating Protocol*." *Archives of Asian Art* 43:38–48 (1990).

Mei Yaochen 梅堯臣 (1002–1060). *Mei Yaochen ji biannian jiaozhu* 梅堯臣集編年校注, edited by Zhu Dongrun 朱東潤. Shanghai: Shanghai guji chubanshe, 1980.

Mencius 孟子. Standard book and paragraph divisions.

Meskill, James, ed. *Wang An-shih: Practical Reformer?* Boston: D. C. Heath, 1963.

Mi Fu 米芾 (1051–1107). *Baojin yingguang ji* 寶晉英光集. In *Congshu jicheng* (q.v.).

————. *Huashi* 畫史. In *Jindai bishu* (q.v.).

Miao Yue 繆鉞. "Lun Su Xin ci yu Zhuang Sao" 論蘇辛詞與《莊》《騷》. In Miao Yue and Ye Jiaying (q.v.), 229–235.

———— and Ye Jiaying. *Lingxi cishuo* 靈溪詞說. Taipei: Guowen tiandi, 1987.

Miaofa lienhua jing 妙法蓮華經. In *Taishō Tripitaka* (q.v.), no. 262, 9:1–62.

Miyazaki Ichisada 宮崎市定. "Ben kan ron no kan o benzu" 辨姦論の姦を辨す. In Kinugawa Tsuyoshi (q.v.), 317–326.

Murakami Tetsumi 村上哲見. "So Tōba shokan no denrai to *Tōbashū* shohon no keifu ni tsuite" 蘇東坡書簡の伝來と東坡集諸本の系譜について. *Chūgoku bungaku hō* 27:51–87 (1977).

Murck, Christian. "Su Shih's Reading of the *Chung yung*." In *Theories of the Arts in China*, edited by Susan Bush and Christian Murck, 267–292. Princeton: Princeton University Press, 1983.

Nakata Yūjirō 中田勇次郎. "So Tōba no sho to shoron" 蘇東坡の書と書論. In *Chūgoku shoron shū* 中國書論集, 195–212. Tokyo: Nigensha, 1970.

Nanshi 南史. Beijing: Zhonghua shuju, 1975.

Needham, Joseph, gen. ed. *Science and Civilisation in China.* See under Kuhn; Needham and Wang.

——— and Wang Ling. *Mechanical Engineering*, pt. 2 of *Physics and Physical Technology*, vol. 4 of *Science and Civilisation in China*, edited by Joseph Needham, gen. ed. Cambridge: Cambridge University Press, 1965.

Nianchang 念常 (fl. 1333). *Fozu lidai tongzai* 佛祖歷代通載. In *Taishō Tripitaka*, no. 2036, 49:477–735.

Nishi Noriaki 西紀昭. "Tōba no shoki no sōbetsu-shi" 東坡の初期の送別詞. *Chūgoku chūsei bungaku kenkyū* 7:64–73 (1968). Translated by Sun Kangyi 孫康宜. "Su Shi chuqi de songbie ci" 蘇軾初期的送別詞. *Zhong-wai wenxue* 7:64–77 (Oct. 1978).

Nishino Teiji 西野貞治. "So Shoku to Genyū tō sōka naka no hitobito" 蘇軾と元祐黨爭渦中の人人. *Jimbun kenkyū* 23.3:200–214 (1972).

———. "So Shoku to sono monka no gesaku shi" 蘇軾とその門下の戲作詩. *Jimbun kenkyū* 16.5:34–50 (1965).

———. "Tōba shi no baiden no go ni tsuite" 東坡詩の買田の語について. *Jimbun kenkyū* 19.10:757–763 (1968).

Ogawa Tamaki 小川環樹. *Kaze to kumo: Chūgoku bungaku ronshū* 風と雲:中國文學論集. Tokyo: Asahi shimbun, 1972.

———. "Shi ni okeru hikaku no kōsetsu to gazoku: So Tōba no baai" 詩における比喩の工拙と雅俗:蘇東坡の場合. *Chūgoku bungaku hō* 2:1–17 (1955). Rpt. in Ogawa, *Kaze to kumo: Chūgoku bungaku ronshū* (q.v.), 145–167.

———. *So Shoku* 蘇軾. 2 vols. Chūgoku shijin senshū, 2nd ser., vols. 5–6. Tokyo: Iwanami shoten, 1962.

——— and Yamamoto Kazuyoshi 山本和義. *So Tōba shishū* 蘇東坡詩集. 4 vols. (of a projected complete translation of Su's *shi* poetry; now through the verse of 1078/6). Tokyo: Chikuma shobō, 1983–1986.

Ouyang Min 歐陽忞 (d. after 1117). *Yudi guangji* 興地廣記. In *Guoxue jiben congshu* (q.v.).

Ouyang Xiu 歐陽修 (1007–1072). *Guitian lu* 歸田錄. In *Ouyang Wenzhong-gong ji* (q.v.), sect. 14.

———. *Jigu lu* 集古錄. In *Ouyang Wenzhonggong ji* (q.v.), sect. 15–16.

————. *Jushi ji* 居士集. In *Ouyang Wenzhonggong ji* (q.v.), sect. 1–6.

————. *Jushi waiji* 居士外集. In *Ouyang Wenzhonggong ji* (q.v.), sect. 6–9.

————. *Ouyang Wenzhonggong ji* 歐陽文忠公集. In *Guoxue jiben congshu* (q.v.).

————. *Shibi* 試筆. In *Ouyang Wenzhonggong ji* (q.v.), sect. 14.

————. *Shujian* 書簡. In *Ouyang Wenzhonggong ji* (q.v.), sect. 16–17.

————. *Zouyi ji* 奏議集. In *Ouyang Wenzhonggong ji* (q.v.), sect. 12–13.

Owen, Stephen. "Meaning the Words: The Genuine as a Value in the Tradition of the Song Lyric." In *Voices in the Song Lyric in China*, edited by Pauline Yu, 30–69. Berkeley: University of California Press, 1994.

Pei Xiu 裴休 (d. 860). *Chuanxin fayao* 傳心法要. *Huangbo shan Duanji chan-shi chuanxin fayao* 黃檗山斷際禪師傳心法要. In *Taishō Tripitaka*, no. 2012A, 48:379–384.

Qi Xia 漆俠. *Wang Anshi bianfa* 王安石變法. Shanghai: Renmin chubanshe, 1979.

Qian Shuoyou 潛說友 (*jinshi* 1244). *Xianchun Lin'an zhi* 咸淳臨安志. In *Siku quanshu* (q.v.).

Qian Zhongshu 錢鍾書. *Guanzhui bian* 管錐編. 4 vols. Beijing: Zhonghua shuju, 1979.

Qin Guan 秦觀 (1049–1100). *Huaihai ji* 淮海集. In *Sibu congkan* (q.v.).

Quan Songci 全宋詞, edited by Tang Guizhang 唐圭璋. 5 vols. Beijing: Zhong-hua shuju, 1965.

Quan Tang Wudai ci 全唐五代詞, edited by Lin Dachun 林大椿. 2 vols. Taipei: Shijie shuju, 1962.

Quan Tangshi 全唐詩. 12 vols. Beijing: Zhonghua shuju, 1960.

Quan Tangwen 全唐文. Neifu, 1814.

Robinet, Isabelle. "Original Contributions of *Neidan* to Taoism and Chinese Thought." In *Taoist Meditation and Longevity Techniques*, edited by Livia Kohn, 297–330. Ann Arbor: Center for Chinese Studies, Univer-sity of Michigan, 1989.

Rong Zhaozu 容肇祖, ed. *Wang Anshi Laozi zhu jiben* 王安石老子註輯本. Beijing: Zhonghua shuju, 1979.

Sargent, Stuart H. "Colophons in Countermotion: Poems by Su Shih and Huang T'ing-chien on Paintings." *Harvard Journal of Asiatic Studies* 52.1:263–302 (1992).

Schneider, Laurence A. *A Madman of Ch'u: The Chinese Myth of Loyalty and Dissent*. Berkeley: University of California Press, 1980.

Sengzhao 僧肇 (384–414). *Zhaolun* 肇論. In *Taishō Tripitaka* (q.v.), no. 1858, 45:150–151.

Shangshu zhushu 尚書註疏. In *Shisan jing zhushu fu jiaokan ji* (q.v.).

Shao Bo 邵博 (d. 1158). *Shaoshi wenjian houlu* 邵氏聞見後錄. Beijing: Zhong-hua shuju, 1983.

Shao Bowen 邵伯溫 (1056–1134). *Shaoshi wenjian lu* 邵氏聞見錄. Beijing: Zhonghua shuju, 1983.

Shi Yuanzhi 施元之 (*jinshi* 1155) and Gu Xi 顧禧, comm. *Shi Gu zhu Sushi* 施顧註蘇詩, edited by Zheng Qian 鄭騫 and Yan Yiping 嚴一萍. Taipei: Yiwen yinshuguan, 1980. Endnote references are to Shi's commentary as quoted in Wang Wen'gao's commentary in *Su Shi shiji*.

Shiba Yoshinobu 斯波義信. *Sōdai Kōnan keizaishi no kenkyū* 宋代江南經濟史の研究. Tokyo: Kyūko shoin, 1988.

———. "Sōdai shiteiku seido no enkaku" 宋代市糴制度の沿革. *Aoyama hakushi koki kinen: Sōdaishi ronsō* (q.v.), 123–159.

Shih, Heng-ch'ing. "The Ch'an-Pure Land Syncretism in China: With Special Reference to Yung-ming Yen-shou." Ph.D. diss., University of Wisconsin-Madison, 1984.

Shiji 史記, by Sima Qian 司馬遷 (145–ca. 87 B.C.). Beijing: Zhonghua shuju, 1959.

Shijing 詩經. Standard ode numbers.

Shisan jing zhushu fu jiaokan ji 十三經註疏附校勘記, edited by Ruan Yuan 阮元 (1764–1849). Nanchang, 1814.

Shou Min 瘦民. "Qiantan Su shi fengge de duoyanghua" 淺談蘇詩風格的多樣化. In *Dongpo shi luncong* (q.v.), 40–53.

Sibu congkan 四部叢刊. Shanghai: Commercial Press, 1929.

Sibu congkan xubian 四部叢刊續編. Shanghai: Commercial Press, 1935.

Siku quanshu 四庫全書. Shanghai: Shanghai guji chubanshe, 1987.

Siku quanshu zongmu tiyao. Heyin Siku quanshu zongmu tiyao ji siku weishou shumu jinhui shumu 合印四庫全書總目提要及四庫未收書目禁燬書目. 5 vols. Taipei: Commercial Press, 1978.

Sima Guang 司馬光 (1019–1086). *Sima Wenzhenggong chuanjia ji* 司馬文正公傳家集. In *Guoxue jiben congshu* (q.v.).

Smith, Paul J. "State Power and Economic Activism During the New Policies, 1068–1085: The Tea and Horse Trade and the 'Green Sprouts' Loan Policy." Presented at the Conference on Sung Dynasty Statecraft in Thought and Action, Scottsdale, Arizona, 1986.

———. *Taxing Heaven's Storehouse: Horses, Bureaucrats, and the Destruction of the Sichuan Tea Industry, 1074–1224.* Harvard-Yenching Institute Monograph Series, no. 32. Cambridge: Council on East Asian Studies, Harvard University, and the Harvard-Yenching Institute, 1991.

Song huiyao jiben 宋會要輯本. Taipei: Shijie shuju, 1964.

Song Qiulong 宋丘龍. *Su Dongpo he Tao Yuanming shi zhi bijiao yanjiu* 蘇東坡和陶淵明詩之比較研究. Taipei: Commercial Press, 1985.

Songren yishi huibian 宋人軼事彙編, compiled by Ding Chuanjing 丁傳靖. Beijing: Zhonghua shuju, 1981.

Songshi 宋史. Bejing: Zhonghua shuju, 1977.

Songshi jishi benmo 宋史紀事本末 (abbreviated *Jishi benmo*), compiled by Chen Bangzhan 陳邦瞻 (*jinshi* 1598). Beijing: Zhonghua shuju, 1977.

Sturman, Peter Charles. "Mi Youren and the Inherited Literati Tradition: Dimensions of Ink-Play." Ph.D. diss., Yale University, 1989.

Su Che 蘇轍 (1039–1112). *Luancheng ji* 欒城集. Shanghai: Shanghai kuji chubanshe, 1987.

Su Huanzhong 蘇寰中. "Qianlun Su Shi Lingnan shi" 淺論蘇軾嶺南詩. In *Lun Su Shi Lingnan shi ji qita* (q.v.), 92–108.

Su Shi 蘇軾 (1037–1101). Primary texts and editions used are listed here. Other editions are listed separately under the name of editor, compiler, or commentator.

―――. *Dongpo shuzhuan* 東坡書傳. In *Xuejin taoyuan* (q.v.).

―――. *Su Dongpo ci* 蘇東坡詞, edited by Cao Shuming 曹樹銘. Hong Kong: Shanghai yinshuguan, 1968.

―――. *Su Shi shiji* 蘇軾詩集, commentary by Wang Wen'gao 王文誥 (b. 1764), edited by Kong Fanli 孔繁禮. Beijing: Zhonghua shuju, 1982.

―――. *Su Shi wenji* 蘇軾文集 (abbreviated *Wenji*), edited by Kong Fanli. Beijing: Zhonghua shuju, 1986.

―――. *Sushi yizhuan* 蘇氏易傳. In *Congshu jicheng* (q.v.).

Su Shi yanjiu zhuanji 蘇軾研究專集. *Sichuan daxue xuebao congkan*, no. 6. Chengdu: Sichuan renmin chubanshe, 1980.

Su Song 蘇頌 (1020–1101). *Su Weigong wenji* 蘇魏公文集. Beijing: Zhonghua shuju, 1988.

Su Xun 蘇洵 (1009–1066). *Jiayou ji* 嘉祐集. In *Guoxue jiben congshu* (q.v.).

Sun Yueban 孫岳頒 (1639–1708), comp. *Peiwen chai shuhua pu* 佩文齋書畫譜. Shanghai: Tongwen tushuguan, 1920.

A Sung Bibliography (Bibliographie des Sung), edited by Yves Hervouet. Hong Kong: The Chinese University Press, 1978.

Sung Biographies, edited by Herbert Franke. Münchener Ostasistische Studien. Wiesbaden: Franz Steiner Verlag, 1976.

Suzuki Chūsei 鈴木中正. "Sōdai ni okeru bukkyō kessha no kakudai to sono seikaku" 宋代における仏教結社の拡大とその性格. In his *Chūgoku shi ni okeru kakumei to shūkyō* 中國史における革命と宗教, 48–65. Kyoto: Kyōto daigaku shuppankai, 1974

Taiping guangji 太平廣記, compiled by Li Fang 李昉 (925–996). Beijing: Renmin wenxue chubanshe, 1959.

Taishō Tripitaka (Taishō shinshū daizōkyō 大正新修大藏經). Tokyo: Daizō Shuppansha, 1924–1932.

Tang Lingling 唐玲玲. "Lun Su Shi de he Tao shi" 論蘇軾的和陶詩. In *Lun Su Shi Lingnan shi ji qita* (q.v.), 166–184.

Tao Daoshu 陶道恕. "*Wutai shian* xinkan" 烏臺詩案新勘. *Wenxue yichan zengkan* 14:290–317 (1982).

Tao Qian 陶潛 (365–427). *Tao Yuanming ji jiaojian* 陶淵明集校箋, edited by Yang Yong 楊勇. Hong Kong: Wuxing ji shuju, 1971.

Tao Wenpeng 陶文鵬. "Shi lun Su Shi de shihua tongyi shuo" 試論蘇軾的詩畫同異說. *Wenxue pinglun congkan* 13:15–37 (1983).

Teiser, Stephen F. *The Ghost Festival in Medieval China*. Princeton: Princeton University Press, 1988.

Thurman, Robert A. F., trans. *The Holy Teaching of Vimalakīrti*. University Park: Pennsylvania State University Press, 1976.

Tomlonovic, Kathleen M. "Poetry of Exile and Return: A Study of Su Shi (1037–1101)." Ph.D. diss., University of Washington, 1989.

Wang Anshi 王安石 (1021–1086). *Linchuan xiansheng wenji* 臨川先生文集. Beijing: Zhonghua shuju, 1964.

——. *Wang Anshi Laozi zhu jiben*. See under Rong Zhaozu.

——. *Wang Linchuan ji* 王臨川集. In *Guoxue jiben congshu* (q.v.).

Wang Baozhen 王保珍. *Zengbu Su Dongpo nianpu huizheng* 增補蘇東坡年譜會證. Taipei: Guoli Taiwan daxue wenxue yuan, 1969.

Wang Cheng 王偁 (d. ca. 1200). *Dongdu shilüe* 東都事略. In *Songshi ziliao cuibian* 宋史資料萃編, compiled by Zhao Tiehan 趙鐵寒. Taipei: Wenhai chubanshe, 1967.

Wang Chong 王充 (b. A.D. 27). *Lunheng jiaoshi* 論衡校釋, edited by Huang Hui 黃暉. In *Guoxue jiben congshu* (q.v.).

Wang Deyi 王德毅. *Songdai xianliang fangzheng ke kao* 宋代賢良方正科考. Hong Kong: Congwen shudian, 1971.

——. *Songdai zaihuang de jiuji zhengce* 宋代災荒的救濟政策. Taipei: Commercial Press, 1970.

Wang Fuzhi 王夫之 (1619–1692). *Jiangzhai shihua* 薑齋詩話. In *Qing shihua* 清詩話. Shanghai: Shanghai guji chubanshe, 1978.

Wang Guowei 王國維 (1877–1927). *Renjian cihua* 人間詞話. Hong Kong: Zhonghua shuju, 1961.

Wang Renyu 王仁裕 (880–956). *Kaiyuan tianbao yishi*. In *Kaiyuan tianbao yishi shizhong* 開元天寶遺事十種. Shanghai: Shanghai guji chubanshe, 1985.

Wang Rixiu 王日休 (d. 1173). *Longshu zengguang jingtu wen* 龍舒增廣淨土文. In *Taishō Tripitaka* (q.v.), no. 1970, 47:251–289.

Wang Ruoxu 王若虛 (1174–1243). *Hunan shihua* 滹南詩話. Beijing: Renmin wenxue chubanshe, 1983.

Wang Shipeng 王十朋 (1112–1171), comm. *Dongpo shizhu* 東坡詩註, edited by Zhu Congyan 朱從延. Shanghai: Saoye shanfang 1914 rpt. of 1698 ed. Endnote references are to Wang's commentary as quoted in Wang Wengao's commentary in *Su Shi shiji*.

Wang Shoumei 王瘦梅. "Su Shi 'Nian nu jiao: Chibi huaigu' yiwen bianxi" 蘇軾《念奴嬌・赤壁懷古》異文辨析. *Sichuan daxue xuebao congkan* 15:90–92 (1982).

Wang Shuizhao 王水照. "Guanyu Shi Shi 'Yu Teng Dadao shu' de xinian he zhuzhi wenti" 關於蘇軾《與滕達道書》的系年和主旨問題. *Wenxue pinglun* 1981.1:58–64.

——. "Lun Su Shi chuangzuo de fazhan jieduan" 論蘇軾創作的發展階段. *Shehui kexue zhanxian* 1984.1:259–269.

——. *Su Shi xuanji* 蘇軾選集. Shanghai: Shanghai guji chubanshe, 1984.

Wang Wen'gao 王文誥 (b. 1764), comm. *Su Wenzhonggong shi bianzhu jicheng* 蘇文忠公詩編註集成. 1819. Endnote references are to Wang's commentary as reproduced in *Su Shi shiji*.

————. *Su Wenzhonggong shi bianzhu jicheng zongan* 蘇文忠公詩編註集成總案 (abbreviated *Zongan*). Chengdu: 1985 rpt. of 1819 ed.

Wang Wenlong 王文龍. "Shi lun Su shi de zheli xing" 試論蘇詩的哲理性. In *Dongpo yanjiu luncong*, 64–78.

Wang Wenru 王文濡, comm. *Pingjian yinzhu guwen ci leizuan* 評校音註古文辭類纂, compiled by Yao Nai 姚鼐 (1732–1815). Taipei: Zhonghua shuju, 1969.

Wang Xuetai 王學泰. "Cong *Wutai shian* kan fengjian zhuanzhi zhuyi dui Songdai shige chuangzuo de yingxiang" 從"烏臺詩案"看封建專制主義對宋代詩歌創作的影響. *Wenxue yichan zengkan* 16:198–220 (1983).

Wang Yu 王煜. "Su Shi de zhexue yu zongjiao" 蘇軾的哲學與宗教. In *Tang Song shi yanjiu* 唐宋史研究, edited by Lin Tienwai 林天蔚 and Joseph Wong 黃約瑟 [Huang Yuesi], 197–215. University of Hong Kong: Centre of Asian Studies, 1987.

Wang Yunsheng 王運生. "Su Dongpo zai Huizhou he Tao shi de sixiang qingxiang" 蘇東坡在惠州和陶詩的傾向. In *Lun Su Shi Lingnan shi ji qita* (q.v.), 185–196.

Watson, Burton, trans. *The Complete Works of Chuang Tzu*. New York: Columbia University Press, 1968.

————. *Records of the Grand Historian of China*. 2 vols. New York: Columbia University Press, 1961.

————. *Su Tung-p'o: Selections from a Sung Dynasty Poet*. New York: Columbia University Press, 1965.

Wei Qingzhi 魏慶之 (fl. 1244). *Shiren yuxie* 詩人玉屑. Shanghai: Shanghai guji chubanshe, 1959.

Wei Xu 韋續 (9th c.). *Mosou* 墨藪. In *Congshu jicheng* (q.v.).

Weimojie suoshuo jing 維摩詰所說經. In *Taishō Tripitaka* (q.v.), no. 475, 14:537–557.

Wen Tong 文同 (1018–1079). *Danyuan ji* 丹淵集. In *Sibu congkan* (q.v.).

Weng Tongwen 翁同文. "Wang Shen shengping kaolüe" 王詵生平考略. In *Songshi yanjiu ji* 宋史研究集, no. 5, pp. 135–168. Taipei: Zhonghua congshu bianshen weiyuanhui, 1970.

Wenji, see Su Shih, *Su Shih wenji*.

Wenxuan 文選, comp. Xiao Tong 蕭統 (501–531). Taipei: Zhengzhong shuju 1971 rpt. of Hu Kejia's 1809 ed.

Williamson, H. R. *Wang An-shih: A Chinese Statesman and Educationalist*, 2 vols. London: Probsthain, 1935–1937.

Wixted, John Timothy. *Poems on Poetry: Literary Criticism by Yuan Hao-wen (1190–1257)*. Wiesbaden: Franz Steiner Verlag, 1982.

Wu Shiduan 吳仕端. "Dongpo zai Huizhou zheju shenghuo tan" 東坡在惠州謫居生活探. In *Lun Su Shi Lingnan shi ji qita* (q.v.), 222–239.

Wu Tingxie 吳廷燮 (b. 1863). *Bei Song jingfu nianbiao* 北宋經撫年表. Beijing: Zhonghua shuju, 1984.

Wu Zeng 吳曾 (d. after 1170). *Nenggai zhai manlu* 能改齋漫錄. Shanghai: Zhonghua shuju, 1960.

Wutai shian 烏臺詩案. Attrib. Peng Jiuwan 朋九萬 (early 12th c.). In *Hanhai* 函海, in *Baibu congshu jicheng* (q.v.).

Xia Changpu 夏長樸. "Wang Anshi sixiang yu Mengzi de guanxi" 王安石思想與孟子的關係. In *Jinian Sima Guang Wang Anshi shishi jiubai zhounian xueshu yantao hui lunwen ji* (q.v.), 295–326.

Xian Qin Han Wei Jin Nanbeichao shi 先秦漢魏晉南北朝詩, edited by Lu Qinli 逯欽立. 3 vols. Beijing: Zhonghua shuju, 1983.

Xiang Chu 項楚. "Su shi biyu suotan" 蘇詩比喻瑣詩. In *Su Shi yanjiu zhuanji* (q.v.), 26–35.

Xiao Gongquan 蕭公權. *Zhongguo zhengzhi sixiang shi* 中國政治思想史. Taipei: Lianjing chubanshe, 1982.

Xie Taofang 謝桃坊. "Su shi fenqi pingyi" 蘇詩分期評議. In *Lun Su Shi Lingnan shi ji qita* (q.v.), 6–23.

Xin Tangshu 新唐書. Beijing: Zhonghua shuju, 1975.

Xu changbian. See Li Tao, *Xu zizhi tongjian changbian*.

Xu Xu 徐續. *Su Shi shixuan* 蘇軾詩選. Hong Kong: Sanlian shuju, 1986.

Xu Yuanhe 徐遠和. *Luoxue yuanliu* 洛學源流. Jinan: Qilu shushe, 1987.

Xuanhe huapu 宣和畫譜. Ca. 1120. In *Congshu jicheng* (q.v.).

Xuanhe shupu 宣和書譜. Ca. 1120. In *Xuejin taoyuan* (q.v.).

Xue Ruisheng 薛瑞生. "Sumen Suxue yu Suti: jianlun Beisong de dangzheng yu wenxue" 蘇門蘇學與蘇體:兼論北宋的黨爭與文學. *Wenxue yichan* 1988.5:60–68.

Xuejin taoyuan 學津討原. In *Baibu congshu jicheng* (q.v.).

Yamamoto Kazuyoshi 山本和義. "Shijin no chō shō—So shi satsuki" 詩人の長嘯:蘇詩劄記. *Nanzan kokubun ronshū* 4:31–46 (1979).

——. "So Shoku shi ronkō" 蘇軾詩論稿. *Chūgoku bungaku hō* 13:76–91 (1961).

——. "Zōbutsu no shosō—So shi satsuki" 造物の諸相—蘇詩劄記. *Nanzan kokubun ronshū* 5:1–13 (1981).

Yamplosky, Philip B., trans. *The Platform Sutra of the Sixth Patriarch*. New York: Columbia University Press, 1967.

Yan Youyi 嚴有翼 (early 12th c.). *Yiyuan cihuang* 藝苑雌黄. In Guo Shaoyu, comp., *Song shihua jiyi* (q.v.), 2:181–234.

Yan Yu 嚴羽 (c. 1200–after 1270). *Conglang shihua* 滄浪詩話. In *Lidai shihua* (q.v.), 2:686–708.

Yan Zhenqing 顏真卿 (709–785). *Wenzhong ji* 文忠集. In *Congshu jicheng* (q.v.).

Yan Zhongqi 顏中其. *Su Dongpo yishi huibian* 蘇東坡軼事匯編. Changsha: Yuelu shushe, 1984.

——. *Su Shi lun wenyi* 蘇軾論文藝. Beijing: Beijing chubanshe, 1985.

Yang Shen 楊慎 (1488–1559), attrib. *(Bai sanshier jia pingzhu) San Su wenfan* (百三十二家評註)三蘇文範. 1914 rpt. of Jiale zhai ed.

Yang Shi 楊時 (1035–1135). *Guishan yulu* 龜山語録. In *Sibu congkan xubian* (q.v.).

Yang, Vincent. *Nature and Self: A Study of the Poetry of Su Dongpo with Comparisons to the Poetry of William Wordsworth*. New York: Peter Lang, 1989.

Yang Wanli 楊萬里 (1127–1206). *Chengzhai shihua* 誠齋詩話. In *Lidai shihua xubian* (q.v.), 1:135–160.

Yang Xiong 揚雄 (53 B.C.–A.D. 18). *Fayan* 法言. In *Congshu jicheng* (q.v.).

Yanshou 延壽 (904–975). *Zongjing lu* 宗鏡録. In *Taishō Tripitaka* (q.v.), no. 2016, 48:415–957.

Ye Jiaying 葉嘉瑩. "Lun Su Shi ci" 論蘇軾詞. In Miao Yue and Ye Jiaying (q.v.), 191–228.

Ye Mengde 葉夢得 (1077–1148). *Bishu luhua* 避暑録話. In *Xuejin taoyuan* (q.v.).

———. *Shilin shihua* 石林詩話. In *Lidai shihua* (q.v.), 1:404–439.

———. *Shilin yanyu* 石林燕語. Beijing: Zhonghua shuju, 1984.

———. *Yanxia fangyan* 巖下放言. In *Siku quanshu* (q.v.).

Yi Shizhen 伊世珍 (14th c.). *Langhuan ji* 瑯嬛記. In *Xuejin taoyuan* (q.v.).

Yokoyama Iseo 橫山伊勢雄. "Shijin ni okeru 'kyō' ni tsuite—So Shoku no baai" 詩人における"狂"について—蘇軾の場合. *Kambun gakkai kaihō* 34:1–12 (1975).

———. "So Shoku no seiji hihan no shi ni tsuite" 蘇軾の政治批判の詩について. *Kambun gakkai kaihō* 31:26–39 (1972).

Yoshida Tora 吉田寅. "Kyūkō katsumin sho to Sōdai no kyūkō seisaku" "救荒活民書"と宋代の救荒政策. In *Aoyama hakushi koki kinen: Sōdaishi ronsō* (q.v.), 447–475.

Yoshikawa Kōjirō 吉川享次郎. *An Introduction to Sung Poetry*, trans. Burton Watson. Harvard-Yenching Institute Monograph Series, no. 17. Cambridge: Harvard-Yenching Institute and Harvard University Press, 1967. Originally published as *Sōshi gaisetsu* 宋詩概說, Chūgoku shijin senshu, 2nd ser., vol. 1. Tokyo: Iwanami shoten, 1962.

———. *Five Hundred Years of Chinese Poetry*, trans. John Timothy Wixted. Princeton: Princeton University Press, 1989. Originally published as *Gen Min shi gaisetsu* 元明詩概說. Chūgoku shijin senshu, 2nd ser., vol. 2. Tokyo: Iwanami shoten, 1963.

Yuan Haowen 元好問 (1190–1257). *Yishan xiansheng wenji* 遺山先生文集. In *Sibu congkan* (q.v.).

Yuan Hong 袁宏 (328–376). *Hou Han ji jiaozhu* 後漢記校註. Tianjin: Tianjin guji chubanshe, 1987.

Yuan Wen 袁文 (1119–1190). *Wengyou xianping* 甕牖閒評. In *Juzhenban congshu* 聚珍版叢書, in *Baibu congshu jicheng* (q.v.).

Yupi zizhi tongjian gangmu xubian 御批資治通鑑綱目續編, edited by Shang Lu 商輅 (1414–1486). In *Siku quanshu* (q.v.).

Zeng Jili 曾季貍 (late 12th c.). *Tingzhai shihua* 艇齋詩話. In *Lidai shihua xubian* (q.v.), 1:281–326.

Zeng Minxing 曾敏行 (1118–1175). *Duxing zazhi* 獨醒雜志. In *Zhibuzu zhai congshu* (q.v.).

Zeng Zao 曾慥 (d. 1115). *Dongpo xiansheng changduan ju* 東坡先生長短句. (Used as the basis for Su's *ci* in *Quan Songci*.)

———. *Gaozhai shihua* 高齋詩話. In Guo Shaoyu, comp., *Song shihua jiyi* (q.v.), 2:129–137.

Zeng Zaozhung 曾棗莊. "Cong *Piling Yizhuan* kan Su Shi de shijie guan" 從《毗陵易傳》看蘇軾的世界觀. In *Su Shi yanjiu zhuanji* (q.v.), 59–66.

———. "Dongpo cizhong de Zhaoyun" 東坡詞中的朝雲. In *Dongpo ci luncong* (q.v.), 214–225.

———. "'Su shi fenqi pingyi' de pingyi" 《蘇詩分期評議》的評議. In *Lun Su Shi Lingnan shi ji qita* (q.v.), 24–41.

———. *Su Shi pingzhuan* 蘇軾評傳. Rev. ed. Chengdu: Sichuan renmin chubanshe, 1984.

———. "Su Xun 'Bianjian lun' zhenwei kao" 蘇洵"辨姦論"真偽考. *Sichuan daxue xuebao congkan* 15:109–116 (1982).

———. *Su Xun pingzhuan* 蘇洵評傳. Chengdu: Sichuan renmin chubanshe, 1983.

Zhang Fangping 張方平 (1007–1091). *Lequan ji* 樂全集. In *Siku quanshu* (q.v.).

Zhang Jie 張戒 (*jinshi* 1124). *Suihan tang shihua* 歲寒堂詩話. In *Lidai shihua xubian* (q.v.), 1:449–476.

Zhang Jie 張介. "Dongpo ci mantan" 東坡詞漫談. In *Dongpo ci luncong* (q.v.), 231–237.

Zhang Peiheng 章培恒. "'Bianjian lun' fei Shao Bowen weizuo" "辨姦論" 非邵伯溫偽作. In *Gudian wenxue luncong* 古典文學論叢, 138–183. Fudan xuebao cengkan 复旦學報增刊. Shanghai: Renmin chubanshe, 1980.

Zhang Sanxi 張三夕. "Lun Su shi zhong de kongjian gan" 論蘇詩中的空間感. *Wenxue yichan* 1982.2:87–96.

Zhang Xiang 張相. *Shi ci qu yuci huishi* 詩詞曲語詞匯釋. 2 vols. Beijing: Zhonghua shuju, 1977.

Zhang Yan 張炎 (b. 1248). *Ciyuan* 詞源. In Tang Guizhang 唐圭璋, comp., *Cihua congbian* 詞話叢編. Taipei: Guangwen shuju, 1967.

Zhang Yanyuan 張彥遠 (b. ca. 815). *Lidai minghua ji* 歷代名畫記. In *Congshu jicheng* (q.v.).

Zhang Zhilie 張志烈. "Su Wang changhe guankui" 蘇王唱和管窺. In *Su Shi yanjiu zhuanji* (q.v.), 93–102.

Zhao Bingwen 趙秉文 (1159–1232). *Xianxian laoren fushui wenji* 閑閑老人滏水文集. In *Sibu congkan* (q.v.).

Zhao Cigong 趙次公 (early 12th c.). Commentary on Su Shi's poetry, quoted by Wang Shipeng.

Zhao Lingzhi 趙令時 (1061–1134). *Houzheng lu* 侯鯖錄. In *Zhibuzu zhai congshu* (q.v.).

Zhao Yi 趙翼 (1724–1814). *Oubei shihua* 甌北詩話. Beijing: Renmin wenxue chubanshe, 1981.

Zheng Zhihui 鄭之惠 (fl. 1602) and Ling Qikang 凌啓康 (fl. 1620). *Su Changgong hezuo* 蘇長公合作. 1620.

Zhibuzu zhai congshu 知不足齋叢書. In *Baibu congshu jicheng* (q.v.).

Zhou Bida 周必大 (1126–1204). *Erlao tang shihua* 二老堂詩話. In *Lidai shihua* (q.v.), 2:655–678.

———. *Yigong tiba* 益公題跋. In *Jindai bishu* (q.v.).

Zhou Hui 周煇 (b. 1126). *Qingbo biezhi* 清波別志. In *Congshu jicheng* (q.v.).

Zhou Xianshen 周先慎. "Manshuo Su Shi zongbi shi: jiantan shiren zai Hui Dan shiqi de chuangzuo xintai shenghuo sixiang" 漫說蘇軾《縱筆》詩：兼談詩人在惠儋時期的創作心態生活思想. *Beijing daxue xuebao* 1988.5: 45–51.

Zhouyi 周易. In *Zhouyi yinde* 周易引得. Harvard-Yenching Sinological Index Series, Supplement no. 10. Taipei: Ch'eng-wen Publishing Co., 1966.

Zhou Zizhi 周紫芝 (b. 1082). *Shiyan* 詩讞. In *Xuehai leibian* 學海類編, in *Baibu congshu jicheng* (q.v.).

Zhu Jinghua 朱靖華. *Su Shi xinlun* 蘇軾新論. Jinan: Qilu shushe, 1983.

Zhu Xi 朱熹 (1137–1200). *Sanchao mingchen yanxing lu* 三朝名臣言行錄. In *Sibu congkan* (q.v.).

———. "Yichuan xiansheng nianpu" 伊川先生年譜. In Cheng Yi and Cheng Hao (q.v.), 1:338–346.

———. *Zhu Wengong wenji* 朱文公文集. In *Sibu congkan* (q.v.).

———. *Zhuzi yulei* 朱子語類. 8 vols. Beijing: Zhonghua shuju, 1986.

Zhuangzi 莊子. In *Zhuangzi yinde* 莊子引得. Harvard-Yenching Institute Sinological Index Series, Supplement no. 20. Cambridge: Harvard University Press, 1956.

Zongan. See Wang Wen'gao, *Su Wenzhonggong shi bianzhu jicheng zongan*.

Zongjian 宗鑑 (fl. 1237). *Shimen zhengtong* 釋門正統. In *Xu zangjing* 續藏經, 130:713–925. Taipei: Xinwenfeng chubanshe, 1977 rpt.

Zongxiao 宗曉 (1151–1224). *Lebang wenlei* 樂邦文類. In *Taishō Tripitaka* (q.v.), no. 1969A, 47:148–231.

Zuozhuan 左傳. In *Chunqiu jingzhuan yinde* 春秋經傳引得. Harvard-Yenching Sinological Index Series, Supplement no. 11. Taipei: Ch'eng-wen Publishing Co., 1966.

Chinese Title Index

This is a list of Su Shi's prose pieces and poems (*shi* and *ci*) that are cited in the preceding chapters, arranged by stroke count. The index does not include every piece cited, only those that are translated or discussed at some length. Works by other writers are not included.

Prose

Poetry (*Shi* and *Ci*)

Glossary-Index

204; on human nature, 10–11, 20, 203–204; on historical figures, 16–20; on recruitment, 15–16; on rites, 8–9; Su's reflections on, 7, 19, 106, 212; on Zhang Liang, 21–26

Examination questions, 98–100, 104, 106, 107

Examination system. *See* Civil service examinations

Exile: of Han Yu, 182, of Yuanyou officials, 105, 213, 216. *See also* Exile (Su's)

Exile (Su's): and blossom metaphor, 250–257; commentaries on classics written during, 68–85, 260; finances during, 208–209, 210–211, 215; illness during, 213, 217, 240; liberating aspects of, 220, 224; to Lingnan, 68, 105, 213, 355; literary work from, xv, 68, 207–208, 220, 411n1; prohibition from speaking out on government affairs, 128, 208, 214; psychological impact of, 211–213, 219–221, 237; search for contentment in, 236–237, 333, 354, 355; search for transcendence during, 161–162, 224, 237–250; visitors during, 217–218. *See also* Hainan Island; Huizhou; Huangzhou exile; *Rhapsody on Red Cliff*

Expedient means, 152

Experience, transitory nature of, 189–191

F

Fa 法 (laws), 274
Fa 法 (policy), 1, 14–15
Fa 發 (release, trigger), 168, 280, 363
Fadu 法度 (institutions), 19
Famine relief, 108–122, 135, 149; policies favored by Su Shi, 110; veracity of Su's reports, 118–121
Fan Chunren 范純仁, 33, 87
Fan Li 范蠡, 171, 316
Fan Zhen 范鎮, 33, 52, 141, 303
Fan Zhongyan 范仲淹, 7, 27, 220, 262
Fan Zuyu 范祖禹, 96, 104, 119–120, 216
Fangbian 方便 (expedient means), 152
Fanxin 凡心 (common mind), 166
Farm, purchase of, 201, 209–210. *See also* Yixing

Farmers, 7, 28, 31, 122, 164, 183–184. *See also* Gentleman farmer; Green Sprouts Policy
Farming, 63, 102, 229, 232, 306, 335–336. *See also* East Slope; Farm, purchase of
Fashe 法杜 (Buddhist societies), 142
Fatie 法帖 (model calligraphic inscriptions), 262
Faxiu 法秀, 163, 361, 429n23
Fayong 法涌, 145
Fayun 法雲, 143
Fei bense 非本色 (untrue to the intrinsic nature), 311
Fei Gun 費袞, 132–133, 135
Fengcai 風采 (manner and bearing), 268
Fengliu 風流 (charm), 356, 362
Fengsu 風俗 (customs), 36
Finance, 6, 7. *See also* Economy
Fire relief, 131, 133
Five phases, 76–77, 167, 239–240, 406n88
Five virtues, 19
Floods: and famine in Hangzhou, 102, 109, 115, 118–119; in Xuzhou, 124, 184, 187–188, 356
Flowing Waters, 145, 146
Fong, Grace, 318
Food and drink, 66–67, 74, 75, 94
Food riots, 120
Forbearance (*ren* 任), 17, 24, 25–26, 147
Foyin 佛印, 140, 142, 197, 357
Friendships, 170, 174, 231. *See also* Su's circle
Fu. See Rhapsody
Fu Bi 富弼, 4, 33, 101, 141
Fu Yaoyu 傅堯俞, 98, 99
Fuller, Michael, xvi, 387n42, 396n95

G

Gao 高, Empress Dowager, 86, 94, 99, 104
Gao Xianzhi 高仙芝, 291
Gaoxian 高閑, 198
Ge 戈 (right-slanting), 273
Ge Hong 葛洪, 242–245
Gen 艮 hexagram, 77–78
Gentleman farmer, 220, 229, 232, 237
Genuineness (*zhen* 真), 318–320
Gimello, Robert, 163–164
Ginsberg, Stanley, xvi
Golden Light Sutra, 145, 153

Lü Bu 呂布, 188
Lü Dafang 呂大防, 216
Lü Gongzhu 呂公著, 33, 94, 104–105
Lü Huiqing 呂惠卿, 47, 48, 61, 91, 104;
demotion of, 87, 103, 105, 308
Lu Shang 呂尚, 355
Lü Zuqian 呂祖謙, 359
Lüqiu Xiaozhong 閭丘孝終, 342–343
Lüshi. See Regulated poetry

M

Ma Mengde 馬夢德, 210–211, 229
Ma Sheng 馬瑊, 120–121
Madness, 176–178, 179
Mahāsattva, 145–146
Mahayana Buddhism, 152, 153, 158, 166
Malaria, 217, 218
Managing wealth. See *Licai*
Manci 慢詞, 339–350. See also *Ci*
Mani 摩尼 gem, 186
Mao Jin 毛晉, 418–419n11
Mao Pang 毛滂, 303
Matching poems, 170, 233–236, 242–243, 258–259, 289, 306, 355
McNair, Amy, 272
Medical care, 125–126. *See also* Hospitals
Meditation, 165, 167, 203, 238, 241
Mei Yaochen 梅堯臣, 5, 265, 408n32
Meishan 眉山, 3, 144, 150, 200–201
Mencius, 6, 18, 30, 70, 74, 127, 319
Meng 盟 (alliance), 365
Meng Ben 孟賁, 23, 387n52
Meng Chang 孟昶, 345, 428n78
Meng Jiao 孟郊, 193
Merchants, 7, 29, 31, 34, 121
Metaphor, 185–186, 192–197
Metaphysics, 65
Mi Fu 米芾, 261, 266, 274, 275, 292, 303, 361, 430n26; centrality of aesthetic expression for, 377, 431n65
Mianyi qian 免役錢, (service exemption tax), 29
Middle way, 18
Military relations, 6, 27–28
Mind, 84–85. *See also* No-mind
Ming 明 (clear-sightedness), 167
Mirrors, 186, 364, 375
Miying 邇英 Palace, 97
Mizhou 密州, 89, 91, 161–162, 207

Mo (extremity). See *Ben* and *mo*
Mobao tang 墨寶堂 (Ink Treasures Hall), 43
Monasteries, 149, 156–157, 165
Monastic rules, 165
Moneylenders, 184
Moonlight, 200, 344–347, 409n57
Moral duty. See *Yi* (duty, rightness)
Mortality, 202, 224, 226, 227, 345–347. *See also* Immortality
Mourning, 5, 27, 94, 98
Moyi 墨義 (elucidation of particular passages), 29
Mozi 墨子, 69, 359
Music, 94
Muyi fa. See Hired Service Policy
Muzong 穆宗, 270

N

Nei/wai. See Inner and outer
New Learning, 60–61, 303; opposed by Su, 63–65, 69, 78, 150, 155, 163, 164, 365
New Policies (*xinfa* 新法): altered attitude toward, 90–92, 389n26, 397n11; criticized by Su Shi, 33–36, 56, 65, 70–71, 79, 106, 176, 203–204, 356; dismantling of, 86, 87–88, 92; effects on commoners, 40–41, 46, 47; and expansion of the bureaucracy, 31; and function of the Censorate, 36–37; mentioned, xiv, 122; opposition to, 32–33, 56, 303, poems of protest against, 39–45; summarized, 28–30. *See also* Civil service examinations; Green Sprouts Policy; Hired Service Policy; New Learning; Poetry, of political protest; Salt regulations; Su Shi (Chronology), arrest and trial of; Wang Anshi
Nie Zheng 聶政, 23, 387n54
Nirmānakāya, 152
Niu Jian 牛戩, 308
No-mind (*wuxin* 無心), 67, 81–83, 153–156, 166
No-thought, 153, 158, 280, 336
Non-abiding, 158, 159, 295
Non-attachment, 157–162, 196, 227
Non-possessiveness, 158, 159, 160
Non-transference, 224, 413n52

HARVARD-YENCHING INSTITUTE MONOGRAPH SERIES
(titles now in print)

11. *Han Shi Wai Chuan: Han Ying's Illustrations of the Didactic Application of the* Classic of Songs, translated and annotated by James Robert Hightower

18. *A History of Japanese Astronomy: Chinese Background and Western Impact,* by Shigeru Nakayama

21. *The Chinese Short Story: Studies in Dating, Authorship, and Composition,* by Patrick Hanan

22. *Songs of Flying Dragons: A Critical Reading,* by Peter H. Lee

23. *Early Chinese Civilization: Anthropological Perspectives,* by K. C. Chang

24. *Population, Disease, and Land in Early Japan, 645–900,* by William Wayne Farris

25. *Shikitei Sanba and the Comic Tradition in Edo Fiction,* by Robert W. Leutner

26. *Washing Silk: The Life and Selected Poetry of Wei Chuang (834?–910),* by Robin D. S. Yates

27. *National Polity and Local Power: The Transformation of Late Imperial China,* by Min Tu-ki

28. *T'ang Transformation Texts: A Study of the Buddhist Contribution to the Rise of Vernacular Fiction and Drama in China,* by Victor H. Mair

29. *Mongolian Rule in China: Local Administration in the Yuan Dynasty,* by Elizabeth Endicott-West

30. *Readings in Chinese Literary Thought,* by Stephen Owen

31. *Remembering Paradise: Nativism and Nostalgia in Eighteenth-Century Japan,* by Peter Nosco

32. *Taxing Heaven's Storehouse: Horses, Bureaucrats, and the Destruction of the Sichuan Tea Industry, 1074–1224,* by Paul J. Smith

33. *Escape from the Wasteland: Romanticism and Realism in the Fiction of Mishima Yukio and Oe Kenzaburo,* by Susan Jolliffe Napier

34. *Inside a Service Trade: Studies in Contemporary Chinese Prose,* by Rudolf G. Wagner

35. *The Willow in Autumn: Ryūtei Tanehiko, 1783–1842,* by Andrew Lawrence Markus

36. *The Confucian Transformation of Korea: A Study of Society and Ideology,* by Martina Deuchler

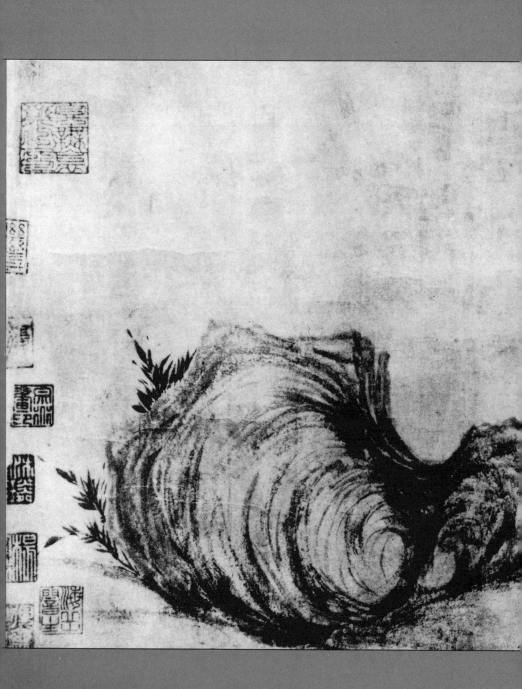